BRITISH

EMPIRICAL PHILOSOPHERS

Locke, Berkeley, Hume,
Reid and J. S. Mill

EDITED BY

A. J. AYER, M.A., F.B.A.

*Wykeham Professor of Logic in the University of Oxford
and Fellow of New College, Oxford*

AND

RAYMOND WINCH, B.A.

*John Stuart Mill
Scholar in the Philosophy of Mind and Logic
at University College, London*

A Clarion Book

PUBLISHED BY

SIMON AND SCHUSTER

A CLARION BOOK
PUBLISHED BY SIMON AND SCHUSTER
ROCKEFELLER CENTER, 630 FIFTH AVENUE
NEW YORK, NEW YORK 10020
REPRINTED BY ARRANGEMENT WITH HUMANITIES PRESS, INC.

FIRST PAPERBACK PRINTING 1968

LIBRARY OF CONGRESS CATALOG CARD NUMBER: 68-19695
MANUFACTURED IN THE UNITED STATES OF AMERICA
PRINTED BY MURRAY PRINTING CO., FORGE VILLAGE, MASS.
BOUND BY ELECTRONIC PERFECT BINDERS, INC., BROOKLYN, N.Y.

CONTENTS

JOHN LOCKE

AN ESSAY CONCERNING HUMAN UNDERSTANDING

CONTENTS

GEORGE BERKELEY

A TREATISE CONCERNING THE PRINCIPLES OF HUMAN KNOWLEDGE

THREE DIALOGUES BETWEEN HYLAS AND PHILONOUS IN OPPOSITION TO SCEPTICS AND ATHEISTS

DAVID HUME

A TREATISE CONCERNING HUMAN NATURE

BOOK I. OF THE UNDERSTANDING

PART I. OF IDEAS, THEIR ORIGIN, COMPOSITION, CONNECTION, ABSTRACTIONS, ETC.

PART II. OF THE IDEAS OF SPACE AND TIME

CONTENTS

THOMAS REID

ESSAY ON THE INTELLECTUAL POWERS OF MAN

JOHN STUART MILL

AN EXAMINATION OF SIR WILLIAM HAMILTON'S PHILOSOPHY

7

INTRODUCTION

This volume has in some degree the character of an anthology. It contains, in chronological order, an abridgement of John Locke's *Essay Concerning Human Understanding*; the whole of Bishop Berkeley's *Principles of Human Knowledge* and of the first of his *Three Dialogues between Hylas and Philonous*, together with extracts from the second and third; very nearly the whole of the first book of David Hume's *Treatise of Human Nature*, as well as a few passages from his *Enquiry Concerning the Human Understanding*; and comparatively brief extracts from Thomas Reid's *Essay on the Intellectual Powers of Man* and John Stuart Mill's *Examination of Sir William Hamilton's Philosophy*. These writings have not, however, been selected at random. The reason for bringing them together is that they all deal with the same type of philosophical question, that they approach these questions from the same general standpoint, and that the various answers which they give to them reflect upon one another. They may thus be regarded as successive contributions to a single philosophical enquiry. The direction is fixed by Locke. Berkeley follows Locke a certain distance, and then diverges from him. Hume, continuing the line of Berkeley, introduces new themes of his own. The passages by Reid are included because they challenge an important assumption which is made by Locke and accepted without question by Berkeley and Hume. The selections from the work of John Stuart Mill are taken from a book in which he is attacking one of the more prominent disciples of Reid. They are not directly polemical, but set out Mill's own views on two of the fundamental points at issue. And these views are in one instance a development of Berkeley's and in the other a development of Hume's.

The branch of philosophy to which these works belong is that which goes by the name of the Theory of Knowledge. And what the Theory of Knowledge is supposed to tell us is first what knowledge is, secondly what it is that can be known, and thirdly how it can be known. More explicitly, it comprises the analysis of the various modes of " cognition," including not only knowledge in the strict sense but also such others as imagination or belief, the discrimination of the various types of proposition which one may claim to believe or know, the analysis of these propositions and of the concepts which occur in them, and the critical examination of the evidence which we may have for holding them. Now it is characteristic of all the philosophers who figure in this volume that, while they may differ in the accounts that they give of the nature of sense experience, and still more in the inferences that they draw from them, they all agree that unless it is validly based upon our sense experience we can have no sufficient ground for maintaining any proposition about a matter of fact. And it is for this reason that they are given the title of Empiricists.

THE PRINCIPLES OF EMPIRICISM

Locke's purpose, as he himself describes it in the first chapter of his *Essay*, is " to enquire into the original, certainty, and extent of human knowledge, together with the grounds and degrees of belief, opinion and assent " : and it is on the enquiry into the " original " of our knowledge that he founds all the rest. He assumes that in order to discover how far knowledge can reach, and in what way anything that passes for knowledge can make its title good, it is necessary first to determine what knowledge consists in; and he thinks that the way to answer this question is to start by showing how knowledge is obtained. What he does, in fact, is to treat knowledge as if it were an article of manufacture; and so we find him asking where the raw material comes from and how it is worked up. It might be thought that there was a preliminary question to be asked about the nature of the raw material, but to Locke this presents no problem. Having given the name of " idea " to " whatsoever is the object of the understanding when a man thinks," he assumes without further ado that the raw material of knowledge consists of ideas. His argument is then devoted to showing how we originally come by our ideas, and what we can subsequently make of them.

Locke's answer to the first of these questions is that all our ideas without exception come to us from Experience. Experience may take the form of Sensation, which gives us such simple ideas as those of " yellow . . . heat . . . soft . . . bitter, and all those which we call sensible qualities," or of Reflection, which is " the perception of the operations of our own minds within us " and yields such simple ideas as those of perception, thinking and willing. All simple ideas are of one or other, or in some cases both, of these two sorts; and all the rest of our ideas are derived from such simple ideas by the operations of combining them, comparing them, or abstracting from them. Further, since anything that comes before the mind must by definition be an idea, it is only with ideas that any cognitive activity can be concerned. And so Locke's definition of knowledge is that it is " nothing but the perception of the connection and agreement, or disagreement and repugnancy, of any of our ideas."

From this brief account of Locke's method it can be seen that he approaches his problem as if it were a problem in psychology. He writes as if he were engaged in compiling a natural history of the mind; and in this he is followed both by Hume and Mill. Indeed, none of the authors with whom we are here concerned makes a very clear distinction between philosophy and psychology. Sometimes the questions that they raise are clearly psychological, but more often a better interpretation is that they are presenting some philosophical thesis in a psychological form.

I think that this is the case here with Locke. If his statements are taken at their face value, as psychological hypotheses, then to the extent to which they are true they are trivial, and in so far as they are not trivial they are not true. It is a trivial proposition that all our ideas are derived from Experience, if this is taken to mean no more than that Experience, in Locke's sense, is a necessary condition of thought. There are certainly no such things as innate ideas, if the assumption of innate ideas is understood to imply that children are capable of using symbols intelligently, and of assenting to propositions, before they have had any sense experience. On the other hand, Locke's atomistic treatment of sensation does not accord with the experiential facts; and the ideas that he regards as " simple " are not psychologically primitive. It is not the case that we begin with the experience of sensible qualities in isolation, and then put them together to obtain our ideas of sensory or perceptual objects. It is not true that we have first to learn the use of words like " yellow " or " sweet " before we can learn the use of words like " sugar " or " ball." If anything, it is the other way round. Neither do we arrive at all our complex ideas in the straightforward manner that Locke suggests. The development of scientific concepts, including the scientific concepts of Locke's own day, show that we have very much greater powers of inventiveness

than his theory allows us. Our imagination is not in fact restricted
to combining, comparing and abstracting from " simple ideas." It
operates very much more freely.

The same objection applies to Hume's theory that " all the perceptions of the human mind resolve themselves into . . . Impressions and Ideas," where Impressions are taken to comprise " all
our sensations, passions and emotions, as they make their first
appearance in the soul," and Ideas are " the faint images of these
in thinking and reasoning." For the psychological difference between thinking and having a sensation is not simply a difference of
vivacity. Neither is our thought limited to going over past impressions, even allowing, as Hume does, that we can imaginatively
re-arrange them. The little latitude that he grants to the imagination does not save Hume's account of the mind's working from
being naïvely photographic; and as such it does not correspond to
the facts.

It is, however, possible to interpret these statements of Locke
and Hume, not as a psychological doctrine about the way in which
our ideas come into being, but as a philosophical doctrine about the
way in which they can be analysed. Thus, even if it is not by
putting together ideas of sensible qualities that we actually form
our conceptions of perceptual objects, it may still be that when we
come to analyse what is meant by a perceptual object we find that
it is nothing but a complex of sensible qualities. And this is what
Berkeley, for example, may be understood to claim. It is not a
point of fact, but a point of logic. The question at issue is whether,
given a suitable notation for describing sensible qualities, we can
by its means say everything that we want to say about perceptual
objects. Berkeley himself does not put the question in this form.
He treats it rather as if it were a question of fact, as if he were
engaged in showing what perceptual objects were made of. But
his treatment of the subject shows that it is the logical question,
which he does not explicitly formulate, that he is interested in
answering. And this question is independent of the psychological
question how our ideas are formed.

Interpreting the statements of Locke and Hume in this way, we
may derive from them the logical thesis that every significant
concept must be analysable in terms of sense impressions, where
these are understood to comprise both " simple ideas of sensation,"
in Locke's sense, and " simple ideas of reflection." And Locke's
account of the way in which complex ideas are formed out of
simple ideas may be regarded, not as a description of any process

that actually takes place, but as specifying the logical relationships that complex ideas must bear to simple ideas if they are to be analysable in terms of them. I do not think that he specifies them correctly, but that is a point that requires to be argued in detail. For the present, I am concerned only with the general principle of empiricism which can be extracted from his work.

This principle may be applied either to concepts or to propositions. In the first case, it states that a concept is legitimate if and only if it either itself stands for something that could be experienced or else is a logical function of concepts which do so stand. In the second case, it states that a complex proposition is significant if and only if it is composed of simple propositions which are significant, and that a simple proposition is significant if and only if it describes what could be experienced. And in both cases the criterion by which it is determined that something could be experienced is that it should be of the same kind as something that has actually been experienced. A further refinement is introduced by Hume, when he draws a distinction between " Relations of Ideas " and " Matters of Fact." Propositions which concern only relations of ideas are purely abstract. Their validity is formal and so " without dependence on what is anywhere existent in the Universe." In the *Treatise*, Hume rightly puts the propositions of arithmetic and algebra into this class and, in the *Enquiry* those of geometry also. To them the empiricist principle does not apply, but it does apply to any other statement whatsoever that purports to be a statement about a matter of fact. Thus the thesis is first that all propositions are either formal or descriptive, and secondly that nothing is a genuinely descriptive proposition unless it describes what could be experienced.

In one form or another, this principle is asserted dogmatically by Locke and Hume, and implicitly accepted by Berkeley and Mill. No attempt is made by them to prove it; and, indeed, it is difficult to see in what way it could be proved. It is put forward as a thesis, but I think it should rather be treated as a definition. As such, it prescribes the conditions under which a symbol or a statement is allowed to have factual content. An argument against it is that it is excessively restrictive. There is a use, in science, for descriptive symbols which do not stand for anything that is directly observable. Consequently, modern empiricists prefer to adopt a more liberal criterion, which requires of a factual statement, not that it must itself describe what could be experienced, but only that some statements which are basic in this sense should, given the appropriate conditions, be derivable from it. The difficulty which then arises is to show exactly what is meant by saying of a statement that it describes " what could be experienced." And here the reference to what has actually been experienced is not an adequate criterion. For this is once again to substitute psychology for logic.

IDEAS : PARTICULAR AND ABSTRACT

The first step in the resolution of this difficulty is to analyse the notion of the " object of experience." We have seen that for Locke the object of experience is necessarily " a simple idea," and that he also makes this " the object of thought." He further assumes that ideas, whether simple or complex, exist only " in the mind," and thereby, as Hume saw, makes them " perishable " and " fleeting." The existence of any given idea is wholly dependent upon the existence of the particular sensation or thought of which it is the object. In this Locke is followed by Berkeley and also by Hume, who clarifies the position by using the term " impression " instead of " simple idea " for the object, or content, of sensation, retaining " idea " for the object of thought. The whole doctrine, at least as regards impressions is, however, challenged by Reid, who protests against it in the name of commonsense. What the ordinary man believes when he looks, for example, at the sun is that he is seeing a real physical object, which goes on existing whether he perceives it or not. He does not believe that the object of his perception is merely an impression or idea in his own mind. And, according to Reid, it is the philosophers who in this case go astray, and the plain man's view which is correct.

Now here it may seem obvious that Reid is in the right. In any ordinary use of the word " perceive," it is absurd to say that, while people may think they perceive physical objects, they are really only perceiving impressions in their own minds. All the same Reid misses the point of what his opponents are saying; and this is not to be wondered at, since they are not at all clear about it themselves. Here again there is a confusion between a question of logic and a question of fact. For while Locke and his followers may seem to be putting forward a factual thesis, and probably themselves believed that this is what they were doing, what they actually do is to introduce a new verbal usage. They do not show that it is factually incorrect to say that we directly perceive physical objects. What they do show is that, in any case in which a person claims that he is directly perceiving a physical object, it is logically possible that he should be mistaken. His perception may be delusive, and whether it is so or not is a matter for further evidence to decide. It is not completely determined by the character of the perception considered by itself. Accordingly, there is a use for a terminology which allows us to give a name to what we are perceiving without prejudging the question whether the perception is veridical or delusive. And it is this purpose that is served by such terms as " impression " or " simple idea of sensation " or the modern " sense-datum." To say that what a man directly sees is not a physical object, such as the sun, but an impression, is thus to create a special use of the word " see "; a use which is characterized by that fact that if something is seen, in this sense, it follows that it exists and that it has whatever properties it appears to have. And the difference between this and the ordinary usage is that in the ordinary usage of perceptual words like " see " it is legitimate to speak of perceiving things that do not exist, or of perceiving things that do not have the properties that they appear to have. We may speak, for example, of seeing the sun in a dream, and it would commonly be said that the sun which we see when we are awake appears to have very different properties from those that it really has. Consequently, the statement that we perceive only impressions does not contradict the statement that we perceive physical objects. For the use of " perceive " is different in each case.

But what sense are we to give to the statement that the immediate objects of perception are " in the mind? " Again, I suggest that this is to be taken, not as an assertion of fact, but as a rule of usage, or at least as the consequence of such a rule. For the reason for which it is said that impressions, or simple ideas of sensation, exist only in the mind is that they exist only while they are being experienced. And that they exist only while they are being experienced is not an additional fact about them but a consequence of the way in which they are defined. It is true that Hume treats this as if it were a scientific question. He adduces facts which go to show that " all our perceptions are dependent upon our organs, and the disposition of our nerves and animal spirits "; and he takes this to be a proof that " our sensible perceptions "—or, in other words, our impressions—" are not possessed of any distinct or independent existence." But all that the premise of this argument establishes is that different sorts of actual or possible impressions are correlated with one another; and from this it does not follow, as a matter of fact, that they cannot also exist independently. We have in any case first to determine what we are going to understand by their " existence." And it is to this that Hume's argument is relevant. Its point is to induce us so to use the word " existence " in connection with impressions that it makes no sense to say of an impression that it exists when it is not experienced. Accordingly, when Berkeley, in this respect preceding Hume, declares that the existence of sensible qualities consists in their being perceived, he must not be understood to be putting forward a factual thesis. What he is doing is to lay down a convention.

This being so, the familiar objection to Berkeley, that he fails to distinguish between the act of sensation and the object which is sensed, misses its aim. It is argued that, while the act of sensation does exist " within the mind," it does not follow that the same is true of its object; and that Berkeley simply takes this for granted because he confuses the object with the act. But if to say that sensible qualities exist only in the mind is merely equivalent to saying that they exist only when perceived, and if to say that they exist only when perceived is not to make a statement of fact but to formulate a convention, then it need make no difference to Berkeley whether the distinction between acts of sensation and their objects is admitted or not. If it is admitted it may supply a motive for adopting a different convention; but it certainly does not show that Berkeley's convention is untenable. And in any case I do not think that it is a valid distinction. I believe that these acts of sensation, conceived as entities distinct from their " objects," are a philosopher's myth.

So far we have been dealing with " ideas " only as objects of perception. But the term is also used by Locke to stand for an object of thought; and in this he is followed by Berkeley and Hume. One disadvantage of this usage is that it makes the word " idea " ambiguous; but a more serious objection is that it is not at all clear in what sense thought can properly be said to have an object at all. An assumption made by Berkeley and Hume, and sometimes also by Locke is that thinking consists in having images; and these images are treated as the immediate, and indeed, in a certain sense, the only, objects of thought. But if thinking is to consist in having images, then it must be assumed that these images are used symbolically, so that some account is required of their symbolic function. And this raises, among others, the problem of generality. For the majority of symbols are general in their reference.

Locke's attempt to deal with this problem of generality is to be found in his doctrine of abstract ideas. He holds that " words become general by being made the signs of general ideas "; and these general ideas he treats sometimes as composite pictures of the particular ideas which fall under them, but more often as abstractions from them, that is, as skeletons from which everything has been stripped away except some character, or set of characters, which is common to the particular ideas in question. This doctrine is attacked by Berkeley on the ground that every idea must have a single determinate set of qualities. It is impossible that an idea should combine inconsistent qualities; an idea of a triangle cannot be both equilateral and scalene : and it is impossible that it should be a mere skeleton; if we form the idea of a man it must be a man of some particular colour, shape and height; there can be no idea of motion " without a body moved and some determinate direction and velocity." Accordingly, Berkeley denies that there are abstract ideas. He does not deny that there are general ideas, but he thinks that what is called a general idea is a particular idea which is made general by being taken as a sign for other particular ideas. " When I demonstrate any proposition concerning triangles . . ., the particular triangle I consider, whether of this or that sort it matters not, doth equally stand for and represent all rectilinear triangles whatsoever, and is, in that sense, *universal*." With this view Hume enthusiastically concurs, saying that he looks upon it " to be one of the greatest and most valuable discoveries that have been made in late years in the republic of letters."

Now, in criticising Locke, Berkeley assumes that an abstract idea must be, if anything, an image, and part of his argument is that no image can be indeterminate. By this he may have meant only that every image has the particular character that it has; a tautology which Locke can hardly have intended to dispute. It is only if it is construed as an empirical statement about images that Berkeley's thesis is controversial; but in that case I think that it is mistaken. It may be assumed that Berkeley himself had strong powers of imagery, and no doubt the images that he formed were very highly articulated. But this is not universally true. My own images, for example, are seldom more than schematic; and in this sense they might very well be said to be indeterminate. Nevertheless, this does not justify Locke. For the strength of Berkeley's case against Locke does not turn upon this empirical question about images. The serious

mistake that Locke made was not empirical, but logical. It was
the mistake of supposing that the " generality " of an idea depended
on its intrinsic character. For the only way in which " ideas," as
images, come into this matter at all is that they may function as
symbols: and to say of a symbol that it is general, as opposed to
particular, is to say something not about its character but about its
use. Thus Berkeley is right to speak of " *universality* not consisting in the absolute, *positive* nature or conception of anything, but
in the *relation* it bears to the particulars signified or represented
by it." Furthermore, since an idea only becomes general by
functioning as a general symbol, it is also a mistake to say, as
Locke does, that " words become general by being made the signs
of general ideas." For, though it is possible that one symbol should
be used to stand for another, it cannot be true in general that what
makes anything a symbol is that it has some other symbol for its
referent; for in that case the second symbol will have to stand for
a third; and so *ad infinitum*. From this it follows that some
symbols must perform their function without the intervention of
other symbols, and, since words can do this just as well as images,
there is no need to reduplicate them by bringing in general ideas
at all. Thus Berkeley's main point against Locke is valid, and
his approach to the problem is correct. But what is required to
solve it is a satisfactory analysis of meaning; and this he does
not give.

THE PROBLEM OF PERCEPTION

Having introduced the convention that what is directly perceived
is an idea, Locke is then faced with the problem of showing how
these ideas are related to physical objects. This problem does not
arise for Reid, since he rejects Locke's convention, but it does arise
for Berkeley, Hume and Mill. The advantage of Reid's position
is that it allows him to say that physical objects are themselves
directly perceived, and so to give a very simple answer to the whole
philosophical question of " our knowledge of the external world."
But just because this type of answer is so simple, it is not philosophically illuminating. The point of introducing a notation such
as Locke's is that it serves to bring out the hidden complexity
of a certain class of propositions. It makes it possible to give an
analysis of propositions about physical objects which throws new
light on their meaning. In refusing to follow Locke, Reid is not in
error. He is merely less ambitious. It is perfectly legitimate to

take one's stand with commonsense. But to do so is not to solve
the problems that Locke raises; it is simply to avoid them.

At the same time, Locke's own treatment of this question is very
far from satisfactory. At some points, indeed, he writes as if he
also held that physical objects were directly perceived without
the intervention of ideas, but in the main he develops a causal
theory of perception. His physical objects are Newtonian particles
whose only intrinsic characteristics are the " primary qualities "
of solidity, extension, figure, motion and rest, and number. The
action of these bodies produces ideas in the percipient's mind; and
these ideas are of two sorts: ideas of primary qualities, which are
resemblances of the primary qualities themselves; and ideas of
secondary qualities, such as colour, taste and sound, which are not
resemblances of any physical qualities, but merely their effects. Thus
the secondary qualities of bodies are " nothing in the bodies themselves, but powers to produce various sensations in us by their
primary qualities, i.e., by the bulk, figure, texture and motion of
their insensible parts." From this it follows that physical objects
are themselves unobservable. Their existence is to be inferred
from the ideas which they cause, and these ideas, besides being
their effects, are to some extent also copies of them.

The obvious objection to this is that if anything that comes
before the mind is, by definition, an idea, then not only have we
no valid reason for believing in the existence of an object which is
not and never could be an idea, but even the conception of such an
object must be unintelligible to us. And this is substantially the
point that Berkeley makes. It is commonly said of him that he
denied the existence of matter, which does indeed sound paradoxical. But, as he himself insists, he does not wish to deny
anything that the ordinary man believes. He does not deny the
existence of tables or chairs or stones or trees or stars. What he
is denying is that their existence implies the existence of " material
substance " when this is defined in such a way that it becomes an
" unknown somewhat " which is not even in principle capable
of being perceived. His contention is that what are called physical
objects are nothing other than collections of sensible qualities; and
this again is not a factual statement but a statement about meaning.
What Berkeley's argument comes to, though he does not put it
in this form, is that the ordinary use of physical-object words like
" tree " or " stone " or " star " is to describe collections of
sensible qualities; in accordance with Locke's convention, these
sensible qualities are classified as ideas, and as such their existence

consists in their being perceived. Neither is there any justification for drawing a distinction in this context between ideas of primary and secondary qualities. For whatever ground there is for saying that ideas of secondary qualities exist only when they are perceived applies equally to ideas of primary qualities. And to assume that ideas of primary qualities are resemblances not of other ideas but of objects lying altogether beyond the reach of the senses is to accept a hypothesis which is not only arbitrary but totally unverifiable.

It seems to me that, as against Locke, Berkeley's argument is sound. But his own analysis of statements about physical objects has a consequence which *is* paradoxical. For if it is the case, as Berkeley seems to imply, that what I am saying when I assert the existence of a physical object which I am now perceiving is simply that I am sensing certain sensible qualities, then, since these sensible qualities do not exist when I am not perceiving them, neither presumably does the physical object. Now this conclusion is certainly not in accordance with commonsense, and Berkeley does not accept it. His way of escaping it is to say that the physical object may still exist as an idea in the mind of some other human being or as an idea in the mind of God. But this raises various difficulties. To begin with, it may be doubted whether the term " God " or the expression " the mind of another person " should have any meaning for Berkeley, since neither stands for an idea. Berkeley's answer to this is that, while we certainly do not have an idea of " spirit " in any sense which would imply that spirits came into the same category as physical objects, yet " in a large sense " we can be said to have it. We have a *notion* of spirit inasmuch as we understand the meaning of the word—" otherwise we could not affirm or deny anything of it." But in this sense Locke might equally well have claimed that he had a notion of matter. And though Berkeley can meet this by arguing that the " notion " of matter corresponds to nothing in our experience, whereas we do in self-knowledge have some experience of spirit, he certainly does not show that we have any such knowledge of ourselves as would provide a model for the spirit of God. But, even if it be allowed that the notion of God can be made intelligible on Berkeley's principles, the existence of God has still to be proved, and for this Berkeley has recourse to a causal argument. He postulates God as the unobserved cause of our ideas. But if the hypothesis that our ideas are caused by matter is to be rejected because it is unverifiable, so also is the hypothesis that they are caused by God. Berkeley's reason for adopting it is that he thinks that he has proved that one's ideas cannot be caused either by matter or by oneself, or by other ideas, so that only God remains; and he support this conclusion by the very weak argument that, since ideas are incorporeal, they must have an incorporeal cause. But the fact is that he is committed to holding, as I think correctly, that ideas cannot in this sense have any external cause at all.

Finally, it may be objected that even if the notion of God were intelligible, and even if his existence could be established, he still would not do the work that Berkeley requires of him. For the world which he keeps alive is not the world that I know; at least I can have no reason to suppose that it is. If Berkeley's arguments are sound I can identify a physical object at any given moment only with the ideas that I am having. And the fact that some other spirit may also be having an idea, which establishes the existence of what he understands by a physical object, is nothing to the purpose.

There is, however, another line of thought in Berkeley which would have enabled him, had he pursued it, to escape the more serious of these difficulties. For he sometimes makes the existence of a physical object depend not upon its actually being perceived, but upon the possibility of perceiving it. This suggestion is taken up by Mill, who defines matter as " Permanent Possibility of Sensation." Thus what constitutes the existence of a physical object is that in certain conditions, which must themselves be describable in sensory terms, certain sorts of sensations regularly occur, and for the truth of this hypothetical proposition it is not necessary that these conditions should actually obtain. The problem then is to show what are the particular features of our sensations that we draw upon for the conception of matter. In modern terms, it is the problem of giving rules for the translation of statements about physical objects into statements about sense-data. Mill is aware of this problem, but he does not solve it. It is not enough merely to invoke the laws of the association of ideas. All the same his treatment of the question is an important development of Berkeley's; and historically it provides the basis for the modern theory of phenomenalism.

To some extent, Mill's discovery was anticipated by Hume. The problem, as Hume saw it, was to give a critical analysis of the belief that the objects of perception have " a continued and distinct existence." He remarks that our natural inclination is to ascribe a continued and distinct existence to our sensible 'perceptions themselves, but " a very little reflection and philosophy is sufficient to make us see the fallacy of this opinion." An impression exists only in so far as it is actually experienced. That our perceptions themselves are fleeting is understood by philosophers; but rather than give up their faith in " continued and distinct existence " they invent external objects and ascribe it to them. But this " philosophical hypothesis of the double existence of perceptions and objects " has nothing to recommend it. " It contains all the difficulties of the vulgar system with some others that are peculiar to itself." For the philosophers' " objects " are either complete fictions or else perceptions in disguise. So long as they are distinguished from · perceptions, their existence is totally unverifiable, and it is only because they are tacitly identified with perceptions that they appeal to the imagination. But as perceptions they do not have a continued and distinct existence, and if they are not perceptions they are nothing at all. It remains then for Hume to show how we came to be deceived into thinking that our perceptions continue to exist when in fact they do not, and his answer to this is that, finding that similar impressions recur in similar situations, we are easily led into regarding them not as merely similar but as identical. In reality, my present perceptions of the table at which I am sitting are numerically different from those that I had an hour ago, but because they are qualitatively similar I look upon them not as new perceptions but as continuations of the old. The difficulty then arises that the continuity may be broken; during the past hour I have left the room and so ceased to have any perception of the table. But if I take my present perceptions of it to be identical with those that I had an hour ago, then I am implying that they persisted throughout the interval; and I try to get over the contradiction by assuming that they persisted unperceived. Thus, the difficulty is met by " supposing that these interrupted perceptions are connected by a real existence of which we are insensible." And it is in this way that we elevate our perceptions into " objects " which continue to exist when no one is perceiving them.

There are other relations, besides qualitative resemblance, which lead us to identify distinct perceptions and to invent fictitious perceptions to fill the gaps between them. Hume lists them under the two headings of constancy and coherence and analyses them in some detail. But what he does not see is that his analysis can be made to serve a different purpose. Instead of saying that our

belief in the continued and distinct existence of what we perceive
is an illusion, for which the constancy and coherence of our perceptions is responsible, he could, and I think should, have taken
these relations of constancy and coherence as the *criterion* of continued and distinct existence. That is, he might have said that
what was meant by the continued and distinct existence of an
object was simply that a certain series of perceptions was obtain-
able, and he could then have brought in constancy and coherence
as indications of the way in which the members of such series were
related. It is true that not all the members of these series would
be actual; some reference to possible perceptions would be needed.
But these possible perceptions would not be required to exist when
no one had them. Only the objects could be said to exist in this
sense, and to say that they existed would simply be equivalent to
saying that certain perceptions were possible. This is, indeed, to
read Mill into Hume; but it is, I think, the correct solution of " the
problem of perception," and it is very largely consistent with
Hume's argument.

<h2 style="text-align:center">HUME'S THEORY OF CAUSATION</h2>

Whatever may be the correct analysis of one's belief in the
existence of a physical object, something more is needed to justify
it than the occurrences of momentary impressions. It may be
true, in fact I think it is true, that in speaking about physical
objects we are referring only to classes of impressions; but the
members of such a class are not all " given " to us simultaneously
—indeed, many of them are never given at all. Of those that have
once been given, some are in a sense " restored " to us by memory,
but many are forgotten, and even if all were remembered they
would not furnish us with what we needed; for we can remember
only what we have in fact experienced, and the physical object is
supposed to be capable of existing unperceived. To complete the
picture we have to bring in *possible* impressions, and these must be
obtained by inference. Now, according to Hume, all inferences
which carry us beyond the present moment, other than the few
that depend only upon memory, are based upon the relation of
cause and effect. It is, therefore, of cardinal importance for the
theory of knowledge to discover what exactly this relation is.

Hume's method is to examine the idea of causation and then to
search for the impression from which it is derived. He begins by
remarking that the cause must be temporarily prior to the effect and
that it must be spatially and temporarily contiguous to it. But

that alone is not sufficient. " An object may be contiguous and prior to another, without being considered as its cause." To these two relations of contiguity and succession a third must be added, that of " Necessary Connection," which is much the most important of the three. But in what does this necessary connection consist? It is not a logical relation. When two objects, or events, are causally connected, it is false to say that one exists without the other, but it is not self-contradictory. " The contrary of every matter of fact is still possible : because it never can imply a contradiction, and is conceived by the mind with the same facility and distinctness, as if ever so conformable to reality." But neither does this idea of necessary connection correspond to anything observable. We may observe that one event immediately succeeds another, or that one object is contiguous to another, but we do not observe any relation of " power " or " force " between them. And the same applies to the impressions of inner sense. It might be thought that the process of volition gave us an immediate impression of necessity; but all that we can observe is that an act of will is followed by certain consequences; what these consequences are we discover by experience, and not by observing any " power " or " energy " in the act, considered by itself. Thus, whether we consider external or internal impressions, there is no single instance of objects standing in a causal relation where " we are able to perceive the tie by which they are united, or (are) able certainly to pronounce that there is a connection betwixt them." And if this is true of single instances, it remains true when the instances are multiplied. For " the repetition of perfectly similar instances can never *alone* give rise to an original idea."

But although the frequent observation of one type of object occurring in conjunction with another does not discover any new quality or relation in the objects themselves, it does produce a new impression in the mind. Because we have so often found that when one of these objects is presented to us the other is presented also, we form the habit of associating them. And it is in this determination, or habit, of our thought " to pass from causes to effects and from effects to causes, according to their experienced union " that Hume finds the source of our idea of necessary connection. All that is to be discovered in the objects themselves is constant conjunction. But this constant conjunction operates upon the mind " by means of custom," which links the two objects in the imagination. And so Hume reaches his definition of a cause as " An object precedent and contiguous to another, and so united

with it in the imagination, that the idea of one determines the mind
to form the idea of the other, and the impression of the one to form
a more lively idea of the other."

There are various defects in this analysis as it stands. To begin
with, Hume does not sufficiently distinguish between impressions
and objects. In the actual series of anyone's impressions there are
indeed a number of recurring patterns; but the repetitions are
neither so numerous nor so exact as Hume would have them. It
is only at a higher logical level, which we reach by classifying
impressions and imaginatively supplementing them, that we find
these constant conjunctions on which Hume's analysis depends.
But in constructing " objects " out of impressions we already make
use of what Hume would regard as relations of cause and effect.
I do not think that this is a very serious difficulty, but it suggests
that our habits of association are not formed in quite the simple
way that Hume describes. What is much more serious is his confusion of psychology and logic. For not only does he give an over-
simplified account of the way in which we actually come by our
idea of necessary connection, but he allows a misplaced element of
psychology to intrude into his definition of cause. It may indeed
be true that our belief that two objects are causally connected
arises in some way out of our imagination; but when we say that
one object, or event, is the cause of another, we are not thereby
referring to our imagination. We are not even saying anything
about our past observation of similar events. Our past observations
may be the ground of our belief in any such causal connection,
but they are not part of its analysis.

All this, however, does not diminish the force of the logical
points that Hume succeeds in making. It is very important to
show, as he does, that there can be no possibility of *deducing* the
occurrence of one event from the occurrence of another. That the
events are connected is a matter of fact which is in no way necessary
a priori. Nor is there any other kind of necessity which this
connection could exemplify. It is not simply that we look to the
objects for an impression of necessity, and fail to find it; it is that
there is nothing that would count as finding such an impression.
Once logical necessity is eliminated, all that can properly be meant
by saying that two objects are necessarily connected is that one is
not in fact to be found without the possibility of finding the other.
And this conclusion is quite independent of any psychological theory
about the nature of experience. Whatever the nature of our
experience, it must still remain true that when two objects or events

are spatio-temporally distinct, the relations which obtain between them are contingent and not necessary.

It seems then that the only reason we can have for supposing that any two objects are connected is that experience shows them to be so. We may indeed arrive at such conclusions, antecedently to our experience of them, by deducing them from valid theories; but then our only reason for holding these theories to be valid is that they conform to our experience. Any given moment, however, what our experience tells us is only, at best, that certain relations between objects have consistently obtained in the past; and the question arises whether this is any guarantee that they will hold good also in the future. As Hume puts it, the question is whether we are justified in believing " that instances of which we have had no experience, must resemble those of which we have had experience, and that the course of nature continues always uniformly the same." He remarks correctly that this principle cannot be demonstrated. That the course of nature will change in this or that respect is a proposition which, whether or not it be true, is certainly not self-contradictory. But neither can the principle be shown to be probable. For " probability is founded on the presumption of a resemblance betwixt those objects of which we have had experience and those of which we have had none; and therefore 'tis impossible this presumption can arise from probability." But if this principle, which is the basis of all our reasoning about matters of fact, can neither be demonstrated nor even shown to be probable, what justification have we for accepting it? Does not this show that any belief which goes beyond the immediate evidence of the senses or of memory is fundamentally irrational?

This problem, which Hume was the first to raise, has come to be known as the Problem of Induction, and, although a great deal of work has since been done on it, it remains to this day very much in the state which Hume left it. In my own view, his arguments are unanswerable. It seems to me quite clear that no inductive principle can be known *a priori*, and any attempt to justify inductive procedure by arguing from experience will obviously be circular, as some inductive principle will always be presupposed. One inductive hypothesis can indeed be used to justify another, but there can be no general justification of induction, any more than there can be a general justification of memory. So far, I think that Hume is clearly right. On the other hand, I think that he is wrong in making this a ground for scepticism. Beliefs which are based upon induction are not irrational in the sense that there is some standard of rationality which they fail to satisfy. For to say that a belief is rational is to say that there is good evidence for it, and in the case of any belief about a matter of fact what counts as good evidence is inductive evidence. So to raise the general question whether inductive evidence is good, is to ask whether what is counted as good evidence really is good evidence; and I do not think that this question is significant.

THE PROBLEM OF THE SELF

It is assumed by both Locke and Berkeley that a man's " self " is an immaterial substance, and Locke explicitly claims that he has an intuitive knowledge of his own existence, meaning by this the existence of his self. Here again, however, Hume shows himself the more consistent empiricist. After remarking that " there are some philosophers who imagine we are every moment intimately conscious of what we call our Self . . . and are certain, beyond the evidence of a demonstration, of its perfect identity and simplicity,'' he once more raises the question from what impression this idea of self can be derived. And his answer is that there is no such impression, if only for the reason that '' there is no impression constant and invariable.'' Further, since all our particular perceptions are " different and distinguishable and separable from each other,'' they all " may exist separately, and have no need of anything to support their existence.'' " For my part,'' he continues, '' when I enter most intimately into what I call *myself*, I always stumble on some particular perception or other, of heat or cold, light or shade, pain or pleasure. I never catch *myself* at any time without a perception, and never can observe anything but the perception.'' He allows that another philosopher may be different from him in this respect. " He may, perhaps, perceive something simple and continued, which he calls *himself*.'' But this is not a serious concession. For Hume concludes that " setting aside some metaphysicians of this kind, I may venture to affirm of the rest of mankind, that they are nothing but a bundle or collection of different perceptions, which succeed each other with an inconceivable rapidity, and are in a perpetual flux and movement.''

Here again I think that Hume is right; but here again he weakens his case by presenting a logical argument as if it were empirical. For the point is not just that the vast majority of men are unable to perform the difficult feat of experiencing themselves as substances. It is rather that such a feat is not conceivable. There is nothing that would count as " stumbling upon " oneself, as opposed to some particular perception. The idea of self as substance is to be discarded not because it is uncommonly difficult to verify in practice but because it is in principle unverifiable.

On the other hand, it is not enough merely to say that the self is a " bundle of perceptions." We want to know how such a bundle holds together; in other words, how a series of perceptions must be related for them to constitute a single self. And at this point Hume, in the appendix to the Treatise, confesses himself to be at a loss. The question is taken up again by Mill, whose views on the nature of the mind are very much the same as Hume's. He improves on Hume by bringing in *possible* perceptions or feelings, and he makes an attempt to deal with the perplexing problem of " our knowledge of other minds." But when he comes to the question of accounting for self-consciousness upon his principles, he weakly resigns himself to talking of a " finally inexplicable fact." What would seem the most promising solution is to try to define personal identity in terms of memory; but it may be that the question is best approached by way of a logical analysis of the use of proper names. Of all the problems of philosophy, this is one of the most difficult. But I think that it is soluble, although I do not think that it has yet been solved.

A. J. AYER.

JOHN LOCKE

*Born in Somerset 1632. Educated at West-
minster School and Christ Church, Oxford.
Senior Student of Christ Church, Oxford,
1659-1684. Fellow of the Royal Society 1668.
Physician and Secretary to first Earl of Shaftesbury 1666-1682. Lived in Exile in Holland
1683-1689. Commissioner of Appeals 1690.
Died 1704.*

Philosophical works include Essay Concerning Human Understanding, *published in* 1690,
three Letters Concerning Toleration, 1689 *and*
1690, Two Treatises of Government, 1690, *and*
An Examination of Malebranche's Opinion of
Seeing all things in God, *published posthumously in* 1706.

IN THE VERSION which follows, the *Essay Concerning Human Understanding* has been reduced to rather less than a quarter of its original length. The numbering shows where whole paragraphs and chapters have been omitted, but for typographical reasons nothing has been done to mark the numerous excisions which occur within a paragraph. A few very slight stylistic alterations have been made to ensure the smooth running of the text, as it is here presented. The chapter and paragraph headings are Locke's own.

In its original form the *Essay* is a very repetitious and discursive work, and it may be hoped that this abridgement of it contains all that is essential to the main argument.

AN ESSAY
CONCERNING HUMAN UNDERSTANDING

BOOK I

OF INNATE NOTIONS

I—INTRODUCTION. II—NO INNATE PRINCIPLES IN THE MIND.
III—NO INNATE PRACTICAL PRINCIPLES. IV—OTHER CONSIDERA-
TIONS CONCERNING INNATE PRINCIPLES

CHAPTER I

INTRODUCTION

1. *An inquiry into the understanding, pleasant and useful.*—
Since it is the understanding that sets man above the rest of
sensible beings, and gives him all the advantage and dominion
which he has over them, it is certainly a subject, even for its
nobleness, worth our labour to inquire into. The understanding,
like the eye, whilst it makes us see and perceive all other things,
takes no notice of itself; and it requires art and pains to set it at
a distance, and make it its own object. But whatever be the
difficulties that lie in the way of this inquiry, whatever it be that
keeps us so much in the dark to ourselves, sure I am that all the
light we can let in upon our own minds, all the acquaintance we
can make with our own understandings, will not only be very
pleasant, but bring us great advantage in directing our thoughts
in the search of other things.

2. *Design.*—This therefore being my purpose, to inquire into
the original, certainty, and extent of human knowledge, together
with the grounds and degrees of belief, opinion and assent, I
shall not at present meddle with the physical consideration of the
mind, or trouble myself to examine wherein its essence consists,

or by what motions of our spirits, or alterations of our bodies, we come to have any sensation by our organs, or any ideas in our understandings; and whether those ideas do, in their formation, any or all of them, depend on matter or no: these are speculations which, however curious and entertaining, I shall decline, as lying out of my way in the design I am now upon. It shall suffice to my present purpose, to consider the discerning faculties of a man as they are employed about the objects which they have to do with; and I shall imagine I have not wholly misemployed myself in the thoughts I shall have on this occasion, if, in this historical, plain method, I can give any account of the ways whereby our understandings come to attain those notions of things we have, and can set down any measures of the certainty of our knowledge, or the grounds of those persuasions which are to be found amongst men, so various, different, and wholly contradictory; and yet asserted somewhere or other with such assurance, and confidence, that he that shall take a view of the opinions of mankind, observe their opposition, and at the same time consider the fondness and devotion wherewith they are embraced, the resolution and eagerness wherewith they are maintained, may perhaps have reason to suspect that either there is no such thing as truth at all, or that mankind hath no sufficient means to attain a certain knowledge of it.

3. *Method.*—It is therefore worth while to search out the bounds between opinion and knowledge, and examine by what measures, in things whereof we have no certain knowledge, we ought to regulate our assent, and moderate our persuasions. In order whereunto, I shall pursue this following method: —

First. I shall inquire into the original of those ideas, notions, or whatever else you please to call them, which a man observes, and is conscious to himself he has in his mind, and the ways whereby the understanding comes to be furnished with them.

Secondly. I shall endeavour to show what knowledge the understanding hath by those ideas, and the certainty, evidence, and extent of it.

Thirdly. I shall make some inquiry into the nature and grounds of faith or opinion; whereby I mean, that assent which we give to any proposition as true, of whose truth yet we have no certain knowledge: and here we shall have occasion to examine the reasons and degrees of assent.

4. *Useful to know the extent of our comprehension.*—If by this inquiry into the nature of the understanding, I can discover

the powers thereof, how far they reach, to what things they are in any degree proportionate, and where they fail us, I suppose it may be of use to prevail with the busy mind of man to be more cautious in meddling with things exceeding its comprehension, to stop when it is at the utmost extent of its tether, and to sit down in a quiet ignorance of those things which, upon examination, are found to be beyond the reach of our capacities. We should not then, perhaps, be so forward, out of an affectation of an universal knowledge, to raise questions, and perplex ourselves and others with disputes, about things to which our understandings are not suited, and of which we cannot frame in our minds any clear or distinct perceptions, or whereof (as it has, perhaps, too often happened) we have not any notions at all. If we can find out how far the understanding can extend its view, how far it has faculties to attain certainty, and in what cases it can only judge and guess, we may learn to content ourselves with what is attainable by us in this state.

6. *Knowledge of our capacity a cure of scepticism and idleness.* —When we know our own strength, we shall the better know what to undertake with hopes of success; and when we have well surveyed the powers of our own minds, and made some estimate what we may expect from them, we shall not be inclined either to sit still, and not set our thoughts on work at all, in despair of knowing anything; nor, on the other side, question everything, and disclaim all knowledge, because some things are not to be understood. It is of great use to the sailor to know the length of his line, though he cannot with it fathom all the depths of the ocean; it is well he knows that it is long enough to reach the bottom at such places as are necessary to direct his voyage, and caution him against running upon shoals that may ruin him. Our business here is not to know all things, but those which concern our conduct. If we can find out those measures whereby a rational creature, put in that state which man is in in this world, may and ought to govern his opinions and actions depending thereon, we need not be troubled that some other things escape our knowledge.

7. *Occasion of this Essay.*—This was that which gave the first rise to this Essay concerning the Understanding. For I thought that the first step towards satisfying several inquiries the mind of man was very apt to run into, was, to take a survey of our own understandings, examine our own powers, and see to what things they were adapted. Till that was done, I suspected we began at

the wrong end, and in vain sought for satisfaction in a quiet and sure possession of truths that most concerned us, whilst we let loose our thoughts into the vast ocean of being; as if all that boundless extent were the natural and undoubted possession of our understandings, wherein there was nothing exempt from its decisions, or that escaped its comprehension. Thus men, extending their inquiries beyond their capacities, and letting their thoughts wander into those depths where they can find no sure footing, it is no wonder that they raise questions and multiply disputes, which, never coming to any clear resolution, are proper only to continue and increase their doubts, and to confirm them at last in perfect scepticism. Whereas, were the capacities of our understandings well considered, the extent of our knowledge once discovered, and the horizon found which sets the bounds between the enlightened and dark parts of things — between what is and what is not comprehensible by us — men would, perhaps, with less scruple, acquiesce in the avowed ignorance of the one, and employ their thoughts and discourse with more advantage and satisfaction in the other.

8. *What " idea " stands for.*—Thus much I thought necessary to say concerning the occasion of this inquiry into human understanding. But, before I proceed on to what I have thought on this subject, I must here, in the entrance, beg pardon of my reader for the frequent use of the word " idea " which he will find in the following treatise. It being that term which, I think, serves best to stand for whatsoever is the object of the understanding when a man thinks, I have used it to express whatever is meant by phantasm, notion, species, or whatever it is which the mind can be employed about in thinking; and I could not avoid frequently using it.

I presume it will be easily granted me, that there are such *ideas* in men's minds. Every one is conscious of them in himself; and men's words and actions will satisfy him that they are in others.

Our first inquiry, then, shall be, how they come into the mind.

CHAPTER II

NO INNATE PRINCIPLES IN THE MIND

1. *The way shown how we come by any knowledge, sufficient to prove it not innate.*—It is an established opinion among some men, that there are in the understanding certain innate principles;

some primary notions, characters, as it were, stamped upon the
mind of man, which the soul receives in its very first being, and
brings into the world with it. It would be sufficient to convince
unprejudiced readers of the falseness of this supposition, if I should
only show (as I hope I shall in the following parts of this discourse)
how men, barely by the use of their natural faculties, may attain
to all the knowledge they have, without the help of any innate
impressions, and may arrive at certainty without any such original
notions or principles.

2. *General assent the great argument.*—There is nothing more
commonly taken for granted, than that there are certain principles,
both speculative and practical (for they speak of both), universally
agreed upon by all mankind; which therefore, they argue, must
needs be constant impressions which the souls of men receive in
their first beings, and which they bring into the world with them,
as necessarily and really as they do any of their inherent faculties.

3. *Universal consent proves nothing innate.*—This argument,
drawn from universal consent, has this misfortune in it, that if
it were true in matter of fact, that there were certain truths wherein
all mankind agreed, it would not prove them innate, if there can
be any other way shown, how men may come to that universal
agreement in the things they do consent in; which I presume may
be done.

4. " *What is, is* "; and, " *It is impossible for the same thing to
be, and not to be,*" *not universally assented to.*—But, which is
worse, this argument of universal consent, which is made use of
to prove innate principles, seems to me a demonstration that there
are none such; because there are none to which all mankind give
an universal assent. I shall begin with the speculative, and
instance in those magnified principles of demonstration: " Whatsoever is, is "; and, " It is impossible for the same thing to be,
and not to be," which, of all others, I think, have the most allowed
title to innate. These have so settled a reputation of maxims
universally received, that it will, no doubt, be thought strange if
anyone should seem to question it. But yet I take liberty to say,
that these propositions are so far from having an universal assent,
that there are a great part of mankind to whom they are not so
much as known.

5. *Not on the mind naturally imprinted, because not known to
children, idiots, etc.*—For it is evident that all children and idiots
have not the least apprehension or thought of them; and the want
of that is enough to destroy that universal assent, which must

needs be the necessary concomitant of all innate truths: it seeming to me near a contradiction to say, that there are truths imprinted on the soul which it perceives or understands not; imprinting, if it signify anything, being nothing else but the making certain truths to be perceived. For to imprint anything on the mind, without the mind's perceiving it, seems to me hardly intelligible. If therefore children and idiots have souls, have minds, with those impressions upon them, they must unavoidably perceive them, and necessarily know and assent to these truths; which since they do not, it is evident that there are no such impressions. For if they are not notions naturally imprinted, how can they be innate? And if they are notions imprinted, how can they be unknown? To say, a notion is imprinted on the mind, and yet at the same time to say that the mind is ignorant of it, and never yet took notice of it, is to make this impression nothing. No proposition can be said to be in the mind which it never yet knew, which it was never yet conscious of.

6. *That men know them when they come to the use of reason, answered.*—To avoid this, it is usually answered, that all men know and assent to them, when they come to the use of reason; and this is enough to prove them innate. I answer,

7. Doubtful expressions, that have scarce any signification, go for clear reasons to those who, being prepossessed, take not the pains to examine even what they themselves say. For, to apply this answer with any tolerable sense to our present purpose, it must signify one of these two things; either, that, as soon as men come to the use of reason, these supposed native inscriptions come to be known and observed by them; or else, that the use and exercise of men's reasons assists them in the discovery of these principles, and certainly makes them known to them.

8. *If reason discovered them, that would not prove them innate.* —If they mean that by the use of reason men may discover these principles, and that this is sufficient to prove them innate, their way of arguing will stand thus: viz., That, whatever truths reason can certainly discover to us, and make us firmly assent to, those are all naturally imprinted on the mind; since that universal assent which is made the mark of them, amounts to no more but this— that by the use of reason we are capable to come to a certain knowledge of, and assent to, them; and by this means there will be no difference between the maxims of the mathematicians and theorems they deduce from them: all must be equally allowed innate, they being all discoveries made by the use of reason, and

truths that a rational creature may certainly come to know, if he apply his thoughts rightly that way.

9. *It is false that reason discovers them.*—But how can these men think the use of reason necessary to discover principles that are supposed innate, when reason (if we may believe them) is nothing else but the faculty of deducing unknown truths from principles or propositions that are already known? That certainly can never be thought innate which we have need of reason to discover, unless, as I have said, we will have all the certain truths that reason ever teaches us to be innate. We may as well think the use of reason necessary to make our eyes discover visible objects, as that there should be need of reason, or the exercise thereof, to make the understanding see what is originally engraven in it, and cannot be in the understanding before it be perceived by it. So that to make reason discover those truths thus imprinted, is to say, that the use of reason discovers to a man what he knew before; and if men have those innate impressed truths originally, and before the use of reason, and yet are always ignorant of them till they come to the use of reason, it is in effect to say that men know, and know them not, at the same time.

11. Those who will take the pains to reflect with a little attention on the operations of the understanding, will find that this ready assent of the mind to some truths, depends not either on native inscription, or the use of reason; but on a faculty of the mind quite distinct from both of them, as we shall see hereafter. Reason therefore having nothing to do in procuring our assent to these maxims, if by saying, that "men know and assent to them when they come to the use of reason," be meant that the use of reason assists us in the knowledge of these maxims, it is utterly false; and, were it true, would prove them not to be innate.

15. *The steps by which the mind attains several truths.*—The senses at first let in particular ideas, and furnish the yet empty cabinet: and the mind by degrees growing familiar with some of them, they are lodged in the memory, and names got to them. Afterwards the mind, proceeding farther, abstracts them, and by degrees learns the use of general names. In this manner the mind comes to be furnished with ideas and language, the materials about which to exercise its discursive faculty; and the use of reason becomes daily more visible, as these materials, that give it employment, increase. But though the having of general ideas, and the use of general words and reason, usually grow together, yet I see not how this any way proves them innate.

17. *Assenting as soon as proposed and understood, proves them not innate.*—This evasion therefore of general assent when men come to the use of reason, failing as it does, and leaving no difference between those supposed innate and other truths that are afterwards acquired and learnt, men have endeavoured to secure an universal assent to those they call maxims, by saying, they are generally assented to as soon as proposed and the terms they are proposed in understood: seeing all men, even children, as soon as they hear and understand the terms, assent to these propositions, they think it is sufficient to prove them innate.

18. In answer to this, I demand whether ready assent, given to a proposition upon first hearing and understanding the terms, be a certain mark of an innate principle ? If it be not, such a general assent is in vain urged as a proof of them: if it be said, that it is a mark of innate, they must then allow all such propositions to be innate which are generally assented to as soon as heard whereby they will find themselves plentifully stored with innate principles. Universal and ready assent upon hearing and understanding the terms, is, I grant, a mark of self-evidence: but self-evidence, depending not on innate impressions, but on something else, belongs to several propositions, which nobody was yet so extravagant as to pretend to be innate.

CHAPTER III

NO INNATE PRACTICAL PRINCIPLES

1. *No moral principles so clear and so generally received as the fore-mentioned speculative maxims.*—If those speculative maxims whereof we discoursed in the foregoing chapter, have not an actual universal assent from all mankind, as we there proved, it is much more visible concerning practical principles, that they come short of an universal reception; and I think it will be hard to instance any one moral rule which can pretend to so general and ready an assent as, " What is, is," or to be so manifest a truth as this, " That it is impossible for the same thing to be, and not to be." Whereby it is evident that they are farther removed from a title to be innate; and the doubt of their being native impressions on the mind is stronger against these moral principles than the other. Not that it brings their truth at all in question. They are equally true, though not equally evident. Those

speculative maxims carry their own evidence with them; but moral principles require reasoning and discourse, and some exercise of the mind, to discover the certainty of their truth.

CHAPTER IV

OTHER CONSIDERATIONS CONCERNING INNATE PRINCIPLES BOTH SPECULATIVE AND PRACTICAL

1. *Principles not innate, unless their ideas be innate.*—Had those who would persuade us that there are innate principles, not taken them together in gross, but considered separately the parts out of which those propositions are made, they would not, perhaps, have been so forward to believe they were innate; since, if the ideas which made up those truths were not, it was impossible that the propositions made up of them should be, innate, or our knowledge of them be born with us. For if the ideas be not innate, there was a time when the mind was without those principles; and then they will not be innate, but be derived from some other original: for where the ideas themselves are not, there can be no knowledge, no assent, no mental or verbal propositions about them.

2. *Ideas, especially those belonging to principles, not born with children.*—If we will attentively consider new-born children, we shall have little reason to think that they bring many ideas into the world with them: for, bating, perhaps, some faint ideas of hunger, and thirst, and warmth, and some pains which they may have felt in the womb, there is not the least appearance of any settled ideas at all in them; especially of ideas answering the terms which make up those universal propositions that are esteemed innate principles. One may perceive how, by degrees, afterwards, ideas come into their minds; and that they get no more, nor no other, than what experience, and the observation of things that come in their way, furnish them with; which might be enough to satisfy us that they are not original characters stamped on the mind.

3. " It is impossible for the same thing to be, and not to be," is certainly (if there be any such) an innate principle. But can anyone think, or will anyone say, that impossibility and identity are two innate ideas? Are they such as all mankind have, and bring into the world with them? And are they those that are the first in children, and antecedent to all acquired ones? If they are innate, they must needs be so. Hath a child an idea of

impossibility and identity before it has of white or black, sweet or bitter?

22. *Difference of men's discoveries depends upon the different application of their faculties.*—To conclude: some ideas forwardly offer themselves to all men's understandings; some sorts of truths result from any ideas as soon as the mind puts them into propositions; other truths require a train of ideas placed in order, a due comparing of them, and deductions made with attention, before they can be discovered and assented to. Some of the first sort, because of their general and easy reception, have been mistaken for innate; but the truth is, ideas and notions are no more born with us than arts and sciences; though some of them, indeed, offer themselves to our faculties more readily than others, and therefore are more generally received.

24. *Whence the opinion of innate principles.*—When men have found some general propositions that could not be doubted of as soon as understood, it was, I know, a short and easy way to conclude them innate. This being once received, it eased the lazy from the pains of search, and stopped the inquiry of the doubtful, concerning all that was once styled innate; and it was of no small advantage to those who affected to be masters and teachers, to make this the principle of principles—that principles must not be questioned; for, having once established this tenet—that there are innate principles, it put their followers upon a necessity of receiving some doctrines as such; which was to take them off from the use of their own reason and judgment, and put them upon believing and taking them upon trust, without farther examination; in which posture of blind credulity, they might be more easily governed by, and made useful to, some sort of men who had the skill and office to principle and guide them. Nor is it a small power it gives one man over another, to have the authority to be the dictator of principles, and teacher of unquestionable truths; and to make a man swallow that for an innate principle which may serve to his purpose who teacheth them. Whereas had they examined the ways whereby men came to the knowledge of many universal truths, they would have found them to result in the minds of men from the being of things themselves, when duly considered; and that they were discovered by the application of those faculties that were fitted by nature to receive and judge of them, when duly employed about them.

25. *Conclusion.*—To show how the understanding proceeds herein, is the design of the following discourse; which I shall

proceed to, when I have first premised, that hitherto, to clear my way to those foundations which I conceive are the only true ones whereon to establish those notions we can have of our own knowledge, it hath been necessary for me to give an account of the reasons I had to doubt of innate principles: and since the arguments which are against them, do, some of them, rise from common received opinions, I have been forced to take several things for granted, which is hardly avoidable to anyone whose task it is to show the falsehood or improbability of any tenet; it happening in controversial discourses, as it does in assaulting of towns; where, if the ground be but firm whereon the batteries are erected, there is no further inquiry of whom it is borrowed, nor whom it belongs to, so it affords but a fit rise for the present purpose. But in the future part of this discourse, designing to raise an edifice uniform and consistent with itself, as far as my own experience and observation will assist me, I hope to erect it on such a basis, that I shall not need to shore it up with props and buttresses, leaning on borrowed or begged foundations; or, at least, if mine prove a castle in the air, I will endeavour it shall be all of a piece, and hang together. Wherein I warn the reader not to expect undeniable cogent demonstrations, unless I may be allowed the privilege, not seldom assumed by others, to take my principles for granted; and then, I doubt not, but I can demonstrate too. All that I shall say for the principles I proceed on, is, that I can only appeal to men's own unprejudiced experience and observation, whether they be true or no; and this is enough for a man who professes no more than to lay down candidly and freely his own conjectures concerning a subject lying somewhat in the dark, without any other design than an unbiassed inquiry after truth.

BOOK II

OF IDEAS

CHAPTER I

OF IDEAS IN GENERAL, AND THEIR ORIGINAL

1. *Idea is the object of thinking.*—Every man being conscious to himself, that he thinks, and that which his mind is applied about, whilst thinking, being the ideas that are there, it is past doubt that men have in their mind several ideas, such as are those expressed by the words, "whiteness," "hardness," "sweetness," "thinking," "motion," "man," "elephant," "army," "drunkenness," and others. It is in the first place then to be inquired, How he comes by them? I know it is a received doctrine, that men have native ideas and original characters stamped upon their minds in their very first being. This opinion I have at large examined already; and, I suppose, what I have said in the foregoing book will be much more easily admitted, when I have shown whence the understanding may get all the ideas it has, and by what ways and degrees they may come into the mind; for which I shall appeal to every one's own observation and experience.

42

2. *All ideas come from sensation or reflection.*—Let us then suppose the mind to be, as we say, white paper, void of all characters, without any ideas; how comes it to be furnished? Whence comes it by that vast store, which the busy and boundless fancy of man has painted on it with an almost endless variety? Whence has it all the materials of reason and knowledge? To this I answer, in one word, From experience : in that all our knowledge is founded, and from that it ultimately derives itself. Our observation, employed either about external sensible objects, or about the internal operations of our minds, perceived and reflected on by ourselves, is that which supplies our understandings with all the materials of thinking. These two are the fountains of knowledge, from whence all the ideas we have, or can naturally have, do spring.

3. *The object of sensation one source of ideas.*—First. Our senses, conversant about particular sensible objects, do convey into the mind several distinct perceptions of things, according to those various ways wherein those objects do affect them; and thus we come by those ideas we have of yellow, white, heat, cold, soft, hard, bitter, sweet, and all those which we call sensible qualities; which when I say the senses convey into the mind, I mean, they from external objects convey into the mind what produces there those perceptions. This great source of most of the ideas we have, depending wholly upon our senses, and derived by them to the understanding, I call " sensation."

4. *The operations of our minds the other source of them.*— Secondly. The other fountain, from which experience furnisheth the understanding with ideas, is the perception of the operations of our own minds within us, as it is employed about the ideas it has got; which operations, when the soul comes to reflect on and consider, do furnish the understanding with another set of ideas which could not be had from things without; and such are perception, thinking, doubting, believing, reasoning, knowing, willing, and all the different actings of our own minds; which we, being conscious of, and observing in ourselves, do from these receive into our understanding as distinct ideas, as we do from bodies affecting our senses. This source of ideas every man has wholly in himself; and though it be not sense as having nothing to do with external objects, yet it is very like it, and might properly enough be called " internal sense." But as I call the other " sensation," so I call this " reflection," the ideas it affords being such only as the mind gets by reflecting on its own operations

within itself. By reflection, then, in the following part of this discourse, I would be understood to mean that notice which the mind takes of its own operations, and the manner of them, by reason whereof there come to be ideas of these operations in the understanding. These two, I say, viz., external material things as the objects of sensation, and the operations of our own minds within as the objects of reflection, are, to me, the only originals from whence all our ideas take their beginnings. The term " operations " here, I use in a large sense, as comprehending not barely the actions of the mind about its ideas, but some sort of passions arising sometimes from them, such as is the satisfaction or uneasiness arising from any thought.

5. *All our ideas are of the one or the other of these.*—The understanding seems to me not to have the least glimmering of any ideas which it doth not receive from one of these two. External objects furnish the mind with the ideas of sensible qualities, which are all those different perceptions they produce in us; and the mind furnishes the understanding with ideas of its own operations.

These, when we have taken a full survey of them, and their several modes, combinations, and relations, we shall find to contain all our whole stock of ideas; and that we have nothing in our minds which did not come in one of these two ways. Let any one examine his own thoughts, and thoroughly search into his understanding, and then let him tell me, whether all the original ideas he has there, are any other than of the objects of his senses, or of the operations of his mind considered as objects of his reflection; and how great a mass of knowledge soever he imagines to be lodged there, he will, upon taking a strict view, see that he has not any idea in his mind but what one of these two hath imprinted, though perhaps with infinite variety compounded and enlarged by the understanding, as we shall see hereafter.

6. *Observable in children.*—He that attentively considers the state of a child at his first coming into the world, will have little reason to think him stored with plenty of ideas that are to be the matter of his future knowledge. It is by degrees he comes to be furnished with them; and though the ideas of obvious and familiar qualities imprint themselves before the memory begins to keep a register of time and order, yet it is often so late before some unusual qualities come in the way, that there are few men that cannot recollect the beginning of their acquaintance with them; and, if it were worth while, no doubt a child might be so ordered as to have but a very few even of the ordinary ideas till he were

grown up to a man. But all that are born into the world being surrounded with bodies that perpetually and diversely affect them, variety of ideas, whether care be taken about it, or no, are imprinted on the minds of children. Light and colours are busy at hand everywhere when the eye is but open; sounds and some tangible qualities fail not to solicit their proper senses, and force an entrance to the mind; but yet I think it will be granted easily, that if a child were kept in a place where he never saw any other but black and white till he were a man, he would have no more ideas of scarlet or green, than he that from his childhood never tasted an oyster or a pine-apple has of those particular relishes.

7. *Men are differently furnished with these according to the different objects they converse with.*—Men then come to be furnished with fewer or more simple ideas from without, according as the objects they converse with afford greater or less variety; and from the operations of their minds within, according as they more or less reflect on them. For, though he that contemplates the operations of his mind cannot but have plain and clear ideas of them; yet, unless he turn his thoughts that way, and considers them attentively, he will no more have clear and distinct ideas of all the operations of his mind, and all that may be observed therein, than he will have all the particular ideas of any landscape, or of the parts and motions of a clock, who will not turn his eyes to it, and with attention heed all the parts of it. The picture or clock may be so placed that they may come in his way every day; but yet he will have but a confused idea of all the parts they are made of, till he applies himself with attention to consider them each in particular.

8. *Ideas of reflection later, because they need attention.*—And hence we see the reason why it is pretty late before most children get ideas of the operations of their own minds; and some have not any very clear or perfect ideas of the greatest part of them all their lives:—because, though they pass there continually, yet like floating visions, they make not deep impressions enough to leave in the mind clear, distinct, lasting ideas, till the understanding turns inwards upon itself, reflects on its own operations, and makes them the object of its own contemplation.

9. *The soul begins to have ideas when it begins to perceive.*—To ask, at what time a man has first any ideas, is to ask when he begins to perceive; having ideas, and perception, being the same thing. I know it is an opinion, that the soul always thinks; and that it has the actual perception of ideas within itself constantly,

as long as it exists; and that actual thinking is as inseparable from the soul, as actual extension is from the body: which, if true, to inquire after the beginning of a man's ideas is the same as to inquire after the beginning of his soul. For, by this account, soul and its ideas, as body and its extension, will begin to exist both at the same time.

10. *The soul thinks not always; for this wants proofs.*—But whether the soul be supposed to exist antecedent to, or coeval with, or some time after, the first rudiments or organisation, or the beginnings of life in the body, I leave to be disputed by those who have better thought of that matter. I confess myself to have one of those dull souls that doth not perceive itself always to contemplate ideas; nor can it conceive it any more necessary for the soul always to think, than for the body always to move.

18. *How knows anyone that the soul always thinks? For if it be not a self-evident proposition, it needs proof.*—I would be glad also to learn from these men, who so confidently pronounce that the human soul, or, which is all one, that a man, always thinks, how they come to know it; nay, how they come to know that they themselves think, when they themselves do not perceive it? This, I am afraid, is to be sure without proofs, and to know without perceiving. It is, I suspect, a confused notion taken up to serve an hypothesis; and none of those clear truths that either their own evidence forces us to admit, or common experience makes it impudence to deny. For the most that can be said of it is, that it is possible the soul may always think, but not always retain it in memory; and I say, it is as possible that the soul may not always think, and much more probable that it should sometimes not think, than that it should often think, and that a long while together, and not be conscious to itself, the next moment after, that it had thought.

23. If it shall be demanded, then, when a man begins to have any ideas? I think, the true answer is, When he first has any sensation. For since there appear not to be any ideas in the mind before the senses have conveyed any in, I conceive that ideas in the understanding are coeval with sensation; which is such an impression or motion made in some part of the body as produces some perception in the understanding. It is about these impressions made on our senses by outward objects, that the mind seems first to employ itself in such operations as we call " perception," " remembering," " consideration," " reasoning," etc.

24. *The original of all our knowledge.*—In time the mind comes

to reflect on its own operations about the ideas got by sensation, and thereby stores itself with a new set of ideas, which I call "ideas of reflection."

25. *In the reception of simple ideas, the understanding is for the most part passive.*—In this part the understanding is merely passive; and whether or not it will have these beginnings and, as it were, materials of knowledge, is not in its own power. For the objects of our senses do many of them obtrude their particular ideas upon our minds, whether we will or no; and the operations of our minds will not let us be without at least some obscure notions of them. No man can be wholly ignorant of what he does when he thinks. These simple ideas, when offered to the mind, the understanding can no more refuse to have, nor alter when they are imprinted, nor blot them out and make new ones itself, than a mirror can refuse, alter or obliterate the images or ideas, which the objects set before it do therein produce. As the bodies that surround us do diversely affect our organs, the mind is forced to receive the impressions, and cannot avoid the perception of those ideas that are annexed to them.

CHAPTER II

OF SIMPLE IDEAS

1. *Uncompounded appearances.*—The better to understand the nature, manner, and extent of our knowledge, one thing is carefully to be observed concerning the ideas we have; and that is, that some of them are simple, and some complex.

Though the qualities that affect our senses are, in the things themselves, so united and blended that there is no separation, no distance between them; yet it is plain the ideas they produce in the mind enter by the senses simple and unmixed. For though the sight and touch often take in from the same object at the same time different ideas — as a man sees at once motion and colour, the hand feels softness and warmth in the same piece of wax—yet the simple ideas thus united in the same subject are as perfectly distinct as those that come in by different senses; the coldness and hardness which a man feels in a piece of ice being as distinct ideas in the mind as the smell and whiteness of a lily, or as the taste of sugar and smell of a rose: and there is nothing can be plainer to a man than the clear and distinct perception he has of those simple ideas; which, being each it itself uncompounded, contains in it nothing but one uniform appearance or conception in the mind, and is not distinguishable into different ideas.

2. *The mind can neither make nor destroy them.*—These simple ideas, the materials of all our knowledge, are suggested and furnished to the mind only by those two ways above mentioned, viz., sensation and reflection. When the understanding is once stored with these simple ideas, it has the power to repeat, compare, and unite them, even to an almost infinite variety, and so can make at pleasure new complex ideas. But it is not in the power of the most exalted wit or enlarged understanding, by any quickness or variety of thoughts, to invent or frame one new simple idea in the mind, not taken in by the ways before mentioned; nor can any force of the understanding destroy those that are there. The same inability will everyone find in himself, who shall go about to fashion in his understanding any simple idea not received in by his senses from external objects, or by reflection from the operations of his own mind about them.

3. I think it is not possible for anyone to imagine any other qualities in bodies, howsoever constituted, whereby they can be taken notice of, besides sounds, tastes, smells, visible and tangible qualities. And had mankind been made with but four senses, the qualities then, which are the objects of the fifth sense, had been as far from our notice, imagination, and conception, as now any belonging to a sixth, seventh, or eighth sense, can possibly be. I have here followed the common opinion of man's having but five senses, though perhaps there may be justly counted more; but either supposition serves equally to my present purpose.

CHAPTER III

OF IDEAS OF ONE SENSE

1. *Division of simple ideas.*—The better to conceive the ideas we receive from sensation, it may not be amiss for us to consider them in reference to the different ways whereby they make their approaches to our minds, and make themselves perceivable by us.

First, then, there are some which come into our minds by one sense only.

Secondly. There are others that convey themselves into the mind by more senses than one.

Thirdly. Others that are had from reflection only.

Fourthly. There are some that make themselves way, and are suggested to the mind, by all the ways of sensation and reflection. We shall consider them apart under these several heads.

1. There are some ideas which have admittance only through one sense, which is peculiarly adapted to receive them. Thus light and colours, as white, red, yellow, blue, with their several degrees or shades and mixtures, as green, scarlet, purple, sea-green, and the rest, come in only by the eyes; all kinds of noises, sounds, and tones, only by the ears; the several tastes and smells, by the nose and palate. And if these organs, or the nerves which are the conduits to convey them from without to their audience in the brain, the mind's presence-room (as I may so call it), are, any of them, so disordered as not to perform their functions, they have no postern to be admitted by, no other way to bring themselves into view, and be received by the understanding.

The most considerable of those belonging to the touch are heat, and cold, and solidity; all the rest—consisting almost wholly in the sensible configuration, as smooth and rough; or else more or less firm adhesion of the parts, as hard and soft, tough and brittle—are obvious enough.

2. I think it will be needless to enumerate all the particular simple ideas belonging to each sense. Nor indeed is it possible if we would, there being a great many more of them belonging to most of the senses than we have names for. I shall therefore, in the account of simple ideas I am here giving, content myself to set down only such as are most material to our present purpose, or are in themselves less apt to be taken notice of, though they are very frequently the ingredients of our complex ideas; amongst which I think I may well account " solidity," which therefore I shall treat of in the next chapter.

CHAPTER IV

OF SOLIDITY

1. *We receive this idea from touch.*—The idea of solidity we receive by our touch; and it arises from the resistance which we find in body to the entrance of any other body into the place it

possesses, till it has left it. There is no idea which we receive
more constantly from sensation than solidity. Whether we move
or rest, in what posture soever we are, we always feel something
under us that supports us, and hinders our farther sinking down-
wards; and the bodies which we daily handle make us perceive
that whilst they remain between them, they do, by an insurmountable force, hinder the approach of the parts of our hands that press
them. That which thus hinders the approach of two bodies, when
they are moving one towards another, I call " solidity." This, of
all other, seems the idea most intimately connected with and
essential to body, so as nowhere else to be found or imagined but
only in matter; and though our senses take no notice of it but in
masses of matter, of a bulk sufficient to cause a sensation in us;
yet the mind, having once got this idea from such grosser sensible
bodies, traces it farther and considers it, as well as figure, in the
minutest particle of matter that can exist, and finds it inseparably
inherent in body, wherever or however modified.

2. *Solidity fills space.*—This is the idea which belongs to body,
whereby we conceive it to fill space. The idea of which filling of
space is, that where we imagine any space taken up by a solid
substance, we conceive it so to possess it that it excludes all other
solid substances.

4. *From hardness.*—Solidity is hereby differenced from hardness,
in that solidity consists in repletion, and so an utter exclusion of
other bodies out of the space it possesses; but hardness, in a firm
cohesion of the parts of matter, making up masses of a sensible
bulk, so that the whole does not easily change its figure. And,
indeed, *hard* and *soft* are names that we give to things only in
relation to the constitutions of our own bodies; that being generally
called " hard " by us which will put us to pain sooner than
change figure by the pressure of any part of our bodies: and that,
on the contrary, " soft " which changes the situation of its parts
upon an easy and unpainful touch.

CHAPTER V

OF SIMPLE IDEAS OF DIVERS SENSES

The ideas we get by more than one sense are of space or
extension, figure, rest and motion: for these make perceivable
impressions both on the eyes and touch; and we can receive and

convey into our minds the ideas of our extension, figure, motion, and rest of bodies, both by seeing and feeling. But having occasion to speak more at large of these in another place, I here only enumerate them.

CHAPTER VI

OF SIMPLE IDEAS OF REFLECTION

1. *Simple ideas of reflection are the operations of the mind about its other ideas.*—The mind, receiving the ideas mentioned in the foregoing chapters from without, when it turns its view inward upon itself, and observes its own actions about those ideas it has, takes from thence other ideas, which are as capable to be the objects of its contemplation as any of those it received from foreign things.

2. *The idea of perception, and idea of willing, we have from reflection.*—The two great and principal actions of the mind, which are most frequently considered, and which are so frequent that everyone that pleases may take notice of them in himself, are these two: perception or thinking, and volition or willing. The power of thinking is called " the understanding," and the power of volition is called " the will "; and these two powers or abilities in the mind are denominated " faculties." Of some of the modes of these simple ideas of reflection, such as are remembrance, discerning, reasoning, judging, knowledge, faith, etc., I shall have occasion to speak hereafter.

CHAPTER VII

OF SIMPLE IDEAS OF BOTH SENSATION AND REFLECTION

1. *Pleasure and pain.*—There be other simple ideas which convey themselves into the mind by all the ways of sensation and reflection; viz., pleasure or delight, and its opposite, pain or uneasiness; power, existence, unity.

2. Delight or uneasiness, one or other of them, join themselves to almost all our ideas both of sensation and reflection; and there is scarce any affection of our senses from without, any retired thought of our mind within, which is not able to produce in us

pleasure or pain. By " pleasure " and " pain," I would be understood to signify whatsoever delights or molests us; whether it arises from the thoughts of our minds, or anything operating on our bodies.

7. *Existence and unity.*—Existence and unity are two other ideas that are suggested to the understanding by every object without, and every idea within. When ideas are in our minds, we consider them as being actually there, as well as we consider things to be actually without us: which is, that they exist, or have existence: and whatever we can consider as one thing, whether a real being or idea, suggests to the understanding the idea of unity.

8. *Power.*—Power also is another of those simple ideas which we receive from sensation and reflection. For, observing in ourselves that we can at pleasure move several parts of our bodies which were at rest, the effects also that natural bodies are able to produce in one another occurring every moment to our senses, we both these ways get the idea of power.

9. *Succession.*—Besides these there is another idea, which though suggested by our senses yet is more constantly offered us by what passes in our own minds; and that is the idea of succession. For if we look immediately into ourselves, and reflect on what is observable there, we shall find our ideas always, whilst we are awake or have any thought, passing in train, one going and another coming without intermission.

10. *Simple ideas the materials of all our knowledge.*—These, if they are not all, are at least (as I think) the most considerable of those simple ideas which the mind has, and out of which is made all its other knowledge: all of which it receives only by the two fore-mentioned ways of sensation and reflection.

Nor let anyone think these too narrow bounds for the capacious mind of man to expatiate in, which takes its flight farther than the stars, and cannot be confined by the limits of the world; that extends its thoughts often even beyond the utmost expansion of matter, and makes excursions into that incomprehensible inane. I grant all this; but desire anyone to assign any simple idea which is not received from one of those inlets before mentioned, or any complex idea not made out of those simple ones. Nor will it be so strange to think these few simple ideas sufficient to employ the quickest thought or largest capacity, and to furnish the materials of all that various knowledge and more various fancies and opinions of all mankind, if we consider how many words may be made out of the various composition of twenty-four letters; or if, going one step farther, we will but reflect on the variety of combinations may be made with barely one of the above-mentioned ideas, viz., number, whose stock is inexhaustible and truly infinite; and what a large and immense field doth extension alone afford the mathematicians !

CHAPTER VIII

SOME FARTHER CONSIDERATIONS CONCERNING OUR SIMPLE IDEAS

1. *Positive ideas from privative causes.*—Concerning the simple ideas of sensation it is to be considered, that whatsoever is so constituted in nature as to be able by affecting our senses to cause any perception in the mind, doth thereby produce in the understanding a simple idea; which, whatever be the external cause of it, when it comes to be taken notice of by our discerning faculty, it is by the mind looked on and considered there to be a real positive idea in the understanding, as much as any other whatsoever; though perhaps the cause of it be but a privation in the subject.

2. Thus the ideas of heat and cold, light and darkness, white and black, motion and rest, are equally clear and positive ideas in the mind; though perhaps some of the causes which produce them are barely privations in those subjects from whence our senses derive those ideas.

7. *Ideas in the mind, qualities in bodies.*—To discover the nature of our ideas the better, and to discourse of them intelligibly, it will be convenient to distinguish them, as they are ideas or perceptions in our minds, and as they are modifications of matter in the bodies that cause such perceptions in us; that so we may not think (as perhaps usually is done) that they are exactly the images and resemblances of something inherent in the subject; most of those of sensation being in the mind no more the likeness of something existing without us than the names that stand for them are the likeness of our ideas, which yet upon hearing they are apt to excite in us.

8. Whatsoever the mind perceives in itself, or is the immediate object of perception, thought, or understanding, that I call " idea "; and the power to produce any idea in our mind, I call " quality " of the subject wherein that power is. Thus a snowball having the power to produce in us the ideas of white, cold, and round, the

powers to produce those ideas in us as they are in the snowball, I call " qualities "; and as they are sensations or perceptions in our understandings, I call them " ideas "; which ideas, if I speak of them sometimes as in the things themselves, I would be understood to mean those qualities in the objects which produce them in us.

9. *Primary qualities.*—Qualities thus considered in bodies are, First, such as are utterly inseparable from the body, in what estate soever it be; such as, in all the alterations and changes it suffers, all the force can be used upon it, it constantly keeps; and such as sense constantly finds in every particle of matter which has bulk enough to be perceived, and the mind finds inseparable from every particle of matter, though less than to make itself singly be perceived by our senses; *v.g.*, take a grain of wheat, divide it into two parts, each part has still solidity, extension, figure, and mobility; divide it again, and it retains still the same qualities; and so divide it on till the parts become insensible, they must retain still each of them all those qualities. For, division (which is all that a mill or pestle or any other body does upon another, in reducing it to insensible parts) can never take away either solidity, extension, figure, or mobility from any body, but only makes two or more distinct separate masses of matter of that which was but one before; all which distinct masses, reckoned as so many distinct bodies, after division, make a certain number. These I call *original* or *primary* qualities of body, which I think we may observe to produce simple ideas in us, viz., solidity, extension, figure, motion or rest, and number.

10. *Secondary qualities.*—Secondly. Such qualities, which in truth are nothing in the objects themselves, but powers to produce various sensations in us by their primary qualities, *i.e.*, by the bulk, figure, texture, and motion of their insensible parts, as colours, sounds, tastes, etc., these I call *secondary* qualities. To these might be added a third sort, which are allowed to be barely powers, though they are as much real qualities in the subject as those which I, to comply with the common way of speaking, call qualities, but, for distinction, *secondary* qualities. For, the power in fire to produce a new colour or consistence in wax or clay by its primary qualities, is as much a quality in fire as the power it has to produce in me a new idea or sensation of warmth or burning, which I felt not before, by the same primary qualities, viz., the bulk, texture, and motion of its insensible parts.

11. *How primary qualities produce their ideas.*—The next thing

to be considered is, how bodies produce ideas in us; and that is manifestly by impulse, the only way which we can conceive bodies operate in.

12. If, then, external objects be not united to our minds when they produce ideas in it, and yet we perceive these original qualities in such of them as singly fall under our senses, it is evident that some motion must be thence continued by our nerves or animal spirits, by some parts of our bodies, to the brain or the seat of sensation, there to produce in our minds the particular ideas we have of them. And since the extension, figure, number, and motion of bodies of an observable bigness, may be perceived at a distance by the sight, it is evident some singly imperceptible bodies must come from them to the eyes, and thereby convey to the brain some motion which produces these ideas which we have of them in us.

13. *How secondary.*—After the same manner that the ideas of these original qualities are produced in us, we may conceive that the ideas of secondary qualities are also produced, viz., by the operation of insensible particles on our senses. For it being manifest that there are bodies, and good store of bodies, each whereof are so small that we cannot by any of our senses discover either their bulk, figure, or motion (as is evident in the particles of the air and water, and other extremely smaller than those, perhaps as much smaller than the particles of air or water as the particles of air or water are smaller than pease or hailstones): let us suppose at present that the different motions and figures, bulk and number, of such particles, affecting the several organs of our senses, produce in us those different sensations which we have from the colours and smells of bodies, *v.g.*, that a violet, by the impulse of such insensible particles of matter of peculiar figures and bulks, and in different degrees and modifications of their motions, causes the ideas of the blue colour and sweet scent of that flower to be produced in our minds; it being no more impossible to conceive that God should annex such ideas to such motions with which they have no similitude, than that He should annex the idea of pain to the motion of a piece of steel dividing our flesh, with which that idea hath no resemblance.

14. What I have said concerning colours and smells may be understood also of tastes and sounds, and other the like sensible qualities; which, whatever reality we by mistake attribute to them, are in truth nothing in the objects themselves, but powers to produce various sensations in us, and depend on those primary

qualities, viz., bulk, figure, texture, and motion of, parts, as I have said.

15. *Ideas of primary qualities are resemblances; of secondary, not.*—From whence I think it is easy to draw this observation, that the ideas of primary qualities of bodies are resemblances of them, and their patterns do really exist in the bodies themselves; but the ideas produced in us by these secondary qualities have no resemblance of them at all. There is nothing like our ideas existing in the bodies themselves. They are, in the bodies we denominate from them, only a power to produce those sensations in us; and what is sweet, blue, or warm in idea, is but the certain bulk, figure, and motion of the insensible parts in the bodies themselves, which we call so.

16. Flame is denominated *hot* and *light;* snow, *white* and *cold;* and manna, *white* and *sweet,* from the ideas they produce in us, which qualities are commonly thought to be the same in those bodies that those ideas are in us, the one the perfect resemblance of the other, as they are in a mirror, and it would by most men be judged very extravagant, if one should say otherwise. And yet he that will consider that the same fire that at one distance produces in us the sensation of warmth, does at a nearer approach produce in us the far different sensation of pain, ought to bethink himself what reason he has to say, that his idea of warmth which was produced in him by the fire, is actually in the fire, and his idea of pain which the same fire produced in him the same way is not in the fire. Why is whiteness and coldness in snow and pain not, when it produces the one and the other idea in us, and can do neither but by the bulk, figure, number, and motion of its solid parts?

17. The particular bulk, number, figure, and motion of the parts of fire or snow are really in them, whether anyone's senses perceive them or no; and therefore they may be called *real* qualities, because they really exist in those bodies. But light, heat, whiteness, or coldness, are no more really in them than sickness or pain is in manna. Take away the sensation of them; let not the eyes see light or colours, nor the ears hear sounds; let the palate not taste, nor the nose smell; and all colours, tastes, odours and sounds, as they are such particular ideas, vanish and cease, and are reduced to their causes, *i.e.,* bulk, figure, and motion of parts.

18. A piece of manna of a sensible bulk is apt to produce in us the idea of a round or square figure; and, by being removed from one place to another, the idea of motion. This idea of motion

represents it as it really is in the manna moving; a circle or square are the same, whether in idea or existence, in the mind or in the manna; and this both motion and figure are really in the manna, whether we take notice of them or no: this everybody is ready to agree to. Besides, manna, by the bulk, figure, texture, and motion of its parts, has a power to produce the sensations of sickness, and sometimes of acute pains or gripings, in us. That these ideas of sickness and pain are not in the manna, but effects of its operations on us, and are nowhere when we feel them not; this also everyone agrees to. And yet men are hardly to be brought to think that sweetness and whiteness are not really in manna, which are but the effects of the operations of manna by the motion, size and figure of its particles on the eyes and palate; as the pain and sickness caused by manna, are confessedly nothing but the effects of its operations on the stomach and guts by the size, motion, and figure of its insensible parts (for by nothing else can a body operate, as has been proved).

22. I have, in what just goes before, been engaged in physical inquiries a little farther than perhaps I intended. But it being necessary to make the nature of sensation a little understood, and to make the difference between the qualities in bodies and the ideas produced by them in the mind to be distinctly conceived, without which it were impossible to discourse intelligibly of them, I hope I shall be pardoned this little excursion into natural philosophy, it being necessary in our present inquiry to distinguish the primary and real qualities of bodies, which are always in them (viz., solidity, extension, figure, number, and motion or rest, and are sometimes perceived by us, viz., when the bodies they are in are big enough singly to be discerned), from those secondary and imputed qualities, which are but the powers of several combinations of those primary ones, when they operate without being distinctly discerned; whereby we also may come to know what ideas are, and what are not, resemblances of something really existing in the bodies we denominate from them.

23. *Three sorts of qualities in bodies.*—The qualities then that are in bodies, rightly considered, are of three sorts:

First. The bulk, figure, number, situation, and motion or rest of their solid parts; those are in them, whether we perceive them or no; and when they are of that size that we can discover them, we have by these an idea of the thing as it is in itself, as is plain in artificial things. These I call *primary* qualities.

Secondly. The power that is in any body by reason of its

insensible primary qualities, to operate after a peculiar manner on any of our senses, and thereby produce in us the different ideas of several colours, sounds, smells, tastes, etc. These are usually called *sensible* qualities.

Thirdly. The power that is in any body, by reason of the particular constitution of its primary qualities, to make such a change in the bulk, figure, texture, and motion of another body, as to make it operate on our senses differently from what it did before. Thus the sun has a power to make wax white, and fire, to make lead fluid. These are usually called " powers."

The first of these, as has been said, I think may be properly called real, original, or primary qualities, because they are in the things themselves, whether they are perceived or no; and upon their different modifications it is that the secondary qualities depend.

The other two are only powers to act differently upon other things, which powers result from the different modifications of those primary qualities.

24. *The first are resemblances; the second thought resemblances, but are not; the third neither are, nor are thought so.*—But though these two latter sorts of qualities are powers barely, and nothing but powers, relating to several other bodies, and resulting from the different modifications of the original qualities, yet they are generally otherwise thought of. For the second sort, viz., the powers to produce several ideas in us by our senses, are looked upon as real qualities in the things thus affecting us; but the third sort are called and esteemed barely powers. *V.g.*, the idea of heat or light which we receive by our eyes or touch from the sun, are commonly thought real qualities existing in the sun, and something more than mere powers in it. But when we consider the sun in reference to wax, which it melts or blanches, we look upon the whiteness and softness produced in the wax, not as qualities in the sun, but effects produced by powers in it: whereas, if rightly considered, these qualities of light and warmth, which are perceptions in me when I am warmed or enlightened by the sun, are no otherwise in the sun than the changes made in the wax, when it is blanched or melted, are in the sun. They are all of them equally powers in the sun, depending on its primary qualities, whereby it is able in the one case so to alter the bulk, figure, texture, or motion of some of the insensible parts of my eyes or hands as thereby to produce in me the idea of light or heat, and in the other it is able so to alter the bulk, figure, texture, or motion of the insensible parts of the wax as to make

them fit to produce in me the distinct ideas of white and fluid.

25. The reason why the one are ordinarily taken for real qualities, and the other only for bare powers, seems to be because the ideas we have of distinct colours, sounds, etc., containing nothing at all in them of bulk, figure, or motion, we are not apt to think them the effects of these primary qualities which appear not to our senses to operate in their production, and with which they have not any apparent congruity, or conceivable connection. Hence it is that we are so forward to imagine that those ideas are the resemblances of something really existing in the objects themselves, since sensation discovers nothing of bulk, figure, or motion of parts, in their production, nor can reason show how bodies by their bulk, figure, and motion, should produce in the mind the ideas of blue or yellow, etc. But, in the other case, in the operations of bodies changing the qualities one of another, we plainly discover that the quality produced hath commonly no resemblance with anything in the thing producing it; wherefore we look on it as a bare effect of power. For though, receiving the idea of heat or light from the sun, we are apt to think it is a perception and resemblance of such a quality in the sun, yet when we see wax or a fair face receive change of colour from the sun, we cannot imagine that to be the perception or resemblance of anything in the sun, because we find not those different colours in the sun itself: for, our senses being able to observe a likeness or unlikeness of sensible qualities in two different external objects, we forwardly enough conclude the production of any sensible quality in any subject to be an effect of bare power, and not the communication of any quality which was really in the efficient, when we find no such sensible quality in the thing that produced it. But our senses not being able to discover any unlikeness between the idea produced in us and the quality of the object producing it, we are apt to imagine that our ideas are resemblances of something in the objects, and not the effects of certain powers placed in the modification of their primary qualities, with which primary qualities the ideas produced in us have no resemblance.

26. *Secondary qualities twofold: first, immediately perceivable; secondly, mediately perceivable.*—To conclude: Besides those before-mentioned primary qualities in bodies, viz., bulk, figure, extension, number, and motion of their solid parts, all the rest whereby we take notice of bodies, and distinguish them one from another, are nothing else but several powers in them depending on those primary qualities, whereby they are fitted, either by

immediately operating on our bodies, to produce several different ideas in us; or else by operating on other bodies, so to change their primary qualities as to render them capable of producing ideas in us different from what before they did. The former of these, I think, may be called secondary qualities immediately perceivable; the latter, secondary qualities mediately perceivable.

CHAPTER IX

OF PERCEPTION

1. *Perception the first simple idea of reflection.*—Perception, as it is the first faculty of the mind exercised about our ideas, so it is the first and simplest idea we have from reflection, and is by some called " thinking " in general. Though thinking, in the propriety of the English tongue, signifies that sort of operation of the mind about its ideas wherein the mind is active; where it, with some degree of voluntary attention, considers anything: for in bare, naked perception, the mind is, for the most part, only passive, and what it perceives it cannot avoid perceiving.

2. *Is only when the mind receives the impression.*—What perception is, everyone will know better by reflecting on what he does himself, when he sees, hears, feels, etc., or thinks, than by any discourse of mine. Whoever reflects on what passes in his own mind, cannot miss it; and if he does not reflect, all the words in the world cannot make him have any notion of it.

3. This is certain, that whatever alterations are made in the body, if they reach not the mind; whatever impressions are made on the outward parts, if they are not taken notice of within; there is no perception. Fire may burn our bodies with no other effect than it does a billet, unless the motion be continued to the brain, and there the sense of heat or idea of pain be produced in the mind, wherein consists actual perception.

4. How often may a man observe in himself, that whilst his mind is intently employed in the contemplation of some objects, and curiously surveying some ideas that are there, it takes no notice of impressions of sounding bodies made upon the organ of hearing with the same alteration that uses to be for the producing the idea of sound ! A sufficient impulse there may be on the organ; but it not reaching the observation of the mind, there follows no perception: and though the motion that uses to produce the

idea of sound be made in the ear, yet no sound is heard. Want of sensation in this case is not through any defect in the organ, or that the man's ears are less affected than at other times when he does hear: but that which uses to produce the idea, though conveyed in by the usual organ, not being taken notice of in the understanding, and so imprinting no idea on the mind, there follows no sensation. So that wherever there is sense or perception, there some idea is actually produced, and present in the understanding.

8. *Ideas of sensation often changed by the judgment.*—We are farther to consider concerning perception, that the ideas we receive by sensation are often in grown people altered by the judgment without our taking notice of it. When we set before our eyes a round globe of any uniform colour, *v.g.*, gold, alabaster, or jet, it is certain that the idea thereby imprinted in our mind is of a flat circle variously shadowed, with several degrees of light and brightness coming to our eyes. But we having by use been accustomed to perceive what kind of appearance convex bodies are wont to make in us, what alterations are made in the reflections of light by the difference of the sensible figures of bodies, the judgment presently, by an habitual custom, alters the appearances into their causes: so that, from that which truly is variety of shadow or colour collecting the figure, it makes it pass for a mark of figure, and frames to itself the perception of a convex figure and an uniform colour; when the idea we receive from thence is only a plane variously coloured, as is evident in painting. To which purpose I shall here insert a problem of that very ingenious and studious promoter of real knowledge, the learned and worthy Mr. Molineux, which he was pleased to send me in a letter some months since: and it is this: " Suppose a man born blind, and now adult, and taught by his touch to distinguish between a cube and a sphere of the same metal, and nighly of the same bigness, so as to tell, when he felt one and the other, which is the cube, which the sphere. Suppose then the cube and sphere placed on a table, and the blind man to be made to see; query, Whether by his sight, before he touched them, he could now distinguish and tell which is the globe, which the cube ? " To which the acute and judicious proposer answers: " Not. For though he has obtained the experience of how a globe, how a cube, affects his touch; yet he has not yet attained the experience, that what affects his touch so or so, must affect his sight so or so; or that a protuberant angle in the cube, that pressed his hand unequally, shall appear

to his eye as it does in the cube.'' I agree with this thinking
gentleman, whom I am proud to call my friend, in his answer to
this his problem; and am of opinion, that the blind man, at first
sight, would not be able with certainty to say which was the
globe, which the cube, whilst he only saw them; though he could
unerringly name them by his touch, and certainly distinguish them
by the difference of their figures felt.

CHAPTER X

OF RETENTION

1. *Contemplation.*—The next faculty of the mind, whereby it
makes a farther progress towards knowledge, is that which I call
retention or the keeping of those simple ideas which from sensation
or reflection it hath received. This is done two ways. First, by
keeping the idea which is brought into it for some time actually
in view, which is called contemplation.

2. *Memory.*—The other way of retention is the power to revive
again in our minds those ideas which after imprinting have
disappeared, or have been as it were laid aside out of sight; and
thus we do, when we conceive heat or light, yellow or sweet, the
object being removed. This is memory, which is, as it were, the
storehouse of our ideas. For the narrow mind of man, not being
capable of having many ideas under view and consideration at
once, it was necessary to have a repository to lay up those ideas,
which at another time it might have use of. But our ideas being
nothing but actual perceptions in the mind, which cease to be
anything when there is no perception of them, this laying up of
our ideas in the repository of the memory signifies no more but
this — that the mind has a power, in many cases, to revive
perceptions which it has once had, with this additional perception
annexed to them—that it has had them before. And in this sense
it is that our ideas are said to be in our memories, when indeed
they are actually nowhere, but only there is an ability in the mind
when it will to revive them again, and, as it were, paint them anew
on itself, though some with more, some with less, difficulty; some
more lively, and others more obscurely.

3. *Attention, repetition, pleasure and pain fix ideas.*—Attention
and repetition help much to the fixing any ideas in the memory;
but those which naturally at first make the deepest and most lasting

impression, are those which are accompanied with pleasure or pain. The great business of the senses being to make us take notice of what hurts or advantages the body, it is wisely ordered by nature (as has been shown) that pain should accompany the reception of several ideas; which, supplying the place of consideration and reasoning in children, and acting quicker than consideration in grown men, makes both the young and old avoid painful objects with that haste which is necessary for their preservation, and in both settles in the memory a caution for the future.

7. *In remembering, the mind is often active.*—In this secondary perception, as I may so call it, or viewing again the ideas that are lodged in the memory, the mind is oftentimes more than barely passive; the appearances of those dormant pictures depending sometimes on the will. The mind very often sets itself on work in search of some hidden idea, and turns, as it were, the eye of the soul upon it; though sometimes too they start up in our minds of their own accord, and offer themselves to the understanding, and very often are roused and tumbled out of their dark cells into open daylight by some turbulent and tempestuous passion; our affections bringing ideas to our memory which had otherwise lain quiet and unregarded. This farther is to be observed concerning ideas lodged in the memory, and upon occasion revived by the mind—that they are not only (as the word " revive " imports) none of them new ones, but also that the mind takes notice of them as of a former impression, and renews its acquaintance with them as with ideas it had known before.

CHAPTER XI

OF DISCERNING, AND OTHER OPERATIONS OF THE MIND

1. *No knowledge without discerning.*—Another faculty we may take notice of in our minds, is that of discerning and distinguishing between the several ideas it has. It is not enough to have a confused perception of something in general: unless the mind had a distinct perception of different objects and their qualities, it would be capable of very little knowledge; though the bodies that affect us were as busy about us as they are now, and the mind were continually employed in thinking. On this faculty of distinguishing one thing from another, depends the evidence and certainty of several even very general propositions, which have

passed for innate truths; because men, overlooking the true cause why those propositions find universal assent, impute it wholly to native uniform impressions: whereas it in truth depends upon this clear discerning faculty of the mind, whereby it perceives two ideas to be the same or different. But of this more hereafter.

2. *The difference of wit and judgment.*—How much the imperfection of accurately discriminating ideas one from another lies either in the dullness or faults of the organs of sense, or want of acuteness, exercise, or attention in the understanding, or hastiness and precipitancy natural to some tempers, I will not here examine; it suffices to take notice, that this is one of the operations that the mind may reflect on and observe in itself. It is of that consequence to its other knowledge, that so far as this faculty is in itself dull, or not rightly made use of for the distinguishing one thing from another, so far our notions are confused, and our reason, and judgment disturbed or misled. If in having our ideas in the memory ready at hand consists quickness of parts; in this of having them unconfused, and being able nicely to distinguish one thing from another where there is but the least difference, consists in a great measure the exactness of judgment and clearness of reason which is to be observed in one man above another. And hence, perhaps, may be given some reason of that common observation—that men who have a great deal of wit and prompt memories, have not always the clearest judgment or deepest reason. For, wit lying most in the assemblage of ideas, and putting those together with quickness and variety wherein can be found any resemblance or congruity, thereby to make up pleasant pictures and agreeable visions in the fancy; judgment, on the contrary, lies quite on the other side, in separating carefully one from another ideas wherein can be found the least difference, thereby to avoid being misled by similitude and by affinity to take one thing for another.

3. *Clearness alone hinders confusion.*—To the well distinguishing our ideas, it chiefly contributes that they be clear and determinate; and when are so, it will not breed any confusion or mistake about them, though the senses should (as sometimes they do) convey them from the same object differently on different occasions, and so seem to err. For though a man in a fever should from sugar have a bitter taste, which at another time would produce a sweet one, yet the idea of bitter in that man's mind would be as clear and distinct from the idea of sweet, as if he had tasted only gall.

4. *Comparing.*—The comparing them one with another, in respect of extent, degrees, time, place, or any other circumstances,

is another operation of the mind about its ideas, and is that upon which depends all that large tribe of ideas, comprehended under relation; which of how vast an extent it is, I shall have occasion to consider hereafter.

6. *Compounding.*—The next operation we may observe in the mind about its ideas is composition; whereby it puts together several of those simple ones it has received from sensation and reflection, and combines them into complex ones. Under this of composition may be reckoned also that of enlarging; wherein though the composition does not so much appear as in more complex ones, yet it is nevertheless a putting several ideas together, though of the same kind. Thus, by adding several units together we make the idea of a dozen, and putting together the repeated ideas of several perches we frame that of a furlong.

8. *Naming.*—When children have by repeated sensations got ideas fixed in their memories, they begin by degrees to learn the use of signs. And when they have got the skill to apply the organs of speech to the framing of articulate sounds, they begin to make use of words to signify their ideas to others. These verbal signs they sometimes borrow from others, and sometimes make themselves, as one may observe among the new and unusual names children often give to things in their first use of language.

9. *Abstracting.*—The use of words then being to stand as outward marks of our internal ideas, and those ideas being taken from particular things, if every particular idea that we take in should have a distinct name, names must be endless. To prevent this, the mind makes the particular ideas, received from particular objects, to become general; which is done by considering them as they are in the mind such appearances separate from all other existences, and the circumstances of real existence, as time, place, or any other concomitant ideas. This is called " abstraction," whereby ideas taken from particular beings become general representatives of all of the same kind; and their names, general names, applicable to whatever exists conformable to such abstract ideas. Such precise, naked appearances in the mind, without considering how, whence, or with what others they came there, the understanding lays up (with names commonly annexed to them) as the standards to rank real existences into sorts, as they agree with these patterns, and to denominate them accordingly. Thus, the same colour being observed to-day in chalk or snow, which the mind yesterday received from milk, it considers that appearance alone, makes it a representative of all of that kind,

and, having given it the name " whiteness," it by that sound signifies the same quality wheresoever to be imagined or met with; and thus universals, whether ideas or terms, are made.

14. *Method.*—These, I think, are the first faculties and operations of the mind which it makes use of in understanding; and though they are exercised about all its ideas in general, yet the instances I have hitherto given have been chiefly in simple ideas; and I have subjoined the explication of these faculties of the mind to that of simple ideas, before I come to what I have to say concerning complex ones, for these following reasons:—

First, Because, several of these faculties being exercised at first principally about simple ideas, we might, by following nature in its ordinary method, trace and discover them in their rise, progress, and gradual improvements.

Secondly, Because, observing the faculties of the mind, how they operate about simple ideas, which are usually in most men's minds much more clear, precise, and distinct than complex ones, we may the better examine and learn how the mind abstracts, denominates, compares, and exercises its other operations about those which are complex, wherein we are much more liable to mistake.

Thirdly, Because these very operations of the mind about ideas received from sensation are themselves, when reflected on, another set of ideas, derived from that other source of our knowledge which I call " reflection "; and therefore fit to be considered in this place after the simple ideas of sensation.

15. *These are the beginnings of human knowledge.*—And thus I have given a short and, I think, true history of the first beginnings of human knowledge, whence the mind has its first objects, and by what steps it makes its progress to the laying in and storing up those ideas out of which is to be framed all the knowledge it is capable of; wherein I must appeal to experience and observation whether I am in the right; the best way to come to truths being to examine things as really they are, and not to conclude they are as we fancy of ourselves, or have been taught by others to imagine.

17. *Dark room.*—I pretend not to teach, but to inquire; and therefore cannot but confess here again, that external and internal sensation are the only passages that I can find of knowledge to the understanding. These alone, as far as I can discover, are the windows by which light is let into this dark room. For methinks the understanding is not much unlike a closet wholly shut from light, with only some little opening left to let in external visible

resemblances or ideas of things without: would the pictures coming into such a dark room but stay there, and lie so orderly as to be found upon occasion, it would very much resemble the understanding of a man in reference to all objects of sight, and the ideas of them.

These are my guesses concerning the means whereby the understanding comes to have and retain simple ideas and the modes of them, with some other operations about them. I proceed now to examine some of these simple ideas and their modes a little more particularly.

CHAPTER XII

OF COMPLEX IDEAS

1. *Made by the mind out of simple ones.*—We have hitherto considered those ideas, in the reception whereof the mind is only passive, which are those simple ones received from sensation and reflection before mentioned, whereof the mind cannot make one to itself, nor have any idea which does not wholly consist of them. But as the mind is wholly passive in the reception of all its simple ideas, so it exerts several acts of its own, whereby out of its simple ideas, as the materials and foundations of the rest, the other are framed. As simple ideas are observed to exist in several combinations united together, so the mind has a power to consider several of them united together as one idea; and that not only as they are united in external objects, but as itself has joined them. Ideas thus made up of several simple ones put together I call " complex "; such as are beauty, gratitude, a man, an army, the universe; which, though complicated of various simple ideas or complex ideas made up of simple ones, yet are, when the mind pleases, considered each by itself as one entire thing, and signified by one name.[1]

2. *Made voluntarily.*—In this faculty of repeating and joining together its ideas, the mind has great power in varying and

[1] In a passage which he introduced into this paragraph in the fourth edition of the Essay, Locke applied the term " complex idea " only to those that were obtained by combining simple ideas with one another, and so distinguished complex ideas from " ideas of relation," which were obtained by comparing simple ideas, and from " general ideas," which were obtained by abstraction. However, since this is at variance with his usual practice, which is to treat ideas of relation, along with substances and modes, as varieties of complex ideas, we omit the passage.—Eds.

multiplying the objects of its thoughts infinitely beyond what sensation or reflection furnished it with; but all this still confined to those simple ideas which it received from those two sources, and which are the ultimate materials of all its compositions. For, simple ideas are all from things themselves; and of these the mind can have no more nor other than what are suggested to it. It can have no other ideas of sensible qualities than what come from without by the senses, nor any ideas of other kind of operations of a thinking substance than what it finds in itself; but when it has once got these simple ideas, it is not confined barely to observation, and what offers itself from without; it can, by its own power, put together those ideas it has, and make new complex ones which it never received so united.

3. *Are either modes, substances, or relations.*—Complex ideas, however compounded and decompounded, though their number be infinite, and the variety endless wherewith they fill and entertain the thoughts of men, yet I think they may be all reduced under these three heads: 1. Modes. 2. Substances. 3. Relations.

4. *Modes.*—First. " Modes " I call such complex ideas which, however compounded, contain not in them the supposition of subsisting by themselves, but are considered as dependencies on or affections of substances; such are the ideas signified by the words, " triangle, gratitude, murder," etc. And if in this I use the word " mode " in somewhat a different sense from its ordinary signification, I beg pardon; it being unavoidable in discourses differing from the ordinary received notions, either to make new words or to use old words in somewhat a new signification: the latter whereof, in our present case, is perhaps the more tolerable of the two.

5. *Simple and mixed modes.*—Of these modes there are two sorts which deserve distinct consideration. First. There are some which are only variations or different combinations of the same simple idea, without the mixture of any other, as a dozen, or score; which are nothing but the ideas of so many distinct units added together: and these I called " simple modes," as being contained within the bounds of one simple idea. Secondly. There are others compounded of simple ideas, of several kinds, put together to make one complex one; *v.g.*, beauty, consisting of a certain composition of colour and figure, causing delight in the beholder; theft, which, being the concealed change of the possession of anything, without the consent of the proprietor, contains, as is visible, a combination of several ideas of several kinds; and these I call " mixed modes."

6. *Substances single or collective.*—Secondly. The ideas of substances are such combinations of simple ideas as are taken to represent distinct particular things subsisting by themselves, in which the supposed or confused idea of substance, such as it is, is always the first and chief. Thus, if to substance be joined the simple idea of a certain dull, whitish colour, with certain degrees of weight, hardness, ductility, and fusibility, we have the idea of lead; and a combination of the ideas of a certain sort of figure, with the powers of motion, thought, and reasoning, joined to substance, make the ordinary idea of a man. Now of substances also there are two sorts of ideas, one of single substances, as they exist separately, as of a man or a sheep; the other of several of those put together, as an army of men or flock of sheep; which collective ideas of several substances thus put together, are as much each of them one single idea as that of a man or an unit.

7. *Relation.*—Thirdly. The last sort of complex ideas is that we call " Relation," which consists in the consideration and comparing one idea with another. Of these several kinds we shall treat in their order.

8. *The abstrusest ideas from the two sources.*—If we will trace the progress of our minds, and with attention observe how it repeats, adds together, and unites its simple ideas received from sensation or reflection, it will lead us farther than at first perhaps we should have imagined. And I believe we shall find, if we warily observe the originals of our notions, that even the most abstruse ideas, how remote soever they may seem from sense, or from any operation of our own minds, are yet only such as the understanding frames to itself, by repeating and joining together ideas that it had either from objects of sense, or from its own operations about them; so that those even large and abstract ideas are derived from sensation or reflection, being no other than what the mind by the ordinary use of its own faculties, employed about ideas received from objects of sense, or from the operations it observes in itself about them, may and does attain unto.

CHAPTER XIII

OF SIMPLE MODES; AND FIRST, OF THE SIMPLE MODES OF SPACE

1. *Simple modes.*—Though in the foregoing part I have often mentioned simple ideas, which are truly the materials of all our knowledge; yet, having treated of them there rather in the way

that they come into the mind than as distinguished from others more compounded, it will not be perhaps amiss to take a view of some of them again under this consideration, and examine those different modifications of the same idea, which the mind either finds in things existing, or is able to make within itself, without the help of any extrinsical object, or any foreign suggestion.

Those modifications of any one simple idea (which, as has been said, I call " simple modes "), are as perfectly different and distinct ideas in the mind as those of the greatest distance or contrariety; for the idea of two is as distinct from that of one as blueness from heat, or either of them from any number; and yet it is made up only of that simple idea of an unit repeated; and repetitions of this kind joined together make those distinct simple modes of a dozen, a gross, a million.

2. *Idea of space.*—I shall begin with the simple idea of space. I have showed above (Chap. IV) that we get the idea of space both by our sight and touch: which I think is so evident that it would be as needless to go to prove that men perceive by their sight a distance between bodies of different colours, or between the parts of the same body, as that they see colours themselves; nor is it less obvious that they can do so in the dark by feeling and touch.

3. *Space and extension.*—This space considered barely in length between any two beings, without considering anything else between them, is called " distance "; if considered in length, breadth, and thickness, I think it may be called " capacity "; the term " extension " is usually applied to it, in what manner soever considered.

4. *Immensity.*—Each different distance is a different modification of space, and each idea of any different distance or space is a simple mode of this idea. Men, for the use and by the custom of measuring, settle in their minds the ideas of certain stated lengths, such as are an inch, foot, yard, fathom, mile, diameter of the earth, etc., which are so many distinct ideas made up only of space. When any such stated lengths or measures of space are made familiar to men's thoughts, they can in their minds repeat them as often as they will, without mixing or joining to them the idea of body or anything else, and frame to themselves the ideas of long, square, or cubic feet, yards, or fathoms, here amongst the bodies of the universe, or else beyond the utmost bounds of all bodies; and, by adding these still one to another, enlarge their idea of space as much as they please. This power of repeating or doubling any idea we have of any distance, and adding it to the former as often as we will, without being ever able to come to

any stop or stint, let us enlarge it as much as we will, is that which gives us the idea of immensity.

5. *Figure.*—There is another modification of this idea, which is nothing but the relation which the parts of the termination of extension or circumscribed space have amongst themselves. This the touch discovers in sensible bodies, whose extremities come within our reach; and the eye takes both from bodies and colours, whose boundaries are within its view: where, observing how the extremities terminate either in straight lines which meet at discernible angles, or in crooked lines wherein no angles can be perceived, by considering these as they relate to one another, in all parts of the extremities of any bodies or space, it has that idea we call " figure," which affords to the mind infinite variety. For, besides the vast number of different figures that do really exist in the coherent masses of matter, the stock that the mind has in its power by varying the idea of space, and thereby making still new compositions, by repeating its own ideas and joining them as it pleases, is perfectly inexhaustible; and so it can multiply figures *in infinitum.*

7. *Place.*—Another idea coming under this head and belonging to this tribe, is that we call " place." As in simple space we consider the relation of distance between any two bodies or points, so in our idea of place we consider the relation of distance betwixt anything and any two or more points, which are considered as keeping the same distance one with another, and so considered as at rest: for when we find anything at the same distance now which it was yesterday from any two or more points, which have not since changed their distance one with another, and with which we then compared it, we say it hath kept the same place; but if it hath sensibly altered its distance with either of those points, we say it hath changed its place; though, vulgarly speaking in the common notion of place, we do not always exactly observe the distance from precise points, but from large portions of sensible objects to which we consider the thing placed to bear relation, and its distance from which we have some reason to observe.

10. That our idea of place is nothing else but such a relative position of anything as I have before mentioned, I think is plain, and will be easily admitted when we consider that we can have no idea of the place of the universe, though we can of all the parts of it; because beyond that we have not the idea of any fixed, distinct, particular beings, in reference to which we can imagine it to have any relation of distance: but all beyond it is one uniform

space or expansion, wherein the mind finds no variety, no marks. For to say that the world is somewhere, means no more than that it does exist: this, though a phrase borrowed from place, signifying only its existence, not location; and when one can find out and frame in his mind clearly and distinctly the place of the universe, he will be able to tell us whether it moves or stands still in the undistinguishable inane of infinite space: though it be true that the word " place " has sometimes a more confused sense, and stands for that space which any body takes up; and so the universe is in a place. The idea therefore of place we have by the same means that we get the idea of space (whereof this is but a particular limited consideration), viz., by our sight and touch, by either of which we receive into our minds the ideas of extension or distance.

11. *Extension and body not the same.*—There are some that would persuade us that body and extension are the same thing. If they mean by body and extension the same that other people do, viz., by body, something that is solid and extended, whose parts are separable and moveable different ways; and by extension, only the space that lies between the extremities of those solid coherent parts, and which is possessed by them, they confound very different ideas one with another. For I appeal to every man's own thoughts, whether the idea of space be not as distinct from that of solidity, as it is from the idea of scarlet colour? It is true, solidity cannot exist without extension, neither can scarlet colour exist without extension; but this hinders not but that they are distinct ideas. Many ideas require others as necessary to their existence or conception, which yet are very distinct ideas. Motion can neither be, nor be conceived, without space; and yet motion is not space, nor space motion; space can exist without it, and they are very distinct ideas; and so, I think, are those of space and solidity. Solidity is so inseparable an idea from body, that upon that depends its filling of space, its contact, impulse, and communication of motion upon impulse. And if it be a reason to prove that spirit is different from body, because thinking includes not the idea of extension in it, the same reason will be as valid, I suppose, to prove that space is not body, because it includes not the idea of solidity in it; space and solidity being as distinct ideas as thinking and extension, and as wholly separable in the mind one from another. Body, then, and extension, it is evident, are two distinct ideas. For,

12. First. Extension includes no solidity nor resistance to the motion of body, as body does.

13. Secondly. The parts of pure space are inseparable one from the other; so that the continuity cannot be separated, neither really nor mentally. For I demand of anyone to remove any part of it from another with which it is continued, even so much as in thought. To divide and separate actually, is as I think, by removing the parts one from another, to make two superfices, where before there was a continuity: and to divide mentally, is to make in the mind two superfices, where before there was a continuity, and consider them as removed one from the other; which can only be done in things considered by the mind as capable of being separated.

14. Thirdly. The parts of pure space are immovable, which follows from their inseparability; motion being nothing but change of distance between any two things: but this cannot be between parts that are inseparable; which therefore must needs be at perpetual rest one amongst another.

Thus the determined idea of simple space distinguishes it plainly and sufficiently from body, since its parts are inseparable, immovable, and without resistance to the motion of body.

CHAPTER XIV

OF DURATION, AND ITS SIMPLE MODES

1. *Duration is fleeting extension.*—There is another sort of distance or length, the idea whereof we get not from the permanent parts of space, but from the fleeting and perpetually perishing parts of succession: this we call "duration," the simple modes whereof are any different lengths of it whereof we have distinct ideas, as hours, days, years, etc., time, and eternity.

2. *Its idea from reflection on the train of our ideas.*—The answer of a great man to one who asked what time was, *Si non rogas intelligo* (which amounts to this: "The more I set myself to think of it the less I understand it"), might perhaps persuade one that time, which reveals all other things, is itself not to be discovered. Duration, time, and eternity are not without reason thought to have something very abstruse in their nature. But however remote these may seem from our comprehension, yet if we trace them right to their originals, I doubt not but one of those sources of all our knowledge, viz., sensation and reflection, will be able to furnish us with these ideas as clear and distinct as many other which are thought much less obscure; and we shall find that the

idea of eternity itself is derived from the same common original with the rest of our ideas.

3. To understand time and eternity aright, we ought with attention to consider what idea it is we have of duration, and how we came by it. It is evident to anyone who will but observe what passes in his own mind, that there is a train of ideas which constantly succeed one another in his understanding as long as he is awake. Reflection on these appearances of several ideas one after another in our minds, is that which furnishes us with the idea of succession; and the distance between any parts of that succession, or between the appearance of any two ideas in our minds, is that we call duration.

4. That we have our notion of succession and duration from this original, viz., from reflection on the train of ideas which we find to appear one after another in our own minds, seems plain to me, in that we have no perception of duration but by considering the train of ideas that take their turns in our understandings. When that succession of ideas ceases, our perception of duration ceases with it; which everyone clearly experiments in himself whilst he sleeps soundly, whether an hour or a day, or a month, or a year; of which duration of things whilst he sleeps or thinks not he has no perception at all, but it is quite lost to him; and the moment wherein he leaves off to think till the moment he begins to think again, seems to him to have no distance. And so I doubt not it would be to a waking man, if it were possible for him to keep only one idea in his mind without variation and the succession of others.

5. *The idea of duration applicable to things whilst we sleep.—* But a man having, from reflection on the succession and number of his own thoughts, got the notion or idea of duration, he can apply that notion to things which exist while he does not think; as he that has got the idea of extension from bodies by his sight or touch, can apply it to distances where no body is seen or felt. And therefore, though a man has no perception of the length of duration which passed whilst he slept or thought not, yet, having observed the revolution of days and nights, and found the length of their duration to be in appearance regular and constant, he can, upon the supposition that that revolution has proceeded after the same manner whilst he was asleep or thought not, as it used to do at other times—he can, I say, imagine and make allowance for the length of duration whilst he slept. But if Adam and Eve (when they were alone in the world), instead of their ordinary night's sleep, had passed the whole twenty-four hours in one

continued sleep, the duration of that twenty-four hours had been irrecoverably lost to them, and been for ever left out of their account of time.

6. *The idea of succession not from motion.*—Thus, by reflecting on the appearance of various ideas one after another in our understandings, we get the notion of succession; which if anyone should think we did rather get from our observation of motion by our senses, he will perhaps be of my mind, when he considers that even motion produces in his mind an idea of succession no otherwise than as it produces there a continued train of distinguishable ideas. For, a man, looking upon a body really moving, perceives yet no motion at all, unless that motion produces a constant train of successive ideas; *v.g.*, a man becalmed at sea, out of sight of land, in a fair day may look on the sun or sea, or ship, a whole hour together, and perceive no motion at all in either: though it be certain that two, and perhaps all of them, have moved during that time a great way; but as soon as he perceives either of them to have changed distance with some other body, as soon as this motion produces any new idea in him, then he perceives that there has been motion. But wherever a man is with all things at rest about him, without perceiving any motion at all, if during this hour of quiet he has been thinking, he will perceive the various ideas of his own thoughts in his own mind appearing one after another, and thereby observe and find succession where he could observe no motion.

7. And this, I think is the reason why motions very slow, though they are constant, are not perceived by us: because, in their remove from one sensible part towards another, their change of distance is so slow that it causes no new ideas in us but a good while one after another; and so, not causing a constant train of new ideas to follow one another immediately in our minds, we have no perception of motion, which, consisting in a constant succession, we cannot perceive that succession without a constant succession of varying ideas arising from it.

8. On the contrary, things that move so swift as not to affect the senses distinctly with several distinguishable distances of their motion, and so cause not any train of ideas in the mind, are not also perceived to move. For anything that moves round about in a circle in less time than our ideas are wont to succeed one another in our minds, is not perceived to move, but seems to be a perfect, entire circle of that matter or colour, and not a part of a circle in motion.

9. *The train of ideas has a certain degree of quickness.*—Hence I leave it to others to judge, whether it be not probable that our ideas do, whilst we are awake, succeed one another in our minds at certain distances, not much unlike the images in the inside of a lantern, turned round by the heat of a candle. This appearance of theirs in train, though perhaps it may be sometimes faster and sometimes slower, yet, I guess, varies not very much in a waking man : there seem to be certain bounds to the quickness and slowness of the succession of those ideas one to another in our minds, beyond which they can neither delay nor hasten.

10. The reason I have for this odd conjecture is from observing that, in the impressions made upon any of our senses, we can but to a certain degree perceive any succession; which if exceeding quick, the sense of succession is lost, even in cases where it is evident that there is a real succession. Let a cannon-bullet pass through a room, and in its way take with it any limb or fleshy parts of a man, it is as clear as any demonstration can be that it must strike successively the two sides of the room; it is also evident that it must touch one part of the flesh first, and another after, and so on in succession : and yet I believe nobody who ever felt the pain of such a shot, or heard the blow against the two distant walls, could perceive any succession either in the pain or sound of so swift a stroke. Such a part of duration as this, wherein we perceive no succession, is that which we may call an instant, and is that which takes up the time of only one idea in our minds without the succession of another, wherein therefore we perceive no succession at all.

12. *This train the measure of other successions.*—So that to me it seems, that the constant and regular succession of ideas in a waking man is, as it were, the measure and standard of all other successions.

13. *The mind cannot fix long on one invariable idea.*—If it be so, that the ideas of our minds, whilst we have any there, do constantly change and shift in a continual succession, it would be impossible, may anyone say, for a man to think long of any one thing : by which if it be meant that a man may have one selfsame single idea a long time alone in his mind, without any variation at all, I think, in matter of fact, it is not possible.

17. *Time is duration set out by measures.*—Having thus got the idea of duration, the next thing natural for the mind to do is, to get some measure of this common duration, whereby it might judge of its different lengths, and consider the distinct order wherein

several things exist: without which a great part of our knowledge would be confused, and a great part of history be rendered very useless. This consideration of duration, as set out by certain periods, and marked by certain measures or epochs, is that, I think, which most properly we call " time."

18. *A good measure of time must divide its whole duration into equal periods.*—In the measuring of extension there is nothing more required but the application of the standard or measure we make use of to the thing of whose extension we would be informed. But in the measuring of duration this cannot be done, because no two different parts of succession can be put together to measure one another: and nothing being a measure of duration but duration, as nothing is of extension but extension, we cannot keep by us any standing unvarying measure of duration, which consists in a constant fleeting succession, as we can of certain lengths of extension, as inches, feet, yards, etc., marked out in permanent parcels of matter. Nothing then could serve well for a convenient measure of time but what has divided the whole length of its duration into apparently equal portions by constantly repeated periods.

19. *The revolutions of the sun and moon the properest measures of time.*—The diurnal and annual revolutions of the sun, as having been from the beginning of nature, constant, regular, and universally observable by all mankind, and supposed equal to one another, have been with reason made use of for the measure of duration. But the distinction of days and years having depended on the motion of the sun, it has brought this mistake with it, that it has been thought that motion and duration were the measure one of another. For men in the measuring of the length of time having been accustomed to the ideas of minutes, hours, days, months, years, etc., which they found themselves upon any mention of time or duration presently to think on (all which portions of time were measured out by the motion of those heavenly bodies), they were apt to confound time and motion, or at least to think that they had a necessary connection one with another; whereas any constant periodical appearance or alteration of ideas in seemingly equidistant spaces of duration, if constant and universally observable, would have as well distinguished the intervals of time as those that have been made use of.

32. And thus I think it is plain, that from those two fountains of all knowledge before mentioned, (viz.) reflection and sensation, we get the ideas of duration, and the measures of it.

For, First, by observing what passes in our minds, how our

ideas there in train constantly some vanish, and others begin to appear, we come by the idea of succession.

Secondly. By observing a distance in the parts of this succession, we get the idea of duration.

Thirdly. By sensation observing certain appearances, at certain regular and seeming equidistant periods, we get the ideas of certain lengths or measures of duration, as minutes, hours, days, years, etc.

Fourthly. By being able to repeat those measures of time, or ideas of stated length of duration in our minds, as often as we will, we can come to imagine duration where nothing does really endure or exist; and thus we imagine to-morrow, next year, or seven years hence.

Fifthly. By being able to repeat any such idea of any length of time, as of a minute, a year, or an age, as often as we will in our own thoughts, and add them one to another, without ever coming to the end of such addition, any nearer than we can to the end of number, to which we can always add, we come by the idea of eternity, as the future eternal duration of our souls, as well as the eternity of that infinite Being which must necessarily have always existed.

Sixthly. By considering any part of infinite duration, as set out by periodical measures, we come by the idea of what we call " time " in general.

CHAPTER XVI

OF NUMBER

1. *Number, the simplest and most universal idea.*—Amongst all the ideas we have, as there is none suggested to the mind by more ways, so there is none more simple, than that of unity, or one. It has no shadow of variety of composition in it; every object our senses are employed about, every idea in our understandings, every thought of our minds, brings this idea along with it : and therefore it is the most intimate to our thoughts, as well as it is, in its agree-ment to all other things, the most universal idea we have. For number applies itself to men, angels, actions, thoughts, everything that either doth exist or can be imagined.

2. *Its modes made by addition.*—By repeating this idea in our minds, and adding the repetitions together, we come by the complex ideas of the modes of it. Thus by adding one to one we have the complex idea of a couple : by putting twelve units together we

have the complex idea of a dozen; and a score, or a million, or any other number.

3. *Each mode distinct.*—The simple modes of number are of all other the most distinct; every the least variation which is an unit, making each combination as clearly different from that which approacheth nearest to it, as the most remote: two being as distinct from one as two hundred; and the idea of two as distinct from the idea of three, as the magnitude of the whole earth is from that of a mite. This is not so in other simple modes, in which it is not so easy, nor perhaps possible, for us to distinguish betwixt two approaching ideas, which yet are really different. For who will undertake to find a difference between the white of this paper and that of the next degree to it? or can form distinct ideas of every the least excess in extension?

5. *Names necessary to numbers.*—By the repeating, as has been said, of the idea of an unit, and joining it to another unit, we make thereof one collective idea, marked by the name " two." And whosoever can do this and proceed on, still adding one more to the last collective idea which he had of any number, and give a name to it, may count, or have ideas for several collections of units, distinguished one from another, as far as he hath a series of names for following numbers, and a memory to retain that series with their several names; all numeration being but still the adding of one unit more, and giving to the whole together, as comprehended in one idea, a new or distinct name or sign, whereby to know it from those before and after, and distinguish it from every smaller or greater multitude of units. So that he that can add one to one, and so to two, and so go on with his tale, taking still with him the distinct names belonging to every progression; and so again by subtracting an unit from each collection, retreat and lessen them; is capable of all the ideas of numbers within the compass of his language, or for which he hath names, though not perhaps of more. For, the several simple modes of numbers being in our minds but so many combinations of units, which have no variety, nor are capable of any other difference but more or less, names or marks for each distinct combination seem more necessary than in any other sort of ideas. For without such names or marks we can hardly well make use of numbers in reckoning, especially where the combination is made up of any great multitudes of units; which put together without a name or mark to distinguish that precise collection, will hardly be kept from being a heap in confusion.

CHAPTER XVII

OF INFINITY

1. *Infinity, in its original intention, attributed to space, duration and number.*—He that would know what kind of idea it is to which we give the name of " infinity," cannot do it better than by considering to what infinity is by the mind more immediately attributed, and then how the mind comes to frame it.

Finite and infinite seem to me to be looked upon by the mind as the modes of quantity, and to be attributed primarily in their first designation only to those things which have parts, and are capable of increase or diminution by the addition or subtraction of any the least part; and such are the ideas of space, duration, and number, which we have considered in the foregoing chapters. It is true that we cannot but be assured that the great God, of Whom and from Whom are all things, is incomprehensibly infinite : but yet when we apply to that first and supreme Being our idea of infinite, in our weak and narrow thoughts, we do it primarily in respect of His duration and ubiquity; and, I think, more figuratively to His power, wisdom, and goodness, and other attributes, which are properly inexhaustible and incomprehensible, etc.

2. *The idea of finite easily got.*—Finite then and infinite being by the mind looked on as modifications of expansion and duration, the next thing to be considered is, how the mind comes by them. As for the idea of finite, there is no great difficulty. The obvious portions of extension that affect our senses carry with them into the mind the idea of finite; and the ordinary periods of succession whereby we measure time and duration, as hours, days and years, are bounded lengths. The difficulty is, how we come by those boundless ideas of eternity and immensity, since the objects which we converse with come so much short of any approach or proportion to that largeness.

3. *How we come by the idea of infinity.*—Everyone that has any idea of any stated lengths of space, as a foot, finds that he can repeat that idea; and, joining it to the former, make the idea of two feet, and, by the addition of a third, three feet, and so on, without ever coming to an end of his additions, whether of the same idea of a foot, or, if he pleases, of doubling it, or any other idea he has of any length, as a mile, or diameter of the earth, or

of the *orbis magnus*; for, whichsoever of these he takes, and how often soever he doubles or any otherwise multiplies it, he finds that, after he has continued this doubling in his thoughts and enlarged his idea as much as he pleases, he has no more reason to stop, nor is one jot nearer the end of such addition than he was at first setting out: the power of enlarging his idea of space by farther additions remaining still the same, he hence takes the idea of infinite space.

4. *Our idea of space boundless.*—This, I think, is the way whereby the mind gets the idea of infinite space. It is a quite different consideration to examine whether the mind has the idea of such a boundless space actually existing, since our ideas are not always proofs of the existence of things; but yet, since this comes here in our way, I suppose I may say that we are apt to think that space in itself is actually boundless, to which imagination the idea of space or expansion of itself naturally leads us. For, it being considered by us either as the extension of body, or as existing by itself, without any solid matter taking it up (for of such a void space we have not only the idea, but I have proved, as I think, from the motion of body, its necessary existence), it is impossible the mind should be ever able to find or suppose any end of it, or be stopped anywhere in its progress in this space, how far soever it extends its thoughts.

5. *And so of duration.*—As, by the power we find in ourselves of repeating as often as we will any idea of space, we get the idea of immensity; so, by being able to repeat the idea of any length of duration we have in our minds, with all the endless addition of number, we come by the idea of eternity. For we find in ourselves, we can no more come to an end of such repeated ideas than we can come to the end of number; which everyone perceives he cannot.

7. *Difference between infinity of space and space infinite.*— Though our idea of infinity arise from the contemplation of quantity, and the endless increase the mind is able to make in quantity by the repeated additions of what portions thereof it pleases; yet, I guess, we cause great confusion in our thoughts when we join infinity to any supposed idea of quantity the mind can be thought to have, and so discourse or reason about an infinite quantity (viz.), an infinite space or an infinite duration. For our idea of infinity being, as I think, an endless growing idea, but the idea of any quantity the mind has being at that time terminated in that idea (for be it as great as it will, it can be no greater than

it is), to join infinity to it, is to adjust a standing measure to a growing bulk; and therefore I think it is not an insignificant subtilty if I say that we are carefully to distinguish between the idea of *the infinity of space* and the idea of *a space infinite*: the first is nothing but a supposed endless progression of the mind over what repeated ideas of space it pleases; but to have actually in the mind the idea of a space infinite, is to suppose the mind already passed over, and actually to have a view of all those repeated ideas of space which an endless repetition can never totally represent to it; which carries in it a plain contradiction.

8. *We have no idea of infinite space.*—This, perhaps, will be a little plainer if we consider it in numbers. The infinity of numbers, to the end of whose addition everyone perceives there is no approach, easily appears to anyone that reflects on it: but how clear soever this idea of the infinity of number be, there is nothing yet more evident than the absurdity of the actual idea of an infinite number. Whatsoever positive ideas we have in our minds of any space, duration, or number, let them be never so great, they are still finite; but when we suppose an inexhaustible remainder, from which we remove all bounds, and wherein we allow the mind an endless progression of thought, without ever completing the idea, there we have our idea of infinity; which though it seems to be pretty clear when we consider nothing else in it but the negation of an end, yet when we would frame in our minds the idea of an infinite space or duration, that idea is very obscure and confused, because it is made up of two parts very different, if not inconsistent. For let a man frame in his mind an idea of any space or number, as great as he will, it is plain the mind rests and terminates in that idea; which is contrary to the idea of infinity, which consists in a supposed endless progression.

9. *Number affords us the clearest idea of infinity.*—But of all other ideas, it is number, as I have said, which, I think, furnishes us with the clearest and most distinct idea of infinity we are capable of. For even in space and duration, when the mind pursues the idea of infinity, it there makes use of the ideas and repetitions of numbers, as of millions of millions of miles or years, which are so many distinct ideas kept best by number from running into a confused heap, wherein the mind loses itself; and when it has added together as many millions, etc., as it pleases of known lengths of space or duration, the clearest idea it can get of infinity is, the confused, incomprehensible remainder of endless addible numbers, which affords no prospect of stop or boundary.

CHAPTER XIX

OF THE MODES OF THINKING

1. *Sensation, remembrance, contemplation, etc.*—When the mind turns its view inwards upon itself, and contemplates its own actions, thinking is the first that occurs. In it the mind observes a great variety of modifications, and from thence receives distinct ideas. Thus the perception which actually accompanies and is annexed to any impression on the body made by an external object, being distinct from all other modifications of thinking, furnishes the mind with a distinct idea which we call " sensation "; which is, as it were, the actual entrance of any idea into the understanding by the senses. The same idea, when it again recurs without the operation of the like object on the external sensory, is " remembrance ": if it be sought after by the mind, and with pain and endeavour found, and brought again in view, it is " recollection ": if it be held there long under attentive consideration, it is " contemplation ": when ideas float in our mind without any reflection or regard of the understanding, it is that which the French call *rêverie;* our language has scarce a name for it: when the ideas that offer themselves (for, as I have observed in another place, whilst we are awake there will always be a train of ideas succeeding one another in our minds) are taken notice of, and, as it were, registered in the memory, it is " attention ": when the mind with great earnestness, and of choice, fixes its view on any idea, considers it on all sides, and will not be called off by the ordinary solicitation of other ideas, it is that we call " intention," or " study ": " sleep " without dreaming is rest from all these: and " dreaming " itself is the having of ideas (whilst the outward senses are stopped, so that they receive not outward objects with their usual quickness) in the mind not suggested by any external objects or known occasion, nor under any choice or conduct of the understanding at all; and whether that which we call " ecstasy " be not dreaming with the eyes open, I leave to be examined.

2. These are some few instances of those various modes of thinking which the mind may observe in itself, and so have as distinct ideas of as it hath of white and red, a square or a circle. I do not pretend to enumerate them all, nor to treat at large of this set of ideas which are got from reflection; that would be to

make a volume. It suffices to my present purpose to have shown here, by some few examples, of what sort these ideas are, and how the mind comes by them.

CHAPTER XXI

OF POWER

1. *This idea how got.*—The mind being every day informed, by the senses, of the alteration of those simple ideas it observes in things without, and taking notice how one comes to an end and ceases to be, and another begins to exist which was not before; reflecting also, on what passes within itself, and observing a constant change of its ideas, sometimes by the impression of outward objects on the senses, and sometimes by the determination of its own choice; and concluding, from what it has so constantly observed to have been, that the like changes will for the future be made in the same things by like agents, and by the like ways; considers in one thing the possibility of having any of its simple ideas changed, and in another the possibility of making that change; and so comes by that idea which we call " power." Thus we say, fire has a power to melt gold; *i.e.,* to destroy the consistency of its insensible parts, and consequently its hardness, and make it fluid; and gold has a power to be melted: that the sun has a power to blanch wax; and wax a power to be blanched by the sun, whereby the yellowness is destroyed, and whiteness made to exist in its room. In which and the like cases, the power we consider is in reference to the change of perceivable ideas: for we cannot observe any alteration to be made in, or operation upon, anything, but by the observable change of its sensible ideas; nor conceive any alteration to be made, but by conceiving a change of some of its ideas.

2. *Power active and passive.*—Power thus considered is twofold; viz., as able to make, or able to receive, any change: the one may be called " active," and the other " passive," power.

4. *The clearest idea of active power had from spirit.*—We are abundantly furnished with the idea of passive power, by almost all sorts of sensible things. In most of them we cannot avoid observing their sensible qualities, nay, their very substances, to be in a continual flux: and therefore with reason we look on them as liable still to the same change. Nor have we of active power (which is the more proper signification of the word " power ")

fewer instances; since, whatever change is observed, the mind must collect a power somewhere, able to make that change, as well as a possibility in the thing itself to receive it. But yet, if we will consider it attentively, bodies, by our senses, do not afford us so clear and distinct an idea of active power, as we have from reflection on the operations of our minds. For, all power relating to action, and there being but two sorts of action whereof we have any idea, viz., thinking and motion, let us consider whence we have the clearest ideas of the powers which produce these actions. (1). Of thinking, body affords us no idea at all: it is only from reflection that we have that. (2). Neither have we from body any idea of the beginning of motion. A body at rest affords us no idea of any active power to move; and when it is set in motion itself, that motion is rather a passion than an action in it. For when the ball obeys the stroke of a billiard stick, it is not any action of the ball, but bare passion: also when by impulse it sets another ball in motion that lay in its way, it only communicates the motion it had received from another, and loses in itself so much as the other received; which gives us but a very obscure idea of an active power moving in body, whilst we observe it only to transfer but not produce any motion. For it is but a very obscure idea of power, which reaches not the production of the action, but the continuation of the passion. For so is motion, in a body impelled by another: The continuation of the alteration made in it from rest to motion being little more an action, than the continuation of the alteration of its figure by the same blow is an action. The idea of the beginning of motion we have only from reflection, on what passes in ourselves, where we find by experience, that, barely by willing it, barely by a thought of the mind, we can move the parts of our bodies which were before at rest. So that it seems to me, we have, from the observation of the operation of bodies by our senses, but a very imperfect, obscure, idea of active power, since they afford us not any idea in themselves of the power to begin any action, either motion or thought. But if from the impulse bodies are observed to make one upon another, anyone thinks he has a clear idea of power, it serves as well to my purpose, sensation being one of those ways whereby the mind comes by its ideas: only I thought it worth while to consider here by the way, whether the mind doth not receive its idea of active power clearer from reflection on its own operations, than it doth from any external sensation.

  5. *Will and understanding two powers.*—This at least I think

evident, that we find in ourselves a power to begin or forbear, continue or end, several actions of our minds and motions of our bodies, barely by a thought or preference of the mind ordering, or, as it were, commanding the doing or not doing such or such a particular action. This power which the mind has thus to order the consideration of any idea, or the forbearing to consider it, or to prefer the motion of any part of the body to its rest, and *vice versa*, in any particular instance, is that which we call " the will." The actual exercise of that power, by directing any particular action or its forbearance, is that which we call " volition " or " willing." The forbearance of that action consequent to such order or command of the mind, is called " voluntary "; and whatsoever action is performed without such a thought of the mind, is called " involuntary." The power of perception is that which we call " the understanding." Perception, which we make the act of the understanding, is of three sorts: (1). The perception of ideas in our minds. (2). The perception of the signification of signs. (3) The perception of the connection or repugnancy, agreement or disagreement, that there is between any of our ideas. All these are attributed to the understanding, or perceptive power, though it be the two latter only that use allows us to say we understand.

6. *Faculties*.—These powers of the mind, viz., of perceiving and of preferring, are usually called by another name : and the ordinary way of speaking, is that the understanding and will are two faculties of the mind; a word proper enough, if it be used, as all words should be, so as not to breed any confusion in men's thoughts by being supposed (as I suspect it has been) to stand for some real beings in the soul, that performed those actions of understanding and volition. For when we say, the will is the commanding and superior faculty of the soul; that it is or is not free; that it determines the inferior faculties; that it follows the dictates of the understanding, etc.; though these and the like expressions, by those that carefully attend to their own ideas, and conduct their thoughts more by the evidence of things than the sound of words, may be understood in a clear and distinct sense : yet I suspect, I say, that this way of speaking of faculties has misled many into a confused notion of so many distinct agents in us, which had their several provinces and authorities, and did command, obey, and perform several actions, as so many distinct beings; which has been no small occasion of wrangling, obscurity, and uncertainty in questions relating to them.

7. *Whence the ideas of liberty and necessity.*—Everyone, I think, finds in himself a power to begin or forbear, continue or put an end to several actions in himself. From the consideration of the extent of this power of the mind over the actions of the man, which everyone finds in himself, arise the ideas of liberty and necessity.

8. *Liberty, what.*—All the actions that we have any idea of, reducing themselves, as has been said, to these two, viz., thinking and motion, so far as a man has a power to think or not to think, to move or not to move, according to the preference or direction of his own mind, so far is a man free. Wherever any performance or forbearance are not equally in a man's power, wherever doing or not doing will not equally follow upon the preference of his mind directing it, there he is not free, though perhaps the action may be voluntary. So that the idea of liberty is the idea of a power in any agent to do or forbear any particular action, according to the determination or thought of the mind, whereby either of them is preferred to the other; where either of them is not in the power of the agent, to be produced by him according to his volition, there he is not at liberty, that agent is under necessity. So that liberty cannot be where there is no thought, no volition, no will; but there may be thought, there may be will, there may be volition, where there is no liberty.

72. It may perhaps be to our purpose, and help to give us clearer conceptions about power, if we make our thoughts take a little more exact survey of action. I have said above, that we have ideas but of two sorts of action, viz., motion and thinking. These, in truth, though called and counted " actions," yet, if nearly considered, will not be found to be always·perfectly so. For, if I mistake not, there are instances of both kinds, which, upon due consideration, will be found rather passions than actions, and consequently so far the effects barely of passive powers in those subjects which yet on their account are thought agents. For in these instances the substance that hath motion or thought receives the same impression, whereby it is put into that action, purely from without, and so acts merely by the capacity it has to receive such an impression from some external agent; and such a power is not properly an active power, but a mere passive capacity in the subject. Sometimes the substance or agent puts itself into action by its own power; and this is properly active power. Whatsoever a modification a substance has whereby it produces any effect, that is called " action "; *v.g.*, a solid substance by motion

operates on or alters the sensible ideas of another substance, and therefore this modification of motion we call " action." But yet this motion in that solid substance is, when rightly considered, but a passion, if it received it only from some external agent. So that the active power of motion is in no substance which cannot begin motion in itself, or in another substance when at rest. So likewise in thinking, a power to receive ideas or thoughts from the operation of any external substance, is called " a power of thinking ": but this is but a passive power or capacity. But to be able to bring into view ideas out of sight at one's own choice, and to compare which of them one thinks fit, this is an active power. This reflection may be of some use to preserve us from mistakes about powers and actions, which grammar and the common frame of languages may be apt to lead us into: since what is signified by verbs that grammarians call " active," does not always signify action; v.g., this proposition, " I see the moon or a star," or, " I feel the heat of the sun," though expressed by a verb active, does not signify any action in me whereby I operate on those substances; but the reception of the ideas of light, roundness, and heat, wherein I am not active, but barely passive, and cannot, in that position of my eyes or body, avoid receiving them. But when I turn my eyes another way, or remove my body out of the sunbeams, I am properly active; because of my own choice, by a power within myself, I put myself into that motion. Such an action is the product of active power.

73. And thus I have, in a short draught, given a view of our original ideas, from whence all the rest are derived, and of which they are made up; which if I would consider as a philosopher, and examine on what causes they depend, and of what they are made, I believe they all might be reduced to these very few primary and original ones, viz., extension, solidity, mobility, or the power of being moved; which by our senses we receive from body: perceptivity, or the power of perception, or thinking; motivity, or the power of moving; which by reflection we receive from our minds. I crave leave to make use of these two new words, to avoid the danger of being mistaken in the use of those which are equivocal. To which if we add existence, duration, number, which belong both to the one and the other, we have perhaps all the original ideas on which the rest depended. For by these, I imagine, might be explained the nature of colours, sounds, tastes, smells, and all other ideas we have, if we had but faculties acute enough to perceive the severally-modified extensions and motions of these minute bodies

which produce those several sensations in us. But my present purpose being only to inquire into the knowledge the mind has of things by those ideas and appearances which God has fitted it to receive from them, and how the mind comes by that knowledge, rather than into their causes or manner of production, I shall not, contrary to the design of this essay, set myself to inquire philosophically into the peculiar constitution of bodies and the configuration of parts, whereby they have the power to produce in us the ideas of their sensible qualities. I shall not enter any farther into that disquisition, it sufficing to my purpose to observe that gold or saffron has a power to produce in us the idea of yellow; and snow or milk, the idea of white; which we can only have by our sight, without examining the texture of the parts of those bodies, or the particular figures or motion of the particles which rebound from them, to cause in us that particular sensation: though when we go beyond the bare ideas in our minds, and would inquire into their causes, we cannot conceive anything else to be in any sensible object whereby it produces different ideas in us, but the different bulk, figure, number, texture, and motion of its insensible parts.

CHAPTER XXII

OF MIXED MODES

1. *Mixed modes, what.*—Having treated of simple modes in the foregoing chapters, and given several instances of some of the most considerable of them, to show what they are, and how we come by them; we are now, in the next place, to consider those we call " mixed modes ": such are the complex ideas we mark by the names " obligation," " drunkenness," " a lie," etc., which, consisting of several combinations of simple ideas of different kinds, I have called " mixed modes," to distinguish them from the more simple modes, which consist only of simple ideas of the same kind. These mixed modes, being also such combinations of simple ideas as are not looked upon to be characteristical marks of any real beings that have a steady existence, but scattered and independent ideas put together by the mind, are thereby distinguished from the complex ideas of substances.

2. *Made by the mind.*—That the mind, in respect of its simple ideas, is wholly passive, and receives them all from the existence

and operations of things, such as sensation or reflection offers them, without being able to make any one idea, experience shows us. But if we attentively consider these ideas I call " mixed modes " we are now speaking of, we shall find their original quite different. The mind often exercises an active power in making these several combinations: for, it being once furnished with simple ideas, it can put them together in several compositions, and so make variety of complex ideas, without examining whether they exist so together in nature.   And hence, I think, it is that these ideas are called " notions "; as if they had their original and constant existence more in the thoughts of men, than in the reality of things; and to form such ideas it sufficed that the mind put the parts of them together, and that they were consistent in the understanding, without considering whether they had any real being: though I do not deny but several of them might be taken from observation, and the existence of several simple ideas so combined as they are put together in the understanding.   For the man who first framed the idea of hypocrisy, might have either taken it at first from the observation of one who made show of good qualities which he had not; or else have framed that idea in his mind without having any such pattern to fashion it by.   For it is evident that, in the beginning of languages and societies of men, several of those complex ideas, which were consequent to the constitutions established amongst them, must needs have been in the minds before they existed anywhere else; and that many names that stood for such complex ideas were in use, and so those ideas framed, before the combinations they stood for ever existed.

3. *Sometimes got by the explication of their names.*—Indeed, now that languages are made, and abound with words standing for such combinations, an usual way of getting these complex ideas is by the explication of those terms that stand for them. For, consisting of a company of simple ideas combined, they may, by words standing for those simple ideas, be represented to the mind of one who understands those words, though that complex combination of simples idea were never offered to his mind by the real existence of things.   Thus a man may come to have the idea of sacrilege or murder, by enumerating to him the simple ideas which these words stand for, without ever seeing either of them committed.

4. *The name ties the parts of mixed modes into one idea.*— Every mixed mode consisting of many distinct simple ideas, it seems reasonable to inquire, whence it has its unity, and how

such a precise multitude comes to make but one idea, since that combination does not always exist together in nature? To which I answer, It is plain it has its unity from an act of the mind combining those several simple ideas together, and considering them as one complex one, consisting of those parts; and the mark of this union, or that which is looked on generally to complete it, is one name given to that combination.

5. *The cause of making mixed modes.*—If we should inquire a little farther, to see what it is that occasions men to make several combinations of simple ideas into distinct and, as it were, settled modes, and neglect others which, in the nature of things themselves, have as much an aptness to be combined and make distinct ideas, we shall find the reason of it to be the end of language; which being to mark or communicate men's thoughts to one another with all the despatch that may be, they usually make such collections of ideas into complex modes, and affix names to them, as they have frequent use of it in their way of living and conversation, leaving others which they have but seldom an occasion to mention loose, and without names that tie them together: they rather choosing to enumerate (when they have need) such ideas as make them up, by the particular names that stand for them, than to trouble their memories by multiplying of complex ideas with names to them, which they shall seldom or never have any occasion to make use of.

CHAPTER XXIII

OF OUR COMPLEX IDEAS OF SUBSTANCES

1. *Ideas of substances, how made.*—The mind being, as I have declared, furnished with a great number of the simple ideas conveyed in by the senses, as they are found in exterior things, or by reflection on its own operations, takes notice, also, that a certain number of these simple ideas go constantly together; which being presumed to belong to one thing, and words being suited to common apprehensions, and made use of for quick despatch, are called, so united in one subject, by one name; which, by inadvertency, we are apt afterward to talk of and consider as one simple idea, which indeed is a complication of many ideas together: because, as I have said, not imagining how these simple ideas can subsist by themselves, we accustom ourselves to suppose

some *substratum* wherein they do subsist, and from which they do result; which therefore we call " substance."

2. *Our idea of substance in general.*—So that if anyone will examine himself concerning his notion of pure substance in general, he will find he has no other idea of it at all, but only a supposition of he knows not what support of such qualities which are capable of producing simple ideas in us; which qualities are commonly called " accidents." If anyone should be asked, " What is the subject wherein colour or weight inheres? " he would have nothing to say but, " The solid extended parts." And if he were demanded " What is it that solidity and extension inhere in? " he would not be in a much better case than the Indian before mentioned, who, saying that the world was supported by a great elephant, was asked, what the elephant rested on? to which his answer was, " A great tortoise ": but being again pressed to know what gave support to the broad-backed tortoise, replied— something, he knew not what. And thus here, as in all other cases where we use words without having clear and distinct ideas, we talk like children; who, being questioned what such a thing is which they know not readily, give this satisfactory answer—that it is something; which in truth signifies no more, when so used, either by children or men, but that they know not what; and that the thing they pretend to know and talk of, is what they have no distinct idea of at all, and so are perfectly ignorant of it, and in the dark. The idea, then, we have, to which we give the general name " substance," being nothing but the supposed, but unknown, support of those qualities we find existing, which we imagine cannot subsist *sine re substante,* " without something to support them," we call that support *substantia*; which, according to the true import of the word, is, in plain English, " standing under," or " upholding."

3. *Of the sorts of substances.*—An obscure and relative idea of substance in general being thus made, we come to have the ideas of particular sorts of substances, by collecting such combinations of simple ideas as are by experience and observation of men's senses taken notice of to exist together, and are therefore supposed to flow from the particular internal constitution or unknown essence of that substance. Thus we come to have the ideas of a man, horse, gold, water, etc., of which substances, whether anyone has any other clear idea, farther than of certain simple ideas co-existing together, I appeal to everyone's own experience. It is the ordinary qualities observable in iron or a diamond, put together, that make

the true complex idea of those substances, which a smith or a jeweller commonly knows better than a philosopher; who, whatever substantial forms he may talk of, has no other idea of those substances than what is framed by a collection of those simple ideas which are to be found in them. Only we must take notice, that our complex ideas of substances, besides all these simple ideas they are made up of, have always the confused idea of something to which they belong and in which they subsist: and therefore, when we speak of any sort of substance we say it is a thing having such or such qualities; as, body is a thing that is extended, figured, and capable of motion; spirit, a thing capable of thinking; and so hardness, friability, and power to draw iron we say, are qualities to be found in a loadstone. These and the like fashions of speaking, intimate that the substance is supposed always something, besides the extension, figure, solidity, motion, thinking, or other observable ideas, though we know not what it is.

4. *No clear idea of substance in general.*—Hence, when we talk or think of any particular sort of corporeal substances, as horse, stone, etc., though the idea we have of either of them be but the complication or collection of those several simple ideas of sensible qualities which we used to find united in the thing called " horse " or " stone "; yet because we cannot conceive how they should subsist alone, nor one in another, we suppose them existing in, and supported by, some common subject; which support we denote by the name " substance," though it be certain we have no clear or distinct idea of that thing we suppose a support.

5. *As clear an idea of spirit as body.*—The same happens concerning the operations of the mind; viz., thinking, reasoning, fearing, etc., which we concluding not to subsist of themselves, nor apprehending how they can belong to body, or be produced by it, we are apt to think these the actions of some other substance, which we call " spirit "; whereby yet it is evident that, having no other idea or notion of matter, but something wherein those many sensible qualities which affect our senses do subsist; by supposing a substance wherein thinking, knowing, doubting, and a power of moving, etc., do subsist; we have as clear a notion of the substance of spirit as we have of body; the one being supposed to be (without knowing what it is) the *substratum* to those simple ideas we have from without; and the other supposed (with a like ignorance of what it is) to be the *substratum* to those operations which we experiment in ourselves within. It is plain, then, that the idea of corporeal substance in matter is as remote from our conceptions

and apprehensions as that of spiritual substance, or spirit; and therefore, from our not having any notion of the substance of spirit, we can no more conclude its non-existence than we can, for the same reason, deny the existence of body: it being as rational to affirm there is no body, because we have no clear and distinct idea of the substance of matter, as to say there is no spirit, because we have no clear and distinct idea of the substance of a spirit.

6. *Of the sorts of substances.*—Whatever therefore be the secret and abstract nature of substance in general, all the ideas we have of particular, distinct sorts of substances, are nothing but several combinations of simple ideas co-existing in such, though unknown, cause of their union, as makes the whole subsist of itself. It is by such combinations of simple ideas, and nothing else, that we represent particular sorts of substances to ourselves; such are the ideas we have of their several species in our minds; and such only do we, by their specific names, signify to others; *v.g.*, man, horse, sun, water, iron: upon hearing which words everyone, who understands the language, frames in his mind a combination of those several simple ideas which he has usually observed or fancied to exist together under that denomination; all which he supposes to rest in, and be, as it were, adherent to, that unknown common subject, which inheres not in anything else; though in the meantime it be manifest, and everyone upon inquiry into his own thoughts will find, that he has no other idea of any substance, *v.g.*, let it be gold, horse, iron, man, vitriol, bread, but what he has barely of those sensible qualities which he supposes to adhere, with a supposition of such a *substratum* as gives, as it were, a support to those qualities, or simple ideas, which he has observed to exist united together. Thus, the idea of the sun, what is it but an aggregate of those several simple ideas — bright, hot, roundish, having a constant regular motion, at a certain distance from us—and perhaps some other? as he who thinks and discourses of the sun has been more or less accurate in observing those sensible qualities, ideas, or properties which are in that thing which he calls the '' sun.''

7. *Power, a great part of our complex ideas of substances.*—For he has the perfectest idea of any of the particular sorts of substances who has gathered and put together most of those simple ideas which do exist in it, among which are to be reckoned its active powers and passive capacities; which, though not simple ideas, yet in this respect, for brevity's sake, may conveniently enough be reckoned amongst them. Thus, the power of drawing iron is one of the ideas

of the complex one of that substance we call a " loadstone," and
a power to be so drawn is a part of the complex one we call " iron ";
which powers pass for inherent qualities in those subjects: because
every subject being as apt, by the powers we observe in it, to
change some sensible qualities in other subjects, as it is to produce
in us those simple ideas which we receive immediately from it,
does, by those new sensible qualities introduced into other subjects,
discover to us those powers which do thereby mediately affect our
senses as regularly as its sensible qualities do it immediately; *v.g.*,
we immediately by our senses perceive in fire its heat and colour;
which are, if rightly considered, nothing but powers in it to produce
those ideas in us: we also by our senses perceive the colour and
brittleness of charcoal, whereby we come by the knowledge of
another power in fire, which it has to change the colour and
consistency of wood. By the former, fire immediately, by the
latter it mediately, discovers to us these several powers, which
therefore we look upon to be a part of the qualities of fire, and so
make them a part of the complex ideas of it.

8. *And why.*—Nor are we to wonder that powers make a great
part of our complex ideas of substances, since their secondary
qualities are those which, in most of them, serve principally to
distinguish substances one from another, and commonly make a
considerable part of the complex idea of the several sorts of them.
For, our senses failing us in the discovery of the bulk, texture,
and figure of the minute parts of bodies, on which their real
constitutions and differences depend, we are fain to make use of
their secondary qualities, as the characteristical notes and marks
whereby to frame ideas of them in our minds, and distinguish them
one from another. All which secondary qualities, as has been
shown, are nothing but bare powers. For the colour and taste of
opium are, as well as its soporific or anodyne virtues, mere powers
depending on its primary qualities, whereby it is fitted to produce
different operations on different parts of our bodies.

9. *Three sorts of ideas make our complex ones of substances.*—
The ideas that make our complex ones of corporeal substances are
of these three sorts. First. The ideas of the primary qualities of
things which are discovered by our senses, and are in them even
when we perceive them not: such are the bulk, figure, number,
situation, and motion of the parts of bodies, which are really in
them, whether we take notice of them or no. Secondly. The
sensible secondary qualities which, depending on these, are nothing
but the powers those substances have to produce several ideas in

us by our senses; which ideas are not in the things themselves otherwise than as anything is in its cause. Thirdly. The aptness we consider in any substance to give or receive such alterations of primary qualities as that the substance so altered should produce in us different ideas from what it did before; these are called '' active and passive powers '': all which powers, as far as we have any notice or notion of them, terminate only in sensible simple ideas. For, whatever alteration a loadstone has the power to make in the minute particles of iron, we should have no notion of any power it had at all to operate on iron, did not its sensible motion discover it; and I doubt not but there are a thousand changes that bodies we daily handle have a power to cause in one another, which we never suspect, because they never appear in sensible effects.

10. *Powers make a great part of our complex idea of substances.* —Powers therefore justly make a great part of our complex ideas of substances. He that will examine his complex idea of gold, will find several of its ideas that make it up to be only powers: as the power of being melted, but of not spending itself in the fire, of being dissolved in *aqua regia*, are ideas as necessary to make up our complex idea of gold, as its colour and weight: which, if duly considered, are also nothing but different powers. For, to speak truly, yellowness is not actually in gold; but is a power in gold to produce that idea in us by our eyes, when placed in a due light: and the heat which we cannot leave out of our idea of the sun, is no more really in the sun than the white colour it introduces into wax. These are both equally powers in the sun, operating, by the motion and figure of its insensible parts, so on a man as to make him have the idea of heat; and so on wax as to make it capable to produce in a man the idea of white.

11. *The now secondary qualities of bodies would disappear, if we could discover the primary ones of their minute parts.*—Had we senses acute enough to discern the minute particles of bodies, and the real constitution on which their sensible qualities depend, I doubt not but they would produce quite different ideas in us, and that which is now the yellow colour of gold would then disappear and instead of it we should see an admirable texture of parts of a certain size and figure. This microscopes plainly discover to us; for, what to our naked eyes produces a certain colour is, by thus augmenting the acuteness of our senses, discovered to be quite a different thing; and the thus altering, as it were, the proportion of the bulk of the minute parts of a coloured object to our usual sight, produces different ideas from what it did before. Thus sand

or pounded glass, which is opaque and white to the naked eye, is pellucid in a microscope; and a hair seen this way loses its former colour, and is in a great measure pellucid, with a mixture of some bright sparkling colours, such as appear from the refraction of diamonds and other pellucid bodies. Blood to the naked eye appears all red; but by a good microscope, wherein its lesser parts appear, shows only some few globules of red, swimming in a pellucid liquor; and how these red globules would appear, if glasses could be found that yet could magnify them one thousand or ten thousand times more, is uncertain.

14. *Complex ideas of substances.*—The ideas we have of substances, and the way come by them; I say, Our specific ideas of substances are nothing else but a collection of a certain number of simple ideas, considered as united in one thing. These ideas of substances, though they are commonly called '' simple apprehensions,'' and the names of them '' simple terms ''; yet, in effect, are complex and compounded. Thus the idea which an Englishman signifies by the name '' swan,'' is white colour, long neck, red beak, black legs, and whole feet, and all these of a certain size, with a power of swimming in the water, and making a certain kind of noise; and perhaps to a man who has long observed those kind of birds, some other properties, which all terminate in sensible simple ideas, all united in one common subject.

15. *Idea of spiritual substances as clear as of bodily substances.*—Besides the complex ideas we have of material sensible substances, of which I have last spoken, by the simple ideas we have taken from those operations of our own minds, which we experiment daily in ourselves, as thinking, understanding, willing, knowing, and power of beginning motion, etc., co-existing in some substance, we are able to frame the complex idea of an immaterial spirit. And thus, by putting together the ideas of thinking, perceiving, liberty, and power of moving themselves and other things, we have as clear a perception and notion of immaterial substances as we have of material. For putting together the ideas of thinking and willing, or the power of moving or quieting corporeal motion, joined to substance, of which we have no distinct idea, we have the idea of an immaterial spirit; and by putting together the ideas of coherent solid parts, and a power of being moved, joined with substance, of which, likewise, we have no positive idea, we have the idea of matter. The one is as clear and distinct an idea as the other; the idea of thinking and moving a body being as clear and distinct ideas as the ideas of extension, solidity, and being moved. For

our idea of substance is equally obscure, or none at all, in both; it is but a supposed I-know-not-what, to support those ideas we call " accidents." It is for want of reflection that we are apt to think that our senses show us nothing but material things. Every act of sensation, when duly considered, gives us an equal view of both parts of nature, the corporeal and spiritual. For, whilst I know, by seeing or hearing, etc., that there is some corporeal being without me, the object of that sensation, I can more certainly know that there is some spiritual being within me that sees and hears. This I must be convinced cannot be the action of bare insensible matter, nor even could be without an immaterial thinking being.

16. *No idea of abstract substance.*—By the complex idea of extended, figured, coloured, and all other sensible qualities which is all that we know of it we are as far from the idea of the substance of body as if we knew nothing at all: nor, after all the acquaintance and familiarity which we imagine we have with matter, and the many qualities men assure themselves they perceive and know in bodies, will it, perhaps, upon examination be found, that they have any more or clearer primary ideas belonging to body than they have belonging to immaterial spirit.

17. *The cohesion of solid parts and impulse, the primary ideas of body.*—The primary ideas we have peculiar to body, as contradistinguished to spirit, are the cohesion of solid, and consequently separable parts, and a power of communicating motion by impulse. These, I think, are the original ideas proper and peculiar to body; for figure is but the consequence of finite extension.

18. *Thinking and motivity, the primary ideas of spirit.*—The ideas we have belonging and peculiar to spirit are thinking, and will, or a power of putting body into motion by thought, and, which is consequent to it, liberty. For as body cannot but communicate its motion by impulse to another body, which it meets with at rest; so the mind can put bodies into motion, or forbear to do so, as it pleases. The ideas of existence, duration, and mobility are common to them both.

22. *Idea of soul and body compared.*—Let us compare, then, our complex idea of an immaterial spirit with our complex idea of body, and see whether there be any more obscurity in one than in the other, and in which most. Our idea of body, as I think, is an extended solid substance, capable of communicating motion by impulse: and our idea of soul, as an immaterial spirit, is of a substance that thinks, and has a power of exciting motion in body,

by will or thought. These, I think, are our complex ideas of soul and body, as contra-distinguished; and now let us examine which has most obscurity in it, and difficulty to be apprehended. I know that people, whose thoughts are immersed in matter, and have so subjected their minds to their senses that they seldom reflect on anything beyond them, are apt to say, they cannot comprehend a thinking thing, which perhaps is true: but I affirm, when they consider it well, they can no more comprehend an extended thing.

30. *Idea of body and spirit compared.*—The idea we have of spirit, compared with the idea we have of body stands thus: The substance of spirit is unknown to us; and so is the substance of body equally unknown to us: two primary qualities or properties of body, viz., solid coherent parts and impulse, we have distinct clear ideas of: so likewise we know and have distinct clear ideas of two primary qualities or properties of spirit, viz., thinking, and a power of action; *i.e.,* a power of beginning or stopping several thoughts or motions. We have also the ideas of several qualities inherent in bodies, and have the clear distinct ideas of them: which qualities are but the various modifications of the extension of cohering solid parts and their motion. We have likewise the ideas of several modes of thinking, viz., believing, doubting, intending, fearing, hoping; all which are but the several modes of thinking. We have also the ideas of willing, and moving the body consequent to it, and with the body itself too; for, as has been showed, spirit is capable of motion.

31. *The notion of spirit involves no more difficulty in it than that of body.*—If this notion of immaterial spirit may have, perhaps, some difficulties in it not easy to be explained, we have therefore no more reason to deny or doubt the existence of such spirits, than we have to deny or doubt the existence of body because the motion of body is cumbered with some difficulties, very hard and perhaps impossible to be explained or understood by us.

32. *We know nothing beyond our simple ideas.*—Which we are not at all to wonder at, since we, having but some few superficial ideas of things, discovered to us only by the senses from without, or by the mind reflecting on what it experiments in itself within, have no knowledge beyond that, much less of the internal constitution and true nature of things, being destitute of faculties to attain it. And therefore experimenting and discovering in ourselves knowledge and the power of voluntary motion, as certainly as we experiment or discover in things without us the cohesion and separation of solid parts, which is the extension and motion of

bodies; we have as much reason to be satisfied with our notion of immaterial spirit, as with our notion of body; and the existence of the one as well as the other. For, it being no more a contradiction that thinking should exist separate and independent from solidity, than it is a contradiction that solidity should exist separate and independent from thinking, they being both but simple ideas, independent one from another; and having as clear and distinct ideas in us of thinking as of solidity, I know not why we may not as well allow a thinking thing without solidity, *i.e.*, immaterial, to exist, as a solid thing without thinking, *i.e.*, matter, to exist; especially since it is no harder to conceive how thinking should exist without matter, than how matter should think. For whensoever we would proceed beyond these simple ideas we have from sensation and reflection, and dive farther into the nature of things, we fall presently into darkness and obscurity, perplexedness and difficulties; and can discover nothing farther but our own blindness and ignorance.

35. *Idea of God.*—Though in His own essence, which certainly we do not know (not knowing the real essence of a pebble, or a fly, or of our own selves), God be simple and uncompounded; yet, I think, I may say we have no other idea of Him but a complex one of existence, knowledge, power, happiness, etc., infinite and eternal: which are all distinct ideas, and some of them being relative are again compounded of others; all which, being, as has been shown, originally got from sensation and reflection, go to make up the idea or notion we have of God.

37. *Recapitulation.*—And thus we have seen what kind of ideas we have of substances of all kinds, wherein they consist, and how we come by them. From whence, I think, it is very evident,

First, That all our ideas of several sorts of substances are nothing but collections of simple ideas, with a supposition of something to which they belong, and in which they subsist; though of this supposed something we have no clear distinct idea at all.

Secondly, That all the simple ideas that, thus united in one common substratum, make up our complex ideas of several sorts of substances, are no other but such as we have received from sensation or reflection. So that even in those which we think we are most intimately acquainted with, and come nearest the comprehension of our most enlarged conceptions, we cannot reach beyond those simple ideas. And even in those which seem most remote from all we have to do with, and do infinitely surpass anything we can perceive in ourselves by reflection, or discover by sensation in other things, we can attain to nothing but those simple ideas which we originally received from sensation or reflection; as is evident in the complex ideas we have of angels, and particularly of God Himself.

Thirdly, That most of the simple ideas that make up our complex ideas of substances, when truly considered, are only powers, however we are apt to take them for positive qualities: *v.g.*, the greatest part of the ideas that make our complex idea of gold are yellowness, great weight, ductility, fusibility, and solubility in *aqua regia*, etc., all united together in an unknown substratum; all which ideas are nothing else but so many relations to other substances, and are not really in the gold considered barely in itself, though they depend on those real and primary qualities of its internal constitution, whereby it has a fitness differently to operate and be operated on by several other substances.

CHAPTER XXV

OF RELATION

1. *Relation, what.*—Besides the ideas, whether simple or complex, that the mind has of things, as they are in themselves, there are others it gets from their comparison one with another. The understanding, in the consideration of anything, is not confined to that precise object: it can carry any idea, as it were, beyond itself, or, at least, look beyond it, to see how it stands in conformity to any other. When the mind so considers one thing, that it does, as it were, bring it to and set it by another, and carry its view from one to the other: this is, as the words import, " relation " and " respect "; and the denominations given to positive things, intimating that respect, and serving as marks to lead the thoughts beyond the subject itself denominated to something distinct from it, are what we call " relatives "; and the things so brought together, " related." Thus, when the mind considers Caius as such a positive being, it takes nothing into that idea, but what really exists in Caius; *v.g.*, when I consider him as man, I have nothing in my mind but the complex idea of the species man. So likewise, when I say, " Caius is a white man," I have nothing but the bare consideration of man who hath that white colour. But when I give Caius the name " husband," I intimate some other person; and when I give him the name " whiter," I intimate some other thing: in both cases my thought is led to something beyond Caius,

and there are two things brought into consideration. And since any idea, whether simple or complex, may be the occasion why the mind thus brings two things together, and as it were, takes a view of them at once, though still considered as distinct; therefore any of our ideas may be the foundation of relation.

6. *Relation only betwixt two things.*—Whatsoever doth or can exist, or be considered as one thing, is positive; and so not only simple ideas and substances, but modes also, are positive beings; though the parts of which they consist are very often relative one to another; but the whole together considered as one thing, and producing in us the complex idea of one thing, which idea is in our minds as one picture, though an aggregate of divers parts and under one name, it is a positive or absolute thing or idea. Thus a triangle, though the parts thereof, compared one to another, be relative, yet the idea of the whole is a positive absolute idea. The same may be said of a family, a tune, etc., for there can be no relation but betwixt two things, considered as two things. There must always be in relation two ideas, or things, either in themselves really separate, or considered as distinct, and then a ground or occasion for their comparison.

8. *The ideas of relations clearer often than of the subjects related.* —The ideas of relations are capable at least of being more perfect and distinct in our minds than those of substances. Because it is commonly hard to know all the simple ideas which are really in any substance, but for the most part easy enough to know the simple ideas that make up any relation.

9. *Relations all terminate in simple ideas.*—Though there be a great number of considerations wherein things may be compared one with another, and so a multitude of relations; yet they all terminate in, and are concerned about, those simple ideas either of sensation or reflection, which I think to be the whole materials of all our knowledge.

11. *Conclusion.*—Having laid down these premises concerning relation in general, I shall now proceed to show in some instances, how all the ideas we have of relation are made up, as the others are, only of simple ideas; and that they all, how refined or remote from sense soever they seem, terminate at last in simple ideas. I shall begin with the most comprehensive relation, wherein all things that do or can exist are concerned; and that is the relation of cause and effect. The idea whereof, how derived from the two fountains of all our knowledge, sensation and reflection, I shall in the next place consider.

CHAPTER XXVI

OF CAUSE AND EFFECT AND OTHER RELATIONS

1. *Whence their ideas got.*—In the notice that our senses take of the constant vicissitude of things, we cannot but observe that several particular both qualities and substances begin to exist; and that they receive this their existence from the due application and operation of some other being. From this observation we get our ideas of cause and effect. That which produces any simple or complex idea, we denote by the general name " cause "; and that which is produced, " effect." Thus finding that in that substance which we call " wax " fluidity, which is a simple idea that was not in it before, is constantly produced by the application of a certain degree of heat, we call the simple idea of heat, in relation to fluidity in wax, *the cause* of it, and fluidity *the effect.* So also finding that the substance, wood, which is a certain collection of simple ideas so called, by the application of fire is turned into another substance called " ashes," *i.e.,* another complex idea, consisting of a collection of simple ideas, quite different from that complex idea which we call " wood," we consider fire, in relation to ashes, as cause, and the ashes, as effect. So that whatever is considered by us to conduce or operate to the producing any particular simple idea, or collection of simple ideas, whether substance or mode, which did not before exist, hath thereby in our minds the relation of a cause, and so is denominated by us.

2. *Creation, generation, making, alteration.*—Having thus, from what our senses are able to discover in the operations of bodies on one another, got the notion of cause and effect, viz., that a cause is that which makes any other thing, either simple idea, substance, or mode, begin to be, and an effect is that which had its beginning from some other thing, the mind finds no great difficulty to distinguish the several originals of things into two sorts:—

First, When the thing is wholly made new, so that no part thereof did ever exist before; as when a new particle of matter doth begin to exist, *in rerum natura,* which had before no being; and this we call " creation."

Secondly, When a thing is made up of particles which did all of them before exist, but that very thing so constituted of pre-existing particles, which, considered all together, make up such a collection of simple ideas, had not any existence before, as this man, this egg, rose, or cherry, etc. And this, when referred to a substance produced in the ordinary course of nature by an internal principle, but set on work by and received from some external agent or cause, and working by insensible ways which we perceive not, we call " generation."

3. *Relations of time.*—Time and place are also the foundations of very large relations, and all finite beings at least are concerned in them. But having already shown in another place how we get these ideas, it may suffice here to intimate, that most of the denominations of things received from time are only relations: thus, when anyone says that " Queen Elizabeth lived sixty-nine, and reigned forty-five years," these words import only the relation of that duration to some other, and means no more but this, that the duration of her existence was equàl to sixty-nine, and the duration of her government to forty-five, annual revolutions of the sun; and so are all words answering *how long.*

CHAPTER XXVII

OF IDENTITY AND DIVERSITY

1. *Wherein identity consists.*—Another occasion the mind often takes of comparing, is, the very being of things, when, considering anything as existing at any determined time and place, we compare it with itself existing at another time, and thereon form the ideas of identity and diversity. When we see anything to be in any place in any instant of time, we are sure (be it what it will) that it is that very thing, and not another, which at that same time exists in another place, how like and undistinguishable soever it may be in all other respects: and in this consists identity, when the ideas it is attributed to, vary not at all from what they were that moment wherein we consider their former existence, and to which we compare the present. For we never finding, nor conceiving it possible, that two things of the same kind should exist in the same place at the same time, we rightly conclude that whatever exists anywhere at any time, excludes all of the same kind, and is there itself alone. When therefore we demand whether anything be the same or no? it refers always to something that existed such a time in such a place, which it was certain at that instant was the same with itself and no other: from whence it follows, that one thing

cannot have two beginnings of existence, nor two things one beginning, it being impossible for two things of the same kind to be or exist in the same instant, in the very same place, or one and the same thing in different places. That therefore that had one beginning, is the same thing; and that which had a different beginning in time and place from that, is not the same, but diverse. That which has made the difficulty about this relation, has been the little care and attention used in having precise notions of the things to which it is attributed.

2. *Identity of substances. Identity of modes.*—We have the ideas but of three sorts of substances: 1. God. 2. Finite intelligences. 3. Bodies. First. God is without beginning, eternal, unalterable, and everywhere; and therefore concerning His identity, there can be no doubt. Secondly. Finite spirits having had each its determinate time and place of beginning to exist, the relation to that time and place will always determine to each of them its identity as long as it exists. Thirdly. The same will hold of every particle of matter, to which no addition or subtraction of matter being made, it is the same. For though these three sorts of substances, as we term them, do not exclude one another out of the same place: yet we cannot conceive but that they must necessarily each of them exclude any of the same kind out of the same place: or else the notions and names of " identity and diversity " would be in vain, and there could be no such distinction of substances, or anything else, one from another.

3. *Principium individuationis.*—From what has been said, it is easy to discover, what is so much inquired after, the *principium individuationis*; and that, it is plain, is existence itself, which determines a being of any sort to a particular time and place incommunicable to two beings of the same kind.

6. *Identity of man.*—The identity of the same man consists in nothing but a participation of the same continued life by constantly fleeting particles of matter, in succession vitally united to the same organized body. He that shall place the identity of man in anything else but, like that of other animals, in one fitly organized body, taken in any one instant, and from thence continued under one organization of life in several successively fleeting particles of matter united to it, will find it hard to make an embryo one of years, mad, and sober, the same man, by any supposition that will not make it possible for Seth, Ismael, Socrates, Pilate, St. Austin, and Cæsar Borgia, to be the same man. For if the identity of soul alone makes the same man, and there be nothing in the

nature of matter why the same individual spirit may not be united
to different bodies, it will be possible that those men living in
distant ages, and of different tempers, may have been the same
man: which way of speaking must be from a very strange use of
the word " man," applied to an idea out of which body and shape
is excluded.

9. *Personal identity.*—This being premised, to find wherein
personal identity consists, we must consider what " person " stands
for; which, I think, is a thinking intelligent being, that has reason
and reflection, and can consider itself as itself, the same thinking
thing, in different times and places; which it does only by that
consciousness which is inseparable from thinking, and it seems to
me essential to it: it being impossible for anyone to perceive,
without perceiving that he does perceive. When we see, hear,
smell, taste, feel, meditate, or will anything, we know that we
do so. Thus it is always as to our present sensations and perceptions: and by this everyone is to himself that which he calls
" self "; it not being considered, in this case, whether the same
self be continued in the same or diverse substances. For since
consciousness always accompanies thinking, and it is that that
makes everyone to be what he calls " self," and thereby distinguishes himself from all other thinking things; in this alone consists
personal identity, *i.e.*, the sameness of a rational being: and as far
as this consciousness can be extended backwards to any past action
or thought, so far reaches the identity of that person; it is the same
self now it was then; and it is by the same self with this present
one that now reflects on it, that that action was done.

23. *Consciousness alone makes self.*—Nothing but consciousness
can unite remote existences into the same person; the identity of
substance will not do it. For, whatever substance there is, however
framed, without consciousness there is no person: and a carcass
may be a person, as well as any sort of substance be so without
consciousness.

CHAPTER XXX

OF REAL AND FANTASTICAL IDEAS

1. *Real ideas are conformable to their archetypes.*—Besides what
we have already mentioned concerning ideas, other considerations
belong to them, in reference to things from whence they are taken,

or which they may be supposed to represent; and thus, I think, they may come under a threefold distinction; and are,

First, Either real or fantastical.

Secondly, Adequate or inadequate.

Thirdly, True or false.

First, By " real ideas," I mean such as have a foundation in nature; such as have a conformity with the real being and existence of things, or with their archetypes. " Fantastical or chimerical," I call such as have no foundation in nature, nor have any conformity with that reality of being to which they are tacitly referred as to their archetypes. If we examine the several sorts of ideas before mentioned, we shall find, that,

2. *Simple ideas all real.*—Our simple ideas are all real, all agree to the reality of things. Not that they are all of them the images or representations of what does exist; the contrary whereof, in all but the primary qualities of bodies, hath been already showed. But though whiteness and coldness are no more in snow than pain is; yet those ideas of whiteness and coldness, pain, etc., being in us the effects of powers in things without us, ordained by our Maker to produce in us such sensations, they are real ideas in us, whereby we distinguish the qualities that are really in things themselves. And thus our simple ideas are all real and true, because they answer and agree to those powers of things which produce them in our minds, that being all that is requisite to make them real, and not fictions at pleasure. For in simple ideas (as has been shown), the mind is wholly confined to the operation of things upon it, and can make to itself no simple idea, more than what it has received.

3. *Complex ideas are voluntary combinations.*—Though the mind be wholly passive in respect of its simple ideas, yet, I think, we may say, it is not so in respect of its complex ideas: for, those being combinations of simple ideas put together, and united under one general name, it is plain that the mind of man uses some kind of liberty in forming those complex ideas: how else comes it to pass, that one man's idea of gold or justice is different from another's, but because he has put in or left out of his some simple idea which the other has not The question then is, Which of these are real, and which barely imaginary, combinations? What collections agree to the reality of things, and what not? And to this, I say, that,

4. *Mixed modes made of consistent ideas are real.*—Mixed modes and relations having no other reality but what they have in the minds of men, there is nothing more required to those kinds of

ideas to make them real but that they be so framed that there be a possibility of existing conformable to them. These ideas, being themselves archetypes, cannot differ from their archetypes, and so cannot be chimerical, unless anyone will jumble together in them inconsistent ideas.

5. *Ideas of substances are real when they agree with the existence of things.*—Our complex ideas of substances, being made all of them in reference to things existing without us, and intended to be representations of substances as they really are, are no farther real than as they are such combinations of simple ideas as are really united, and co-exist in things without us. Ideas of substances being made conformable to no pattern existing that we know, and consisting of such collections of ideas as no substance ever showed us united together, they ought to pass with us for barely imaginary; but much more are those complex ideas so, which contain in them any inconsistency or contradiction of their parts.

CHAPTER XXXI

OF ADEQUATE AND INADEQUATE IDEAS

1. *Adequate ideas are such as perfectly represent their archetypes.* —Of our real ideas, some are adequate, and some are inadequate. Those I call " adequate " which perfectly represent those archetypes which the mind supposes them taken from; which it intends them to stand for, and to which it refers them. Inadequate ideas are such which are but a partial or incomplete representation of those archetypes to which they are referred.

2. *Simple ideas all adequate.*—First, That all our simple ideas are adequate. Because being nothing but the effects of certain powers in things, fitted and ordained by God to produce such sensations in us, they cannot but be correspondent and adequate to those powers : and we are sure they agree to the reality of things. For if sugar produce in us the ideas which we call " whiteness," and " sweetness," we are sure there is a power in sugar to produce those ideas in our minds, or else they could not have been produced by it.

12. *Simple ideas and adequate.*—The mind has three sorts of abstract ideas, or nominal essences :

First, Simple ideas which are ἔκτυπα, or " copies "; but yet

certainly adequate. Because being intended to express nothing
but the power in things to produce in the mind such a sensation,
that sensation, when it is produced, cannot but be the effect of
that power. So the paper I write on, having the power, in the
light (I speak according to the common notion of light), to produce
in me the sensation which I call " white," it cannot but be the effect
of such a power in something without the mind, since the mind has
not the power to produce any such idea in itself; and being meant
for nothing else but the effect of such a power, that simple idea is
real and adequate: the sensation of " white " in my mind being
the effect of that power which is in the paper to produce it, is
perfectly adequate to that power; or else that power would produce
a different idea.

13. *Ideas of substances are* εκτυπα, *inadequate.*—Secondly, The
complex ideas of substances are *ectypes* or " copies," too; but not
perfect ones, not adequate; which is very evident to the mind, in
that it plainly perceives that whatever collection of simple ideas it
makes of any substance that exists, it cannot be sure that it exactly
answers all that are in that substance: since, not having tried
all the operations of all other substances upon it, and found all the
alterations it would receive from or cause in other substances, it
cannot have an exact adequate collection of all its active and
passive capacities; and so not have an adequate complex idea of
the powers of any substance existing and its relations, which is
that sort of complex idea of substances we have. And after all, if
we could have, and actually had, in our complex idea, an exact
collection of all the secondary qualities or powers of any substance,
we should not yet thereby have an idea of the essence of that thing.
For since the powers or qualities that are observable by us are not
the real essence of that substance, but depend on it, and flow from
it, any collection whatsoever of these qualities cannot be the real
essence of that thing. Whereby it is plain that our ideas of substances are not adequate; are not what the mind intends them to be.
Besides, a man has no idea of substance in general, nor knows
what substance is in itself.

14. *Ideas of modes and relations are archetypes, and cannot but
be adequate.*—Thirdly, Complex ideas of modes and relations are
originals and archetypes; are not copies, nor made after the pattern
of any real existence, to which the mind intends them to be
conformable, and exactly to answer. These being such collections
of simple ideas that the mind itself puts together, and such collections that each of them contains in it precisely all that the mind

intends it should, they are archetypes and essences of modes that may exist.

CHAPTER XXXII

OF TRUE AND FALSE IDEAS

1. *Truth and falsehood properly belong to propositions.*— Though truth and falsehood belong, in propriety of speech, only to propositions, yet ideas are oftentimes termed " true or false " (as what words are there that are not used with great latitude, and with some deviation from their strict and proper significations?) though I think, that when ideas themselves are termed " true or false," there is still some secret or tacit proposition which is the foundation of that denomination: as we shall see, if we examine the particular occasions wherein they come to be called " true or false." In all which we shall find some kind of affirmation or negation, which is the reason of that denomination. For our ideas being nothing but bare appearances or perceptions in our minds, cannot properly and simply in themselves be said to be true or false, no more than a single name of anything can be said to be true or false.

4. *Ideas referred to anything may be true or false.*—Whenever the mind refers any of its ideas to anything extraneous to them, they are then capable to be called true or false. Because the mind in such a reference makes a tacit supposition of their conformity to that thing; which supposition, as it happens to be true or false, so the ideas themselves come to be denominated. The most usual cases wherein this happens are these following:

5. *Other men's ideas, real existence, and supposed real essences, are what men usually refer ideas to.*—First, When the mind supposes any idea it has conformable to that in other men's minds, called by the same common name; *v.g.,* when the mind intends or judges its ideas of justice, temperance, religion, to be the same with what other men give those names to.

Secondly, When the mind supposes any idea it has in itself to be conformable to some real existence. Thus the two ideas of a man and a centaur, supposed to be the ideas of real substances, are the one true and the other false; the one having a conformity to what has really existed, the other not.

Thirdly, When the mind refers any of its ideas to that real

constitution and essence of anything, whereon all its properties depend: and thus the greatest part, if not all our ideas of substances, are false.

CHAPTER XXXIII

OF THE ASSOCIATION OF IDEAS

5. Some of our ideas have a natural correspondence and connection one with another; it is the office and excellency of our reason to trace these, and hold them together in that union and correspondence which is founded in their peculiar beings. Besides this, there is another connection of ideas wholly owing to chance or custom: ideas that in themselves are not at all of kin, come to be so united in some men's minds that it is very hard to separate them; they always keep in company, and the one no sooner at any time comes into the understanding, but its associate appears with it; and if they are more than two which are thus united, the whole gang, always inseparable, show themselves together.

6. *This connection, how made.*—This strong combination of ideas, not allied by nature, the mind makes in itself either voluntarily or by chance; and hence it comes in different men to be very different, according to their different inclinations, educations, interests, etc. Custom settles habits of thinking in the understanding, as well as of determining in the will, and of motions in the body; all which seem to be but trains of motion in the animal spirits, which, once set a-going, continue in the same steps they have been used to, which, by often treading, are worn into a smooth path, and the motion in it becomes easy, and as it were natural. As far as we can comprehend thinking, thus ideas seem to be produced in our minds; or if they are not, this may serve to explain their following one another in an habitual train, when once they are put into that track, as well as it does to explain such motions of the body. A musician used to any tune will find, that, let it but once begin in his head, the ideas of the several notes will follow one another orderly in his understanding, without any care or attention, as regularly as his fingers move orderly over the keys of the organ to play out the tune he has begun, though his unattentive thoughts be elsewhere a-wandering.

19. *Conclusion.*—Having thus given an account of the original sorts and extent of our ideas, with several other considerations

about these (I know not whether I may say) instruments, or materials, of our knowledge: the method I at first proposed to myself, would now require that I should immediately proceed to show what use the understanding makes of them, and what knowledge we have by them. This was that which, in the first general view I had of this subject, was all that I thought I should have to do: but upon a nearer approach, I find that there is so close a connection between ideas and words, and our abstract ideas and general words have so constant a relation one to to another, that it is impossible to speak clearly and distinctly of our knowledge, which all consists in propositions, without considering first the nature, use, and signification of language; which therefore must be the business of the next book.

BOOK III

OF WORDS

CHAPTER I

OF WORDS OR LANGUAGE IN GENERAL

6. To understand the use and force of language as subservient to instruction and knowledge, it will be convenient to consider,

First, To what it is that names, in the use of language, are immediately applied.

Secondly, Since all (except proper) names are general, and so stand not particularly for this or that single thing, but for sorts and ranks of things, it will be necessary to consider, in the next place, what the sorts and kinds, or, if you rather like the Latin names, what the *species* and *genera* of things are, wherein they consist, and how they come to be made. These being (as they ought) well looked into, we shall the better come to find the right use of words, the natural advantages and defects of language, and the remedies that ought to be used to avoid the inconveniences of obscurity or uncertainty in the signification of words; without which it is impossible to discourse with any clearness or order concerning knowledge : which being conversant about propositions, and those most commonly universal ones, has greater connection with words than perhaps is suspected.

These considerations, therefore, shall be the matter of the following chapters.

CHAPTER II

OF THE SIGNIFICATION OF WORDS

1. *Words are sensible signs necessary for communication.*—Man, though he have great variety of thoughts, and such from which others as well as himself might receive profit and delight, yet they are all within his own breast, invisible, and hidden from others, nor can of themselves be made appear. The comfort and advantage of society not being to be had without communication of thoughts, it was necessary that man should find out some external sensible signs, whereby those invisible ideas which his thoughts are made up of might be made known to others. For this purpose nothing was so fit, either for plenty or quickness, as those articulate sounds which, with so much ease and variety, he found himself able to make. The use, then, of words is to be sensible marks of ideas, and the ideas they stand for are their proper and immediate signification.

2. *Words are the sensible signs of his ideas who uses them.*—The use men have of these marks being either to record their own thoughts for the assistance of their own memory, or, as it were, to bring out their ideas, and lay them before the view of others: words in their primary or immediate signification stand for nothing but the ideas in the mind of him that uses them, how imperfectly soever or carelessly those ideas are collected from the things which they are supposed to represent. Words being voluntary signs, they cannot be voluntary signs imposed by a man on things he knows not. That would be to make them signs of nothing, sounds without signification. A man cannot make his words the signs either of qualities in things, or of conceptions in the mind of another, whereof he has none in his own.

3. Words, in every man's mouth, stand for the ideas he has, and which he would express by them. A child having taken notice of nothing in the metal he hears called " gold," but the bright shining yellow colour, he applies the word " gold " only to his own idea of that colour, and nothing else; and therefore calls the same colour in a peacock's tail, " gold." Another, that hath better observed, adds to shining yellow great weight: and then the sound " gold," when he uses it, stands for a complex idea of a shining yellow and very weighty substance. Another adds to those qualities

fusibility: and then the word "gold" to him signifies a body, bright, yellow, fusible, and very heavy. Another adds malleability. Each of these uses equally the word "gold," when they have occasion to express the idea which they have applied it to: but it is evident that each can apply it only to his own idea; nor can he make it stand as a sign of such a complex idea as he has not.

4. *Words often secretly referred.*—But though words, as they are used by men, can properly and immediately signify nothing but the ideas that are in the mind of the speaker, yet they in their thoughts give them a secret reference to two other things.

First, To the ideas in other men's minds.—First, They suppose their words to be marks of the ideas in the minds also of other men, with whom they communicate: for else they should talk in vain, and could not be understood, if the sounds they applied to one idea were such as by the hearer were applied to another, which is to speak two languages.

5. *Secondly, To the reality of things.*—Secondly, Because men would not be thought to talk barely of their own imaginations, but of things as really they are; therefore they often suppose their words to stand also for the reality of things.

6. *Words by use readily excite ideas.*—Concerning words also it is farther to be considered: First, That they being immediately the signs of men's ideas, and by that means, the instruments whereby men communicate their conceptions, and express to one another those thoughts and imaginations they have within their own breasts, there comes, by constant use, to be such a connection between certain sounds and the ideas they stand for, that the names heard almost as readily excite certain ideas, as if the objects themselves which are apt to produce them did actually affect the senses. Which is manifestly so in all obvious sensible qualities, and in all substances that frequently and familiarly occur to us.

7. *Words often used without signification.*—Secondly, That though the proper and immediate signification of words are ideas in the mind of the speaker, yet because, by familiar use from our cradles, we come to learn certain articulate sounds very perfectly, and have them readily on our tongues, and always at hand in our memories, but yet are not always careful to examine or settle their significations perfectly; it often happens that men, even when they would apply themselves to an attentive consideration, do set their thoughts more on words than things.

8. *Their signification perfectly arbitrary.*—Words, by long and familiar use, as has been said, come to excite in men certain ideas

so constantly and readily, that they are apt to suppose a natural connexion between them. But that they signify only men's peculiar ideas, and that by a perfectly arbitrary imposition, is evident in that they often fail to excite in others (even that use the same language) the same ideas we take them to be the signs of: and every man has so inviolable a liberty to make words stand for what ideas he pleases, that no one hath the power to make others have the same ideas in their minds that he has, when they use the same words that he does. Whatever be the consequence of any man's using of words differently, either from their general meaning, or the particular sense of the person to whom he addresses them, this is certain, their signification, in his use of them, is limited to his ideas, and they can be signs of nothing else.

CHAPTER III

OF GENERAL TERMS

1. *The greatest part of words general.*—All things that exist being particulars, it may perhaps be thought reasonable that words, which ought to be conformed to things, should be so too, I mean in their signification: but yet we find the quite contrary. The far greatest part of words, that make all languages, are general terms: which has not been the effect of neglect or chance, but of reason and necessity.

2. *For every particular thing to have a name is impossible.*— First, It is impossible that every particular thing should have a distinct peculiar name. For the signification and use of words depending on that connexion which the mind makes between its ideas and the sounds it uses as signs of them, it is necessary, in the application of names to things, that the mind should have distinct ideas of the things, and retain also the particular name that belongs to every one, with its peculiar appropriation to that idea. But it is beyond the power of human capacity to frame and retain distinct ideas of all the particular things we meet with: every bird and beast men saw, every tree and plant that affected the senses, could not find a place in the most capacious understanding.

3. *And useless.*—Secondly, If it were possible, it would yet be useless, because it would not serve to the chief end of language. Men would in vain heap up names of particular things, that would not serve them to communicate their thoughts. Men learn names,

and use them in talk with others, only that they may be understood: which is then only done when, by use or consent, the sound I make by the organs of speech excites, in another man's mind who hears it, the idea I apply it to in mine when I speak it. This cannot be done by names applied to particular things, whereof I alone having the ideas in my mind, the names of them could not be significant or intelligible to another who was not acquainted with all those very particular things which had fallen under my notice.

4. Thirdly, But yet granting this also feasible (which I think is not), yet a distinct name for every particular thing would not be of any great use for the improvement of knowledge: which, though founded in particular things, enlarges itself by general views; to which things reduced into sorts under general names, are properly subservient.

6. *How general words are made.*—The next thing to be considered is, how general words come to be made. For, since all things that exist are only particulars, how come we by general terms, or where find we those general natures they are supposed to stand for? Words become general by being made the signs of general ideas: and ideas become general by separating from them the circumstances of time, and place, and any other ideas that may determine them to this or that particular existence. By this way of abstraction they are made capable of representing more individuals than one; each of which, having in it a conformity to that abstract idea, is (as we call it) of that sort.

7. But to deduce this a little more distinctly, it will not perhaps be amiss to trace our notions and names from their beginning, and observe by what degrees we proceed, and by what steps we enlarge our ideas from our first infancy. There is nothing more evident than that the ideas of the persons children converse with (to instance in them alone), are, like the persons themselves, only particular. The ideas of the nurse and the mother are well framed in their minds; and, like pictures of them there, represent only those individuals. The names they first gave to them are confined to these individuals; and the names of " nurse " and " mamma " the child uses, determine themselves to those persons. Afterwards, when time and a larger acquaintance has made them observe that there are a great many other things in the world, that, in some common agreements of shape and several other qualities, resemble their father and mother, and those persons they have been used to, they frame an idea which they find those many particulars do

partake in; and to that they give, with others, the name " man,"
for example. And thus they come to have a general name, and a
general idea. Wherein they make nothing new, but only leave out
of the complex idea they had of Peter and James, Mary and Jane,
that which is peculiar to each, and retain only what is common to
them all.

9. *General natures are nothing but abstract ideas.*—He that
thinks general natures or notions are anything else but abstract and
partial ideas of more complex ones, taken at first from particular
existences, will, I fear, be at a loss where to find them. For, let
anyone reflect, and then tell me wherein does his idea of " man "
differ from that of " Peter " and " Paul," or his idea of " horse "
from that of " Bucephalus," but in the leaving out something
that is peculiar to each individual, and retaining so much of those
particular complex ideas of several particular existences as they
are found to agree in? Of the complex ideas signified by the
names " man " and " horse," leaving out but those particulars
wherein they differ, and retaining only those wherein they agree,
and of those making a new distinct complex idea, and giving the
name " animal " to it, one has a more general term, that comprehends with man, several other creatures. Leave out of the idea of
" animal " sense and spontaneous motion, and the remaining
complex idea, made up of the remaining simple ones of " body,
life, and nourishment," becomes a more general one under the
more comprehensive term, *vivens*.

11. *General and universal are creatures of the understanding.*—
It is plain, by what has been said, that general and universal
belong not to the real existence of things; but are the inventions
and creatures of the understanding, made by it for its own use,
and concern only signs, whether words or ideas. Words are
general, as has been said, when used for signs of general ideas,
and so are applicable indifferently to many particular things; and
ideas are general when they are set up as the representatives of
many particular things: but universality belongs not to things
themselves, which are all of them particular in their existence, even
those words and ideas which in their signification are general.
When therefore we quit particulars, the generals that rest are only
creatures of our own making, their general nature being nothing
but the capacity they are put into by the understanding of signifying or representing many particulars. For the signification they
have is nothing but a relation that by the mind of man is added
to them.

12. *Abstract ideas are the essences of the* genera *and* species.—
The next thing therefore to be considered, is, what kind of signification it is that general words have. For as it is evident that they do
not signify barely one particular thing, for then they would not
be general terms, but proper names; so on the other side it is as
evident they do not signify a plurality; for " man " and " men "
would then signify the same, and the distinction of " numbers "
(as grammarians call them) would be superfluous and useless. That
then which general words signify, is a sort of things; and each of
them does that by being a sign of an abstract idea in the mind;
to which idea as things existing are found to agree, so they come to
be ranked under that name; or, which is all one, be of that sort.
Whereby it is evident, that the essences of the sorts, or (if the
Latin word pleases better) *species* of things, are nothing else but
these abstract ideas. For the having the essence of any species,
being that which makes any thing to be of that species, and the
conformity to the idea to which the name is annexed being that
which gives a right to that name, the having the essence, and the
having that conformity, must needs be the same thing : since to
be of any species, and to have a right to the name of that species,
is all one. As, for example : to be a man or of the species man,
and to have right to the name " man," is the same thing. Again :
to be a man, or of the species man, and have the essence of a
man, is the same thing. Now, since nothing can be a man, or
have a right to the name " man," but what has a conformity to
the abstract idea the name " man " stands for; nor any thing be
a man, or have a right to the species man, but what has the essence
of that species; it follows, that the abstract idea for which the
name stands, and the essence of the species, is one and the same.
From whence it is easy to observe, that the essences of the sorts
of things, and consequently the sorting of this, is the workmanship
of the understanding that abstracts and makes those general ideas.

13. *They are the workmanship of the understanding, but have
their foundation in the similitude of things.*—I would not here be
thought to forget, much less to deny, that nature, in the production
of things, makes several of them alike : there is nothing more
obvious, especially in the races of animals, and all things propagated
by seed. But yet, I think, we may say, the sorting of them under
names is the workmanship of the understanding, taking occasion,
from the similitude it observes amongst them, to make abstract
general ideas, and set them up in the mind with names annexed to
them, as patterns or forms; for in that sense the word " form "

has a very proper signification, to which as particular things existing are found to agree, so they come to be of that species, have that denomination, or are put into that *classis*. And when general names have any connection with particular beings, these abstract ideas are the medium that unites them: so that the essence of species, as distinguished and denominated by us, neither are nor can be anything but those precise abstract ideas we have in our minds. And therefore the supposed real essences of substances, if different from our abstract ideas, cannot be the essences of the species we rank things into. For two species may be one as rationally as two different essences be the essences of one species; and I demand, what are the alterations may or may not be in a horse or lead, without making either of them to be of another species? In determining the species of things by our abstract ideas, this is easy to resolve. But if any one will regulate himself herein by supposed real essences, he will, I suppose, be at a loss: and he will never be able to know when anything precisely ceases to be of the species of a horse or lead.

14. *Each distinct abstract idea is a distinct essence.*—Nor will any one wonder that I say, these essences, or abstract ideas (which are the measures of name, and the boundaries of species), are the workmanship of the understanding, who considers that at least the complex ones are often, in several men, different collections of simple ideas: and therefore that is covetousness to one man, which is not so to another. Nay, even in substances, where their abstract ideas seem to be taken from the things themselves, they are not constantly the same; no, not in that species which is most familiar to us, and with which we have the most intimate acquaintance: it having been more than once doubted, whether the fœtus born of a woman were a man, even so far as that it hath been debated whether it were or were not to be nourished and baptized; which could not be if the abstract idea or essence to which the name " man " belonged were of nature's making, and were not the uncertain and various collection of simple ideas, which the understanding puts together, and then, abstracting it, affixed a name to it. So that in truth every distinct abstract idea is a distinct essence: and the names that stand for such distinct ideas, are the names of things essentially different. Thus, a circle is as essentially different from an oval as a sheep from a goat, and rain is as essentially different from snow as water from earth; that abstract idea which is the essence of one, being impossible to be communicated to the other. And thus any two abstract ideas, that in any

part vary one from another, with two distinct names annexed to them, constitute two distinct sorts, or, if you please, *species*, as essentially different as any two the most remote or opposite in the world.

15. *Real and nominal essence.*—But since the essences of things are thought, by some (and not without reason), to be wholly unknown; it may not be amiss to consider the several significations of the word " essence."

First, Essence may be taken for the being of any thing, whereby it is what it is. And thus the real internal (but generally in substances unknown) constitution of things, whereon their discoverable qualities depend, may be called their " essence." This is the proper original signification of the word.

Secondly, The learning and disputes of the schools having been much busied about *genus* and *species*, the word " essence " has almost lost its primary signification; and, instead of the real constitution of things, has been almost wholly applied to the artificial constitution of *genus* and *species*. It is true there is ordinarily supposed a real constitution of the sorts of things: and it is past doubt there must be some real constitution, on which any collection of simple ideas co-existing must depend. But it being evident that things are ranked under names into sorts or species only as they agree to certain abstract ideas to which we have annexed those names, the essence of each genus or sort comes to be nothing but that abstract idea, which the general or " sortal " (if I may have leave so to call it from " sort," as I do " general " from *genus*) name stands for. And this we shall find to be that which the word " essence " imports in its most familiar use. These two sorts of essences, I suppose, may not unfitly be termed, the one the " real," the other the " nominal," essence.

18. *Real and nominal essence the same in simple ideas and modes different in substances.*—Essences being thus distinguished into nominal and real, we may further observe, that in the species of simple ideas and modes, they are always the same: but in substances, always quite different. Thus a figure including a space between three lines, is the real as well as nominal essence of a triangle; it being not only the abstract idea to which the general name is annexed, but the very *essentia*, or " being," of the thing itself, that foundation from which all its properties flow, and to which they are all inseparably annexed. But it is far otherwise concerning that parcel of matter which makes the ring on my finger, wherein these two essences are apparently different. For it is the

real constitution of its insensible parts, on which depend all those properties of colour, weight, fusibility, fixedness, etc., which makes it to be gold, or gives it a right to that name, which is therefore its nominal essence; since nothing can be called " gold " but what has a conformity of qualities to that abstract complex idea, to which that name is annexed. But this distinction of essences, belonging particularly to substances, we shall, when we come to consider their names, have an occasion to treat of more fully.

20. *Recapitulation.*—To conclude: This is that which in short I would say, viz., that all the great business of *genera* and *species*, and their essences, amounts to no more but this—that men making abstract ideas, and settling them in their minds, with names annexed to them, do thereby enable themselves to consider things, and discourse of them, as it were, in bundles, for the easier and readier improvement and communication of their knowledge; which would advance but slowly, were their words and thoughts confined only to particulars.

CHAPTER IV

OF THE NAMES OF SIMPLE IDEAS

1-4. *Names of simple ideas, modes, and substances, have each something peculiar.*—Though all words, as I have shown, signify nothing immediately but the ideas in the mind of the speaker, yet, upon a nearer survey, we shall find that the names of simple ideas, mixed modes (under which I comprise relations too), and natural substances, have each of them something peculiar, and different from the other. For example:—

First, The names of simple ideas and substances, with the abstract ideas in the mind which they immediately signify, intimate also some real existence, from which was derived their original pattern. But the names of mixed modes terminate in the idea that is in the mind, and lead not the thoughts any farther, as we shall see more at large in the following chapter.

Secondly, The names of simple ideas and modes signify always the real as well as nominal essence of their species. But the names of natural substances signify rarely, if ever, any thing but barely the nominal essences of those species, as we shall show in the chapter that treats of the names of substances in particular.

Thirdly, The names of simple ideas are not capable of any definitions; the names of all complex ideas are.

5. *If all were definable, it would be a process* in infinitum.—I will not here trouble myself to prove that all terms are not definable, from that progress, *in infinitum*, which it will visibly lead us into if we should allow that all names could be defined. For if the terms of one definition were still to be defined by another, where at last should we stop? But I shall, from the nature of our ideas, and the signification of our words, show why some names can, and others cannot, be defined, and which they are.

6. *What a definition is.*—I think it is agreed, that a definition is nothing else but " the showing the meaning of one word by several other not synonymous terms." The meaning of words being only the ideas they are made to stand for by him that uses them, the meaning of any term is then showed, or the word is defined, when by other words the idea it is made the sign of and annexed to in the mind of the speaker is, as it were, represented or set before the view of another; and thus its signification ascertained. This is the only use and end of definitions; and therefore the only measure of what is or is not a good definition.

11. *Simple ideas, why undefinable, farther explained.*—Simple ideas, as has been shown, are only to be got by those impressions objects themselves make on our minds by the proper inlets appointed to each sort. If they are not received this way, all the words in the world made use of to explain or define any of their names, will never be able to produce in us the idea it stands for. For words, being sounds, can produce in us no other simple ideas than of those very sounds; nor excite any in us but by that voluntary connexion which is known to be between them and those simple ideas which common use has made them signs of. He that thinks otherwise, let him try if any words can give him the taste of a pine-apple, and make him have the true idea of the relish of that celebrated delicious fruit. So far as he is told it has a resemblance with any tastes whereof he has the ideas already in his memory, imprinted there by sensible objects not strangers to his palate, so far may he approach that resemblance in his mind. But this is not giving us that idea by a definition, but exciting in us other simple ideas by their known names; which will be still very different from the true taste of that fruit itself. In light and colours, and all other simple ideas, it is the same thing: for the signification of sounds is not natural, but only imposed and arbitrary.

12. *The contrary showed in complex ideas.*—The case is quite otherwise in complex ideas, which consisting of several simple ones, it is in the power of words, standing for the several ideas that make

that composition, to imprint complex ideas in the mind which were never there before, and so make their names be understood. In such collections of ideas passing under one name, definition, or the teaching the signification of one word by several others, has place, and may make us understand the names of things which never came within the reach of our senses, and frame ideas suitable to those in other men's minds, when they use those names: provided that none of the terms of the definition stand for any such simple ideas which he to whom the explication is made has never yet had in his thought. Thus the word " statue " may be explained to a blind man by other words, when " picture " cannot; his senses having given him the idea of figure, but not of colours, which therefore words cannot excite in him.

14. *The names of complex ideas, when to be made intelligible by words.*—Simple ideas, as has been showed, can only be got by experience from those objects which are proper to produce in us those perceptions. When by this means we have our minds stored with them, and know the names for them, then we are in a condition to define, and by definition to understand, the names of complex ideas that are made up of them.

CHAPTER VI

OF THE NAMES OF SUBSTANCES

1. *The common names of substances stand for sorts.*—The common names of substances, as well as other general terms, stand for sorts: which is nothing else but the being made signs of such complex ideas, wherein several particular substances do or might agree, by virtue of which they are capable of being comprehended in one common conception, and be signified by one name. I say, " do or might agree ": for though there be but one sun existing in the world, yet the idea of it being abstracted, so that more substances (if there were several) might each agree in it; it is as much a sort as if there were as many suns as there are stars.

2. *The essence of each sort is the abstract idea.*—The measure and boundary of each sort or species whereby it is constituted that particular sort and distinguished from others, is that we call its " essence," which is nothing but that abstract idea to which that name is annexed: so that everything contained in that idea is essential to that sort. This, though it be all the essence of natural

substances that we know, or by which we distinguish them into sorts; yet I call it by a peculiar name, the " nominal essence," to distinguish it from that real constitution of substances upon which depends this nominal essence, and all the properties of that sort; which therefore, as has been said, may be called the " real essence ": *v.g.*, the nominal essence of gold is that complex idea the word " gold " stands for, let it be, for instance, a body yellow, of a certain weight, malleable, fusible, and fixed. But the real essence is the constitution of the insensible parts of that body, on which those qualities and all the other properties of gold depend. How far these two are different, though they are both called " essence," is obvious, at first sight to discover.

3. *The nominal and real essence different.*—For though, perhaps, voluntary motion, with sense and reason, joined to a body of a certain shape, be the complex idea to which I and others annex the name " man," and so be the nominal essence of the species so called: yet nobody will say that that complex idea is the real essence and source of all those operations which are to be found in any individual of that sort. The foundation of all those qualities which are the ingredients of our complex idea, is something quite different: and had we such a knowledge of that constitution of man from which his faculties of moving, sensation, and reasoning, and other powers flow, and on which his so regular shape depends, as it is possible angels have, and it is certain his Maker has, we should have a quite other idea of his essence than what now is contained in our definition of that species.

4. *Nothing essential to individuals.*—That " essence," in the ordinary use of the word, relates to sorts, and that it is considered in particular beings no farther than they are ranked into sorts, appears from hence: that take but away the abstract ideas by which we sort individuals, and rank them under common names, and then the thought of anything essential to any of them instantly vanishes: we have no notion of the one without the other; which plainly shows their relation. It is necessary for me to be as I am: God and nature has made me so: but there is nothing I have is essential to me. An accident or disease may very much alter my colour or shape; a fever or fall may take away my reason or memory, or both; and an apoplexy leave neither sense nor under-standing, no, nor life. Other creatures of my shape may be made with more and better, or fewer and worse, faculties than I have: and others may have reason and sense in a shape and body very different from mine. None of these are essential to the one or the

other, or to any individual whatsoever, till the mind refers it to some sort or species of things; and then presently, according to the abstract idea of that sort, something is found essential. Let any one examine his own thoughts, and he will find, that as soon as he supposes or speaks of essential, the consideration of some species, or the complex idea, signified by some general name, comes into his mind: and it is in reference to that, that this or that quality is said to be essential. So that if it be asked, whether it be essential to me, or any other particular corporeal being, to have reason? I say, No; no more than it is essential to this white thing I write on to have words in it. But if that particular being be to be counted of the sort "man," and to have the name "man" given it, then reason is essential to it, supposing reason to be a part of the complex idea the name "man" stands for: as it is essential to this thing I write on to contain words, if I will give it the name "treatise," and rank it under that species. So that "essential" and "not essential" relate only to our abstract ideas, and the names annexed to them; which amounts to no more but this, that whatever particular thing has not in it those qualities which are contained in the abstract idea which any general term stands for, cannot be ranked under that species, nor be called by that name, since that abstract idea is the very essence of that species.

5. Thus, if the idea of body, with some people, be bare extension or space, then solidity is not essential to body: if others make the idea to which they give the name "body," to be solidity and extension, then solidity is essential to body. That therefore, and that alone, is considered as essential which makes a part of the complex idea the name of a sort stands for, without which no particular thing can be reckoned of that sort, nor be entitled to that name. Should there be found a parcel of matter that had all the other qualities that are in iron, but wanted obedience to the loadstone, and would neither be drawn by it, nor receive direction from it; would any one question whether it wanted any thing essential? It would be absurd to ask, whether a thing really existing wanted any thing essential to it? Or could it be demanded, whether this made an essential or specific difference or no? since we have no other measure of essential or species but our abstract ideas. And to talk of specific differences in nature, without reference to general ideas and names, is to talk unintelligibly. For, I would ask any one, What is sufficient to make an essential difference in nature between any two particular beings, without any regard had to some abstract idea, which is looked upon as the essence and

standard of a species? All such patterns and standards being quite laid aside, particular beings, considered barely in themselves, will be found to have all their qualities equally essential; and every thing in each individual will be essential to it, or, which is more, nothing at all. For though it may be reasonable to ask, whether obeying the magnet be essential to iron? yet, I think, it is very improper and insignificant to ask, whether it be essential to the particular parcel of matter I cut my pen with? without considering it under the name " iron," or as being of a certain species. And if, as has been said, our abstract ideas which have names annexed to them, are the boundaries of species, nothing can be essential but what is contained in those ideas.

6. It is true I have often mentioned a real essence, distinct in substances from those abstract ideas of them, which I call their " nominal essence." By this " real essence," I mean that real constitution of any thing which is the foundation of all those properties that are combined in, and are constantly found to co-exist with, the nominal essence; that particular constitution which every thing has within itself, without any relation to any thing without it. But essence, even in this sense, relates to a sort, and supposes a species: for, being that real constitution on which the properties depend, it necessarily supposes a sort of things, properties belonging only to species, and not to individuals; *v.g.*, supposing the nominal essence of gold to be body of such a peculiar colour and weight, with malleability and fusibility, the real essence is that constitution of the parts of matter on which these qualities and their union depend; and is also the foundation of its solubility in *aqua regia,* and other properties accompanying that complex idea. Here are essences and properties, but all upon supposition of a sort, or general abstract idea, which is considered as immutable; but there is no individual parcel of matter to which any of these qualities are so annexed as to be essential to it or inseparable from it. That which is essential belongs to it as a condition whereby it is of this or that sort: but take away the consideration of its being ranked under the name of some abstract idea, and then there is nothing necessary to it, nothing inseparable from it. Indeed, as to the real essences of substances, we only suppose their being, without precisely knowing what they are: but that which annexes them still to the species is the nominal essence, of which they are the supposed foundation and cause.

7. *The nominal essence bounds the species.*—The next thing to be considered is, by which of those essences it is that substances

are determined into sorts or species; and that, it is evident, is by the nominal essence. For it is that alone that the name, which is the mark of the sort, signifies. It is impossible therefore that any thing should determine the sorts of things which we rank under general names, but that idea which that name is designed as a mark for; which is that, as has been shown, which we call the " nominal essence." Why do we say, " This is a horse, and that a mule; this is an animal, that an herb? " How comes any particular thing to be of this or that sort, but because it has that nominal essence, or, which is all one, agrees to that abstract idea that name is annexed to ?

9. *Not the real essence, which we know not.*—Nor, indeed, can we rank and sort things, and consequently (which is the end of sorting) denominate them, by their real essences, because we know them not. Our faculties carry us no farther towards the knowledge and distinction of substances than a collection of those sensible ideas which we observe in them; which, however made with the greatest diligence and exactness we are capable of, yet is more remote from the true internal constitution from which those qualities flow than, as I said, a countryman's idea is from the inward contrivance of that famous clock at Strasburg, whereof he only sees the outward figure and motions.

21. But since, as has been remarked, we have need of general words, though we know not the real essences of things; all we can do is to collect such a number of simple ideas as by examination we find to be united together in things existing, and thereof to make one complex idea. Which, though it be not the real essence of any substance that exists, is yet the specific essence to which our name belongs, and is convertible with it; by which we may at least try the truth of these nominal essences.

28. But though these nominal essences of substances are made by the mind, they are not yet made so arbitrarily as those of mixed modes. To the making of any nominal essence, it is necessary, First, that the ideas whereof it consists, have such an union as to make but one idea, how compounded soever. Secondly, That the particular ideas so united be exactly the same, neither more nor less. For if two abstract complex ideas differ either in number or sorts of their component parts, they make two different, and not one and the same essence. In the first of these, the mind, in making its complex ideas of substances, only follows nature: and puts none together, which are not supposed to have an union in nature. Nobody joins the voice of a sheep with the shape of a horse, nor

the colour of lead with the weight and fixedness of gold, to be the complex ideas of any real substances; unless he has a mind to fill his head with chimeras, and his discourse with unintelligible words. Men, observing certain qualities always joined and existing together, therein copied nature; and of ideas so united made their complex ones of substances. For though men may make what complex ideas they please, and give what names to them they will; yet, if they will be understood when they speak of things really existing, they must, in some degree, conform their ideas to the things they would speak of: or else men's language will be like that of Babel; and every man's words, being intelligible only to himself, would no longer serve to conversation and the ordinary affairs of life, if the ideas they stand for be not some way answering the common appearances and agreement of substances as they really exist.

36. *Nature makes the similitude.*—This, then, in short, is the case: nature makes many particular things which do agree one with another in many sensible qualities, and probably, too, in their internal frame and constitution; but it is not this real essence that distinguishes them into species; it is men, who taking occasion from the qualities they find united in them, and wherein they observe often several individuals to agree, range them into sorts in order to their naming, for the convenience of comprehensive signs; under which, individuals, according to their conformity to this or that abstract idea, come to be ranked as under ensigns; so that this is of the blue, that the red, regiment; this is a man, that a drill: and in this, I think, consists the whole business of *genus* and *species*.

BOOK IV

OF KNOWLEDGE AND OPINION

CHAPTER I

OF KNOWLEDGE IN GENERAL

1. *Our knowledge conversant about our ideas.*—Since the mind, in all its thoughts and reasonings, hath no other immediate object but its own ideas, which it alone does or can contemplate, it is evident that our knowledge is only conversant about them.

2. *Knowledge is the perception of the agreement or disagreement of two ideas.*—Knowledge then seems to me to be nothing but the perception of the connection and agreement, or disagreement and repugnancy, of any of our ideas. In this alone it consists. Where this perception is, there is knowledge; and where it is not, there, though we may fancy, guess, or believe, yet we always come short of knowledge. For, when we know that white is not black, what do we else but perceive that these two ideas do not agree? When we possess ourselves with the utmost security of the demonstration that the three angles of a triangle are equal to two right ones, what do we more but perceive, that equality to two right ones does necessarily agree to, and is inseparable from, the three angles of a triangle?

3. *This agreement fourfold.*—But, to understand a little more

distinctly, wherein this agreement or disagreement consists, I think we may reduce it all to these four sorts: (1). Identity, or diversity. (2). Relation. (3). Co-existence, or necessary connection. (4). Real existence.

4. *First, Of identity or diversity.*—First, As to the first sort of agreement or disagreement, viz., identity or diversity. It is the first act of the mind, when it has any sentiments or ideas at all, to perceive its ideas, and, so far as it perceives them, to know that one is not another. This is so absolutely necessary, that without it there could be no knowledge, no reasoning, no imagination, no distinct thoughts at all. By this the mind clearly and infallibly perceives each idea to agree with itself, and to be what it is; and all distinct ideas to disagree, *i.e.*, the one not to be the other: and this it does without pains, labour, or deduction, but at first view, by its natural power of perception and distinction.

5. *Secondly, Relative.*—Secondly, The next sort of agreement or disagreement the mind perceives in any of its ideas may, I think, be called " relative," and is nothing but the perception of the relation between any two ideas, of what kind soever, whether substances, modes, or any other. For, since all distinct ideas must eternally be known not to be the same, and so be universally and constantly denied one of another: there could be no room for any positive knowledge at all, if we could not perceive any relation between our ideas, and find out the agreement or disagreement they have one with another, in several ways the mind takes of comparing them.

6. *Thirdly, Of co-existence.*—Thirdly, The third sort of agreement or disagreement to be found in our ideas, which the perception of the mind is employed about, is co-existence, or non-co-existence in the same subject; and this belongs particularly to substances. Thus when we pronounce concerning " gold " that it is fixed, our knowledge of this truth amounts to no more but this, that fixedness, or a power to remain in the fire unconsumed, is an idea that always accompanies and is joined with that particular sort of yellowness, weight, fusibility, malleableness and solubility in *aqua regia*, which make our complex idea, signified by the word " gold."

7. *Fourthly, Of real existence.*—Fourthly, The fourth and last sort is that of actual real existence agreeing to any idea. Within these four sorts of agreement or disagreement is, I suppose, contained all the knowledge we have or are capable of; for, all the inquiries that we can make concerning any of our ideas, all that we know or can affirm concerning any of them, is that it is or is not

the same with some other; that it does or does not always co-exist
with some other idea in the same subject; that it has this or that
relation to some other idea; or that it has a real existence without
the mind.   Thus, " Blue is not yellow," is of identity.   " Two
triangles upon equal bases between two parallels are equal," is of
relation.   " Iron is susceptible of magnetical impressions," is of
co-existence.   " God is," is of real existence.   Though identity
and co-existence are truly nothing but relations, yet they are so
peculiar ways of agreement or disagreement of our ideas, that they
deserve well to be considered as distinct heads, and not under
relation in general; since they are so different grounds of affirmation
and negation, as will easily appear to any one who will but reflect
on what is said in several places of this Essay.

CHAPTER II

OF THE DEGREES OF OUR KNOWLEDGE

    1. *Intuitive.*—All our knowledge consisting, as I have said, in
the view the mind has of its own ideas, which is the utmost light
and greatest certainty we, with our faculties and in our way of
knowledge, are capable of, it may not be amiss to consider a little
the degrees of its evidence.   The different clearness of our knowledge
seems to me to lie in the different way of perception the mind has
of the agreement or disagreement of any of its ideas.   For if we
will reflect on our own ways of thinking, we shall find that sometimes the mind perceives the agreement or disagreement of two
ideas immediately by themselves, without the intervention of any
other: and this, I think, we may call " intuitive knowledge."   For
in this the mind is at no pains of proving or examining, but
perceives the truth, as the eye doth light, only by being directed
towards it.   Thus the mind perceives that white is not black, that
a circle is not a triangle, that three are more than two, and equal
to one and two.   Such kind of truths the mind perceives at the
first sight of the ideas together, by bare intuition, without the
intervention of any other idea; and this kind of knowledge is the
clearest and most certain that human frailty is capable of.   This
part of knowledge is irresistible, and, like bright sunshine, forces
itself immediately to be perceived as soon as ever the mind turns
its view that way; and leaves no room for hesitation, doubt, or
examination, but the mind is presently filled with the clear light of

it. It is on this intuition that depends all the certainty and evidence of all our knowledge, which certainty every one finds to be so great that he cannot imagine, and therefore not require, a greater: for a man cannot conceive himself capable of a greater certainty, than to know that any idea in his mind is such as he perceives it to be; and that two ideas, wherein he perceives a difference, are different, and not precisely the same. He that demands a greater certainty than this demands he knows not what, and shows only that he has a mind to be a sceptic without being able to be so. Certainty depends so wholly on this intuition, that in the next degree of knowledge, which I call "demonstrative," this intuition is necessary in all the connections of the intermediate ideas, without which we cannot attain knowledge and certainty.

2. *Demonstrative.*—The next degree of knowledge is, where the mind perceives the agreement or disagreement of any ideas, but not immediately. Though wherever the mind perceives the agreement or disagreement of any of its ideas, there be certain knowledge; yet it does not always happen that the mind sees that agreement or disagreement which there is between them, even where it is discoverable; and in that case remains in ignorance, and at most gets no farther that a probable conjecture. The reason why the mind cannot always perceive presently the agreement or disagreement of two ideas, is, because those ideas concerning whose agreement or disagreement the inquiry is made, cannot by the mind be so put together as to show it. In this case, then, when the mind cannot so bring its ideas together as, by their immediate comparison and, as it were, juxtaposition or application one to another, to perceive their agreement or disagreement, it is fain, by the intervention of other ideas (one or more, as it happens), to discover the agreement or disagreement which it searches; and this is that which we call "reasoning." Thus the mind, being willing to know the agreement or disagreement in bigness between the three angles of a triangle and two right ones, cannot, by an immediate view and comparing them, do it: because the three angles of a triangle cannot be brought at once, and be compared with any one or two angles; and so of this the mind has no immediate, no intuitive knowledge. In this case the mind is fain to find out some other angles, to which the three angles of a triangle have an equality; and finding those equal to two right ones, comes to know their equality to two right ones.

3. *Depends on proofs.*—Those intervening ideas which serve to show the agreement of any two others, are called "proofs"; and

where the agreement or disagreement is by this means plainly and clearly perceived, it is called " demonstration."

4. *But not so easy.*—This knowledge by intervening proofs, though it be certain, yet the evidence of it is not altogether so clear and bright, nor the assent so ready, as in intuitive knowledge. For though in demonstration the mind does at last perceive the agreement or disagreement of the ideas it considers, yet it is not without pains and attention: there must be more than one transient view to find it. A steady application and pursuit is required to this discovery: and there must be a progression by steps and degrees before the mind can in this way arrive at certainty, and come to perceive the agreement or repugnancy between two ideas that need proofs and the use of reason to show it.

5. *Not without precedent doubt.*—Another difference between intuitive and demonstrative knowledge, is, that though in the latter all doubt be removed, when by the intervention of the intermediate ideas the agreement or disagreement is perceived; yet before the demonstration there was a doubt; which in intuitive knowledge cannot happen to the mind that has its faculty of perception left to a degree capable of distinct ideas, no more than it can be a doubt to the eye (that can distinctly see white and black), whether this ink and this paper be all of a colour.

6. *Not so clear.*—It is true, the perception produced by demonstration is also very clear; yet it is often with a great abatement of that evident lustre and full assurance that always accompany that which I call " intuitive "; like a face reflected by several mirrors one to another, where, as long as it retains the similitude and agreement with the object, it produces a knowledge; but it is still in every successive reflection with a lessening of that perfect clearness and distinctness which is in the first, till at last, after many removes, it has a great mixture of dimness, and is not at first sight so knowable, especially to weak eyes. Thus it is with knowledge made out by a long train of proofs.

7. *Each step must have intuitive evidence.*—Now, in every step reason makes in demonstrative knowledge, there is an intuitive knowledge of that agreement or disagreement it seeks with the next intermediate idea, which it uses as a proof: for if it were not so, that yet would need a proof; since without the perception of such agreement or disagreement there is no knowledge produced. If it be perceived by itself, it is intuitive knowledge: if it cannot be perceived by itself, there is need of some intervening idea, as a common measure, to show their agreement or disagreement. By

which it is plain, that every step in reasoning that produces knowledge has intuitive certainty; which when the mind perceives, there is no more required but to remember it, to make the agreement or disagreement of the ideas, concerning which we inquire, visible and certain. So that to make any thing a demonstration, it is necessary to perceive the immediate agreement of the intervening ideas, whereby the agreement or disagreement of the two ideas under examination (whereof the one is always the first, and the other the last in the account) is found. This intuitive perception of the agreement or disagreement of the intermediate ideas, in each step and progression of the demonstration, must also be carried exactly in the mind, and a man must be sure that no part is left out: which, because in long deductions, and the use of many proofs, the memory does not always so readily and exactly retain; therefore it comes to pass, that this is more imperfect than intuitive knowledge, and men embrace often falsehood for demonstrations.

14. *Sensitive knowledge of particular existence.*—These two, viz., intuition and demonstration, are the degrees of our knowledge; whatever comes short of one of these, with what assurance soever embraced, is but faith or opinion, but not knowledge, at least in all general truths. There is, indeed another perception of the mind employed about the particular existence of finite beings without us; which, going beyond bare probability, and yet not reaching perfectly to either of the foregoing degrees of certainty, passes under the name of " knowledge." There can be nothing more certain, than that the idea we receive from an external object is in our minds; this is intuitive knowledge. But whether there be any thing more than barely that idea in our minds, whether we can thence certainly infer the existence of any thing without us which corresponds to that idea, is that whereof some men think there may be a question made; because men may have such ideas in their minds when no such thing exists, no such object affects their senses. But yet here, I think, we are provided with an evidence that puts us past doubting; for I ask any one, whether he be not invincibly conscious to himself of a different perception when he looks on the sun by day, and thinks on it by night; when he actually tastes wormwood, or smells a rose, or only thinks on that savour or odour? We as plainly find the difference there is between any idea revived in our minds by our own memory, and actually coming into our minds by our senses, as we do between any two distinct ideas. If any one say, " A dream may do the same thing, and all these ideas may be produced in us without any external

objects "; he may please to dream that I make him this answer:
(1). That it is no great matter whether I remove his scruple or no:
where all is but dream, reasoning and arguments are of no use,
truth and knowledge nothing. (2). That I believe he will allow a
very manifest difference between dreaming of being in the fire,
and being actually in it. But yet if he be resolved to appear so
sceptical as to maintain, that what I call " being actually in the
fire " is nothing but a dream; and that we cannot thereby certainly
know that any such thing as fire actually exists without us; I
answer, that we certainly finding that pleasure or pain follows upon
the application of certain objects to us, whose existence we perceive,
or dream that we perceive, by our senses: this certainty is as great
as our happiness or misery, beyond which we have no concernment
to know or to be. So that, I think, we may add to the two former
sorts of knowledge this also, of the existence of particular external
objects by that perception and consciousness we have of the actual
entrance of ideas from them, and allow these three degrees of
knowledge, viz., intuitive, demonstrative, and sensitive: in each of
which there are different degrees and ways of evidence and
certainty.

CHAPTER III

OF THE EXTENT OF HUMAN KNOWLEDGE

1. Knowledge, as has been said, lying in the perception of the
agreement or disagreement of any of our ideas, it follows from
hence, that,

First, We can have knowledge no farther than we have ideas.

2. Secondly, That we can have no knowledge farther than we can
have perception of that agreement or disagreement: which perception being, (1). Either by intuition, or the immediate comparing
any two ideas; or, (2). By reason, examining the agreement or
disagreement of two ideas by the intervention of some others; or,
(3). By sensation, perceiving the existence of particular things;
hence it also follows,

3. Thirdly, that we cannot have an intuitive knowledge that shall
extend itself to all our ideas, and all that we would know about
them; because we cannot examine and perceive all the relations
they have one to another by juxtaposition, or an immediate
comparison one with another. Thus having the ideas of an obtuse

and an acute-angled triangle, both drawn from equal bases, and between parallels, I can by intuitive knowledge perceive the one not to be the other; but cannot that way know whether they be equal or no; because their agreement or disagreement in equality can never be perceived by an immediate comparing them; the difference of figure makes their parts uncapable of an exact immediate application; and therefore there is need of some intervening qualities to measure them by, which is demonstration or rational knowledge.

4. Fourthly, It follows also, from what is above observed, that our rational knowledge cannot reach to the whole extent of our ideas: because between two different ideas we would examine, we cannot always find such mediums as we can connect one to another with an intuitive knowledge, in all the parts of the deduction; and wherever that fails, we come short of knowledge and demonstration.

5. Fifthly, Sensitive knowledge, reaching no farther than the existence of things actually present to our senses, is yet much narrower than either of the former.

6. From all which it is evident, that the extent of our knowledge comes not only short of the reality of things, but even of the extent of our own ideas. Though our knowledge be limited to our ideas. and cannot exceed them either in extent or perfection: and though these be very narrow bounds in respect of the extent of all being, and far short of what we may justly imagine to be in some even created understandings not tied down to the dull and narrow information is to be received from some few and not very acute ways of perception, such as are our senses; yet it would be well with us if our knowledge were but as large as our ideas, and there were not many doubts and inquiries concerning the ideas we have, whereof we are not, nor I believe ever shall be in this world, resolved. Nevertheless, I do not question but that human knowledge, under the present circumstances of our beings and constitutions, may be carried much farther than it hitherto has been, if men would sincerely, and with freedom of mind, employ all that industry and labour of thought in improving the means of discovering truth which they do for the colouring or support of falsehood, to maintain a system, interest, or party they are once engaged in. But yet, after all, I think I may, without injury to human perfection, be confident that our knowledge would never reach to all we might desire to know concerning those ideas we have; nor be able to surmount all the difficulties, and resolve all the questions, might arise concerning any of them. We have the

ideas of a square, a circle, and equality: and yet, perhaps, shall never be able to find a circle equal to a square, and certainly know that it is so. We have the ideas of matter and thinking, but possibly shall never be able to know whether any mere material being thinks or no.

7. *How far our knowledge reaches.*—The affirmations or negations we make concerning the ideas we have, may, as I have before intimated in general, be reduced to these four sorts, viz., identity, co-existence, relation, and real existence. I shall examine how far our knowledge extends in each of these:—

8. *First. Our knowledge of identity and diversity, as far as our ideas.*—First, As to identity and diversity, in this way of the agreement or disagreement of ideas, our intuitive knowledge is as far extended as our ideas themselves; and there can be no idea in the mind which does not presently, by an intuitive knowledge, perceive to be what it is, and be different from any other.

9. *Secondly. Of co-existence, a very little way.*—Secondly, As to the second sort, which is the agreement or disagreement of our ideas in co-existence, in this our knowledge is very short, though in this consists the greatest and most material part of our knowledge concerning substances. For our ideas of the species of substances being, as I have showed, nothing but certain collections of simple ideas united in one subject, and so co-existing together:—*v.g.*, our idea of " flame " is a body hot, luminous, and moving upward; of " gold," a body heavy to a certain degree, yellow, malleable, and fusible. These, or some such complex ideas as these in men's minds, do these two names of the different substances, " flame " and " gold," stand for. When we would know any thing farther concerning these, or any other sort of substances, what do we inquire but what other qualities or powers these substances have or have not? which is nothing else but to know what other simple ideas do or do not co-exist with those that make up that complex idea.

10. This, how weighty and considerable a part soever of human science, is yet very narrow, and scarce any at all. The reason whereof is, that the simple ideas whereof our complex ideas of substances are made up are, for the most part, such as carry with them, in their own nature, no visible necessary connection or inconsistency with any other simple ideas, whose co-existence with them we would inform ourselves about.

11. *Especially of secondary qualities.*—The ideas that our complex ones of substances are made up of, and about which our

knowledge concerning substances is most employed, are those of their secondary qualities; which depending all (as has been shown) upon the primary qualities of their minute and insensible parts, or, if not upon them, upon something yet more remote from our comprehension, it is impossible we should know which have a necessary union or inconsistency one with another: for, not knowing the root they spring from, not knowing what size, figure, and texture of parts they are on which depend and from which result those qualities which make our complex idea of gold, it is impossible we should know what other qualities result from or are incompatible with the same constitution of the insensible parts of gold; and so, consequently, must always co-exist with that complex idea we have of it, or else are inconsistent with it.

12. *Because all connection between any secondary and primary qualities is undiscoverable.*—Besides this ignorance of the primary qualities of the insensible parts of bodies, on which depend all their secondary qualities, there is yet another and more incurable part of ignorance, which sets us more remote from a certain knowledge of the co-existence or in-co-existence (if I may so say) of different ideas in the same subject; and that is, that there is no discoverable connection between any secondary quality and those primary qualities that it depends on.

14. Thus, though we see the yellow colour, and upon trial find the weight, malleableness, fusibility, and fixedness that are united in a piece of gold; yet, because no one of these ideas has any evident dependence or necessary connection with the other, we cannot certainly know that where any four of these are the fifth will be there also, how highly probable soever it may be: because the highest probability amounts not to certainty; without which there can be no true knowledge. For this co-existence can be no farther known than it is perceived: and it cannot be perceived but either in particular subjects by the observation of our senses, or in general by the necessary connection of the ideas themselves.

18. *Thirdly, Of other relations, it is not easy to say how far.*— As to the third sort of our knowledge, viz., the agreement or disagreement of any of our ideas in any other relation: this, as it is the largest field of our knowledge, so it is hard to determine how far it may extend: because the advances that are made in this part of knowledge depending on our sagacity in finding inter-mediate ideas that may show the relations and habitudes of ideas, whose co-existence is not considered, it is a hard matter to tell when we are at an end of such discoveries, and when reason has

all the helps it is capable of for the finding of proofs, or examining the agreement or disagreement of remote ideas. They that are ignorant of algebra, cannot imagine the wonders in this kind are to be done by it: and what farther improvements and helps, advantageous to other parts of knowledge, the sagacious mind of man may yet find out, it is not easy to determine.

21. *Fourthly, Of real existence.*—As to the fourth sort of our knowledge, viz., of the real actual existence of things, we have an intuitive knowledge of our own existence; a demonstrative knowledge of the existence of a God; of the existence of anything else, we have no other but a sensitive knowledge, which extends not beyond the objects present to our senses.

CHAPTER IV

OF THE REALITY OF HUMAN KNOWLEDGE

1. *Objection. Knowledge placed in ideas may be all bare vision.* —I doubt not but my reader by this time may be apt to think that I have been all this while only building a castle in the air; and be ready to say to me, " To what purpose all this stir? ' Knowledge,' say you, ' is only the perception of the agreement or disagreement of our own ideas '; but who knows what those ideas may be? Is there any thing so extravagant as the imaginations of men's brains? Where is the head that has no chimeras in it? Or if there be a sober and a wise man, what difference will there be, by your rules, between his knowledge, and that of the most extravagant fancy in the world? They both have their ideas, and perceive their agreement and disagreement one with another. If there be any difference between them, the advantage will be on the warm-headed man's side, as having the more ideas, and the more lively. And so, by your rules, he will be the more knowing. If it be true, that all knowledge lies only in the perception of the agreement or disagreement of our own ideas, the visions of an enthusiast, and the reasonings of a sober man, will be equally certain. It is no matter how things are: so a man observe but the agreement of his own imaginations, and talk conformably, it is all truth, all certainty. Such castles in the air will be as strongholds of truth as the demonstrations of Euclid. That an harpy is not a centaur, is by this way as certain knowledge, and as much a truth, as that a square is not a circle.

" But of what use is all this fine knowledge of men's own

imaginations to a man that inquires after the reality of things?
It matters not what men's fancies are, it is the knowledge of things
that is only to be prized: it is this alone gives a value to our
reasonings, and preference to one man's knowledge over another's,
that it is of things as they really are, and not of dreams and fancies.''

2. *Answer. Not so where ideas agree with things.*—To which I
answer, That if our knowledge of our ideas terminate in them, and
reach no farther, where there is something farther intended, our
most serious thoughts will be of little more use than the reveries of
a crazy brain: and the truths built thereon of no more weight
than the discourses of a man who sees things clearly in a dream, and
with great assurance utters them. But I hope before I have done
to make it evident that this way of certainty, by the knowledge of
our own ideas, goes a little farther than bare imagination; and I
believe it will appear, that all the certainty of general truths a
man has lies in nothing else.

3. It is evident the mind knows not things immediately, but only
by the intervention of the ideas it has of them. Our knowledge
therefore is real only so far as there is a conformity between our
ideas and the reality of things. But what shall be here the
criterion? How shall the mind, when it perceives nothing but its
own ideas, know that they agree with things themselves? This,
though it seems not to want difficulty, yet I think there be two
sorts of ideas that we may be assured agree with things.

4. *As, First, all simple ideas do.*—First, The first are simple
ideas, which since the mind, as has been showed, can by no means
make to itself, must necessarily be the product of things operating
on the mind in a natural way, and producing therein those perceptions which by the wisdom and will of our Maker they are ordained
and adapted to. From whence it follows, that simple ideas are not
fictions of our fancies, but the natural and regular productions of
things without us really operating upon us; and so carry with them
all the conformity which is intended, or which our state requires;
for they represent to us things under those appearances which they
are fitted to produce in us, whereby we are enabled to distinguish
the sorts of particular substances, to discern the states they are in,
and so to take them for our necessities, and apply them to our
uses. Thus the idea of whiteness or bitterness, as it is in the mind,
exactly answering that power which is in any body to produce it
there, has all the real conformity it can or ought to have with
things without us. And this conformity between our simple ideas
and the existence of things is sufficient for real knowledge.

5. *Secondly, All complex ideas except of substances.*—Secondly, All our complex ideas except those of substances being archetypes of the mind's own making, not intended to be the copies of any thing, nor referred to the existence of any thing, as to their originals, cannot want any conformity necessary to real knowledge. For that which is not designed to represent any thing but itself, can never be capable of a wrong representation, nor mislead us from the true apprehension of any thing by its dislikeness to it; and such, excepting those of substances, are all our complex ideas: which, as I have showed in another place, are combinations of ideas which the mind by its free choice puts together without considering any connection they have in nature. And hence it is, that in all these sorts the ideas themselves are considered as the archetypes, and things no otherwise regarded but as they are conformable to them. So that we cannot but be infallibly certain, that all the knowledge we attain concerning these ideas is real, and reaches things themselves; because in all our thoughts, reasonings, and discourses of this kind, we intend things no farther than as they are conformable to our ideas. So that in these we cannot miss of a certain and undoubted reality.

6. *Hence the reality of mathematical knowledge.*—I doubt not but it will be easily granted that the knowledge we have of mathematical truths, is not only certain but real knowledge; and not the bare empty vision of vain, insignificant chimeras of the brain: and yet, if we will consider, we shall find that it is only of our own ideas. The mathematician considers the truth and properties belonging to a rectangle or circle, only as they are an idea in his own mind. For it is possible he never found either of them existing mathematically, *i.e.*, precisely true, in his life. But yet the knowledge he has of any truths or properties belonging to a circle, or any other mathematical figure, are never the less true and certain even of real things existing: because real things are no farther concerned, nor intended to be meant by any such propositions, than as things really agree to those archetypes in his mind. Is it true of the idea of a triangle, that its three angles are equal to two right ones? It is true also of a triangle wherever it really exists.

7. *And of moral.*—And hence it follows that moral knowledge is as capable of real certainty as mathematics. For, certainty being but the perception of the agreement or disagreement of our ideas, and demonstration nothing but the perception of such agreement by the intervention of other ideas or mediums, our moral ideas as well as mathematical being archetypes themselves, and so adequate

and complete ideas, all the agreement or disagreement which we shall find in them will produce real knowledge, as well as in mathematical figures.

11. *Ideas of substances have their archetypes without us.*— Thirdly, There is another sort of complex ideas, which being referred to archetypes without us may differ from them, and so our knowledge about them may come short of being real. Such are our ideas of substances, which consisting of a collection of simple ideas, supposed taken from the works of nature, may yet vary from them, by having more or different ideas united in them that are to be found united in the things themselves: from whence it comes to pass, that they may and often do fail of being exactly conformable to things themselves.

12. Whatever ideas we have, the agreement we find they have with others will still be knowledge. If those ideas be abstract, it will be general knowledge. But to make it real concerning substances, the ideas must be taken from the real existence of things. Whatever simple ideas have been found to co-exist in any substance, these we may with confidence join together again, and so make abstract ideas of substances. For whatever have once had an union in nature, may be united again.

18. *Recapitulation.*—Wherever we perceive the agreement or disagreement of any of our ideas, there is certain knowledge: and wherever we are sure those ideas agree with the reality of things, there is certain real knowledge. Of which agreement of our ideas with the reality of things having here given the marks, I think I have shown wherein it is that certainty, real certainty, consists. Which, whatever it was to others, was, I confess, to me heretofore one of those *desiderata* which I found great want of.

CHAPTER V

OF TRUTH IN GENERAL

2. *A right joining or separating of signs; i.e., ideas or words.*— Truth seems to me, in the proper import of the word, to signify nothing but the joining or separating of signs, as the things signified by them do agree or disagree one with another. The joining or separating of signs here meant, is what by another name we call " proposition." So that truth properly belongs only to propositions: whereof there are two sorts, viz., mental and verbal; as there are two sorts of signs commonly made use of, viz., ideas and words.

5. We must observe two sorts of propositions that we are capable of, making,

First, Mental, wherein the ideas in our understandings are, without the use of words, put together or separated by the mind perceiving or judging of their agreement or disagreement.

Secondly, Verbal propositions, which are words, the signs of our ideas, put together or separated in affirmative or negative sentences. By which way of affirming or denying, these signs, made by sounds, are as it were put together or separated one from another. So that proposition consists in joining or separating signs, and truth consists in the putting together or separating these signs, according as the things which they stand for agree or disagree.

9. *Falsehood is the joining of names otherwise than their ideas agree.*—Truth is the marking down in words the agreement or disagreement of ideas as it is. Falsehood is the marking down in words the agreement or disagreement of ideas otherwise than it is. And so far as these ideas thus marked by sounds agree to their archetypes, so far only is the truth real. The knowledge of this truth consists in knowing what ideas the words stand for, and the perception of the agreement or disagreement of those ideas, according as it is marked by those words.

11. *Moral and metaphysical truth.*—Besides truth taken in the strict sense before mentioned, there are other sorts of truths; as, (1). Moral truth, which is speaking things according to the persuasion of our own minds, though the proposition we speak agree not to the reality of things. (2). Metaphysical truth, which is nothing but the real existence of things conformable to the ideas to which we have annexed their names. This, though it seems to consist in the very beings of things, yet when considered a little nearly will appear to include a tacit proposition, whereby the mind joins that particular thing to the idea it had before settled with a name to it. But these considerations of truth, either having been before taken notice of, or not being much to our present purpose, it may suffice here only to have mentioned them.

CHAPTER VII

OF MAXIMS

1. *They are self-evident.*—There are a sort of propositions which under the name of "maxims and axioms," have passed for principles of science: and, because they are self-evident, have been

supposed innate, although nobody (that I know) ever went about to show the reason and foundation of their clearness or cogency.

2. *Wherein that self-evidence consists.*—Knowledge, as has been shown, consists in the perception of the agreement or disagreement of ideas: now where that agreement or disagreement is perceived immediately by itself, without the intervention or help of any other, there our knowledge is self-evident. This will appear to be so to any one who will but consider any of those propositions which, without any proof, he assents to at first sight; for in all of them he will find that the reason of his assent is from that agreement or disagreement which the mind, by an immediate comparing them, finds in those ideas, answering the affirmation or negation in the proposition.

3. *Self-evidence not peculiar to received axioms.*—This being so, in the next place let us consider whether this self-evidence be peculiar only to those propositions which commonly pass under the name of "maxims," and have the dignity of axioms allowed them. And here it is plain, that several other truths, not allowed to be axioms, partake equally with them in this self-evidence.

4. *First, As to identity and diversity, all propositions are equally self-evident.*—For, First, the immediate perception of the agreement or disagreement of identity being founded in the mind's having distinct ideas, this affords us as many self-evident propositions as we have distinct ideas. Every one that has any knowledge at all has, as the foundation of it, various and distinct ideas: and it is the first act of the mind (without which it can never be capable of any knowledge) to know every one of its ideas by itself, and distinguish it from others.

5. *Secondly, In co-existence we have few self-evident propositions.*—Secondly, As to co-existence, or such necessary connection between two ideas, that, in the subject where one of them is supposed, there the other must necessarily be also; of such agreement or disagreement as this the mind has an immediate perception but in very few of them; and therefore in this sort we have but very little intuitive knowledge. Nor are there to be found very many propositions that are self-evident, though some there are; *v.g.*, the idea of filling a place equal to the contents of its superficies, being annexed to our idea of body, I think it is a self-evident proposition, that "two bodies cannot be in the same place."

6. *Thirdly, In other relations we may have.*—Thirdly, As to the relations of modes, mathematicians have framed many axioms concerning that one relation of equality: As, "Equals taken from

equals, the remainder will be equals." These and a thousand other such propositions may be found in numbers which, at the very first hearing, force the assent, and carry with them an equal, if not a greater clearness than those mathematical axioms.

7. *Fourthly, Concerning real existence we have none.*—Fourthly, As to real existence, since that has no connection with any other of our ideas but that of ourselves and of a first being, we have in that concerning the real existence of all other beings not so much as demonstrative, much less a self-evident, knowledge, and therefore concerning those there are no maxims.

8. In the next place let us consider what influence these received maxims have upon the other parts of our knowledge.

9. *They are not the truths we first knew.*—First, That they are not the truths first known to the mind is evident to experience, as we have shown in another place. (Book i., chap. ii.) Thus particular ideas are first received and distinguished, and so knowledge got about them; and next to them the less general or specific, which are next to particular: for, abstract ideas are not so obvious or easy to children or the yet unexercised mind, as particular ones. If they seem so to grown men, it is only because by constant and familiar use they are made so: for when we nicely reflect upon them, we shall find that general ideas are fictions and contrivances of the mind, that carry difficulty with them, and do not so easily offer themselves as we are apt to imagine. For example: Does it not require some pains and skill to form the general idea of a triangle? (which is yet none of the most abstract, comprehensive, and difficult); for it must be neither oblique, nor rectangle, neither equilateral, equicrural, nor scalenon; but all and none of these at once. In effect, it is something imperfect, that cannot exist; an idea wherein some parts of several different and inconsistent ideas are put together.

10. *On them the other parts of our knowledge do not depend.*— Secondly, From what has been said, it plainly follows that these magnified maxims are not the principles and foundations of all our other knowledge. For, if there be a great many other truths which have as much self-evidence as they, and a great many that we know before them, it is impossible they should be the principles from which we deduce all other truths. Is it impossible to know that one and two are equal to three, but by virtue of this or some such axiom, viz., "The whole is equal to all its parts taken together?" Many a one knows that one and two are equal to three, without having heard or thought on that or any other axiom

by which it might be proved; and knows it as certainly as any other man knows that " the whole is equal to all its parts," or any other maxim; and all from the same reason of self-evidence, the quality of those ideas being as visible and certain to him without that or any other axiom as with it, it needing no proof to make it perceived.

CHAPTER IX

OF OUR KNOWLEDGE OF EXISTENCE

1. *General certain propositions concern not existence.*—Hitherto we have only considered the essences of things, which, being only abstract ideas, and thereby removed in our thoughts from particular existence (that being the proper operation of the mind in abstraction, to consider an idea under no other existence but what it has in the understanding), give us no knowledge of real existence at all. Where, by the way, we may take notice, that universal propositions, of whose truth or falsehood we can have certain knowledge, concern not existence; and farther, that all particular affirmations or negations that would not be certain if they were made general, are only concerning existence; they declaring only the accidental union or separation of ideas in things existing, which in their abstract natures have no known necessary union or repugnancy.

2. *A threefold knowledge of existence.*—But leaving the nature of propositions, and different ways of predication, to be considered more at large in another place, let us proceed now to inquire concerning our knowledge of the existence of things, and how we come by it. I say then, that we have the knowledge of our own existence by intuition; of the existence of God by demonstration; and of other things by sensation.

3. *Our knowledge of our own existence is intuitive.*—As for our own existence, we perceive it so plainly and so certainly that it neither needs nor is capable of any proof. For nothing can be more evident to us than our own existence. I think, I reason, I feel pleasure and pain: can any of these be more evident to me than my own existence? If I doubt of all other things, that very doubt makes me perceive my own existence, and will not suffer me to doubt of that. For, if I know I feel pain, it is evident I have as certain perception of my own existence, as of the existence of the pain I feel: or if I know I doubt, I have as certain perception

of the existence of the thing doubting, as of that thought which I call "doubt." Experience, then, convinces us that we have an intuitive knowledge of our own existence, and an internal infallible perception that we are. In every act of sensation, reasoning, or thinking, we are conscious to ourselves of our own being; and, in this matter, come not short of the highest degree of certainty.

CHAPTER X

OF OUR KNOWLEDGE OF THE EXISTENCE OF A GOD

1. *We are capable of knowing certainly that there is a God.*— Though God has given us no innate ideas of Himself; though He has stamped no original characters on our minds, wherein we may read His being; yet, having furnished us with those faculties our minds are endowed with, He hath not left Himself without witness; since we have sense, perception, and reason, and cannot want a clear proof of Him as long as we carry ourselves about us. Nor can we justly complain of our ignorance in this great point, since He has so plentifully provided us with the means to discover and know Him, so far as is necessary to the end of our being, and the great concernment of our happiness. But though this be the most obvious truth that reason discovers, and though its evidence be (if I mistake not) equal to mathematical certainty; yet it requires thought and attention, and the mind must apply itself to a regular deduction of it from some part of our intuitive knowledge, or else we shall be as uncertain and ignorant of this as of other propositions which are in themselves capable of clear demonstration. To show, therefore, that we are capable of knowing, *i.e.,* being certain, that there is a God, and how we may come by this certainty, I think we need go no farther than ourselves, and that undoubted knowledge we have of our own existence.

2. *Man knows that he himself is.*—I think it is beyond question, that man has a clear perception of his own being; he knows certainly that he exists, and that he is something. He that can doubt whether he be any thing or no, I speak not to; no more than I would argue with pure nothing, or endeavour to convince nonentity that it were something. If any one pretends to be so sceptical as to deny his own existence (for really to doubt of it is manifestly impossible), let him, for me, enjoy his beloved happiness of being nothing, until hunger or some other pain convince him of the

contrary. This, then, I think I may take for a truth, which every one's certain knowledge assures him of beyond the liberty of doubting, viz., that he is something that actually exists.

3. *He knows also that nothing cannot produce a being, therefore something eternal.*—In the next place, man knows by an intuitive certainty that bare nothing can no more produce any real being, than it can be equal to two right angles. If a man knows not that nonentity, or the absence of all being, cannot be equal to two right angles, it is impossible he should know any demonstration in Euclid. If therefore we know there is some real being, and that nonentity cannot produce any real being, is it an evident demonstration, that from eternity there has been something; since what was not from eternity had a beginning; and what had a beginning must be produced by something else.

4. *That Eternal Being must be most powerful.*—Next, it is evident, that what had its being and beginning from another, must also have all that which is in and belongs to its being from another too. All the powers it has, must be owing to and received from the same source. This eternal source, then, of all being, must also be the source and original of all power; and so this Eternal Being must be also the most powerful.

5. *And most knowing.*—Again: a man finds in himself perception and knowledge. We have then got one step farther; and we are certain now that there is not only some being, but some knowing, intelligent being in the world.

There was a time, then, when there was no knowing being, and when knowledge began to be; or else there has been also a knowing Being from eternity. If it be said, " There was a time when no being had any knowledge, when that Eternal Being was void of all understanding "; I reply, that then it was impossible there should ever have been any knowledge; it being as impossible that things wholly void of knowledge, and operating blindly and without any perception, should produce a knowing being, as it is impossible that a triangle should make itself three angles bigger than two right ones. For it is as repugnant to the idea of senseless matter that it should put into itself sense, perception, and knowledge, as it is repugnant to the idea of a triangle that it should put into itself greater angles than two right ones.

6. *And therefore God.*—Thus from the consideration of ourselves, and what we infallibly find in our own constitutions, our reason leads us to the knowledge of this certain and evident truth, that there is an eternal, most powerful, and most knowing Being; which

whether any one will please to call " God," it matters not. The thing is evident; and from this idea, duly considered, will easily be deduced all those other attributes which we ought to ascribe to this Eternal Being.

8. *Something from eternity.*—There is no truth more evident than that something must be from eternity. I never yet heard of any one so unreasonable, or that could suppose so manifest a contradiction, as a time wherein there was perfectly nothing; this being of all absurdities the greatest, to imagine that pure nothing, the perfect negation and absence of all beings, should ever produce any real existence.

It being then unavoidable for all rational creatures to conclude that something has existed from eternity, let us next see what kind of thing that must be.

9. *Two sorts of beings cogitative and incogitative.*—There are but two sorts of beings in the world that man knows or conceives :—

First, Such as are purely material, without sense, perception, or thought, as the clippings of our beards and parings of our nails.

Secondly, Sensible, thinking, perceiving beings, such as we find ourselves to be; which, if you please, we will hereafter call " cogitative and incogitative beings "; which, to our present purpose, if for nothing else, are perhaps better terms than " material and immaterial."

10. *Incogitative being cannot produce a cogitative.*—If then there must be something eternal, let us see what sort of being it must be. And to that it is very obvious to reason, that it must necessarily be a cogitative being. For it is as impossible to conceive that ever bare incogitative matter should produce a thinking intelligent being, as that nothing should of itself produce matter. Let us suppose any parcel of matter eternal, great or small, we shall find it in itself able to produce nothing. For example : Let us suppose the matter of the next pebble we meet with, eternal, closely united, and the parts firmly at rest together; if there were no other being in the world, must it not eternally remain so, a dead, inactive lump? Is it possible to conceive it can add motion to itself, being purely matter, or produce any thing? Matter, then, by its own strength, cannot produce in itself so much as motion : the motion it has must also be from eternity, or else be produced and added to matter by some other being more powerful than matter : matter, as is evident, having not power to produce motion in itself. But let us suppose motion eternal too; yet matter, incogitative matter and motion, whatever changes it might produce of figure and bulk,

could never produce thought. Knowledge will still be as far beyond the power of motion and matter to produce, as matter is beyond the power of nothing or nonentity to produce. And I appeal to every one's own thoughts, whether he cannot as easily conceive matter produced by nothing, as thought to be produced by pure matter, when before there was no such thing as thought or an intelligent being existing. So that, if we will suppose nothing first or eternal, matter can never begin to be: if we will suppose bare matter without motion, eternal motion can never begin to be: if we suppose only matter and motion first, or eternal, thought can never begin to be.

11. *Therefore there has been an eternal wisdom.*—If, therefore, it be evident that something necessarily must exist from eternity, it is also as evident that that something must necessarily be a cogitative being: for it is as impossible that incogitative matter should produce a cogitative being, as that nothing, or the negation of all being, should produce a positive being or matter.

12. Though this discovery of the necessary existence of an eternal mind does sufficiently lead us into the knowledge of God, since it will hence follow that all other knowing beings that have a beginning must depend on him, and have no other ways of knowledge or extent of power than what he gives them; and therefore if he made those, he made also the less excellent pieces of this universe, all inanimate beings, whereby his omniscience, power, and providence will be established, and all his other attributes necessarily follow.

CHAPTER XI

OF OUR KNOWLEDGE OF THE EXISTENCE OF OTHER THINGS

1. *It is to be had only by sensation.*—The knowledge of our own being we have by intuition. The existence of a God reason clearly makes known to us, as has been shown.

The knowledge of the existence of any other thing, we can have only by sensation: for, there being no necessary connection of real existence with any idea a man hath in his memory, nor of any other existence but that of God with the existence of any particular man, no particular man can know the existence of any other being, but only when by actual operating upon him it makes itself perceived by him. For, the having the idea of any thing in

our mind no more proves the existence of that thing than the
picture of a man evidences his being in the world, or the visions
of a dream make thereby a true history.

2. *Instance whiteness of this paper.*—It is therefore the actual
receiving of ideas from without that gives us notice of the existence
of other things, and makes us know that something doth exist at
that time without us which causes that idea in us, though perhaps
we neither know nor consider how it does it: for it takes not from
the certainty of our senses, and the idea we receive by them, that
we know not the manner wherein they are produced; *v.g.*, whilst I
write this, I have, by the paper affecting my eyes, that idea
produced in my mind which whatever object causes, I call
" white "; by which I know that that quality or accident (*i.e.*,
whose appearance before my eyes always causes that idea) doth
really exist and hath a being without me. And of this the greatest
assurance I can possibly have, and to which my faculties can
attain, is the testimony of my eyes, which are the proper and sole
judges of this thing; whose testimony I have reason to rely on as
so certain that I can no more doubt, whilst I write this, that I see
white and black, and that something really exists that causes that
sensation in me, than that I write or move my hand; which is a
certainty as great as human nature is capable of concerning the
existence of any thing but a man's self alone and of God.

3. *This, though not so certain as demonstration, yet may be
called " knowledge," and proves the existence of things without
us.*—The notice we have by our senses of the existing of things
without us, though it be not altogether so certain as our intuitive
knowledge, or the deductions of our reason employed about the
clear abstract ideas of our own minds; yet it is an assurance that
deserves the name of knowledge. If we persuade ourselves that
our faculties act and inform us right concerning the existence of
those objects that affect them, it cannot pass for an ill-grounded
confidence: for I think nobody can, in earnest, be so sceptical as
to be uncertain of the existence of those things which he sees and
feels. This is certain, the confidence that our faculties do not
herein deceive us is the greatest assurance we are capable of
concerning the existence of material beings. For we cannot act
any thing but by our faculties, nor talk of knowledge itself but by
the help of those faculties which are fitted to apprehend even
what knowledge is. But, besides the assurance we have from our
senses themselves, that they do not err in the information they
give us of the existence of things without us, when they are affected

by them, we are farther confirmed in this assurance by other concurrent reasons.

4. *First, Because we cannot have them but by the inlet of the senses*.—First, It is plain those perceptions are produced in us by exterior causes affecting our senses, because those that want the organs of any sense never can have the ideas belonging to that sense produced in their minds. This is too evident to be doubted: and therefore we cannot but be assured that they come in by the organs of that sense, and no other way. The organs themselves, it is plain, do not produce them; for then the eyes of a man in the dark would produce colours, and his nose smell roses in the winter: but we see nobody gets the relish of a pine-apple till he goes to the Indies where it is, and tastes it.

5. *Secondly, Because an idea from actual sensation, and another from memory are very distinct perceptions*.—Secondly, Because sometimes I find that I cannot avoid the having those ideas produced in my mind: for though when my eyes are shut, or windows fast, I can at pleasure recall to my mind the ideas of light or the sun, which former sensations had lodged in my memory: so I can at pleasure lay by that idea, and take into my view that of the smell of a rose, or taste of sugar. But if I turn my eyes at noon towards the sun, I cannot avoid the ideas which the light or sun then produces in me. So that there is a manifest difference between the ideas laid up in my memory (over which, if they were there only, I should have constantly the same power to dispose of them, and lay them by at pleasure), and those which force themselves upon me and I cannot avoid having. And therefore it must needs be some exterior cause, and the brisk acting of some objects without me, whose efficacy I cannot resist, that produces those ideas in my mind, whether I will or no. Besides, there is nobody who doth not perceive the difference in himself between contemplating the sun as he hath the idea of it in his memory, and actually looking upon it: of which two his perception is so distinct, that few of his ideas are more distinguishable one from another: and therefore he hath certain knowledge that they are not both memory, or the actions of his mind and fancies only within him; but that actual seeing hath a cause without.

6. *Thirdly, Pleasure or pain, which accompanies actual sensation, accompanies not the returning of those ideas without the external objects*.—Thirdly, Add to this, that many of those ideas are produced in us with pain, which afterwards we remember without

the least offence. Thus the pain of heat or cold, when the idea of it is revived in our minds, gives us no disturbance; which, when felt, was very troublesome.

7. *Fourthly, Our senses assist one another's testimony of the existence of outward things.*—Fourthly, Our senses, in many cases, bear witness to the truth of each other's report concerning the existence of sensible things without us. He that sees a fire may, if he doubt whether it be any thing more than a bare fancy, feel it too, and be convinced by putting his hand in it; which certainly could never be put into such exquisite pain by a bare idea or phantom, unless that the pain be a fancy too; which yet he cannot, when the burn is well, by raising the idea of it, bring upon himself again.

8. *This certainty is as great as our condition needs.*—But yet, if after all this any one will be so sceptical as to distrust his senses, and affirm that all we see and hear, feel and taste, think and do, during our whole being, is but the series and deluding appearances of a long dream whereof there is no reality, and therefore will question the existence of all things or our knowledge of any thing; I must desire him to consider, that if all be a dream, then he doth but dream that he makes the question; and so it is not much matter that a waking man should answer him. But yet, if he pleases, he may dream that I make him this answer, that the certainty of things existing *in rerum natura,* when we have the testimony of our senses for it, is not only as great as our frame can attain to, but as our condition needs.

9. *But reaches no farther than actual sensation.*—In fine, then when our senses do actually convey into our understandings any idea, we cannot but be satisfied that there doth something at that time really exist without us which doth affect our senses, and by them give notice of itself to our apprehensive faculties, and actually produce that idea which we then perceive: and we cannot so far distrust their testimony as to doubt that such collections of simple ideas as we have observed by our senses to be united together, do really exist together. But this knowledge extends as far as the present testimony of our senses, employed about particular objects that do then affect them, and no farther. For if I saw such a collection of simple ideas as is wont to be called " man " existing together one minute since, and am now alone; I cannot be certain that the same man exists now, since there is no necessary connection of his existence a minute since with his existence now: by a thousand ways he may cease to be, since I had the testimony of my senses

for his existence. And if I cannot be certain that the man I saw last to-day is now in being, I can less be certain that he is so who hath been longer removed from my senses, and I have not seen since yesterday, or since the last year, and much less can I be certain of the existence of men that I never saw. And therefore, though it be highly probable that millions of men do now exist, yet, whilst I am alone writing this, I have not that certainty of it which we strictly call " knowledge "; though the great likelihood of it puts me past doubt, and it be reasonable for me to do several things upon the confidence that there are men (and men also of my acquaintance, with whom I have to do) now in the world: but this is but probability, not knowledge.

12. *The existence of spirits not knowable.*—What ideas we have of spirits, and how we come by them, I have already shown. But though we have those ideas in our minds, and know we have them there, the having the ideas of spirits does not make us know that any such things do exist without us, or that there are any finite spirits, or any other spiritual beings but the eternal God. We have ground from revelation, and several other reasons, to believe with assurance that there are such creatures; but, our senses not being able to discover them, we want the means of knowing their particular existences. For we can no more know that there are finite spirits really existing by the idea we have of such beings in our minds, than by the ideas any one has of fairies or centaurs he can come to know that things answering those ideas do really exist.

And therefore concerning the existence of finite spirits, as well as several other things, we must content ourselves with the evidence of faith; but universal certain propositions concerning this matter are beyond our reach. For, however true it may be, *v.g.*, that all the intelligent spirits that God ever created do still exist, yet it can never make a part of our certain knowledge. These and the like propositions we may assent to as highly probable, but are not, I fear, in this state capable of knowing.

13. *Particular propositions concerning existences are knowable.* —By which it appears that there are two sorts of propositions. (1). There is one sort of propositions concerning the existence of any thing answerable to such an idea: as having the idea of an elephant, phœnix, motion, or an angel in my mind, the first and natural inquiry is, whether such a thing does any where exist. And this knowledge is only of particulars. No existence of any thing without us, but only of God, can certainly be known farther than

our senses inform us. (2). There is another sort of propositions, wherein is expressed the agreement or disagreement of our abstract ideas, and their dependence one on another. Such propositions may be universal and certain. So having the idea of God and myself, of fear and obedience, I cannot but be sure that God is to be feared and obeyed by me: and this proposition will be certain concerning man in general, if I have made an abstract idea of such a species, whereof I am one particular. But yet this proposition, how certain soever, that men ought to fear and obey God, proves not to me the existence of men in the world, but will be true of all such creatures whenever they do exist: which certainty of such general propositions depends on the agreement or disagreement is to be discovered in those abstract ideas.

CHAPTER XIV

OF JUDGMENT

1. *Our knowledge being short, we want something else.*—The understanding faculties being given to man, not barely for speculation, but also for the conduct of his life, man would be at a great loss if he had nothing to direct him but what has the certainty of true knowledge. For, that being very short and scanty, as we have seen, he would be often utterly in the dark, and in most of the actions of his life perfectly at a stand, had he nothing to guide him in the absence of clear and certain knowledge. He that will not eat till he has demonstration that it will nourish him, he that will not stir till he infallibly knows the business he goes about will succeed, will have little else to do but sit still and perish.

2. *What use to be made of this twilight state.*—Therefore, as God has set some things in broad daylight, as he has given us some certain knowledge, though limited to a few things in comparison, probably as a taste of what intellectual creatures are capable of, to excite in us a desire and endeavour after a better state; so, in the greatest part of our concernment, he has afforded us only in twilight, as I may so say, of probability, suitable, I presume, to that state of mediocrity and probationership he has been pleased to place us in here.

3. *Judgment supplies the want of knowledge.*—The faculty which God has given man to supply the want of clear and certain knowledge, in cases where that cannot be had, is judgment: whereby the mind takes its ideas to agree or disagree; or, which is the same,

any proposition to be true or false, without perceiving a demonstrative evidence in the proofs.

4. *Judgment is the presuming things to be so without perceiving it.*—Thus the mind has two faculties conversant about truth and falsehood:—

First, Knowledge, whereby it certainly perceives, and is undoubtedly satisfied of the agreement or disagreement of any ideas.

Secondly, Judgment, which is the putting ideas together, or separating them from one another in the mind, when their certain agreement or disagreement is not perceived, but presumed to be so; which is, as the word imports, taken to be so before it certainly appears. And if it so unites or separates them as in reality things are, it is right judgment.

CHAPTER XV

OF PROBABILITY

1. *Probability is the appearance of agreement upon fallible proofs.* —As demonstration is the showing the agreement or disagreement of two ideas by the intervention of one or more proofs, which have a constant, immutable, and visible connection one with another; so probability is nothing but the appearance of such an agreement or disagreement by the intervention of proofs, whose connection is not constant and immutable, or at least is not perceived to be so; but is, or appears for the most part to be so, and is enough to induce the mind to judge the proposition to be true or false, rather than the contrary. For example: In the demonstration of it, a man perceives the certain immutable connection there is of equality between the three angles of a triangle, and those intermediate ones which are made use of to show their equality to two right ones; and so, by an intuitive knowledge of the agreement or disagreement of the intermediate ideas in each step of the progress, the whole series is continued with an evidence which clearly shows the agreement or disagreement of those three angles in equality to two right ones: and thus he has certain knowledge that it is so. But another man, who never took the pains to observe the demonstration, hearing a mathematician, a man of credit, affirm " the three angles of a triangle to be equal to two right ones," assents to it, *i.e.*, receives it for true. In which case the foundation of his assent is the probability of the thing, the proof being such as for

the most part carries truth with it: the man on whose testimony he receives it not being wont to affirm any thing contrary to or besides his knowledge, especially in matters of this kind. So that that which causes his assent to this proposition, that " the three angles of a triangle are equal to two right ones," that which makes him take these ideas to agree without knowing them to do so, is the wonted veracity of the speaker in other cases, or his supposed veracity in this.

3. *Being that which makes us presume things to be true before we know them to be so.*—Probability is likeliness to be true; the very notation of the word signifying such a proposition for which there be arguments or proofs to make it pass, or be received, for true. The entertainment the mind gives this sort of propositions is called " belief," " assent," or " opinion," which is the admitting or receiving any proposition for true, upon arguments or proofs that are found to persuade us to receive it as true, without certain knowledge that it is so. And herein lies the difference between probability and certainty, faith and knowledge, that in all the parts of knowledge there is intuition; each immediate idea, each step has its visible and certain connection: in belief not so. That which makes me believe, is something extraneous to the thing I believe; something not evidently joined on both sides to, and so not manifestly showing the agreement or disagreement, of those ideas that are under consideration.

4. *The grounds of probability are two; conformity with our own experience, or the testimony of others' experience.*—Probability, then, being to supply the defect of our knowledge, and to guide us where that fails, is always conversant about propositions whereof we have no certainty, but only some inducements to receive them for true. The grounds of it are, in short, these two following:—

First, The conformity of any thing with our own knowledge, observation, and experience.

Secondly, The testimony of others, vouching their observation and experience.

CHAPTER XXI

OF THE DIVISION OF THE SCIENCES

1. *Three sorts.*—All that can fall within the compass of human understanding being either, First, The nature of things as they are in themselves, their relations, and their manner of operation:

or, Secondly, That which man himself ought to do, as a rational and voluntary agent, for the attainment of any end, especially happiness: or, Thirdly, The ways and means whereby the knowledge of both the one and the other of these are attained and communicated: I think science may be divided properly into these three sorts: —

2. *First*, Physica.—First, The knowledge of things as they are in their own proper beings, their constitutions, properties, and operations, whereby I mean not only matter and body, but spirits also, which have their proper natures, constitutions, and operations, as well as bodies. This, in a little more enlarged sense of the word, I call, φυσική, or " natural philosophy." The end of this is bare speculative truth: and whatsoever can afford the mind of man any such falls under this branch, whether it be God Himself, angels, spirits, bodies, or any of their affections, as number and figure, etc.

3. *Secondly*, Practica.—Secondly, πρακτική, the skill of right applying our own powers and actions for the attainment of things good and useful. The most considerable under this head is ethics, which is the seeking out those rules and measures of human actions which lead to happiness, and the means to practise them. The end of this is not bare speculation and the knowledge of truth; but right, and a conduct suitable to it.

4. *Thirdly*, σημιωτική.—Thirdly, The third branch may be called σημιωτική or, the " doctrine of signs," the most usual whereof being words, it is aptly enough termed also λογική, " logic "; the business whereof is to consider the nature of signs the mind makes use of for the understanding of things, or conveying its knowledge to others. For, since the things the mind contemplates are none of them, besides itself, present to the understanding, it is necessary that something else, as a sign or representation of the thing it considers, should be present to it: and these are ideas. And because the scene of ideas that makes one man's thoughts cannot be laid open to the immediate view of another, nor laid up any where but in the memory, a no very sure repository; therefore, to communicate our thoughts to one another, as well as record them for our own use, signs of our ideas are also necessary. Those which men have found most convenient, and therefore generally make use of, are articulate sounds. The consideration, then, of ideas and words as the great instruments of knowledge, makes no despicable part of their contemplation who would take a view of human knowledge in the whole extent of it. And perhaps, if they were distinctly weighed and duly considered, they would afford

us another sort of logic and critic than what we have been hitherto
acquainted with.

5. *This is the first division of the objects of knowledge.*—This
seems to me the first and most general, as well as natural, division
of the objects of our understanding. For a man can employ his
thoughts about nothing but either the contemplation of things
themselves for the discovery of truth; or about the things in his
own power, which are his own actions, for the attainment of his
own ends; or the signs the mind makes use of, both in the one and
the other, and the right ordering of them for its clearer information.
All which three, viz., things as they are in themselves knowable,
actions as they depend on us in order to happiness, and the right
use of signs in order to knowledge, being *toto cælo* different, they
seemed to me to be the three great provinces of the intellectual
world, wholly separate and distinct one from another.

GEORGE BERKELEY

Born in County Kilkenny, 1685. *Educated
at Trinity College, Dublin. Fellow of Trinity
College, Dublin,* 1707. *Dean of Dromore,*
1721. *Dean of Derry,* 1724. *Bishop of
Cloyne,* 1734-1752. *Died at Oxford,* 1753.
Philosophical works include An Essay To-
wards a New Theory of Vision, 1707, A
Treatise Concerning the Principles of Human
Knowledge, 1708, Three Dialogues between
Hylas and Philonous, 1713, Alciphron, 1732,
The Analyst, 1734, *and* Siris, 1744.

WITH THE exception of a few unimportant footnotes, the *Treatise Concerning the Principles of Human Knowledge* is reprinted here in full. Of the *Three Dialogues between Hylas and Philonous,* only the first is reprinted in full; the greater part of the second and third has been omitted, as they add little to the argument, but space has been found for a few passages which bring out certain points that are not so clearly made by Berkeley elsewhere.

A TREATISE CONCERNING THE PRINCIPLES OF HUMAN KNOWLEDGE

wherein the chief causes of error and difficulty
in the sciences, with the grounds of scepticism
atheism, and irreligion, are inquired into.

INTRODUCTION

1. PHILOSOPHY being nothing else but *the study of wisdom and truth*, it may with reason be expected, that those who have spent most time and pains in it should enjoy a greater calm and serenity of mind, a greater clearness and evidence of knowledge, and be less disturbed with doubts and difficulties than other men. Yet so it is, we see the illiterate bulk of mankind, that walk the high road of plain, common sense, and are governed by the dictates of nature, for the most part easy and undisturbed. To them nothing *that is familiar* appears unaccountable or difficult to comprehend. They complain not of any want of evidence in their senses, and are out of all danger of becoming *sceptics*. But no sooner do we depart from sense and instinct to follow the light of a superior principle, to reason, meditate, and reflect on the nature of things, but a thousand scruples spring up in our minds, concerning those things which before we seemed fully to comprehend. Prejudices and errors of sense do from all parts discover themselves to our view; and endeavouring to correct these by reason, we are insensibly drawn into uncouth paradoxes, difficulties, and inconsistences, which multiply and grow upon us as we advance in speculation; till at length, having wandered through many intricate mazes, we find ourselves just where we were, or, which is worse, sit down in a forlorn scepticism.

2. The cause of this is thought to be (1) the obscurity of things, or the natural weakness and imperfection of our understandings. It is said the faculties we have are few, and those designed by

nature for the *support* and comfort of life, and not to penetrate into the *inward essence* and constitution of things. Besides, (2) the mind of man being finite, when it treats of things which partake of infinity, it is not to be wondered at if it run into absurdities and contradictions; out of which it is impossible it should ever extricate itself, it being of the nature of infinite not to be comprehended by that which is finite.

3. But perhaps we may be too partial to ourselves in placing the fault originally in our faculties, and not rather in the wrong use we make of them. *It is a hard thing to suppose, that right deductions from true principles should ever end in consequences which cannot be maintained* or made consistent. We should believe that God has dealt more bountifully with the sons of men, than to give them a strong desire for that knowledge which he had placed quite out of their reach. This were not agreeable to the wonted indulgent methods of Providence, which, whatever appetites it may have implanted in the creatures, doth usually furnish them with such means as, if rightly made use of, will not fail to satisfy them. Upon the whole I am inclined to think that the far greater part, if not all, of those difficulties which have hitherto amused philosophers, and blocked up the way to knowledge, are entirely owing to ourselves. That we have first raised a dust, and then complain we cannot see.

4. My purpose therefore is, to try if I can discover what those principles are, which have introduced all that doubtfulness and uncertainty, those absurdities and contradictions into the several sects of philosophy; insomuch that the wisest men have thought our ignorance incurable, conceiving it to arise from the natural dulness and limitation of our faculties. And surely it is a work well deserving our pains, to make a strict inquiry concerning the first principles of human knowledge, to sift and examine them on all sides: especially since there may be some grounds to suspect that those lets and difficulties, which stay and embarrass the mind in its search after truth, do not spring from any darkness and intricacy in the objects, or natural defect in the understanding, so much as from false principles which have been insisted on, and might have been avoided.

5. How difficult and discouraging soever this attempt may seem, when I consider how many great and extraordinary men have gone before me in the same designs: yet I am not without some hopes, upon the consideration that the largest views are not always the clearest, and that he who is short-sighted will be obliged to

draw the object nearer, and may, perhaps, by a close and narrow survey, discern that which had escaped far better eyes.

6. *A chief source of error in all parts of knowledge.*—In order to prepare the mind of the reader for the easier conceiving what follows, it is proper to premise somewhat, by way of introduction, concerning the nature and abuse of language. But the unravelling this matter leads me in some measure to anticipate my design, by taking notice of what seems to have had a chief part in rendering speculation intricate and perplexed, and to have occasioned innumerable errors and difficulties in almost all parts of knowledge. And that is the opinion that the mind hath a power of framing *abstract ideas* or notions of things. He who is not a perfect stranger to the writings and disputes of philosophers, must needs acknowledge that no small part of them are spent about abstract ideas. These are, in a more especial manner, thought to be the object of those sciences which go by the name of *logic* and *metaphysics*, and of all that which passes under the notion of the most abstracted and sublime learning, in all which one shall scarce find any question handled in such a manner, as does not suppose their existence in the mind, and that it is well acquainted with them.

7. *Proper acceptation of abstraction.*—It is agreed, on all hands, that the qualities or modes of things do never *really exist each of them apart by itself*, and separated from all others, but are mixed, as it were, and blended together, several in the same object. But we are told, the mind being able to consider each quality singly, or abstracted from those other qualities with which it is united, does by that means frame to itself abstract ideas. For example, there is perceived by sight an object extended, coloured, and moved : this mixed or compound idea the mind resolving into its simple, constituent parts, and viewing each by itself, exclusive of the rest, does frame the abstract ideas of extension, colour, and motion. Not that it is possible for colour or motion to exist without extension : but only that the mind can frame to itself by *abstraction* the idea of colour exclusive of extension, and of motion exclusive of both colour and extension.

8. *Of generalizing.*—Again, the mind having observed that in the particular extensions perceived by sense, there is something *common* and alike in *all*, and some other things peculiar, as this or that figure or magnitude, which distinguish them one from another; it considers apart or singles out by itself that which is common, making thereof a most abstract idea of extension, which is neither line, surface, nor solid, nor has any figure of magnitude,

but is an idea entirely prescinded from all these. So likewise the mind, by leaving out of the particular colours perceived by sense, that which distinguishes them one from another, and retaining only that which is *common to all*, makes an idea of colour in abstract, which is neither red, nor blue, nor white, nor any other determinate colour. And in like manner, by considering motion abstractedly not only from the body moved, but likewise from the figure it describes, and all particular directions and velocities, the abstract idea of motion is framed; which equally corresponds to all particular motions whatsoever that may be perceived by sense.

9. *Of compounding.*—And as the mind frames to itself abstract ideas of qualities or *modes*, so does it, by the same precision or mental separation, attain abstract ideas of the more compounded *being*s, which include several coexistent qualities. For example, the mind having observed that Peter, James, and John resemble each other, in certain common agreements of shape and other qualities, leaves out of the complex or compounded idea it has of Peter, James, and any other particular man, that which is peculiar to each, retaining only what is common to all; and so makes an abstract idea wherein all the particulars equally partake, abstracting entirely from and cutting off all those circumstances and differences, which might determine it to any particular existence. And after this manner it is said we come by the abstract idea of *man*, or, if you please, humanity or human nature; wherein it is true there is included colour, because there is no man but has some colour, but then it can be neither white, nor black, nor any particular colour; because there is no one particular colour wherein all men partake. So likewise there is included stature, but then it is neither tall stature nor low stature, nor yet middle stature, but something abstracted from all these. And so of the rest. Moreover, there being a great variety of other creatures that partake in some parts, but not all, of the complex idea of *man*, the mind leaving out those parts which are peculiar to men, and retaining those only which are common to all the living creatures, frameth the idea of *animal*, which abstracts not only from all particular men, but also birds, beasts, fishes, and insects. The constituent parts of the abstract idea of animal are body, life, sense, and spontaneous motion. By *body* is meant, body without any particular shape or figure, there being no one shape or figure common to all animals, without covering, either of hair or feathers, or scales, etc., nor yet naked: hair, feathers, scales, and nakedness, being the distinguishing properties of particular animals, and for

that reason left out of the *abstract idea*. Upon the same account the spontaneous motion must be neither walking, nor flying, nor creeping; it is nevertheless a motion, but what that motion is, it is not easy to conceive.

10. *Two objections to the existence of abstract ideas.*—Whether others have this wonderful faculty of *abstracting their ideas*, they best can tell: for myself I find indeed I have a faculty of imagining, or representing to myself the ideas of those particular things I have perceived, and of variously compounding and dividing them. I can imagine a man with two heads, or the upper parts of a man joined to the body of a horse. I can consider the hand, the eye, the nose, each by itself abstracted or separated from the rest of the body. But then whatever hand or eye I imagine, it must have some particular shape and colour. Likewise the idea of man that I frame to myself, must be either of a white, or a black, or a tawny, a straight, or a crooked, a tall, or a low, or a middle-sized man. I cannot by any effort of thought conceive the abstract idea above described. And it is equally impossible for me to form the abstract idea of motion distinct from the body moving, and which is neither swift nor slow, curvilinear nor rectilinear; and the like may be said of all other abstract general ideas whatsoever. To be plain, I own myself able to abstract *in one sense,* as when I consider some particular parts or qualities separated from others, with which though they are united in some object, yet it is possible they may really exist without them. But I deny that I can abstract one from another, or conceive separately, those qualities which it is impossible should exist so separated; or that I can frame a general notion by abstracting from particulars in the manner aforesaid. Which two last are the proper acceptations of *abstraction*. And there are grounds to think most men will acknowledge themselves to be in my case. The generality of men which are simple and illiterate never pretend to *abstract notions*. It is said they are difficult, and not to be attained without pains and study. We may therefore reasonably conclude that, if such there be, they are confined only to the learned.

11. I proceed to examine what can be alleged in *defence of the doctrine of abstraction,* and try if I can discover what it is that inclines the men of speculation to embrace an opinion so remote from common sense as that seems to be. There has been a late deservedly esteemed philosopher, who, no doubt, has given it very much countenance by seeming to think the having abstract general ideas is what puts the widest difference in point of understanding

betwixt man and beast. " The having of general ideas," saith he, " is that which puts a perfect distinction betwixt man and brutes, and is an excellency which the faculties of brutes do by no means attain unto. For it is evident we observe no footsteps in them of making use of general signs for universal ideas; from which we have reason to imagine that they have not the faculty of *abstracting,* or making general ideas, since they have no use of words or any other general signs." And a little after: " Therefore, I think, we may suppose that it is in this that the species of brutes are discriminated from men and it is that proper difference wherein they are wholly separated, and which at last widens to so wide a distance. For if they have any ideas at all, and are not bare machines (as some would have them), we cannot deny them to have some reason. It seems as evident to me that they do some of them in certain instances reason as that they have sense, but it is only in particular ideas, just as they receive them from their senses. They are the best of them tied up within those narrow bounds, and have not (as I think) the faculty to enlarge them by any kind of *abstraction*." (Essay on Hum. Underst., b. ii., ch. xi., sect. 10, 11.) I readily agree with this learned author, that the faculties of brutes can by no means attain to *abstraction*. But then if this be made the distinguishing property of that sort of animals, I fear a great many of those that pass for men must be reckoned into their number. The reason that is here assigned why we have no grounds to think brutes have abstract general ideas, is that we observe in them no use of words or any other general signs: which is built on this supposition, to wit, that the making use of words implies the having general ideas. From which it follows that men who use language are able to *abstract* or *generalize* their ideas. That this is the sense and arguing of the author will further appear by his answering the question he in another place puts. " Since all things that exist are only particulars, how come we by general terms? " His answer is, " Words become general by being made the signs of general ideas." (Essay on Hum. Underst., b. iii., ch. iii., sect. 6.) But it seems that a word becomes general by being made the sign, not of an *abstract* general idea, but of several particular ideas, any one of which it indifferently suggests to the mind. For example, when it is said *the change of motion is proportional to the impressed force,* or that *whatever has extension is divisible;* these propositions are to be understood of motion and extension in general, and nevertheless it will not follow that they suggest to my thoughts an idea of motion without a body moved, or any determinate direction and velocity, or that I must conceive an abstract general idea of extension, which is neither line, surface, nor solid, neither great nor small, black, white, nor red, nor of any other determinate colour. It is only implied that whatever motion I consider, whether it be swift or slow, perpendicular, horizontal, or oblique, or in whatever object, the axiom concerning it holds equally true. As does the other of every particular extension, it matters not whether line, surface, or solid, whether of this or that magnitude or figure.

12. *Existence of general ideas admitted.*—By observing how ideas become general, we may the better judge how words are made so. And here it is to be noted that I do not deny absolutely there are general ideas, but only that there are any *abstract general ideas*: for in the passages above quoted, wherein there is mention of general ideas, it is always supposed that they are formed by *abstraction,* after the manner set forth in Sects. VIII and IX. Now if we will annex a meaning to our words, and speak only of what we can conceive, I believe we shall acknowledge, that an idea, which considered in itself is particular, becomes general, by being made to represent or stand for all other particular ideas of the *same sort.* To make this plain by an example, suppose a geometrician is demonstrating the method of cutting a line in two equal parts. He draws, for instance, a black line of an inch in length; this, which in itself is a particular line, is nevertheless with regard to its signification general, since, as it is there used, it represents all particular lines whatsoever; so that what is demonstrated of it, is demonstrated of all lines, or, in other words, of a line in general. And as that particular line becomes general, by being made a sign, so the name *line*, which taken absolutely is *particular*, by being a sign is made *general*. And as the former owes its generality, not to its being the sign of an abstract or general, but of *all particular* right lines that may possibly exist; so the latter must be thought to derive its generality from the same cause, namely, the *various particular* lines which it indifferently denotes.

13. *Abstract general ideas necessary, according to Locke.*—To give the reader a yet clearer view of the nature of abstract ideas, and the uses they are thought necessary to, I shall add one more passage out of the Essay on Human Understanding, which is as follows. " *Abstract ideas* are not so obvious or easy to children or the yet unexercised mind as particular ones. If they seem so to grown men, it is only because by constant and familiar use they are made so. For when we nicely reflect upon them, we shall find

that general ideas are fictions and contrivances of the mind, that carry difficulty with them, and do not so easily offer themselves as we are apt to imagine. For example, does it not require some pains and skill to form the general idea of a triangle? (which is yet none of the most abstract, comprehensive and difficult); for it must be neither oblique nor rectangle, neither equilateral, equicrural, nor scalenon, but *all and none* of these at once. In effect, it is something imperfect that cannot exist, an idea wherein some parts of several different and *inconsistent* ideas are put together. It is true the mind in this imperfect state has need of such ideas, and makes all the haste to them it can, for the (1) *conveniency of communication* and (2) *enlargement of knowledge,* to both which it is naturally very much inclined. But yet one has reason to suspect such ideas are marks of our imperfection. At least this is enough to show that the most abstract and general ideas are not those that the mind is first and most easily acquainted with, nor such as its earliest knowledge is conversant about.'' (Book iv., ch. vii., sect. 9.) If any man has the faculty of framing in his mind such an idea of a triangle as is here described, it is in vain to pretend to dispute him out of it, nor would I go about it. All I desire is, that the reader would fully and certainly inform himself whether he has such an idea or no. And this, methinks, can be no hard task for any one to perform. What more easy than for any one to look a little into his own thoughts, and there try whether he has, or can attain to have, an idea that shall correspond with the description that is here given of the general idea of a triangle, which is, *neither oblique, nor rectangle, equilateral, equicrural, nor scalenon, but all and none of these at once?*

14. *But they are not necessary for communication.*—Much is here said of the difficulty that abstract ideas carry with them, and the pains and skill requisite to the forming them. And it is on all hands agreed that there is need of great toil and labour of the mind to emancipate our thoughts from particular objects, and raise them to those sublime speculations that are conversant about abstract ideas. From all which the natural consequence should seem to be, that so *difficult* a thing as the forming abstract ideas was not necessary for *communication,* which is so *easy* and familiar to *all sorts of men.* But we are told, if they seem obvious and easy to grown men, *it is only because by constant and familiar use they are made so.* Now I would fain know at what time it is men are employed in surmounting that difficulty, and furnishing themselves with those necessary helps for discourse. It cannot be when they are grown-

up, for then it seems they are not conscious of any such painstaking; it remains therefore to be the business of their childhood. And surely, the great and multiplied labour of framing abstract notions will be found a hard task for that tender age. Is it not a hard thing to imagine, that a couple of children cannot prate together of their sugar-plums, and rattles, and the rest of their little trinkets, till they have first tacked together numberless inconsistencies, and so framed in their minds *abstract general ideas*, and annexed them to every common name they make use of?

15. *Nor for the enlargement of knowledge.*—Nor do I think them a whit more needful for the *enlargement of knowledge* than for *communication*. It is, I know, a point much insisted on, that all knowledge and demonstration are about universal notions, to which I fully agree: but then it doth not appear to me that these notions are formed by *abstraction* in the manner premised; *universality*, so far as I can comprehend, not consisting in the absolute, *positive* nature or conception of any thing, but in the *relation* it bears to the particulars signified or represented by it, by virtue whereof it is that things, names, or notions, being in their own nature *particular*, are rendered *universal*. Thus when I demonstrate any propositions concerning triangles, it is to be supposed that I have in view the universal idea of a triangle; which ought not to be understood as if I could frame an idea of a triangle which was neither equilateral, nor scalenon, nor equicrural. But only that the particular triangle I consider, whether of this or that sort it matters not, doth equally stand for and represent all rectilinear triangles whatsoever, and is, in that sense, *universal*. All which seems very plain, and not to include any difficulty in it.

16. *Objection.—Answer.*—But here it will be demanded, *how can we know any proposition to be true of all particular triangles, except* we have first seen it *demonstrated of the abstract idea of a triangle* which equally agrees to all? For, because a property may be demonstrated to agree to some one particular triangle, it will not thence follow that it equally belongs to any other triangle, which in all respects is not the same with it. For example, having demonstrated that the three angles of an isosceles rectangular triangle are equal to two right ones, I cannot therefore conclude this affection agrees to all other triangles, which have neither a right angle, nor two equal sides. It seems therefore that, to be certain this proposition is universally true, we must either make a particular demonstration for every particular triangle, which is impossible, or once for all demonstrate it of the *abstract idea of a triangle*, in which all

the particulars do indifferently partake, and by which they are all equally represented. To which I answer, that though the idea I have in view whilst I make the demonstration, be, for instance, that of an isosceles rectangular triangle, whose sides are of a determinate length, I may nevertheless be certain it extends to all other rectilinear triangles, of what sort or bigness soever. And that, because neither the right angle, nor the equality, nor determinate length of the sides, are at all concerned in the demonstration It is true, the diagram I have in view includes all these particulars, but then there is not the least mention made of them in the proof of the proposition. It is not said, the three angles are equal to two right ones, because one of them is a right angle, or because the sides comprehending it are of the same length. Which sufficiently shows that the right angle might have been oblique, and the sides unequal, and for all that the demonstration have held good. And for this reason it is, that I conclude that to be true of any obliqu-angular or scalenon, which I had demonstrated of a particular right-angled, equicrural triangle; and not because I demonstrated the proposition of the abstract idea of a triangle. And here it must be acknowledged, that a man may consider a figure merely as triangular, without attending to the particular qualities of the angles, or relations of the sides. So far he may abstract : but this will never prove that he can frame an abstract general inconsistent idea of a triangle. In like manner we may consider Peter so far forth as man, or so far forth as animal, without framing the fore-mentioned abstract idea, either of man or of animal, inasmuch as all that is perceived is not considered.

17. *Advantage of investigating the doctrine of abstract general ideas.*—It were an endless, as well as a useless thing, to trace the *schoolmen,* those great masters of abstraction, through all the manifold, inextricable labyrinths of error and dispute, which their doctrine of abstract natures and notions seems to have led them into. What bickerings and controversies, and what a learned dust have been raised about those matters, and what mighty advantage hath been from thence derived to mankind, are things at this day too clearly known to need being insisted on. And it had been well if the ill effects of that doctrine were confined to those only who make the most avowed profession of it. When men consider the great pains, industry, and parts, that have, for so many ages, been laid out on the cultivation and advancement of the sciences, and that notwithstanding all this, the far greater part of them remain full of darkness and uncertainty, and disputes that are like never

to have an end, and even those that are thought to be supported by the most clear and cogent demonstrations, contain in them paradoxes which are perfectly irreconcilable to the understandings of men, and that, taking all together, a small portion of them doth supply any real benefit to mankind, otherwise than by being an innocent diversion and amusement: I say, the consideration of all this is apt to throw them into a despondency, and perfect contempt of all study. But this may perhaps cease, upon a view of the false principles that have obtained in the world, amongst all which there is none, methinks, hath a more wide influence over the thoughts of speculative men, than this of abstract general ideas.

18. I come now to consider the *source of this prevailing notion*, and that seems to me to be *language*. And surely nothing of less extent than reason itself could have been the source of an opinion so universally received. The truth of this appears as from other reasons, so also from the plain confession of the ablest patrons of abstract ideas, who acknowledge that they are made in order to naming; from which it is a clear consequence, that if there had been no such thing as speech or universal signs, there never had been any thought of abstraction. See book iii., ch. vi., sect. 39, and elsewhere, of the Essay on Human Understanding. Let us therefore examine the manner wherein words have contributed to the origin of that mistake. First, then, it is thought that every name hath, or ought to have, *one only* precise and settled signification, which inclines men to think there are certain *abstract, determinate ideas*, which constitute the true and only immediate signification of each general name. And that it is by the mediation of these abstract ideas, that a general name comes to signify any particular thing. Whereas, in truth, there is no such thing as one precise and definite signification annexed to any general name, they all signifying indifferently a great number of particular ideas. All which doth evidently follow from what has been already said, and will clearly appear to any one by a little reflection. To this it will be *objected*, that every name that has a definition, is thereby restrained to one certain signification. For example, a *triangle* is defined to be a *plain surface comprehended by three right lines;* by which that name is limited to denote one certain idea and no other. To which I answer, that in the definition it is not said whether the surface be great or small, black or white, nor whether the sides are long or short, equal or unequal, nor with what angles they are inclined to each other; in all which there may be great variety, and consequently there is *no one settled idea* which limits the signification

of the word *triangle*. It is one thing for to keep a name constantly to the same definition, and another to make it stand every where for the same idea: the one is necessary, the other useless and impracticable.

19. *Secondly,* But to give a further account how *words* came to *produce the doctrine of abstract ideas,* it must be observed that it is a received opinion, that language has *no other end* but the communicating our ideas, and that every significant name stands for an idea. This being so, and it being withal certain, that names, which yet are not thought altogether insignificant, do not always mark out *particular* conceivable ideas, it is straightway concluded that *they stand for abstract notions.* That there are many names in use amongst speculative men, which do not always suggest to others determinate particular ideas, is what nobody will deny. And a little attention will discover, that it is not necessary (even in the strictest reasonings) significant names which stand for ideas should, every time they are used, excite in the understanding the ideas they are made to stand for: in reading and discoursing, names being, for the most part, used as letters are in *algebra,* in which, though a particular quantity be marked by each letter, yet to proceed right it is not requisite that in every step each letter suggest to your thoughts that particular quantity it was appointed to stand for.

20. *Some of the ends of language.*—Besides, the (1) communicating of ideas marked by words is not the chief and only end of language, as is commonly supposed. There are other ends, as the (2) raising of some passion, the exciting to, or (3) deterring from an action, the (4) putting the mind in some particular disposition; to which the former, is in many cases, barely subservient, and sometimes entirely omitted, when these can be obtained without it, as I think doth not infrequently happen in the familiar use of language. I entreat the reader to reflect with himself, and see if it doth not often happen, either in hearing or reading a discourse, that the passions of fear, love, hatred, admiration, disdain, and the like, arise immediately in his mind upon the perception of certain words, without any ideas coming between. At first, indeed, the words might have occasioned ideas that were fit to produce those emotions; but, if I mistake not, it will be found that when language is once grown familiar, the hearing of the sounds or sight of the characters is oft immediately attended with those passions, which at first were wont to be produced by the intervention of ideas, that are now quite omitted. May we not, for example, be affected with

the promise of a *good thing,* though we have not an idea of what
it is? Or is not the being threatened with danger sufficient to excite
a dread, though we think not of any particular evil likely to befall
us, nor yet frame to ourselves an idea of danger in abstract? If
any one shall join ever so little reflection of his own to what has
been said, I believe it will evidently appear to him, that general
names are often used in the propriety of language without the
speaker's designing them for marks of ideas in his own, which he
would have them raise in the mind of the hearer. Even proper
names themselves do not seem always spoken with a design to
bring into our view the ideas of those individuals that are supposed
to be marked by them. For example, when a schoolman tells me,
" Aristotle hath said it," all I conceive he means by it, is to dispose
me to embrace his opinion with the deference and submission which
custom has annexed to that name. And this effect may be so
instantly produced in the minds of those who are accustomed to
resign their judgment to the authority of that philosopher, as it
is impossible any idea either of his person, writings, or reputation,
should go before. Innumerable examples of this kind may be
given, but why should I insist on those things which every one's
experience will, I doubt not, plentifully suggest unto him?

   21. *Caution in the use of language necessary.*—We have, I think,
shown (1) the impossibility of *abstract ideas*. We have considered
(2) what has been said for them by their ablest patrons; and
endeavoured to show they are of no use for those ends to which
they are thought necessary. And lastly, we have (3) traced them
to the source from whence they flow, which appears to be language.
It cannot be denied that words are of excellent use; in that, by
their means, all that stock of knowledge, which has been purchased
by the joint labours of inquisitive men in all ages and nations, may
be drawn into the view and made the possession of one single
person. But at the same time it must be owned that most parts of
knowledge have been strangely perplexed and darkened by the
abuse of words, and general ways of speech wherein they are
delivered. Since, therefore, words are so apt to impose on the
understanding, whatever ideas I consider, I shall endeavour to take
them bare and naked into my view, keeping out of my thoughts,
so far as I am able, those names which long and constant use hath
so strictly united with them; from which I may expect to derive
the following advantages : —

   22. *First,* I shall be sure to get clear of all controversies *purely
verbal;* the springing up of which weeds in almost all the sciences

has been a main hindrance to the growth of true and sound knowledge. *Secondly*, this seems to be a sure way to extricate myself out of that fine and subtle net of *abstract ideas,* which has so miserably perplexed and entangled the minds of men, and that with this peculiar circumstance, that by how much the finer and more curious was the wit of any man, by so much the deeper was he like to be ensnared, and faster held therein. *Thirdly*, so long as I confine my thoughts to my own ideas divested of words, I do not see how I can be easily mistaken. The objects, I consider, I clearly and adequately know. I cannot be deceived in thinking I have an idea which I have not. It is not possible for me to imagine, that any of my own ideas are like or unlike, that are not truly so. To discern the agreements or disagreements that are between my ideas, to see what ideas are included in any compound idea, and what not, there is nothing more requisite, than an attentive perception of what passes in my own understanding.

23. But the attainment of all *these advantages* doth *presuppose an entire deliverance from the deception of words*, which I dare hardly promise myself; so difficult a thing it is to dissolve a union so early begun, and confirmed by so long a habit as that betwixt words and ideas. Which difficulty seems to have been very much increased by the doctrine of *abstraction*. For so long as men thought abstract ideas were annexed to their words, it doth not seem strange that they should use words for ideas: it being found an impracticable thing to lay aside the word, and *retain the abstract idea in the mind, which in itself was perfectly inconceivable*. This seems to me the principal cause, why those men who have so emphatically recommended to others the laying aside all use of words in their meditations, and contemplating their bare ideas, have yet failed to perform it themselves. Of late many have been very sensible of the absurd opinions and insignificant disputes, which grow out of the abuse of words. And in order to remedy these evils they advise well, that we attend to the ideas signified, and draw off our attention from the words which signify them. But how good soever this advice may be they have given others, it is plain they could not have a due regard to it themselves, so long as they thought (1) the only immediate use of words was to signify ideas, and that (2) the immediate signification of every general name was a *determinate abstract idea*.

24. But *these being known to be mistakes, a man may* with greater ease *prevent his being imposed on by words*. He that knows he has no other than particular ideas, will not puzzle himself in

vain to find out and conceive the abstract idea, annexed to any name. And he that knows names do not always stand for ideas, will spare himself the labour of looking for ideas, where there are none to be had. It were therefore to be wished that every one would use his utmost endeavours, to obtain a clear view of the ideas he would consider, separating from them all that dress and encumbrance of words which so much contribute to blind the judgment and divide the attention. In vain do we extend our view into the heavens, and pry into the entrails of the earth; in vain do we consult the writings of learned men, and trace the dark footsteps of antiquity; we need only draw the curtain of words, to behold the fairest tree of knowledge, whose fruit is excellent, and within the reach of our hand.

25. Unless we take care *to clear the first principles of knowledge, from the* embarrass and *delusion of words,* we may make infinite reasonings upon them to no purpose: we may draw consequences from consequences, and be never the wiser. The further we go, we shall only lose ourselves the more irrecoverably, and be the deeper entangled in difficulties and mistakes Whoever therefore designs to read the following sheets, I entreat him to make my words the occasion of his own thinking, and endeavour to attain the same train of thoughts in reading, that I had in writing them. By this means it will be easy for him to discover the truth or falsity of what I say. He will be out of all danger of being deceived by my words, and I do not see how he can be led into an error by considering his own naked, undisguised ideas.

OF THE
PRINCIPLES OF HUMAN KNOWLEDGE

PART I

1. *Objects of human knowledge.*—It is evident to any one who takes a survey of the objects of human knowledge, that they are either *ideas* actually (1) imprinted on the senses, or else such as (2) perceived by attending to the passions and operations of the mind, or lastly, ideas (3) formed by help of memory and imagination, either compounding, dividing, or barely representing those originally perceived in the aforesaid ways. By sight I have the ideas of light and colours with their several degrees and variations. By touch I perceive, for example, hard and soft, heat and cold, motion and resistance, and of all these more and less either as to quantity or degree. Smelling furnishes me with odours; the palate with tastes; and hearing conveys sounds to the mind in all their variety of tone and composition. And as several of these are observed to accompany each other, they come to be marked by one name, and so to be reputed as one thing. Thus, for example, a certain colour, taste, smell, figure, and consistence having been observed to go together, are accounted one distinct thing, signified by the name *apple*. Other collections of ideas constitute a stone, a tree, a book, and the like sensible things; which, as they are pleasing or disagreeable, excite the passions of love, hatred, joy, grief, and so forth.

2. *Mind — spirit — soul.*—But besides all that endless variety of ideas or objects of knowledge, there is likewise something which knows or perceives them, and exercises divers operations, as willing, imagining, remembering about them. This perceiving, active being is what I call *mind, spirit, soul,* or *myself.* By which words I do not denote any one of my ideas, but a thing entirely distinct from them, *wherein they exist,* or, which is the same thing, whereby they are perceived; for the existence of an idea consists in being perceived.

3. *How far the assent of the vulgar conceded.*—That neither our thoughts, nor passions, nor ideas formed by the imagination, exist

without the mind, is what *every body will allow*. And (to me) **it** seems no less evident that the various sensations or ideas imprinted on the sense, however blended or combined together (that is, whatever objects they compose), cannot exist otherwise than *in* a mind perceiving them. I think an intuitive knowledge may be obtained of this, by any one that shall attend to *what is meant by the term " exist,"* when applied to sensible things. The table I write on, I say, exists, that is, I see and feel it; and if I were out of my study I should say it existed, meaning thereby that if I was in my study I might perceive it, or that some other spirit actually does perceive it. There was an odour, that is, it was smelled; there was a sound, that is to say, it was heard; a colour or figure, and it was perceived by sight or touch. This is all that I can understand by these and the like expressions. For as to what is said of the absolute existence of unthinking things without any relation to their being perceived, that seems perfectly unintelligible. Their *esse* is *percipi*, nor is it possible they should have any existence, out of the minds or thinking things which perceive them.

4. *The vulgar opinion involves a contradiction.*—It is indeed an opinion *strangely* prevailing amongst men, that houses, mountains, rivers, and in a word all sensible objects have an existence natural or real, distinct from their being perceived by the understanding. But with how great an assurance and acquiescence soever this principle may be entertained in the world; yet whoever shall find in his heart to call it in question, may, if I mistake not, perceive it to involve a manifest contradiction. For what are the forementioned objects but the things we *perceive* by sense, and what do we perceive *besides our own ideas or sensations;* and is it not plainly repugnant that any one of these or any combination of them should exist unperceived?

5. *Cause of this prevalent error.*—If we thoroughly examine this tenet, it will, perhaps, be found at bottom to depend on the doctrine of *abstract ideas*. For can there be a nicer strain of abstraction than to distinguish the existence of sensible objects from their being perceived, so as to conceive them existing unperceived? Light and colours, heat and cold, extension and figures, in a word the things we see and feel, what are they but so many sensations, notions, ideas, or impressions on the sense; and is it possible to separate, even in thought, any of these from perception? For my part I might as easily divide a thing from itself. I may indeed divide in my thoughts or conceive apart from each other those things which, perhaps, I never perceived by sense so divided. Thus I imagine

the trunk of a human body without the limbs, or conceive the smell of a rose without thinking on the rose itself. So far I will not deny I can abstract, if that may properly be called *abstraction*, which extends only to the conceiving separately such objects as it is possible may really exist or be actually perceived asunder. But my conceiving or imagining power does not extend beyond the possibility of real existence or perception. Hence as it is impossible for me to see or feel any thing without an actual sensation of that thing, so is it impossible for me to conceive in my thoughts any sensible thing or object distinct from the sensation or perception of it.

6. Some truths there are so near and obvious to the mind, that a man need only open his eyes to see them. Such I take this important one to be, to wit, that all the choir of heaven and furniture of the earth, in a word all those bodies which compose the mighty frame of the world, have not any subsistence without a mind, that their *being* (*esse*) is to be perceived or known; that consequently so long as they are not actually perceived by me, or do not exist in my mind or that of any other *created spirit*, they must either have no existence at all, *or else subsist in the mind of some eternal spirit*: it being perfectly unintelligible and involving all the absurdity of abstraction, to attribute to any single part of them an existence independent of a spirit. To be convinced of which, the reader need only reflect and try to separate in his own thoughts the being of a sensible thing from its being perceived.

7. *Second argument.*—From what has been said, it follows, there is *not any other substance than spirit*, or that which perceives. But for the fuller proof of this point, let it be considered, the sensible qualities are colour, figure, motion, smell, taste, and such like, that is, the ideas perceived by sense. Now for an idea to exist in an unperceiving thing, is a manifest contradiction; for *to have an idea is all one as to perceive*: that therefore wherein colour, figure, and the like qualities exist, must perceive them; hence it is clear there can be no *unthinking* substance or *substratum* of those ideas.

8. *Objection.*—*Answer.*—But say you, though the ideas themselves do not exist without the mind, yet there may be things *like* them whereof they are copies or resemblances, which things exist without the mind, in an unthinking substance. I *answer*, an idea can be like nothing but an idea; a colour or figure can be like nothing but another colour or figure. If we look but ever so little into our thoughts, we shall find it impossible for us to conceive a likeness except only between our ideas. Again, I ask whether those

supposed originals or external things, of which our ideas are the pictures or representations, be themselves perceivable or no? if they are, *then they are ideas*, and we have gained our point; but if you say they are not, I appeal to any one whether it be sense, to assert a colour is like something which is invisible; hard or soft, like something which is intangible; and so of the rest.

9. *The philosophical notion of matter involves a contradiction.*— Some there are who make a *distinction* betwixt *primary* and *secondary* qualities: by the former, they mean extension, figure, motion, rest, solidity or impenetrability, and number: by the latter they denote all other sensible qualities, as colours, sounds, tastes, and so forth. The ideas we have of these they acknowledge not to be the resemblances of any things existing without the mind or unperceived; but they will have our ideas of the primary qualities to be patterns or images of things which exist without the mind, in an unthinking substance which they call *matter*. By *matter* therefore we are to understand an inert, senseless substance, in which extension, figure, and motion, *do actually subsist*. But it is evident from what we have already shown, that extension, figure, and motion, are *only ideas existing in the mind*, and that an idea can be like nothing but another idea, and that consequently neither they nor their archetypes can exist in an *unperceiving substance*. Hence it is plain, that the very notion of what is called *matter*, or *corporeal substance*, involves a contradiction in it.

10. *Argumentum ad hominem.*—They who assert that figure, motion, and the rest of the primary or original qualities, do exist without the mind, in unthinking substances, do at the same time acknowledge that colours, sounds, heat, cold, and such like secondary qualities, do not, which they tell us are sensations existing *in the mind alone*, that depend on and are occasioned by the different size, texture, and motion of the minute particles of matter. This they take for an undoubted truth, which they can demonstrate beyond all exception. Now if it be certain, that those original qualities *are inseparably united with the other sensible qualities*, and not, even in thought, capable of being abstracted from them, it plainly follows that they exist only in the mind. But I desire any one to reflect and try, whether he can, by any abstraction of thought, conceive the extension and motion of a body, without all other sensible qualities. For my own part, I see evidently that it is not in my power to frame an idea of a body extended and moved, but I must withal give it some colour or other sensible quality which is *acknowledged* to exist only in the mind. In short, extension,

figure, and motion, abstracted from all other qualities, are inconceivable. Where therefore the other sensible qualities' are, there
must these be also, to wit, in the mind and nowhere else.

11. *A second argumentum ad hominem.*—Again, *great* and *small,*
swift and *slow,* are *allowed to exist no where without the mind,*
being entirely *relative,* and changing as the frame or position of
the organs of sense varies. The extension therefore which exists
without the mind, is neither great nor small, the motion neither
swift nor slow, that is, they are nothing at all. But, say you, they
are extension in general, and motion in general: thus we see how
much the tenet of extended, moveable substances existing without
the mind, depends on that strange doctrine of *abstract ideas.* And
here I cannot but remark, how nearly the vague and indeterminate
description of matter or corporeal substance, which the modern
philosophers are run into by their own principles, resembles that
antiquated and so much ridiculed notion of *materia prima,* to be
met with in Aristotle and his followers. Without extension solidity
cannot be conceived; since therefore it has been shown that extension exists not in an unthinking substance, the same must also be
true of solidity.

12. That *number* is entirely *the creature of the mind,* even though
the other qualities be allowed to exist without, will be evident to
whoever considers, that the same thing bears a different denomination of number, as the mind views it with different respects. Thus,
the same extension is one, or three, or thirty-six, according as the
mind considers it with reference to a yard, a foot, or an inch.
Number is so visibly relative, and dependent on men's understanding, that it is strange to think how any one should give it an
absolute existence without the mind. We say, one book, one page,
one line; all these are equally units, though some contain several
of the others. And in each instance it is plain, the unit relates to
some particular combination of ideas arbitrarily put together by
the mind. .

13. *Unity,* I know, some will have to be a *simple* or *uncom-*
pounded idea, accompanying all other ideas into the mind. That
I have any such idea, answering the word *unity,* I do not find;
and if I had, methinks I could not miss finding it; on the contrary,
it should be the most familiar to my understanding, since it is said
to accompany all other ideas, and to be perceived by all the ways
of sensation and reflection. To say no more, it is an *abstract idea.*

14. *A third argumentum ad hominem.*—I shall further add, that
after the same manner as modern philosophers prove certain

sensible qualities to have no existence in matter, or without the mind, the same thing may be likewise proved of all other sensible qualities whatsoever. Thus, for instance, it is said that heat and cold are affections only of the mind, and not at all patterns of real beings, existing in the corporeal substances which excite them, for that the same body which appears cold to one hand, seems warm to another. Now why may we not as well argue that figure and extension are not patterns or resemblances of qualities existing in matter, because to the same eye at different stations, or eyes of a different texture at the same station, they appear various, and cannot therefore be the images of any thing *settled and determinate without the mind*? Again, it is proved that *sweetness* is not really in the sapid thing, because, the thing remaining unaltered, the sweetness is changed into bitter, as in case of a fever or otherwise vitiated palate. Is it not as reasonable to say, that *motion* is not without the mind, since if the succession of ideas in the mind become swifter, the motion, it is acknowledged, shall appear slower without any alteration in any external object.

15. *Not conclusive as to extension.*—In short, let any one consider those arguments which are thought manifestly to prove that colours and tastes exist only in the mind, and he shall find they may with equal force be brought to prove the same thing of extension, figure, and motion. Though it must be confessed, this method of arguing doth not so much prove that there is no extension or colour in an outward object, as that we do not know by *sense* which is the *true* extension or colour of the object. But the arguments foregoing plainly show it to be impossible that any colour or extension at all, or other sensible quality whatsoever, should exist in an *unthinking* subject without the mind, or in truth, that there should be any such thing as an outward object.

16. But let us examine a little the received opinion. It is said *extension* is a *mode* or accident of *matter*, and that matter is the *substratum* that supports it. Now I desire that you would explain what is meant by matter's *supporting* extension: say you, I have no idea of matter, and therefore cannot explain it. I answer, though you have no positive, yet if you have any meaning at all, you must at least have a relative idea of matter; though you know not what it is, yet you must be supposed to know what relation it bears to accidents, and what is meant by its supporting them. It is evident *support* cannot here be taken in its usual or literal sense, as when we say that pillars support a building: in what sense therefore must it be taken ?

17. *Philosophical meaning of " material substance " divisible into two parts.*—If we inquire into what the most accurate philosophers declare themselves to mean by *material substance,* we shall find them acknowledge, they have no other meaning annexed to those sounds, but the idea of *being in general,* together *with the relative notion of its supporting accidents.* The general idea of being appeareth to me the most abstract and incomprehensible of all other; and as for its supporting accidents, this, as we have just now observed, cannot be understood in the common sense of those words; it must therefore be taken in some other sense, but what that is they do not explain. So that when I consider the *two parts* or branches which make the signification of the words *material substance,* I am convinced there is no distinct meaning annexed to them. But why should we trouble ourselves any further in discussing this material *substratum* or support of figure and motion, and other sensible qualities? does it not suppose they have an existence without the mind? and is not this a direct repugnancy, and altogether inconceivable?

18. *The existence of external bodies wants proof.*—But though it were possible that solid, figured, moveable substances may exist without the mind, corresponding to the ideas we have of bodies, yet *how is it possible for us to know this?* either we must know it by sense, or by reason. As for our senses, by them we have the knowledge *only of our sensations,* ideas, or those things that are immediately perceived by sense, call them what you will: but they do not inform us that things exist without the mind, or unperceived, like to those which are perceived. This the materialists themselves acknowledge. It remains therefore that if we have any knowledge at all of external things, it must be by *reason,* inferring their existence from what is immediately perceived by sense. But (I do not see) what reason can induce us to believe the existence of bodies without the mind, from what we perceive, since the very patrons of matter themselves do not pretend, there is *any necessary connection betwixt them and our ideas.* I say, it is granted on all hands (and what happens in dreams, frenzies, and the like, puts it beyond dispute) that *it is possible we might be affected with all the ideas we have now, though no bodies existed without, resembling them.* Hence it is evident the supposition of external bodies is not necessary for the producing our ideas: since it is granted they are produced sometimes, and might possibly be produced always, in the same order we see them in at present, without their concurrence.

19. *The existence of external bodies affords no explication of the manner in which our ideas are produced.*—But though we might possibly have all our sensations without them, yet perhaps it may be thought *easier* to conceive and explain the *manner* of their production, by supposing external bodies in their likeness rather than otherwise; and so it might be at least probable there are such things as bodies that excite their ideas in our minds. But neither can this be said; for though we give the materialists their external bodies, they, by their own confession, are never the nearer knowing how our ideas are produced: since they own themselves unable to comprehend in what manner *body can act upon spirit,* or how it is possible it should imprint any idea in the mind. Hence it is evident, the production of ideas or sensations in our minds, can be no reason why we should suppose matter or corporeal substances, *since that is acknowledged to remain equally inexplicable with or without this supposition.* If therefore it were possible for bodies to exist without the mind, yet to hold they do so must needs be a very precarious opinion; since it is to suppose, without any reason at all, that God has created innumerable beings *that are entirely useless, and serve to no manner of purpose.*

20. *Dilemma.*—In short, if there were external bodies, it is impossible we should ever come to know it; and if there were not, we might have the very same reasons to think there were that we have now. Suppose, what no one can deny possible, an intelligence, without the help of external bodies, to be affected with the same train of sensations or ideas that you are, imprinted in the same order and with like vividness in his mind. I ask, whether that intelligence hath not all the reason to believe the existence of corporeal substances, represented by his ideas, and exciting them in his mind, that you can possibly have for believing the same thing? Of this there can be no question; which one consideration is enough to make any reasonable person suspect the strength of whatever arguments he may think himself to have for the existence of bodies without the mind.

21. Were it necessary to add any *further proof against the existence of matter,* after what has been said, I could instance several of those errors and difficulties (not to mention impieties) which have sprung from that tenet. It has occasioned numberless controversies and disputes in philosophy, and not a few of greater moment in religion. But I shall not enter into the detail of them in this place, as well because I think arguments *a posteriori* are unnecessary for confirming what has been, if I mistake not, suffi-

ciently demonstrated *a priori*, as because I shall hereafter find occasion to say somewhat of them.

22. I am afraid I have given cause to think me needlessly prolix in handling this subject. For to what purpose is it to dilate on that which may be demonstrated with the utmost evidence in a line or two, to any one that is capable of the least reflection? it is but looking into your own thoughts, and so trying whether you can conceive it possible for a sound, or figure, or motion, or colour, to exist without the mind, or unperceived. This easy trial may make you see, that what you contend for is a downright contradiction. Insomuch that I am content to put the whole upon this issue; if you can but *conceive* it possible for one extended moveable substance, or in general, for any one idea, or any thing like an idea, to exist otherwise than in a mind perceiving it, I shall readily give up the cause: and as for all that *compages* of external bodies which you contend for, I shall grant you its existence, though (1) *you cannot either give me any reason why you believe it exists; or* (2) *assign any use to it when it is supposed to exist.* I say, the bare possibility of your opinion's being true, shall pass for an argument that it so.

23. But say you, surely there is nothing easier than to imagine trees, for instance, in a park, or books existing in a closet, and nobody to perceive them. I answer, you may so, there is no difficulty in it: but what is all this, I beseech you, more than framing in your mind certain ideas which you call *books* and *trees*, and at the same time omitting to frame the idea of any one that may perceive them? *but do not you yourself perceive or think of them all the while?* This therefore is nothing to the purpose; it only shows you have the power of imagining or forming ideas in your mind; but it doth not show that you can conceive it possible the objects of your thought may exist without the mind: to make out this, *it is necessary that you conceive them existing unconceived or unthought-of, which is a manifest repugnancy.* When we do our utmost to conceive the existence of external bodies, we are all the while only contemplating our own ideas. But the mind, taking no notice of itself, is deluded to think it can and doth conceive bodies existing unthought-of or without the mind; though at the same time they are apprehended by or exist in itself. A little attention will discover to any one the truth and evidence of what is here said, and make it unnecessary to insist on any other proofs against the existence of material substance.

24. *The absolute existence of unthinking things are words*

without a meaning.—It is very obvious, upon the least inquiry into our own thoughts, to know whether it be possible for us to understand what is meant by the *absolute existence of sensible objects in themselves or without the mind.* To me it is evident those words mark out either a direct contradiction, or else nothing at all. And to convince others of this, I know no readier or fairer way, than to entreat they would calmly attend to their own thoughts: and if by this attention the emptiness or repugnancy of those expressions does appear, surely nothing more is requisite for their conviction. It is on this therefore that I insist, to wit, that the *absolute* existence of unthinking things are words without a meaning, or which include a contradiction. This is what I repeat and inculcate, and earnestly recommend to the attentive thoughts of the reader.

25. *Third argument.—Refutation of Locke.*—All our ideas, sensations, or the things which we perceive, by whatsoever names they may be distinguished, are visibly inactive; there is nothing of power or agency included in them. So that *one idea* or object of thought *cannot produce,* or make *any alteration in another.* To be satisfied of the truth of this, there is nothing else requisite but a bare observation of our ideas. For since they and every part of them exist only in the mind, it follows that there is nothing in them but what is perceived. But whoever shall attend to his ideas, whether of sense or reflection, will not perceive in them any power or activity; there is therefore no such thing contained in them. A little attention will discover to us that the very being of an idea implies passiveness and inertness in it, insomuch that it is impossible for an idea to do any thing, or, strictly speaking, to be the cause of any thing: neither can it be the resemblance or pattern of any active being, as is evident from Sect. VIII. Whence it plainly follows that extension, figure, and motion, cannot be the cause of our sensations. To say, therefore, that these are the effects of powers resulting from the configuration, number, motion, and size of corpuscles, must certainly be false.

26. *Cause of ideas.*—We perceive a continual succession of ideas, some are anew excited, others are changed or totally disappear. There is therefore some cause of these ideas whereon they depend, and which produces and changes them. That this cause cannot be any quality or idea or combination of ideas, is clear from the preceding section. It must therefore be a substance; but it has been shown that there is no corporeal or material substance: it remains therefore that the *cause of ideas* is an incorporeal active substance or spirit.

27. *No idea of spirit.*—A spirit is one simple, undivided, active being: as it perceives ideas, it is called the *understanding*, and as it produces or otherwise operates about them, it is called the *will*. Hence there can be no idea formed of a soul or spirit: for all ideas whatever, being passive and inert (vide Sect. xxv.), they cannot represent unto us, by way of image or *likeness*, that which acts. A little attention will make it plain to any one, that to have an idea which shall be like that active principle of motion and change of ideas, is absolutely impossible. Such is the nature of *spirit*, or that which acts, that it cannot be of itself perceived *but only by the effects which it produceth*. If any man shall doubt of the truth of what is here deelivered, let him but reflect and try if he can frame the idea of any power or active being; and whether he hath ideas of two principal powers, marked by the names *will* and *understanding*, distinct from each other as well as from a third idea of substance or being in general, with a relative notion of its supporting or being the subject of the aforesaid powers, which is signified by the name *soul* or *spirit*. This is what some hold; but so far as I can see, the words *will, soul, spirit*, do not stand for different ideas, or in truth, for any idea at all, but for something which is very different from ideas, and which being an agent cannot be like unto, or represented by, any idea whatsoever. Though it must be owned at the same time, that we have some notion of soul, spirit, and the operations of the mind, such as willing, loving, hating, inasmuch as we know or understand the meaning of those words.

28. I find I can excite ideas in my mind at pleasure, and vary and shift the scene as oft as I think fit. It is no more than willing, and straightway this or that idea arises in my fancy: and by the same power it is obliterated, and makes way for another. This making and unmaking of ideas doth very properly denominate the mind active. Thus much is certain, and grounded on experience: but when we talk of unthinking agents, or of exciting ideas exclusive of volition, we only amuse ourselves with words.

29. *Ideas of sensation differ from those of reflection or memory.* —But whatever power I may have over *my own* thoughts, I find the ideas actually perceived by sense have not a like dependence on my will. When in broad daylight I open my eyes, it is not in my power to choose whether I shall see or no, or to determine what particular objects shall present themselves to my view; and so likewise as to the hearing and other senses, the ideas imprinted on

them are not creatures of my will. There is *therefore some other will or spirit* that *produces them.*

30. *Laws of nature.*—The ideas of sense are more strong, lively, and *distinct* than those of the imagination; they have likewise a steadiness, order, and coherence, and are not excited at random, as those which are the effects of human wills often are, but in a regular train or series, the admirable connection whereof sufficiently testifies the wisdom and benevolence of its author. Now *the set rules or established methods, wherein the mind we depend on excites in us the ideas of sense, are called the laws of nature*: and these we learn by experience, which teaches us that such and such ideas are attended with such and such other ideas, in the ordinary course of things.

31. *Knowledge of them necessary for the conduct of worldly affairs.*—This gives us a sort of foresight, which enables us to regulate our actions for the benefit of life. And without this we should be eternally at a loss: we could not know how to act any thing that might procure us the least pleasure, or remove the least pain of sense. That food nourishes, sleep refreshes, and fire warms us; that to sow in the seed-time is the way to reap in the harvest, and, in general, that to obtain such or such ends, such or such means are conducive, all this we know, *not by discovering any necessary connection between our ideas,* but only by the observation of the settled laws of nature, without which we should be all in uncertainty and confusion, and a grown man no more know how to manage himself in the affairs of life than an infant just born.

32. And yet *this* consistent, *uniform working,* which so evidently displays the goodness and wisdom of that governing Spirit whose will constitutes the laws of nature, is so far from leading our thoughts to Him, that it rather *sends them a wandering after second causes.* For when we perceive certain ideas of sense constantly followed by other ideas, and *we know this is not of our own doing,* we forthwith attribute power and agency to the ideas themselves, and make one the cause of another, than which nothing can be more absurd and unintelligible. Thus, for example, having observed that when we perceive by sight a certain round luminous figure, we at the same time perceive by touch the idea or sensation called *heat,* we do from thence conclude the sun to be the cause of heat. And in like manner perceiving the motion and collision of bodies to be attended with sound, we are inclined to think the latter an effect of the former.

33. *Of real things and ideas or chimeras.*—The ideas imprinted

on the senses by the author of nature are called *real things*: and those excited in the imagination, being less regular, vivid, and constant, are more properly termed *ideas, or images of things,* which they copy and represent. But then our sensations, be they never so vivid and distinct, are nevertheless *ideas,* that is, they exist in the mind, or are perceived by it, as truly as the ideas of its own framing. The ideas of sense are allowed to have more reality in them, that is, to be more (1) *strong,* (2) *orderly,* and (3) *coherent* than the creatures of the mind: but this is no argument that they exist without the mind. They are also (4) *less dependent on the spirit,* or thinking substance which perceives them, in that they are excited by the will of another and more powerful spirit: yet still they are *ideas,* and certainly no *idea,* whether faint or strong, can exist otherwise than in a mind perceiving it.

34. *First general objection.—Answer.*—Before we proceed any further, it is necessary to spend some time in answering objections which may probably be made against the principles hitherto laid down. In doing of which, if I seem too prolix to those of quick apprehensions, I hope it may be pardoned, since all men do not equally apprehend things of this nature; and I am willing to be understood by every one. *First* then it will be objected that by the foregoing principles, *all that is real and substantial in nature is banished out of the world*: and instead thereof a chimerical scheme of ideas takes place. All things that exist, exist only in the mind, that is, they are purely notional. What therefore becomes of the sun, moon, and stars? What must we think of houses, rivers, mountains, trees, stones; nay, even of our own bodies? Are all these but so many chimeras and illusions on the fancy? To all which, and whatever else of the same sort may be objected, I *answer,* that by the principles premised, we are not deprived of any one thing in nature. Whatever we see, feel, hear, or any wise conceive or understand, remains as secure as ever, and is as real as ever. There is a *rerum natura,* and the distinction between realities and chimeras retains its full force. This is evident from Sect. XXIX, XXX and XXXIII, where we have shown what is meant by *real things* in opposition to *chimeras,* or ideas of our own framing; but then they both equally exist in the mind, and in that sense are like *ideas.*

35. *The existence of matter, as understood by philosophers, denied.*—I do not argue against the existence of any one thing that we can apprehend, either by sense or reflection. That the things I see with mine eyes and touch with my hands do exist,

really exist, I make not the least question. The only thing whose existence we deny, *is that which philosophers call matter* or corporeal substance. And in doing of this, there is no damage done to the rest of mankind, who, I dare say, will never miss it. The atheist indeed will want the colour of an empty name to support his impiety; and the philosophers may possibly find, they have lost a great handle for trifling and disputation.

36. *Reality explained.*—If any man thinks this detracts from the existence or reality of things, he is very far from understanding what hath been premised in the plainest terms I could think of. Take here an abstract of what has been said. There are spiritual substances, minds, or human souls, which will or excite ideas in themselves at pleasure: but these are faint, weak, and unsteady in respect of others they perceive by sense, which being impressed upon them according to certain rules or laws of nature, speak themselves the effects of a mind more powerful and wise than human spirits. These latter are said to have more *reality* in them than the former: by which is meant that they are affecting, orderly, and distinct, and that they are not fictions of the mind perceiving them. And in this sense, the sun that I see by day is the real sun, and that which I imagine by night is the idea of the former. In the sense here given of *reality*, it is evident that every vegetable, star, mineral, and in general each part of the mundane system, is as much a *real being* by our principles as by any other. Whether others mean any thing by the term *reality* different from what I do, I entreat them to look into their own thoughts and see.

37. *The philosophic, not the vulgar substance, taken away.*— It will be urged that thus much at least is true, to wit, that we take away all corporeal substances. To this my answer is, that if the word *substance* be taken in the vulgar sense, for a combination of sensible qualities, such as extension, solidity, weight, and the like: this we cannot be accused of taking away. But if it be taken in a philosophic sense, for the *support* of accidents or *qualities without the mind;* then indeed I acknowledge that we take it away, if one may be said to take away that which never had any existence, not even in the imagination.

38. But, say you, it sounds very harsh to say we eat and drink ideas, and are clothed with ideas. I acknowledge it does so, the word *idea* not being used in common discourse to signify the several combinations of sensible qualities, which are called *things*: and it is certain that any expression which varies from the familiar use of language, will seem harsh and ridiculous. But this doth not

concern the truth of the proposition, which in other words is no more than to say, we are fed and clothed with those things which we perceive immediately by our senses. The hardness or softness, the colour, taste, warmth, figure, and such like qualities, which combined together constitute the several sorts of victuals and apparel, have been shown to exist only in the mind that perceives them; and this is all that is meant by calling them *ideas*; which word, if it was as ordinarily used as *thing,* would sound no harsher nor more ridiculous than it. I am not for disputing about the propriety, but the truth of that expression. If therefore you agree with me that we eat, and drink, and are clad with the immediate objects of sense, which cannot exist unperceived or without the mind; I shall readily grant it is more proper or conformable to custom, that they should be called things rather than ideas.

39. *The term idea preferable to thing.*—If it be demanded why I make use of the word *idea,* and do not rather in compliance with custom call them *things,* I answer, I do it for two reasons: first because the term *thing,* in contradistinction to *idea,* is generally supposed to denote somewhat existing without the mind: secondly, because *thing* hath a more comprehensive signification than *idea,* including *spirits,* or thinking things, as well as *ideas.* Since therefore the objects of sense exist only in the mind, and are withal thoughtless and inactive, I chose to mark them by the word *idea,* which implies those properties.

40. *The evidence of the senses not discredited.*—But, say what we can, some one perhaps may be apt to reply, he will still believe his senses, and never suffer any arguments, how plausible soever, to prevail over the certainty of them. Be it so, assert the evidence of sense as high as you please, we are willing to do the same. That what I see, hear, and feel *doth exist, that is* to say, *is perceived by me,* I no more doubt than I do of my own being. But I do not see how the testimony of sense can be alleged as a proof for the existence of any thing which is not perceived by sense. We are not for having any man turn *sceptic,* and disbelieve his senses; on the contrary, we give them all the stress and assurance imaginable; nor are there any principles more opposite to scepticism than those we have laid down, as shall be hereafter clearly shown.

41. *Second objection.—Answer.*—Secondly, it will be *objected* that there is a great difference between real fire, for instance, and the idea of fire, betwixt dreaming or imagining one's self burnt, and actually being so: this and the like may be urged in opposition to our tenets. To all which the *answer* is evident from what hath

been already said, and I shall only add in this place, that if real fire be very different from the idea of fire, so also is the real pain that it occasions, very different from the idea of the same pain: and yet nobody will pretend that real pain either is, or can possibly be, in an unperceiving thing or without the mind, any more than its idea.

42. *Third objection.—Answer.*—Thirdly, it will be objected that we see things actually without or at a distance from us, and which consequently do not exist in the mind, it being absurd that those things which are seen at the distance of several miles, should be as near to us as our own thoughts. In answer to this, I desire it may be considered, that in a *dream* we do oft perceive things as existing at a great distance off, and yet for all that, those things are acknowledged to have their existence only in the mind.

43. But for the fuller clearing of this point, it may be worth while to consider, how it is that we perceive distance and things placed at a distance by sight. For that we should in truth see *external space,* and bodies actually existing in it, some nearer, others further off, seems to carry with it some opposition to what hath been said, of their existing nowhere without the mind. The consideration of this difficulty it was that gave birth to my Essay towards a new Theory of Vision, which was published not long since. Wherein it is shown (1) that *distance* or outness is *neither immediately* of itself *perceived* by sight, nor yet apprehended or judged of by lines and angles, or any thing that hath a necessary connection with it: but (2) that it is *only suggested* to our thoughts, by certain visible ideas and sensations attending vision, which in their own nature have no manner of similitude or relation, either with distance, or things placed at a distance. But by a connection taught us *by experience,* they come to signify and suggest them to us, after the same manner that *words* of any language suggest the ideas they are made to stand for. Insomuch that a man *born* blind, and afterwards made to see, would not, at first sight, think the things he saw to be without his mind, or at any distance from him. See Sect. XLI of the forementioned treatise.

44. The ideas of sight and touch make two species, entirely distinct and heterogeneous. *The former are marks and prognostics of the latter.* That the proper objects of sight neither exist without the mind, nor are the images of external things, was shown even in that treatise. Though throughout the same, the contrary be supposed true of tangible objects: not that to suppose that vulgar error was necessary for establishing the notions therein laid down,

but because it was beside my purpose to examine and refute it in a discourse concerning *vision*. So that in strict truth the ideas of sight, when we apprehend by them distance and things placed at a distance, do not suggest or mark out to us things *actually* existing at a distance, but only admonish us what ideas of touch will be imprinted in our minds at such and such distances of time, and in consequence of such and such actions. It is, I say, evident from what has been said in the foregoing parts of this treatise, and in Sect. CXLVII, and elsewhere of the essay concerning vision, that visible ideas are the language whereby the governing Spirit, on whom we depend, informs us what tangible ideas he is about to imprint upon us, in case we excite this or that motion in our own bodies. But for a fuller information in this point, I refer to the essay itself.

45. *Fourth objection, from perpetual annihilation and creation.* *—Answer.*—Fourthly, it will be objected, that from the foregoing principles it follows, things are every moment annihilated and created anew. The objects of sense exist only when they are perceived: the trees therefore are in the garden, or the chairs in the parlour, no longer than while there is somebody by to perceive them. Upon *shutting my eyes,* all the furniture in the room is reduced to nothing, and barely upon opening them it is again created. In *answer* to all which, I refer the reader to what has been said in Sec. III, IV, etc., and desire he will consider whether he means any thing by the actual existence of an idea, distinct from its being perceived. For my part, after the nicest inquiry I could make, I am not able to discover that any thing else is meant by those words. And I once more entreat the reader to sound his own thoughts, and not suffer himself to be imposed on by words. If he can conceive it possible either for his ideas or their archetypes to exist without being perceived, then I give up the cause: but if he cannot, he will acknowledge it is unreasonable for him to stand up in defence of he knows not what, and pretend to charge on me as an absurdity the not assenting to those propositions which at bottom have no meaning in them.

46. *Argumentum ad hominem.*—It will not be amiss to observe, how far the received principles of philosophy are themselves chargeable with those pretended absurdities. (1) It is thought strangely absurd that upon closing my eyelids all the visible objects round me should be reduced to nothing; and yet is not this what philosophers commonly acknowledge when they agree on all hands, that light and colours, which alone are the proper and immediate

objects of sight, are mere sensations, that exist no longer than they are perceived? (2) Again, it may to some perhaps seem very incredible, that things should be every moment creating; yet this very notion is commonly taught in the schools. For the *schoolmen*, though they acknowledge the existence of matter, and that the whole mundane fabric is framed out of it, are nevertheless of opinion that it cannot subsist without the divine conservation, which by them is expounded to be a continual creation.

47. (3) Further, a little thought will discover to us, that though we allow the existence of matter or corporeal substances, yet it will unavoidably follow *from the principles which are now generally admitted,* that the *particular* bodies, of what kind soever, do none of them exist whilst they are not perceived. For (1) it is evident from Sect. xi and the following sections, that the matter philosophers contend for is an incomprehensible somewhat, *which hath none of those particular qualities whereby the bodies falling under our senses are distinguished one from another.* (2) But to make this more plain, it must be remarked, that the infinite divisibility of matter is now universally allowed, at least by the most approved and considerable philosophers, who, on the received principles, demonstrate it beyond all exception. Hence it follows, that there is an infinite number of parts in each particle of matter, which are not perceived by sense. The reason, therefore, that any particular body seems to be of a finite magnitude, or exhibits only a finite number of parts to sense, is, not because it contains no more, since in itself it contains an infinite number of parts, *but because the sense is not acute enough to discern them.* In proportion, therefore, as the sense is rendered more acute, it perceives a greater number of parts in the object; that is, the object appears greater, and its figure varies, those parts in its extremities which were before unperceivable, appearing now to bound it in very different lines and angles from those perceived by an obtuser sense. And, at length, after various changes of size and shape, when the sense becomes infinitely acute, the body shall seem infinite. During all which, there is no alteration in the body, but only in the sense. *Each body, therefore, considered in itself, is infinitely extended, and consequently void of all shape or figure.* From which it follows, that though we should grant the existence of matter to be ever so certain, yet it is withal as certain, the materialists themselves are by their own principles forced to acknowledge, that neither the particular bodies perceived by sense, nor any thing like them, exist without the mind. Matter, I say, and each particle thereof, is

according to them infinite and shapeless, *and it is the mind that frames all that variety of bodies which compose the visible world, any one whereof does not exist longer than it is perceived.*

48. If we consider it, the objection proposed in Sect. xlv will not be found reasonably charged on the principles we have premised, so as in truth to make any objection at all against our notions. For though we hold, indeed, the objects of sense to be nothing else but ideas which cannot exist unperceived, yet we may not hence conclude they have no existence, except only while they are perceived by *us*, since *there may be some other spirit that perceives them, though we do not.* Wherever bodies are said to have no existence without the mind, I would not be understood to mean this or that particular mind, but *all minds whatsoever.* It does not therefore follow from the foregoing principles, that bodies are annihilated and created every moment, or exist not at all during the intervals between our perception in them.

49. *Fifth objection.—Answer.*—Fifthly, it may perhaps be *objected*, that if extension and figure exist only in the mind, it follows that the mind is extended and figured; since extension is a mode or attribute, which (to speak with the schools) is predicated of the subject in which it exists. I *answer*, (1) Those qualities are in the mind *only as they are perceived by it*, that is, not by way of *mode* or *attribute*, but only by way of *idea;* and it no more follows, that the soul or mind is extended because extension exists in it alone, than it does that it is red or blue, because those colours are *on all hands* acknowledged to exist in it, and nowhere else. (2) As to what philosophers say of subject and mode, that seems very groundless and unintelligible. For instance, in this proposition, a die is hard, extended, and square; they will have it that the word die denotes a subject or substance, distinct from the hardness, extension, and figure, which are predicated of it, and in which they exist. This I cannot comprehend: to me a die seems to be nothing distinct from those things which are termed its modes or accidents. And to say a die is hard, extended, and square, is not to attribute those qualities to a subject distinct from and supporting them, but only an explication of the meaning of the word *die*.

50. *Sixth objection, from natural philosophy.—Answer.*—Sixthly, you will say there have been a great many things explained by matter and motion: take away these, and you destroy the whole corpuscular philosophy, and undermine those mechanical principles which have been applied with so much success to account for the

phenomena. In short, whatever advances have been made, either by ancient or modern philosophers, in the study of nature, do all proceed on the supposition, that corporeal substance or matter doth really exist. To this I *answer,* that there is not any one *phenomenon* explained on that supposition, which may not as well be explained without it, as might easily be made appear by an *induction of particulars.* To explain the *phenomena,* is all one as to show, why upon such and such occasions we are affected with such and such ideas. But (1) how matter should operate on a spirit, or produce any idea in it, is what no philosopher will pretend to explain. It is therefore evident, there can be no use of matter in natural philosophy. Besides, (2) they who attempt to account for things, do it not by *corporeal substance,* but by figure, motion, and other qualities, which are in truth no more than mere ideas, and therefore cannot be the cause of any thing, as hath been already shown. See Sect. xxv.

51. *Seventh objection.—Answer.*—Seventhly, it will upon this be demanded whether it does not seem *absurd to take away natural causes, and ascribe every thing to the immediate operation of spirits?* We must no longer say upon these principles that fire heats, or water cools, but that a spirit heats, and so forth. Would not a man be deservedly laughed at, who should talk after this manner? I *answer,* he would so; in such things we ought to *think with the learned, and speak with the vulgar.* They who to demonstration are convinced of the truth of the Copernican system, do nevertheless say the sun rises, the sun sets, or comes to the meridian: and if they affected a contrary style in common talk, it would without doubt appear very ridiculous. A little reflection on what is here said will make it manifest, that the common use of language would receive no manner of alteration or disturbance from the admission of our tenets.

52. *In the ordinary affairs of life, any phrases may be retained,* so long as they excite in us proper sentiments, or dispositions to act in such a manner as is necessary for our *well-being,* how false soever they may be, if taken in a strict and *speculative sense.* Nay, this is unavoidable, since propriety being regulated by *custom,* language is suited to the *received* opinions, which are not always the truest. Hence it is impossible, even in the most rigid philosophic reasonings, so far to alter the bent and genius of the tongue we speak, as never to give a handle for cavillers to pretend difficulties and inconsistencies. But a fair and ingenuous reader will collect the sense from the scope and tenor and connection of a discourse,

making allowances for those inaccurate modes of speech which use has made inevitable.

53. *As to the opinion that there are no corporeal causes,* this has been heretofore maintained by some of the schoolmen, as it is of late by others among the modern philosophers, who though they allow matter to exist, yet will have God alone to be the immediate efficient cause of all things. These men saw, that amongst all the objects of sense, there was none which had any power or activity included in it, and that by consequence this was likewise true of whatever bodies they supposed to exist without the mind, like unto the immediate objects of sense. But then, that they should suppose an innumerable multitude of created beings, which they acknowledge are not capable of producing any one effect in nature, and which therefore are made to no manner of purpose, since God might have done every thing as well without them; this I say, though we should allow it possible, must yet be a very unaccountable and extravagant supposition.

54. *Eighth objection.—Twofold answer.*—In the eighth place, the universal concurrent assent of mankind may be thought by some an invincible argument in behalf of matter, or the existence of external things. Must we suppose the whole world to be mistaken? and if so, what cause can be assigned of so widespread and predominant an error? I answer, *first,* That upon a narrow inquiry, it will not perhaps be found, so many as is imagined do really believe the existence of matter or things without the mind. Strictly speaking, to believe that which involves a contradiction, or has no meaning at all, is impossible: and whether the foregoing expressions are not of that sort, I refer it to the impartial examination of the reader. In one sense indeed, men may be said to believe that matter exists, that is, they *act* as if the immediate cause of their sensations, which affects them every moment and so is nearly present to them, were some senseless, unthinking being. But that they should clearly apprehend any meaning marked by those words, and form thereof a settled *speculative* opinion, is what I am not able to conceive. This is not the only instance wherein men impose upon themselves, by imagining they believe those propositions they have often heard, though at bottom they have no meaning in them.

55. But *secondly,* though we should grant a notion to be ever so universally and stedfastly adhered to, yet this is but a weak argument of its truth, to whoever considers what a vast number of prejudices and false opinions are every where embraced with

the utmost tenaciousness, by the unreflecting (which are the far greater) part of mankind. There was a time when the antipodes and motion of the earth were looked upon as monstrous absurdities, even by men of learning: and if it be considered what a small proportion they bear to the rest of mankind, we shall find that at this day, those notions have gained but a very inconsiderable footing in the world.

56. *Ninth objection.—Answer.*—But it is demanded. that we assign *a cause of this prejudice,* and account for its obtaining in the world. To this I *answer,* That men knowing they perceived several ideas, *whereof they themselves were not the authors,* as not being excited from within, nor depending on the operation of their wills, this made them maintain, those ideas or objects of perception had an *existence independent of, and without the mind,* without ever dreaming that a contradiction was involved in those words. But philosophers having plainly seen that the immediate objections of perception do not exist without the mind, *they in some degree* corrected the mistake of the vulgar, but at the same time run into another which seems no less absurd, to wit, that there are certain objects really existing without the mind, or having a subsistence distinct from being perceived, *of which our ideas are only images* or resemblances, imprinted by those objects on the mind. And this notion of the philosophers owes its origin to the same cause with the former, namely, their being conscious that they were not the authors of their own sensations, which they evidently knew were imprinted from without, and which therefore must have some cause distinct from the minds on which they are imprinted.

57. But *why they should suppose the ideas of sense to be excited in us by things in their likeness,* and not rather have recourse to *spirit* which alone can act, may be accounted for, *first,* because they were not aware of the repugnancy there is, (1) as well in supposing things like unto our ideas existing without, as (2) attributing to them *power or activity. Secondly,* because the supreme spirit, which excites those ideas in our minds, is not marked out and limited to our view *by any particular finite collection of sensible ideas,* as human agents are by their size, complexion, limbs, and motions. And *thirdly,* because his operations are regular and uniform. Whenever the course of nature is interrupted by a miracle, men are ready to own the presence of a superior agent. But when we see things go on in the ordinary course, they do not excite in us any reflection; their order and concatenation, though it be an argument of the greatest wisdom, power, and

goodness in their creator, is yet so constant and familiar to us, that we do not think them the immediate effects of a *free spirit*: especially since inconstancy and mutability in acting, though it be an imperfection, is looked on as a mark of *freedom*.

58. *Tenth objection.—Answer.*—Tenthly, it will be objected, that the notions we advance are inconsistent with several sound truths in philosophy and mathematics. For example, *the motion of the earth* is now universally admitted by astronomers, as a truth grounded on the clearest and most convincing reasons; but on the foregoing principles, there can be no such thing. For motion being only an idea, it follows that if it be not perceived, it exists not; but the motion of the earth is not perceived by sense. I *answer*, that tenet, if rightly understood, will be found to agree with the principles we have premised; for the question, whether the earth moves or no, amounts in reality to no more than this; to wit, whether we have reason to conclude from what hath been observed by astronomers, that if we were placed in such and such circumstances, and such or such a position and distance, both from the earth and sun, we should perceive the former to move among the choir of the planets, and appearing in all respects like one of them: and this, by the established rules of nature, which we have no reason to mistrust, is reasonably collected from the phenomena.

59. We may, from the experience we have had of the train and succession of ideas in our minds, often make, I will not say uncertain conjectures, but sure and well-grounded predictions, concerning the ideas we shall be affected with, pursuant to a great train of actions, and be enabled to pass a right judgment of what would have appeared to us, in case we were in circumstances very different from those we are in at present. Herein consists the knowledge of nature, which may preserve its use and certainty very consistently with what hath been said. It will be easy to apply this to whatever objections of the like sort may be drawn from the magnitude of the stars, or any other discoveries in astronomy or nature.

60. *Eleventh objection.*—In the eleventh place, it will be demanded *to what purpose serves that curious organization of plants,* and *the admirable mechanism in the parts of animals?* Might not vegetables grow, and shoot forth leaves and blossoms, and animals perform all their motions, as well without as with all that variety of internal parts so elegantly contrived and put together, *which being ideas have nothing powerful or operative in them, nor have any necessary connection with the effects ascribed*

to them? If it be a spirit that immediately produces every effect by a *fiat*, or act of his will, we must think all that is fine and artificial in the works, whether of man or nature, to be made in vain. By this doctrine, though an *artist* hath made the spring and every movement of a watch, and adjusted them in such a manner as he knew would produce the motions he designed; yet he must think all this done to no purpose, and that it is an intelligence which directs the index, and points to the hour of the day. If so, why may not the intelligence do it, without his being at the pains of making the movements, and putting them together? Why does not an empty case serve as well as another? And how comes it to pass, that whenever there is any fault in the going of a watch, there is some corresponding disorder to be found in the movements, which being mended by a skilful hand, all is right again?

The like may be said of all the clock-work of nature, the great part whereof is so wonderfully fine and subtile, as scarce to be discerned by the best microscope. In short it will be asked, how upon our principles any tolerable account can be given, or any final cause assigned of an innumerable multitude of bodies and machines framed with the most exquisite art, which in the common philosophy have very apposite uses assigned them, and serve to explain abundance of phenomena.

61. *Answer*.—To all which I answer, *first*, that though there were some difficulties relating to the administration of providence, and the uses by it assigned to the several parts of nature, which I could not solve by the foregoing principles, yet this objection could be of small weight against the truth and certainty of those things which may be proved *a priori*, with the utmost evidence. *Secondly*, but neither are the received principles free from the like difficulties; for it may still be demanded, to what end God should take those roundabout methods of effecting things by instruments and machines, which no one can deny might have been effected by the *mere command of His will*, without all that *apparatus*: nay, (*thirdly*), if we narrowly consider it, we shall find the objection may be retorted with greater force on those who hold the existence of those machines without the mind; for it has been made evident, that solidity, bulk, figure, motion, and the like, *have no activity or efficacy* in them, so as to be capable of producing any one effect in nature. See Sect. xxv. Whoever therefore supposes them to exist (allowing the supposition possible) when they are not perceived, does it manifestly to no purpose; since the only use that is assigned to them, as they exist unperceived, is that they produce

those perceivable effects, which in truth cannot be ascribed to any thing but spirit.

62. (*Fourthly*.)—But to come nearer the difficulty, it must be observed, that though the fabrication of all those parts and organs be not absolutely necessary to the *producing any effect*, yet it is necessary to the producing of things *in a constant, regular way, according to the laws of nature*. There are certain general laws that run through the whole chain of natural effects: these are learned by the observation and study of nature, and are by men applied (1) as well to the framing artificial things for the use and ornament of life, as (2) to the explaining the various *phenomena*: which explication consists only in showing the conformity any particular phenomenon hath to the general laws of nature, or which is the same thing, in discovering the *uniformity* there is in the production of natural effects; as will be evident to whoever shall attend to the several instances, wherein philosophers pretend to account for appearances.   That there is a great and conspicuous use in these regular constant methods of working observed by the supreme agent, hath been shown in Sect. XXXVI. And it is no less visible, that a particular size, figure, motion, and disposition of parts are necessary, though not absolutely to the producing any effect, yet to the producing it according to the standing mechanical laws of nature. Thus, for instance, it cannot be denied that God, or the intelligence which sustains and rules the ordinary course of things, might, if he were minded to produce a miracle, cause all the motions on the dial-plate of a watch, though nobody had ever made the movements, and put them in it: but yet if he will act agreeably to the rules of mechanism, by him for wise ends established and maintained in the creation, it is necessary that those actions of the watchmaker, whereby he makes the movements and rightly adjusts them, precede the production of the aforesaid motions; as also that any disorder in them be attended with the perception of some corresponding disorder in the movements, which being once corrected, all is right again.

63. It may indeed on some occasions be *necessary, that the author of nature display his overruling power* in producing some appearance out of his ordinary series of things.   Such exceptions from the general rules of nature are proper to *surprise and awe men* into an acknowledgment of the divine being: but then they are to be used but seldom, (1) otherwise there is a plain reason why they should fail of that effect.   (2) Besides, God seems to choose the *convincing our reason* of His attributes by the works of nature,

which discover so much harmony and contrivance in their make, and are such plain indications of wisdom and beneficence in their author, rather than to *astonish* us into a belief of his being by anomalous and surprising events.

64. *To set this matter in a yet clearer light*, I shall observe that what has been objected to in Sect. LX amounts in reality to no more than this: ideas are not any how and at random produced, there being a certain order and connection between them, like to that of cause and effect: there are also several combinations of them, made in a very regular and artificial manner, which seem like so many instruments in the hand of nature, that being hid, as it were, behind the scenes, have a secret operation in producing those appearances which are seen on the theatre of the world, being themselves discernible only to the curious eye of the philosopher. But since one idea cannot be the cause of another, to what purpose is that connection? and since those instruments, being barely *inefficacious perceptions* in the mind, are not subservient to the production of natural effects: it is demanded why they are made, or, in other words, what reason can be assigned why God should make us, upon a close inspection into his works, behold so great variety of ideas, so artfully laid together, and so much according to rule; it not being credible that he would be at the expense (if one may so speak) of all that art and regularity to no purpose.

65. To all which my *answer* is, *first*, that the connection of ideas does not imply the relation of *cause* and *effect*, but only of a mark or *sign* with the thing *signified*. The *fire* which I see is not the cause of the pain I suffer upon my approaching it, but the mark that forewarns me of it. In like manner, the noise that I hear is not the effect of this or that motion or collision of the ambient bodies, but the sign thereof. *Secondly*, the reason why ideas are formed into machines, that is, artificial and regular combinations, is the same with that for combining letters into words. That a few original ideas may be made to signify a *great number of effects and actions*, it is necessary they be variously combined together: and to the end their use be *permanent and universal*, these combinations must by made by *rule*, and with *wise contrivance*. By this means abundance of information is conveyed unto us concerning what we are to expect from such and such actions, and what methods are proper to be taken, for the exciting such and such ideas: which in effect is all that I conceive to be distinctly meant, when it is said that by discerning the figure, texture, and mechanism of the inward parts of bodies, whether natural or artificial, we may

attain to know the several uses and properties depending thereon, or the nature of the thing.

66. *Proper employment of the natural philosopher.*—Hence it is evident, that those *things* which, *under the notion of a cause co-operating* or concurring *to the production of effects, are altogether inexplicable,* and run us into great absurdities, may be very naturally explained, and have a proper and obvious use assigned them, when they are considered only as marks or signs for our information. And it is the *searching after, and endeavouring to understand those signs* (this language, if I may so call it) *instituted by the author of nature,* that ought to be the employment of the natural philosopher, and not the pretending to explain things by corporeal causes; which doctrine seems to have too much estranged the minds of men from that active principle, that supreme and wise spirit, " in whom we live, move, and have our being."

67. *Twelfth objection.—Answer.*—In the twelfth place, it may perhaps be objected, that though it be clear from what has been said, that there can be no such thing as an inert, senseless, extended, solid, figured, moveable substance, existing without the mind, such as philosophers describe matter: yet if any man shall leave out of his idea of *matter,* the positive ideas of extension, figure, solidity, and motion, and say that he means only by that word an inert senseless substance, that exists without the mind, or unperceived, which is the *occasion of our ideas,* or at the presence whereof God is pleased to excite ideas in us: it doth not appear, but that matter taken in this sense may possibly exist. In *answer* to which I say, *first,* that it seems no less absurd to suppose a substance without accidents than it is to suppose accidents without a substance. But *secondly,* though we should grant this unknown substance may possibly exist, yet *where can it be supposed to be?* that it exists not in the mind is agreed, and that it exists not in place is no less certain; *since all* (place or) *extension exists only in the mind,* as hath been already proved. It remains therefore that it exists no where at all.

68. *Matter supports nothing, an argument against its existence.* —Let us examine a little the description that is here given us of *matter.* It neither acts, nor perceives, nor is perceived: for this is all that is meant by saying it is an *inert, senseless, unknown* substance; which is a definition entirely made up of negatives, excepting only the relative notion of its standing under or supporting: but then it must be observed, that it *supports* nothing at all; and how nearly this comes to the description of a *nonenity,* I desire may be

considered. But, say you, it is the *unknown occasion, at the presence of which* ideas are excited in us by the will of God. Now I would fain know how any thing can be *present* to us, which is neither perceivable by sense nor reflection, nor capable of producing any idea in our minds, nor is at all extended, nor hath any form, nor exists in any place. The words *to be present*, when thus applied, must needs be taken in some abstract and strange meaning, and which I am not able to comprehend.

69. Again, let us examine what is meant by *occasion;* so far as I can gather from the common use of language, that word signifies, either the agent which *produces any effect*, or else something that is *observed to accompany*, or go before it, in the ordinary course of things. But when it is applied to matter as above described, it can be taken in neither of those senses. For matter is said to be passive and inert, and so cannot be an *agent* or efficient cause. It is also *unperceivable*, as being devoid of all sensible qualities, and so cannot be the occasion of our perceptions in the latter sense : as when the *burning my finger* is said to be the occasion of the pain that attends it. What therefore can be meant by calling matter an occasion? this term is either used in no sense at all, or else in some sense very distant from its received signification.

70. You will perhaps say that *matter*, though it be not perceived by us, *is* nevertheless *perceived by God*, to Whom it is the occasion of exciting ideas in our minds. For, say you, since we observe our sensations to be imprinted in an *orderly and constant manner*, it is but reasonable to suppose there are certain constant and regular occasions of their being produced. That is to say, that there are certain permanent and distinct parcels of matter, cor-responding to our ideas, which, though they do not excite them in our minds, or any ways immediately affect us, as being altogether passive and unperceivable to us, they are nevertheless to God, by Whom they are perceived, as it were so many occasions to remind Him when and what ideas to imprint on our minds : *that so things may go on in a constant, uniform manner.*

71. In *answer* to this I observe, that as the notion of matter is here stated, the question is no longer concerning the existence of a thing distinct from *spirit* and *idea*, from perceiving and being perceived : but whether there are not certain ideas, of I know not what sort, in the mind of God, which are so many marks or notes that direct him how to produce sensations in our minds, in a constant and regular method : much after the same manner as a musician is directed by the notes of music to produce that

harmonious train and composition of sound, which is called a *tune*; though they who hear the music do not perceive the notes, and may be entirely ignorant of them.   But this notion of matter seems too extravagant to deserve a confutation.   Besides, it is in effect no objection against what we have advanced to wit, that there is no senseless, *unperceived substance.*

72. *The order of our perceptions shows the goodness of God, but affords no proof of the existence of matter.*—If we follow the light of reason, we shall, from the constant, uniform method of our sensations, collect the goodness and wisdom of the *spirit* who excites them in our minds.   But this is all that I can see reasonably concluded from thence.   To me, I say, it is evident that the being of a *spirit infinitely wise, good, and powerful* is abundantly sufficient to explain all the appearances of nature.   But as for *inert, senseless matter*, nothing that I perceive has any the least connection with it, or leads to the thoughts of it.   And I would fain see any one explain any the meanest *phenomenon* in nature by it, or show any manner of reason, though in the lowest rank of probability, that he can have for its existence; or even make any tolerable sense or meaning of that supposition.   For as to its being an occasion, we have, I think, evidently shown that with regard to us it is no occasion : it remains therefore that it must be, if at all, the occasion to God of exciting ideas in us; and what this amounts to, we have just now seen.

73. It is worth while to reflect a little on the *motives* which induced men *to suppose the existence of material substance;* that so having observed the gradual ceasing and expiration of those motives or reasons, we may proportionately withdraw the assent that was grounded on them.   *First*, therefore, it was thought that colour, figure, motion, and the rest of the sensible qualities or accidents, did really exist without the mind; and for this reason, it *seemed needful to suppose some unthinking substratum or sub-stance wherein they did exist, since they could not be conceived to exist by themselves.   Afterwards*, (*secondly*) in process of time, men being convinced that colours, sounds, and the rest of the sensible secondary qualities had no existence without the mind, they stripped this *substratum* or material substance of those qualities, leaving only the *primary ones,* figure, motion, and such like, which they still conceived to exist without the mind, and consequently to stand in need of a material support.   But it having been shown, that none, even of these, can possibly exist otherwise than in a spirit or mind which perceives them, it follows that we

have no longer any reason to suppose the being of *matter*. Nay
that it is utterly impossible there should be any such thing, so
long as that word is taken to denote an *unthinking substratum*
of qualities or accidents, wherein they exist without the mind.

74. But though it be allowed by the *materialists* themselves, that
matter was thought of only for the sake of supporting accidents;
and the reason entirely ceasing, one might expect the mind should
naturally, and without any reluctance at all, quit the belief of
what was solely grounded thereon. Yet the prejudice is riveted
so deeply in our thoughts, that we can scarce tell how to part
with it, and are therefore inclined, since the *thing* itself is indefen-
sible, at least to retain the *name*; which we apply to I know not
what abstracted and indefinite notions of *being* or *occasion*, though
without any show of reason, at least so far as I can see. For what
is there on our part, or what do we perceive amongst all the ideas,
sensations, notions, which are imprinted on our minds, either by
sense or reflection, from whence may be inferred the existence of
an inert, thoughtless, unperceived occasion? and on the other
hand, on the part of an *all-sufficient spirit*, what can there be that
should make us believe, or even suspect, He is *directed* by an inert
occasion to excite ideas in our minds?

75. *Absurdity of contending for the existence of matter as the
occasion of ideas.*—It is a very extraordinary instance of the force
of prejudice, and much to be lamented, that the mind of man
retains so great a fondness, against all the evidence of reason, for
a stupid, thoughtless *somewhat*, by the interposition whereof it
would, as it were, screen itself from the providence of God, and
remove Him further off from the affairs of the world. But though
we do the utmost we can, to secure the belief of *matter*, though
when reason forsakes us, we endeavour to support our opinion on
the bare possibility of the thing, and though we indulge ourselves
in the full scope of an imagination not regulated by reason, to
make out that poor *possibility*, yet the upshot of all is, that there
are certain *unknown ideas* in the mind of God; for this, if any
thing, is all that I conceive to be meant by *occasion* with regard
to God. And this, at the bottom, is no longer contending for the
thing, but for the *name*.

76. Whether therefore there are such ideas in the mind of God,
and whether they may be called by the name *matter*, I shall not
dispute. But if you stick to the notion of an *unthinking* substance,
or support of extension, motion, and other sensible qualities, then
to me is it most evidently impossible there should be any such

thing. Since is it a plain repugnancy, that those qualities should exist in or be supported by an unperceiving substance.

77. *That a substratum not perceived, may exist, unimportant.*— But say you, though it be granted that there is no thoughtless support of extension, and the other qualities or accidents *which we perceive;* yet there may, perhaps, be some inert unperceiving substance, or *substratum* of *some other qualities,* as incomprehensible to us as colours are to a man born blind, *because we have not a sense adapted to them.* But if we had a new sense, we should possibly no more doubt of their existence, than a blind man made to see does of the existence of light and colours. I answer, *first,* if what you mean by the word *matter* be only the *unknown support of unknown qualities,* it is no matter whether there is such a thing or not, since it no way concerns us: and I do not see the advantage there is in disputing about we know not *what,* and we know not *why.*

78. But *secondly,* if we had *a new sense,* it *could only furnish us with new ideas or sensations*: and then we should have the same reason against their existing in an unperceiving substance, that has been already offered with relation to figure, motion, colour, and the like. Qualities, aas hath been shown, are nothing else but *sensations* or *ideas,* which exist only in a *mind* perceiving them and this is true not only of the ideas we are acquainted with at present, but likewise of all possible ideas whatsoever.

79. But you will *insist,* what if (1) I have no reason to believe the existence of matter, what if (2) I can assign any use to it, or (3) explain any thing by it, or even (4) conceive what is meant by that word? yet still it is no contradiction to say that matter exists, and that this matter is *in general a substance,* or *occasion of ideas*; though, indeed, to go about to unfold the meaning, or adhere to any particular explication of those words, may be attended with great difficulties. I *answer,* when words are used without a meaning, you may put them together as you please, without danger of running into a contradiction. You may say, for example, that *twice two* is equal to *seven,* so long as you declare you do not take the words of that proposition in their usual acceptation, but for marks of you know not what. And by the same reason you may say, there is an inert thoughtless substance without accidents, which is the occasion of our ideas. And we shall understand just as much by one proposition, as the other.

80. In the last place, you will *say,* what if we give up the cause of material substance, and assert, that matter is an unknown

somewhat, neither substance nor accident, spirit nor idea, inert, thoughtless, indivisible, immoveable, unextended, existing in no place? for, say you, whatever may be urged against *substance* or *occasion*, or any other positive or relative notion of matter, hath no place at all, so long as this *negative definition of matter* is adhered to. I *answer*, you may, if so it shall seem good, use the word *matter* in the same sense that other men use *nothing*, and so make those terms convertible in your style. For after all, this is what appears to me to be the result of that definition, the parts whereof when I consider with attention, either collectively, or separate from each other, I do not find that there is any kind of effect or impression made on my mind, different from what is excited by the term *nothing*.

81. You will *reply* perhaps, that in the foresaid definition is included, what doth *sufficiently* distinguish it from nothing, the positive, abstract idea of *quiddity, entity,* or *existence*. I own indeed, that those who pretend to the faculty of framing abstract general ideas, do talk as if they had such an idea, which is, say they, the most abstract and general notion of all, that is to me the most incomprehensible of all others. That there are a great variety of spirits of different orders and capacities, whose faculties, both in number and extent, are far exceeding those the author of my being has bestowed on me, I see no reason to deny. And for me to pretend to determine by my own few, stinted, narrow inlets of perception, what ideas the inexhaustible power of the supreme spirit may imprint upon them, were certainly the utmost folly and presumption. Since there may be, for ought that I know, innumerable sorts of ideas or sensations, as different from one another, and from all that I have perceived, as colours are from sounds. But how ready soever I may be to acknowledge the scantiness of my comprehension, with regard to the endless variety of spirits and ideas, that might possibly exist, yet for any one to pretend to a notion of entity or existence, *abstracted* from *spirit* and *idea*, from perceiving and being perceived, is, I suspect, a downright repugnancy and trifling with words. It remains that we consider the objections which may possibly be made on the part of religion.

82. *Objections derived from the scriptures answered.*—Some there are who think, that though the arguments for the real existence of bodies, which are drawn from reason, be allowed not to amount to demonstration, yet (first) the *holy scriptures* are so clear in the point, as will sufficiently convince every good Christian,

that bodies do really exist, and are something more than mere ideas; there being in holy writ innumerable facts related, which evidently suppose the reality of timber, and stone, mountains, and rivers, and cities, and human bodies. To which I *answer*, that no sort of writings whatever, sacred or profane, which use those and the like words in the *vulgar acceptation*, or so as to have a meaning in them, are in danger of having their truth called in question by our doctrine. That all those things do really exist, that there are bodies, even corporeal substances, when taken *in the vulgar sense*, has been shown to be agreeable to our principles: and the difference betwixt *things* and *idea*, *realities* and *chimeras*, has been distinctly explained. And I do not think, that either what philosophers call *matter*, or the existence of objects without the mind, is any where mentioned in scripture.

83. *No objection as to language tenable.*—Again, whether there be or be not external things, it is agreed on all hands, that the proper use of words is the marking our conceptions, or things *only as they are known and perceived by us*; whence it plainly follows, that in the tenets we have laid down, there is nothing inconsistent with the right use and significancy of *language*, and that discourse of what kind soever, so far as it is intelligible, remains undisturbed. But all this seems so manifest, from what hath been set forth in the premises, that it is needless to insist any further on it.

84. But (secondly) it will be urged, that *miracles do*, at least, *lose much of their* stress and *import by our principles*. What must we think of Moses' rod, was it not *really* turned into a serpent, or was there only a change of *ideas* in the minds of the spectators? And can it be supposed, that our Saviour did no more at the marriage-feast in Cana, than impose on the sight, and smell, and taste of the guests, so as to create in them the appearance or idea only of wine? The same may be said of all other miracles: which, in consequence of the foregoing principles, must be looked upon only as so many cheats, or illusions of fancy. To this I reply, that the rod was changed into a real serpent, and the water into real wine. That this doth not, in the least, contradict what I have elsewhere said, will be evident from Sect. xxxiv, xxxv. But this business of *real* and *imaginary* hath been already so plainly and fully explained, and so often referred to, and the difficulties about it are so easily answered from what hath gone before, that it were an affront to the reader's understanding, to resume the explication of it in this place. I shall only observe, that if at table all who

were present should see, and smell, and taste, and drink wine, and find the effects of it, with me there could be no doubt of its reality. So that at bottom, the scruple concerning real miracles hath no place at all on ours, but only on the received principles, and, consequently, maketh rather *for*, than *against*, what hath been said.

85. *Consequences of the preceding tenets.*—Having done with the objections, which I endeavoured to propose in the clearest light, and given them all the force and weight I could, we proceed in the next place to take a view of our tenets *in their consequences*. Some of these appear at first sight, as that several difficult and obscure questions, on which abundance of speculation hath been thrown away, are entirely banished from philosophy. Whether (1) corporeal substance can think? whether (2) matter be infinitely divisible? and (3) how it operates on spirit? These, and the like inquiries, have given infinite amusement to philosophers in all ages. But depending on the existence of *matter*, they have no longer any place on our principles. Many other advantages there are, as well with regard to *religion* as the *sciences*, which it is easy for any one to deduce from what hath been premised. But this will appear more plainly in the sequel.

86. *The removal of matter gives certainty to knowledge.*—From the principles we have laid down, it follows, human knowledge may naturally be reduced to two heads, that of *ideas* and that of spirits. Of each of these I shall treat in order. And first, as to ideas or unthinking things, our knowledge of these hath been very much obscured and confounded, and we have been led into very dangerous errors, by supposing a two-fold existence of the objects of sense, the one *intelligible*, or in the mind, the other *real* and without the mind: whereby unthinking things are thought to have a natural subsistence of their own, distinct from being perceived by spirits. This, which, if I mistake not, hath been shown to be a most groundless and absurd notion, is *the very root of scepticism*: for so long as men thought that real things subsisted without the mind, and that their knowledge was only so far forth *real* as it was conformable to *real things*, it follows, they could not be certain that they had any real knowledge at all. For how can it be known, that the things which are perceived are conformable to those which are not perceived, or exist without the mind?

87. Colour, figure, motion, extension and the like, considered only as so many *sensations* in the mind, are perfectly known, there being nothing in them which is not perceived. But if they

are looked on as notes or images, referred to *things* or *archetypes* existing without the mind, then are we involved all in *scepticism*. We see only the appearances, and not the real qualities of things. What may be the extension, figure, or motion of any thing really and absolutely, or in itself, it is impossible for us to know, but only the *proportion* or the *relation* they bear to our senses. Things remaining the same, our ideas vary, and which of them, or even whether any of them at all represent the true quality really existing in the thing, it is out of our reach to determine. So that, for ought we know, all we see, hear, and feel, may be only phantóm and vain chimera, and not at all agree with the real things, existing in *rerum natura*. All this scepticism follows, from our supposing a difference between *things* and *ideas*, and that the former have a subsistence without the mind, or unperceived. It were easy to dilate on this subject, and show how the arguments urged by sceptics in all ages, depend on the supposition of external objects.

88. *If there be external matter, neither the nature nor existence of things can be known.*—So long as we attribute a real existence to unthinking things, distinct from their being perceived, it is not only impossible for us to know with evidence (1) the nature of any real unthinking being, but even (2) that it exists. Hence it is, that we see philosophers distrust their senses, and doubt of the existence of heaven and earth, of every thing they see or feel, even of their own bodies. And after all their labour and struggle of thought, they are forced to own, we cannot attain to any self-evident or demonstrative knowledge of the existence of sensible things. But all this doubtfulness, which so bewilders and confounds the mind, and makes *philosophy* ridiculous in the eyes of the world, vanishes, if we annex a meaning to our words, and do not amuse ourselves with the terms *absolute, external, exist,* and such like, signifying we know not what. I can as well doubt of my own being, as of the being of those things which I actually perceive by sense: it being a manifest contradiction, that any sensible object should be immediately perceived by sight or touch, and, at the same time, have no existence in nature, since the very existence of an unthinking being consists in *being perceived*.

89. *Of thing or being.*—Nothing seems of more importance, towards erecting a firm system of sound and real knowledge, which may be proof against the assaults of scepticism, than to lay the beginning in a distinct explication of what is meant by *thing, reality, existence*: for in vain shall we dispute concerning the real

existence of things, or pretend to any knowledge thereof, so long
as we have not fixed the meaning of those words. *Thing* or *being*
is the most general name of all; it comprehends under it two kinds
entirely distinct and heterogeneous, and which have nothing
common but the name, to wit, *spirits* and *ideas*. The former are
active, indivisible (incorruptible) *substances*: the latter are *inert,
fleeting* (perishable passions) or *dependent beings,* which subsist
not by themselves, but are supported by, or exist in minds or
spiritual substances. We comprehend our own existence by inward
feeling or reflection, and that of other spirits by reason. We may
be said to have some knowledge or notion of our own minds, of
spirits and active beings, whereof, in a strict sense, we have not
ideas. In like manner we know and have a notion of relations
between things or ideas, which relations are distinct from the ideas
or things related, inasmuch as the latter may be perceived by us
without our perceiving the former. To me it seems that ideas,
spirits, and relations, are all, in their respective kinds, the object
of human knowledge and subject of discourse: and that the term
idea would be improperly extended to signify every thing we know
or have any notion of.

90. *External things either imprinted by or perceived by some other
mind.*—Ideas imprinted on the senses are real things, or do really
exist; this we do not deny, but we deny (1) they can subsist without
the minds which perceive them, or (2) that they are resemblances
of any archetypes existing without the mind: (1) since the very
being of a sensation or idea consists in being perceived, and (2)
an idea can be like nothing but an idea. Again, the *things perceived by sense may be termed external,* with regard to their
origin, in that they are not generated from within, by the mind
itself, but (1) *imprinted by a spirit distinct from that which perceives
them.* Sensible objects may likewise be said to be without the
mind, in another sense, namely (2) *when they exist in some other
mind.* Thus when I shut my eyes, the things I saw may still exist,
but it must be in another mind.

91. *Sensible qualities real.*—It were a mistake to think, that
what is here said derogates in the least from the reality of things.
It is acknowledged, on the received principles, that extension,
motion, and, in a word, all sensible qualities, have need of a
support, as not being able to subsist by themselves. But the
objects perceived by sense are allowed to be nothing but combinations of those qualities, and, consequently, cannot subsist by
themselves. *Thus far it is agreed on all hands.* So that in denying

the things perceived by sense, an existence independent of a substance, or support wherein they may exist, we detract nothing from the received opinion of their *reality,* and are guilty of no innovation in that respect.   All the difference is, that according to us the unthinking beings perceived by sense have no existence distinct from being perceived, and cannot therefore exist in any other substance, than those *unextended, indivisible substances,* or *spirits, which act, and think, and perceive them*: whereas philosophers vulgarly hold, that the sensible qualities exist in an *inert, extended, unperceiving substance,* which they call *matter,* to which they attribute a natural subsistence, exterior to all thinking beings, or distinct from being perceived by any mind whatsoever, even the eternal mind of the Creator, wherein they suppose only ideas of the corporeal substances created by him: if indeed they allow them to be at all *created.*

92. *Objections of atheists overturned.*—For as we have shown the doctrine of matter, or corporeal substance, to have been the main pillar and support of scepticism, so likewise upon the same foundation have been raised all the impious schemes of atheism and irreligion.   Nay, so great a difficulty hath it been thought, *to conceive matter produced out of nothing,* that the most celebrated among the ancient philosophers, even of these who maintained the being of a God, have thought matter to be uncreated and coeternal with him.   How great a friend material substance hath been to atheists in all ages, were needless to relate.   All their monstrous systems have so visible and necessary a dependence on it, that when this corner-stone is once removed, the whole fabric cannot choose but fall to the ground; insomuch that it is no longer worth while to bestow a particular consideration on the absurdities of every wretched sect of atheists.

93. *And of fatalists also.*—That impious and profane persons should readily fall in with those systems which favour their inclinations, by deriding immaterial substance, and supposing the soul to be divisible and subject to corruption as the body; which exclude all freedom, intelligence, and design from the formation of things, and instead thereof make a self-existent, stupid, unthinking substance, the root and origin of all beings.   That they should hearken to those who deny a Providence, or inspection of a superior mind over the affairs of the world, attributing the whole series of events either to *blind chance* or *fatal necessity,* arising *from the impulse of one body on another.*   All this is very natural. And on the other hand, when men of better principles observe the

enemies of religion lay so great a stress on *unthinking matter*, and all of them use so much industry and artifice to reduce everything to it; methinks they should rejoice to see them deprived of their grand support, and driven from that only fortress, without which your Epicureans, Hobbists, and the like, have not even the shadow of a pretence, but become the most cheap and easy triumph in the world.

94. *Of Idolaters.*—The existence of matter, or bodies unperceived, has not only been the main support of atheists and fatalists, but on the same principle doth *idolatry* likewise in all its various forms depend. Did men but consider that the sun, moon, and stars, and every other object of the senses, are only so many sensations in their minds, which have no other existence but barely being perceived, doubtless they would never fall down and worship their own *ideas*; but rather address their homage to that eternal invisible Mind which produces and sustains all things.

95. *And Socinians.*—The same absurd principle, by mingling itself with the articles of our faith, hath occasioned no small difficulties to Christians. For example, about the Resurrection, how many scruples and objections have been raised by Socinians and others? But do not the most plausible of them depend on the supposition, that a body is denominated the same, with regard not to the form or *that which is perceived by sense,* but the material substance which remains the same under several forms? Take away this *material substance*, about the identity whereof all the dispute is, and mean by *body* what every plain ordinary person means by that word, to wit, that which is immediately seen and felt, which is only a combination of sensible qualities, or ideas: and then their most unanswerable objections come to nothing.

96. *Summary of the consequences of expelling matter.*—Matter being once expelled out of nature, drags with it so many sceptical and impious notions, such an incredible number of disputes and puzzling questions, which have been thorns in the sides of divines, as well as philosophers, and made so much fruitless work for mankind; that if the arguments we have produced against it are not found equal to demonstration (as to me they evidently seem), yet I am sure all friends to knowledge, peace, and religion, have reason to wish they were.

97. Beside the external existence of the objects of perception, another great source of errors and difficulties, with regard to ideal knowledge, is the doctrine of *abstract ideas*, such as it hath been set forth in the introduction. The plainest things in the world,

those we are most intimately acquainted with, and perfectly know, when they are considered in an abstract way, appear strangely difficult and incomprehensible. Time, place, and motion, taken in particular or concrete, are what every body knows; but having passed through the hands of a metaphysician, they become too abstract and fine to be apprehended by men of ordinary sense. Bid your servant meet you at such a *time*, in such a *place*, and he shall never stay to deliberate on the meaning of those words: in conceiving that particular time and place, or the motion by which he is to get hither, he finds not the least difficulty. But if *time* be taken, exclusive of all those particular actions and ideas that diversify the day, merely for the *continuation of existence*, or duration in abstract, then it will perhaps gravel even a philosopher to comprehend it.

98. *Dilemma.*—For my own part, whenever I attempt to frame a simple idea of time, abstracted from the succession of ideas in my mind, which flows uniformly, and is participated by all beings, I am lost and embrangled in inextricable difficulties. I have no notion of it at all, only I hear others say, it is infinitely divisible, and speak of it in such a manner as leads me to entertain odd thoughts of my existence; since that doctrine lays one under an absolute necessity of thinking, either (1) that he passes away innumerable ages without a thought, or else (2) that he is annihilated every moment of his life: both of which seem equally absurd. Time therefore being nothing, *abstracted from the succession of ideas in our minds*, it follows that the duration of any finite spirit must be estimated *by the number of ideas or actions* succeeding each other in that spirit or mind. Hence it is a plain consequence that the soul always thinks: and in truth, whoever shall go about to divide in his thoughts, or abstract the *existence* of a spirit from its *cogitation*, will, I believe, find it no easy task.

99. So likewise, when we attempt to abstract *extension* and *motion* from all other qualities, and consider them by themselves, we presently lose sight of them, and run into great extravagancies. All which depend on a twofold abstraction: first, it is supposed that extension, for example, may be abstracted from all other sensible qualities; and secondly, that the entity of extension may be abstracted from its being perceived. But whoever shall reflect, and take care to understand what he says, will, if I mistake not, acknowledge that all sensible qualities are alike *sensations*, and alike *real*; that where the extension is, there is the colour too, to wit, in his mind, and that their archetypes can exist only in some

other *mind*: and that the objects of sense are nothing but those
sensations combined, blended, or (if one may so speak) concreted
together: none of all which can be supposed to exist unperceived.

100. What it is for a man to be happy, or an object of good, of
happiness, prescinded from all particular pleasure, or of *goodness*,
from every thing that is good, this is what few can pretend to. So
likewise, a man may be just and virtuous, without having precise
ideas of *justice* and *virtue*. The opinion that those and the like
words stand for general notions *abstracted from all particular
persons and actions*, seems to have rendered morality difficult, and
the study thereof of less use to mankind. And in effect, the
doctrine of *abstraction* has not a little contributed towards spoiling
the most useful parts of knowledge.

101. *Of natural philosophy and mathematics.*—The two great
provinces of speculative science, conversant about ideas received
from sense and their relations, are *natural philosophy* and
mathematics; with regard to each of these I shall make some
observations. And first, I shall say somewhat of natural philosophy. On this subject it is that the sceptics triumph: all that
stock of arguments they produce to depreciate our faculties, and
make mankind appear ignorant and low, are drawn principally
from this head, to wit, that we are under an invincible blindness
as to the *true* and *real* nature of things. This they exaggerate, and
love to enlarge on. We are miserably bantered, say they, by our
senses, and amused only with the outside and show of things.
The real essence, the internal qualities, and constitution of every
the meanest object, is hid from our view; something there is in
every drop of water, every grain of sand, which it is beyond the
power of human understanding to fathom or comprehend. But it
is evident from what has been shown, that all this complaint is
groundless, and that we are influenced by false principles to that
degree as to mistrust our senses, and think we know nothing of
those things which we perfectly comprehend.

102. One great inducement to our pronouncing ourselves
ignorant of the nature of things, is the current opinion *that every
thing includes within itself the cause of its properties*: or that there
is in each object an inward essence, which is the source whence its
discernible qualities flow, and whereon they depend. Some have
pretended to account for appearances by *occult qualities*, but of
late they are mostly resolved into *mechanical causes*, to wit, the
figure, *motion, weight,* and such like qualities of insensible particles:
whereas in truth there is no other agent or efficient cause than

spirit, it being evident that motion, as well as all other *ideas*, is perfectly inert. See Sect. xxv. Hence, to endeavour to explain the production of colours or sounds, by figure, motion, every one may think he knows. But to frame an abstract idea magnitude, and the like, must needs be labour in vain. And accordingly, we see the attempts of that kind are not at all satisfactory. Which may be said, in general, of those instances, wherein one *idea* or *quality* is assigned for the cause of another. I need not say, how many hypotheses and speculations are left out, and how much the study of nature is abridged by this doctrine.

103. *Attraction signifies the effect, not the manner or cause.*— The great mechanical principle now in vogue is *attraction*. That a stone falls to the earth, or the sea swells towards the moon, may to some appear sufficiently explained thereby. But how are we enlightened by being told this is done by attraction? Is it that that word signifies the manner of the tendency, and that it is by the mutual drawing of bodies, instead of their being impelled or protruded towards each other? but nothing is determined of the manner or action, and it may as truly (for ought we know) be termed *impulse*, or *protrusion*, as *attraction*. Again, the parts of steel we see cohere firmly together, and this also is accounted for by attraction; but in this, as in the other instances, I do not perceive that any thing is signified besides the *effect* itself: for as to the *manner* of the action, whereby it is produced, or the *cause* which produces it, these are not so much as aimed at.

104. Indeed, if we take a view of the several phenomena, and compare them together, we may observe some likeness and conformity between them. For example, in the falling of a stone to the ground, in the rising of the sea towards the moon, in cohesion and crystallization, there is something alike, namely a union or mutual approach of bodies. So that any one of these or the like phenomena, may not seem strange or surprising to a man who hath nicely observed and compared the effects of nature. For that only is thought so which is uncommon, or a thing by itself, and out of the ordinary course of our observation. That bodies should tend towards the centre of the earth, is not thought strange, because it is what we perceive every moment of our lives. But that they should have a like gravitation towards the centre of the moon, may seem odd and unaccountable to most men, because it is discerned only in the tides. But a philosopher, whose thoughts take in a larger compass of nature, having observed a certain similitude of appearances, as well in the heavens as the earth, that

argue innumerable bodies to have a mutual tendency towards each other, which he denotes by the general name *attraction*, whatever can be reduced to that, he thinks justly accounted for. Thus he explains the tides by the attraction of the terraqueous globe towards the moon, which to him doth not appear odd or anomalous, but only a particular example of a general rule or law of nature.

105. If therefore we consider the *difference* there is *betwixt natural philosophers and other men*, with regard to their knowledge of the phenomena, we shall find it consists, not in an exacter knowledge of the *efficient cause* that produces them, for that can be no other than the *will of a spirit*, but only in *a greater largeness of comprehension, whereby analogies, harmonies, and agreements are discovered in the works of nature, and the particular effects explained*, that is, reduced to general rules (see Sect. LXII), which rules, grounded on the analogy and uniformness observed in the production of natural effects, are most agreeable, and sought after by the mind; for that they extend our prospect beyond what is present, and near to us, and enable us to make *very probable conjectures*, touching things that may have happened at very great distances of time and place, as well as to predict things to come; which sort of endeavour towards omniscience is much affected by the mind.

106. *Caution as to the use of analogies.*—But we should proceed warily in such things: for we are apt to lay too great a stress on analogies, and to the prejudice of truth, humour that eagerness of the mind, whereby it is carried to extend its knowledge into general theorems. For example, gravitation, or mutual attraction, because it appears in many instances, some are straightway for pronouncing *universal*; and that to *attract, and be attracted by every other body, is an essential quality inherent in all bodies whatsoever*. Whereas it appears the *fixed stars* have no such tendency towards each other: and so far is that gravitation from being *essential* to bodies, that in some instances a quite contrary principle seems to show itself; as in the perpendicular *growth of plants*, and the *elasticity of the air*. There is nothing *necessary or essential in the case*, but it depends entirely on the will of the *governing spirit*, who causes certain bodies to cleave together, or tend towards each other, according to various laws, whilst he keeps others at a fixed distance; and to some he gives a quite contrary tendency to fly asunder, just as he sees convenient.

107. After what has been premised, I think we may lay down *the following conclusions. First*, it is plain philosophers amuse

themselves in vain, when they inquire for any natural efficient cause distinct from a *mind* or *spirit*. *Secondly*, considering the whole creation is the workmanship of a *wise and good agent*, it should seem to become philosophers to employ their thoughts (contrary to what some hold) about the *final causes of things*: and I must confess, I see no reason why pointing out *the various ends* to which natural things are adapted, and for which they were originally with unspeakable wisdom contrived, should not be thought one good way of accounting for them, and altogether worthy a philosopher. *Thirdly*, from what hath been premised no reason can be drawn, why the *history of nature should* not still *be studied*, and observations and experiments made, which, that they are of use to mankind, and enable us to draw any general conclusions, is not the result of any *immutable habitudes*, or relations between things themselves, but only of God's goodness and kindness to men in the administration of the world.   (See Sect. xxx, xxxi.) *Fourthly*, by a diligent observation of the phenomena within our view, we may *discover the general laws of nature, and from them deduce the other phenomena*, I do not say *demonstrate*; for all deductions of that kind depend on a supposition that the Author of nature always operates uniformly, and in a constant observance of those rules we take for principles: *which we cannot evidently know*.

108. *Three analogies.*—Those men who frame general rules from the phenomena, and afterwards derive the phenomena from those rules, seem to consider signs rather than causes.   A man may well understand natural signs without knowing their *analogy* or being able to (1) *say* by what rule a thing is so or so.   And as it is very possible (2) to *write* improperly *through too strict an observance of general grammar rules*: so in arguing from general rules of nature, it is not impossible we may extend the analogy too far, and by that means run into mistakes.

109. As in (3) *reading* other books, a wise man will choose to fix his thoughts on the *sense* and apply it to use, rather than lay them out in *grammatical remarks* on the language; so in perusing the volume of nature, it seems beneath the dignity of the mind to affect an exactness in reducing *each particular phenomenon to general rules*, or showing how it follows from them.   We should propose to ourselves nobler views, such as (1) to recreate and exalt the mind, with a prospect of the beauty, *order*, extent, and variety of natural things: hence, by proper inferences, (2) to enlarge our notions of the grandeur, wisdom, and beneficence of the Creator:

and lastly, (3) to make the several parts of the creation, so far as in us lies, subservient to the ends they were designed for, God's glory, and the sustentation and comfort of ourselves and fellow-creatures.

110. The best key for the aforesaid analogy, or natural science, will be easily acknowledged to be a certain celebrated treatise of *mechanics*: in the entrance of which justly admired treatise, time, space, and motion, are distinguished into *absolute* and *relative, true* and *apparent, mathematical* and *vulgar*: which distinction, as it is at large explained by the author, doth suppose those quantities to have an existence without the mind: and that they are ordinarily conceived with relation to sensible things, to which nevertheless, in their own nature, they bear no relation at all.

111. As for *time*, as it is there taken in an absolute or abstracted sense, for the duration or perseverance of the existence of things, I have nothing more to add concerning it, after what hath been already said on that subject, Sect. xcvii, xcviii. For the rest, this celebrated author holds there is an *absolute space*, which, being unperceivable to sense, remains in itself similar and immoveable: and relative space to be the measure thereof, which being moveable, and defined by its situation in respect of sensible bodies, is vulgarly taken for immoveable space. *Place* he defines to be that part of space which is occupied by any body. And according as the space is absolute or relative, so also is the place. *Absolute motion* is said to be the translation of a body from absolute place to absolute place, as relative motion is from one relative place to another. And because the parts of absolute space do not fall under our senses, instead of them we are obliged to use their sensible measures: and so define both place and motion with respect to bodies, which we regard as immoveable. But it is said, in philosophical matters we must *abstract* from our senses, since it may be, that none of those bodies which seem to be quiescent, are truly so: and the same thing which is moved relatively, may be really at rest. As likewise one and the same body may be in relative rest and motion, or even moved with contrary relative motions at the same time, according as its place is variously defined. All which ambiguity is to be found in the apparent motions, but not at all in the true or absolute, which should therefore be alone regarded in philosophy. And the true, we are told, are distinguished from apparent or relative motions by the following properties. First, in true or absolute motion, all *parts* which preserve the same position with respect to the whole, partake of

the motions of the whole. Secondly, the *place* being moved, that which is placed therein is also moved: so that a body moving in a place which is in motion, doth participate the motion of its place. Thirdly, *true motion* is never generated or changed, otherwise than by force impressed on the *body itself*. Fourthly, true motion is always changed by *force impressed* on the *body moved*. Fifthly, in circular motion *barely relative*, there is no centrifugal force, which nevertheless in that which is true or absolute, is proportional to the quantity of motion.

112. *Motion, whether real or apparent, relative.*—But notwithstanding what hath been said, it doth not appear to me, that there can be any motion other than *relative*: so that to conceive motion, there must be at least two conceived bodies, whereof the distance or position in regard to each other is varied. Hence if there was one only body in being, it could not possibly be moved. This seems evident, in that the idea I have of motion doth necessarily include relation.

113. *Apparent motion denied.*—But though in every motion it be necessary to conceive more bodies than one, yet it may be that one only is moved, namely that on which the force causing the change of distance is impressed, or in other words, that to which the action is applied. For however some may define relative motion, so as to term that body *moved,* which changes its distance from some other body, whether the force or action causing that change were applied to it, or no: yet as relative motion is that which is perceived by sense, and regarded in the ordinary affairs of life, it should seem that every man of common sense knows what it is, as well as the best philosopher: now I ask any one, whether in this sense of motion as he walks along the streets, the stones he passes over may be said to *move,* because they change distance with his feet? To me it seems, that though motion includes a relation of one thing to another, yet *it is not necessary that each term of the relation be denominated from it.* As a man may think of somewhat which doth not think, so a body may be moved to or from another body, which is not therefore itself in motion.

114. As the *place* happens to be variously defined, the motion which is related to it varies. A man in a ship may be said to be quiescent, with relation to the sides of the vessel, and yet move with relation to the land. Or he may move eastward in respect of the one, and westward in respect of the other. In the common affairs of life, men never go beyond the earth to define the place

of any body: and what is quiescent in respect of that, is accounted *absolutely* to be so. But philosophers, who have a greater extent of thought, and juster notions of the system of things, discover even the earth itself to be moved. In order therefore to fix their notions, they seem to conceive the corporeal world as finite, and the utmost unmoved walls or shell thereof to be the place whereby they estimate true motions. If we sound our own conceptions, I believe we may find all the absolute motion we can frame an idea of, to be at bottom no other than relative motion thus defined. For as hath been already observed, absolute motion exclusive of all external relation is incomprehensible: and to this kind of relative motion, all the above-mentioned properties, causes, and effects ascribed to absolute motion, will, if I mistake not, be found to agree. As to what is said of the centrifugal force, that it doth not at all belong to circular relative motion: I do not see how this follows from the experiment which is brought to prove it. See *Philosophiæ Naturalis Principia Mathematica, in Schol. Def. VIII.* For the water in the vessel, at that time wherein it is said to have the greatest relative circular motion, hath, I think, no motion at all; as is plain from the foregoing section.

115. For to denominate a body *moved*, it is requisite, *first*, that it change its distance or situation with regard to some other body: and *secondly*, that the force or action occasioning that change be applied to it. If either of these be wanting, I do not think that agreeable to the sense of mankind, or the propriety of language, a body can be said to be in motion. I grant indeed, that it is possible for us to think a body, which we see change its distance from some other, to be moved, though it have no force applied to it (in which sense there may be apparent motion), but then it is, because the force causing the change of distance is *imagined* by us to be applied or impressed on that body thought to move. Which indeed shows we are capable of mistaking a thing to be in motion which is not, and that is all; but does not prove that, in the common acceptation of *motion*, a body is moved merely because it changes distance from another; since as soon as we are undeceived, and find that the moving force was not communicated to it, we no longer hold it to be moved. So on the other hand, when one only body, the parts whereof preserve a given position between themselves, is imagined to exist; some there are who think that it can be moved all manner of ways, though without any change of distance or situation to any other bodies; which we should not deny if they meant only that it might have an impressed

force, which, *upon the bare creation of other bodies, would produce a motion of some certain quantity* and determination. But that an actual motion (distinct from the impressed force, or power productive of change of place, in case there were bodies present whereby to define it) can exist in such a single body, I must confess I am not able to comprehend.

116. *Any idea of pure space relative.*—From what hath been said, it follows that *the philosophic consideration of motion doth not imply the being of an absolute space,* distinct from that which is perceived by sense, and related to bodies : which that it cannot exist without the mind, is clear upon the same principles, that demonstrate the like of all other objects of sense. And perhaps, if we inquire narrowly, we shall find we cannot even frame an idea of *pure space exclusive of all body.* This, I must confess, seems impossible, as being a most abstract idea. When I excite a motion in some part of my body, if it be free or without resistance, I say there is *space* : but if I find a resistance, then I say there is *body* : and in proportion as the resistance to motion is lesser or greater, I say the *space* is more or less *pure.* So that when I speak of pure or empty space, it is not to be supposed, that the word *space* stands for an idea distinct from, or conceivable without body and motion. Though indeed *we are apt to think every noun substantive stands for a distinct idea,* that may be separated from all others : which hath occasioned infinite mistakes. When therefore supposing, all the world to be annihilated besides my own body, I say there still remains *pure space* : thereby nothing else is meant, but only that I conceive it possible for the limbs of my body to be moved on all sides without the least resistance : but if that too were annihilated, then there could be no motion, and consequently no space. Some perhaps may think the sense of seeing doth furnish them with the idea of pure space; but it is plain from what we have elsewhere shown, that the ideas of space and distance are not obtained by that sense. See the Essay concerning Vision.

117. What is here laid down seems to put an end to all those disputes and difficulties which have sprung up amongst the learned concerning the nature of *pure space.* But the chief advantage arising from it is, that we are freed from that dangerous dilemma, to which several who have employed their thoughts on this subject imagine themselves reduced, to wit, of thinking either that real space is God, or else that there is something beside God which is eternal, uncreated, infinite, indivisible, immutable. Both which

may justly be thought pernicious and absurd notions. It is certain that not a few divines, as well as philosophers of great note, have, from the difficulty they found in conceiving either limits or annihilation of space, concluded it must be *divine*. And some of late have set themselves particularly to show, that the incommunicable attributes of God agree to it. Which doctrine, how unworthy soever it may seem of the divine nature, yet I do not see how we can get clear of it, so long as we adhere to the received opinions.

118. *The errors arising from the doctrines of abstraction and external material existences, influence mathematical reasonings.*— Hitherto of *natural philosophy*: we come now to make some inquiry concerning that other great branch of speculative knowledge, to wit, *mathematics*. These, how celebrated soever they may be for their clearness and certainty of demonstration, which is hardly any where else to be found, cannot nevertheless be supposed altogether free from mistakes, if in their principles there lurks some secret error, which is common to the professors of those sciences with the rest of mankind. Mathematicians, though they deduce their theorems from a great height of evidence, yet their first principles are limited by the consideration of quantity; and they do not ascend into any inquiry concerning those transcendental maxims, which influence all the particular sciences, each part whereof, mathematics not excepted, doth consequently participate of the errors involved in them. That the principles laid down by mathematicians are true, and their way of deduction from those principles clear and incontestable, we do not deny. But we hold, there may be certain erroneous maxims of greater extent than the object of mathematics, and for that reason not expressly mentioned, though tacitly supposed throughout the whole progress of that science; and that the ill effects of those secret, unexamined errors are diffused through all the branches thereof. To be plain, we suspect the mathematicians are, as well as other men, concerned in the errors (1) arising from the doctrine of abstract general ideas, and (2) the existence of objects without the mind.

119. *Arithmetic* hath been thought to have for its object *abstract* ideas of *number*. Of which to understand the properties and mutual habitudes is supposed no mean part of speculative knowledge. The opinion of the pure and intellectual nature of numbers in abstract, hath made them in esteem with those philosophers, who seem to have affected an uncommon fineness and elevation of thought. It hath set a price on the most trifling numerical speculations, which in practice are of no use, but serve only for amusement: and hath

therefore so far infected the minds of some, that they have dreamt of mighty *mysteries* involved in numbers, and attempted the explication of natural things by them. But if we inquire into our own thoughts, and consider what hath been premised, we may perhaps entertain a low opinion of those high flights and abstractions, and look on all inquiries about numbers, only as so many *difficiles nugæ*, so far as they are not subservient to practice, and promote the benefit of life.

120. *Unity in abstract* we have before considered in Sect. XIII, from which and what has been said in the Introduction, it plainly follows *there is not any such idea.* But number being defined a *collection of units*, we may conclude that, if there be no such thing as unity or unit in abstract, there are no ideas of number *in abstract* denoted by the numeral names and figures. The theories therefore in arithmetic, if they are abstracted from the names and figures, as likewise from all use and practice, as well as from the particular things numbered, can be supposed to have nothing at all for their object. Hence we may see, how entirely the science of numbers is subordinate to practice, and how jejune and trifling it becomes, when considered as a matter of mere speculation.

121. However since there may be some, who, deluded by the specious show of discovering abstracted verities, waste their time in arithmetical theorems and problems, which have not any use: it will not be amiss, if we more fully consider, and expose the vanity of that pretence; and this will plainly appear, by taking a view of arithmetic in its infancy, and observing what it was that originally put men on the study of that science, and to what scope they directed it. It is natural to think that at first men, for ease of memory and help of computation, made use of counters, or in writing of single strokes, points, or the like, each whereof was made to signify a unit, that is, some one thing of whatever kind they had occasion to reckon. Afterwards they found out the more compendious ways, of making one character stand in place of several strokes, or points. And lastly, the notation of the Arabians or Indians came into use, wherein, by the repetition of a few characters or figures, and varying the signification of each figure according to the place it obtains, all numbers may be most aptly expressed: which seems to have been done in imitation of language, so that an exact analogy is observed betwixt the notation by figures and names, the nine simple figures answering the nine first numeral names and places in the former, corresponding to denominations in the latter. And agreeably to those conditions

of the simple and local value of figures, were contrived methods of finding from the given figures or marks of the parts, what figures, and how placed, are proper to denote the whole, or *vice versa*. And having found the sought figures, the same rule or analogy being observed throughout, it is easy to read them into words; and so the number becomes perfectly known. For then the number of any particular things is said to be known, when we know the names or figures (with their due arrangement) that according to the standing analogy belong to them. For these signs being known, we can, by the operations of arithmetic, know the signs of any part of the particular sums signified by them; and thus computing in signs (because of the connection established betwixt them and the distinct multitudes of things, whereof one is taken for a unit), we may be able rightly to sum up, divide, and proportion the things themselves that we intend to number.

122. In *arithmetic* therefore we regard not the *things* but the *signs,* which nevertheless are not regarded for their own sake, but because they *direct us how to act* with relation to things, and dispose rightly of them. Now agreeably to what we have before observed of words in general (Sect. xix Introd.), it happens here likewise, that abstract ideas are thought to be signified by numeral names or characters, while they do not suggest *ideas of particular things* to our minds. I shall not at present enter into a more particular dissertation on this subject; but only observe that it is evident from what hath been said, those things which pass for abstract truths and theorems concerning numbers are, in reality, conversant about no object distinct from particular numerable things, except only names and characters; which originally came to be considered on no other account but their being *signs,* or capable to represent aptly whatever particular things men had need to compute. Whence it follows, that to study them for their own sake would be just as wise, and to as good purpose, as if a man, neglecting the true use or original intention and subserviency of language, should spend his time in impertinent criticisms upon words, or reasonings and controversies purely verbal.

123. From numbers we proceed to speak of *extension,* which considered as relative, is the object of *geometry*. The *infinite* divisibility of *finite* extension, though it is not expressly laid down, either as an axiom or theorem in the elements of that science, yet is throughout the same every where supposed, and thought to have so inseparable and essential a connection with the principles and demonstrations in geometry, that mathematicians never admit it

into doubt, or make the least question of it.   And as this notion
is the source from whence do spring all those amusing geometrical
paradoxes, which have such a direct repugnancy to the plain
common sense of mankind, and are admitted with so much reluctance into a mind not yet debauched by learning; so is it the
principal occasion of all that nice and extreme subtilty, which
renders the study of *mathematics* so difficult and tedious.   Hence,
if we can make it appear that no finite extension contains
innumerable parts, or is infinitely divisible, it follows that we shall
at once clear the science of geometry from a great number of
difficulties and contradictions, which have ever been esteemed a
reproach to human reason, and withal make the attainment thereof
a business of much less time and pains than it hitherto hath been.

124. Every particular *finite extension*, which may possibly be
the object of our thought, is an *idea* existing only in the mind,
and consequently *each part thereof* must be perceived.   If therefore
I cannot perceive innumerable parts in any finite extension that I
consider, it is certain that they are not contained in it: but it is
evident, that I cannot distinguish innumerable parts in any
particular line, surface, or solid, which I either perceive by sense,
or figure to myself in my mind: wherefore I conclude they are not
contained in it.   Nothing can be plainer to me, than that the
extensions I have in view are no other than my own ideas, and it
is no less plain, that I cannot resolve any one of my ideas into
an infinite number of other ideas, that is, that they are not infinitely
indivisible.   If by *finite extension* be meant something distinct
from a finite idea, I declare I do not know what that is, and so
cannot affirm or deny any thing of it.   But if the terms *extension,
parts*, and the like, are taken in any sense conceivable, that is, for
ideas; then to say a finite quantity or extension consists of parts
infinite in number, is so manifest a contradiction, that every one
at first sight acknowledges it to be so.   And it is impossible it
should ever gain the assent of any reasonable creature, who is not
brought to it by gentle and slow degrees, as a converted gentile
to the belief of *transubstantiation*.   Ancient and rooted prejudices
do often pass into principles: and those propositions which once
obtain the force and credit of a *principle*, are not only themselves,
but likewise whatever is deducible from them, thought privileged
from all examination.   And there is no absurdity so gross, which
by this means the mind of man may not be prepared to swallow.

125. (1) He whose understanding is prepossessed with the *doctrine
of abstract general ideas*, may be persuaded, that (whatever be

thought of the ideas of sense) extension in *abstract* is infinitely divisible. (2) And one who thinks the objects of sense exist *without the mind*, will perhaps in virtue thereof be brought to admit, that a line but an inch long may contain innumerable parts really existing, though too small to be discerned. These errors are grafted as well in the minds of *geometricians*, as of other men, and have a like influence on their reasonings; and it were no difficult thing, to show how the arguments from geometry, made use of to support the infinite divisibility of extension, are bottomed on them. At present we shall only observe in general, whence it is that the mathematicians are all so fond and tenacious of this doctrine.

126. It hath been observed in another place, that the theorems and demonstrations in geometry are conversant about *universal* ideas. (Sect. xv. Intro.) Where it is explained in what sense this *ought* to be understood, to wit, that the particular lines and figures included in the diagram, are supposed to stand for innumerable others of different sizes: or in other words, the geometer considers them abstracting from their magnitude: which doth not imply that he forms an abstract idea, but only that he cares not what the particular magnitude is, whether great or small, but looks on that as a thing indifferent to the demonstration: hence it follows, that a line in the scheme, but an inch long, must be spoken of as though it contained ten thousand parts, since it is regarded not in itself, but as it is universal; and it is universal only in its signification, whereby it represents innumerable lines greater than itself, in which may be distinguished ten thousand parts or more, though there may not be above an inch in it. After this manner *the properties of the lines signified are* (*by a very usual figure*) *transferred to the sign,* and thence through mistake thought to appertain to it considered in its own nature.

127. Because there is no number of parts so great, but it is possible there may be a line containing more, the inch-line is said to contain parts more than any assignable number; which is true, not of the inch taken absolutely, but only for the things signified by it. But men not retaining that distinction in their thoughts, slide into a belief that the small particular line described on paper contains in itself parts innumerable. There is no such thing as the ten-thousandth part of an *inch*; but there is of a *mile* or *diameter of the earth*, which may be signified by that inch. When therefore I delineate a triangle on paper, and take one side not above an inch, for example, in length, to be the *radius*; this I consider as divided into ten thousand or a hundred thousand parts, or more.

For though the ten-thousandth part of that line, considered in itself, is nothing at all, and consequently may be neglected without any error or inconveniency; yet these described lines being only marks standing for greater quantities, whereof it may be the ten-thousandth part is very considerable, it follows, that to prevent notable errors in practice, the *radius* must be taken of ten thousand parts, or more.

128. *Lines which are infinitely divisible.*—From what hath been said the reason is plain why, to the end any theorem may become universal in its use, it is necessary we speak of the lines described on paper, as though they contained parts which really they do not. In doing of which, if we examine the matter throughly, we shall perhaps discover that we cannot conceive an inch itself as consisting of, or being divisible into a thousand parts, but only some other line which is far greater than an inch, and represented by it. And that when we say a line is *infinitely divisible*, we must mean a line which is *infinitely great*. What we have here observed seems to be the chief cause, why to suppose the infinite divisibility of finite extension hath been thought necessary in geometry.

129. The several *absurdities* and contradictions which flowed *from this false principle* might, one would think, have been esteemed so many demonstrations against it. But by I know not what *logic*, it is held that proofs *a posteriori* are not to be admitted against propositions relating to infinity. As though it were not impossible even for an infinite mind to reconcile contradictions. Or as if any thing absurd and repugnant could have a necessary connection with truth, or flow from it. But whoever considers the weakness of this pretence, will think it was contrived on purpose to humour the laziness of the mind, which had rather acquiesce in an indolent scepticism, than be at the pains to go through with a severe examination of those principles it hath ever embraced for true.

130. Of late the *speculations about infinites* have run so high, and grown to such strange notions, as have occasioned no small scruples and disputes among the geometers of the present age. Some there are of great note, who, not content with holding that finite lines may be divided into an infinite number of parts, do yet further maintain, that each of those infinitesimals is itself sub-divisible into an infinity of other parts, or infinitesimals of a second crder, and so on *ad infinitum*. These, I say, assert there are infinitesimals of infinitesimals of infinitesimals, without ever coming to an end. So that according to them an inch doth not

barely contain an infinite number of parts, but an infinity of an infinity *ad infinitum* of parts.   Others there be who hold all orders of infinitesimals below the first to be nothing at all, thinking it with good reason absurd, to imagine there is any positive quantity or part of extension, which though multiplied infinitely, can ever equal to the smallest given extension.   And yet on the other hand it seems no less absurd, to think the square, cube, or other power of a positive real root, should itself be nothing at all; which they who hold infinitesimals of the first order, denying all of the subsequent orders, are obliged to maintain.

131. *Objection of mathematicians.—Answer.*—Have we not therefore reason to conclude, that they are *both* in the wrong, and that there is in effect no such thing as parts infinitely small, or an infinite number of parts contained in any finite quantity?   But you will say, that if this doctrine obtains, it will follow (1) that the very *foundations of geometry are destroyed*: and those great men who have raised that science to so astonishing a height, have been all the while building a castle in the air.   To this it may be *replied*, that whatever is useful in geometry and promotes the benefit of human life, doth still remain firm and unshaken on our principles. That science, considered as *practical*, will rather receive advantage than any prejudice from what hath been said.   But to set this in a due light, may be the subject of a distinct inquiry.   For the rest, though it should follow that some of the more intricate and subtle parts of *speculative mathematics* may be pared off without any prejudice to truth; yet I do not see what damage will be thence derived to mankind.   On the contrary, it were highly to be wished, that men of great abilities and obstinate application would draw off their thoughts from those amusements, and employ them in the study of such things as lie nearer the concerns of life, or have a more direct influence on the manners.

132. *Second objection of mathematicians.—Answer.*—If it be said that several theorems undoubtedly true, are discovered by methods in which *infinitesimals* are made use of, which could never have been, if their existence included a contradiction in it.   I *answer*, that upon a thorough examination it will not be found, that in any instance it is necessary to make use of or conceive infinitesimal parts of finite lines, or even quantities less than the *minimum sensibile*: nay, it will be evident this is never done, it being impossible.

133. *If the doctrine were only an hypothesis it should be respected for its consequences.*—By what we have premised, it is

plain that very numerous and *important errors have taken their rise from those false principles*, which were impugned in the foregoing parts of this treatise. And the opposites of those erroneous tenets at the same time appear to be most fruitful principles, from whence do flow innumerable consequences highly advantageous to true philosophy as well as to religion. Particularly, *matter or the absolute existence of corporeal objects*, hath been shown to be that wherein the most avowed and pernicious enemies of all knowledge, whether human or divine, have ever placed their chief strength and confidence. And surely, if by distinguishing the real existence of unthinking things from their being perceived, and allowing them a substance of their own out of the minds of spirits, (1) *no one thing is explained in nature*; but on the contrary a great many inexplicable difficulties arise: if (2) *the supposition of matter is barely precarious*, as not being grounded on so much as one single reason: if (3) *its consequences cannot endure the light of examination* and free inquiry, but screen themselves under the dark and general pretence of *infinites being incomprehensible*: if withal (4) the removal of this *matter* be not attended with the least evil consequence, if it be not even missed in the world, but every thing as well, nay much easier conceived without it: if lastly (5) both *sceptics* and *atheists* are for ever silenced upon supposing only spirits and ideas, and this scheme of things is perfectly agreeable both to *reason and religion*: methinks we may expect it should be admitted and firmly embraced, though it were proposed only as an *hypothesis*, and the existence of matter had been allowed possible, which yet I think we have evidently demonstrated that it is not.

134. True it is, that in consequence of the foregoing principles, several disputes and speculations, which are esteemed no mean parts of learning, are rejected as useless. But how great a prejudice soever against our notions, this may give to those who have already been deeply engaged, and made large advances in studies of that nature: yet by others, we hope it will not be thought any just ground of dislike to the principles and tenets herein laid down, that they abridge the labour of study, and make human sciences more clear, compendious, and attainable, than they were before.

135. HAVING despatched what we intended to say concerning the knowledge of *ideas*, the method we proposed leads us, in the next place, to treat of *spirits*: with regard to which, perhaps human knowledge is not so deficient as is vulgarly imagined. The great

reason that is assigned for our being thought ignorant of the nature of spirits, is, our not having an idea of it. But surely it ought not to be looked on as a defect in a human understanding, that it does not perceive the idea of *spirit*, if it is *manifestly impossible there should be any such idea*. And this, if I mistake not, has been demonstrated in Sect. XXVII; to which I shall here add that a spirit has been shown to be the only substance or support, wherein the unthinking beings or ideas can exist: but that this *substance* which supports or perceives ideas should itself be an *idea*, or like an *idea*, is evidently absurd.

136. *Objection.—Answer.*—It will perhaps be said, that we want a sense (as some have imagined) proper to know substances withal, which if we had, we might know our own soul, as we do a triangle. To this I *answer*, that in case we had a new sense bestowed upon us, we could only receive thereby *some new sensations or ideas of sense*. But I believe nobody will say, that what he means by the terms *soul* and *substance,* is only some particular sort of idea or sensation. We may therefore infer, that all things duly considered, it is not more reasonable to think our faculties defective, in that they do not furnish us with an idea of spirit or *active thinking* substance, than it would be if we should blame them for not being able to comprehend a *round square*.

137. From the opinion (1) that *spirits are to be known after the manner of an idea* or sensation, have risen many absurd and heterodox tenets, and much scepticism about the nature of the soul. It is even probable, that this opinion may have produced a doubt in some, whether they had any soul at all distinct from their body, since upon inquiry they could not find *they had an idea of it*. That an *idea*, which is inactive, and the existence whereof consists in being perceived, should be the image or likeness of an agent subsisting by itself, seems to need no other refutation, than barely attending to what is meant by those words. But perhaps you will say, that though an *idea* cannot resemble a *spirit*, in its thinking, acting, or subsisting by itself, yet it may in some other respects: and it is not necessary that an idea or image be in all respects like the original.

138. *I answer*, if it does not in those mentioned, it is impossible it should represent it in any other thing. Do but leave out the power of willing, thinking, and perceiving ideas, and there remains nothing else wherein the idea can be like a spirit. For by the word *spirit* we mean only that which thinks, wills, and perceives; this, and this alone, constitutes the signification of that term. If

therefore, it is impossible that any degree of those powers should be represented in an idea, it is evident there can be no idea of a spirit.

139. But it will be objected (2) that if there is no *idea* signified by the terms *soul, spirit,* and *substance,* they are wholly insignificant, or have no meaning in them. I answer, those words do mean or signify a real thing, which is neither an idea nor like an idea, but that which perceives ideas, and wills, and reasons about them. What I am myself, that which I denote by the term I, is the same with what is meant by *soul* or *spiritual substance.* If it be said that this is only quarrelling at a word, and that since the immediate significations of other names are, by common consent, called *ideas,* no reason can be assigned, why that which is signified by the name *spirit* or *soul,* may not partake in the same appellation. I answer, all the unthinking objects of the mind agree, in that they are *entirely passive,* and their existence consists only in being perceived: whereas a soul or spirit is an active being, whose existence consists not in being perceived, but *in perceiving ideas* and thinking. It is therefore necessary, *in order to prevent equivocation,* and confounding natures perfectly disagreeing and unlike, that we distinguish between *spirit* and *idea.* (See Sect. xxvii.)

140. *Our idea of spirit.*—In a large sense indeed, we may be said to have an idea, or rather a notion of *spirit,* that is (1) we understand the meaning of the word, otherwise we could not affirm or deny any thing of it. Moreover (2) as we conceive the ideas that are in the minds of other spirits by means of our own, which we suppose to be *resemblances* of them: so we know other spirits by means of our own soul, which in that sense is the image or idea of them, having a like respect to other spirits, that blueness or heat by me perceived hath to those ideas perceived by another.

141. *The natural immortality of the soul is a necessary consequence of the foregoing doctrine.*—It must not be supposed, that they who assert the natural immortality of the soul are of opinion that it is *absolutely incapable of annihilation,* even by the infinite power of the Creator who first gave it being: but only that it is not liable to be broken or dissolved by the *ordinary laws of nature or motion.* They, indeed, who hold the soul of man to be only a thin vital flame, or system of animal spirits, make it perishing and corruptible as the body, since there is nothing more easily dissipated than such a being, which it is naturally impossible should survive the ruin of the tabernacle wherein it is enclosed. And this notion hath been greedily embraced and cherished by the worst part of

mankind, as the most effectual antidote against all impressions of virtue and religion. But it hath been made evident, that bodies, of what frame or texture soever, are barely passive ideas in the mind, which is more distant and heterogeneous from them, than light is from darkness. We have shown that the soul is indivisible, incorporeal, unextended, and it is consequently *incorruptible*. Nothing can be plainer, than that the motions, changes, decays, and dissolutions, which we hourly see befall natural bodies (and which is what we mean by the *course of nature*), cannot possibly affect an *active, simple, uncompounded* substance: such a being therefore is indissoluble by the force of nature, that is to say, *the soul of man is* naturally *immortal*.

142. After what hath been said, it is I suppose plain, that *our souls are not be known in the same manner as senseless*, inactive *objects*, or by way of *idea*. *Spirits* and *ideas* are things so wholly different, that when we say *they exist, they are known*, or the like, these words must not be thought to signify any thing common to both natures. There is nothing alike or common in them: and to expect that by any multiplication or enlargement of our faculties, we may be enabled to know a spirit as we do a triangle, seems as absurd as if we should hope to *see a sound*. This is inculcated because I imagine it may be of moment towards clearing several important questions, and preventing some very dangerous errors concerning the nature of the soul. We may not, I think, strictly be said to have an idea of an active being, or of an action, although we may be said to have a notion of them. I have some knowledge or notion of my mind, and its acts about ideas, inasmuch as I know or understand what is meant by those words. What I know, that I have some notion of. I will not say that the terms *idea* and *notion* may not be used convertibly, if the world will have it so. But yet it conduceth to clearness and propriety, that we distinguish things very different by different names. It is also to be remarked, that, all relations including an act of the mind, we cannot so properly be said to have an idea, but rather a notion of the relations or habitudes between things. But if, in the modern way, the word *idea* is extended to spirits, and relations, and acts; this is, after all, an affair of verbal concern.

143. It will not be amiss to add, that the doctrine of *abstract ideas* hath had no small share in *rendering those sciences intricate* and obscure, *which are* particularly *conversant about spiritual things*. Men have imagined they could frame abstract notions of the *powers and acts of the mind*, and consider them prescinded, as

well from the mind or spirit itself, as from their respective objects and effects. Hence a great number of dark and ambiguous terms, presumed to stand for abstract notions, have been introduced into metaphysics and morality, and from these have grown infinite distractions and disputes amongst the learned.

144. But nothing seems more to have contributed towards engaging men in controversies and mistakes, with regard to the nature and operations of the mind, *than the being used to speak of those things in terms borrowed from sensible ideas*. For example, the will is termed the *motion* of the soul: this infuses a belief that the mind of man is as a ball in motion, impelled and determined by the objects of sense, as necessarily as that is by the stroke of a racket. Hence arise endless scruples and errors of dangerous consequence in morality. All which, I doubt not, may be cleared and truth appear plain, uniform, and consistent, could but philosophers be prevailed on to retire into themselves, and attentively consider their own meaning.

145. *Knowledge of spirits not immediate.*—From what hath been said, it is plain that *we* cannot *know the existence of other spirits* otherwise than *by their operations,* or *the ideas by them excited in us.* I perceive several motions, changes, and combinations of ideas, that inform me there are certain particular agents *like myself,* which accompany them, and concur in their production. Hence the knowledge I have of other spirits is *not immediate,* as is the knowledge of my ideas; but depending on the intervention of ideas, by me referred to *agents or spirits* distinct from myself, as effects or concomitant signs.

146. But though there be some things which convince us human agents are concerned in producing them; yet it is evident to every one, that those things which are called the works of nature, that is, the far greater part of the ideas or sensations perceived by us, are not produced by, or dependent on, the wills of men. There is therefore some other spirit that causes them, since it is repugnant that they should subsist by themselves. See Sect. xxix. But if we attentively consider the constant regularity, order, and concatenation of natural things, the surprising magnificence, beauty, and perfection of the larger, and the exquisite contrivance of the smaller parts of the creation, together with the exact harmony and correspondence of the whole, but, above all, the never enough admired laws of pain and pleasure, and the instincts or natural inclinations, appetites, and passions of animals; I say if we consider all these things, and at the same time attend to the

meaning and import of the attributes, one, eternal, infinitely wise, good, and perfect, we shall clearly perceive that they belong to the aforesaid spirit, *who works in all, and by whom all things consist.*

147. *The existence of God more evident than that of man.*— Hence it is evident, that God is known as certainly and immediately as any other mind or spirit whatsoever, distinct from ourselves. We may even assert, that the existence of God is far more evidently perceived than the existence of men; because the effects of nature are infinitely *more numerous and considerable* than those ascribed to human agents.   There is not any one mark that denotes a man, or effect produced by him, which doth not more strongly evince the being of that Spirit who is the *Author of nature.*   For it is evident that in affecting other persons, the will of man hath no other object than barely the *motion of the limbs of his body*; but that such a motion should be attended by, or excite *any idea in the mind of another,* depends wholly on the will of the Creator. He alone it is who, " upholding all things by the word of His power," maintains that intercourse between spirits, whereby they are able to perceive the existence of each other.   And yet this pure and clear light, which enlightens every one, is itself invisible to the greatest part of mankind.

148. It seems to be a *general pretence of the unthinking* herd, that *they cannot see God.*   Could we but see Him, say they, as we see a man, we should believe that He is, and believing obey His commands.   But, alas, we need only open our eyes to see the sovereign Lord of all things with a more full and clear view, than we do any one of our fellow-creatures.   Not that I imagine we see God (as some will have it) by a direct and immediate view, or see corporeal things, not by themselves, but by seeing that which represents them in the essence of God, which doctrine is, I must confess, to me incomprehensible.   But I shall explain my meaning. A human spirit or person is not perceived by sense, as not being an idea; when therefore we see the colour, size, figure, and motions of a man, we perceive only certain sensations or ideas excited in our own minds: and these being exhibited to our view in sundry distinct collections, serve to mark out unto us the existence of finite and created spirits like ourselves.   Hence it is plain, we do not see a man, if by *man* is meant that which lives, moves, perceives, and thinks as we do: but only such a certain collection of ideas, as directs us to think there is a distinct principle of thought and motion like to ourselves, accompanying and represented by it.   And

after the same manner we see God; all the difference is, that whereas
some one finite and narrow assemblage of ideas denotes a particular
human mind, whithersoever we direct our view, we do at all times
and in all places perceive manifest tokens of the divinity: every
thing we see, hear, feel, or anywise perceive by sense, being a sign
or effect of the power of God; as is our perception of those very
motions which are produced by men.

149. It is therefore plain, that *nothing can be more evident* to
any one that is capable of the least reflection, *than the existence
of God,* or a Spirit who is intimately present to our minds, producing
in them all that variety of ideas or sensations, which continually
affect us, on whom we have an absolute and entire dependence, in
short, *in whom we live, and move, and have our being.* That the
discovery of this great truth, which lies so near and obvious to the
mind, should be attained to by the reason of so very few, is a sad
instance of the stupidity and inattention of men, who, though they
are surrounded with such clear manifestations of the Deity, are
yet so little affected by them, that they seem as it were blinded
with excess of light.

150. *Objection on behalf of nature.—Answer.—*But you will say,
hath nature no share in the production of natural things, and
must they be all ascribed to the immediate and sole operation of
God? I answer, if by *nature* is meant only the visible *series* of
effects, or sensations imprinted on our minds according to certain
fixed and general laws: then it is plain, that nature taken in this
sense cannot produce any thing at all. But if by *nature* is meant
some being distinct from God, as well as from the laws of nature,
and things perceived by sense, I must confess that word is to me
an empty sound, without any intelligible meaning annexed to it.
Nature in this acceptation is a vain *chimera,* introduced by those
heathens, who had not just notions of the omnipresence and infinite
perfection of God. But it is more unaccountable, that it should
be received among Christians professing belief in the holy scriptures, which constantly ascribe those effects to the *immediate hand
of God,* that heathen philosophers are wont to impute to *nature.*
'' The Lord, He causeth the vapours to ascend; He maketh light-
nings with rain; He bringeth forth the wind out of His treasures,''
(Jer. x, 13.) '' He turneth the shadow of death into the morning,
and maketh the day dark with night '' (Amos v, 8). '' He visiteth
the earth, and maketh it soft with showers: He blesseth the
springing thereof, and crowneth the year with His goodness, so
that the pastures are clothed with flocks, and the valleys are covered

with corn." See Psalm lxv. But notwithstanding that this is the constant language of scripture; yet we have I know not what aversion from believing that God concerns Himself so nearly in our affairs. Fain would we suppose Him at a great distance off, and substitute some blind unthinking deputy in His stead, though (if we may believe St. Paul) He be " not far from every one of us."

151. *Objection to the hand of God being the immediate cause, threefold.—Answer.*—It will I doubt not be objected (1) that the slow and gradual methods observed in the production of natural things, do not seem to have for their cause the *immediate* hand of an *almighty agent.* (2) Besides, monsters, untimely births, fruits blasted in the blossom, rains falling in desert places, (3) miseries incident to human life, are so many arguments that the whole frame of nature is not immediately actuated and superintended by a spirit of infinite wisdom and goodness. But the answer to this objection is in a good measure plain from Sect. LXII, it being visible, that the aforesaid methods of nature are absolutely necessary, in order to working by the most simple and general rules, and after *a steady and consistent manner*; which argues both the *wisdom* and *goodness* of God. Such is the artificial contrivance of this mighty machine of nature, that whilst its motions and various phenomena strike on our senses, the hand which actuates the whole is itself unperceivable to men of flesh and blood. " Verily," saith the prophet, " Thou art a God that hidest Thyself " (Isaiah xlv, 15). But though God conceal Himself from the eyes of the sensual and lazy, who will not be at the least expense of thought; yet to an unbiassed and attentive mind, nothing can be more plainly legible, than the intimate presence of an all-wise Spirit, Who fashions, regulates, and sustains the whole system of being. (*Secondly*), it is clear from what we have elsewhere observed, that the operating according to general and stated laws, is so necessary *for our guidance in the affairs of life,* and letting us into the secret of nature, that without it, all reach and compass of thought, all human sagacity and design could serve to no manner of purpose: it were even impossible there should be any such faculties or powers in the mind. See Sect. XXXI. Which one consideration abundantly outbalances whatever particular inconveniences may thence arise.

152. We should *further consider* (1) that the very blemishes and defects of nature are not without their use, in that they make an agreeable sort of variety, and augment the beauty of the rest of the creation, as shades in a picture serve to set off the brighter

and more enlightened parts. (2) We would likewise do well to examine, whether our taxing the waste of seeds and embryos, and accidental destruction of plants and animals, before they come to full maturity, as an *imprudence* in the author of nature, be not the effect of *prejudice* contracted by our familiarity with impotent and saving mortals. In *man* indeed a thrifty management of those things, which *he cannot procure without much pains* and industry, may be esteemed *wisdom*. But we must not imagine, that the inexplicably fine machine of an animal or vegetable costs the great Creator any more pains or trouble in its production than a pebble doth: nothing being more evident, than that an omnipotent spirit can indifferently produce every thing by a mere *fiat* or act of his will. Hence it is plain, that the splendid profusion of natural things should not be interpreted weakness or prodigality in the agent who produces them, but rather be looked on as an argument of the riches of his power.

153. As for the *mixture of pain*, or uneasiness which is *in the world*, pursuant to the general laws of nature, and the actions of finite imperfect spirits: this, in the state we are in at present, is indispensably necessary to our well-being. But our prospects are *too narrow*: we take, for instance, the idea of *some one particular pain* into our thoughts, and account it *evil*; whereas if we enlarge our view, so as to comprehend the various ends, connections, and dependencies of things, on what occasions and in what proportions we are affected with pain and pleasure, the nature of human freedom, and the design with which we are put into the world; we shall be forced to acknowledge that those particular things, which considered in themselves appear to be *evil*, have the nature of *good*, when considered as *linked with the whole system of beings*.

154. *Atheism and Manicheism would have few supporters if mankind were in general attentive.*—From what hath been said it will be manifest to any considering person, that it is merely for want of attention and comprehensiveness of mind, that there are any favourers of *atheism* or the *Manichean heresy* to be found. Little and unreflecting souls may indeed burlesque the works of Providence, the beauty and order whereof they have not capacity, or will not be at the pains, to comprehend. But those who are masters of any justness and extent of thought, and are withal used to reflect, can never sufficiently admire the divine traces of wisdom and goodness that shine throughout the economy of nature. But what truth is there which shineth so strongly on the mind, that by an aversion of thought, a wilful shutting of the eyes, we may

not escape seeing it? Is it therefore to be wondered at, if the generality of men, who are ever intent on business or pleasure, and little used to fix or open the eye of their mind, should not have all that conviction and evidence of the being of God, which might be expected in reasonable creatures?

155. We should rather *wonder, that men can be found so stupid as to neglect,* than that neglecting they should be unconvinced of such an evident and momentous truth. And yet it is to be feared that too many of parts and leisure, who live in Christian countries, are merely through a supine and dreadful negligence sunk into a sort of *atheism.* Since it is downright impossible, that a soul pierced and enlightened with a thorough sense of the omnipresence, holiness, and justice of that Almighty Spirit, should persist in a remorseless violation of His laws. We ought therefore earnestly to meditate and dwell on those important points; that so we may attain conviction without all scruple, that " the eyes of the Lord are in every place beholding the evil and the good "; that He is with us and keepeth us in all places whither we go, and giveth us bread to eat, and raiment to put on; that He is present and conscious to our innermost thoughts; and that we have a most absolute and immediate dependence on Him. A clear view of which great truths cannot choose but fill our heart with an awful circumspection and holy fear, which is the strongest incentive to *virtue*, and the best guard against *vice*.

156. For after all, what deserves the first place in our studies, is the consideration of God, and our *duty*; which to promote, as it was, the main drift and design of my labours, so shall I esteem them altogether useless and ineffectual if by what I have said I cannot inspire my readers with a pious sense of the presence of God: and having shown the falseness or vanity of those barren speculations, which make the chief employment of learned men, the better dispose them to reverence and embrace the salutary truths of the gospel, which to know and to practise is the highest perfection of human nature.

THREE DIALOGUES
BETWEEN HYLAS AND PHILONOUS, IN OPPOSITION TO SCEPTICS AND ATHEISTS

THE FIRST DIALOGUE

Philonous. GOOD morrow, Hylas: I did not expect to find you abroad so early.

Hylas. It is indeed something unusual: but my thoughts were so taken up with a subject I was discoursing of last night, that finding I could not sleep, I resolved to rise and take a turn in the garden.

Phil. It happened well, to let you see what innocent and agreeable pleasures you lose every morning. Can there be a pleasanter time of the day, or a more delightful season of the year? That purple sky, those wild but sweet notes of birds, the fragrant bloom upon the trees and flowers, the gentle influence of the rising sun these and a thousand nameless beauties of nature inspire the soul with secret transports; its faculties too being at this time fresh and lively, are fit for these meditations, which the solitude of a garden and tranquillity of the morning naturally dispose us to. But I am afraid I interrupt your thoughts; for you seemed very intent on something.

Hyl. It is true, I was, and shall be obliged to you if you will permit me to go on in the same vein; not that I would by any means deprive myself of your company, for my thoughts always flow more easily in conversation with a friend, than when I am alone: but my request is, that you would suffer me to impart my reflections to you.

Phil. With all my heart, it is what I should have requested myself, if you had not prevented me.

Hyl. I was considering the odd fate of those men who have in all ages, through an affectation of being distinguished from the vulgar, or some unaccountable turn of thought, pretended either to believe nothing at all, or to believe the most extravagant things in the world. This however might be borne, if their paradoxes and scepticism did not draw after them some consequences of general disadvantage to mankind. But the mischief lieth here; that when men of less leisure see them who are supposed to have spent their whole time in the pursuits of knowledge, professing an entire ignorance of all things, or advancing such notions as are repugnant to plain and commonly received principles, they will be tempted to entertain suspicions concerning the most important truths, which they had hitherto held sacred and unquestionable.

Phil. I entirely agree with you, as to the ill tendency of the affected doubts of some philosophers, and fantastical conceits of others. I am even so far gone of late in this way of thinking, that I have quitted several of the sublime notions I had got in their schools for vulgar opinions. And I give it you on my word, since this revolt from metaphysical notions to the plain dictates of nature and common sense, I find my understanding strangely enlightened, so that I can now easily comprehend a great many things which before were all mystery and riddle.

Hyl. I am glad to find there was nothing in the accounts I heard of you.

Phil. Pray, what were those?

Hyl. You were represented in last night's conversation, as one who maintained the most extravagant opinion that ever entered into the mind of man, to wit, that there is no such thing as *material substance* in the world.

Phil. That there is no such thing as what philosophers call *material substance*, I am seriously persuaded: but if I were made to see any thing absurd or sceptical in this, I should then have the same reason to renounce this, that I might imagine I have now to reject the contrary opinion.

Hyl. What! can any thing be more fantastical, more repugnant to common sense, or a more manifest piece of scepticism, than to believe there is no such thing as *matter*?

Phil. Softly, good Hylas. What if it should prove, that you who hold there is, are by virtue of that opinion a greater sceptic, and maintain more paradoxes and repugnancies to common sense, than I who believe no such thing?

Hyl. You may as soon persuade me, the part is greater than the whole, as that, in order to avoid absurdity and scepticism, I should ever be obliged to give up my opinion in this point.

Phil. Well then, are you content to admit that opinion for true, which upon examination shall appear most agreeable to common sense, and remote from scepticism?

Hyl. With all my heart. Since you are for raising disputes about the plainest things in nature, I am content for once to hear what you have to say.

Phil. Pray, Hylas, what do you mean by a *sceptic*?

Hyl. I mean what all men mean, one that doubts of every thing.

Phil. He then who entertains no doubt concerning some particular point, with regard to that point cannot be thought a *sceptic*?

Hyl. I agree with you.

Phil. Whether doth doubting consist in embracing the affirmative or negative side of a question?

Hyl. In neither; for whoever understands English, cannot but know that *doubting* signifies a suspense between both.

Phil. He then that denieth any point, can no more be said to doubt of it than he who affirmeth it with that same degree of assurance.

Hyl. True.

Phil. And consequently, for such his ·denial is no more to be esteemed a *sceptic* than the other.

Hyl. I acknowledge it.

Phil. How cometh it to pass then, Hylas, that you pronounce me a *sceptic*, because I deny what you affirm, to wit, the existence of matter? Since, for ought you can tell, I am as peremptory in my denial, as you in your affirmation.

Hyl. Hold, Philonous, I have been a little out in my definition; but every false step a man makes in discourse is not to be insisted on. I said, indeed, that a *sceptic* was one who doubted of every thing; but I should have added, or who denies the reality and truth of things.

Phil. What things? Do you mean the principles and theorems of sciences? but these you know are universal intellectual notions, and consequently independent of matter; the denial therefore of this doth not imply the denying them.

Hyl. I grant it. But are there no other things? What think you of distrusting the senses, of denying the real existence of sensible things, or pretending to know nothing of them? Is not this sufficient to denominate a man a *sceptic*?

Phil. Shall we therefore examine which of us it is that denies the reality of sensible things, or professes the greatest ignorance of them; since, if I take you rightly, he is to be esteemed the greatest *sceptic*?

Hyl. That is what I desire.

Phil. What mean you by sensible things?

Hyl. Those things which are perceived by the senses. Can you imagine that I mean any thing else?

Phil. Pardon me, Hylas, if I am desirous clearly to apprehend your notions, since this may much shorten our inquiry. Suffer me then to ask you this further question. Are those things only perceived by the senses which are perceived immediately? or may those things properly be said to be *sensible*, which are perceived mediately, or not without the intervention of others?

Hyl. I do not sufficiently understand you.

Phil. In reading a book, what I immediately perceive are the letters, but mediately, or by means of these, are suggested to my mind the notions of God, virtue, truth, etc. Now that the letters are truly sensible things, or perceived by sense, there is no doubt: but I would know whether you take the things suggested by them to be so too.

Hyl. No, certainly, it were absurd to think *God* or *virtue* sensible things, though they may be signified and suggested to the mind by sensible marks, with which they have an arbitrary connection.

Phil. It seems then, that by *sensible things* you mean those only which can be perceived immediately by sense.

Hyl. Right.

Phil. Doth it not follow from this, that though I see one part of the sky red, and another blue, and that my reason doth thence evidently conclude there must be some cause of that diversity of colours, yet that cause cannot be said to be a sensible thing, or perceived by the sense of seeing?

Hyl. It doth.

Phil. In like manner, though I hear variety of sounds, yet I cannot be said to hear the causes of those sounds.

Hyl. You cannot.

Phil. And when by my touch I perceive a thing to be hot and heavy, I cannot say with any truth or propriety, that I feel the cause of its heat or weight.

Hyl. To prevent any more questions of this kind, I tell you once for all, that by *sensible things* I mean those only which are perceived by sense, and that in truth the senses perceive nothing which they do not perceive immediately: for they make no inferences. The deducing therefore of causes or occasions from effects and appearances, which alone are perceived by sense, entirely relates to reason.

Phil. This point then is agreed between us, that *sensible things are those only which are immediately perceived by sense.* You will further inform me, whether we immediately perceive by sight any thing beside light, and colours, and figures: or by hearing any thing but sounds: by the palate, any thing besides tastes: by the smell, besides odours: or by the touch, more than tangible qualities.

Hyl. We do not.

Phil. It seems therefore, that if you take away all sensible qualities, there remains nothing sensible.

Hyl. I grant it.

Phil. Sensible things therefore are nothing else but so many sensible qualities, or combinations of sensible qualities.

Hyl. Nothing else.

Phil. Heat then is a sensible thing.

Hyl. Certainly.

Phil. Doth the reality of sensible things consist in being perceived? or, is it something distinct from their being perceived, and that bears no relation to the mind?

Hyl. To *exist* is one thing, and to be *perceived* is another.

Phil. I speak with regard to sensible things only; and of these I ask, whether by their real existence you mean a subsistence exterior to the mind, and distinct from their being perceived?

Hyl. I mean a real absolute being, distinct from, and without any relation to their being perceived.

Phil. Heat, therefore, if it be allowed a real being, must exist without the mind.

Hyl. It must.

Phil. Tell me, Hylas, is this real existence equally compatible to all degrees of heat, which we perceive: or is there any reason why we should attribute it to some, and deny it others? and if there be, pray let me know that reason.

Hyl. Whatever degree of heat we perceive by sense, we may be sure the same exists in the object that occasions it.

Phil. What, the greatest as well as the least?

Hyl. I tell you, the reason is plainly the same in respect of both: they are both perceived by sense; nay, the greater degree of heat is more sensibly perceived; and consequently, if there is any difference, we are more certain of its real existence than we can can be of the reality of a lesser degree.

Phil. But is not the most vehement and intense degree of heat a very great pain?

Hyl. No one can deny it.

Phil. And is any unperceiving thing capable of pain or pleasure?

Hyl. No certainly.

Phil. Is your material substance a senseless being, or a being endowed with sense and perception?

Hyl. It is senseless without doubt.

Phil. It cannot therefore be the subject of pain.

Hyl. By no means.

Phil. Nor consequently of the greatest heat perceived by sense, since you acknowledge this to be no small pain.

Hyl. I grant it.

Phil. What shall we say then of your external object; is it a material substance, or no?

Hyl. It is a material substance with the sensible qualities inhering in it.

Phil. How then can a great heat exist in it, since you own it cannot in a material substance? I desire you would clear this point.

Hyl. Hold, Philonous; I fear I was out in yielding intense heat to be a pain. It should seem rather, that pain is something distinct from heat, and the consequence or effect of it.

Phil. Upon putting your hand near the fire, do you perceive one simple uniform sensation, or two distinct sensations?

Hyl. But one simple sensation.

Phil. Is not the heat immediately perceived?

Hyl. It is.

Phil. And the pain.

Hyl. True.

Phil. Seeing therefore they are both immediately perceived at the same time, and the fire affects you only with one simple, or uncompounded idea, it follows that this same simple idea is both the intense heat immediately perceived, and the pain; and consequently, that the intense heat immediately perceived, is nothing distinct from a particular sort of pain.

Hyl. It seems so.

Phil. Again, try in your thoughts, Hylas, if you can conceive a vehement sensation to be without pain, or pleasure.

Hyl. I cannot.

Phil. Or can you frame to yourself an idea of sensible pain or pleasure in general, abstracted from every particular idea of heat, cold, tastes, smells, etc.?

Hyl. I do not find that I can.

Phil. Doth it not therefore follow, that sensible pain is nothing distinct from those sensations, or ideas, in an intense degree?

Hyl. It is undeniable; and to speak the truth, I begin to suspect a very great heat cannot exist but in a mind perceiving it.

Phil. What! are you then in that *sceptical* state of suspense, between affirming and denying?

Hyl. I think I may be positive in the point. A very violent and painful heat cannot exist without the mind.

Phil. It hath not therefore, according to you, any real being.

Hyl. I own it.

Phil. Is it therefore certain, that there is no body in nature really hot?

Hyl. I have not denied there is any real heat in bodies. I only say, there is no such thing as an intense real heat.

Phil. But did you not say before, that all degrees of heat were equally real: or if there was any difference, that the greater were more undoubtedly real than the lesser?

Hyl. True: but it was, because I did not then consider the ground there is for distinguishing between them, which I now plainly see. And it is this: because intense heat is nothing else but a particular kind of painful sensation; and pain cannot exist but in a perceiving being; it follows that no intense heat can really exist in an unperceiving corporeal substance. But this is no reason why we should deny heat in an inferior degree to exist in such a substance.

Phil. But how shall we able to discern those degrees of heat which exist only in the mind, from those which exist without it?

Hyl. That is no difficult matter. You know, the least pain cannot exist unperceived; whatever therefore degree of heat is a pain, exists only in the mind. But as for all other degrees of heat, nothing obliges us to think the same of them.

Phil. I think you granted before, that no unperceiving being was capable of pleasure, any more than of pain.

Hyl. I did.

Phil. And is not warmth, or a more gentle degree of heat than what causes uneasiness, a pleasure?

Hyl. What then?

Phil. Consequently it cannot exist without the mind in any unperceiving substance, or body.

Hyl. So it seems.

Phil. Since therefore, as well those degrees of heat that are not painful, as those that are, can exist only in a thinking substance;

may we not conclude that external bodies are absolutely incapable of any degree of heat whatsoever?

Hyl. On second thoughts, I do not think it so evident that warmth is a pleasure, as that a great degree of heat is a pain.

Phil. I do not pretend that warmth is as great a pleasure as heat is a pain. But if you grant it to be even a small pleasure, it serves to make good my conclusion.

Hyl. I could rather call it an *indolence.* It seems to be nothing more than a privation of both pain and pleasure. And that such a quality or state as this may agree to an unthinking substance, I hope you will not deny.

Phil. If you are resolved to maintain that warmth, or a gentle degree of heat, is no pleasure, I know not how to convince you otherwise, than by appealing to your own sense. But what think you of cold?

Hyl. The same that I do of heat. An intense degree of cold is a pain; for to feel a very great cold, is to perceive a great uneasiness: it cannot therefore exist without the mind; but a lesser degree of cold may, as well as a lesser degree of heat.

Phil. Those bodies therefore, upon whose application to our own we perceive a moderate degree of heat, must be concluded to have a moderate degree of heat or warmth in them; and those, upon whose application we feel a like degree of cold, must be thought to have cold in them.

Hyl. They must.

Phil. Can any doctrine be true that necessarily leads a man into an absurdity?

Hyl. Without doubt it cannot.

Phil. Is it not an absurdity to think that the same thing should be at the same time both cold and warm?

Hyl. It is.

Phil. Suppose now one of your hands hot, and the other cold, and that they are both at once put into the same vessel of water, in an intermediate state; will not the water seem cold to one hand, and warm to the other?

Hyl. It will.

Phil. Ought we not therefore by your principles to conclude, it is really both cold and warm at the same time, that is, according to your own concession, to believe an absurdity?

Hyl. I confess it seems so.

Phil. Consequently, the principles themselves are false, since you have granted that no true principle leads to an absurdity.

Hyl. But after all, can any thing be more absurd than to say, *there is no heat in the fire?*

Phil. To make the point still clearer; tell me, whether in two cases exactly alike, we ought not to make the same judgment?

Hyl. We ought.

Phil. When a pin pricks your finger, doth it not rend and divide the fibres of your flesh?

Hyl. It doth.

Phil. And when a coal burns your finger, doth it any more?

Hyl. It doth not.

Phil. Since therefore you neither judge the sensation itself occasioned by the pin, nor any thing like it to be in the pin; you should not, conformably to what you have now granted, judge the sensation occasioned by the fire, or any thing like it, to be in the fire.

Hyl. Well, since it must be so, I am content to yield this point, and acknowledge, that heat and cold are only sensations existing in our minds: but there still remain qualities enough to secure the reality of external things.

Phil. But what will you say, Hylas, if it shall appear that the case is the same with regard to all other sensible qualities, and that they can no more be supposed to exist without the mind, than heat and cold?

Hyl. Then indeed you will have done something to the purpose; but that is what I despair of seeing proved.

Phil. Let us examine them in order. What think you of tastes, do they exist without the mind, or no?

Hyl. Can any man in his senses doubt whether sugar is sweet, or wormwood bitter?

Phil. Inform me, Hylas. Is a sweet taste a particular kind of pleasure or pleasant sensation, or is it not?

Hyl. It is.

Phil. And is not bitterness some kind of uneasiness or pain?

Hyl. I grant it.

Phil. If therefore sugar and wormwood are unthinking corporeal substances existing without the mind, how can sweetness and bitterness, that is, pleasure and pain, agree to them?

Hyl. Hold, Philonous; I now see what it was deluded me all this time. You asked whether heat and cold, sweetness and bitterness, were not particular sorts of pleasure and pain; to which I answered simply, that they were. Whereas I should have thus distinguished: those qualities, as perceived by us, are pleasures or pains, but not as existing in the external objects. We must not therefore conclude absolutely, that there is no heat in the fire, or sweetness in the sugar, but only that heat or sweetness, as perceived by us, are not in the fire or sugar. What say you to this?

Phil. I say it is nothing to the purpose. Our discourse proceeded altogether concerning sensible things, which you defined to be the things we *immediately perceive by our senses*. Whatever other qualities therefore you speak of, as distinct from these, I know nothing of them, neither do they at all belong to the point in dispute. You may indeed pretend to have discovered certain qualities which you do not perceive, and assert those insensible qualities exist in fire and sugar. But what use can be made of this to your present purpose, I am at a loss to conceive. Tell me then once more, do you acknowledge that heat and cold, sweetness and bitterness (meaning those qualities which are perceived by the senses), do not exist without the mind?

Hyl. I see it is to no purpose to hold out, so I give up the cause as to those mentioned qualities. Though I profess it sounds oddly, to say that sugar is not sweet.

Phil. But for your further satisfaction, take this along with you: that which at other times seems sweet, shall to a distempered palate appear bitter. And nothing can be plainer, than that divers persons perceive different tastes in the same food, since that which one man delights in, another abhors. And how could this be, if the taste was something really inherent in the food?

Hyl. I acknowledge I know not how.

Phil. In the next place, odours are to be considered. And with regard to these, I would fain know, whether what hath been said of tastes doth not exactly agree to them? Are they not so many pleasing or displeasing sensations?

Hyl. They are.

Phil. Can you then conceive it possible that they should exist in an unperceiving thing?

Hyl. I cannot.

Phil. Or can you imagine, that filth and ordure affect those brute animals that feed on them out of choice, with the same smells which we perceive in them?

Hyl. By no means.

Phil. May we not therefore conclude of smells, as of the other forementioned qualities, that they cannot exist in any but a perceiving substance or mind?

Hyl. I think so.

Phil. Then as to sounds, what must we think of them: are they accidents really inherent in external bodies, or not?

Hyl. That they inhere not in the sonorous bodies, is plain from hence; because a bell struck in the exhausted receiver of an air-pump, sends forth no sound. The air therefore must be thought the subject of sound.

Phil. What reason is there for that, Hylas?

Hyl. Because when any motion is raised in the air, we perceive a sound greater or lesser, in proportion to the air's motion; but without some motion in the air, we never hear any sound at all.

Phil. And granting that we never hear a sound but when some motion is produced in the air, yet I do not see how you can infer from thence, that the sound itself is in the air.

Hyl. It is this very motion in the external air, that produces in the mind the sensation of *sound*. For striking on the drum of the ear, it causeth a vibration, which by the auditory nerves being communicated to the brain, the soul is thereupon affected with the sensation called *sound*.

Phil. What! is sound then a sensation ?

Hyl. I tell you, as perceived by us, it is a particular sensation in the mind.

Phil. And can any sensation exist without the mind?

Hyl. No, certainly.

Phil. How then can sound, being a sensation, exist in the air, if by the *air* you mean a senseless substance existing without the mind.

Hyl. You must distinguish, Philonous, between sound, as it is perceived by us, and as it is in itself; or (which is the same thing) between the sound we immediately perceive, and that which exists without us. The former indeed is a particular kind of sensation, but the latter is merely a vibrative or undulatory motion in the air.

Phil. I thought I had already obviated that distinction by the answer I gave when you were applying it in a like case before. But to say no more of that; are you sure then that sound is really nothing but motion?

Hyl. I am.

Phil. Whatever therefore agrees to real sound, may with truth be attributed to motion.

Hyl. It may.

Phil. It is then good sense to speak of *motion*, as of a thing that is *loud, sweet, acute,* or *grave.*

Hyl. I see you are resolved not to understand me. Is it not evident, those accidents or modes belong only to sensible sound, or *sound* in the common acceptation of the word, but not to *sound* in the real and philosophic sense, which, as I just now told you, is nothing but a certain motion of the air?

Phil. It seems then there are two sorts of sound, the one vulgar, or that which is heard, the other philosophical and real.

Hyl. Even so.

Phil. And the latter consists in motion.

Hyl. I told you so before.

Phil. Tell me, Hylas, to which of the senses, think you, the idea of motion belongs: to the hearing?

Hyl. No, certainly, but to the sight and touch.

Phil. It should follow then, that according to you, real sounds may possibly be *seen* or *felt*, but never *heard*.

Hyl. Look you, Philonous, you may if you please make a jest of my opinion, but that will not alter the truth of things. I own, indeed, the inferences you draw me into sound something oddly: but common language, you know, is framed by, and for the use of the vulgar: we must not therefore wonder, if expressions adapted to exact philosophic notions, seem uncouth and out of the way.

Phil. Is it come to that? I assure you, I imagine myself to have gained no small point, since you make so light of departing from common phrases and opinions; it being a main part of our inquiry to examine whose notions are widest of the common road, and most repugnant to the general sense of the world. But can you think it no more than a philosophical paradox, to say that *real sounds are never heard,* and that the idea of them is obtained by some other sense. And is there nothing in this contrary to nature and the truth of things?

Hyl. To deal ingenuously, I do not like it. And after the concessions already made, I had as well grant that sounds too have no real being without the mind.

Phil. And I hope you will make no difficulty to acknowledge the same of colours.

Hyl. Pardon me; the case of colours is very different. Can any thing be plainer, than that we see them on the objects?

Phil. The objects you speak of are, I suppose, corporeal substances existing without the mind.

Hyl. They are.

Phil. And have true and real colours inhering in them?

Hyl. Each visible object hath that colour which we see in it.

Phil. How! is there any thing visible but what we perceive by sight.

Hyl. There is not.

Phil. And do we perceive any thing by sense, which we do not perceive immediately?

Hyl. How often must I be obliged to repeat the same thing? I tell you, we do not.

Phil. Have patience, good Hylas; and tell me once more whether there is any thing immediately perceived by the senses, except sensible qualities. I know you asserted there was not: but I would now be informed, whether you still persist in the same opinion.

Hyl. I do.

Phil. Pray, is your corporeal substance either a sensible quality or made up of sensible qualities?

Hyl. What a question that is! who ever thought it was?

Phil. My reason for asking was, because in saying, *each visible object hath that colour which we see in it,* you make visible objects to be corporeal substances; which implies either that corporeal substances are sensible qualities, or else that there is something beside sensible qualities perceived by sight: but as this point was formerly agreed between us, and is still maintained by you, it is a clear consequence, that your corporeal substance is nothing distinct from sensible qualities.

Hyl. You may draw as many absurd consequences as you please, and endeavour to perplex the plainest things; but you shall never persuade me out of my senses. I clearly understand my own meaning.

Phil. I wish you would make me understand it too. But since you are unwilling to have your notion of corporeal substance examined, I shall urge that point no further. Only be pleased to let me know, whether the same colours which we see, exist in external bodies, or some other.

Hyl. The very same.

Phil. What! are then the beautiful red and purple we see on yonder clouds, really in them? Or do you imagine they have in themselves any other form than that of a dark mist or vapour?

Hyl. I must own, Philonous, those colours are not really in the clouds as they seem to be at this distance. They are only apparent colours.

Phil. *Apparent* call you them? how shall we distinguish these apparent colours from real?

Hyl. Very easily. Those are to be thought apparent, which, appearing only at a distance, vanish upon a nearer approach.

Phil. And those I suppose are to be thought real, which are discovered by the most near and exact survey.

Hyl. Right.

Phil. Is the nearest and exactest survey made by the help of a microscope, or by the naked eye?

Hyl. By a microscope, doubtless.

Phil. But a microscope often discovers colours in an object different from those perceived by the unassisted sight. And in case we had microscopes magnifying to any assigned degree; it is certain, that no object whatsoever viewed through them, would appear in the same colour which it exhibits to the naked eye.

Hyl. And what will you conclude from all this? You cannot argue that there are really and naturally no colours on objects; because by artificial managements they may be altered, or made to vanish.

Phil. I think it may evidently be concluded from your own concessions, that all the colours we see with our naked eyes, are only apparent as those on the clouds, since they vanish upon a more close and accurate inspection, which is afforded by a microscope. Then as to what you say by way of prevention; I ask you, whether the real and natural state of an object is better discovered by a very sharp and piercing sight, or by one which is less sharp?

Hyl. By the former without doubt.

Phil. Is it not plain from *dioptrics,* that microscopes make the sight more penetrating, and represent objects as they would appear to the eye, in case it were naturally endowed with a most exquisite sharpness?

Hyl. It is.

Phil. Consequently the microscopical representation is to be thought that which best sets forth the real nature of the thing, or what it is in itself. The colours therefore by it perceived, are more genuine and real, than those perceived otherwise.

Hyl. I confess there is something in what you say.

Phil. Besides, it is not only possible but manifest, that there actually are animals, whose eyes are by nature framed to perceive those things, which by reason of their minuteness escape our sight. What think you of those inconceivably small animals perceived by glasses? must we suppose they are all stark blind? Or, in case they see, can it be imagined their sight hath not the same use in preserving their bodies from injuries, which appears in that of other animals? And if it hath, is it not evident, they must see particles less than their own bodies, which will present them with a far different view in each object, from that which strikes our senses? Even our own eyes do not always represent objects to us after the same manner. In the *jaundice*, every one knows that all things seem yellow. Is it not therefore highly probable, those animals in whose eyes we discern a very different texture from that of ours, and whose bodies abound with different humours, do not see the same colours in every object that we do? From all of which, should it not seem to follow that all colours are equally apparent, and that none of those which we perceive are really inherent in any outward object?

Hyl. It should.

Phil. The point will be past all doubt, if you consider, that in case colours were real properties or affections inherent in external bodies, they could admit of no alteration, without some change wrought in the very bodies themselves; but is it not evident from what hath been said, that upon the use of microscopes, upon a change happening in the humours of the eye, or a variation of distance, without any manner of real alteration in the thing itself, the colours of any object are either changed, or totally disappear? Nay, all other circumstances remaining the same, change but the situation of some objects, and they shall present different colours to the eye. The same thing happens upon viewing an object in various degrees of light. And what is more known, than that the same bodies appear differently coloured by candle-light from what they do in the open day? Add to these the experiment of a prism, which, separating the heterogeneous rays of light, alters the colour of any object; and will cause the whitest to appear of a deep blue or red to the naked eye. And now tell me, whether you are still of opinion, that every body hath its true, real colour inhering in it; and if you think it hath, I would fain know further from you, what certain distance and position of the object, what peculiar texture and formation of the eye, what degree or kind of light is necessary for ascertaining that true colour, and distinguishing it from apparent ones?

Hyl. I own myself entirely satisfied, that they are all equally apparent; and that there is no such thing as colour really inhering in external bodies, but that it is altogether in the light. And what confirms me in this opinion, is, that in proportion to the light, colours are still more or less vivid; and if there be no light, then are there no colours perceived. Besides, allowing there are colours on external objects, yet how is it possible for us to perceive them? For no external body affects the mind, unless it act first on our organs of sense. But the only action of bodies is motion; and motion cannot be communicated otherwise than by impulse. A distant object therefore cannot act on the eye, nor consequently make itself or its properties perceivable to the soul. Whence it plainly follows, that it is immediately some contiguous substance, which operating on the eye occasions a perception of colours: and such is light.

Phil. How! is light then a substance?

Hyl. I tell you, Philonous, external light is nothing but a thin fluid substance, whose minute particles being agitated with a brisk motion, and in various manners reflected from the different surfaces of outward objects to the eyes, communicate different motions to the optic nerves; which being propagated to the brain, cause therein various impressions: and these are attended with the sensations of red, blue, yellow, etc.

Phil. It seems, then, the light doth no more than shake the optic nerves.

Hyl. Nothing else.

Phil. And consequent to each particular motion of the nerves the mind is affected with a sensation, which is some particular colour.

Hyl. Right.

Phil. And these sensations have no existence without the mind.

Hyl. They have not.

Phil. How then do you affirm that colours are in the light, since by light you understand a corporeal substance external to the mind?

Hyl. Light and colours, as immediately perceived by us, I grant cannot exist without the mind. But in themselves they are only the motions and configurations of certain insensible particles of matter.

Phil. Colours then, in the vulgar sense, or taken for the immediate objects of sight, cannot agree to any but a perceiving substance.

Hyl. That is what I say.

Phil. Well then, since you give up the point as to those sensible qualities, which are alone thought colours by all mankind beside, you may hold what you please with regard to those invisible ones of the philosophers. It is not my business to dispute about them; only I would advise you to bethink yourself, whether, considering the inquiry we are upon, it be prudent for you to affirm *the red and blue which we see are not real colours, but certain unknown*

motions and figures which no man ever did or can see, are truly so.
Are not these shocking notions, and are not they subject to as
many ridiculous inferences, as those you were obliged to renounce
before in the case of sounds?

Hyl. I frankly own, Philonous, that it is in vain to stand out
any longer. Colours, sounds, tastes, in a word, all those termed
secondary qualities, have certainly no existence without the mind.
But by this acknowledgment I must not be supposed to derogate
any thing from the reality of matter or external objects, seeing
it is no more than several philosophers maintain, who nevertheless
are the furthest imaginable from denying matter. For the clearer
understanding of this, you must know sensible qualities are by
philosophers divided into *primary* and *secondary*. The former are
extension, figure, solidity, gravity, motion, and rest. And these
they hold exist really in bodies. The latter are those above
enumerated; or briefly, all sensible qualities beside the primary,
which they assert are only so many sensations or ideas existing
no where but in the mind. But all this, I doubt not, you are
already apprised of. For my part, I have been a long time
sensible there was such an opinion current among philosophers,
but was never thoroughly convinced of its truth till now.

Phil. You are still then of opinion, that extension and figures
are inherent in external unthinking substances.

Hyl. I am.

Phil. But what if the same arguments which are brought against
secondary qualities, will hold proof against these also?

Hyl. Why then I shall be obliged to think, they too exist only
in the mind.

Phil. Is it your opinion, the very figure and extension which you
perceive by sense, exist in the outward object or material substance?

Hyl. It is.

Phil. Have all other animals as good grounds to think the same
of the figure and extension which they see and feel?

Hyl. Without doubt, if they have any thought at all.

Phil. Answer me, Hylas. Think you the senses were bestowed
upon all animals for their preservation and well-being in life? or
were they given to men alone for this end?

Hyl. I make no question but they have the same use in all other
animals.

Phil. If so, is it not necessary they should be enabled by them
to perceive their own limbs, and those bodies which are capable
of harming them?

Hyl. Certainly.

Phil. A mite therefore must be supposed to see his own foot, and things equal or even less than it, as bodies of some considerable dimension; though at the same time they appear to you scarce discernible, or at best as so many visible points.

Hyl. I cannot deny it.

Phil. And to creatures less than the mite they will seem yet larger.

Hyl. They will.

Phil. Insomuch that what you can hardly discern, will to another extremely minute animal appear as some huge mountain.

Hyl. All this I grant.

Phil. Can one and the same thing be at the same time in itself of different dimensions?

Hyl. That were absurd to imagine.

Phil. But from what you have laid down it follows, that both the extension by you perceived, and that perceived by the mite itself, as likewise all those perceived by lesser animals, are each of them the true extension of the mite's foot, that is to say, by your own principles you are led into an absurdity.

Hyl. There seems to be some difficulty in the point.

Phil. Again, have you not acknowledged that no real inherent property of any object can be changed, without some change in the thing itself?

Hyl. I have.

Phil. But as we approach to or recede from an object, the visible extension varies, being at one distance ten or a hundred times greater than at another. Doth it not therefore follow from hence likewise, that it is not really inherent in the object?

Hyl. I own I am at a loss what to think.

Phil. Your judgment will soon be determined, if you will venture to think as freely concerning this quality, as you have done concerning the rest. Was it not admitted as a good argument, that neither heat nor cold was in the water, because it seemed warm to one hand, and cold to the other?

Hyl. It was.

Phil. Is it not the very same reasoning to conclude, there is no extension or figure in an object, because to one eye it shall seem little, smooth, and round, when at the same time it appears to the other, great, uneven, and angular?

Hyl. The very same. But doth this latter fact ever happen?

Phil. You may at any time make the experiment, by looking

with one eye bare, and with the other through a microscope.

Hyl. I know not how to maintain it, and yet I am loath to give up *extension*, I see so many odd consequences following upon such a concession.

Phyl. Odd, say you? After the concessions already made, I hope you will stick at nothing for its oddness. But on the other hand should it not seem very odd, if the general reasoning which includes all other sensible qualities did not also include extension? If it be allowed that no idea nor any thing like an idea can exist in an unperceiving substance, then surely it follows, that no figure or mode of extension, which we can either perceive or imagine, or have any idea of, can be really inherent in matter; not to mention the peculiar difficulty there must be, in conceiving a material substance, prior to and distinct from extension, to be the *substratum* of extension. Be the sensible quality what it will, figure, or sound, or colour; it seems alike impossible it should subsist in that which doth not perceive it.

Hyl. I give up the point for the present, reserving still a right to retract my opinion, in case I shall hereafter discover any false step in my progress to it.

Phil. That is a right you cannot be denied. Figures and extension being despatched, we proceed next to *motion*. Can a real motion in any external body be at the same time both very swift and very slow?

Hyl. It cannot.

Phil. Is not the motion of a body swift in a reciprocal proportion to the time it takes up in describing any given space? Thus a body that describes a mile in an hour, moves three times faster than it would in case it described only a mile in three hours.

Hyl. I agree with you.

Phil. And is not time measured by the succession of ideas in our minds?

Hyl. It is.

Phil. And is it not possible ideas should succeed one another twice as fast in your mind, as they do in mine, or in that of some spirit of another kind.

Hyl. I own it.

Phil. Consequently the same body may to another seem to perform its motion over any space in half the time that it doth to you. And the same reasoning will hold as to any other proportion: that is to say, according to your principles (since the motions perceived are both really in the object) it is possible one and the same body shall be really moved the same way at once, both very swift and very slow. How is this consistent either with common sense, or with what you just now granted?

Hyl. I have nothing to say to it.

Phil. Then as for *solidity*: either you do not mean any sensible quality by that word, and so it is beside our inquiry: or if you do, it must be either hardness or resistance. But both the one and the other are plainly relative to our senses: it being evident, that what seems hard to one animal, may appear soft to another, who hath greater force and firmness of limbs. Nor is it less plain, that the resistance I feel is not in the body.

Hyl. I own the very sensation of resistance, which is all you immediately perceive, is not in the *body*, but the cause of that sensation is.

Phil. But the causes of our sensations are not things immediately perceived, and therefore not sensible. This point I thought had been already determined.

Hyl. I own it was; but you will pardon me if I seem a little embarrassed: I know not how to quit my old notions.

Phil. To help you out, do but consider, that if extension be once acknowledged to have no existence without the mind, the same must necessarily be granted of motion, solidity, and gravity, since they all evidently suppose extension. It is therefore superfluous to inquire particularly concerning each of them. In denying extension, you have denied them all to have any real existence.

Hyl. I wonder, Philonous, if what you say be true, why those philosophers who deny the secondary qualities any real existence, should yet attribute it to the primary. If there is no difference between them, how can this be accounted for?

Phil. It is not my business to account for every opinion of the philosophers. But among other reasons which may be assigned for this, it seems probable, that pleasure and pain being rather annexed to the former than the latter, may be one. Heat and cold, tastes and smells, have something more vividly pleasing or disagreeable than the ideas of extension, figure, and motion, affect us with. And it being too visibly absurd to hold, that pain or pleasure can be in an unperceiving substance, men are more easily weaned from believing the external existence of the secondary, than the primary qualities. You will be satisfied there is something in this, if you recollect the difference you made between an intense and more moderate degree of heat, allowing the one a real existence, while you denied it to the other. But after all, there is no rational ground for that distinction; for surely an indifferent sensation is as truly *a sensation*, as one more pleasing or painful; and consequently should not any more than they be supposed to exist in an unthinking subject.

Hyl. It is just come into my head, Philonous, that I have somewhere heard of a distinction between absolute and sensible extension. Now though it be acknowledged that *great* and *small*, consisting merely in the relation which other extended beings have to the parts of our own bodies, do not really inhere in the substances themselves; yet nothing obliges us to hold the same with regard to *absolute extension*, which is something abstracted from *great* and *small*, from this or that particular magnitude or figure. So likewise as to motion, *swift* and *slow* are altogether relative to the succession of ideas in our own minds. But it doth not follow, because those modifications exist not without the mind, that therefore absolute motion abstracted from them doth not.

Phil. Pray what is it that distinguishes one motion, or one part of extension from another? Is it not something sensible, as some degree of swiftness or slowness, some certain magnitude or figure peculiar to each?

Hyl. I think so.

Phil. These qualities therefore, stripped of all sensible properties, are without all specific and numerical differences, as the schools call them.

Hyl. They are.

Phil. That is to say, they are extension in general, and motion in general.

Hyl. Let it be so.

Phil. But it is a universally received maxim, that *every thing which exists is particular*. How then can motion in general, or extension in general, exist in any corporeal substance?

Hyl. I will take time to solve your difficulty.

Phil. But I think the point may be speedily decided. Without doubt you can tell, whether you are able to frame this or that idea. Now I am content to put our dispute on this issue. If you can frame in your thoughts a distinct abstract idea of motion or extension, divested of all those sensible modes, as swift and slow, great and small, round and square, and the like, which are acknowledged to exist only in the mind, I will then yield the point you contend for. But if you cannot, it will be unreasonable on your side to insist any longer upon what you have no notion of.

Hyl. To confess ingenuously, I cannot.

Phil. Can you even separate the ideas of extension and motion, from the ideas of all those qualities which they who make the distinction term *secondary*?

Hyl. What! is it not an easy matter, to consider extension and motion by themselves, abstracted from all other sensible qualities? Pray how do the mathematicians treat of them?

Phil. I acknowledge, Hylas, it is not difficult to form general propositions and reasonings about those qualities, without mentioning any other; and in this sense to consider or treat of them abstractedly. But how doth it follow that because I can pronounce the word *motion* by itself, I can form the idea of it in my mind exclusive of body? Or because theorems may be made of extension and figures, without any mention of *great* or *small*, or any other sensible mode or quality; that therefore it is possible such an abstract idea of extension, without any particular size or figure, or sensible quality, should be distinctly formed, and apprehended by the mind? Mathematicians treat of quantity, without regarding what other sensible qualities it is attended with, as being altogether indifferent to their demonstrations. But when laying aside the words, they contemplate the bare ideas, I believe you will find, they are not the pure abstracted ideas of extension.

Hyl. But what say you to *pure intellect*? May not abstracted ideas be framed by that faculty?

Phil. Since I cannot frame abstract ideas at all, it is plain, I cannot frame them by the help of *pure intellect*, whatsoever faculty you understand by those words. Besides—not to inquire into the nature of pure intellect and its spiritual objects, as *virtue—reason, God*, or the like, thus much seems manifest, that sensible things are only to be perceived by sense, or represented by the imagination. Figures therefore and extension, being originally perceived by sense, do not belong to pure intellect. But for your further satisfaction, try if you can frame the idea of any figure, abstracted from all particularities of size, or even from other sensible qualities.

Hyl. Let me think a little——I do not find that I can.

Phil. And can you think it possible, that should really exist in nature, which implies a repugnancy in its conception?

Hyl. By no means.

Phil. Since therefore it is impossible even for the mind to disunite the ideas of extension and motion from all other sensible qualities, doth it not follow, that where the one exist, there necessarily the other exist likewise?

Hyl. It should seem so.

Phil. Consequently the very same arguments which you admitted, as conclusive against the secondary qualities, are without any further application of force against the primary too. Besides, if you will trust your senses, is it not plain all sensible qualities co-exist, or to them appear as being in the same place? Do they ever represent a motion, or figure, as being divested of all other visible and tangible qualities?

Hyl. You need say no more on this head. I am free to own, if there be no secret error or oversight in our proceedings hitherto, that all sensible qualities are alike to be denied existence without the mind. But my fear is, that I have been too liberal in my former concessions, or overlooked some fallacy or other. In short, I did not take time to think.

Phil. For that matter, Hylas, you may take what time you please in reviewing the progress of our inquiry. You are at liberty to recover any slips you might have made, or offer whatever you have omitted, which makes for your first opinion.

Hyl. One great oversight I take to be this: that I did not sufficiently distinguish the *object* from the *sensation*. Now though this latter may not exist without the mind, yet it will not thence follow that the former cannot.

Phil. What object do you mean? The object of the senses?

Hyl. The same.

Phil. It is then immediately perceived?

Hyl. Right.

Phil. Make me to understand the difference between what is immediately perceived, and a sensation.

Hyl. The sensation I take to be an act of the mind perceiving; beside which, there is something perceived; and this I call the *object.* For example, there is red and yellow on that tulip. But then the act of perceiving those colours is in me only, and not in the tulip.

Phil. What tulip do you speak of? is it that which you see?

Hyl. The same.

Phil. And what do you see beside colour, figure, and extension?

Hyl. Nothing.

Phil. What you would say then is, that the red and yellow are co-existent with the extension; is it not?

Hyl. That is not all: I would say, they have a real existence without the mind, in some unthinking substance.

Phil. That the colours are really in the tulip which I see, is manifest. Neither can it be denied, that this tulip may exist independent of your mind or mine; but that any immediate object of the senses, that is, any idea, or combination of ideas, should exist in an unthinking substance, or exterior to all minds, is in itself an evident contradiction. Nor can I imagine how this follows from what you said just now, to wit that the red and yellow were on the tulip *you saw*, since you do not pretend to *see* that unthinking substance.

Hyl. You have an artful way, Philonous, of diverting our inquiry from the subject.

Phil. I see you have no mind to be pressed that way. To return then to your distinction between *sensation* and *object*; if I take you right, you distinguish in every perception two things, the one an action of the mind, the other not.

Hyl. True.

Phil. And this action cannot exist in, or belong to any unthinking thing; but whatever beside is implied in a perception, may.

Hyl. That is my meaning.

Phil. So that if there was a perception without any act of the mind, it were possible such a perception should exist in an unthinking substance.

Hyl. I grant it. But it is impossible there should be such a perception.

Phil. When is the mind said to be active?

Hyl. When it produces, puts an end to, or changes any thing.

Phil. Can the mind produce, discontinue, or change any thing but by an act of the will?

Hyl. It cannot.

Phil. The mind therefore is to be accounted active in its perceptions, so far forth as volition is included in them.

Hyl. It is.

Phil. In plucking this flower, I am active, because I do it by the motion of my hand, which was consequent upon my volition; so likewise in applying it to my nose. But is either of these smelling?

Hyl. No.

Phil. I act too in drawing the air through my nose; because my breathing so rather than otherwise, is the effect of my volition. But neither can this be called *smelling*: for if it were, I should smell every time I breathed in that manner.

Hyl. True

Phil. Smelling then is somewhat consequent to all this.

Hyl. It is.

Phil. But I do not find my will concerned any further. Whatever

266   BRITISH EMPIRICAL PHILOSOPHERS

more there is, as that I perceive such a particular smell or any smell at all, this is independent of my will, and therein I am altogether passive. Do you find it otherwise with you, Hylas?

Hyl. No, the very same.

Phil. Then as to seeing, is it not in your power to open your eyes, or keep them shut; to turn them this or that way?

Hyl. Without doubt.

Phil. But doth it in like manner depend on your will, that in looking on this flower, you perceive *white* rather than any other colour? Or directing your open eyes towards yonder part of the heaven, can you avoid seeing the sun? Or is light or darkness the effect of your volition?

Hyl. No, certainly.

Phil. You are then in these respects altogether passive.

Hyl. I am.

Phil. Tell me now, whether *seeing* consists in perceiving light and colours, or in opening and turning the eyes?

Hyl. Without doubt, in the former.

Phil. Since, therefore, you are in the very perception of light and colours altogether passive, what is become of that action you were speaking of, as an ingredient in every sensation? And doth it not follow from your own concessions, that the perception of light and colours, including no action in it, may exist in an unperceiving substance? And is not this a plain contradiction?

Hyl. I know not what to think of it.

Phil. Besides, since you distinguish the *active* and *passive* in every perception, you must do it in that of pain. But how is it possible that pain, be it as little active as you please, should exist in an unperceiving substance? In short, do but consider the point, and then confess ingenuously, whether light and colours, tastes, sounds, etc., are not all equally passions or sensations in the soul. You may indeed call them *external objects,* and give them in words what subsistence you please. But examine your own thoughts, and then tell me whether it be not as I say?

Hyl. I acknowledge, Philonous, that upon a fair observation of what passes in my mind, I can discover nothing else, but that I am a thinking being, affected with variety of sensations; neither is it possible to conceive how a sensation should exist in an unperceiving substance. But then on the other hand, when I look on sensible things in a different view, considering them as so many modes and qualities, I find it necessary to suppose a material *substratum,* without which they cannot be conceived to exist.

Phil. Material substratum call you it? Pray, by which of your senses came you acquainted with that being?

Hyl. It is not itself sensible; its modes and qualities only being perceived by the senses.

Phil. I presume then, it was by reflection and reason you obtained the idea of it.

Hyl. I do not pretend to any proper positive idea of it. However I conclude it exists, because qualities cannot be conceived to exist without a support.

Phil. It seems then you have only a relative notion of it, or that you conceive it not otherwise than by conceiving the relation it bears to sensible qualities.

Hyl. Right.

Phil. Be pleased therefore to let me know wherein that relation consists.

Hyl. Is it not sufficiently expressed in the term *substratum*, or *substance*?

Phil. If so, the word *substratum* should import, that it is spread under the sensible qualities or accidents.

Hyl. True.

Phil. And consequently under extension.

Hyl. I own it.

Phil. It is therefore somewhat in its own nature entirely distinct from extension.

Hyl. I tell you, extension is only a mode, and matter is something that supports modes. And is it not evident the thing supported is different from the thing supporting?

Phil. So that something distinct from, and exclusive of extension, is supposed to be the *substratum* of extension?

Hyl. Just so.

Phil. Answer me, Hylas. Can a thing be spread without extension? or is not the idea of extension necessarily included in *spreading*?

Hyl. It is.

Phil. Whatsoever therefore you suppose spread under any thing, must have in itself an extension distinct from the extension of that thing under which it is spread.

Hyl. It must.

Phil. Consequently every corporeal substance being the *substratum* of extension, must have in itself another extension by which it is qualified to be a *substratum*: and so on to infinity. And I ask whether this be not absurd in itself, and repugnant to what you granted just now, to wit, that the *substratum* was something distinct from, and exclusive of extension.

Hyl. Aye but Philonous, you take me wrong. I do not mean that matter is *spread* in a gross literal sense under extension. The word *substratum* is used only to express in general the same thing with *substance*.

Phil. Well then, let us examine the relation implied in the term *substance*. Is it not that it stands under accidents?

Hyl. The very same.

Phil. But that one thing may stand under or support another, must it not be extended?

Hyl. It must.

Phil. Is not therefore this supposition liable to the same absurdity with the former?

Hyl. You still take things in a strict literal sense: that is not fair, Philonous.

Phil. I am not for imposing any sense on your words: you are at liberty to explain them as you please. Only I beseech you, make me understand something by them. You tell me, matter supports or stands under accidents. How! is it as your legs support your body?

Hyl. No; that is the literal sense.

Phil. Pray let me know any sense, literal or not literal, that you understand it in.——How long must I wait for an answer, Hylas?

Hyl. I declare I know not what to say. I once thought I understood well enough what was meant by matter's supporting accidents. But now the more I think on it, the less can I comprehend it; in short, I find that I know nothing of it.

Phil. It seems then you have no idea at all, neither relative nor positive, of matter; you know neither what it is in itself, nor what relation it bears to accidents.

Hyl. I acknowledge it.

Phil. And yet you asserted, that you could not conceive how qualities or accidents should really exist, without conceiving at the same time a material support of them.

Hyl. I did.

Phil. That is to say, when you conceive the real existence of qualities, you do withal conceive something which you cannot conceive.

Hyl. It was wrong, I own. But still I fear there is some fallacy or other. Pray what think you of this? It is just come into my head, that the ground of all our mistake lies in your treating of each quality by itself. Now, I grant that each quality cannot singly subsist without the mind. Colour cannot without extension, neither can figure without some other sensible quality. But as the several qualities united or blended together form entire sensible things, nothing hinders why such things may not be supposed to exist without the mind.

Phil. Either, Hylas, you are jesting, or have a very bad memory. Though indeed we went through all the qualities by name one after another; yet my arguments, or rather your concessions no where tended to prove, that the secondary qualities did not subsist each alone by itself: but that they were not *at all* without the mind. Indeed in treating of figure and motion, we concluded they could not exist without the mind, because it was impossible even in thought to separate them from all secondary qualities, so as to conceive them existing by themselves. But then this was not the only argument made use of upon that occasion. But (to pass by all that hath been hitherto said, and reckon it for nothing, if you will have it so) I am content to put the whole upon this issue. If you can conceive it possible for any mixture or combination of qualities, or any sensible object whatever, to exist without the mind, then I will grant it actually to be so.

Hyl. If it comes to that, the point will soon be decided. What more easy than to conceive a tree or house existing by itself, independent of, and unperceived by any mind whatsoever? I do at this present time conceive them existing after that manner.

Phil. How say you, Hylas, can you see a thing which is at the same time unseen?

Hyl. No, that were a contradiction.

Phil. Is it not as great a contradiction to talk of *conceiving* a thing which is *unconceived*?

Hyl. It is.

Phil. The tree or house therefore which you think of, is conceived by you.

Hyl. How should it be otherwise?

Phil. And what is conceived is surely in the mind.

Hyl. Without question, that which is conceived is in the mind.

Phil. How then came you to say, you conceived a house or tree existing independent and out of all minds whatsoever?

Hyl. That was, I own, an oversight: but stay, let me consider what led me into it.—It is a pleasant mistake enough. As I was thinking of a tree in a solitary place, where no one was present to see it, methought that was to conceive a tree as existing unperceived or unthought of, not considering that I myself conceived it all the while. But now I plainly see, that all I can do is to frame ideas in my own mind. I may indeed conceive in my own thoughts the idea of a tree, or a house, or a mountain, but that is all. And this is far from proving, that I can conceive them *existing out of the minds of all spirits*.

Phil. You acknowledge then that you cannot possibly conceive how any one corporeal sensible thing should exist otherwise than in a mind.

Hyl. I do.

Phil. And yet you will earnestly contend for the truth of that which you cannot so much as conceive.

Hyl. I profess I know not what to think, but still there are some scruples remain with me. Is it not certain I see things at a distance? Do we not perceive the stars and moon, for example, a great way off? Is not this, I say, manifest to the senses?

Phil. Do you not in a dream too perceive those or the like objects?

Hyl. I do.

Phil. And have they not then the same appearance of being distant?

Hyl. They have.

Phil. But you do not thence conclude the apparitions in a dream to be without the mind?

Hyl. By no means.

Phil. You ought not therefore to conclude that sensible objects are without the mind, from their appearance or manner wherein they are perceived.

Hyl. I acknowledge it. But doth not my sense deceive me in those cases?

Phil. By no means. The idea or thing which you immediately perceive, neither sense nor reason inform you that it actually exists without the mind. By sense you only know that you are affected with such certain sensations of light and colours, etc. And these you will not say are without the mind.

Hyl. True: but beside all that, do you not think the sight suggests something of *outness* or *distance*?

Phil. Upon approaching a distant object, do the visible size and figure change perpetually, or do they appear the same at all distances?

Hyl. They are in a continual change.

Phil. Sight therefore doth not suggest or in any way inform you, that the visible object you immediately perceive, exists at a distance, or will be perceived when you advance further onward, there being a continued series of visible objects succeeding each other, during the whole time of your approach.

Hyl. It doth not; but still I know, upon seeing an object, what object I shall perceive after having passed over a certain distance: no matter whether it be exactly the same or no: there is still something of distance suggested in the case.

Phil. Good Hylas, do but reflect a little on the point, and then tell me whether there be any more in it than this. From the ideas you actually perceive by sight, you have by experience learned to collect what other ideas you will (according to the standing order of nature) be affected with, after such a certain succession of time and motion.

Hyl. Upon the whole, I take it to be nothing else.

Phil. Now is it not plain, that if we suppose a man born blind was on a sudden made to see, he could at first have no experience of what may be suggested by sight.

Hyl. It is.

Phil. He would not then, according to you, have any notion of distance annexed to the things he saw; but would take them for a new set of sensations existing only in his mind.

Hyl. It is undeniable.

Phil. But to make it still more plain: is not *distance* a line turned endwise to the eye?

Hyl. It is.

Phil. And can a line so situated be perceived by sight?

Hyl. It cannot.

Phil. Doth it not therefore follow that distance is not properly and immediately perceived by sight?

Hyl. It should seem so.

Phil. Again, is it your opinion that colours are at a distance?

Hyl. It must be acknowledged, they are only in the mind.

Phil. But do not colours appear to the eye as co-existing in the same place with extension and figures?

Hyl. They do.

Phil. How can you then conclude from sight, that figures exist without, when you acknowledge colours do not; the sensible appearance being the very same with regard to both?

Hyl. I know not what to answer.

Phil. But allowing that distance was truly and immediately perceived by the mind, yet it would not thence follow it existed out of the mind. For whatever is immediately perceived is an idea: and can any *idea* exist out of the mind?

Hyl. To suppose that were absurd: but inform me, Philonous, can we perceive or know nothing beside our ideas?

Phil. As for the rational deducing of causes from effects, that is beside our inquiry. And by the senses you can best tell, whether you perceive anything which is not immediately perceived. And I ask you, whether the things immediately perceived, are other than your own sensations or ideas? You have indeed more than once, in the course of this conversation, declared yourself on these points; but you seem, by this last question, to have departed from what you then thought.

Hyl. To speak the truth, Philonous, I think there are two kinds of objects, the one perceived immediately, which are likewise called *ideas*; the other are real things or external objects perceived by the mediation of ideas, which are their images and representations. Now I own, ideas do not exist without the mind; but the latter sort of objects do. I am sorry I did not think of this distinction sooner; it would probably have cut short your discourse.

Phil. Are those external objects perceived by sense, or by some other faculty?

Hyl. They are perceived by sense.

Phil. How! is there any thing perceived by sense, which is not immediately perceived?

Hyl. Yes, Philonous, in some sort there is. For example, when I look on a picture or statue of Julius Cæsar, I may be said, after a manner to perceive him (though not immediately) by my senses.

Phil. It seems, then, you will have our ideas, which alone are immediately perceived, to be pictures of external things: and that these also are perceived by sense, inasmuch as they have a conformity or resemblance to our ideas.

Hyl. That is my meaning.

Phil. And in the same way that Julius Cæsar, in himself invisible, is nevertheless perceived by sight; real things, in themselves imperceptible, are perceived by sense.

Hyl. In the very same.

Phil. Tell me, Hylas, when you behold the picture of Julius Cæsar, do you see with your eyes any more than some colours and figures, with a certain symmetry and composition of the whole.

Hyl. Nothing else.

Phil. And would not a man, who had never known any thing of Julius Cæsar, see as much?

Hyl. He would.

Phil. Consequently he hath his sight, and the use of it, in as perfect a degree as you.

Hyl. I agree with you.

Phil. Whence comes it then that your thoughts are directed to the Roman Emperor and his are not. This cannot proceed from the sensations or ideas of sense by you then perceived; since you acknowledge you have no advantage over him in that respect. It should seem therefore to proceed from reason and memory: should it not?

Hyl. It should.

Phil. Consequently it will not follow from that instance, that any thing is perceived by sense which is not immediately perceived. Though I grant we may in one acceptation be said to perceive sensible things mediately by sense: that is, when from a frequently perceived connection, the immediate perception of ideas by one sense suggests to the mind others perhaps belonging to another sense, which are wont to be connected with them. For instance, when I hear a coach drive along the streets, immediately I perceive only the sound; but from the experience I have had that such a sound is connected with a coach, I am said to hear the coach. It is nevertheless evident, that in truth and strictness, nothing can be *heard* but *sound*; and the coach is not then properly perceived by sense, but suggested from experience. So likewise when we are said to see a red-hot bar of iron; the solidity and heat of the iron are not the objects of sight, but suggested to the imagination by the colour and figure, which are properly perceived by that sense. In short, those things alone are actually and strictly perceived by any sense, which would have been perceived, in case that same sense had then been first conferred on us. As for other things, it is plain they are only suggested to the mind by experience grounded on former perceptions. But to return to your comparison of Cæsar's picture, it is plain, if you keep to that, you must hold the real things or archetypes of our ideas are not perceived by sense, but by some internal faculty of the soul, as reason or memory. I would therefore fain know, what arguments you can draw from reason for the existence of what you call *real things or material objects*; or whether you remember to have seen them formerly as they are in themselves; or if you have heard or read of any one that did.

Hyl. I see, Philonous, you are disposed to raillery; but that will never convince me.

Phil. My aim is only to learn from you the way to come at the knowledge of *material beings.* Whatever we perceive, is perceived either immediately or mediately: by sense, or by reason and reflection. But as you have excluded sense, pray show me what reason you have to believe their existence; or what *medium* you can possibly make use of to prove it, either to mine or your own understanding.

Hyl. To deal ingenuously, Philonous, now I consider the point, I do not find I can give you any good reason for it. But thus much seems pretty plain, that it is at least possible such things may really exist; and as long as there is no absurdity in supposing them, I am resolved to believe as I did, till you bring good reasons to the contrary.

Phil. What! is it come to this, that you only believe the existence of material objects, and that your belief is founded barely on the possibility of its being true? Then you will have me bring reasons against it: though another would think it reasonable, the proof should lie on him who holds the affirmative. And after all, this very point which you are now resolved to maintain without any reason, is, in effect, what you have more than once, during this discourse, seen good reason to give up. But to pass over all this; if I understand you rightly, you say our ideas do not exist without the mind; but that they are copies, images, or representations of certain originals that do.

Hyl. You take me right.

Phil. They are then like external things.

Hyl. They are.

Phil. Have those things a stable and permanent nature independent of our senses; or are they in a perpetual change, upon our producing any motions in our bodies, suspending, exerting, or altering our faculties or organs of sense?

Hyl. Real things, it is plain, have a fixed and real nature, which remains the same, notwithstanding any change in our senses, or in the posture and motion of our bodies; which, indeed, may affect the ideas in our minds, but it were absurd to think they had the same effect on things existing without the mind.

Phil. How then is it possible, that things perpetually fleeting and variable as our ideas, should be copies or images of any thing fixed and constant? or in other words, since all sensible qualities, as size, figure, colour, etc., that is, our ideas, are continually changing upon every alteration in the distance, medium, or instruments of sensation; how can any determinate material objects be properly represented or painted forth by several distinct things, each of which is so different from and unlike the rest? Or if you say it resembles some one only of our ideas, how shall we be able to distinguish the true copy from all the false ones?

Hyl. I profess, Philonous, I am at a loss. I know not what to say to this.

Phil. But neither is this all. Which are material objects in themselves, perceptible or imperceptible?

Hyl. Properly and immediately nothing can be perceived but ideas. All material things therefore are in themselves insensible, and to be perceived only by their ideas.

Phil. Ideas then are sensible, and their archetypes or originals insensible.

Hyl. Right.

Phil. But how can that which is sensible be like that which is insensible? Can a real thing in itself *invisible* be like a *colour*; or a real thing which is not *audible,* be like a *sound?* In a word, can any thing be like a sensation or idea, but another sensation or idea?

Hyl. I must own, I think not.

Phil. Is it possible there should be any doubt in the point? Do you not perfectly know your own ideas?

Hyl. I know them perfectly; since what I do not perceive or know, can be no part of my idea.

Phil. Consider therefore and examine them, and then tell me it there be any thing in them which can exist without the mind: or if you can conceive any thing like them existing without the mind.

Hyl. Upon inquiry, I find it is impossible for me to conceive or understand how any thing but an idea can be like an idea. And it is most evident, that *no idea can exist without the mind.*

Phil. You are therefore by your principles forced to deny the reality of sensible things, since you made it to consist in an absolute existence exterior to the mind. That is to say, you are a downright sceptic. So I have gained my point, which was to show your principles led to scepticism.

Hyl. For the present I am, if not entirely convinced, at least silenced.

Phil. I would fain know what more you would require in order to a perfect conviction. Have you not had the liberty of explaining yourself all manner of ways?   Were any little slips in discourse laid hold and insisted on?   Or were you not allowed to retract or reinforce any thing you had offered, as best served your purpose? Hath not every thing you could say been heard and examined with all the fairness imaginable?   In a word, have you not in every point been convinced out of your own mouth?   And if you can at present discover any flaw in any of your former concessions, or think of any remaining subterfuge, any new distinction, colour, or comment whatsoever, why do you not produce it?

Hyl. A little patience, Philonous.   I am at present so amazed tc see myself ensnared, and as it were imprisoned in the labyrinths you have drawn me into, that on the sudden it cannot be expected I should find my way out.   You must give me time to look about me, and recollect myself.

Phil. Hark; is not this the college-bell?

Hyl. It rings for prayers.

Phil. We will go in then if you please, and meet here again to-morrow morning.   In the mean time you may employ your thoughts on this morning's discourse, and try if you can find any fallacy in it, or invent any new means to extricate yourself.

Hyl. Agreed.

THE SECOND DIALOGUE

Hyl. I own there is a great deal in what you say.   Nor can any one be more entirely satisfied of the truth of those odd consequences, so long as I have in view the reasonings that lead to them.   But when these are out of my thoughts, there seems on the other hand something so satisfactory, so natural and intelligible in the modern way of explaining things, that I profess I know not how to reject it.

Phil. I know not what way you mean.

Hyl. I mean the way of accounting for our sensations or ideas.

Phil. How is that?

Hyl. It is supposed the soul makes her residence in some part of the brain, from which the nerves take their rise, and are thence extended to all parts of the body: and that outward objects, by the different impressions they make on the organs of sense, communicate certain vibrative motions to the nerves; and these being filled with spirits, propagate them to the brain or seat of the soul, which according to the various impressions or traces thereby made in the brain, is variously affected with ideas.

Phil. And you call this an explication of the manner whereby we are affected with ideas?

Hyl. Why not, Philonous? have you any thing to object against it?

Phil. I would first know whether I rightly understand your hypothesis. You make certain traces in the brain to be the causes or occasions of our ideas. Pray tell me, whether by the *brain* you mean any sensible thing?

Hyl. What else think you I could mean?

Phil. Sensible things are all immediately perceivable; and those things which are immediately perceivable, are ideas; and these exist only in the mind. Thus much you have, if I mistake not, long since agreed to.

Hyl. I do not deny it.

Phil. The brain therefore you speak of, being a sensible thing, exists only in the mind. Now, I would fain know whether you think it reasonable to suppose, that one idea or thing existing in the mind, occasions all other ideas. And if you think so, pray how do you account for the origin of that primary idea or brain itself?

Hyl. I do not explain the origin of our ideas by that brain which is perceivable to sense, this being itself only a combination of sensible ideas, but by another which I imagine.

Phil. But are not things imagined as truly in the mind as things perceived?

Hyl. I must confess they are.

Phil. It comes therefore to the same thing; and you have been all this while accounting for ideas, by certain motions or impressions in the brain, that is, by some alterations in an idea, whether sensible or imaginable, it matters not.

Hyl. I begin to suspect my hypothesis.

Phil. Beside spirits, all that we know or conceive are our own ideas. When therefore you say, all ideas are occasioned by impressions in the brain, do you conceive this brain or no? If you do, then you talk of ideas imprinted in an idea, causing that same idea, which is absurd. If you do not conceive it, you talk unintelligibly, instead of forming a reasonable hypothesis.

Hyl. I now clearly see it was a mere dream. There is nothing in it.

Phil. You need not be much concerned at it; for after all, this way of explaining things, as you called it, could never have satisfied any reasonable man. What connection is there between a motion in the nerves, and the sensations of sound or colour in the mind? Or how is it possible these should be the effect of that?

Hyl. But I could never think it had so little in it, as now it seems to have.

Phil. Well then, are you at length satisfied that no sensible things have a real existence; and that you are in truth an arrant *sceptic*?

Hyl. It is too plain to be denied.

THE THIRD DIALOGUE

Phil. I am of a vulgar cast, simple enough to believe my senses, and leave things as I find them. To be plain, it is my opinion, that the real things are those very things I see and feel, and perceive by my senses. These I know, and finding they answer all the necessities and purposes of life, have no reason to be solicitous about any other unknown beings. A piece of sensible bread, for instance, would stay my stomach better than ten thousand times as much of that insensible, unintelligible, real bread you speak of. It is likewise my opinion, that colours and other sensible qualities are on the objects. I cannot for my life help thinking that snow is white, and fire hot. You indeed, who by *snow* and *fire* mean certain external, unperceived, unperceiving substances, are in the right to deny whiteness or heat to be affections inherent in them. But I, who understand by those words the things I see and feel, am obliged to think like other folks. And as I am no sceptic with regard to the nature of things, so neither am I as to their existence. That a thing should be really perceived by my senses, and at the same time not really exist, is to me a plain contradiction; since I cannot prescind or abstract, even in thought, the existence of a sensible thing from its being perceived. Wood, stones, fire, water, flesh, iron, and the like things, which I name and discourse of, are things that I know. And I should not have known them, but that I perceived them by my senses; and things perceived by the senses are immediately perceived; and things immediately perceived are ideas; and ideas cannot exist without the mind; their existence therefore consists in being perceived; when therefore they are actually perceived, there can be no doubt of their existence. Away then with all that scepticism, all those ridiculous philosophical doubts. What a jest is it for a philosopher to question the existence of sensible things, till he hath it proved to him from the veracity of God: or to pretend our knowledge in this point falls short of intuition or demonstration! I might as well doubt of my own being, as of the being of those things I actually see and feel.

Hyl. Not so fast, Philonous: you say you cannot conceive how sensible things should exist without the mind. Do you not?

Phil. I do.

Hyl. Supposing you were annihilated, cannot you conceive it possible that things perceivable by sense may still exist?

Phil. I can; but then it must be in another mind. When I deny sensible things an existence out of the mind, I do not mean my mind in particular, but all minds. Now it is plain they have an existence exterior to my mind, since I find them by experience to be independent of it. There is therefore some other mind wherein they exist, during the intervals between the times of my perceiving them: as likewise they did before my birth, and would do after my supposed annihilation. And as the same is true with regard to all other finite created spirits, it necessarily follows, there is an *omnipresent, eternal Mind,* which knows and comprehends all things, and exhibits them to our view in such a manner, and according to such rules as he himself hath ordained, and are by us termed the *laws of nature.*

Hyl. Answer me, Philonous. Are all our ideas perfectly inert beings? Or have they any agency included in them?

Phil. They are altogether passive and inert.

Hyl. And is not God an agent, a being purely active?

Phil. I acknowledge it.

Hyl. No idea therefore can be like unto, or represent the nature of God.

Phil. It cannot.

Hyl. Since therefore you have no idea of the mind of God, how can you conceive it possible, that things should exist in his mind? Or, if you can conceive the mind of God without having an idea of it, why may not I be allowed to conceive the existence of matter, notwithstanding that I have no idea of it ?

Phil. As to your first question: I own I have properly no idea, either of God or any other spirit; for these being active, cannot be represented by things perfectly inert, as our ideas are. I do nevertheless know, that I, who am a spirit or thinking substance, exist as certainly, as I know my ideas exist. Further, I know what I mean by the terms *I* and *myself*; and I know this immediately, or intuitively, though I do not perceive it as I perceive a triangle, a colour, or a sound. The mind, spirit, or soul, is that indivisible, unextended thing, which thinks, acts, and perceives. I say *indivisible*, because unextended, and *unextended*; because extended, figured, moveable things, are ideas; and that which perceives ideas, which thinks and wills, is plainly itself no idea, nor like an idea. Ideas are things inactive, and perceived: and spirits a sort of beings altogether different from them. I do not therefore say my soul is an idea, or like an idea. However, taking the word *idea* in a large sense, my soul may be said to furnish me with an idea, that is, an image, or likeness of God, though indeed extremely inadequate. For all the notion I have of God, is obtained by reflecting on my own soul, heightening its powers, and removing its imperfections. I have therefore, though not an inactive idea, yet in myself some sort of an active thinking image of the Deity. And though I perceive him not by sense, yet I have a notion of Him, or know Him by reflection and reasoning. My own mind and my own ideas I have an immediate knowledge of; and by the help of these, do mediately apprehend the possibility of the existence of other spirits and ideas. Further, from my own being, and from the dependency I find in myself and my ideas, I do by an act of reason necessarily infer the existence of a God, and of all created things in the mind of God. So much for your first question. For the second: I suppose by this time you can answer it yourself. For you neither perceive matter objectively, as you do an inactive being or idea, nor know it, as you do yourself, by a reflex act: neither do you mediately apprehend it by similitude of the one or the other: nor yet collect it by reasoning from that which you know immediately. All which makes the case of *matter* widely different from that of the *Deity*.

Hyl. You say your own soul supplies you with some sort of an idea or image of God. But at the same time you acknowledge you have, properly speaking, no idea of your own soul. You even affirm that spirits are a sort of beings altogether different from ideas. Consequently that no idea can be like a spirit. We have therefore no idea of any spirit. You admit nevertheless that there is spiritual substance, although you have no idea of it; while you deny there can be such a thing as material substance, because you have no notion or idea of it. Is this fair dealing? To act consistently, you must either admit matter or reject spirit. What say you to this?

Phil. I say in the first place, that I do not deny the existence of material substance merely because I have no notion of it, but because the notion of it is inconsistent, or in other words, because it is repugnant that there should be a notion of it. Many things, for aught I know, may exist, whereof neither I nor any other man hath or can have any idea or notion whatsoever. But then those things must be possible, that is, nothing inconsistent must be included in their definition. I say secondly, that although we believe things to exist which we do not perceive; yet we may not believe that any particular thing exists, without some reason for such belief: but I have no reason for believing the existence of matter. I have no immediate intuition thereof: neither can I mediately from my sensations, ideas, notions, actions, or passions, infer an unthinking, unperceiving, inactive substance, either by probable deduction, or necessary consequence. Whereas the being of myself, that is, my own soul, mind, or thinking principle, I evidently know by reflection. You will forgive me if I repeat the same things in answer to the same objections. In the very notion or definition of material substance, there is included a manifest repugnance and inconsistency. But this cannot be said of the notion of spirit. That ideas should exist in what doth not perceive, or be produced by what doth not act, is repugnant. But it is no repugnancy to say, that a perceiving thing should be the subject of ideas, or an active thing the cause of them. It is granted we have neither an immediate evidence nor a demonstrative knowledge of the existence of other finite spirits; but it will not thence follow that such spirits are on a foot with material substances: if to suppose the one be inconsistent, and it be not inconsistent to suppose the other; if the one can be inferred by no argument, and there is a probability for the other; if we see signs and effects indicating distinct finite agents like ourselves, and see no sign or symptom whatever that leads to a rational belief of matter. I say lastly, that I have a notion of spirit, though I have not, strictly speaking, an idea of it. I do not perceive it as an idea or by means of an idea, but know it by reflection.

Hyl. Notwithstanding all you have said, to me it seems, that according to your own way of thinking, and in consequence of your own principles, it should follow that you are only a system of floating ideas, without any substance to support them. Words are not to be used without a meaning. And as there is no more meaning in spiritual substance than in material substance, the one is to be exploded as well as the other.

Phil. How often must I repeat, that I know or am conscious of my own being; and that I myself am not my ideas, but somewhat else, a thinking, active principle that perceives, knows, wills, and operates about ideas? I know that I, one and the same self, perceive both colours and sounds: that a colour cannot perceive a sound, nor a sound a colour: that I am therefore one individual principle, distinct from colour and sound; and, for the same reason, from all other sensible things and inert ideas. But I am not in like manner conscious either of the existence or essence of matter. On the contrary, I know that nothing inconsistent can exist, and that the existence of matter implies an inconsistency. Further, I know what I mean, when I affirm that there is a spiritual substance or support of ideas, that is, that a spirit knows and perceives ideas. But I do not know what is meant, when it is said, that an unperceiving substance hath inherent in it and supports either ideas or the archetypes of ideas. There is therefore upon the whole no parity of case between spirit and matter.

Hyl. I own myself satisfied in this point. But do you in earnest think, the real existence of sensible things consists in their being actually perceived? If so, how comes it that all mankind distinguish between them? Ask the first man you meet, and he shall tell you, *to be perceived* is one thing, and *to exist* is another.

Phil. I am content, Hylas, to appeal to the common sense of the world for the truth of my notion. Ask the gardener, why he thinks yonder cherry-tree exists in the garden, and he shall tell you, because he sees and feels it; in a word, because he perceives it by his senses. Ask him, why he thinks an orange-tree not to be there, and he shall tell you, because he does not perceive it. What he perceives by sense, that he terms a real being, and saith it *is*, or *exists*; but that which is not perceivable, the same, he saith, hath no being.

Hyl. Yes, Philonous, I grant the existence of a sensible thing actually consists in being perceivable, but not in being actually perceived.

Phil. And what is perceivable but an idea? And can an idea exist without being actually perceived? These are points long since agreed between us.

Hyl. But be your opinion never so true, yet surely you will not deny it is shocking, and contrary to the common sense of men. Ask the fellow, whether yonder tree hath an existence out of his mind: what answer, think you, he would make?

Phil. The same that I should myself, to wit, that it doth exist out of his mind. But then to a Christian it cannot surely be shocking to say, the real tree existing without his mind is truly known and comprehended by (that is, *exists in*) the infinite mind of God. Probably he may not at first glance be aware of the direct and immediate proof there is of this, inasmuch as the very being of a tree, or any other sensible thing, implies a mind wherein it is. But the point itself he cannot deny. The question between the materialists and me is not, whether things have a real existence out of the mind of this or that person, but whether they have an absolute existence, distinct from being perceived by God, and exterior to all minds. This indeed some heathens and philosophers have affirmed, but whoever entertains notions of the Deity suitable to the holy scriptures, will be of another opinion.

Hyl. But according to your notions, what difference is there between real things, and chimeras formed by the imagination, or the visions of a dream, since they are all equally in the mind?

Phil. The ideas formed by the imagination are faint and indistinct; they have besides an entire dependence on the will. But the ideas perceived by sense, that is, real things, are more vivid and clear, and being imprinted on the mind by a spirit distinct from us, have not a like dependence on our will. There is therefore no danger of confounding these with the foregoing: and there is as little of confounding them with the visions of a dream, which are dim, irregular, and confused. And though they should happen to be never so lively and natural, yet by their not being connected, and of a piece with the preceding and subsequent transactions of our lives, they might easily be distinguished from realities. In short, by whatever method you distinguish *things* from *chimeras* on your own scheme, the same, it is evident, will hold also upon mine. For it must be, I presume, by some perceived difference, and I am not for depriving you of any one thing that you perceive.

Hyl. But still, Philonous, you hold, there is nothing in the world but spirits and ideas. And this, you must needs acknowledge, sounds very oddly.

Phil. I own the word *idea*, not being commonly used for *thing*, sounds something out of the way. My reason for using it was, because a necessary relation to the mind is understood to be implied by that term; and it is now commonly used by philosophers, to denote the immediate objects of the understanding. But however oddly the proposition may sound in words, yet it includes nothing so very strange or shocking in its sense, which in effect amounts to no more than this, to wit, that there are only things perceiving, and things perceived; or that every unthinking being is necessarily, and from the very nature of its existence, perceived by some mind; if not by any finite created mind, yet certainly by the infinite mind of God, in whom " we live, and move, and have our being." Is this as strange as to say, the sensible qualities are not on the objects : or, that we cannot be sure of the existence of things, or know any thing of their real natures, though we both see and feel them, and perceive them by all our senses?

Hyl. And in consequence of this, must we not think there are no such things as physical or corporeal causes; but that a spirit is the immediate cause of all the phenomena in nature? Can there be any thing more extravagant than this?

Phil. Yes, it is infinitely more extravagant to say, a thing which is inert, operates on the mind, and which is unperceiving, is the cause of our perceptions. Besides, that which to you, I know not for what reason, seems so extravagant, is no more than the holy scriptures assert in a hundred places. In them God is represented as the sole and immediate author of all those effects, which some heathens and philosophers are wont to ascribe to nature, matter, fate, or the like unthinking principle. This is so much the constant language of scripture, that it were needless to confirm it by citations.

*   *   *   *   *   *

Hyl. What say you to this? Since, according to you, men judge of the reality of things by their senses, how can a man be mistaken in thinking the moon a plain lucid surface, about a foot in diameter; or a square tower, seen at a distance, round; or an oar, with one end in the water, crooked?

Phil. He is not mistaken with regard to the ideas he actually perceives; but in the inferences he makes from his present perceptions. Thus in the case of the oar, what he immediately perceives by sight in certainly crooked; and so far he is in the right. But if he thence conclude, that upon taking the oar out of the water, he shall perceive the same crookedness, or that it would affect his touch as crooked things are wont to do, in that he is mistaken. In like manner, if he should conclude from what he perceives in one station, that in case he advances toward the moon or tower, he should still be affected with the like ideas, he is mistaken. But his mistake lies not in what he perceives immediately and at present (it being a manifest contradiction to suppose he should err in respect of that), but in the wrong judgment he makes concerning the ideas he apprehends to be connected with those immediately perceived : or concerning the ideas that, from what he preceives at present, he imagines would be perceived in other circumstances. The case is the same with regard to the Copernican system. We do not here perceive any motion of the earth : but it were erroneous thence to conclude, that in case we were placed at as great a distance from that, as we are now from the other planets, we should not then perceive its motion.

*   *   *   *   *   *

Phil. I am not for changing things into ideas, but rather ideas into things; since those immediate objects of perception, which, according to you, are only appearances of things, I take to be the real things themselves.

Hyl. Things! you may pretend what you please; but it is certain, you leave us nothing but the empty forms of things, the outside only which strikes the senses.

Phil. What you call the empty forms and outside of things, seems to me the very things themselves.   Nor are they empty or incomplete otherwise, than upon your supposition, that matter is an essential part of all corporeal things.   We both therefore agree in this, that we perceive only sensible forms : but herein we differ, you will have them to be empty appearances, I real beings.   In short you do not trust your senses, I do.

*   *   *   *   *   *

Hyl. But the same idea which is in my mind, cannot be in yours, or in any other mind.   Doth it not therefore follow from your principles, that no two can see the same thing?   And is not this highly absurd?

Phil. If the term *same* be taken in the vulgar acceptation, it is certain (and not at all repugnant to the principles I maintain) that different persons may perceive the same thing; or the same thing or idea exist in different minds.   Words are of arbitrary imposition; and since men are used to apply the word *same* where no distinction or variety is perceived, and I do not pretend to alter their perceptions, it follows, that as men have said before, *several saw the same thing*, so they may upon like occasions still continue to use the same phrase, without any deviation either from propriety of language, or the truth of things.   But if the term *same* be used in the acceptation of philosophers, who pretend to an abstracted notion of identity, then, according to their sundry definitions of this notion (for it is not yet agreed wherein that philosophic identity consists), it may or may not be possible for divers persons

to perceive the same thing.   But whether philosophers shall think
fit to call a thing the *same* or no, is, I conceive, of small importance.
Let us suppose several men together, all endued with the same
faculties, and consequently affected in like sort by their senses,
and who had yet never known the use of language; they would
without question agree in their perceptions.   Though perhaps, when
they came to the use of speech, some regarding the uniformness
of what was perceived, might call it the *same* thing: others
especially regarding the diversity of persons who perceived, might
choose the denomination of different things.   But who sees not that
all the dispute is about a word; to wit, whether what is perceived
by different persons, may yet have the term *same* applied to it?
Or suppose a house, whose walls or outward shell remaining
unaltered, the chambers are all pulled down, and new ones built
in their place; and that you should call this the *same*, and I should
say it was not the *same* house: would we not for all this perfectly
agree in our thoughts of the house, considered in itself?   And
would not all the difference consist in a sound?   If you should
say, we differ in our notions; for that you super-added to your
idea of a house the simple abstracted idea of identity, whereas I
did not; I would tell you I know not what you mean by that
abstracted idea of identity; and should desire you to look into
your own thoughts, and be sure you understood yourself.——Why
so silent, Hylas?   Are you not yet satisfied, men may dispute
about identity and diversity, without any real difference in their
thoughts and opinions, abstracted from names?   Take this further
reflection with you: that whether matter be allowed to exist or
no, the case is exactly the same as the point in hand.   For the
materialists themselves acknowledge what we immediately perceive
by our senses to be our own ideas.   Your difficulty therefore, that
no two see the same thing, makes equally against the materialists
and me.

*   *   *   *   *   *

Hyl. I own myself entirely satisfied for the present in all respects.
But what security can I have that I shall still continue the same
full assent to your opinion, and that no unthought-of objection or
difficulty will occur hereafter?

Phil. Pray, Hylas, do you in other cases, when a point is once
evidently proved, withhold your assent on account of objections or
difficulties it may be liable to?   Are the difficulties that attend
the doctrine of incommensurable quantities, of the angle of contact,

of the asymptotes to curves, or the like, sufficient to make you hold out against mathematical demonstration? Or will you disbelieve the providence of God, because there may be some particular things which you know not how to reconcile with it? If there are difficulties attending immaterialism, there are at the same time direct and evident proofs for it. But for the existence of matter there is not one proof, and far more numerous and insurmountable objections lie against it. But where are those mighty difficulties you insist on? Alas! you know not where or what they are; something which may possibly occur hereafter. If this be a sufficient pretence for withholding your full assent, you should never yield it to any proposition, how free soever from exceptions, how clearly and solidly soever demonstrated.

Hyl. You have satisfied me, Philonous.

Phil. But to arm you against all future objections, do but consider, that which bears equally hard on two contradictory opinions, can be a proof against neither. Whenever therefore any difficulty occurs, try if you can find a solution for it on the hypothesis of the *materialists.* Be not deceived by words; but sound your own thoughts. And in case you cannot conceive it easier by the help of *materialism,* it is plain it can be no objection against *immaterialism.* Had you proceeded all along by this rule, you would probably have spared yourself abundance of trouble in objecting; since of all your difficulties I challenge you to show one that is explained by matter; nay, which is not more unintelligible with, than without that supposition, and consequently makes rather *against* than *for* it. You should consider in each particular, whether the difficulty arises from the *non-existence of matter.* If it doth not, you might as well argue from the infinite divisibility of extension against the divine prescience, as from such a difficulty against *immaterialism.* And yet upon recollection I believe you will find this to have been often, if not always the case. You should likewise take heed not to argue on a *petitio principii.* One is apt to say, the unknown substances ought to be esteemed real things, rather than the ideas in our minds: and who can tell but the unthinking external substance may concur as a cause or instrument in the production of our ideas? But is not this proceeding on a supposition that there are such external substances? And to suppose this, is it not begging the question? But above all things you should beware of imposing on yourself by that vulgar sophism, which is called *ignoratio elenchi.* You talked often as if you thought I maintained the non-existence of sensible things:

whereas in truth no one can be more thoroughly assured of their existence than I am, and it is you who doubt; I should have said, positively deny it. Every thing that is seen, felt, heard, or any way perceived by the senses, is, on the principles I embrace, a real being, but not on yours. Remember the matter you contend for is an unknown somewhat (if indeed it may be termed *somewhat*), which is quite stripped of all sensible qualities, and can neither be perceived by sense, nor apprehended by the mind. Remember, I say, that it is not any object which is hard or soft, hot or cold, blue or white, round or square, etc. For all these things I affirm do exist. Though indeed I deny they have any existence distinct from being perceived; or that they exist out of all minds whatsoever. Think on these points; let them be attentively considered and still kept in view. Otherwise you will not comprehend the state of the question; without which your objections will always be wide of the mark, and instead of mine, may possibly be directed (as more than once they have been) against your own notions.

Hyl. I must needs own, Philonous, nothing seems to have kept me from agreeing with you more than this same *mistaking the question*. In denying matter, at first glimpse I am tempted to imagine you deny the things we see and feel; but upon reflection find there is no ground for it. What think you therefore of retaining the name *matter*, and applying it to sensible things? This may be done without any change in your sentiments: and believe me it would be a means of reconciling them to some persons, who may be more shocked at an innovation in words than in opinion.

Phil. With all my heart: retain the word *matter*, and apply it to the objects of sense, if you please, provided you do not attribute to them any subsistence distinct from their being perceived. I shall never quarrel with you for an expression. *Matter*, or *material substance*, are terms introduced by philosophers; and as used by them, imply a sort of independency, or a subsistence distinct from being perceived by a mind: but are never used by common people; or if ever, it is to signify the immediate objects of sense. One would think therefore, so long as the names of all particular things, with the terms *sensible*, *substance*, *body*, *stuff*, and the like, are retained, the word *matter* should be never missed in common talk. And in philosophical discourses it seems the best way to leave it quite out; since there is not perhaps any one thing that hath more favoured and strengthened the depraved bent of the mind toward *atheism*, than the use of that general confused term.

Hyl. Well but, Philonous, since I am content to give up the notion of an unthinking substance exterior to the mind, I think you ought not to deny me the privilege of using the word *matter* as I please, and annexing it to a collection of sensible qualities subsisting only in the mind. I freely own there is no other substance in a strict sense, than *spirit*. But I have been so long accustomed to the term *matter*, that I know not how to part with it. To say, there is no *matter* in the world, is still shocking to me. Whereas to say, there is no *matter*, if by that term be meant an unthinking substance existing without the mind; but if by matter is meant some sensible thing, whose existence consists in being perceived, then there is *matter*: this distinction gives it quite another turn: and men will come into your notions with small difficulty, when they are proposed in that manner. For after all, the controversy about matter, in the strict acceptation of it, lies altogether between you and the philosophers, whose principles, I acknowledge, are not near so natural, or so agreeable to the common sense of mankind, and holy scripture, as yours. There is nothing we either desire or shun, but as it makes, or is apprehended to make some part of our happiness or misery. But what hath happiness or misery, joy or grief, pleasure or pain, to do with absolute existence, or with unknown entities, abstracted from all relation to us? It is evident, things regard us only as they are pleasing or displeasing: and they can please or displease only so far forth as they are perceived. Further therefore we are not concerned; and thus far you leave things as you found them. Yet still there is something new in this doctrine. It is plain, I do not now think with the philosophers, nor yet altogether with the vulgar. I would know how the case stands in that respect: precisely, what you have added to, or altered in my former notions.

Phil. I do not pretend to be a setter-up of *new notions*. My endeavours tend only to unite and place in a clearer light that truth, which was before shared between the vulgar and the philosophers: the former being of opinion, that *those things they immediately perceive are the real things*: and the latter, that *the things immediately perceived are ideas which exist only in the mind*. Which two notions put together, do in effect constitute the substance of what I advance.

Hyl. I have been a long time distrusting my senses; methought I saw things by a dim light, and through false glasses. Now the glasses are removed, and a new light breaks in upon my understanding. I am clearly convinced that I see things in their native forms; and am no longer in pain about their unknown natures or absolute existence. This is the state I find myself in at present: though indeed the course that brought me to it I do not yet thoroughly comprehend. You set out upon the same principles that Academics, Cartesians, and the like sects, usually do; and for a long time it looked as if you were advancing their philosophical scepticism; but in the end your conclusions are directly opposite to theirs.

Phil. You see, Hylas, the water of yonder fountain, how it is forced upwards, in a round column, to a certain height; at which it breaks and falls back into the basin from whence it rose: its ascent, as well as descent, proceeding from the same uniform law or principle of *gravitation*. Just so, the same principles which at first view lead to scepticism, pursued to a certain point, bring men back to common sense.

DAVID HUME

Born at Edinburgh, 1711. Attended University of Edinburgh. Retired to France to write Treatise, 1734-1737. Judge-advocate-general to General St. Clair, 1747. Librarian to Faculty of Advocates in Edinburgh, 1752. Write History of England. Secretary to the Embassy in Paris, 1765, and for a short time chargé d'affaires. Under-Secretary to the Secretary of State, 1767-68. Died at Edinburgh, 1776.

Philosophical works include A Treatise of Human Nature, *Books 1 and 2, 1739, Book 3, 1740,* An Enquiry Concerning Human Understanding, *1748,* An Enquiry Concerning the Principles of Morals, *1751, and the posthumously published* Dialogues Concerning Natural Religion.

THE FIRST book of the *Treatise* is reprinted here in full, with the exception of a short chapter on *the Reason of Animals*, which contains little of interest, and a rather long chapter on *the Immateriality of the Soul*, in which Hume maintains among other things that the notion of Substance, as something underlying either perceptions or objects, is unintelligible, that the supposed distinction between " extended " matter and " unextended " thought reduces to the fact that some perceptions are spatial and others not, that we have " no idea of a Being endowed with any power," and *a fortiori* no idea of a Supreme Being endowed with infinite power, and that since, " to consider the matter *a priori*, anything may produce anything," there is no reason why there should not be casual relations between " matter " and " thought." The chapter as a whole is well worth reading, but it was thought possible to omit it as it is largely an application of doctrines which are developed elsewhere in the book. The second and third books of the *Treatise*, which are not reprinted here, deal with questions of psychology and moral philosophy.

The *Enquiry Concerning Human Understanding* covers very much the same ground as the first book of the *Treatise*. It is better written, but for the most part of smaller philosophical interest. The few passages which are here included either introduce new material or else re-state certain points in a more effective way.

A TREATISE OF HUMAN NATURE

INTRODUCTION

NOTHING is more usual and more natural for those, who pretend to discover anything new to the world in philosophy and the sciences, than to insinuate the praises of their own systems, by decrying all those which have been advanced before them. And indeed were they content with lamenting that ignorance, which we still lie under in the most important questions that can come before the tribunal of human reason, there are few, who have an acquaintance with the sciences, that would not readily agree with them. It is easy for one of judgment and learning, to perceive the weak foundation even of those systems, which have obtained the greatest credit, and have carried their pretensions highest to accurate and profound reasoning. Principles taken upon trust, consequences lamely deduced from them, want of coherence in the parts, and of evidence in the whole, these are everywhere to be met with in the systems of the most eminent philosophers, and seem to have drawn disgrace upon philosophy itself.

Nor is there required such profound knowledge to discover the present imperfect condition of the sciences, but even the rabble without doors may judge from the noise and clamour which they hear, that all goes not well within. There is nothing which is not the subject of debate, and in which men of learning are not of contrary opinions. The most trivial question escapes not our controversy, and in the most momentous we are not able to give any certain decision. Disputes are multiplied, as if everything was uncertain. Amidst all this bustle, it is not reason which carries the pride, but eloquence; and no man needs ever despair of gaining proselytes to the most extravagant hypothesis, who has art enough to represent it in any favourable colours. The victory is not gained by the men at arms, who manage the pike and the sword, but by the trumpeters, drummers, and musicians of the army.

From hence, in my opinion, arises that common prejudice against

293

metaphysical reasonings of all kinds, even amongst those who profess themselves scholars, and have a just value for every other part of literature. By metaphysical reasonings, they do not understand those on any particular branch of science, but every kind of argument which is any way abstruse, and requires some attention to be comprehended. We have so often lost our labour in such researches, that we commonly reject them without hesitation, and resolve, if we must for ever be a prey to errors and delusions, that they shall at least be natural and entertaining. And, indeed, nothing but the most determined scepticism, along with a great degree of indolence, can justify this aversion to metaphysics. For, if truth be at all within the reach of human capacity, it is certain it must lie very deep and abstruse; and to hope we shall arrive at it without pains, while the greatest geniuses have failed with the utmost pains, must certainly be esteemed sufficiently vain and presumptuous. I pretend to no such advantage in the philosophy I am going to unfold, and would esteem it a strong presumption against it, were it so very easy and obvious.

It is evident, that all the sciences have a relation, greater or less, to human nature; and that, however wide any of them may seem to run from it, they still return back by one passage or another. Even *Mathematics*, *Natural Philosophy*, and *Natural Religion*, are in some measure dependent on the science of MAN; since they lie under the cognisance of men, and are judged of by their powers and faculties. It is impossible to tell what changes and improvements we might make in these sciences were we thoroughly acquainted with the extent and force of human understanding, and could explain the nature of the ideas we employ, and of the operations we perform in our reasonings. And these improvements are the more to be hoped for in natural religion, as it is not content with instructing us in the nature of superior powers, but carries its views further, to their disposition towards us, and our duties towards them; and consequently, we ourselves are not only the beings that reason, but also one of the objects concerning which we reason.

If, therefore, the sciences of mathematics, natural philosophy, and natural religion, have such a dependence on the knowledge of man, what may be expected in the other sciences, whose connection with human nature is more close and intimate? The sole end of logic is to explain the principles and operations of our reasoning faculty, and the nature of our ideas; morals and criticism regard our tastes and sentiments; and politics consider men as united in

society, and dependent on each other. In these four sciences of
Logic, Morals, Criticism, and *Politics,* is comprehended almost
everything which it can anyway import us to be acquainted with,
or which can tend either to the improvement or ornament of the
human mind.

Here then is the only expedient, from which we can hope for
success in our philosophical researches, to leave the tedious linger-
ing method, which we have hitherto followed, and, instead of
taking now and then a castle or village on the frontier, to march
up directly to the capital or centre of these sciences, to human
nature itself; which being once masters of, we may everywhere
else hope for an easy victory. From this station we may extend
our conquests over all those sciences, which more intimately concern
human life, and may afterwards proceed at leisure to discover
more fully those which are the objects of pure curiosity. There is
no question of importance, whose decision is not comprised in the
science of man; and there is none, which can be decided with any
certainty, before we become acquainted with that science. In
pretending, therefore, to explain the principles of human nature,
we in effect propose a complete system of the sciences, built on a
foundation almost entirely new, and the only one upon which they
can stand with any security.

And, as the science of man is the only solid foundation for the
other sciences, so, the only solid foundation we can give to this
science itself must be laid on experience and observation. It is no
astonishing reflection to consider, that the application of experimental philosophy to moral subjects should come after that to
natural, at the distance of above a whole century; since we find
in fact, that there was about the same interval betwixt the origins
of these sciences; and that, reckoning from Thales to Socrates,
the space of time is nearly equal to that betwixt my Lord Bacon
and some late philosophers[1] in England, who have begun to put
the science of man on a new footing, and have engaged the attention,
and excited the curiosity of the public. So true it is, that however
other nations may rival us in poetry, and excel us in some other
agreeable arts, the improvements in reason and philosophy can
only be owing to a land of toleration and of liberty.

Nor ought we to think, that this latter improvement in the science
of man will do less honour to our native country than the former
in natural philosophy, but ought rather to esteem it a greater glory,

[1] Mr. Locke, my Lord Shaftesbury, Dr. Mandeville, Mr. Hutchinson,
Dr. Butler, etc.

upon account of the greater importance of that science, as well as the necessity it lay under of such a reformation. For to me it seems evident, that the essence of the mind being equally unknown to us with that of external bodies, it must be equally impossible to form any notion of its powers and qualities otherwise than from careful and exact experiments, and the observation of those particular effects, which result from its different circumstances and situations. And though we must endeavour to render all our principles as universal as possible, by tracing up our experiments to the utmost, and explaining all effects from the simplest and fewest causes, it is still certain we cannot go beyond experience; and any hypothesis, that pretends to discover the ultimate original qualities of human nature, ought at first to be rejected as presumptuous and chimerical.

I do not think a philosopher, who would apply himself so earnestly to the explaining the ultimate principles of the soul, would show himself a great master in that very science of human nature, which he pretends to explain, or very knowing in what is naturally satisfactory to the mind of man. For nothing is more certain, than that despair has almost the same effect upon us with enjoyment, and that we are no sooner acquainted with the impossibility of satisfying any desire, than the desire itself vanishes. When we see, that we have arrived at the utmost extent of human reason, we sit down contented; though we be perfectly satisfied in the main of our ignorance, and perceive that we can give no reason for our most general and most refined principles, beside our experience of their reality; which is the reason of the mere vulgar, and what it required no study at first to have discovered for the most particular and most extraordinary phenomenon. And as this impossibility of making any further progress is enough to satisfy the reader, so the writer may derive a more delicate satisfaction from the free confession of his ignorance, and from his prudence in avoiding that error, into which so many have fallen, of imposing their conjectures and hypotheses on the world for the most certain principles. When this mutual contentment and satisfaction can be obtained betwixt the master and scholar, I know not what more we can require of our philosophy.

But if this impossibility of explaining ultimate principles should be esteemed a defect in the science of man, I will venture to affirm, that it is a defect common to it with all the sciences, and all the arts, in which we can employ ourselves, whether they be such as are cultivated in the schools of the philosophers, or practised in the shops of the meanest artisans. None of them can go beyond experience, or establish any principles which are not founded on that authority. Moral philosophy has, indeed, this peculiar disadvantage, which is not found in natural, that in collecting its experiments, it cannot make them purposely, with premeditation, and after such a manner as to satisfy itself concerning every particular difficulty which may arise. When I am at a loss to know the effects of one body upon another in any situation, I need only put them in that situation, and observe what results from it. But should I endeavour to clear up after the same manner any doubt in moral philosophy, by placing myself in the same case with that which I consider, it is evident this reflection and premeditation would so disturb the operation of my natural principles, as must render it impossible to form any just conclusion from the phenomenon. We must, therefore, glean up our experiments in this science from a cautious observation of human life, and take them as they appear in the common cause of the world, by men's behaviour in company, in affairs, and in their pleasures. Where experiments of this kind are judiciously collected and compared, we may hope to establish on them a science which will not be inferior in certainty, and will be much superior in utility, to any other of human comprehension.

BOOK 1—OF THE UNDERSTANDING.

PART I

OF IDEAS, THEIR ORIGIN, COMPOSITION, CONNECTION, ABSTRACTION, ETC.

I—OF THE ORIGIN OF OUR IDEAS. II—DIVISION OF THE SUBJECT. III—OF THE IDEAS OF MEMORY AND IMAGINATION. IV—OF THE CONNECTION OR ASSOCIATION OF IDEAS. V—OF RELATIONS. VI—OF MODES AND SUBSTANCES. VII—OF ABSTRACT IDEAS.

SECTION I

OF THE ORIGIN OF OUR IDEAS

ALL the perceptions of the human mind resolve themselves into two distinct kinds, which I shall call *impressions* and *ideas*. The difference betwixt these consists in the degrees of force and liveliness, with which they strike upon the mind, and make their way into our thought or consciousness. Those perceptions which enter with most force and violence, we may name *impressions*; and, under this name, I comprehend all our sensations, passions, and emotions, as they make their first appearance in the soul. By *ideas*, I mean the faint images of these in thinking and reasoning; such as, for instance, are all the perceptions excited by the present discourse, excepting only those which arise from the sight and touch, and excepting the immediate pleasure or uneasiness it may occasion. I believe it will not be very necessary to employ many words in explaining this distinction. Every one of himself will readily perceive the difference betwixt feeling and thinking. The common degrees of these are easily distinguished; though it is not impossible but, in particular instances, they may very nearly approach to each other. Thus, in sleep, in a fever, in madness, or in any very violent emotions of soul, our ideas may approach to our impressions: as, on the other hand, it sometimes happens, that our impressions are so faint and low that we cannot distinguish them from our ideas. But, notwithstanding this near resemblance in a few instances, they are in general so very different, that no one can make a scruple to rank them under distinct heads, and assign to each a peculiar name to mark the difference.[1]

There is another division of our perceptions, which it will be convenient to observe, and which extends itself both to our impressions and ideas. This division is into *simple* and *complex*. Simple perceptions, or impressions and ideas, are such as admit of no distinction nor separation. The complex are the contrary to these, and may be distinguished into parts. Though a particular colour, taste, and smell, are qualities all united together in this apple, it is easy to perceive they are not the same, but are at least distinguishable from each other.

Having, by these divisions, given an order and arrangement to our objects, we may now apply ourselves to consider, with the more accuracy, their qualities and relations. The first circumstance that strikes my eye, is the great resemblence betwixt our impressions and ideas in every other particular, except their degree of force and vivacity. The one seems to be, in a manner, the reflection of the other; so that all the perceptions of the mind are double, and appear both as impressions and ideas. When I shut my eyes, and think of my chamber, the ideas I form are exact representations of the impressions I felt; nor is there any circumstance of the one, which is not to be found in the other. In running over my other perceptions, I find still the same resemblance and representation. Ideas and impressions appear always to correspond to each other. This circumstance seems to me remarkable, and engages my attention for a moment.

Upon a more accurate survey I find I have been carried away too far by the first appearance, and that I must make use of the distinction of perceptions into *simple* and *complex*, to limit this

---

[1] I here make use of these terms, *impression* and *idea*, in a sense different from what is usual, and I hope this liberty will be allowed me. Perhaps I rather restore the word idea to its original sense, from which Mr. Locke had perverted it, in making it stand for all our perceptions. By the term of impression, I would not be understood to express the manner in which our lively perceptions are produced in the soul, but merely the perceptions themselves; for which there is no particular name, either in the English or any other language that I know of.

general decision, *that all our ideas and impressions are resembling.*
I observe that many of our complex ideas never had impressions
that corresponded to them, and that many of our complex impressions never are exactly copied in ideas. I can imagine to myself
such a city as the New Jerusalem, whose pavement is gold, and
walls are rubies, though I never saw any such. I have seen Paris;
but shall I affirm I can form such an idea of that city, as will
perfectly represent all its streets and houses in their real and just
proportions?

I perceive, therefore, that though there is, in general, a great
resemblance betwixt our *complex* impressions and ideas, yet the
rule is not universally true, that they are exact copies of each other.
We may next consider, how the case stands with our *simple* perceptions. After the most accurate examination of which I am capable,
I venture to affirm, that the rule here holds without any exception,
and that every simple idea has a simple impression, which resembles
it, and every simple impression a correspondent idea. That idea of
red, which we form in the dark, and that impression which strikes
our eyes in sunshine, differ only in degree, not in nature. That
the case is the same with all our simple impressions and ideas, it
is impossible to prove by a particular enumeration of them. Every
one may satisfy himself in this point by running over as many
as he pleases. But if any one should deny this universal
resemblance, I know no way of convincing him, but by desiring
him to show a simple impression that has not a correspondent idea,
or a simple idea that has not a correspondent impression. If he
does not answer this challenge, as it is certain he cannot, we may,
from his silence and our own observation, establish our conclusion.

Thus we find, that all simple ideas and impressions resemble each
other; and, as the complex are formed from them, we may affirm
in general, that these two species of perception are exactly
correspondent. Having discovered this relation, which requires
no further examination, I am curious to find some other of their
qualities. Let us consider, how they stand with regard to their
existence, and which of the impressions and ideas are causes, and
which effects.

The full examination of this question is the subject of the present
treatise; and, therefore, we shall here content ourselves with establishing one general proposition, *That all our simple ideas in their
first appearance, are derived from simple impressions, which are
correspondent to them, and which they exactly represent.*

In seeking for phenomena to prove this proposition, I find only those of two kinds; but, in each kind the phenomena are obvious, numerous, and conclusive. I first make myself certain, by a new review, of what I have already asserted, that every simple impression is attended with a correspondent idea, and every simple idea with a correspondent impression. From this constant conjunction of resembling perceptions I immediately conclude, that there is a great connection betwixt our correspondent impressions and ideas, and that the existence of the one has a considerable influence upon that of the other. Such a constant conjunction, in such an infinite number of instances, can never arise from chance; but clearly proves a dependence of the impressions on the ideas, or of the ideas on the impressions. That I may know on which side this dependence lies, I consider the order of their *first appearance*; and find, by constant experience, that the simple impressions always take the precedence of their correspondent ideas, but never appear in the contrary order. To give a child an idea of scarlet or orange, of sweet or bitter, I present the objects, or, in other words, convey to him these impressions; but proceed not so absurdly, as to endeavour to produce the impressions by exciting the ideas. Our ideas, upon their appearance, produce not their correspondent impressions, nor do we perceive any colour, or feel any sensation merely upon thinking of them. On the other hand we find, that any impression, either of the mind or body, is constantly followed by an idea, which resembles it, and is only different in the degrees of force and liveliness. The constant conjunction of our resembling perceptions, is a convincing proof, that the one are the causes of the other; and this priority of the impressions is an equal proof, that our impressions are the causes of our ideas, not our ideas of our impressions.

To confirm this, I consider another plain and convincing phenomenon; which is, that wherever, by any accident, the faculties which give rise to any impressions are obstructed in their operations, as when one is born blind or deaf, not only the impressions are lost, but also their correspondent ideas; so that there never appear in the mind the least trace of either of them. Nor is this only true, where the organs of sensation are entirely destroyed, but likewise where they have never been put in action to produce a particular impression. We cannot form to ourselves a just idea of the taste of a pine-apple, without having actually tasted it.

There is, however, one contradictory phenomenon, which may prove, that it is not absolutely impossible for ideas to go before their correspondent impressions. I believe it will readily be allowed, that the several distinct ideas of colours, which enter by the eyes, or those of sounds, which are conveyed by the hearing, are really different from each other, though, at the same time, resembling. Now, if this be true of different colours, it must be no less so of the different shades of the same colour, that each of them produces a distinct idea, independent of the rest. For if this should be denied, it is possible, by the continual gradation of shades, to run a colour insensibly into what is most remote from it; and, if you will not allow any of the means to be different, you cannot, without absurdity, deny the extremes to be the same. Suppose, therefore, a person to have enjoyed his sight for thirty years, and to have become perfectly well acquainted with colours of all kinds, excepting one particular shade of blue, for instance, which it never has been his fortune to meet with. Let all the different shades of that colour except that single one, be placed before him, descending gradually from the deepest to the lightest; it is plain, that he will perceive a blank, where that shade is wanting, and will be sensible that there is a greater distance in that place, betwixt the contiguous colours, than in any other. Now I ask, whether it is possible for him, from his own imagination, to supply this deficiency, and raise up to himself the idea of that particular shade, though it had never been conveyed to him by his senses? I believe there are few but will be of opinion that he can; and this may serve as a proof, that the simple ideas are not always derived from the correspondent impressions; though the instance is so particular and singular, that it is scarce worth our observing, and does not merit that, for it alone, we should alter our general maxim.

But, besides this exception, it may not be amiss to remark, on this head, that the principle of the priority of impressions to ideas, must be understood with another limitation, viz., that as our ideas are images of our impressions, so we can form secondary ideas, which are images of the primary, as appears from this very reasoning concerning them. This is not, properly speaking, an exception to the rule so much as an explanation of it. Ideas produce the images of themselves in new ideas; but as the first ideas are supposed to be derived from impressions, it still remains true, that all our simple ideas proceed, either mediately or immediately, from their correspondent impressions.

This, then, is the first principle I establish in the science of human nature; nor ought we to despise it because of the simplicity of its appearance. For it is remarkable, that the present question concerning the precedency of our impressions or ideas, is the same with what has made so much noise in other terms, when it has been disputed whether there be any *innate ideas*, or whether all ideas be derived from sensation and reflection. We may observe, that in order to prove the ideas of extension and colour not to be innate, philosophers do nothing but show that they are conveyed by our senses. To prove the ideas of passion and desire not to be innate, they observe, that we have a preceding experience of these emotions in ourselves. Now, if we carefully examine these arguments, we shall find that they prove nothing but that ideas are preceded by other more lively perceptions, from which they are derived, and which they represent. I hope this clear stating of the question will remove all disputes concerning it, and will render this principle of more use in our reasonings, than it seems hitherto to have been.

SECTION II

DIVISION OF THE SUBJECT

SINCE it appears, that our simple impressions are prior to their correspondent ideas, and that the exceptions are very rare, method seems to require we should examine our impressions before we consider our ideas. Impressions may be divided into two kinds, those of *sensation*, and those of *reflection*. The first kind arises in the soul originally, from unknown causes. The second is derived, in a great measure, from our ideas, and that in the following order. An impression first strikes upon the senses, and makes us perceive heat or cold, thirst or hunger, pleasure or pain, of some kind or other. Of this impression there is a copy taken by the mind, which remains after the impression ceases; and this we call an idea. This idea of pleasure or pain, when it returns upon the soul, produces the new impressions of desire and aversion, hope and fear, which may properly be called impressions of reflection, because derived from it. These again are copied by the memory and imagination, and become ideas: which, perhaps, in their turn, give rise to other impressions and ideas; so that the impressions of reflection are not only antecedent to their correspondent ideas, but posterior to those of sensation, and derived from them. The examination of our sensations belongs more to anatomists and natural philosophers than to moral; and, therefore, shall not at present be entered upon. And, as the impressions of reflection,

viz., pasions, desires, and emotions, which principally deserve our
attention, arise mostly from ideas, it will be necessary to reverse
that method, which at first sight seems most natural; and, in order
to explain the nature and principles of the human mind, give a
particular account of ideas, before we proceed to impressions. For
this reason, I have here chosen to begin with ideas.

SECTION III

OF THE IDEAS OF THE MEMORY AND IMAGINATION

WE find, by experience, that when any impression has been present
with the mind, it again makes its appearance there as an idea; and
this it may do after two different ways: either when, in its new
appearance, it retains a considerable degree of its first vivacity,
and is somewhat intermediate betwixt an impression and an idea;
or when it entirely loses that vivacity, and is a perfect idea. The
faculty by which we repeat our impressions in the first manner, is
called the *memory*, and the other the *imagination*. It is evident,
at first sight, that the ideas of the memory are much more lively
and strong than those of the imagination, and that the former
faculty paints its objects in more distinct colours than any which
are employed by the latter. When we remember any past event,
the idea of it flows in upon the mind in a forcible manner; whereas,
in the imagination, the perception is faint and languid, and cannot,
without difficulty, be preserved by the mind steady and uniform
for any considerable time. Here, then, is a sensible difference
betwixt one species of ideas and another. But of this more fully
hereafter.[1]

There is another difference betwixt these two kinds of ideas,
which is no less evident, namely, that though neither the ideas of
the memory nor imagination, neither the lively nor faint ideas,
can make their appearance in the mind, unless their correspondent
impressions have gone before to prepare the way for them, yet
the imagination is not restrained to the same order and form with
the original impressions; while the memory is in a manner tied down
in that respect, without any power of variation.

It is evident, that the memory preserves the original form in
which its objects were presented, and that wherever we depart

[1] Part III. Sect. 5.

from it in recollecting anything, it proceeds from some defect or imperfection in that faculty. An historian may, perhaps, for the more convenient carrying on of his narration, relate an event before another to which it was in fact posterior; but then, he takes notice of this disorder, if he be exact; and, by that means, replaces the idea in its due position. It is the same case in our recollection of those places and persons, with which we were formerly acquainted. The chief exercise of the memory is not to preserve the simple ideas, but their order and position. In short, this principle is supported by such a number of common and vulgar phenomena, that we may spare ourselves the trouble of insisting on it any further.

The same evidence follows us in our second principle, *of the liberty of the imagination to transpose and change its ideas.* The fables we meet with in poems and romances put this entirely out of question. Nature there is totally confounded, and nothing mentioned but winged horses, fiery dragons, and monstrous giants. Nor will this liberty of the fancy appear strange, when we consider that all our ideas are copied from our impressions, and that there are not any two impressions which are perfectly inseparable. Not to mention, that this is an evident consequence of the division of ideas into simple and complex. Wherever the imagination perceives a difference among ideas, it can easily produce a separation.

SECTION IV

OF THE CONNECTION OR ASSOCIATION OF IDEAS

As all simple ideas may be separated by the imagination, and may be united again in what form it pleases, nothing would be more unaccountable than the operations of that faculty, were it not guided by some universal principles, which render it, in some measure, uniform with itself in all times and places. Were ideas entirely loose and unconnected, chance alone would join them; and it is impossible the same simple ideas should fall regularly into complex ones (as they commonly do), without some bond of union among them, some associating quality, by which one idea naturally introduces another. This uniting principle among ideas is not to be considered as an inseparable connection; for that has been already excluded from the imagination: nor yet are we to conclude that without it the mind cannot join two ideas; for nothing is more free than that faculty: but we are only to regard it as a gentle force, which commonly prevails, and is the cause why, among other things, languages so nearly correspond to each other; Nature, in a manner, pointing out to every one those simple ideas, which are most proper to be united into a complex one. The qualities, from which this association arises, and by which the mind is, after this manner, conveyed from one idea to another, are three, viz., *resemblance, contiguity* in time or place, and *cause* and *effect*.

I believe it will not be very necessary to prove, that these qualities produce an association among ideas, and, upon the appearance of one idea, naturally introduce another. It is plain, that, in the course of our thinking, and in the constant revolution of our ideas, our imagination runs easily from one idea to any other that *resembles* it, and that this quality alone is to the fancy a sufficient bond and association. It is likewise evident, that as the senses, in changing their objects, are necessitated to change them regularly, and take them as they lie *contiguous* to each other, the imagination must, by long custom, acquire the same method of thinking, and run along the parts of space and time in conceiving its objects. As to the connection that is made by the relation of *cause and effect*, we shall have occasion afterwards to examine it to the bottom, and therefore shall not at present insist upon it. It is sufficient to observe, that there is no relation, which produces a stronger connection in the fancy, and makes one idea more readily recall another, than the relation of cause and effect betwixt their objects.

That we may understand the full extent of these relations, we must consider, that two objects are connected together in the imagination, not only when the one is immediately resembling, contiguous to, or the cause of the other, but also when there is interposed betwixt them a third object, which bears to both of them any of these relations. This may be carried on to a great length; though, at the same time we may observe, that each remove considerably weakens the relation. Cousins in the fourth degree are connected by *causation*, if I may be allowed to use that term; but not so closely as brothers, much less as child and parent. In general, we may observe, that all the relations of blood depend upon cause and effect, and are esteemed near or remote, according to the number of connecting causes interposed betwixt the persons.

Of the three relations above mentioned, this of causation is the most extensive. Two objects may be considered as placed in this relation, as well when one is the cause of any of the actions or motions of the other, as when the former is the cause of the existence of the latter. For as that action or motion is nothing but the object itself, considered in a certain light, and as the object continues the same in all its different situations, it is easy to imagine how such an influence of objects upon one another may connect them in the imagination.

We may carry this further, and remark, not only that two objects are connected by the relation of cause and effect, when the one produces a motion or any action in the other, but also when it has a power of producing it. And this we may observe to be the source of all the relations of interest and duty, by which men influence each other in society, and are placed in the ties of government and subordination. A master is such a one as, by his situation, arising either from force or agreement, has a power of directing in certain particulars the actions of another, whom we call servant. A judge is one, who, in all disputed cases, can fix by his opinion the possession or property of anything betwixt any members of the society. When a person is possessed of any power, there is no more required to convert it into action, but the exertion of the will; and *that* in every case is considered as possible, and in many as probable; especially in the case of authority, where the obedience of the subject is a pleasure and advantage to the superior.

These are, therefore the principles of union or cohesion among our simple ideas, and in the imagination supply the place of that inseparable connection, by which they are united in our memory. Here is a kind of *attraction*, which in the mental world will be found to have as extraordinary effects as in the natural, and to show itself in as many and as various forms. Its effects are everywhere conspicuous; but, as to its causes, they are mostly unknown, and must be resolved into *original* qualities of human nature, which I pretend not to explain. Nothing is more requisite for a true philosopher, than to restrain the intemperate desire of searching into causes; and, having established any doctrine upon a sufficient number of experiments, rest contented with that, when he sees a further examination would lead him into obscure and uncertain speculations. In that case his inquiry would be much better employed in examining the effects than the causes of his principle.

Amongst the effects of this union or association of ideas, there are none more remarkable than those complex ideas, which are the common subjects of our thoughts and reasoning, and generally arise from some principle of union among our simple ideas. These complex ideas may be divided into *relations, modes,* and *substances.* We shall briefly examine each of these in order, and shall subjoin some considerations concerning our *general* and *particular* ideas, before we leave the present subject, which may be considered as the elements of this philosophy

SECTION V

OF RELATIONS

THE word relation is commonly used in two senses considerably different from each other. Either for that quality, by which two ideas are connected together in the imagination, and the one naturally introduces the other, after the manner above explained; or for that particular circumstance, in which, even upon the arbitrary union of two ideas in the fancy, we may think proper to compare them. In common language, the former is always the sense in which we use the word relation; and it is only in philosophy that we extend it to mean any particular subject of comparison, without a connecting principle. Thus, distance will be allowed by philosophers to be a true relation, because we acquire an idea of it by the comparing of objects: but in a common way we say, *that nothing can be more distant than such or such things from each other, nothing can have less relation*; as if distance and relation were incompatible.

It may, perhaps, be esteemed an endless task to enumerate all those qualities, which make objects admit of comparison, and by which the ideas of *philosophical* relation are produced. But if we diligently consider them we shall find, that without difficulty they may be comprised under seven general heads, which may be considered as the sources of all philosophical relation.

1. The first is *resemblance*: and this is a relation, without which no philosophical relation can exist, since no objects will admit of comparison, but what have some degree of resemblance. But though resemblance be necessary to all philosophical relation, it does not follow that it always produces a connection or association of ideas. When a quality becomes very general, and is common to a great many individuals, it leads not the mind directly to any one of them; but, by presenting at once too great a choice, does thereby prevent the imagination from fixing on any single object.

2. *Identity* may be esteemed a second species of relation. This relation I here consider as applied in its strictest sense to constant and unchangeable objects; without examining the nature and

foundation of personal identity, which shall find its place afterwards. Of all relations the most universal is that of identity, being common to every being, whose existence has any duration.

3. After identity the most universal and comprehensive relations are those of *space* and *time*, which are the sources of an infinite number of comparisons, such as *distant, contiguous, above, below, before, after,* etc.

4. All those objects, which admit of *quantity* or *number*, may be compared in that particular, which is another very fertile source of relation.

5. When any two objects possess the same *quality* in common, the *degrees* in which they possess it form a fifth species of relation. Thus, of two objects which are both heavy, the one may be either of greater or less weight than the other. Two colours, that are of the same kind, may yet be of different shades, and in that respect admit of comparison.

6. The relation of *contrariety* may at first sight be regarded as an exception to the rule, *that no relation of any kind can subsist without some degree of resemblance.* But let us consider that no two ideas are in themselves contrary, except those of existence and non-existence, which are plainly resembling, as implying both of them an idea of the object; though the latter excludes the object from all times and places, in which it is supposed not to exist.

7. All other objects, such as fire and water, heat and cold, are only found to be contrary from experience, and from the contrariety of their *causes* or *effects*; which relation of cause and effect is a seventh philosophical relation, as well as a natural one. The resemblance implied in this relation shall be explained afterwards.

It might naturally be expected that I should join *difference* to the other relations; but that I consider rather as a negation of relation than as anything real or positive. Difference is of two kinds, as opposed either to identity or resemblance. The first is called a difference of *number*; the other of *kind*.

SECTION VI

OF MODES AND SUBSTANCES

I would fain ask those philosophers, who found so much of their reasonings on the distinction of substance and accident, and imagine we have clear ideas of each, whether the idea of *substance* be derived from the impressions of sensation or reflection? If it be conveyed to us by our senses, I ask, which of them, and after what manner? If it be perceived by the eyes, it must be a colour; it by the ears, a sound; if by the palate, a taste; and so of the other senses. But I believe none will assert, that substance is either a colour, or sound, or a taste. The idea of substance must, therefore, be derived from an impression of reflection, if it really exist. But the impressions of reflection resolve themselves into our passions and emotions; none of which can possibly represent a substance. We have, therefore, no idea of substance, distinct from that of a collection of particular qualities, nor have we any other meaning when we either talk or reason concerning it.

The idea of a substance as well as that of a mode, is nothing but a collection of simple ideas, that are united by the imagination, and have a particular name assigned them, by which we are able to recall, either to ourselves or others, that collection. But the difference betwixt these ideas consists in this, that the particular qualities which form a substance, are commonly referred to an unknown *something*, in which they are supposed to inhere; or granting this fiction should not take place, are at least supposed to be closely and inseparably connected by the relations of contiguity and causation. The effect of this is, that whatever new simple quality we discover to have the same connection with the rest, we immediately comprehend it among them, even though it did not enter into the first conception of the substance. Thus our idea of gold may at first be a yellow colour, weight, malleableness, fusibility; but upon the discovery of its dissolubility in *aqua regia*, we join that to the other qualities, and suppose it to belong to the substance as much as if its idea had from the beginning made a part of a compound one. The principle of union being regarded as the chief part of the complex idea, gives entrance to whatever quality afterwards occurs, and is equally comprehended by it, as are the others, which first presented themselves.

That this cannot take place in modes, is evident from considering their nature. The simple ideas of which modes are formed, either represent qualities, which are not united by contiguity and causation, but are dispersed in different subjects; or if they be all united together, the uniting principle is not regarded as the foundation of the complex idea. The idea of a dance is an instance of the first kind of modes; that of beauty of the second. The reason is obvious, why such complex ideas cannot receive any new idea, without changing the name, which distinguishes the mode.

SECTION VII

OF ABSTRACT IDEAS

A VERY material question has been started concerning *abstract* or *general* ideas, *whether they be general or particular in the mind's conception of them.* A great philosopher[1] has disputed the received opinion in this particular, and has asserted, that all general ideas are nothing but particular ones annexed to a certain term, which gives them a more extensive signification, and makes them recall upon occasion other individuals, which are similar to them. As I look upon this to be one of the greatest and most valuable discoveries that has been made of late years in the republic of letters, I shall here endeavour to confirm it by some arguments, which I hope will put it beyond all doubt and controversy.

It is evident, that, in forming most of our general ideas, if not all of them, we abstract from every particular degree of quantity and quality, and that an object ceases not to be of any particular species on account of every small alteration in its extension, duration, and other properties. It may, therefore, be thought, that here is a plain dilemma, that decides concerning the nature of those abstract ideas, which have afforded so much speculation to philosophers. The abstract idea of a man represents men of all sizes and all qualities, which it is concluded it cannot do, but either by representing at once all possible sizes and all possible qualities, or by representing no particular one at all. Now, it having been esteemed absurd to defend the former proposition, as implying an infinite capacity in the mind, it has been commonly inferred in favour of the latter; and our abstract ideas have been supposed to represent no particular degree either of quantity or quality. But that this inference is erroneous, I shall endeavour to make appear, *first*, by proving, that it is utterly impossible to conceive any quantity or quality, without forming a precise notion of its degrees; and, *secondly*, by showing, that though the capacity of the mind be not infinite, yet we can at once form a notion of all possible degrees of quantity and quality, in such a manner at least, as, however imperfect, may serve all the purposes of reflection and conversation.

To begin with the first proposition, *that the mind cannot form any notion of quantity or quality without forming a precise notion of degrees of each,* we may prove this by the three following arguments. First, we have observed, that whatever objects are different

[1] Dr. Berkeley.

are distinguishable, and that whatever objects are distinguishable are separable by the thought and imagination. And we may here add, that these propositions are equally true in the *inverse*, and that whatever objects are separable are also distinguishable, and that whatever objects are distinguishable are also different. For how is it possible we can separate what is not distinguishable, or distinguish what is not different? In order, therefore, to know whether abstraction implies a separation, we need only consider it in this view, and examine, whether all the circumstances, which we abstract from in our general ideas, be such as are distinguishable and different from those, which we retain as essential parts of them. But it is evident at first sight, that the precise length of a line is not different nor distinguishable from the line itself; nor the precise degree of any quality from the quailty. These ideas, therefore, admit no more of separation than they do of distinction and difference. They are, consequently, conjoined with each other in the conception; and the general idea of a line, notwithstanding all our abstractions and refinements, has, in its appearance in the mind, a precise degree of quantity and quality; however it may be made to represent others which have different degrees of both.

Secondly, it is confessed, that no object can appear to the senses; or in other words, that no impression can become present to the mind, without being determined in its degrees both of quantity and quality. The confusion, in which impressions are sometimes involved, proceeds only from their faintness and unsteadiness, not from any capacity in the mind to receive any impression, which in its real existence has no particular degree nor proportion. That is a contradiction in terms, viz., that it is possible for the same thing both to be and not to be.

Now, since all ideas are derived from impressions, and are nothing but copies and representations of them, whatever is true of the one must be acknowledged concerning the other. Impressions and ideas differ only in their strength and vivacity. The foregoing conclusion is not founded on any particular degree of vivacity. It cannot, therefore, be affected by any variation in that particular. An idea is a weaker impression; and, as a strong impression must necessarily have a determinate quantity and quality, the case must be the same with its copy or representative.

Thirdly, it is a principle generally received in philosophy, that everything in nature is individual, and that it is utterly absurd to suppose a triangle really existent, which has no precise proportion of sides and angles. If this, therefore, be absurd in *fact and reality*, it must also be absurd *in idea*; since nothing of which we can form a clear and distinct idea is absurd and impossible. But to form the idea of an object, and to form an idea simply, is the same thing; the reference of the idea to an object being an extraneous denomination, of which in itself it bears no mark or character. Now, as it is impossible to form an idea of an object that is possessed of quantity and quality, and yet is possessed of no precise degree of either, it follows, that there is an equal impossibility of forming an idea, that is not limited and confined in both these particulars. Abstract ideas are, therefore, in themselves individual, however they may become general in their representation. The image in the mind is only that of a particular object, though the application of it in our reasoning be the same as if it were universal.

This application of ideas, beyond their nature, proceeds from our collecting all their possible degrees of quantity and quality in such an imperfect manner as may serve the purposes of life, which is the second proposition I proposed to explain. When we have found a resemblance[1] among several objects, that often occur to us, we apply the same name to all of them, whatever differences we may observe in the degrees of their quantity and quality, and whatever other differences may appear among them. After we have acquired a custom of this kind, the hearing of that name revives the idea of one of these objects, and makes the imagination conceive it with all its particular circumstances and proportions. But as the same word is supposed to have been frequently applied to other individuals, that are different in many respects from that idea, which is immediately present to the mind; the word not being able to revive the idea of all these individuals, only touches the soul, if I may be allowed so to speak, and revives that custom,

---

[1] It is evident, that even different simple ideas may have a similarity or resemblance to each other; nor is it necessary, that the point or circumstance of resemblance should be distinct or separable from that in which they differ. *Blue* and *green* are different simple ideas, but are more resembling than *blue* and *scarlet*; though their perfect simplicity excludes all possibility of separation or distinction. It is the same case with particular sounds, and tastes, and smells. These admit of infinite resemblances upon the general appearance and comparison, without having any common circumstance the same And of this we may be certain, even from the very abstract terms *simple idea*. They comprehend all simple ideas under them. These resemble each other in their simplicity. And yet from their very nature, which excludes all composition, this circumstance, in which they resemble, is not distinguishable or separate from the rest. It is the same case with all the degrees in any quality. They are all resembling, and yet the quality, in any individual, is not distinct from the degree.

which we have acquired by surveying them. They are not really and in fact present to the mind, but only in power; nor do we draw them all out distinctly in the imagination, but keep ourselves in a readiness to survey any of them, as we may be prompted by a present design or necessity. The word raises up an individual idea, along with a certain custom, and that custom produces any other individual one, for which we may have occasion. But as the production of all the ideas, to which the name may be applied, is in most cases impossible, we abridge that work by a more partial consideration, and find but few inconveniences to arise in our reasoning from that abridgment.

For this is one of the most extraordinary circumstances in the present affair, that after the mind has produced an individual idea, upon which we reason, the attendant custom, revived by the general or abstract term, readily suggests any other individual, if by chance we form any reasoning that agrees not with it. Thus, should we mention the word triangle, and form the idea of a particular equilateral one to correspond to it, and should we afterwards assert, *that the three angles of a triangle are equal to each other*, the other individuals of a scalenum and isosceles, which we overlooked at first, immediately crowd in upon us, and make us perceive the falsehood of this proposition, though it be true with relation to that idea which we had formed. If the mind suggests not always these ideas upon occasion, it proceeds from some imperfection in its faculties; and such a one as is often the source of false reasoning and sophistry. But this is principally the case with those ideas which are abstruse and compounded. On other occasions the custom is more entire, and it is seldom that we run into such errors.

Nay so entire is the custom, that the very same idea may be annexed to several different words, and may be employed in different reasonings, without any danger of mistake. Thus the idea of an equilateral triangle of an inch perpendicular may serve us in talking of a figure, of a rectilineal figure, of a regular figure, of a triangle, and of an equilateral triangle. All these terms, therefore, are in this case attended with the same idea; but as they are wont to be applied in a greater or lesser compass, they excite their particular habits, and thereby keep the mind in a readiness to observe, that no conclusion be formed contrary to any ideas, which are usually comprised under them.

Before those habits have become entirely perfect, perhaps the mind may not be content with forming the idea of only one individual, but may run over several, in order to make itself comprehend its own meaning, and the compass of that collection, which it intends to express by the general term. That we may fix the meaning of the word, figure, we may revolve in our mind the ideas of circles, squares, parallelograms, triangles of different sizes and proportions, and may not rest on one image or idea. However this may be, it is certain *that* we form the idea of individuals whenever we use any general term; *that* we seldom or never can exhaust these individuals; and *that* those which remain, are only represented by means of that habit by which we recall them, whenever any present occasion requires it. This then is the nature of our abstract ideas and general terms; and it is after this manner we account for the foregoing paradox, *that some ideas are particular in their nature, but general in their representation*. A particular idea becomes general by being annexed to a general term; that is, to a term which, from a customary conjunction, has a relation to many other particular ideas, and readily recalls them in the imagination.

The only difficulty that can remain on this subject, must be with regard to that custom, which so readily recalls every particular idea for which we may have occasion, and is excited by any word or sound to which we commonly annex it. The most proper method, in my opinion, of giving a satisfactory explication of this act of the mind, is by producing other instances which are analogous to it, and other principles which facilitate its operation. To explain the ultimate causes of our mental actions is impossible. It is sufficient if we can give any satisfactory account of them from experience and analogy.

First, then, I observe, that when we mention any great number, such as a thousand, the mind has generally no adequate idea of it, but only a power of producing such an idea, by its adequate idea of the decimals under which the number is comprehended. This imperfection, however, in our ideas, is never felt in our reasonings, which seems to be an instance parallel to the present one of universal ideas.

Secondly, we have several instances of habits which may be revived by one single word; as when a person who has, by rote, any periods of a discourse, or any number of verses, will be put in remembrance of the whole, which he is at a loss to recollect, by that single word or expression with which they begin.

Thirdly, I believe every one who examines the situation of his mind in reasoning, will agree with me, that we do not annex distinct and complete ideas to every term we make use of, and that in talking of *government, church, negotiation, conquest,* we seldom spread out in our minds all the simple ideas of which these complex ones are composed. It is however observable, that notwithstanding this imperfection we may avoid talking nonsense on these subjects, and may perceive any repugnance among the ideas as well as if we had a full comprehension of them. Thus, if instead of saying, *that in war the weaker have always recourse to negotiations,* we should say, *that they have always recourse to conquest,* the custom which we have acquired of attributing certain relations to ideas, still follows the words, and makes us immediately perceive the absurdity of that proposition; in the same manner as one particular idea may serve us in reasoning concerning other ideas, however different from it in several circumstances.

Fourthly, as the individuals are collected together, and placed under a general term with a view to that resemblance which they bear to each other, this relation must facilitate their entrance in the imagination, and make them be suggested more readily upon occasion. And, indeed, if we consider the common progress of the thought, either in reflection or conversation, we shall find great reason to be satisfied in this particular. Nothing is more admirable than the readiness with which the imagination suggests its ideas, and presents them at the very instant in which they become necessary or useful. The fancy runs from one end of the universe to the other, in collecting those ideas which belong to any subject. One would think the whole intellectual world of ideas was at once subjected to our view, and that we did nothing but pick out such as were most proper for our purpose. There may not, however, be any present, beside those very ideas, that are thus collected by a kind of magical faculty in the soul, which, though it be always most perfect in the greatest geniuses, and is properly what we call a genius, is however inexplicable by the utmost efforts of human understanding.

Perhaps these four reflections may help to remove all difficulties to the hypothesis I have proposed concerning abstract ideas, so contrary to that which has hitherto prevailed in philosophy. But to tell the truth, I place my chief confidence in what I have already proved concerning the impossibility of general ideas, according to the common method of explaining them. We must certainly seek some new system on this head, and there plainly is none beside what I have proposed. If ideas be particular in their nature, and at the same time finite in their number, it is only by custom they can become general in their representation, and contain an infinite number of other ideas under them.

Before I leave this subject, I shall employ the same principles to explain that *distinction of reason*, which is so much talked of, and is so little understood in the schools. Of this kind is the distinction betwixt figure and the body figured; motion and the body moved. The difficulty of explaining this distinction arises from the principle above explained, *that all ideas which are different are separable.* For it follows from thence, that if the figure be different from the body, their ideas must be separable as well as distinguishable; if they be not different, their ideas can neither be separable nor distinguishable. What then is meant by a distinction of reason, since it implies neither a difference nor separation?

To remove this difficulty, we must have recourse to the foregoing explication of abstract ideas. It is certain that the mind would never have dreamed of distinguishing a figure from the body figured, as being in reality neither distinguishable, nor different, nor separable, did it not observe, that even in this simplicity there might be contained many different resemblances and relations. Thus, when a globe of white marble is presented, we receive only the impression of a white colour disposed in a certain form, nor are we able to separate and distinguish the colour from the form. But observing afterwards a globe of black marble and a cube of white, and comparing them with our former object, we find two separate resemblances, in what formerly seemed, and really is, perfectly inseparable. After a little more practice of this kind, we begin to distinguish the figure from the colour by a *distinction of reason*; that is, we consider the figure and colour together, since they are, in effect, the same and undistinguishable; but still view them in different aspects, according to the resemblances of which they are susceptible. When we would consider only the figure of the globe of white marble, we form in reality an idea both of the figure and colour, but tacitly carry our eye to its resemblance with the globe of black marble: and in the same manner, when we would consider its colour only, we turn our view to its resemblance with the cube of white marble. By this means we accompany our ideas with a kind of reflection, of which custom renders us, in a great measure, insensible. A person who desires us to consider the figure of a globe of white marble without thinking on its colour, desires an impossibility; but his meaning is, that we should consider the colour and figure together, but still keep in our eye the resemblance to the globe of black marble, or that to any other globe of whatever colour or substance.

PART II

OF THE IDEAS OF SPACE AND TIME

I—Of the Infinite Divisibility of Our Ideas of Space and Time. II—Of the Infinite Divisibility of Space and Time. III—Of the Other Qualities of Our Ideas of Space and Time. IV—Objections Answered. V—The Same Subject Continued. VI—Of the Ideas of Existence and of External Existence.

SECTION I

OF THE INFINITE DIVISIBILITY OF OUR IDEAS OF SPACE AND TIME

Whatever has the air of a paradox, and is contrary to the first and most unprejudiced notions of mankind, is often greedily embraced by philosophers, as showing the superiority of their science, which could discover opinions so remote from vulgar conception. On the other hand, anything proposed to us, which causes surprise and admiration, gives such a satisfaction to the mind, that it indulges itself in those agreeable emotions, and will never be persuaded that its pleasure is entirely without foundation. From these dispositions in philosophers and their disciples, arises that mutual complaisance betwixt them; while the former furnish such plenty of strange and unaccountable opinions, and the latter so readily believe them. Of this mutual complaisance I cannot give a more evident instance than in the doctrine of infinite divisibility, with the examination of which I shall begin this subject of the ideas of space and time.

It is universally allowed, that the capacity of the mind is limited, and can never attain a full and adequate conception of infinity: and though it were not allowed, it would be sufficiently evident from the plainest observation and experience. It is also obvious, that whatever is capable of being divided *in infinitum*, must consist of an infinite number of parts, and that it is impossible to set any bounds to the number of parts, without setting bounds at the same time to the division. It requires scarce any induction to conclude from hence, that the *idea* which we form of any finite quality, is not infinitely divisible, but that by proper distinctions and separations we may run up this idea to inferior ones, which will be perfectly simple and indivisible. In rejecting the infinite capacity of the mind, we suppose it may arrive at an end in the division of its ideas; nor are there any possible means of evading the evidence of this conclusion.

It is therefore certain, that the imagination reaches a *minimum*, and may raise up to itself an idea, of which it cannot conceive any subdivision, and which cannot be diminished without a total annihilation. When you tell me of the thousandth and ten-thousandth part of a grain of sand, I have a distinct idea of these numbers and of their different proportions; but the images which I form in my mind to represent the things themselves, are nothing different from each other, nor inferior to that image, by which I represent the grain of sand itself, which is supposed so vastly to exceed them. What consists of parts is distinguishable into them, and what is distinguishable is separable. But, whatever we may imagine of the thing, the idea of a grain of sand is not distinguishable nor separable into twenty, much less into a thousand, ten thousand, or an infinite number of different ideas.

It is the same case with the impressions of the senses, as with the ideas of the imagination. Put a spot of ink upon paper, fix your eye upon that spot, and retire to such a distance that at last you lose sight of it; it is plain, that the moment before it vanished, the image, or impression, was perfectly indivisible. It is not for want of rays of light striking on our eyes, that the minute parts of distant bodies convey not any sensible impression; but because they are removed beyond that distance, at which their impressions were reduced to a *minimum*, and were incapable of any further diminution. A microscope or telescope, which render them visible, produces not any new rays of light, but only spreads those which always flowed from them; and, by that means, both gives parts to impressions, which to the naked eye appear simple and uncompounded, and advances to a *minimum* what was formerly imperceptible.

We may hence discover the error of the common opinion, that the capacity of the mind is limited on both sides, and that it is impossible for the imagination to form an adequate idea of what goes beyond a certain degree of minuteness as well as of greatness. Nothing can be more minute than some ideas which we form in the fancy, and images which appear to the senses; since there are ideas and images perfectly simple and indivisible. The only defect of our senses is, that they give us disproportioned images of things, and represent as minute and uncompounded what is really great and composed of a vast number of parts. This mistake we are not sensible of; but, taking the impressions of those minute objects, which appear to the senses to be equal, or nearly equal to the objects, and finding, by reason, that there are other objects vastly more minute, we too hastily conclude, that these are inferior to any idea of our imagination or impression of our senses. This, however, is certain, that we can form ideas, which shall be no greater than the smallest atom of the animal spirits of an insect a thousand times less than a mite: and we ought rather to conclude, that the difficulty lies in enlarging our conceptions so much as to form a just notion of a mite, or even of an insect a thousand times less than a mite. For, in order to form a just notion of these animals, we must have a distinct idea representing every part of them; which, according to the system of infinite divisibility, is utterly impossible, and according to that of indivisible parts or atoms, is extremely difficult, by reason of the vast number and multiplicity of these parts.

SECTION II

OF THE INFINITE DIVISIBILITY OF SPACE AND TIME

WHEREVER ideas are adequate representations of objects, the relations, contradictions, and agreements of the ideas are all applicable to the objects; and this we may, in general, observe to be the foundation of all human knowledge. But our ideas are adequate representations of the most minute parts of extension; and, through whatever divisions and subdivisions we may suppose these parts to be arrived at, they can never become inferior to some ideas which we form. The plain consequence is, that whatever *appears* impossible and contradictory upon the comparison of these ideas, must be *really* impossible and contradictory, without any further excuse or evasion.

Everything capable of being infinitely divided contains an infinite number of parts; otherwise the division would be stopped short by the indivisible parts, which we should immediately arrive at. If therefore any finite extension be infinitely divisible, it can be no contradiction to suppose, that a finite extension contains an infinite number of parts: and *vice versa*, if it be a contradiction to suppose, that a finite extension contains an infinite number of parts, no finite extension can be infinitely divisible. But that this latter supposition is absurd, I easily convince myself by the consideration of my clear ideas. I first take the least idea I can form of a part of extension, and being certain that there is nothing more minute than this idea, I conclude, that whatever I discover by its means, must be a real quality of extension. I then repeat this idea once, twice, thrice, etc., and find the compound idea of extension, arising from its repetition, always to augment, and become double, triple, quadruple, etc., till at last it swells up to a considerable bulk, greater or smaller, in proportion as I repeat more or less the same idea. When I stop in the addition of parts, the idea of extension ceases to augment; and were I to carry on the addition *in infinitum*, I clearly perceive, that the idea of extension must also become infinite. Upon the whole, I conclude, that the idea of an infinite number of parts is individually the same idea with that of an infinite extension; that no finite extension is capable of containing an infinite number of parts; and, consequently, that no finite extension is infinitely divisible.[1]

I may subjoin another argument proposed by a noted author,[2] which seems to me very strong and beautiful. It is evident, that existence in itself belongs only to unity, and is never applicable to number, but on account of the units of which the number is composed. Twenty men may be said to exist; but it is only because one, two, three, four, etc., are existent; and if you deny the existence of the latter, that of the former falls of course. It is therefore utterly absurd to suppose any number to exist, and yet deny the existence of units; and as extension is always a number, according to the common sentiment of metaphysicians, and never dissolves itself into any unit or indivisible quantity, it follows that extension can never at all exist. It is in vain to reply, that any determinate quantity of extension is a unit; but such a one as

[1] It has been objected to me, that infinite divisibility supposes only an infinite number of *proportional* not of *aliquot* parts, and that an infinite number of proportional parts does not form an infinite extension. But this distinction is entirely frivolous. Whether these parts be called *aliquot* or *proportional*, they cannot be inferior to those minute parts, we conceive; and therefore, cannot form a less extension by their conjunction.

[2] Mons. Malezieu.

admits of an infinite number of fractions, and is inexhaustible in its subdivisions. For by the same rule, these twenty men *may be considered as a unit*. The whole globe of the earth, nay, the whole universe *may be considered as a unit*. That term of unity is merely a fictitious denomination, which the mind may apply to any quantity of objects it collects together; nor can such a unity any more exist alone than number can, as being in reality a true number. But the unity, which can exist alone, and whose existence is necessary to that of all number, is of another kind, and must be perfectly indivisible, and incapable of being resolved into any lesser unity.

All this reasoning takes place with regard to time; along with an additional argument, which it may be proper to take notice of. It is a property inseparable from time, and which in a manner constitutes its essence, that each of its parts succeeds another, and that none of them, however contiguous, can ever be coexistent. For the same reason that the year 1737 cannot concur with the present year 1738, every moment must be distinct from, and posterior or antecedent to another. It is certain then, that time, as it exists, must be composed of indivisible moments. For if in time we could never arrive at an end of division, and if each moment, as it succeeds another, were not perfectly single and indivisible, there would be an infinite number of coexistent moment, or parts of time; which I believe will be allowed to be an arrant contradiction.

The infinite divisibility of space implies that of time, as is evident from the nature of motion.. If the latter, therefore, be impossible, the former must be equally so.

I doubt not but it will readily be allowed by the most obstinate defender of the doctrine of infinite divisibility, that these arguments are difficulties, and that it is impossible to give any answer to them which will be perfectly clear and satisfactory. But here we may observe, that nothing can be more absurd than this custom of calling a *difficulty* what pretends to be a *demonstration*, and endeavouring by that means to elude its force and evidence. It is not in demonstrations, as in probabilities, that difficulties can take place, and one argument counterbalance another, and diminish its authority. A demonstration, if just, admits of no opposite difficulty; and if not just, it is a mere sophism, and consequently can never be a difficulty. It is either irresistible, or has no manner of force. To talk therefore of objections and replies, and balancing of arguments in such a question as this, is to confess, either that human reason is nothing but a play of words, or that the person himself, who talks so, has not a capacity equal to such subjects. Demonstrations may be difficult to be comprehended, because of the abstractedness of the subject; but can never have any such difficulties as will weaken their authority, when once they are comprehended.

It is true, mathematicians are wont to say, that there are here equally strong arguments on the other side of the question, and that the doctrine of indivisible points is also liable to unanswerable objections. Before I examine these arguments and objections in detail, I will here take them in a body, and endeavour, by a short and decisive reason, to prove, at once, that it is utterly impossible they can have any just foundation.

It is an established maxim in metaphysics, *That whatever the mind clearly conceives includes the idea of possible existence,* or, in other words, *that nothing we imagine is absolutely impossible.* We can form the idea of a golden mountain, and from thence conclude, that such a mountain may actually exist. We can form no idea of a mountain without a valley, and therefore regard it as impossible.

Now it is certain we have an idea of extension; for otherwise, why do we talk and reason concerning it? It is likewise certain, that this idea, as conceived by the imagination, though divisible into parts or inferior ideas, is not infinitely divisible, nor consists of an infinite number of parts: for that exceeds the comprehension of our limited capacities. Here then is an idea of extension, which consists of parts or inferior ideas, that are perfectly indivisible: consequently this idea implies no contradiction: consequently it is possible for extension really to exist conformable to it: and consequently, all the arguments employed against the possibility of mathematical points are mere scholastic quibbles, and unworthy of our attention.

These consequences we may carry one step further, and conclude that all the pretended demonstrations for the infinite divisibility of extension are equally sophistical; since it is certain these demonstrations cannot be just without proving the impossibility of mathematical points; which it is an evident absurdity to pretend to.

SECTION III

OF THE OTHER QUALITIES OF OUR IDEAS OF SPACE AND TIME

No discovery could have been made more happily for deciding all controversies concerning ideas, than that above mentioned, that impressions always take the precedency of them, and that every idea, with which the imagination is furnished, first makes its appearance in a correspondent impression. These latter perceptions are all so clear and evident, that they admit of no controversy; though many of our ideas are so obscure, that it is almost impossible even for the mind, which forms them, to tell exactly their nature and composition. Let us apply this principle, in order to discover further the nature of our ideas of space and time.

Upon opening my eyes and turning them to the surrounding objects, I perceive many visible bodies; and upon shutting them again, and considering the distance betwixt these bodies, I acquire the idea of extension. As every idea is derived from some impression which is exactly similar to it, the impressions similar to this idea of extension, must either be some sensations derived from the sight, or some internal impressions arising from these sensations.

Our internal impressions are our passions, emotions, desires, and aversions; none of which, I believe, will ever be asserted to be the model from which the idea of space is derived. There remains, therefore, nothing but the senses which can convey to us this original impression. Now, what impression do our senses here convey to us? This is the principal question, and decides without appeal concerning the nature of the idea.

The table before me is alone sufficient by its view to give me the idea of extension. This idea, then, is borrowed from, and represents some impression which this moment appears to the senses. But my senses convey to me only the impressions of coloured points, disposed in a certain manner. If the eye is sensible of anything further, I desire it may be pointed out to me. But, if it be impossible to show anything further, we may conclude with certainty, that the idea of extension is nothing but a copy of these coloured points, and of the manner of their appearance.

Suppose that, in the extended object, or composition of coloured points, from which we first received the idea of extension, the points were of a purple colour; it follows, that in every repetition of that idea we would not only place the points in the same order with respect to each other, but also bestow on them that precise colour with which alone we are acquainted. But afterwards, having experience of the other colours of violet, green, red, white, black, and of all the different compositions of these, and finding a resemblance in the disposition of coloured points, of which they are composed, we omit the peculiarities of colour, as far as possible, and found an abstract idea merely on that disposition of points, or manner of appearance, in which they agree. Nay, even when the resemblance is carried beyond the objects of one sense, and the impressions of touch are found to be similar to those of sight in the disposition of their parts; this does not hinder the abstract idea from representing both, upon account of their resemblance. All abstract ideas are really nothing but particular ones, considered in a certain light; but being annexed to general terms, they are able to represent a vast variety, and to comprehend objects, which, as they are alike in some particulars, are in others vastly wide of each other.

The idea of time, being derived from the succession of our perceptions of every kind, ideas as well as impressions, and impressions of reflection as well as of sensation, will afford us an instance of an abstract idea, which comprehends a still greater variety than that of space, and yet is represented in the fancy by some particular individual idea of a determined quantity and quality.

As it is from the disposition of visible and tangible objects we receive the idea of space, so, from the succession of ideas and impressions we form the idea of time; nor is it possible for time alone ever to make its appearance, or be taken notice of by the mind. A man in a sound sleep, or strongly occupied with one thought, is insensible of time; and according as his perceptions succeed each other with greater or less rapidity, the same duration appears longer or shorter to his imagination. It has been remarked by a great philosopher,[1] that our perceptions have certain bounds in this particular, which are fixed by the original nature and constitution of the mind, and beyond which no influence of external objects on the senses is ever able to hasten or retard our thought. If you wheel about a burning coal with rapidity, it will present to the senses an image of a circle of fire; nor will there seem to be any interval of time betwixt its revolutions; merely because it is

[1] Mr. Locke.

impossible for our perceptions to succeed each other, with the same rapidity that motion may be communicated to external objects. Wherever we have no successive perceptions, we have no notion of time, even though there be a real succession in the objects. From these phenomena, as well as from many others, we may conclude, that time cannot make its appearance to the mind, either alone or attended with a steady unchangeable object, but is always discovered by some *perceivable* succession of changeable objects.

To confirm this we may add the following argument, which to me seems perfectly decisive and convincing. It is evident, that time or duration consists of different parts: for otherwise, we could not conceive a longer or shorter duration. It is also evident, that these parts are not co-existent: for that quality of the co-existence of parts belongs to extension, and is what distinguishes it from duration. Now as time is composed of parts that are not coexistent, an unchangeable object, since it produces none but coexistent impressions, produces none that can give us the idea of time; and, consequently, that idea must be derived from a succession of changeable objects, and time in its first appearance can never be severed from such a succession.

Having therefore found, that time in its first appearance to the the mind is always conjoined with a succession of changeable objects, and that otherwise it can never fall under our notice, we must now examine, whether it can be *conceived* without our conceiving any succession of objects, and whether it can alone form a distinct idea in the imagination.

In order to know whether any objects, which are joined in impression, be separable in idea, we need only consider if they be different from each other; in which case it is plain they may be conceived apart. Everything that is different is distinguishable, and everything that is distinguishable may be separated, according to the maxims above explained. If, on the contrary, they be not different they are not distinguishable; and if they be not distinguishable, they cannot be separated. But this is precisely the case with respect to time, compared with successive perceptions. The idea of time is not derived from a particular impression mixed up with others, and plainly distinguishable from them, but arises altogether from the manner in which impressions appear to the mind, without making one of the number. Five notes played on a flute give us the impression and idea of time, though time be not a sixth impression which presents itself to the hearing or any other of the senses. Nor is it a sixth impression which the mind by reflection finds in itself. These five sounds making their appearance in this particular manner, excite no emotion in the mind, nor produce an affection of any kind, which being observed by it can give rise to a new idea. For *that* is necessary to produce a new idea of reflection; nor can the mind, by revolving over a thousand times all its ideas of sensation, ever extract from them any new original idea, unless nature has so framed its faculties, that it feels some new original impression arise from such a contemplation. But here it only takes notice of the *manner* in which the different sounds make their appearance, and that it may afterwards consider without considering these particular sounds, but may conjoin it with any other objects. The ideas of some objects it certainly must have, nor is it possible for it without these ideas ever to arrive at any conception of time; which, since it appears not as any primary distinct impression, can plainly be nothing but different ideas, or impressions, or objects disposed in a certain manner, that is, succeeding each other.

I know there are some who pretend that the idea of duration is applicable in a proper sense to objects which are perfectly unchangeable; and this I take to be the common opinion of philosophers as well as of the vulgar. But to be convinced of its falsehood, we need but reflect on the foregoing conclusion, that the idea of duration is always derived from a succession of changeable objects, and can never be conveyed to the mind by anything steadfast and unchangeable. For it inevitably follows from thence, that since the idea of duration cannot be derived from such an object, it can never in any propriety or exactness be applied to it, nor can anything unchangeable be ever said to have duration. Ideas always represent the objects or impressions from which they are derived, and can never, without a fiction, represent or be applied to any other. By what fiction we apply the idea of time, even to what is unchangeable, and suppose, as is common, that duration is a measure of rest as well as of motion, we shall consider afterwards.[1]

There is another very decisive argument, which establishes the present doctrine concerning our ideas of space and time, and is founded only on that simple principle, *that our ideas of them are compounded of parts, which are indivisible.* This argument may be worth the examining.

Every idea that is distinguishable being also separable, let us take one of those simple indivisible ideas, of which the compound

[1] Sect. 5.

one of *extension* is formed, and separating it from all others, and considering it apart, let us form a judgment of its nature and qualities.

It is plain it is not the idea of extension: for the idea of extension consists of parts; and this idea, according to the supposition, is perfectly simple and indivisible. Is it, therefore, nothing? That is absolutely impossible. For as the compound idea of extension, which is real, is composed of such ideas, were these so many nonentities there would be a real existence composed of nonentities, which is absurd. Here, therefore, I must ask, *What is our idea of a simple and indivisible point*? No wonder if my answer appear somewhat new, since the question itself has scarce ever yet been thought of. We are wont to dispute concerning the nature of mathematical points, but seldom concerning the nature of their ideas.

The idea of space is conveyed to the mind by two senses, the sight and touch; nor does anything ever appear extended, that is not either visible or tangible. That compound impression, which represents extension, consists of several lesser impressions, that are indivisible to the eye or feeling, and may be called impressions of atoms or corpuscles endowed with colour and solidity. But this is not all. It is not only requisite that these atoms should be coloured or tangible, in order to discover themselves to our senses; it is also necessary we should preserve the idea of their colour or tangibility, in order to comprehend them by our imagination. There is nothing but the idea of their colour or tangibility which can render them conceivable by the mind. Upon the removal of the ideas of these sensible qualities, they are utterly annihilated to the thought or imagination.

Now, such as the parts are, such is the whole. If a point be not considered as coloured or tangible, it can convey to us no idea; and consequently the idea of extension, which is composed of the ideas of these points, can never possibly exist: but if the idea of extension really can exist, as we are conscious it does, its parts must also exist; and in order to that, must be considered as coloured or tangible. We have, therefore, no idea of space or extension, but when we regard it as an object either of our sight or feeling.

The same reasoning will prove, that the indivisible moments of time must be filled with some real object or existence, whose succession forms the duration, and makes it be conceivable by the mind.

SECTION IV

OBJECTIONS ANSWERED

OUR system concerning space and time consists of two parts, which are intimately connected together. The first depends on this chain of reasoning. The capacity of the mind is not infinite, consequently no idea of extension or duration consists of an infinite number of parts or inferior ideas, but of a finite number, and these simple and indivisible: it is, therefore, possible for space and time to exist conformable to this idea: and if it be possible, it is certain they actually do exist conformable to it, since their infinite divisibility is utterly impossible and contradictory.

The other part of our system is a consequence of this. The parts, into which the ideas of space and time resolve themselves, become at last indivisible; and these indivisible parts, being nothing in themselves, are inconceivable when not filled with something real and existent. The ideas of space and time are, therefore, no separate or distinct ideas, but merely those of the manner or order in which objects exist; or, in other words, it is impossible to conceive either a vacuum and extension without matter, or a time when there was no succession or change in any real existence. The intimate connection betwixt these parts of our system is the reason why we shall examine together the objections which have been urged against both of them, beginning with those against the finite divisibility of extension.

1. The first of these objections which I shall take notice of, is more proper to prove this connection and dependence of the one part upon the other than to destroy either of them. It has often been maintained in the schools, that extension must be divisible, *in infinitum*, because the system of mathematical points is absurd; and that system is absurd, because a mathematical point is a nonentity, and consequently can never, by its conjunction with others, form a real existence. This would be perfectly decisive, were there no medium betwixt the infinite divisibility of matter, and the nonentity of mathematical points. But there is evidently a medium, viz., the bestowing a colour or solidity on these points; and the absurdity of both the extremes is a demonstration of the truth and reality of this medium. The system of *physical* points. which is another medium, is too absurd to need a refutation. A

real extension, such as a physical point is supposed to be, can never exist without parts different from each other; and wherever objects are different, they are distinguishable and separable by the imagination.

2. The second objection is derived from the necessity there would be of *penetration*, if extension consisted of mathematical points. A simple and indivisible atom that touches another must necessarily penetrate it; for it is impossible it can touch it by its external parts, from the very supposition of its perfect simplicity, which excludes all parts. It must therefore touch it intimately, and in its whole essence, *secundum se, tota, et totaliter*; which is the very definition of penetration. But penetration is impossible: mathematical points are of consequence equally impossible.

I answer this objection by substituting a juster idea of penetration. Suppose two bodies, containing no void within their circumference, to approach each other, and to unite in such a manner that the body, which results from their union, is no more extended than either of them; it is this we must mean when we talk of penetration. But it is evident this penetration is nothing but the annihilation of one of these bodies, and the preservation of the other, without being able to distinguish particularly which is preserved and which annihilated. Before the approach we have the idea of two bodies; after it we have the idea only of one. It is impossible for the mind to preserve any notion of difference betwixt two bodies of the same nature existing in the same place at the same time.

Taking then penetration in this sense, for the annihilation of one body upon its approach to another, I ask any one if he sees a necessity that a coloured or tangible point should be annihilated upon the approach of another coloured or tangible point? On the contrary, does he not evidently perceive, that, from the union of these points, there results an object which is compounded and divisible, and may be distinguished into two parts, of which each preserves its existence, distinct and separate, notwithstanding its contiguity to the other? Let him aid his fancy by conceiving these points to be of different colours, the better to prevent their coalition and confusion. A blue and a red point may surely lie contiguous without any penetration or annihilation. For if they cannot, what possibly can become of them? Whether shall the red or the blue be annihilated? Or if these colours unite into one, what new colour will they produce by their union?

What chiefly gives rise to these objections, and at the same time renders it so difficult to give a satisfactory answer to them, is the natural infirmity and unsteadiness both of our imagination and senses when employed on such minute objects. Put a spot of ink upon paper, and retire to such a distance that the spot becomes altogether invisible, you will find, that, upon your return and nearer approach, the spot first becomes visible by short intervals, and afterwards becomes always visible; and afterwards acquires only a new force in its colouring, without augmenting its bulk; and afterwards, when it has increased to such a degree as to be really extended, it is still difficult for the imagination to break it into its component parts, because of the uneasiness it finds in the conception of such a minute object as a single point. This infirmity affects most of our reasonings on the present subject, and makes it almost impossible to answer in an intelligible manner, and in proper expressions, many questions which may arise concerning it.

3. There have been many objections drawn from the *mathematics* against the indivisibility of the parts of extension, though at first sight that science seems rather favourable to the present doctrine; and if it be contrary in its *demonstrations*, it is perfectly conformable in its *definitions*. My present business then must be, to defend the definitions and refute the demonstrations.

A surface is *defined* to be length and breadth without depth; a line to be length without breadth or depth; a point to be what has neither length, breadth, nor depth. It is evident that this is perfectly unintelligible upon any other supposition than that of the composition of extension by indivisible points or atoms. How else could anything exist without length, without breadth, or without depth?

Two different answers, I find, have been made to this argument, neither of which is, in my opinion, satisfactory. The first is, that the objects of geometry, those surfaces, lines, and points, whose proportions and positions it examines, are mere ideas in the mind; and not only never did, but never can exist in nature. They never did exist; for no one will pretend to draw a line or make a surface entirely conformable to the definition: they never can exist; for we may produce demonstrations from these very ideas to prove that they are impossible.

But can anything be imagined more absurd and contradictory than this reasoning? Whatever can be conceived by a clear and distinct idea, necessarily implies the possibility of existence; and he who pretends to prove the impossibility of its existence by any argument derived from the clear idea, in reality asserts that we have no clear idea of it, because we have a clear idea. It is in vain to search for a contradiction in anything that is distinctly conceived by the mind. Did it imply any contradiction, it is impossible it could ever be conceived.

There is therefore no medium betwixt allowing at least the possibility of indivisible points, and denying their ideas; and it is on this latter principle that the second answer to the foregoing argument is founded. It has been pretended, that though it be impossible to conceive a length without any breadth, yet by an abstraction without a separation we can consider the one without regarding the other; in the same manner as we may think of the length of the way betwixt two towns and overlook its breadth. The length is inseparable from the breadth both in nature and in our minds; but this excludes not a partial consideration, and a *distinction of reason*, after the manner above explained.

In refuting this answer I shall not insist on the argument, which I have already sufficiently explained, that if it be impossible for the mind to arrive at a *minimum* in its ideas, its capacity must be infinite in order to comprehend the infinite number of parts, of which its idea of any extension would be composed. I shall here endeavour to find some new absurdities in this reasoning.

A surface terminates a solid; a line terminates a surface; a point terminates a line; but I assert, that if the *ideas* of a point, line, or surface, were not indivisible, it is impossible we should ever conceive these terminations. For let these ideas be supposed infinitely divisible, and then let the fancy endeavour to fix itself on the idea of the last surface, line, or point, it immediately finds this idea to break into parts; and upon its seizing the last of these parts, it loses its hold by a new division, and so on *in infinitum*, without any possibility of its arriving at a concluding idea. The number of fractions bring it no nearer the last division than the first idea it formed. Every particle eludes the grasp by a new fraction, like quicksilver, when we endeavour to seize it. But as in fact there must be something which terminates the idea of every finite quantity, and as this terminating idea cannot itself consist of parts of inferior ideas, otherwise it would be the last of its parts, which finished the idea, and so on; this is a clear proof, that the ideas of surfaces, lines, and points, admit not of any division; those of surfaces in depth, of lines in breadth and depth, and of points in any dimension.

The *schoolmen* were so sensible of the force of this argument, that some of them maintained that nature has mixed among those

particles of matter, which are divisible *in infinitum,* a number of
mathematical points in order to give a termination to bodies; and
others eluded the force of this reasoning by a heap of unintelligible
cavils and distinctions. Both these adversaries equally yield the
victory. A man who hides himself confesses as evidently the
superiority of his enemy, as another, who fairly delivers his arms.

Thus it appears, that the definitions of mathematics destroy the
pretended demonstrations; and that if we have the idea of indivisible points, lines, and surfaces, conformable to the definition,
their existence is certainly possible; but if we have no such idea,
it is impossible we can ever conceive the termination of any
figure, without which conception there can be no geometrical
demonstration.

But I go further, and maintain, that none of these demonstrations
can have sufficient weight to establish such a principle as this of
infinite divisibility; and that because with regard to such minute
objects, they are not properly demonstrations, being built on ideas
which are not exact, and maxims which are not precisely true.
When geometry decides anything concerning the proportions of
quantity, we ought not to look for the utmost *precision* and
exactness. None of its proofs extend so far; it takes the dimensions
and proportions of figures justly; but roughly, and with some
liberty. Its errors are never considerable, nor would it err at all,
did it not aspire to such an absolute perfection.

I first ask mathematicians what they mean when they say one
line or surface is *equal* to, or *greater*, or *less* than another? Let
any of them give an answer, to whatever sect he belongs, and
whether he maintains the composition of extension by indivisible
points, or by quantities divisible *in infinitum.* This question will
embarrass both of them.

There are few or no mathematicians who defend the hypothesis
of indivisible points, and yet these have the readiest and justest
answer to the present question. They need only reply, that lines
or surfaces are equal, when the numbers of points in each are equal;
and that as the proportion of the numbers varies, the proportion
of the lines and surfaces is also varied. But though this answer
be *just* as well as obvious, yet I may affirm, that this standard
of equality is entirely *useless,* and that it never is from such a
comparison we determine objects to be equal or unequal with
respect to each other. For as the points which enter into the
composition of any line or surface, whether perceived by the sight
or touch, are so minute and so confounded with each other that it

is utterly impossible for the mind to compute their number, such a computation will never afford us a standard by which we may judge of proportions. No one will ever be able to determine, by an exact enumeration, that an inch has fewer points than a foot, or a foot fewer than an ell, or any greater measure; for which reason, we seldom or never consider this as the standard of equality or inequality.

As to those who imagine that extension is divisible *in infinitum*, it is impossible they can make use of this answer, or fix the equality of any line or surface by a numeration of its component parts. For since, according to their hypothesis, the least as well as greatest figures contain an infinite number of parts, and since infinite numbers, properly speaking, can neither be equal nor unequal with respect to each other, the equality or inequality of any portions of space can never depend on any proportion in the number of their parts. It is true, it may be said, that the inequality of an ell and a yard consists in the different numbers of the feet of which they are composed, and that of a foot and a yard in the number of inches. But as that quantity we call an inch in the one is supposed equal to what we call an inch in the other, and as it is impossible for the mind to find this equality by proceeding *in infinitum* with these references to inferior quantities, it is evident that at last we must fix some standard of equality different from an enumeration of the parts.

There are some who pretend, that equality is best defined by *congruity*, and that any two figures are equal, when upon the placing of one upon the other, all their parts correspond to and touch each other. In order to judge of this definition let us consider, that since equality is a relation, it is not, strictly speaking, a property in the figures themselves, but arises merely from the comparison which the mind makes betwixt them. If it consists, therefore, in this imaginary application and mutual contact of parts, we must, at least, have a distinct notion of these parts, and must conceive their contact. Now it is plain, that in this conception we would run up these parts to the greatest minuteness which can possibly be conceived, since the contact of large parts would never render the figures equal. But the minutest parts we can conceive are mathematical points, and consequently this standard of equality is the same with that derived from the equality of the number of points, which we have already determined to be a just but useless standard. We must therefore look to some other quarter for a solution of the present difficulty.

There are many philosophers, who refuse to assign any standard of *equality*, but assert, that it is sufficient to present two objects that are equal in order to give us a just notion of this proportion. All definitions, say they, are fruitless without the perception of such objects; and where we perceive such objects we no longer stand in need of any definition. To this reasoning I entirely agree; and assert, that the only useful notion of equality, or inequality, is derived from the whole united appearance and the comparison of particular objects.

It is evident that the eye, or rather the mind, is often able at one view to determine the proportions of bodies, and pronounce them equal to, or greater or less than each other, without examining or comparing the number of their minute parts. Such judgments are not only common, but in many cases certain and infallible. When the measure of a yard and that of a foot are presented, the mind can no more question, that the first is longer than the second, than it can doubt of those principles which are the most clear and self-evident.

There are therefore three proportions, which the mind distinguishes in the general appearance of its objects, and calls by the names of *greater*, *less*, and *equal*. But though its decisions concerning these proportions be sometimes infallible, they are not always so; nor are our judgments of this kind more exempt from doubt and error than those on any other subject. We frequently correct our first opinion by a review and reflection; and pronounce those objects to be equal, which at first we esteemed unequal; and regard an object as less, though before it appeared greater than another. Nor is this the only correction which these judgments of our senses undergo; but we often discover our error by a juxtaposition of the objects; or, where that is impracticable, by the use of some common and invariable measure, which, being successively applied to each, informs us of their different proportions. And even this correction is susceptible of a new correction, and of different degrees of exactness, according to the nature of the instrument by which we measure the bodies, and the care which we employ in the comparison.

When therefore the mind is accustomed to these judgments and their corrections, and finds that the same proportion which makes two figures have in the eye that appearance, which we call *equality*, makes them also correspond to each other, and to any common measure with which they are compared, we form a mixed notion of equality derived both from the looser and stricter methods of comparison. But we are not content with this. For as sound reason convinces us that there are bodies *vastly* more minute than those which appear to the senses; and as a false reason would persuade us, that there are bodies *infinitely* more minute, we clearly perceive that we are not possessed of any instrument or art of measuring which can secure us from all error and uncertainty. We are sensible that the addition or removal of one of these minute parts is not discernible either in the appearance or measuring; and as we imagine that two figures, which were equal before, cannot be equal after this removal or addition, we therefore suppose some imaginary standard of equality, by which the appearances and measuring are exactly corrected, and the figures reduced entirely to that proportion. This standard is plainly imaginary. For as the very idea of equality is that of such a particular appearance, corrected by juxtaposition or a common measure, the notion of any correction beyond what we have instruments and art to make, is a mere fiction of the mind, and useless as well as incomprehensible. But though this standard be only imaginary, the fiction however is very natural; nor is anything more usual, than for the mind to proceed after this manner with any action, even after the reason has ceased, which first determined it to begin. This appears very conspicuously with regard to time; where, though it is evident we have no exact method of determining the proportions of parts, not even so exact as in extension, yet the various corrections of our measures, and their different degrees of exactness, have given us an obscure and implicit notion of a perfect and entire equality. The case is the same in many other subjects. A musician, finding his ear become every day more delicate, and correcting himself by reflection and attention, proceeds with the same act of the mind even when the subject fails him, and entertains a notion of a complete *tierce* or *octave*, without being able to tell whence he derives his standard. A painter forms the same fiction with regard to colours; a mechanic with regard to motion. To the one *light* and *shade*, to the other *swift* and *slow*, are imagined to be capable of an exact comparison and equality beyond the judgments of the senses.

We may apply the same reasoning to *curve* and *right* lines. Nothing is more apparent to the senses than the distinction betwixt a curve and a right line; nor are there any ideas we more easily form than the ideas of these objects. But however easily we may form these ideas, it is impossible to produce any definition of them, which will fix the precise boundaries betwixt them. When we draw lines upon paper or any continued surface, there is a certain order by which the lines run along from one point to another, that they may produce the entire impression of a curve or right line; but this order is perfectly unknown, and nothing is observed but the united appearance. Thus, even upon the system of indivisible points, we can only form a distant notion of some unknown standard to these objects. Upon that of infinite divisibility we cannot go even this length, but are reduced merely to the general appearance, as the rule by which we determine lines to be either curve or right ones. But though we can give no perfect definition of these lines, nor produce any very exact method of distinguishing the one from the other, yet this hinders us not from correcting the first appearance by a more accurate consideration, and by a comparison with some rule, of whose rectitude, from repeated trials, we have a greater assurance. And it is from these corrections, and by carrying on the same action of the mind, even when its reason fails us, that we form the loose idea of a perfect standard to these figures, without being able to explain or comprehend it.

It is true, mathematicians pretend they give an exact definition of a right line when they say, *it is the shortest way betwixt two points*. But in the first place I observe, that this is more properly the discovery of one of the properties of a right line, than a just definition of it. For I ask any one, if, upon mention of a right line, he thinks not immediately on such a particular appearance, and if it is not by accident only that he considers this property? A right line can be comprehended alone; but this definition is unintelligible without a comparison with other lines, which we conceive to be more extended. In common life, it is established as a maxim, that the straightest way is always the shortest; which would be as absurd as to say, the shortest way is always the shortest, if our idea of a right line was not different from that of the shortest way betwixt two points.

Secondly, I repeat, what I have already established, that we have no precise idea of equality and inequality, shorter and longer, more than of a right line or a curve; and consequently that the one can never afford us a perfect standard for the other. An exact idea can never be built on such as are loose and undeterminate.

The idea of a *plain surface* is as little susceptible of a precise standard as that of a right line; nor have we any other means of distinguishing such a surface, than its general appearance. It is in vain that mathematicians represent a plain surface as produced by the flowing of a right line. It will immediately be objected, that our idea of a surface is as independent of this method of forming a surface, as our idea of an ellipse is of that of a cone; that the idea of a right line is no more precise than that of a plain surface; that a right line may flow irregularly, and by that means form a figure quite different from a plane; and that therefore we must suppose it to flow along two right lines parallel to each other and on the same plane; which is a description that explains a thing by itself, and returns in a circle.

It appears, then, that the ideas which are most essential to geometry, viz., those of equality and inequality, of a right line and a plain surface, are far from being exact and determinate, according to our common method of conceiving them. Not only we are incapable of telling if the case be in any degree doubtful, when such particular figures are equal; when such a line is a right one, and such a surface a plain one; but we can form no idea of that proportion, or of these figures, which is firm and invariable. Our appeal is still to the weak and fallible judgment, which we make from the appearance of the objects, and correct by a compass, of common measure; and if we join the supposition of any further correction, it is of such a one as is either useless or imaginary. In vain should we have recourse to the common topic, and employ the supposition of a Deity, whose omnipotence may enable him to form a perfect geometrical figure, and describe a right line without any curve or inflection. As the ultimate standard of these figures is derived from nothing but the senses and imagination, it is absurd to talk of any perfection beyond what these faculties can judge of; since the true perfection of anything consists in its conformity to its standard.

Now, since these ideas are so loose and uncertain, I would fain ask any mathematician, what infallible assurance he has, not only of the more intricate and obscure propositions of his science, but of the most vulgar and obvious principles? How can he prove to me, for instance, that two right lines cannot have one common segment? Or that it is impossible to draw more than one right line betwixt any two points? Should he tell me, that these opinions are obviously absurd, and repugnant to our clear ideas; I would answer, that I do not deny, where two right lines incline upon each other with a sensible angle, but it is absurd to imagine them to have a common segment. But supposing these two lines to approach at the rate of an inch in twenty leagues, I perceive no absurdity in asserting, that upon their contact they become one. For, I beseech you, by what rule or standard do you judge, when you assert that the line, in which I have supposed them to concur, cannot make the same right line with those two, that form so small an angle betwixt them? You must surely have some idea of a right line, to which this line does not agree. Do you therefore mean, that it takes not the points in the same order and by the same rule, as is peculiar and essential to a right line? If so, I must inform you, that besides that, in judging after this manner, you allow that extension is composed of indivisible points (which, perhaps, is more than you intend), besides this, I say, I must inform you, that neither is this the standard from which we form the idea of a right line; nor, if it were, is there any such firmness in our senses or imagination, as to determine when such an order is violated or preserved. The original standard of a right line is in reality nothing but a certain general appearance; and it is evident right lines may be made to concur with each other, and yet correspond to this standard, though corrected by all the means either practicable or imaginable.

To whatever side mathematicians turn, this dilemma still meets them. If they judge of equality, or any other proportion, by the accurate and exact standard, viz., the enumeration of the minute indivisible parts, they both employ a standard, which is useless in practice, and actually establish the indivisibility of extension, which they endeavour to explode. Or if they employ, as is usual, the inaccurate standard, derived from a comparison of objects, upon their general appearance, corrected by measuring and juxtaposition; their first principles, though certain and infallible, are too coarse to afford any such subtile inference as they commonly draw from them. The first principles are founded on the imagination and senses; the conclusion therefore can never go beyond, much less contradict, these faculties.

This may open our eyes a little, and let us see, that no geometrical demonstration for the infinite divisibility of extension can have so much force as what we naturally attribute to every argument, which is supported by such magnificent pretensions. At the same time we may learn the reason, why geometry fails of evidence in this single point, while all its other reasonings command our fullest assent and approbation. And indeed it seems more requisite to give the reason of this exception, than to show that we really must make such an exception, and regard all the mathematical arguments for infinite divisibility as utterly sophistical. For it is evident, that as no idea of quantity is infinitely divisible, there cannot be imagined a more glaring absurdity, than to endeavour to prove, that quantity itself admits of such a division; and to prove this by means of ideas, which are directly opposite in that particular. And as this absurdity is very glaring in itself, so there is no argument founded on it, which is not attended with a new absurdity, and involves not an evident contradiction.

I might give as instances those arguments for infinite divisibility which are derived from the *point of contact.* I know there is no mathematician, who will not refuse to be judged by the diagrams he describes upon paper, these being loose draughts, as he will tell us, and serving only to convey with greater facility certain ideas, which are the true foundation of all our reasoning. This I am satisfied with, and am willing to rest the controversy merely upon these ideas. I desire therefore our mathematician to form, as accurately as possible, the ideas of a circle and a right line; and then I ask, if upon the conception of their contact he can conceive them as touching in a mathematical point, or if he must necessarily imagine them to concur for some space. Whichever side he chooses, he runs himself into equal difficulties. If he affirms, that in tracing these figures in his imagination, he can imagine them to touch only in a point, he allows the possibility of that idea, and consequently of the thing. If he says, that in his conception of the contact of those lines, he must make them concur, he thereby acknowledges the fallacy of geometrical demonstrations, when carried beyond a certain degree of minuteness; since, it is certain he has such demonstrations against the concurrence of a circle and a right line; that is, in other words, he can prove an idea, viz., that of concurrence, to be *incompatible* with two other ideas, viz., those of a circle and right line; though at the same time he acknowledges these ideas to be *inseparable.*

SECTION V

THE SAME SUBJECT CONTINUED

IF the second part of my system be true, *that the idea of space or extension is nothing but the idea of visible or tangible points distributed in a certain order,* it follows, that we can form no idea of a vacuum, or space, where there is nothing visible or tangible. This gives rise to three objections, which I shall examine together, because the answer I shall give to one is a consequence of that which I shall make use of for the others.

First, it may be said, that men have disputed for many ages

concerning a vacuum and a plenum, without being able to bring the affair to a final decision: and philosophers, even at this day, think themselves at liberty to take party on either side, as their fancy leads them. But whatever foundation there may be for a controversy concerning the things themselves, it may be pretended that the very dispute is decisive concerning the idea, and that it is impossible men could so long reason about a vacuum, and either refute or defend it, without having a notion of what they refuted or defended.

Secondly, if this argument should be contested, the reality, or at least possibility, of the *idea* of a vacuum, may be proved by the following reasoning. Every idea is possible which is a necessary and infallible consequence of such as are possible. Now, though we allow the world to be at present a plenum, we may easily conceive it to be deprived of motion; and this idea will certainly be allowed possible. It must also be allowed possible, to conceive the annihilation of any part of matter by the omnipotence of the Deity, while the other parts remain at rest. For as every idea that is distinguishable is separable by the imagination, and as every idea that is separable by the imagination may be conceived to be separately existent, it is evident, that the existence of one particle of matter no more implies the existence of another, than a square figure in one body implies a square figure in every one. This being granted, I now demand what results from the concurrence of these two possible ideas of *rest* and *annihilation*, and what must we conceive to follow upon the annihilation of all the air and subtile matter in the chamber, supposing the walls to remain the same, without any motion or alteration? There are some metaphysicians who answer, that since matter and extension are the same, the annihilation of the one necessarily implies that of the other; and there being now no distance betwixt the walls of the chamber, they touch each other; in the same manner as my hand touches the paper which is immediately before me. But though this answer be very common, I defy these metaphysicians to conceive the matter according to their hypothesis, or imagine the floor and roof, with all the opposite sides of the chamber, to touch each other, while they continue in rest, and preserve the same position. For how can the two walls, that run from south to north, touch each other, while they touch the opposite ends of two walls that run from east to west? And how can the floor and roof ever meet, while they are separated by the four walls that lie in a contrary position? If you change their position, you suppose a motion. If you conceive anything betwixt them, you suppose a new creation. But keeping strictly to the two ideas of *rest* and *annihilation*, it is evident, that the idea which results from them is not that of a contact of parts, but something else, which is concluded to be the idea of a vacuum.

The third objection carries the matter still further, and not only asserts, that the idea of a vacuum is real and possible, but also necessary and unavoidable. This assertion is founded on the motion we observe in bodies, which, it is maintained, would be impossible and inconceivable without a vacuum, into which one body must move in order to make way for another. I shall not enlarge upon this objection, because it principally belongs to natural philosophy, which lies without our present sphere.

In order to answer these objections, we must take the matter pretty deep, and consider the nature and origin of several ideas, lest we dispute without understanding perfectly the subject of the controversy. It is evident the idea of darkness is no positive idea, but merely the negation of light, or, more properly speaking, of coloured and visible objects. A man who enjoys his sight, receives no other perception from turning his eyes on every side, when entirely deprived of light, than what is common to him with one born blind; and it is certain such a one has no idea either of light or darkness. The consequence of this is, that it is not from the mere removal of visible objects we receive the impression of extension without matter; and that the idea of utter darkness can never be the same with that of vacuum.

Suppose, again, a man to be supported in the air, and to be softly conveyed along by some invisible power; it is evident he is sensible of nothing, and never receives the idea of extension, nor indeed any idea, from this invariable motion. Even supposing he moves his limbs to and fro, this cannot convey to him that idea. He feels in that case a certain sensation or impression, the parts of which are successive to each other, and may give him the idea of time, but certainly are not disposed in such a manner as is necessary to convey the idea of space or extension.

Since, then, it appears that darkness and motion, with the utter removal of everything visible and tangible, can never give us the idea of extension without matter, or of a vacuum; the next question is, whether they can convey this idea, when mixed with something visible and tangible?

It is commonly allowed by philosophers, that all bodies which discover themselves to the eye, appear as if painted on a plain surface, and that their different degrees of remoteness from our-selves are discovered more by reason than by the senses. When I hold up my hand before me, and spread my fingers, they are separated as perfectly by the blue colour of the firmament, as they could be by any visible object which I could place betwixt them. In order, therefore, to know whether the sight can convey the impression and idea of a vacuum, we must suppose, that amidst an entire darkness, there are luminous bodies presented to us, whose light discovers only these bodies themselves, without giving us any impression of the surrounding objects.

We must form a parallel supposition concerning the objects of our feeling. It is not proper to suppose a perfect removal of all tangible objects: we must allow something to be perceived by the feeling; and after an interval and motion of the hand or other organ of sensation, another object of the touch to be met with, and upon leaving that, another; and so on, as often as we please. The question is, whether these intervals do not afford us the idea of extension without body?

To begin with the first case; it is evident, that when only two luminous bodies appear to the eye, we can perceive whether they be conjoined or separate; whether they be separated by a great or small distance; and if this distance varies, we can perceive its increase or diminution, with the motion of the bodies. But as the distance is not in this case anything coloured or visible, it may be thought that there is here a vacuum or pure extension, not only intelligible to the mind, but obvious to the very senses.

This is our natural and most familiar way of thinking, but which we shall learn to correct by a little reflection. We may observe, that when two bodies present themselves, where there was formerly an entire darkness, the only change that is discoverable is in the appearance of these two objects, and that all the rest continues to be as before, a perfect negation of light, and of every coloured or visible object. This is not only true of what may be said to be remote from these bodies, but also of the very distance which is interposed betwixt them; *that* being nothing but darkness, or the negation of light; without parts, without composition, invariable and indivisible. Now, since this distance causes no perception different from what a blind man receives from his eyes, or what is conveyed to us in the darkest night, it must partake of the same properties; and as blindness and darkness afford us no ideas of extension, it is impossible that the dark and undistinguishable distance betwixt two bodies can ever produce that idea.

The sole difference betwixt an absolute darkness and the appearance of two or more visible luminous objects consists, as I said, in the objects themselves, and in the manner they affect our senses. The angles, which the rays of light flowing from them form with each other; the motion that is required in the eye, in its passage from one to the other; and the different parts of the organs which are affected by them; these produce the only perceptions from which we can judge of the distance. But as these perceptions are each of them simple and indivisible, they can never give us the idea of extension.

We may illustrate this by considering the sense of feeling, and the imaginary distance or interval interposed betwixt tangible or solid objects. I suppose two cases, viz., that of a man supported in the air, and moving his limbs to and fro, without meeting anything tangible; and that of a man, who, feeling something tangible, leaves it, and, after a motion of which he is sensible, perceives another tangible object; and I then ask, wherein consists the difference betwixt these two cases? No one will make any scruple to affirm, that it consists merely in the perceiving those objects, and that the sensation, which arises from the motion, is in both cases the same; and as that sensation is not capable of conveying to us an idea of extension, when unaccompanied with some other perception, it can no more give us that idea, when mixed with the impressions of tangible objects, since that mixture produces no alteration upon it.

But though motion and darkness, either alone or attended with tangible and visible objects, convey no idea of a vacuum or extension without matter, yet they are the causes why we falsely imagine we can form such an idea. For there is a close relation betwixt that motion and darkness, and a real extension, or composition of visible and tangible objects.

First, we may observe, that two visible objects, appearing in the midst of utter darkness, affect the senses in the same manner, and form the same angle by the rays which flow from them, and meet in the eye, as if the distance betwixt them were filled with visible objects, that give us a true idea of extension. The sensation of motion is likewise the same, when there is nothing tangible interposed betwixt two bodies, as when we feel a compounded body, whose different parts are placed beyond each other.

Secondly, we find by experience, that two bodies, which are so placed as to effect the senses in the same manner with two others, that have a certain extent of visible objects interposed betwixt them, are capable of receiving the same extent, without any sensible impulse or penetration, and without any change on that angle, under which they appear to the senses. In like manner, where there is one object, which we cannot feel after another without an interval, and the perceiving of that sensation we call motion in our hand or organ of sensation; experience shows us, that it is possible the same object may be felt with the same sensation of motion, along with the interposed impression of solid and tangible objects, attending the sensation. That is, in other words, an invisible and intangible distance may be converted into a visible and tangible one, without any change on the distant objects.

Thirdly, we may observe, as another relation betwixt these two kinds of distance, that they have nearly the same effects on every natural phenomenon. For as all qualities, such as heat, cold, light, attraction, etc., diminish in proportion to the distance; there is but little difference observed, whether this distance be marked out by compounded and sensible objects, or be known only by the manner in which the distant objects affect the senses.

Here then are three relations betwixt that distance, which conveys the idea of extension, and that other, which is not filled with any coloured or solid object. The distant objects affect the senses in the same manner, whether separated by the one distance or the other; the second species of distance is found capable of receiving the first; and they both equally diminish the force of every quality.

These relations betwixt the two kinds of distance, will afford us an easy reason why the one has so often been taken for the other, and why we imagine we have an idea of extension without the idea of any object either of the sight or feeling. For we may establish it as a general maxim in this science of human nature, that wherever there is a close relation betwixt two ideas, the mind is very apt to mistake them, and in all its discourses and reasonings to use the one for the other. This phenomenon occurs on so many occasions, and is of such consequence, that I cannot forbear stopping a moment to examine its causes. I shall only premise, that we must distinguish exactly betwixt the phenomenon itself, and the causes which I shall assign for it; and must not imagine, for any uncertainty in the latter, that the former is also uncertain. The phenomenon may be real, though my explication be chimerical. The falsehood of the one is no consequence of that of the other; though at the same time we may observe, that it is very natural for us to draw such a consequence; which is an evident instance of that very principle, which I endeavour to explain.

When I received the relations of *resemblance, contiguity,* and *causation,* as principles of union among ideas, without examining into their causes, it was more in prosecution of my first maxim, that we must in the end rest contented with experience, than for want of something specious and plausible, which I might have displayed on that subject. It would have been easy to have made an imaginary dissection of the brain, and have shown, why, upon our conception of any idea, the animal spirits run into all the contiguous traces, and rouse up the other ideas that are related to it. But though I have neglected any advantage, which I might have drawn from this topic in explaining the relations of ideas, I am afraid I must here have recourse to it, in order to account for the mistakes that arise from these relations. I shall therefore observe, that as the mind is endowed with a power of exciting any idea it pleases; whenever it despatches the spirits into that region of the brain, in which the idea is placed; these spirits always excite the idea, when they run precisely into the proper traces, and rummage that cell, which belongs to the idea. But as their motion is seldom direct, and naturally turns a little to the one side or the other; for this reason the animal spirits, falling into the contiguous traces, present other related ideas, in lieu of that which the mind desired at first to survey. This change we are not always sensible of; but continuing still the same train of thought, make use of the related idea, which is presented to us, and employ it in our reasoning, as if it were the same with what we demanded. This is the cause of many mistakes and sophisms in philosophy; as will naturally be imagined, and as it would be easy to show, if there was occasion.

Of the three relations above mentioned that of resemblance is the most fertile source of error; and indeed there are few mistakes in reasoning, which do not borrow largely from that origin. Resembling ideas are not only related together, but the actions of the mind, which we employ in considering them, are so little different, that we are not able to distinguish them. This last circumstance is of great consequence; and we may in general observe, that wherever the actions of the mind in forming any two ideas are the same or resembling, we are very apt to confound these ideas, and take the one for the other. Of this we shall see many instances in the progress of this treatise. But though resemblance be the relation, which most readily produces a mistake in ideas, yet the others of causation and contiguity may also concur in the same influence. We might produce the figures of poets and orators, as sufficient proofs of this, were it as usual as it is reasonable, in metaphysical subjects, to draw our arguments from that quarter. But lest metaphysicians should esteem this below their dignity, I shall borrow a proof from an observation, which may be made on most of their own discourses, viz., that it is usual for men to use words for ideas, and to talk instead of thinking in their reasonings. We use words for ideas, because they are commonly so closely connected, that the mind easily mistakes them. And this likewise is the reason, why we substitute the idea of a distance, which is not considered either as visible or tangible, in the room of extension, which is nothing but a composition of visible or tangible points disposed in a certain order. In causing this mistake there concur both the relations of *causation* and *resemblance*. As the first species of distance is found to be convertible into the second, it is in this respect a kind of cause; and the similarity of their manner of affecting the senses, and diminishing every quality, forms the relation of resemblance.

After this chain of reasoning and explication of my principles, I am now prepared to answer all the objections that have been offered, whether derived from *metaphysics* or *mechanics*. The frequent disputes concerning a vacuum, or extension without matter, prove not the reality of the idea, upon which the dispute turns; there being nothing more common, than to see men deceive themselves in this particular; especially when, by means of any close relation, there is another idea presented, which may be the occasion of their mistake.

We may make almost the same answer to the second objection, derived from the conjunction of the ideas of rest and annihilation. When everything is annihilated in the chamber, and the walls continue immovable, the chamber must be conceived much in the same manner as at present, when the air that fills it is not an object of the senses. This annihilation leaves to the *eye* that fictitious distance, which is discovered by the different parts of the organ that are affected, and by the degrees of light and shade; and to the *feeling*, that which consists in a sensation of motion in the hand, or other member of the body. In vain should we search any further. On whichever side we turn this subject, we shall find that these are the only impressions such an object can produce after the supposed annihilation; and it has already been remarked, that impressions can give rise to no ideas, but to such as resemble them.

Since a body interposed betwixt two others may be supposed to be annihilated, without producing any change upon such as lie on each hand of it, it is easily conceived how it may be created anew, and yet produce as little alteration. Now the motion of a body has much the same effect as its creation. The distant bodies are no more affected in the one case, than in the other. This suffices to satisfy the imagination, and proves there is no repugnance in such a motion. Afterwards experience comes in play to persuade us that two bodies, situated in the manner above described, have really such a capacity of receiving body betwixt them, and that there is no obstacle to the conversion of the invisible and intangible distance into one that is visible and tangible. However natural that conversion may seem, we cannot be sure it is practicable, before we have had experience of it.

Thus I seem to have answered the three objections above mentioned; though at the same time I am sensible, that few will be satisfied with these answers, but will immediately propose new objections and difficulties. It will probably be said, that my reasoning makes nothing to the matter in hand, and that I explain only the manner in which objects affect the senses, without endeavouring to account for their real nature and operations. Though there be nothing visible or tangible interposed betwixt two bodies, yet we find by experience, that the bodies may be placed in the same manner, with regard to the eye, and require the same motion of the hand in passing from one to the other, as if divided by something visible and tangible. This invisible and intangible distance is also found by experience to contain a capacity of receiving body, or of becoming visible and tangible. Here is the whole of my system; and in no part of it have I endeavoured to explain the cause which separates bodies after this manner, and gives them a capacity of receiving others betwixt them, without any impulse or penetration.

I answer this objection by pleading guilty, and by confessing that my intention never was to penetrate into the nature of bodies, or explain the secret causes of their operations. For, besides that this belongs not to my present purpose, I am afraid, that such an enterprise is beyond the reach of human understanding, and that we can never pretend to know body otherwise than by those external properties, which discover themselves to the senses. As to those who attempt anything further, I cannot approve of their ambition, till I see, in some one instance at least, that they have met with success. But at present I content myself with knowing perfectly the manner in which objects affect my senses, and their connections with each other, as far as experience informs me of them. This suffices for the conduct of life; and this also suffices for my philosophy, which pretends only to explain the nature and causes of our perceptions, or impressions and ideas.[1]

I shall conclude this subject of extension with a paradox, which will easily be explained from the foregoing reasoning. This paradox is, that if you are pleased to give to the invisible and intangible distance, or, in other words, to the capacity of becoming a visible and tangible distance, the name of a vacuum, extension and matter are the same, and yet there is a vacuum. If you will not give it that name, motion is possible in a plenum, without any impulse *in infinitum,* without returning in a circle, and without penetration. But however we may express ourselves, we must always confess that we have no idea of any real extension without filling it with sensible objects, and conceiving its parts as visible or tangible.

As to the doctrine, that time is nothing but the manner in which some real objects exist, we may observe, that it is liable to the

---

[1] As long as we confine our speculations to *the appearances* of objects to our senses, without entering into disquisitions concerning their real nature and operations, we are safe from all difficulties, and can never be embarrassed by any question. Thus, if it be asked, if the invisible and intangible distance interposed betwixt two objects, be something or nothing: it is easy to answer, that it is *something,* viz., a property of the objects, which affect the *senses* after such a particular manner. If it be asked, whether two objects having such a distance betwixt them, touch or not: it may be answered, that this depends upon the definition of the word *touch.* If objects be said to touch, when there is nothing *sensible* interposed betwixt them, these objects touch. If objects be said to touch, when their *images* strike contiguous parts of the eye, and when the hand *feels* both objects successively, without any interposed motion, these objects do not touch. The appearances of objects to our senses are all consistent; and no difficulties can ever arise, but from the obscurity of the terms we make use of.

If we carry our inquiry beyond the appearances of objects to the senses, I am afraid that most of our conclusions will be full of scepticism and uncertainty. Thus, if it be asked, whether or not the invisible and intangible distance be always full of *body,* or of something that by an improvement of our organs might become visible or tangible, I must acknowledge, that I find no very decisive arguments on either side: though I am inclined to the contrary opinion, as being more suitable to vulgar and popular notions. If *the Newtonian* philosophy be rightly understood, it will be found to mean no more. A vacuum is asserted; that is, bodies are said to be placed after such a manner, as to receive bodies betwixt them, without impulsion or penetration. The real nature of this position of bodies is unknown. We are only acquainted with its effects on the senses, and its power of receiving body. Nothing is more suitable to that philosophy, than a modest scepticism to a certain degree, and a fair confession of ignorance in subjects that exceed all human capacity.

same objections as the similar doctrine with regard to extension. If it be a sufficient proof, that we have the idea of a vacuum, because we dispute and reason concerning it; we must for the same reason have the idea of time without any changeable existence; since there is no subject of dispute more frequent and common. But that we really have no such idea, is certain. For whence should it be derived? Does it arise from an impression of sensation or of reflection? Point it out distinctly to us, that we may know its nature and qualities. But if you cannot point out *any such impression*, you may be certain you are mistaken, when you imagine you have *any such idea*.

But though it be impossible to show the impression, from which the idea of time without a changeable existence is derived, yet we can easily point out those appearances, which make us fancy we have that idea. For we may observe, that there is a continual succession of perceptions in our mind; so that the idea of time being for ever present with us, when we consider a steadfast object at five o'clock, and regard the same at six, we are apt to apply to it that idea in the same manner as if every moment were distinguished by a different position, or an alteration of the object. The first and second appearances of the object, being compared with the succession of our perceptions, seem equally removed as if the object had really changed. To which we may add, what experience shows us, that the object was susceptible of such a number of changes betwixt these appearances; as also that the unchangeable or rather fictitious duration has the same effect upon every quality, by increasing or diminishing it, as that succession which is obvious to the senses. From these three relations we are apt to confound our ideas, and imagine we can form the idea of a time and duration, without any change or succession.

SECTION VI

OF THE IDEAS OF EXISTENCE, AND OF EXTERNAL EXISTENCE

IT may not be amiss, before we leave this subject, to explain the ideas of *existence* and of *external existence;* which have their difficulties, as well as the ideas of space and time. By this means we shall be the better prepared for the examination of knowledge and probability, when we understand perfectly all those particular ideas, which may enter into our reasoning.

There is no impression nor idea of any kind, of which we have any consciousness or memory, that is not conceived as existent; and it is evident that, from this consciousness, the most perfect idea and assurance of *being* is derived. From hence we may form a dilemma, the most clear and conclusive that can be imagined, viz., that since we never remember any idea or impression without attributing existence to it, the idea of existence must either be derived from a distinct impression, conjoined with every perception or object of our thought, or must be the very same with the idea of the perception or object.

As this dilemma is an evident consequence of the principle, that every idea arises from a similar impression, so our decision betwixt the propositions of the dilemma is no more doubtful. So far from there being any distinct impression attending every impression and every idea, that I do not think there are any two distinct impressions which are inseparably conjoined. Though certain sensations may at one time be united, we quickly find they admit of a separation, and may be presented apart. And thus, though every impression and idea we remember be considered as existent, the idea of existence is not derived from any particular impression.

The idea of existence, then, is the very same with the idea of what we conceive to be existent. To reflect on anything simply, and to reflect on it as existent, are nothing different from each other. That idea, when conjoined with the idea of any object, makes no addition to it. Whatever we conceive, we conceive to be existent. Any idea we please to form is the idea of a being; and the idea of a being is any idea we please to form.

Whoever opposes this, must necessarily point out that distinct impression, from which the idea of entity is derived, and must prove, that this impression is inseparable from every perception be believe to be existent. This we may without hesitation conclude to be impossible.

Our foregoing reasoning[1] concerning the *distinction* of ideas, without any real *difference*, will not here serve us in any stead. That kind of distinction is founded on the different resemblances, which the same simple idea may have to several different ideas. But no object can be presented resembling some object with respect to its existence, and different from others in the same particular; since every object that is presented, must necessarily be existent.

A like reasoning will account for the idea of *external existence*. We may observe, that it is universally allowed by philosophers,

[1] Part I. Sect. 7.

and is besides pretty obvious of itself, that nothing is ever really present with the mind but its perceptions or impressions and ideas, and that external objects become known to us only by those perceptions they occasion. To hate, to love, to think, to feel, to see; all this is nothing but to perceive.

Now since nothing is ever present to the mind but perceptions, and since all ideas are derived from something antecedently present to the mind; it follows, that it is impossible for us so much as to conceive or form an idea of anything specifically different from ideas and impressions. Let us fix our attention out of ourselves as much as possible; let us chase our imagination to the heavens, or to the utmost limits of the universe; we never really advance a step beyond ourselves, nor can conceive any kind of existence, but those perceptions, which have appeared in that narrow compass. This is the universe of the imagination, nor have we any idea but what is there produced.

The furthest we can go towards a conception of external objects, when supposed *specifically* different from our perceptions, is to form a relative idea of them, without pretending to comprehend the related objects. Generally speaking, we do not suppose them specifically different; but only attribute to them different relations, connections, and durations. But of this more fully hereafter.[1]

[1] Part IV. Sect. 2.

PART III

OF KNOWLEDGE AND PROBABILITY

I—OF KNOWLEDGE. II—OF PROBABILITY, AND OF THE IDEA OF CAUSE AND EFFECT. III—WHY A CAUSE IS ALWAYS NECESSARY. IV—OF THE COMPONENT PARTS OF OUR REASONINGS CONCERNING THE CAUSE AND EFFECT. V—OF THE IMPRESSIONS OF THE SENSES AND OF MEMORY. VI—OF THE INFERENCE FROM THE IMPRESSION TO THE IDEA. VII—OF THE NATURE OF THE IDEA OF BELIEF. VIII—OF THE CAUSES OF BELIEF. IX—OF THE EFFECTS OF OTHER RELATIONS AND OTHER HABITS. X—OF THE INFLUENCE OF BELIEF. XI—OF THE PROBABILITY OF CHANCES. XII—OF THE PROBABILITY OF CAUSES. XIII—OF UNPHILOSOPHICAL PROBABILITY. XIV—OF THE IDEA OF NECESSARY CONNECTION. XV—RULES BY WHICH TO JUDGE OF CAUSES AND EFFECTS.

SECTION I

OF KNOWLEDGE

THERE are seven different kinds of philosophical relation,[1] viz., *resemblance, identity, relations of time and place, proportion in quantity or number, degrees in any quality, contrariety, and causation.* These relations may be divided into two classes; into such as depend entirely on the ideas, which we compare together, and such as may be changed without any change in the ideas. It is from the idea of a triangle, that we discover the relation of equality, which its three angles bear to two right ones; and this relation is invariable, as long as our idea remains the same. On the contrary, the relations of *contiguity* and *distance* betwixt two objects may be changed merely by an alteration of their place,

[1] Part I. Sect. 5.

without any change on the objects themselves or on their ideas, and the place depends on a hundred different accidents, which cannot be foreseen by the mind. It is the same case with *identity* and *causation*. Two objects, though perfectly resembling each other, and even appearing in the same place at different times, may be numerically different: and as the power, by which one object produces another, is never discoverable merely from their idea, it is evident *cause* and *effect* are relations, of which we receive information from experience, and not from any abstract reasoning or reflection. There is no single phenomenon, even the most simple, which can be accounted for from the qualities of the objects, as they appear to us; or which we could foresee without the help of our memory and experience.

It appears therefore that of these seven philosophical relations, there remain only four, which depending solely upon ideas, can be the objects of knowledge and certainty. These four are *resemblance, contrariety, degrees in quality, and proportions in quantity or number*. Three of these relations are discoverable at first sight, and fall more properly under the province of intuition than demonstration. When any objects *resemble* each other, the resemblance will at first strike the eye, or rather the mind; and seldom requires a second examination. The case is the same with *contrariety*, and with the *degrees* of any *quality*. No one can once doubt but existence and non-existence destroy each other, and are perfectly incompatible and contrary. And though it be impossible to judge exactly of the degrees of any quality, such as colour, taste, heat, cold, when the difference betwixt them is very small; yet it is easy to decide, that any of them is superior or inferior to another, when their difference is considerable. And this decision we always pronounce at first sight, without any inquiry or reasoning.

We might proceed, after the same manner, in fixing the *proportions* of *quantity* or *number*, and might at one view observe a superiority, or inferiority betwixt any numbers, or figures; especially where the difference is very great and remarkable. As to equality or any exact proportion, we can only guess at it from a single consideration; except in very short numbers, or very limited portions of extension; which are comprehended in an instant, and where we perceive an impossibility of falling into any considerable error. In all other cases we must settle the proportions with some liberty, or proceed in a more *artificial* manner.

I have already observed, that geometry, or the *art* by which we fix the proportions of figures; though it much excels both in universality and exactness, the loose judgments of the senses and imagination; yet never attains a perfect precision and exactness. Its first principles are still drawn from the general appearance of the objects; and that appearance can never afford us any security, when we examine the prodigious minuteness of which nature is susceptible. Our ideas seem to give a perfect assurance, that no two right lines can have a common segment; but if we consider these ideas, we shall find, that they always suppose a sensible inclination of the two lines, and that where the angle they form is extremely small, we have no standard of a right line so precise as to assure us of the truth of this proposition. It is the same case with most of the primary decisions of the mathematics.

There remain therefore algebra and arithmetic as the only sciences, in which we can carry on a chain of reasoning to any degree of intricacy, and yet preserve a perfect exactness and certainty. We are possessed of a precise standard, by which we can judge of the equality and proportion of numbers; and according as they correspond or not to that standard, we determine their relations, without any possibility of error. When two numbers are so combined, as that the one has always an unit answering to every unit of the other, we pronounce them equal; and it is for want of such a standard of equality in extension, that geometry can scarce be esteemed a perfect and infallible science.[1]

But here it may not be amiss to obviate a difficulty, which may arise from my asserting, that though geometry falls short of that perfect precision and certainty, which are peculiar to arithmetic and algebra, yet it excels the imperfect judgments of our senses and imagination. The reason why I impute any defect to geometry is, because its original and fundamental principles are derived merely from appearances; and it may perhaps be imagined, that this defect must always attend it, and keep it from ever reaching a greater exactness in the comparison of objects or ideas, than what our eye or imagination alone is able to attain. I own that this defect so far attends it, as to keep it from ever aspiring to a full certainty: but since these fundamental principles depend on the easiest and least deceitful appearances, they bestow on their consequences a degree of exactness, of which these consequences are singly incapable. It is impossible for the eye to determine the

[1] As regards pure geometry this distinction is not tenable and Hume abandoned it in the *Enquiry*, where he classifies geometry with arithmetic and algebra as exact sciences. Vide *Enquiry* Sect. 4 and Sect. 12, part 3.
—[ED.]

angles of a chiliagon to be equal to 1996 right angles, or make any conjecture, that approaches this proportion; but when it determines, that right lines cannot concur; that we cannot draw more than one right line between two given points; its mistakes can never be of any consequence. And this is the nature and use of geometry, to run us up to such appearances, as, by reason of their simplicity, cannot lead us into any considerable error.

I shall here take occasion to propose a second observation concerning our demonstrative reasonings, which is suggested by the same object of the mathematics. It is usual with mathematicians to pretend, that those ideas, which are their objects, are of so refined and spiritual a nature, that they fall not under the conception of the fancy, but must be comprehended by a pure and intellectual view, of which the superior faculties of the soul are alone capable. The same notion runs through most parts of philosophy, and is principally made use of to explain our abstract ideas, and to show how we can form an idea of a triangle, for instance, which shall neither be an isosceles nor scalenum, nor be confined to any particular length and proportion of sides. It is easy to see why philosophers are so fond of this notion of some spiritual and refined perceptions; since by that means they cover many of their absurdities, and may refuse to submit to the decisions of clear ideas, by appealing to such as are obscure and uncertain. But to destroy this artifice, we need but reflect on that principle so oft insisted on, *that all our ideas are copied from our impressions.* For from thence we may immediately conclude, that since all impressions are clear and precise, the ideas, which are copied from them, must be of the same nature, and can never, but from our fault, contain anything so dark and intricate. An idea is by its very nature weaker and fainter than an impression; but being in every other respect the same, cannot imply any very great mystery. If its weakness render it obscure, it is our business to remedy that defect, as much as possible, by keeping the idea steady and precise; and till we have done so, it is in vain to pretend to reasoning and philosophy.

SECTION II

OF PROBABILITY, AND OF THE IDEA OF CAUSE AND EFFECT

THIS is all I think necessary to observe concerning those four relations, which are the foundation of science; but as to the other three, which depend not upon the idea, and may be absent or present even while *that* remains the same, it will be proper to explain them more particularly. These three relations are *identity, the situations in time and place, and causation.*

All kinds of reasoning consist in nothing but a *comparison*, and a discovery of those relations, either constant or inconstant, which two or more objects bear to each other. This comparison we may make, either when both the objects are present to the senses, or when neither of them is present, or when only one. When both the objects are present to the senses along with the relation, we call *this* perception rather than reasoning; nor is there in this case any exercise of the thought, or any action, properly speaking, but a mere passive admission of the impressions through the organs of sensation. According to this way of thinking, we ought not to receive as reasoning any of the observations we may make concerning *identity* and the *relations* of *time* and *place*; since in none of them the mind can go beyond what is immediately present to the senses, either to discover the real existence or the relations of objects. It is only *causation*, which produces such a connection, as to give us assurance from the existence or action of one object, that it was followed or preceded by any other existence or action; nor can the other two relations ever be made use of in reasoning, except so far as they either affect or are affected by it. There is nothing in any objects to persuade us, that they are either always *remote* or always *contiguous;* and when from experience and observation we discover, that their relation in this particular is is invariable, we always conclude there is some secret *cause* which separates or unites them. The same reasoning extends to *identity.* We readily suppose an object may continue individually the same, though several times absent from and present to the senses; and ascribe to it an identity, notwithstanding the interruption of the perception, whenever we conclude, that if we had kept our eye or hand constantly upon it, it would have conveyed an invariable and uninterrupted perception. But this conclusion beyond the impressions of our senses can be founded only on the connection of *cause and effect*; nor can we otherwise have any security that the object is not changed upon us, however much the new object may resemble that which was formerly present to the senses. Whenever we discover such a perfect resemblance, we consider whether it be common in that species of objects; whether possibly or probably any cause could operate in producing the change and resemblance; and according as we determine concerning these causes and effects, we form our judgment concerning the identity of the object.

Here then it appears, that of those three relations, which depend not upon the mere ideas, the only one that can be traced beyond our senses, and informs us of existences and objects, which we do not see or feel, is *causation*. This relation therefore we shall endeavour to explain fully before we leave the subject of the understanding.

To begin regularly, we must consider the idea of *causation*, and see from what origin it is derived. It is impossible to reason justly, without understanding perfectly the idea concerning which we reason; and it is impossible perfectly to understand any idea, without tracing it up to its origin, and examining that primary impression, from which it arises. The examination of the impression bestows a clearness on the idea; and the examination of the idea bestows a like clearness on all our reasoning.

Let us therefore cast our eye on any two objects, which we call cause and effect, and turn them on all sides, in order to find that impression, which produces an idea of such prodigious consequence. At first sight I perceive, that I must not search for it in any of the particular *qualities* of the objects; since, whichever of these qualities I pitch on, I find some object that is not possessed of it, and yet falls under the denomination of cause or effect. And indeed there is nothing existent, either externally or internally, which is not to be considered either as a cause or an effect; though it is plain there is no one quality which universally belongs to all beings, and gives them a title to that denomination.

The idea then of causation must be derived from some *relation* among objects; and that relation we must now endeavour to discover. I find in the first place, that whatever objects are considered as causes or effects, are *contiguous*; and that nothing can operate in a time or place, which is ever so little removed from those of its existence. Though distant objects may sometimes seem productive of each other, they are commonly found upon examination to be linked by a chain of causes, which are contiguous among themselves, and to the distant objects; and when in any particular instance we cannot discover this connection, we still presume it to exist. We may therefore consider the relation of *contiguity* as essential to that of causation; at least may suppose it such, according to the general opinion, till we can find a more proper occasion[1] to clear up this matter, by examining what objects are or are not susceptible of juxtaposition and conjunction.

The second relation I shall observe as essential to causes and effects, is not so universally acknowledged, but is liable to some controversy. It is that of *priority* of time in the cause before the effect. Some pretend that it is not absolutely necessary, a cause should precede its effect; but that any object or action, in the very first moment of its existence, may exert its productive quality, and give rise to another object or action, perfectly contemporary with itself. But beside that experience in most instances seems to contradict this opinion, we may establish the relation of priority by a kind of inference or reasoning. It is an established maxim, both in natural and moral philosophy, that an object which exists for any time in its full perfection without producing another, is not its sole cause; but is assisted by some other principle which pushes it from its state of inactivity, and makes it exert that energy, of which it was secretly possessed. Now if any cause may be perfectly contemporary with its effect, it is certain, according to this maxim, that they must all of them be so; since any one of them, which retards its operation for a single moment, exerts not itself at that very individual time, in which it might have operated; and therefore is no proper cause. The consequence of this would be no less than the destruction of that succession of causes, which we observe in the world; and indeed the utter annihilation of time. For if one cause were contemporary with its effect, and this effect with *its* effect, and so on, it is plain there would be no such thing as succession, and all objects must be coexistent.

If this argument appear satisfactory, it is well. If not, I beg the reader to allow me the same liberty, which I have used in the preceding case, of supposing it such. For he shall find, that the affair is of no great importance.

Having thus discovered or supposed the two relations of *contiguity* and *succession* to be essential to causes and effects, I find I am stopped short, and can proceed no further in considering any single instance of cause and effect. Motion in one body is

[1] Part IV. Sect. 5.

regarded upon impulse as the cause of motion in another. When we consider these objects with the utmost attention, we find only that the one body approaches the other; and that the motion of it precedes that of the other, but without any sensible interval. It is in vain to rack ourselves with *further* thought and reflection upon this subject. We can go no *further* in considering this particular instance.

Should any one leave this instance, and pretend to define a cause, by saying it is something productive of another, it is evident he would say nothing. For what does he mean by *production?* Can he give any definition of it, that will not be the same with that of causation? If he can, I desire it may be produced. If he cannot, he here runs in a circle, and gives a synonymous term instead of a definition.

Shall we then rest contented with these two relations of contiguity and succession, as affording a complete idea of causation? By no means. An object may be contiguous and prior to another, without being considered as its cause. There is a *necessary connection* to be taken into consideration; and that relation is of much greater importance, than any of the other two above mentioned.

Here again I turn the object on all sides, in order to discover the nature of this necessary connection, and find the impression, or impressions, from which its idea may be derived. When I cast my eye on the *known qualities* of objects, I immediately discover that the relation of cause and effect depends not in the least on *them.* When I consider their *relations,* I can find none but those of contiguity and succession; which I have already regarded as imperfect and unsatisfactory. Shall the despair of success make me assert, that I am here possessed of an idea, which is not preceded by any similar impression? This would be too strong a proof of levity and inconstancy; since the contrary principle has been already so firmly established, as to admit of no further doubt; at least, till we have more fully examined the present difficulty.

We must therefore proceed like those who, being in search of anything that lies concealed from them, and not finding it in the place they expected, beat about all the neighbouring fields, without any certain view or design, in hopes their good fortune will at last guide them to what they search for. It is necessary for us to leave the direct survey of this question concerning the nature of that *necessary connection,* which enters into our idea of cause and effect; and endeavour to find some other questions, the

examination of which will perhaps afford a hint, that may serve
to clear up the present difficulty. Of these questions there occur
two, which I shall proceed to examine, viz.,

First, for what reason we pronounce it *necessary*, that everything
whose existence has a beginning, should also have a cause?

Secondly, why we conclude, that such particular causes must
necessarily have such particular effects; and what is the nature
of that *inference* we draw from the one to the other, and of the
belief we repose in it?

I shall only observe before I proceed any further, that though
the ideas of cause and effect be derived from the impressions of
reflection as well as from those of sensation, yet for brevity's sake,
I commonly mention only the latter as the origin of these ideas;
though I desire that, whatever I say of them, may also extend
to the former. Passions are connected with their objects and with
one another; no less than external bodies are connected together.
The same relation then of cause and effect, which belongs to one,
must be common to all of them.

SECTION III

WHY A CAUSE IS ALWAYS NECESSARY

To begin with the first question concerning the necessity of a
cause: It is a general maxim in philosophy, that *whatever begins
to exist, must have a cause of existence*. This is commonly taken
for granted in all reasonings, without any proof given or demanded.
It is supposed to be founded on intuition, and to be one of those
maxims which, though they may be denied with the lips, it is
impossible for men in their hearts really to doubt of. But if we
examine this maxim by the idea or knowledge above explained,
we shall discover in it no mark of any such intuitive certainty;
but on the contrary shall find, that it is of a nature quite foreign
to that species of conviction.

All certainty arises from the comparison of ideas, and from the
discovery of such relations as are unalterable, so long as the ideas
continue the same. These relations are *resemblance, proportions
in quantity and number, degrees of any quality, and contrariety;*
none of which are implied in this proposition, *Whatever has a
beginning has also a cause of existence*. That proposition therefore

is not intuitively certain. At least any one, who would assert it to be intuitively certain, must deny these to be the only infallible relations, and must find some other relation of that kind to be implied in it; which it will then be time enough to examine.

But here is an argument, which proves at once, that the foregoing proposition is neither intuitively nor demonstrably certain. We can never demonstrate the necessity of a cause to every new existence, or new modification of existence, without showing at the same time the impossibility there is, that anything can ever begin to exist without some productive principle; and where the latter proposition cannot be proved, we must despair of ever being able to prove the former. Now that the latter proposition is utterly incapable of a demonstrative proof, we may satisfy ourselves by considering, that as all distinct ideas are separable from each other, and as the ideas of cause and effect are evidently distinct, it will be easy for us to conceive any object to be non-existent this moment, and existent the next, without conjoining to it the distinct idea of a cause or productive principle. The separation therefore of the idea of a cause from that of a beginning of existence, is plainly possible for the imagination; and consequently the actual separation of these objects is so far possible, that it implies no contradiction nor absurdity; and is therefore incapable of being refuted by any reasoning from mere ideas, without which it is impossible to demonstrate the necessity of a cause.

Accordingly, we shall find upon examination, that every demonstration, which has been produced for the necessity of a cause, is fallacious and sophistical. All the points of time and place, say some philsophers,[1] in which we can suppose any object to begin to exist, are in themselves equal; and unless there be some cause, which is peculiar to one time and to one place, and which by that means determines and fixes the existence, it must remain in eternal suspense; and the object can never begin to be, for want of something to fix its beginning. But I ask, is there any more difficulty in supposing the time and place to be fixed without a cause, than to suppose the existence to be determined in that manner! The first question that occurs on this subject is always, *whether* the object shall exist or not: the next, *when* and *where* it shall begin to exist. If the removal of a cause be intuitively absurd in the one case, it must be so in the other; and if that absurdity be not clear without a proof in the one case, it will equally require one in the other. The absurdity then of the one supposition

[1] Mr. Hobbes.

can never be a proof of that of the other; since they are both upon the same footing, and must stand or fall by the same reasoning.

The second argument,[1] which I find used on this head, labours under an equal difficulty. Everything, it is said, must have a cause; for if anything wanted a cause, *it* would produce *itself*, that is, exist before it existed, which is impossible. But this reasoning is plainly unconclusive; because it supposes that, in our denial of a cause, we still grant what we expressly deny, viz., that there must be a cause; which therefore is taken to be the object itself; and *that*, no doubt, is an evident contradiction. But to say that anything is produced, or, to express myself more properly, comes into existence, without a cause, is not to affirm that it is itself its own cause; but, on the contrary, in excluding all external causes, excludes *a fortiori* the thing itself which is created. An object that exists absolutely without any cause, certainly is not its own cause; and when you assert, that the one follows from the other, you suppose the very point in question, and take it for granted that it is utterly impossible anything can ever begin to exist without a cause, but that, upon the exclusion of one productive principle, we must still have recourse to another.

It is exactly the same case with the third argument,[2] which has been employed to demonstrate the necessity of a cause. Whatever is produced without any cause, is produced by *nothing*; or, in other words, has nothing for its cause. But nothing can never be a cause, nor more than it can be something, or equal to two right angles. By the same intuition, that we perceive nothing not to be equal to two right angles, or not to be something, we perceive, that it can never be a cause; and consequently must perceive, that every object has a real cause of its existence.

I believe it will not be necessary to employ many words in showing the weakness of this argument, after what I have said of the foregoing. They are all of them founded on the same fallacy, and are derived from the same turn of thought. It is sufficient only to observe, that when we exclude all causes we really do exclude them, and neither suppose nothing nor the object itself to be the cause of the existence; and consequently can draw no argument from the absurdity of these suppositions to prove the absurdity of that exclusion. If everything must have a cause, it follows, that, upon the exclusion of other causes, we must accept of the object itself or of nothing as causes. But it is the very point in question, whether everything must have a cause or not; and

[1] Dr. Clarke and others.   [2] Mr. Locke.

therefore, according to all just reasoning, it ought never to be taken for granted.

They are still more frivolous who say, that every effect must have a cause, because it is implied in the very idea of effect. Every effect necessarily presupposes a cause; effect being a relative term, of which cause is the correlative. But this does not prove that every being must be preceded by a cause; no more than it follows, because every husband must have a wife, that therefore every man must be married. The true state of the question is, whether every object which begins to exist, must owe its existence to a cause; and this I assert neither to be intuitively nor demonstratively certain, and hope to have proved it sufficiently by the foregoing arguments.

Since it is not from knowledge or any scientific reasoning, that we derive the opinion of the necessity of a cause to every new production, that opinion must necessarily arise from observation and experience. The next question, then, should naturally be, *how experience gives rise to such a principle?* But as I find it will be more convenient to sink this question in the following, *why we conclude, that such particular causes must necessarily have such particular effects, and why we form an inference from one to another?* we shall make that the subject of our future inquiry. It will, perhaps, be found in the end, that the same answer will serve for both questions.

SECTION IV

OF THE COMPONENT PARTS OF OUR REASONINGS CONCERNING CAUSE AND EFFECT

THOUGH the mind in its reasonings from causes or effects, carries its view beyond those objects which it sees or remembers, it must never lose sight of them entirely, nor reason merely upon its own ideas, without some mixture of impressions, or at least of ideas of the memory, which are equivalent to impressions. When we infer effects from causes, we must establish the existence of these causes; which we have only two ways of doing, either by an immediate perception of our memory or senses, or by an inference from other causes; which causes again we must ascertain in the same manner, either by a present impression or by an inference from *their* causes, and so on, till we arrive at some object, which we see or remember.

It is impossible for us to carry on our inferences *in infinitum*; and the only thing that can stop them, is an impression of the memory or senses, beyond which is no room for doubt or inquiry. To give an instance of this, we may choose any point of history, and consider for what reason we either believe or reject it. Thus, we believe that Cæsar was killed in the senate-house on the *ides* of *March*, and that because this fact is established on the unanimous testimony of historians, who agree to assign this precise time and place to that event. Here are certain characters and letters present either to our memory or senses; which characters we likewise remember to have been used as the signs of certain ideas; and these ideas were either in the minds of such as were immediately present at that action, and received the ideas directly from its existence; or they were derived from the testimony of others, and that again from another testimony, by a visible gradation, till we arrive at those who were eye-witnesses and spectators of the event. It is obvious all this chain of argument or connection of causes and effects, is at first founded on those characters or letters, which are seen or remembered, and that without the authority either of the memory or senses, our whole reasoning would be chimerical and without foundation. Every link of the chain would in that case hang upon another; but there would not be anything fixed to one end of it, capable of sustaining the whole; and consequently there would be no belief nor evidence. And this actually is the case with all *hypothetical* arguments, or reasonings upon a supposition; there being in them neither any present impression, nor belief of a real existence.

I need not observe, that it is no just objection to the present doctrine, that we can reason upon our past conclusions or principles, without having recourse to those impressions, from which they first arose. For even supposing these impressions should be entirely effaced from the memory, the conviction they produced may still remain; and it is equally true, that all reasonings concerning causes and effects are originally derived from some impression; in the same manner, as the assurance of a demonstration proceeds always from a comparison of ideas, though it may continue after the comparison is forgot.

SECTION V

OF THE IMPRESSIONS OF THE SENSES AND MEMORY

In this kind of reasoning, then, from causation, we employ materials, which are of a mixed and heterogeneous nature, and which, however connected, are yet essentially different from each other. All our arguments concerning causes and effects consist both of an impression of the memory or senses, and of the idea of that existence, which produces the object of the impression, or is produced by it. Here, therefore, we have three things to explain, viz., *first*, the original impression. *Secondly*, the transition to the idea of the connected cause or effect. *Thirdly*, the nature and qualities of that idea.

As to those *impressions*, which arise from the *senses*, their ultimate cause is, in my opinion, perfectly inexplicable by human reason, and it will always be impossible to decide with certainty, whether they arise immediately from the object, or are produced by the creative power of the mind, or are derived from the Author of our being. Nor is such a question any way material to our present purpose. We may draw inferences from the coherence of our perceptions, whether they be true or false; whether they represent nature justly, or be mere illusions of the senses.

When we search for the characteristic, which distinguishes the *memory* from the imagination, we must immediately perceive, that it cannot lie in the simple ideas it presents to us; since both these faculties borrow their simple ideas from the impressions, and can never go beyond these original perceptions. These faculties are as little distinguished from each other by the arrangement of their complex ideas. For, though it be a peculiar property of the memory to preserve the original order and position of its ideas, while the imagination transposes and changes them as it pleases; yet this difference is not sufficient to distinguish them in their operation, or make us know the one from the other; it being impossible to recall the past impressions, in order to compare them with our present ideas, and see whether their arrangement be exactly similar. Since therefore the memory is known, neither by the order of its *complex* ideas, nor the nature of its *simple* ones; it follows, that the difference betwixt it and the imagination lies in its superior force and vivacity. A man may indulge his fancy in feigning any past scene of adventures; nor would there be any possibility of distinguishing this from a remembrance of a like kind, were not the ideas of the imagination fainter and more obscure.

It frequently happens, that when two men have been engaged in any scene of action, the one shall remember it much better than the other, and shall have all the difficulty in the world to make his companion recollect it. He runs over several circumstances in vain; mentions the time, the place, the company, what was said, what was done on all sides; till at last he hits on some lucky circumstance, that revives the whole, and gives his friend a perfect memory of everything. Here the person that forgets, receives at first all the ideas from the discourse of the other, with the same circumstances of time and place; though he considers them as mere fictions of the imagination. But as soon as the circumstance is mentioned that touches the memory, the very same ideas now appear in a new light, and have, in a manner, a different feeling from what they had before. Without any other alteration, beside that of the feeling, they become immediately ideas of the memory, and are assented to.

Since therefore the imagination can represent all the same objects that the memory can offer to us, and since those faculties are only distinguished by the different *feeling* of the ideas they present, it may be proper to consider what is the nature of that feeling. And here I believe every one will readily agree with me, that the ideas of the memory are more *strong* and *lively* than those of the fancy.

A painter, who intended to represent a passion or emotion of any kind, would endeavour to get a sight of a person actuated by a like emotion, in order to enliven his ideas, and give them a force and vivacity superior to what is found in those, which are mere fictions of the imagination. The more recent this memory is, the clearer is the idea; and when, after a long interval, he would return to the contemplation of his object, he always finds its idea to be much decayed, if not wholly obliterated. We are frequently in doubt concerning the ideas of the memory, as they become very weak and feeble; and are at a loss to determine whether any image proceeds from the fancy or the memory, when it is not drawn in such lively colours as distinguish that latter faculty. I think I remember such an event, says one; but am not sure. A long tract of time has almost worn it out of my memory, and leaves me uncertain whether or not it be the pure offspring of my fancy.

And as an idea of the memory, by losing its force and vivacity, may degenerate to such a degree, as to be taken for an idea of the imagination; so, on the other hand, an idea of the imagination may acquire such a force and vivacity, as to pass for an idea of the memory, and counterfeit its effects on the belief and judgment. This is noted in the case of liars; who by the frequent repetition of their lies, come at last to believe and remember them, as realities; custom and habit having, in this case, as in many others, the same influence on the mind as nature, and infixing the idea with equal force and vigour.

Thus it appears, that the *belief* or *assent*, which always attends the memory and senses, is nothing but the vivacity of those perceptions they present; and that this alone distinguishes them from the imagination. To believe is in this case to feel an immediate impression of the senses, or a repetition of that impression in the memory. It is merely the force and liveliness of the perception, which constitutes the first act of the judgment, and lays the foundation of that reasoning, which we build upon it, when we trace the relation of cause and effect.

SECTION VI

OF THE INFERENCE FROM THE IMPRESSION TO THE IDEA

It is easy to observe, that in tracing this relation, the inference we draw from cause to effect, is not derived merely from a survey of these particular objects, and from such a penetration into their essences as may discover the dependence of the one upon the other. There is no object which implies the existence of any other, if we consider these objects in themselves, and never look beyond the ideas which we form of them. Such an inference would amount to knowledge, and would imply the absolute contradiction and impossibility of conceiving anything different. But as all distinct ideas are separable, it is evident there can be no impossibility of that kind. When we pass from a present impression to the idea of any object, we might possibly have separated the idea from the impression, and have substituted any other idea in its room.

It is therefore by *experience* only that we can infer the existence of one object from that of another. The nature of experience is this. We remember to have had frequent instances of the existence of one species of objects; and also remember, that the individuals of another species of objects have always attended them, and have existed in a regular order of contiguity and succession with regard to them. Thus we remember to have seen that species of object we call *flame*, and to have felt that species of sensation we call *heat*. We likewise call to mind their constant conjunction in all past instances. Without any further ceremony, we call the one *cause*, and the other *effect*, and infer the existence of the one from that of the other. In all those instances from which we learn the conjunction of particular causes and effects, both the causes and effects have been perceived by the senses, and are remembered: but in all cases, wherein we reason concerning them, there is only one perceived or remembered, and the other is supplied in conformity to our past experience.

Thus, in advancing, we have insensibly discovered a new relation betwixt cause and effect when we least expected it, and were entirely employed upon another subject. This relation is their *constant conjunction*. Contiguity and succession are not sufficient to make us pronounce any two objects to be cause and effect, unless we perceive that these two relations are preserved in several instances. We may now see the advantage of quitting the direct survey of this relation, in order to discover the nature of that *necessary connection* which makes so essential a part of it. There are hopes, that by this means we may at last arrive at our proposed end; though, to tell the truth, this new-discovered relation of a constant conjunction seems to advance us but very little in our way. For it implies no more than this, that like objects have always been placed in like relations of contiguity and succession; and it seems evident, at least at first sight, that by this means we can never discover any new idea, and can only multiply, but not enlarge, the objects of our mind. It may be thought, that what we learn not from one object, we can never learn from a hundred, which are all of the same kind, and are perfectly resembling in every circumstance. As our senses show us in one instance two bodies, or motions, or qualities, in certain relations of succession and contiguity, so our memory presents us only with a multitude of instances wherein we always find like bodies, motions, or qualities, in like relations. From the mere repetition of any past impression, even to infinity, there never will arise any new original idea, such as that of a necessary connection; and the number of impressions has in this case no more effect than if we confined ourselves to one only. But though this reasoning seems just and obvious, yet, as it would be folly to despair too soon, we shall continue the thread of our discourse; and having found, that after the discovery of the constant conjunction of any objects, we always draw an inference from one object to another, we shall now examine the nature of that inference, and of the transition from the impression to the idea. Perhaps it will appear in the end, that the necessary connection depends on the inference, instead of the inference's depending on the necessary connection.

Since it appears, that the transition from an impression present to the memory or senses to the idea of an object, which we call cause or effect, is founded on past *experience*, and on our remembrance of their *constant conjunction*, the next question is, whether experience produces the idea by means of the understanding or imagination; whether we are determined by reason to make the transition, or by a certain association and relation of perceptions. If reason determined us, it would proceed upon that principle, *that instances, of which we have had no experience, must resemble those of which we have had experience, and that the course of nature continues always uniformly the same.* In order, therefore, to clear up this matter, let us consider all the arguments upon which such a proposition may be supposed to be founded; and as these must be derived either from *knowledge* or *probability*, let us cast our eye on each of these degrees of evidence, and see whether they afford any just conclusion of this nature.

Our foregoing method of reasoning will easily convince us, that there can be no *demonstrative* arguments to prove, *that those instances of which we have had no experience resemble those of which we have had experience.* We can at least conceive a change in the course of nature; which sufficiently proves that such a change is not absolutely impossible. To form a clear idea of anything is an undeniable argument for its possibility, and is alone a refutation of any pretended demonstration against it.

Probability, as it discovers not the relations of ideas, considered as such, but only those of objects, must, in some respects, be founded on the impressions of our memory and senses, and in some respects on our ideas. Were there no mixture of any impression in our probable reasonings, the conclusion would be entirely chimerical: and were there no mixture of ideas, the action of the mind, in observing the relation, would, properly speaking, be sensation, not reasoning. It is, therefore, necessary, that in all probable reasonings there be something present to the mind, either seen or remembered; and that from this we infer something connected with it, which is not seen nor remembered.

The only connection or relation of objects, which can lead us beyond the immediate impressions of our memory and senses, is that of cause and effect; and that because it is the only one, on which we can found a just inference from one object to another. The idea of cause and effect is derived from *experience*, which informs us, that such particular objects, in all past instances, have been constantly conjoined with each other: and as an object similar to one of these is supposed to be immediately present in its impression, we thence presume on the existence of one similar to its usual attendant. According to this account of things, which is, I think, in every point unquestionable, probability is founded on the presumption of a resemblance betwixt those objects of which we have had experience, and those of which we have had none; and, therefore, it is impossible this presumption can arise from probability. The same principle cannot be both the cause and effect of another; and this is, perhaps, the only proposition concerning that relation, which is either intuitively or demonstratively certain.

Should any one think to elude this argument; and without determining whether our reasoning on this subject be derived from demonstration or probability, pretend that all conclusions from causes and effects are built on solid reasoning: I can only desire that this reasoning may be produced, in order to be exposed to our examination. It may perhaps be said, that after experience of the constant conjunction of certain objects, we reason in the following manner. Such an object is always found to produce another. It is impossible it could have this effect, if it was not endowed with a power of production. The power necessarily implies the effect; and therefore there is a just foundation for drawing a conclusion from the existence of one object to that of its usual attendant. The past production implies a power: the power implies a new production: and the new production is what we infer from the power and the past production.

It were easy for me to show the weakness of this reasoning, were I willing to make use of those observations I have already made, that the idea of *production* is the same with that of *causation*, and that no existence certainly and demonstratively implies a power in any other object; or were it proper to anticipate what I shall have occasion to remark afterwards concerning the idea we form of *power* and *efficacy*. But as such a method of proceeding may seem either to weaken my system, by resting one part of it on another, I shall endeavour to maintain my present assertion without any such assistance.

It shall therefore be allowed for a moment, that the production of one object by another in any one instance implies a power; and that this power is connected with its effect. But it having been already proved, that the power lies not in the sensible qualities of the cause; and there being nothing but the sensible qualities present to us; I ask, why in other instances you presume that the same power still exists, merely upon the appearance of these qualities? Your appeal to past experience decides nothing in the present case; and at the utmost can only prove, that that very object, which produced any other, was at that very instant endowed with such a power; but can never prove, that the same power must continue in the same object or collection of sensible qualities; much less, that a like power is always conjoined with like sensible qualities. Should it be said, that we have experience, that the same power continues united with the same object, and that like objects are endowed with like powers, I would renew my question, *why from this experience we form any conclusion beyond those past instances, of which we have had experience?* If you answer this question in the same manner as the preceding, your answer gives still occasion to a new question of the same kind, even *in infinitum*; which clearly proves, that the foregoing reasoning had no just foundation.

Thus, not only our reason fails us in the discovery of the *ultimate connection* of causes and effects, but even after experience has informed us of their *constant conjunction,* it is impossible for us to satisfy ourselves by our reason, why we should extend that experience beyond those particular instances which have fallen under our observation. We suppose, but are never able to prove, that there must be a resemblance betwixt those objects, of which we have had experience, and those which lie beyond the reach of our discovery.

We have already taken notice of certain relations, which make us pass from one object to another, even though there be no reason to determine us to that transition; and this we may establish for a general rule, that wherever the mind constantly and uniformly makes a transition without any reason, it is influenced by these relations. Now, this is exactly the present case. Reason can never show us the connection of one object with another, though aided by experience, and the observation of their constant conjunction in all past instances. When the mind therefore passes from the idea or impression of one object to the idea or belief of another, it is not determined by reason, but by certain principles, which associate together the ideas of these objects, and unite them in the imagination. Had ideas no more union in the fancy, than objects seem to have to the understanding, we could never draw any inference from causes to effects, nor repose belief in any matter of fact. The inference therefore depends solely on the union of ideas.

The principles of union among ideas, I have reduced to three general ones, and have asserted, that the idea or impression of any object naturally introduces the idea of any other object, that is resembling, contiguous to, or connected with it. These principles I allow to be neither the *infallible* nor the *sole* causes of a union among ideas. They are not the infallible causes. For one may fix his ·attention during some time on any one object without looking further. They are not the sole causes. For the thought has evidently a very irregular motion in running along its objects, and may leap from the heavens to the earth, from one end of the creation to the other, without any certain method or order. But though I allow this weakness in these three relations, and this irregularity in the imagination; yet I assert, that the only *general* principles which associate ideas, are resemblance, contiguity, and causation.

There is indeed a principle of union among ideas, which at first sight may be esteemed different from any of these, but will be found at the bottom to depend on the same origin. When every individual of any species of objects is found by experience to be constantly united with an individual of another species, the appearance of any new individual of either species naturally conveys the thought to its usual attendant. Thus, because such a particular idea is commonly annexed to such a particular word, nothing is required but the hearing of that word to produce the correspondent idea; and it will scarce be possible for the mind, by its utmost efforts, to prevent that transition. In this case it is not absolutely necessary, that upon hearing such a particular sound, we should reflect on any past experience, and consider what idea has been usually connected with the sound. The imagination of itself supplies the place of this reflection, and is so accustomed to pass from the word to the idea, that it interposes not a moment's delay betwixt the hearing of the one, and the conception of the other.

But though I acknowledge this to be a true principle of association among ideas, I assert it to be the very same with that betwixt the ideas of cause and effect, and to be an essential part in all our reasonings from that relation. We have no other notion of cause and effect, but that of certain objects, which have been *always conjoined* together, and which in all past instances have been found inseparable. We cannot penetrate into the reason of the conjunction. We only observe the thing itself, and always find that, from the constant conjunction, the objects require a union in the imagination. When the impression of one becomes present to us, we immediately form an idea of its usual attendant; and consequently we may establish this as one part of the definition of an opinion or belief, that it is *an idea related to or associated with a present impression*.

Thus, though causation be a *philosophical* relation, as implying contiguity, succession, and constant conjunction, yet it is only so far as it is a *natural* relation, and produces a union among our ideas, that we are able to reason upon it, or draw any inference from it.

SECTION VII

OF THE NATURE OF THE IDEA OR BELIEF

THE idea of an object is an essential part of the belief of it, but not the whole. We conceive many things which we do not believe. In order, then, to discover more fully the nature of belief, or the qualities of those ideas we assent to, let us weigh the following considerations.

It is evident, that all reasonings from causes or effects terminate in conclusions concerning matter of fact; that is, concerning the existence of objects or of their qualities. It is also evident, that the idea of existence is nothing different from the idea of any object, and that when after the simple conception of anything we would conceive it as existent, we in reality make no addition to or alteration on our first idea. Thus, when we affirm that God is existent, we simply form the idea of such a Being as he is represented to us: nor is the existence, which we attribute to him, conceived by a particular idea, which we join to the idea of his other qualities, and can again separate and distinguish from them. But I go further; and, not content with asserting, that the conception of the existence of any object is no addition to the simple conception of it, I likewise maintain, that the belief of the existence joins no new ideas to those, which compose the idea of the object. When I think of God, when I think of him as existent, and when I believe him to be existent, my idea of him neither increases nor diminishes. But as it is certain there is a great difference betwixt the simple conception of the existence of an object, and the belief of it, and as this difference lies not in the parts or composition of the idea which we conceive; it follows, that it must lie in the *manner* in which we conceive it.

Suppose a person present with me, who advances propositions, to which I do not assent, *that Cæsar died in his bed, that silver is more fusible than lead, or mercury heavier than gold;* it is evident that, notwithstanding my incredulity, I clearly understand his meaning, and form all the same ideas which he forms. My imagination is endowed with the same powers as his; nor is it possible for him to conceive any idea, which I cannot conceive; or conjoin any, which I cannot conjoin. I therefore ask, wherein consists the difference betwixt believing and disbelieving any proposition? The answer is easy with regard to propositions, that are proved by intuition or demonstration. In that case, the person who assents not only conceives the ideas according to the proposition, but is necessarily determined to conceive them in that particular manner, either immediately, or by the interposition of other ideas. Whatever is absurd is unintelligible; nor is it possible for the imagination to conceive anything contrary to a demonstration. But as, in reasonings from causation, and concerning matters of fact, this absolute necessity cannot take place, and the imagination is free to conceive both sides of the question, I still ask, *wherein consists the difference betwixt incredulity and belief?* since, in both cases the conception of the idea is equally possible and requisite.

It will not be a satisfactory answer to say, that a person, who does not assent to a proposition you advance; after having conceived the object in the same manner with you, immediately conceives it in a different manner, and has different ideas of it. This answer is unsatisfactory; not because it contains any falsehood, but because it discovers not all the truth. It is confessed that, in all cases wherein we dissent from any person, we conceive both sides of the question; but as we can believe only one, it evidently follows, that the belief must make some difference betwixt that conception to which we assent, and that from which we dissent. We may mingle, and unite, and separate, and confound, and vary our ideas in a hundred different ways; but until there appears some principle, which fixes one of these different situations, we have in reality no opinion: and this principle, as it plainly makes no addition to our precedent ideas, can only change the *manner* of our conceiving them.

All the perceptions of the mind are of two kinds, viz., impressions and ideas, which differ from each other only in their different degrees of force and vivacity. Our ideas are copied from our impressions, and represent them in all their parts. When you would any way vary the idea of a particular object, you can only increase or diminish its force and vivacity. If you make any other change on it, it represents a different object or impression. The case is the same as in colours. A particular shade of any colour may acquire a new degree of liveliness or brightness without any other variation. But when you produce any other variation, it is no longer the same shade or colour; so that as belief does nothing but vary the manner in which we conceive any object, it can only bestow on our ideas an additional force and vivacity. An opinion, therefore, or belief, may be most accurately defined, *a lively idea related to or associated with a present impression.*[1]

[1] We may here take occasion to observe a very remarkable error, which, being frequently inculcated in the schools, has become a kind of established maxim, and is universally received by all logicians. This error consists in the vulgar division of the acts of the understanding into *conception, judgment,* and *reasoning,* and in the definitions we give of them. Conception is defined to be the simple survey of one or more ideas: judgment to be the separating or uniting of different ideas: reasoning to be the separating or uniting of different ideas by the interposition of others, which show the relation they bear to each other. But these distinctions and definitions are faulty in very considerable articles. For, *first,* it is far from being true, that, in every judgment which we form, we unite two different ideas; since in that proposition, *God is,* or indeed, any other, which regards existence, the idea of existence is no distinct idea, which we unite with that of the object, and which is capable of forming a compound idea by the union. *Secondly,* as we can thus form a proposition, which contains only one idea, so we may exert our reason without employing more than two ideas, and without having recourse to a third to serve as a medium betwixt them. We infer a cause immediately from its effect; and this inference is not only a true species of reasoning, but the strongest of all others, and more convincing than when we interpose another idea to connect the two extremes. What we may in general affirm concerning these three acts of the understanding is, that taking them in a proper light, they all resolve themselves into the first, and are nothing but particular ways of conceiving our objects. Whether we consider a single object or several; whether we dwell on these objects, or run from them to others; and in whatever form or order we survey them, the act of the mind exceeds not a simple conception; and the only remarkable difference, which occurs on this occasion, is, when we join belief to the conception, and are persuaded of the truth of what we conceive. This act of the mind has never yet been explained by any philosopher; and therefore I am at liberty to propose my hypothesis concerning it; which is, that it is only a strong and steady conception of any idea, and such as approaches in some measure to an immediate impression.

Here are the heads of those arguments, which lead us to this conclusion. When we infer the existence of an object from that of others, some object must always be present either to the memory or senses, in order to be the foundation of our reasoning; since the mind cannot run up with its inferences *in infinitum*. Reason can never satisfy us that the existence of any one object does ever imply that of another; so that when we pass from the impression of one to the idea or belief of another, we are not determined by reason, but by custom, or a principle of association. But belief is somewhat more than a simple idea. It is a particular manner of forming an idea; and as the same idea can only be varied by a variation of its degrees of force and vivacity; it follows upon the whole, that belief is a lively idea produced by a relation to a present impression, according to the foregoing definition.

This operation of the mind, which forms the belief of any matter of fact, seems hitherto to have been one of the greatest mysteries of philosophy; though no one has so much as suspected, that there was any difficulty in explaining it. For my part, I must own, that I find a considerable difficulty in the case; and that even when I think I understand the subject perfectly, I am at a loss for terms to express my meaning. I conclude, by an induction which seems to me very evident, that an opinion or belief is nothing but an idea, that is different from a fiction, not in the nature, or the order of its parts, but in the *manner* of its being conceived. But when I would explain this *manner*, I scarce find any word that fully answers the case, but am obliged to have recourse to every one's feeling, in order to give him a perfect notion of this operation of the mind. An idea assented to *feels* different from a fictitious idea, that the fancy alone presents to us: and this different feeling I endeavour to explain by calling it a superior *force*, or *vivacity*, or *solidity*, or *firmness*, or *steadiness*. This variety of terms, which may seem so unphilosophical, is intended only to express that act of the mind, which renders realities more present to us than fictions, causes them to weigh more in the thought, and gives them a superior influence on the passions and imagination. Provided we agree about the thing, it is needless to dispute about the terms. The imagination has the command over all its ideas, and can join, and mix, and vary them in all the ways possible. It may conceive objects with all the circumstances of place and time. It may set them, in a manner, before our eyes in their true colours, just as they might have existed. But as it is impossible that that faculty can ever of itself reach belief, it is

evident, that belief consists not in the nature and order of our
ideas, but in the manner of their conception, and in their feeling
to the mind. I confess, that it is impossible to explain perfectly
this feeling or manner of conception. We may make use of words
that express something near it. But its true and proper name is
belief, which is a term that every one sufficiently understands in
common life. And in philosophy, we can go no further than
assert, that it is something *felt* by the mind, which distinguishes
the ideas of the judgment from the fictions of the imagination. It
gives them more force and influence; makes them appear of greater
importance; infixes them in the mind; and renders them the
governing principles of all our actions.

This definition will also be found to be entirely conformable to
every one's feeling and experience. Nothing is more evident, than
that those ideas, to which we assent, are more strong, firm, and
vivid, than the loose reveries of a castle-builder. If one person
sits down to read a book as a romance, and another as a true
history, they plainly receive the same ideas, and in the same order;
nor does the incredulity of the one, and the belief of the other,
hinder them from putting the very same sense upon their author.
His words produce the same ideas in both; though his testimony
has not the same influence on them. The latter has a more lively
conception of all the incidents. He enters deeper into the concerns
of the persons: represents to himself their actions, and characters,
and friendships, and enmities: he even goes so far as to form a
notion of their features, and air, and person. While the former,
who gives no credit to the testimony of the author, has a more
faint and languid conception of all these particulars, and, except
on account of the style and ingenuity of the composition, can
receive little entertainment from it.

SECTION VIII

OF THE CAUSES OF BELIEF

HAVING thus explained the nature of belief, and shown that it
consists in a lively idea related to a present impression; let us now
proceed to examine from what principles it is derived, and what
bestows the vivacity on the idea.

I would willingly establish it as a general maxim in the science
of human nature, *that when any impression becomes present to us,*

*it not only transports the mind to such ideas as are related to it,
but likewise communicates to them a share of its force and vivacity.*
All the operations of the mind depend, in a great measure, on its
disposition when it performs them; and according as the spirits are
more or less elevated, and the attention more or less fixed, the
action will always have more or less vigour and vivacity. When
therefore, any object is presented which elevates and enlivens the
thought, every action, to which the mind applies itself, will be
more strong and vivid, as long as that disposition continues. Now,
it is evident the continuance of the disposition depends entirely on
the objects about which the mind is employed; and that any new
object naturally gives a new direction to the spirits, and changes
the disposition; as on the contrary, when the mind fixes constantly
on the same object, or passes easily and insensibly along related
objects, the disposition has a much longer duration. Hence it
happens, that when the mind is once enlivened by a present
impression, it proceeds to form a more lively idea of the related
objects, by a natural transposition of the disposition from the one
to the other. The change of the objects is so easy, that the mind
is scarce sensible of it, but applies itself to the conception of the
related idea with all the force and vivacity it acquired from the
present impression.

If, in considering the nature of relation, and that facility of
transition which is essential to it, we can satisfy ourselves concerning the reality of this phenomenon, it is well: but I must confess
I place my chief confidence in experience to prove so material a
principle. We may therefore observe, as the first experiment to
our present purpose, that upon the appearance of the picture of an
absent friend, our idea of him is evidently enlivened by the
resemblance, and that every passion which that idea occasions,
whether of joy or sorrow, acquires new force and vigour. In
producing this effect there concur both a relation and a present
impression. Where the picture bears him no resemblance, or at
least was not intended for him, it never so much as conveys our
thought to him: and where it is absent as well as the person; though
the mind may pass from the thought of the one to that of the other;
it feels its idea to be rather weakened than enlivened by that
transition. We take a pleasure in viewing the picture of a friend,
when it is set before us; but when it is removed, rather choose to
consider him directly, than by reflection in an image, which is
equally distant and obscure.

The ceremonies of the Roman Catholic religion may be

considered as experiments of the same nature. The devotees of
that strange superstition usually plead in excuse of the mummeries
with which they are upbraided, that they feel the good effect of
those external motions, and postures, and actions, in enlivening
their devotion, and quickening their fervour, which otherwise
would decay away, if directed entirely to distant and immaterial
objects. We shadow out the objects of our faith, say they, in
sensible types and images, and render them more present to us
by the immediate presence of these types, than it is possible for
us to do, merely by an intellectual view and contemplation.
Sensible objects have always a greater influence on the fancy than
any other; and this influence they readily convey to those ideas
to which they are related, and which they resemble. I shall only
infer from these practices, and this reasoning, that the effect of
resemblance in enlivening the idea is very common; and as in
every case a resemblance and a present impression must concur,
we are abundantly supplied with experiments to prove the reality
of the foregoing principle.

We may add force to these experiments by others of a different
kind, in considering the effects of *contiguity*, as well as of *resemblance*. It is certain that distance diminishes the force of every
idea; and that, upon our approach to any object, though it does
not discover itself to our senses, it operates upon the mind with an
influence that imitates an immediate impression. The thinking on
any object readily transports the mind to what is contiguous; but
it is only the actual presence of an object, that transports it with
a superior vivacity. When I am a few miles from home, whatever
relates to it touches me more nearly than when I am two hundred
leagues distant; though even at that distance the reflecting on
anything in the neighbourhood of my friends and family naturally
produces an idea of them. But as in this latter case, both the
objects of the mind are ideas; notwithstanding there is an easy
transition betwixt them; that transition alone is not able to give a
superior vivacity to any of the ideas, for want of some immediate
impression.

No one can doubt but causation has the same influence as the
other two relations of resemblance and contiguity. Superstitious
people are fond of the relics of saints and holy men, for the same
reason that they seek after types and images, in order to enliven
their devotion, and give them a more intimate and strong conception
of those exemplary lives, which they desire to imitate. Now, it is
evident one of the best relics a devotee could procure would be

DAVID HUME

the handywork of a saint; and if his clothes and furniture are ever to be considered in this light, it is because they were once at his disposal, and were moved and affected by him; in which respect they are to be considered as imperfect effects, and as connected with him by a shorter chain of consequences than any of those, from which we learn the reality of his existence. This phenomenon clearly proves, that a present impression with a relation of causation may enliven any idea, and consequently produce belief or assent, according to the precedent definition of it.

But why need we seek for other arguments to prove, that a present impression with a relation or transition of the fancy may enliven any idea, when this very instance of our reasonings from cause and effect will alone suffice to that purpose? It is certain we must have an idea of every matter of fact which we believe. It is certain that this idea arises only from a relation to a present impression. It is certain that the belief superadds nothing to the idea, but only changes our manner of conceiving it, and renders it more strong and lively. The present conclusion concerning the influence of relation is the immediate consequence of all these steps; and every step appears to be sure and infallible. There enters nothing into this operation of the mind but a present impression, a lively idea, and a relation or association in the fancy betwixt the impression and idea; so that there can be no suspicion of mistake.

In order to put this whole affair in a fuller light, let us consider it as a question in natural philosophy, which we must determine by experience and observation. I suppose there is an object presented, from which I draw a certain conclusion, and form to myself ideas, which I am said to believe or assent to. Here it is evident, that however that object, which is present to my senses, and that other, whose existence I infer by reasoning, may be thought to influence each other by their particular powers or qualities; yet as the phenomenon of belief, which we at present examine, is merely internal, these powers and qualities being entirely unknown, can have no hand in producing it. It is the present impression which is to be considered as the true and real cause of the idea, and of the belief which attends it. We must therefore endeavour to discover, by experiments, the particular qualities by which it is enabled to produce so extraordinary an effect.

First then I observe, that the present impression has not this effect by its own proper power and efficacy, and, when considered alone as a single perception, limited to the present moment. I find that an impression, from which, on its first appearance, I can draw no conclusion, may afterwards become the foundation of belief, when I have had experience of its usual consequences. We must in every case have observed the same impression in past instances, and have found it to be constantly conjoined with some other impression. This is confirmed by such a multitude of experiments, that it admits not of the smallest doubt.

From a second observation I conclude, that the belief which attends the present impression, and is produced by a number of past impressions and conjunctions; that this belief, I say, arises immediately, without any new operation of the reason or imagination. Of this I can be certain, because I never am conscious of any such operation, and find nothing in the subject on which it can be founded. Now, as we call everything *custom* which proceeds from a past repetition, without any new reasoning or conclusion, we may establish it as a certain truth, that all the belief, which follows upon any present impression, is derived solely from that origin. When we are accustomed to see two impressions conjoined together, the appearance or idea of the one immediately carries us to the idea of the other.

Being fully satisfied on this head, I make a third set of experiments, in order to know whether anything be requisite, beside the customary transition, towards the production of this phenomenon of belief. I therefore change the first impression into an idea; and observe, that though the customary transition to the correlative idea still remains, yet there is in reality no belief nor persuasion. A present impression, then, is absolutely requisite to this whole operation; and when after this I compare an impression with an idea, and find that their only difference consists in their different degrees of force and vivacity, I conclude upon the whole, that belief is a more vivid and intense conception of an idea, proceeding from its relation to a present impression.

Thus, all probable reasoning is nothing but a species of sensation. It is not solely in poetry and music we must follow our taste and sentiment, but likewise in philosophy. When I am convinced of any principle, it is only an idea which strikes more strongly upon me. When I give the preference to one set of arguments above another, I do nothing but decide from my feeling concerning the superiority of their influence. Objects have no discoverable connection together; nor is it from any other principle but custom operating upon the imagination, that we can draw any inference from the appearance of one to the existence of another.

It will be here worth our observation, that the past experience, on which all our judgments concerning cause and effect depend, may operate on our mind in such an insensible manner as never to be taken notice of, and may even in some measure be unknown to us. A person, who stops short in his journey upon meeting a river in his way, foresees the consequences of his proceeeding forward; and his knowledge of these consequences is conveyed to him by past experience, which informs him of such certain conjunctions of causes and effects. But can we think, that on this occasion he reflects on any past experience, and calls to remembrance instances that he has seen or heard of, in order to discover the effects of water on animal bodies? No, surely; this is not the method, in which he proceeds in his reasoning. The idea of sinking is so closely connected with that of water, and the idea of suffocating with that of sinking, that the mind makes the transition without the assistance of the memory. The custom operates before we have time for reflection. The objects seem so inseparable, that we interpose not a moment's delay in passing from the one or the other. But as this transition proceeds from experience, and not from any primary connection betwixt the ideas, we must necessarily acknowledge, that experience may produce a belief and a judgment of causes and effects by a separate operation, and without being once thought of. This removes all pretext, if there yet remains any, for asserting that the mind is convinced by reasoning of that principle, *that instances of which we have no experience, must necessarily resemble those of which we have.* For we here find, that the understanding or imagination can draw inferences from past experience, without reflecting on it; much more without forming any principle concerning it, or reasoning upon that principle.

In general we may observe, that in all the most established and uniform conjunctions of causes and effects, such as those of gravity, impulse, solidity, etc., the mind never carries its view expressly to consider any past experience: though in other associations of objects, which are more rare and unusual, it may assist the custom and transition of ideas by this reflection. Nay, we find in some cases, that the reflection produces the belief without the custom; or, more properly speaking, that the reflection produces the custom in an *oblique* and *artificial* manner. I explain myself. It is certain, that not only in philosophy, but even in common life, we may attain the knowledge of a particular cause merely by one experiment, provided it be made with judgment, and after a careful removal of all foreign and superfluous circumstances. Now, as after one experiment of this kind, the mind, upon the appearance either of the cause or the effect, can draw an inference concerning the existence of its correlative, and as a habit can never be acquired merely by one instance, it may be thought that belief cannot in this case be esteemed the effect of custom. But this difficulty will vanish, if we consider, that, though we are here supposed to have had only one experiment of a particular effect, yet we have many millions to convince us of this principle, *that like objects, placed in like circumstances, will always produce like effects*; and as this principle has established itself by a sufficient custom, it bestows an evidence and firmness on any opinion to which it can be applied. The connection of the ideas is not habitual after one experiment; but this connection is comprehended under another principle that is habitual; which brings us back to our hypothesis. In all cases we transfer our experience to instances of which we have no experience, either *expressly* or *tacitly*, either *directly* or *indirectly*.

I must not conclude this subject without observing, that it is very difficult to talk of the operations of the mind with perfect propriety and exactness; because common language has seldom made any very nice distinctions among them, but has generally called by the same term all such as nearly resemble each other. And as this is a source almost inevitable of obscurity and confusion in the author, so it may frequently give rise to doubts and objections in the reader, which otherwise he would never have dreamed of. Thus, my general position that an opinion or belief is *nothing but a strong and lively idea derived from a present impression related to it*, may be liable to the following objection, by reason of a little ambiguity in those words *strong* and *lively*. It may be said, that not only an impression may give rise to reasoning, but that an idea may also have the same influence; especially upon my principle, *that all our ideas are derived from correspondent impressions*. For, suppose I form at present an idea, of which I have forgot the correspondent impression, I am able to conclude, from this idea, that such an impression did once exist; and as this conclusion is attended with belief, it may be asked, from whence are the qualities of force and vivacity derived which constitute this belief? And to this I answer very readily, *from the present idea*. For as this idea is not here considered as the representation of any absent object, but as a real perception in the mind, of which we are intimately conscious, it must be able to bestow, on whatever is related to it, the same quality, call it *firmness*, or *solidity*, or *force*, or *vivacity*, with which the mind reflects upon it, and is assured of its present existence. The idea here supplies the place of an impression, and is entirely the same, so far as regards our present purpose.

Upon the same principles we need not be surprised to hear of the remembrance of an idea; that is, of the idea of an idea, and of its force and vivacity superior to the loose conceptions of the imagination. In thinking of our past thoughts we not only delineate out the objects of which we were thinking, but also conceive the action of the mind in the meditation, that certain *je-ne-scai-quoi*, of which it is impossible to give any definition or description, but which every one sufficiently understands. When the memory offers an idea of this, and represents it as past, it is easily conceived how that idea may have more vigour and firmness than when we think of a past thought of which we have no remembrance.

After this, any one will understand how we may form the idea of an impression and of an idea, and how we may believe the existence of an impression and of an idea.

SECTION IX

OF THE EFFECTS OF OTHER RELATIONS AND OTHER HABITS

HOWEVER convincing the foregoing arguments may appear, we must not rest contented with them, but must turn the subject on every side, in order to find some new points of view, from which we may illustrate and confirm such extraordinary and such fundamental principles. A scrupulous hesitation to receive any new hypothesis is so laudable a disposition in philosophers, and so necessary to the examination of truth, that it deserves to be complied with, and requires that every argument be produced which may tend to their satisfaction, and every objection removed which may stop them in their reasoning.

I have often observed, that, beside cause and effect, the two relations of resemblance and contiguity are to be considered as associating principles of thought, and as capable of conveying the imagination from one idea to another. I have also observed, that when of two objects, connected together by any of these relations, one is immediately present to the memory or senses, not only the mind is conveyed to its co-relative by means of the associating principle, but likewise conceives it with an additional force and

386 BRITISH EMPIRICAL PHILOSOPHERS

vigour, by the united operation of that principle, and of the present impression. All this I have observed, in order to confirm, by analogy, my explication of our judgments concerning cause and effect. But this very argument may perhaps be turned against me, and instead of a confirmation of my hypothesis, may become an objection to it. For it may be said, that, if all the parts of that hypothesis be true, viz., *that* these three species of relation are derived from the same principles; *that* their effects, in enforcing and enlivening our ideas, are the same; and *that* belief is nothing but a more forcible and vivid conception of an idea; it should follow, that that action of the mind may not only be derived from the relation of cause and effect, but also from those of contiguity and resemblance. But as we find by experience that belief arises only from causation, and that we can draw no inference from one object to another, except they be connected by this relation, we may conclude, that there is some error in that reasoning which leads us into such difficulties.

This is the objection: let us now consider its solution. It is evident, that whatever is present to the memory, striking upon the mind with a vivacity which resembles an immediate impression, must become of considerable moment in all the operations of the mind, and must easily distinguish itself above the mere fictions of the imagination. Of these impressions or ideas of the memory we form a kind of system, comprehending whatever we remember to have been present, either to our internal perception or senses; and every particular of that system, joined to the present impressions, we are pleased to call a *reality*. But the mind stops not here. For finding, that with this system of perceptions there is another connected by custom, or, if you will, by the relation of cause or effect, it proceeds to the consideration of their ideas; and as it feels that it is in a manner necessarily determined to view these particular ideas, and that the custom or relation, by which it is determined, admits not of the least change, it forms them into a new system, which it likewise dignifies with the title of *realities*. The first of these systems is the object of the memory and senses; the second of the judgment.

It is this latter principle which peoples the world, and brings us acquainted with such existences as, by their removal in time and place, lie beyond the reach of the senses and memory. By means of it I paint the universe in my imagination, and fix my attention on any part of it I please. I form an idea of Rome, which I neither see nor remember, but which is connected with such impressions as I remember to have received from the conversation and books of travellers and historians. This idea of Rome I placed in a certain situation on the idea of an object which I call the globe. I join to it the conception of a particular government, and religion, and manners. I look backward and consider its first foundation, its several revolutions, successes, and misfortunes. All this, and everything else which I believe, are nothing but ideas, though, by their force and settled order, arising from custom and the relation of cause and effect, they distinguish themselves from the other ideas, which are merely the offspring of the imagination.

As to the influence of contiguity and resemblance, we may observe, that if the contiguous and resembling object be comprehended in this system of realities, there is no doubt but these two relations will assist that of cause and effect, and infix the related idea with more force in the imagination. This I shall enlarge upon presently. Meanwhile I shall carry my observation a step further, and assert, that even where the related object is but feigned, the relation will serve to enliven the idea, and increase its influence. A poet, no doubt, will be the better able to form a strong description of the Elysian fields, that he prompts his imagination by the view of a beautiful meadow or garden; as at another time he may, by his fancy, place himself in the midst of these fabulous regions, that by the feigned contiguity he may enliven his imagination.

But though I cannot altogether exclude the relations of resemblance and contiguity from operating on the fancy in this manner, it is observable that, when single, their influence is very feeble and uncertain. As the relation of cause and effect is requisite to persuade us of any real existence, so is this persuasion requisite to give force to these other relations. For where upon the appearance of an impression we not only feign another object, but likewise arbitrarily, and of our mere goodwill and pleasure give it a particular relation to the impression, this can have but a small effect upon the mind; nor is there any reason, why, upon the return of the same impression, we should be determined to place the same object in the same relation to it. There is no manner of necessity for the mind to feign any resembling and contiguous objects; and if it feigns such, there is as little necessity for it always to confine itself to the same, without any difference or variation. And indeed such a fiction is founded on so little reason, that nothing but pure *caprice* can determine the mind to form it; and that principle being fluctuating and uncertain, it is impossible it can ever operate with any considerable degree of force and constancy. The mind foresees and anticipates the change; and even from the very first instant feels the looseness of its actions, and the weak hold it has of its objects. And as this imperfection is very sensible in every single instance, it still increases by experience and observation, when we compare the several instances we may remember, and form a *general rule* against the reposing any assurance in those momentary glimpses of light, which arise in the imagination from a feigned resemblance and contiguity.

The relation of cause and effect has all the opposite advantages. The objects it presents are fixed and unalterable. The impressions of the memory never change in any considerable degree; and each impression draws along with it a precise idea, which takes its place in the imagination, as something solid and real, certain and invariable. The thought is always determined to pass from the impression to the idea, and from that particular impression to that particular idea, without any choice or hesitation.

But not content with removing this objection, I shall endeavour to extract from it a proof of the present doctrine. Contiguity and resemblance have an effect much inferior to causation; but still have some effect, and augment the conviction of any opinion, and the vivacity of any conception. If this can be proved in several new instances, beside what we have already observed, it will be allowed no inconsiderable argument, that belief is nothing but a lively idea related to a present impression.

To begin with contiguity; it has been remarked among the Mohametans as well as Christians, that those *pilgrims*, who have seen Mecca or the Holy Land, are ever after more faithful and zealous believers, than those who have not had that advantage. A man, whose memory presents him with a lively image of the Red Sea, and the Desert, and Jerusalem, and Galilee, can never doubt of any miraculous events, which are related either by Moses or the Evangelists. The lively idea of the places passes by an easy transition to the facts, which are supposed to have been related to them by contiguity, and increases the belief by increasing the vivacity of the conception. The remembrance of these fields and rivers has the same influence on the vulgar as a new argument, and from the same causes.

We may form a like observation concerning *resemblance*. We have remarked, that the conclusion which we draw from a present object to its absent cause or effect, is never founded on any qualities which we observe in that object, considered in itself; or, in other words, that it is impossible to determine otherwise than by experience, what will result from any phenomenon, or what has preceded it. But though this be so evident in itself, that it seemed not to require any proof, yet some philosophers have imagined that there is an apparent cause for the communication of motion, and that a reasonable man might immediately infer the motion of one body from the impulse of another, without having recourse to any past observation. That this opinion is false will admit of an easy proof. For if such an inference may be drawn merely from the ideas of body, of motion, and of impulse, it must amount to a demonstration, and must imply the absolute impossibility of any contrary supposition. Every effect, then, beside the communication of motion, implies a formal contradiction; and it is impossible not only that it can exist, but also that it can be conceived. But we may soon satisfy ourselves of the contrary, by forming a clear and consistent idea of one's body moving upon another, and of its rest immediately upon the contact; or of its returning back in the same line in which it came; or of its annihilation, or circular or elliptical motion; and in short, of an infinite number of other changes, which they may suppose it to undergo. These suppositions are all consistent and natural; and the reason why we imagine the communication of motion to be more consistent and natural, not only than those suppositions, but also than any other natural effect, is founded on the relation of *resemblance* betwixt the cause and effect, which is here united to experience, and binds the objects in the closest and most intimate manner to each other, so as to make us imagine them to be absolutely inseparable. Resemblance, then, has the same or a parallel influence with experience; and as the only immediate effect of experience is to associate our ideas together, it follows that all belief arises from the association of ideas, according to my hypothesis.

It is universally allowed by the writers on optics, that the eye at all times sees an equal number of physical points, and that a man on the top of a mountain has no larger an image presented to his senses, than when he is cooped up in the narrowest court or chamber. It is only by experience that he infers the greatness of the object from some peculiar qualities of the image; and this inference of the judgment he confounds with sensation, as is common on other occasions. Now it is evident, that the inference of the judgment is here much more lively than what is usual in our common reasonings, and that a man has a more vivid conception of the vast extent of the ocean from the image he receives by the eye, when he stands on the top of the high promontory, than merely from hearing the roaring of the waters. He feels a more sensible pleasure from its magnificence, which is a proof of a more lively idea; and he confounds his judgment with sensation, which is another proof of it. But as the inference is equally certain and immediate in both cases, this superior vivacity of our conception in one case can proceed from nothing but this, that in drawing an inference from the sight, beside the customary conjunction, there is also a resemblance betwixt the image and the object we infer, which strengthens the relation, and conveys the vivacity of the impression to the related idea with an easier and more natural movement.

No weakness of human nature is more universal and conspicuous than what we commonly call *credulity*, or a too easy faith in the testimony of others; and this weakness is also very naturally accounted for from the influence of resemblance. When we receive any matter of fact upon human testimony, our faith arises from the very same origin as our inferences from causes to effects, and from effects to causes; nor is there anything but our *experience* of the governing principles of human nature, which can give us any assurance of the veracity of men. But though experience be the true standard of this, as well as of all other judgments, we seldom regulate ourselves entirely by it, but have a remarkable propensity to believe whatever is reported, even concerning apparitions, enchantments, and prodigies, however contrary to daily experience and observation. The words or discourses of others have an intimate connection with certain ideas in their mind; and these ideas have also a connection with the facts or objects which they represent. This latter connection is generally much overrated, and commands our assent beyond what experience will justify, which can proceed from nothing beside the resemblance betwixt the ideas and the facts. Other effects only point out their causes in an oblique manner; but the testimony of men does it directly, and is to be considered as an image as well as an effect. No wonder, therefore, we are so rash in drawing our inferences from it, and are less guided by experience in our judgments concerning it, than in those upon any other subject.

As resemblance, when conjoined with causation, fortifies our reasonings, so the want of it in any very great degree is able almost entirely to destroy them. Of this there is a remarkable instance in the universal carelessness and stupidity of men with regard to a future state, where they show as obstinate an incredulity, as they do a blind credulity on other occasions. There is not indeed a more ample matter of wonder to the studious, and of regret to the pious man, than to observe the negligence of the bulk of mankind concerning their approaching condition; and it is with reason, that many eminent theologians have not scrupled to affirm, that though the vulgar have no formal principles of infidelity, yet they are really infidels in their hearts, and have nothing like what we can call a belief of the eternal duration of their souls. For let us consider on the one hand what divines have displayed with such eloquence concerning the importance of eternity; and at the same time reflect, that though in matters of rhetoric we ought to lay our account with some exaggeration, we must in this case allow, that the strongest figures are infinitely inferior to the subject: and after this, let us view on the other hand the prodigious security of men in this particular: I ask, if these people really believe what is inculcated on them, and what they pretend to affirm; and the answer is obviously in the negative. As belief is an act of the mind arising from custom, it is not strange the want of resemblance should overthrow what custom has established, and diminish the force of the idea, as much as that latter principle increases it. A future state is so far removed from our comprehension, and we have so obscure an idea of the manner in which we shall exist after the dissolution of the body, that all the reasons we can invent, however strong in themselves, and however much assisted by education, are never able with slow imaginations to surmound this difficulty, or bestow a sufficient authority and force on the idea. I rather choose to ascribe this incredulity to the faint idea we form of our future condition, derived from its want of resemblance to the present life, than to that derived from its remoteness. For I observe, that men are everywhere concerned about what may happen after their death, provided it regard this world; and that there are few to whom their name, their family, their friends, and their country are in any period of time entirely indifferent.

And indeed the want of resemblance in this case so entirely destroys belief, that except those few who, upon cool reflection on the importance of the subject, have taken care by repeated meditation to imprint in their minds the arguments for a future state, there scarce are any who believe the immortality of the soul with a true and established judgment; such as is derived from the testimony of travellers and historians. This appears very conspicuously wherever men have occasion to compare the pleasures and pains, the rewards and punishments of this life with those of a future; even though the case does not concern themselves, and there is no violent passion to disturb their judgment. The Roman Catholics are certainly the most zealous of any sect in the Christian world; and yet you will find few among the more sensible part of that communion who do not blame the Gunpowder Treason, and the massacre of St. Bartholomew, as cruel and barbarous, though projected or executed against those very people, whom without any scruple they condemn to eternal and infinite punishments. All we can say in excuse for this inconsistency is, that they really do not believe what they affirm concerning a future state; nor is there any better proof of it than the very inconsistency.

We may add to this a remark, that in matters of religion men take a pleasure in being terrified, and that no preachers are so popular as those who excite the most dismal and gloomy passions. In the common affairs of life, where we feel and are penetrated with the solidity of the subject, nothing can be more disagreeable than fear and terror; and it is only in dramatic performances and in religious discourses that they ever give pleasure. In these latter cases the imagination reposes itself indolently on the idea; and the passion being softened by the want of belief in the subject, has no more than the agreeable effect of enlivening the mind and fixing the attention.

The present hypothesis will receive additional confirmation, if we examine the effects of other kinds of custom, as well as of other relations. To understand this, we must consider that custom, to which I attribute all belief and reasoning, may operate upon the mind in invigorating an idea after two several ways. For supposing that, in all past experience, we have found two objects to have been always conjoined together, it is evident, that upon the appearance of one of these objects in an impression, we must, from custom, make an easy transition to the idea of that object, which usually attends it; and by means of the present impression and easy transition must conceive that idea in a stronger and more lively manner than we do any loose floating image of the fancy. But let us next suppose, that a mere idea alone, without any of this curious and almost artificial preparation, should frequently make its appearance in the mind, this idea must, by degrees, acquire a facility and force; and both by its firm hold and easy introduction distinguish itself from any new and unusual idea. This is the only particular in which these two kinds of custom agree; and if it appear that their effects on the judgment are similar and proportionable, we may certainly conclude, that the foregoing explication of that faculty is satisfactory. But can we doubt of this agreement in their influence on the judgment, when we consider the nature and effects of *education*?

All those opinions and notions of things, to which we have been accustomed from our infancy, take such deep root, that it is impossible for us, by all the powers of reason and experience, to eradicate them; and this habit not only approaches in its influence, but even on many occasions prevails over that which arises from the constant and inseparable union of causes and effects. Here we must not be contented with saying, that the vividness of the idea produces the belief: we must maintain that they are individually the same. The frequent repetition of any idea infixes it in the imagination; but could never possibly of itself produce belief, if that act of the mind was, by the original constitution of our natures, annexed only to a reasoning and comparison of ideas. Custom may lead us into some false comparison of ideas: This is the utmost effect we can conceive of it; but it is certain it could never supply the place of that comparison, nor produce any act of the mind which naturally belonged to that principle.

A person that has lost a leg or an arm by amputation endeavours for a long time afterwards to serve himself with them. After the death of any one, it is a common remark of the whole family, but especially the servants, that they can scarce believe him to be dead, but still imagine him to be in his chamber or in any other place, where they were accustomed to find him. I have often heard in conversation, after talking of a person that is in any way celebrated, that one, who has no acquaintance with him, will say, *I have never seen such a one, but almost fancy I have, so often have I heard talk of him.* All these are parallel instances.

If we consider this argument from *education* in a proper light, it will appear very convincing; and the more so, that it is founded on one of the most common phenomena that is anywhere to be met with. I am persuaded that, upon examination, we shall find more than one half of those opinions that prevail among mankind to be owing to education, and that the principles which are thus implicitly embraced, overbalance those, which are owing either to abstract reasoning or experience. As liars, by the frequent repetition of their lies, come at last to remember them; so the judgment, or rather the imagination, by the like means, may have ideas so strongly imprinted on it, and conceive them in so full a light, that they may operate upon the mind in the same manner with those which the senses, memory, or reason present to us. But as education is an artificial and not a natural cause, and as its maxims are frequently contrary to reason, and even to themselves in different times and places, it is never upon that account recognised by philosophers; though in reality it be built almost on the same foundation of custom and repetition as our reasonings from causes and effects.[1]

SECTION X

OF THE INFLUENCE OF BELIEF

BUT though education be disclaimed by philosophy, as a fallacious ground of assent to any opinion, it prevails nevertheless in the world, and is the cause why all systems are apt to be rejected at first as new and unusual. This, perhaps, will be the fate of what I have here advanced concerning *belief*; and though the proofs I have produced appear to me perfectly conclusive, I expect not to make many proselytes to my opinion. Men will scarce ever be persuaded, that effects of such consequence can flow from principles which are seemingly so inconsiderable, and that the far greatest part of our reasonings, with all our actions and passions, can be derived from nothing but custom and habit. To obviate this objection, I shall here anticipate a little what would more properly fall under our consideration afterwards, when we come to treat of the Passions and the Sense of Beauty.

There is implanted in the human mind a perception of pain and pleasure as the chief spring and moving principle of all its actions. But pain and pleasure have two ways of making their appearance in the mind; of which the one has effects very different from the other. They may either appear an impression to the actual feeling, or only in idea, as at present when I mention them. It is evident

---

[1] In general we may observe, that as our assent to all probable reasonings is founded on the vivacity of ideas, it resembles many of those whimsies and prejudices which are rejected under the opprobrious character of being the offspring of the imagination. By this expression it appears, that the word imagination, is commonly used in two different senses; and though nothing be more contrary to true philosophy than this inaccuracy, yet, in the following reasonings, I have often been obliged to fall into it. When I oppose the imagination to the memory, I mean the faculty by which we form our fainter ideas. When I oppose it to reason, I mean the same faculty, excluding only our demonstrative and probable reasonings. When I oppose it to neither, it is indifferent whether it be taken in the larger or more limited sense, or at least the context will sufficiently explain the meaning.

the influence of these upon our actions is far from being equal. Impressions always actuate the soul, and that in the highest degree; but it is not every idea which has the same effect. Nature has proceeded with caution in this case, and seems to have carefully avoided the inconveniences of two extremes. Did impressions alone influence the will, we should every moment of our lives be subject to the greatest calamities; because, though we foresaw their approach, we should not be provided by nature with any principle of action, which might impel us to avoid them. On the other hand, did every idea influence our actions, our condition would not be much mended. For such is the unsteadiness and activity of thought, that the images of everything, especially of goods and evils, are always wandering in the mind; and were it moved by every idle conception of this kind, it would never enjoy a moment's peace and tranquillity.

Nature has therefore chosen a medium, and has neither bestowed on every idea of good and evil the power of actuating the will, nor has yet entirely excluded them from this influence. Though an idle fiction has no efficacy, yet we find by experience, that the ideas of those objects which we believe either are or will be existent, produce in a lesser degree the same effect with those impressions, which are immediately present to the senses and perception. The effect then of belief, is to raise up a simple idea to an equality with our impressions, and bestow on it a like influence on the passions. This effect it can only have by making an idea approach an impression in force and vivacity. For as the different degrees of force make all the original difference betwixt an impression and an idea, they must of consequence be the source of all the differences in the effects of these perceptions, and their removal, in whole or in part, the cause of every new resemblance they acquire. Wherever we can make an idea approach the impressions in force and vivacity, it will likewise imitate them in its influence on the mind; and *vice versa*, where it imitates them in that influence, as in the present case, this must proceed from its approaching them in force and vivacity. Belief, therefore, since it causes an idea to imitate the effects of the impressions, must make it resemble them in these qualities, and is nothing but *a more vivid and intense conception of any idea*. This then may both serve as an additional argument for the present system, and may give us a notion after what manner our reasonings from causation are able to operate on the will and passions.

As belief is almost absolutely requisite to the exciting our passions, so the passions, in their turn, are very favourable to belief; and not only such facts as convey agreeable emotions, but very often such as give pain, do upon that account become more readily the objects of faith and opinion. A coward, whose fears are easily awakened, readily assents to every account of danger he meets with; as a person of a sorrowful and melancholy disposition is very credulous of everything that nourishes his prevailing passion. When any affecting object is presented, it gives the alarm, and excites immediately a degree of its proper passion; especially in persons who are naturally inclined to that passion. This emotion passes by an easy transition to the imagination; and, diffusing itself over the idea of the affecting object, makes us form that idea with greater force and vivacity, and consequently assent to it, according to the precedent system. Admiration and surprise have the same effect as the other passions; and accordingly we may observe, that among the vulgar, quacks and projectors meet with a more easy faith upon account of their magnificent pretensions, than if they kept themselves within the bounds of moderation. The first astonishment, which naturally attends their miraculous relations, spreads itself over the whole soul, and so vivifies and enlivens the idea, that it resembles the inferences we draw from experience. This is a mystery, with which we may be already a little acquainted, and which we shall have further occasion to be let into in the progress of this Treatise.

After this account of the influence of belief on the passions, we shall find less difficulty in explaining its effects on the imagination, however extraordinary they may appear. It is certain we cannot take pleasure in any discourse, where our judgment gives no assent to those images which are presented to our fancy. The conversation of those, who have acquired a habit of lying, though in affairs of no moment, never gives any satisfaction; and that because those ideas they present to us, not being attended with belief, make no impression upon the mind. Poets themselves, though liars by profession, always endeavour to give an air of truth to their fictions; and where that is totally neglected, their performances, however ingenious, will never be able to afford much pleasure. In short, we may observe, that even when ideas have no manner of influence on the will and passions, truth and reality are still requisite, in order to make them entertaining to the imagination.

But if we compare together all the phenomena that occur on this head, we shall find, that truth, however necessary it may seem in all works of genius, has no other effect than to procure an easy reception for the ideas, and to make the mind acquiesce in them with satisfaction, or at least without reluctance. But as this is an effect, which may easily be supposed to flow from that solidity and force, which, according to my system, attend those ideas that are established by reasonings from causation; it follows, that all the influence of belief upon the fancy may be explained from that system. Accordingly we may observe, that wherever that influence arises from any other principles beside truth or reality, they supply its place, and give an equal entertainment to the imagination. Poets have formed what they call a poetical system of things, which, though it be believed neither by themselves nor readers, is commonly esteemed a sufficient foundation for any fiction. We have been so much accustomed to the names of Mars, Jupiter, Venus, that in the same manner as education infixes any opinion, the constant repetition of these ideas makes them enter into the mind with facility, and prevail upon the fancy, without influencing the judgment. In like manner tragedians always borrow their fable, or at least the names of their principal actors, from some known passage in history; and that not in order to deceive the spectators; for they will frankly confess, that truth is not in any circumstance inviolably observed, but in order to procure a more easy reception into the imagination for those extraordinary events, which they represent. But this is a precaution which is not required of comic poets, whose personages and incidents, being of a more familiar kind, enter easily into the conception, and are received without any such formality, even though at first sight they be known to be fictitious, and the pure offspring of the fancy.

This mixture of truth and falsehood in the fables of tragic poets not only serves our present purpose, by showing that the imagination can be satisfied without any absolute belief or assurance; but may in another view be regarded as a very strong confirmation of this system. It is evident, that poets make use of this artifice of borrowing the names of their persons, and the chief events of their poems, from history, in order to procure a more easy reception for the whole, and cause it to make a deeper impression on the fancy and affections. The several incidents of the piece acquire a kind of relation by being united into one poem or representation; and if any of these incidents be an object of belief, it bestows a force and vivacity on the others, which are related to it. The vividness of the first conception diffuses itself along the relations, and is conveyed, as by so many pipes or canals, to every idea that has any communication with the primary one. This indeed can never amount to a perfect assurance; and that because the union among the ideas is in a manner accidental: but still it approaches so near in its influence, as may convince us that they are derived from the same origin. Belief must please the imagination by means of the force and vivacity which attends it; since every idea which has force and vivacity, is found to be agreeable to that faculty.

To confirm this we may observe, that the assistance is mutual betwixt the judgment and fancy, as well as betwixt the judgment and passion; and that belief not only gives vigour to the imagination, but that a vigorous and strong imagination is of all talents the most proper to procure belief and authority. It is difficult for us to withhold our assent from what is painted out to us in all the colours of eloquence; and the vivacity produced by the fancy is in many cases greater than that which arises from custom and experience. We are hurried away by the lively imagination of our author or companion; and even he himself is often a victim to his own fire and genius.

Nor will it be amiss to remark, that as a lively imagination very often degenerates into madness or folly, and bears it a great resemblance in its operations; so they influence the judgment after the same manner, and produce belief from the very same principles. When the imagination, from any extraordinary ferment of the blood and spirits, acquires such a vivacity as disorders all its powers and faculties, there is no means of distinguishing betwixt truth and falsehood; but every loose fiction or idea, having the same influence as the impressions of the memory, or the conclusions of the judgment, is received on the same footing, and operates with equal force on the passions. A present impression and a customary transition are now no longer necessary to enliven our ideas. Every chimera of the brain is as vivid and intense as any of those inferences, which we formerly dignified with the name of conclusions concerning matters of fact, and sometimes as the present impressions of the senses.

We may observe the same effect of poetry in a lesser degree; and this is common both to poetry and madness, that the vivacity they bestow on the ideas is not derived from the particular situations or connections of the objects of these ideas, but from the present temper and disposition of the person. But how great soever the pitch may be to which this vivacity rise, it is evident, that in poetry it never has the same *feeling* with that which arises in the mind, when we reason, though even upon the lowest species of probability.

The mind can easily distinguish betwixt the one and the other; and whatever emotion the poetical enthusiasm may give to the spirits, it is still the mere phantom of belief or persuasion. The case is the same with the idea as with the passion it occasions. There is no passion of the human mind but what may arise from poetry; though, at the same time, the *feelings* of the passions are very different when excited by poetical fictions, from what they are when they arise from belief and reality. A passion which is disagreeable in real life, may afford the highest entertainment in a tragedy or epic poem. In the latter case it lies not with that weight upon us: it feels less firm and solid, and has no other than the agreeable effect of exciting the spirits, and rousing the attention. The difference in the passions is a clear proof of a like difference in those ideas from which the passions are derived. Where the vivacity arises from a customary conjunction with a present impression, though the imagination may not, in appearance, be so much moved, yet there is always something more forcible and real in its actions than in the fervours of poetry and eloquence. The force of our mental actions in this case, no more than in any other, is not to be measured by the apparent agitation of the mind. A poetical description may have a more sensible effect on the fancy than an historical narration. It may collect more of those circumstances that form a complete image or picture. It may seem to set the object before us in more lively colours. But still the ideas it presents are different to the *feeling* from those which arise from the memory and the judgment. There is something weak and imperfect amidst all that seeming vehemence of thought and sentiment which attends the fictions of poetry.

We shall afterwards have occasion to remark both the resemblances and differences betwixt a poetical enthusiasm and a serious conviction. In the meantime, I cannot forbear observing, that the great difference in their feeling proceeds, in some measure, from reflection and *general rules*. We observe, that the vigour of conception which fictions receive from poetry and eloquence, is a circumstance merely accidental, of which every idea is equally susceptible; and that such fictions are connected with nothing that is real. This observation makes us only lend ourselves, so to speak, to the fiction, but causes the idea to feel very different from the eternal established persuasions founded on memory and custom. They are somewhat of the same kind; but the one is much inferior to the other, both in its causes and effects.

A like reflection on *general rules* keeps us from augmenting our belief upon every increase of the force and vivacity of our ideas. Where an opinion admits of no doubt, or opposite probability, we attribute to it a full conviction; though the want of resemblance, or contiguity, may render its force inferior to that of other opinions. It is thus the understanding corrects the appearances of the senses, and makes us imagine, that an object at twenty foot distance seems even to the eye as large as one of the same dimensions at ten.

We may observe the same effect of poetry in a lesser degree; only with this difference, that the least reflection dissipates the illusions of poetry, and places the objects in their proper light. It is however certain, that in the warmth of a poetical enthusiasm, a poet has a counterfeit belief, and even a kind of vision of his objects; and if there be any shadow of argument to support this belief, nothing contributes more to his full conviction than a blaze of poetical figures and images, which have their effect upon the poet himself, as well as upon his readers.

SECTION XI

OF THE PROBABILITY OF CHANCES

But in order to bestow on this system its full force and evidence, we must carry our eye from it a moment to consider its consequences, and explain, from the same principles, some other species of reasoning which are derived from the same origin.

Those philosophers who have divided human reason into *knowledge and probability*, and have defined the first to be *that evidence which arises from the comparison of ideas*, are obliged to comprehend all our arguments from causes or effects under the general term of probability. But though every one be free to use his terms in what sense he pleases; and accordingly, in the precedent part of this discourse, I have followed this method of expression; it is however certain, that in common discourse we readily affirm, that many arguments from causation exceed probability, and may be received as a superior kind of evidence. One would appear ridiculous who would say, that it is only probable the sun will rise to-morrow, or that all men must die; though it is plain we have no further assurance of these facts than what experience affords us. For this reason it would perhaps be more convenient, in order at once to preserve the common signification of words, and mark the several degrees of evidence, to distinguish human reason into three kinds, viz., *that from knowledge, from proofs, and from probabilities*. By knowledge, I mean the assurance arising from the comparison of ideas. By proofs, those arguments which are derived from the relation of cause and effect, and which are entirely free from doubt and uncertainty. By probability, that evidence which is still attended with uncertainty. It is this last species of reasoning I proceed to examine.

Probability or reasoning from conjecture may be divided into two kinds, viz., that which is founded on *chance*, and that which arises from *causes*. We shall consider each of these in order.

The idea of cause and effect is derived from experience, which, presenting us with certain objects constantly conjoined with each other, produces such a habit of surveying them in that relation, that we cannot, without a sensible violence, survey them in any other. On the other hand, as chance is nothing real in itself, and, properly speaking, is merely the negation of a cause, its influence on the mind is contrary to that of causation; and it is essential to it to leave the imagination perfectly indifferent, either to consider the existence or non-existence of that object which is regarded as contingent. A cause traces the way to our thought, and in a manner forces us to survey such certain objects in such certain relations. Chance can only destroy this determination of the thought, and leave the mind in its native situation of indifference; in which, upon the absence of a cause, it is instantly reinstated.

Since, therefore, an entire indifference is essential to chance, no one chance can possibly be superior to another, otherwise than as it is composed of a superior number of equal chances. For if we affirm that one chance can, after any other manner, be superior to another, we must at the same time affirm, that there is something which gives it the superiority, and determines the event rather to that side than the other: that is, in other words, we must allow of a cause, and destroy the supposition of chance, which we had before established. A perfect and total indifference is essential to chance, and one total indifference can never in itself be either superior or inferior to another. This truth is not peculiar to my system, but is acknowledged by every one that forms calculations concerning chances.

And here it is remarkable, that though chance and causation be directly contrary, yet it is impossible for us to conceive this combination of chances, which is requisite to render one hazard superior to another, without supposing a mixture of causes among the chances, and a conjunction of necessity in some particulars, with a total indifference in others. Where nothing limits the chances, every notion that the most extravagant fancy can form is upon a footing of equality; nor can there be any circumstance to give one the advantage above another. Thus, unless we allow that there are some causes to make the dice fall, and preserve their form in their fall, and lie upon some one of their sides, we can form no calculation concerning the laws of hazard. But supposing these causes to operate, and supposing likewise all the rest to be indifferent and to be determined by chance, it is easy to arrive at a notion of a superior combination of chances. A die that has four sides marked with a certain number of spots, and only two with another, affords us an obvious and easy instance of this superiority. The mind is here limited by the causes to such a precise number and quality of the events; and, at the same time, is undetermined in its choice of any particular event.

Proceeding, then, in that reasoning, wherein we have advanced three steps; *that* chance is merely the negation of a cause, and produces a total indifference in the mind; *that* one negation of a cause and one total indifference can never be superior or inferior to another; *that* there must always be a mixture of causes among the chances, in order to be the foundation of any reasoning. We are next to consider what effect a superior combination of chances can have upon the mind, and after what manner it influences our judgment and opinion. Here we may repeat all the same arguments we employed in examining that belief which arises from causes; and may prove, after the same manner, that a superior number of chances produces our assent neither by *demonstration* nor *probability*. It is indeed evident, that we can never, by the comparison of mere ideas, make any discovery which can be of consequence in this affair, and that it is impossible to prove with certainty that any event must fall on that side where there is a superior number of chances. To suppose in this case any certainty, were to overthrow what we have established concerning the opposition of chances, and their perfect equality and indifference.

Should it be said, that though in an opposition of chances, it is impossible, to determine with *certainty* on which side the event will fall, yet we can pronounce with certainty, that it is more likely and probable it will be on that side where there is a superior number of chances, than where there is an inferior: should this be said, I would ask, what is here meant by *likelihood and probability*? The likelihood and probability of chances is a superior number of equal chances; and consequently, when we say it is likely the event will fall on the side which is superior, rather than on the inferior, we do no more than affirm, that where there is a superior number of chances there is actually a superior, and where there is an inferior there is an inferior, which are identical propositions, and of no consequence. The question is, by what means a superior number of equal chances operates upon the mind, and produces belief or assent, since it appears that it is neither by arguments derived from demonstration, nor from probability.

In order to clear up this difficulty, we shall suppose a person to take a die, formed after such a manner as that four of its sides are marked with one figure, or one number of spots, and two with another; and to put this die into the box with an intention of throwing it: it is plain, he must conclude the one figure to be more probable than the other, and give the preference to that which is inscribed on the greatest number of sides. He in a manner believes that this will lie uppermost; though still with hesitation and doubt in proportion to the number of chances which are contrary: and according as these contrary chances diminish, and the superiority increases on the other side, his belief acquires new degrees of stability and assurance. This belief arises from an operation of the mind upon the simple and limited object before us; and therefore its nature will be the more easily discovered and explained. We have nothing but one single die to contemplate, in order to comprehend one of the most curious operations of the understanding.

This die formed as above, contains three circumstances worthy of our attention. First, certain causes, such as gravity, solidity, a cubical figure, etc., which determine it to fall, to preserve its form in its fall, and to turn up one of its sides. Secondly, a certain number of sides, which are supposed indifferent. Thirdly, a certain figure inscribed on each side. These three particulars form the whole nature of the die, so far as relates to our present purpose; and consequently are the only circumstances regarded by the mind in its forming a judgment concerning the result of such a throw. Let us therefore consider gradually and carefully what must be the influence of these circumstances on the thought and imagination.

First, we have already observed, that the mind is determined by custom to pass from any cause to its effect, and that upon the appearance of the one, it is almost possible for it not to form an idea of the other. Their constant conjunction in past instances has produced such a habit in the mind, that it always conjoins them in its thought, and infers the existence of the one from that of its usual attendant. When it considers the die as no longer supported by the box, it cannot without violence regard it as suspended in the air; but naturally places it on the table, and views it as turning up one of its sides. This is the effect of the intermingled causes, which are requisite to our forming any calculation concerning chances.

Secondly, it is supposed, that though the die be necessarily determined to fall, and turn up one of its sides, yet there is nothing to fix the particular side, but that this is determined entirely by chance. The very nature and essence of chance is a negation of causes, and the leaving the mind in a perfect indifference among those events which are supposed contingent. When, therefore, the thought is determined by the causes to consider the die as falling and turning up one of its sides, the chances present all these sides as equal, and make us consider every one of them, one after another, as alike probable and possible. The imagination passes from the cause, viz., the throwing of the die, to the effect, viz., the turning up one of the six sides; and feels a kind of impossibility both of stopping short in the way, and of forming any other idea. But as all these six sides are incompatible, and the die cannot turn up above one at once, this principle directs us not to consider all of them at once as lying uppermost, which we look upon as impossible: neither does it direct us with its entire force to any particular side; for in that case this side would be considered as certain and inevitable; but it directs us to the whole six sides after such a manner as to divide its force equally among them. We conclude in general, that some one of them must result from the throw: we run all of them over in our minds: the determination of the thought is common to all; but no more of its force falls to the share of any one, than what is suitable to its proportion with the rest. It is after this manner the original impulse, and consequently the vivacity of thought arising from the causes, is divided and split in pieces by the intermingled chances.

We have already seen the influence of the two first qualities of the die, viz., the *causes*, and the *number*, and *difference* of the sides, and have learned how they give an impulse to the thought, and divide that impulse into as many parts as there are units in the number of sides. We must now consider the effects of the third particular, viz., the *figures* inscribed on each side. It is evident that where several sides have the same figure inscribed on them, they must concur in their influence on the mind, and must unite upon one image or idea of a figure, all those divided

impulses that were dispersed over the several sides upon which
that figure is inscribed. Were the question only what side will be
turned up, these are all perfectly equal, and no one could ever
have any advantage above another. But as the question is concerning the figure, and as the same figure is presented by more
than one side, it is evident that the impulses belonging to all these
sides must reunite in that one figure, and become stronger and
more forcible by the union. Four sides are supposed in the present
case to have the same figure inscribed on them, and two to have
another figure. The impulses of the former are therefore superior
to those of the latter. But as the events are contrary, and it is
impossible both these figures can be turned up; the impulses,
likewise, become contrary, and the inferior destroys the superior,
as far as its strength goes. The vivacity of the idea is always
proportionable to the degrees of the impulse or tendency to the
transition; and belief is the same with the vivacity of the idea,
according to the precedent doctrine.

SECTION XII

OF THE PROBABILITY OF CAUSES

What I have said concerning the probability of chances, can serve
to no other purpose than to assist us in explaining the probability
of causes; since it is commonly allowed by philosophers, that what
the vulgar call chance is nothing but a secret and concealed cause.
That species of probability, therefore, is what we must chiefly
examine.

The probabilities of causes are of several kinds; but are all
derived from the same origin, viz., *the association of ideas to a
present impression.* As the habit which produces the association
arises from the frequent conjunction of objects, it must arrive at
its perfection by degrees, and must acquire new force from each
instance that falls under our observation. The first instance has
little or no force: the second makes some addition to it: the third
becomes still more sensible; and it is by these slow steps that our
judgment arrives at a full assurance. But before it attains this
pitch of perfection, it passes through several inferior degrees, and
in all of them is only to be esteemed a presumption or probability.
The gradation, therefore, from probabilities to proofs, is in many
cases insensible; and the difference betwixt these kinds of evidence

is more easly perceived in the remote degrees, than in, the near and contiguous.

It is worthy of remark on this occasion, that though the species of probability here explained be the first in order, and naturally takes place before any entire proof can exist, yet no one, who is arrived at the age of maturity, can any longer be acquainted with it. It is true, nothing is more common than for people of the most advanced knowledge to have attained only an imperfect experience of many particular events; which naturally produces only an imperfect habit and transition: but then we must consider that the mind, having formed another observation concerning the connection of causes and effects, gives new force to its reasoning from that observation; and by means of it can build an argument on one single experiment, when duly prepared and examined. What we have found once to follow from any object, we conclude will for ever follow from it; and if this maxim be not always built upon as certain, it is not for want of a sufficient number of experiments, but because we frequently meet with instances to the contrary; which leads us to the second species of probability, where there is a *contrariety* in our experience and observation.

It would be very happy for men in the conduct of their lives and actions, were the same objects always conjoined together, and we had nothing to fear but the mistakes of our own judgment, without having any reason to apprehend the uncertainty of nature. But as it is frequently found that one observation is contrary to another, and that causes and effects follow not in the same order, of which we have had experience, we are obliged to vary our reasoning on account of this uncertainty, and take into consideration the contrariety of events. The first question that occurs on this head is concerning the nature and causes of the contrariety.

The vulgar, who take things according to their first appearance, attribute the uncertainty of events to such an uncertainty in the causes, as makes them often fail of their usual influence, though they meet with no obstacle nor impediment in their operation. But philosophers observing that almost in every part of nature there is contained a vast variety of springs and principles, which are hid, by reason of their minuteness or remoteness, find that it is at least possible the contrariety of events may not proceed from any contingency in the cause, but from the secret operation of contrary causes. This possibility is converted into certainty by further observation, when they remark, that upon an exact scrutiny, a contrariety of effects always betrays a contrariety of causes, and proceeds from their mutual hinderance and opposition. A peasant can give no better reason for the stopping of any clock or watch than to say, that commonly it does not go right: but an artisan easily perceives that the same force in the spring or pendulum has always the same influence on the wheels; but fails of its usual effect, perhaps by reason of a grain of dust, which puts a stop to the whole movement. From the observation of several parallel instances, philosophers form a maxim, that the connection betwixt all causes and effects is equally necessary, and that its seeming uncertainty in some instances proceeds from the secret opposition of contrary causes.

But however philosophers and the vulgar may differ in their explication of the contrariety of events, their inferences from it are always of the same kind, and founded on the same principles. A contrariety of events in the past may give us a kind of hesitating belief for the future, after two several ways. First, by producing an imperfect habit and transition from the present impression to the related idea. When the conjunction of any two objects is frequent, without being entirely constant, the mind is determined to pass from one object to the other; but not with so entire a habit as when the union is uninterrupted, and all the instances we have ever met with are uniform and of a piece. We find from common experience, in our actions as well as reasonings, that a constant perseverance in any course of life produces a strong inclination and tendency to continue for the future; though there are habits of inferior degrees of force, proportioned to the inferior degrees of steadiness and uniformity in our conduct.

There is no doubt but this principle sometimes takes place, and produces those inferences we draw from contrary phenomena; though I am persuaded that, upon examination, we shall not find it to be the principle that most commonly influences the mind in this species of reasoning. When we follow only the habitual determination of the mind, we make the transition without any reflection, and interpose not a moment's delay betwixt the view of one object, and the belief of that which is often found to attend it. As the custom depends not upon any deliberation, it operates immediately, without allowing any time for reflection. But this method of proceeding we have but few instances of in our probable reasonings; and even fewer than in those, which are derived from the uninterrupted conjunction of objects. In the former species of reasoning we commonly take knowingly into consideration the contrariety of past events; we compare the different sides of the contrariety, and carefully weigh the experiments, which we have on each side: whence we may conclude, that our reasonings of this kind arise not *directly* from the habit, but in an *oblique* manner; which we must now endeavour to explain.

It is evident that when an object is attended with contrary effects, we judge of them only by our past experience, and always consider those as possible, which we have observed to follow from it. And as past experience regulates our judgment concerning the possibility of these effects, so it does that concerning their probability; and that effect, which has been the most common, we always esteem the most likely. Here then are two things to be considered, viz., the *reasons* which determine us to make the past a standard for the future, and the *manner* how we extract a single judgment from a contrariety of past events.

First we may observe, that the supposition, *that the future resembles the past,* is not founded on arguments of any kind, but is derived entirely from habit, by which we are determined to expect for the future the same train of objects to which we have been accustomed. This habit or determination to transfer the past to the future is full and perfect; and consequently the first impulse of the imagination in this species of reasoning is endowed with the same qualities.

But, *secondly*, when in considering past experiments we find them of a contrary nature, this determination, though full and perfect in itself, presents us with no steady object, but offers us a number of disagreeing images in a certain order and proportion. The first impulse therefore is here broke into pieces, and diffuses itself over all those images, of which each partakes an equal share of that force and vivacity that is derived from the impulse. Any of these past events may again happen; and we judge that when they do happen, they will be mixed in the same proportion as in the past.

If our intention, therefore, be to consider the proportions of contrary events in a great number of instances, the images presented by our past experience must remain in their *first form*, and preserve their first proportions. Suppose, for instance, I have found, by long observation, that of twenty ships which go to sea, only nineteen return. Suppose I see at present twenty ships that leave the port: I transfer my past experience to the future, and represent to myself nineteen of these ships as returning in safety, and one as perishing. Concerning this there can be no difficulty. But as we frequently run over those several ideas of past events, in order to form a judgment concerning one single event, which appears uncertain; this consideration must change the *first form* of our ideas, and draw together the divided images presented by experience; since it is to *it* we refer the determination of that particular event, upon which we reason. Many of these images are supposed to concur, and a superior number to concur on one side. These agreeing images unite together, and render the idea more strong and lively, not only than a mere fiction of the imagination, but also than any idea, which is supported by a lesser number of experiments. Each new experiment is as a new stroke of the pencil, which bestows an additional vivacity on the colours, without either multiplying or enlarging the figure. This operation of the mind has been so fully explained in treating of the probability of chance, that I need not here endeavour to render it more intelligible. Every past experiment may be considered as a kind of chance; it being uncertain to us, whether the object will exist conformable to one experiment or another: and for this reason everything that has been said on the one subject is applicable to both.

Thus, upon the whole, contrary experiments produce an imperfect belief, either by weakening the habit, or by dividing and afterwards joining in different parts, that *perfect habit*, which makes us conclude in general, that instances, of which we have no experience, must necessarily resemble those of which we have.

To justify still further this account of the second species of probability, where we reason with knowledge and reflection from a contrariety of past experiments, I shall propose the following considerations, without fearing to give offence by that air of subtilty which attends them. Just reasoning ought still, perhaps, to retain its force, however subtle; in the same manner as matter preserves its solidity in the air, and fire, and animal spirits, as well as in the grosser and more sensible forms.

First, we may observe, that there is no probability so great as not to allow of a contrary possibility; because otherwise it would cease to be a probability, and would become a certainty. That probability of causes, which is most extensive, and which we at present examine, depends on a contrariety of experiments; and it is evident an experiment in the past proves at least a possibility for the future.

Secondly, the component parts of this possibility and probability are of the same nature, and differ in number only, but not in kind. It has been observed, that all single chances are entirely equal, and that the only circumstance, which can give any event that is contingent a superiority over another, is a superior number of chances. In like manner, as the uncertainty of causes is discovered by experience, which presents us with a view of contrary events, it is plain that, when we transfer the past to the future, the known to the unknown, every past experiment has the same weight, and that it is only a superior number of them, which can throw the balance on any side. The possibility, therefore, which enters into every reasoning of this kind, is composed of parts, which are of the same nature both among themselves, and with those that compose the opposite probability.

Thirdly, we may establish it as a certain maxim, that in all moral as well as natural phenomena, wherever any cause consists of a number of parts, and the effect increases or diminishes, according to the variation of that number, the effect, properly speaking, is a compounded one, and arises from the union of the several effects, that proceed from each part of the cause. Thus, because the gravity of a body increases or diminishes by the increase or diminution of its parts, we conclude that each part contains this quality, and contributes to the gravity of the whole. The absence or presence of a part of the cause is attended with that of a proportionable part of the effect. This connection or constant conjunction sufficiently proves the one part to be the cause of the other. As the belief, which we have of any event, increases or diminishes according to the number of chances or past experiments, it is to be considered as a compounded effect, of which each part arises from a proportionable number of chances or experiments.

Let us now join these three observations, and see what conclusion we can draw from them. To every probability there is an opposite possibility. This possibility is composed of parts that are entirely of the same nature with those of the probability; and consequently have the same influence on the mind and understanding. The belief which attends the probability is a compounded effect, and is formed by the concurrence of the several effects, which proceed from each part of the probability. Since, therefore, each part of the probability contributes to the production of the belief, each part of the possibility must have the same influence on the opposite side; the nature of these parts being entirely the same. The contrary belief attending the possibility implies a view of a certain object, as well as the probability does an opposite view. In this particular both these degrees of belief are alike. The only manner then, in which the superior number of similar component parts in the one can exert its influence, and prevail above the inferior in the other, is by producing a stronger and more lively view of its object. Each part presents a particular view; and all these views uniting together produce one general view, which is fuller and more distinct by the greater number of causes or principles from which it is derived.

The component parts of the probability and possibility being alike in their nature, must produce like effects; and the likeness of their effects consists in this, that each of them presents a view of a particular object. But though these parts be alike in their nature, they are very different in their quantity and number; and this difference must appear in the effect as well as the similarity. Now, as the view they present is in both cases full and entire, and comprehends the object in all its parts, it is impossible that, in this particular, there can be any difference; nor is there anything but a superior vivacity in the probability, arising from the concurrence of a superior number of views, which can distinguish these effects.

Here is almost the same argument in a different light. All our reasonings concerning the probability of causes are founded on the transferring of past to future. The transferring of any past experiment to the future is sufficient to give us a view of the object; whether that experiment be single or combined with others of the same kind; whether it be entire, or opposed by others of a contrary kind. Suppose then it acquires both these qualities of combination and opposition, it loses not, upon that account, its former power of presenting a view of the object, but only concurs with and opposes other experiments that have a like influence. A question, therefore, may arise concerning the manner both of the concurrence and opposition. As to the *concurrence* there is only the choice left betwixt these two hypotheses. *First*, that the view of the object, occasioned by the transference of each past experiment, preserves itself entire, and only multiplies the number of views. Or, *secondly*, that it runs into the other similar and correspondent views, and gives them a superior degree of force and vivacity. But that the first hypothesis is erroneous is evident from experience, which informs us that the belief attending any reasoning consists in one conclusion, not in a multitude of similar ones, which would only distract the mind, and, in many cases, would be too numerous to be comprehended distinctly by any finite capacity. It remains, therefore, as the only reasonable opinion, that these similar views run into each other and unite their forces; so as to produce a stronger and clearer view than what arises from any one alone.

This is the manner in which past experiments concur when they are transferred to any future event. As to the manner of their *opposition*, it is evident that, as the contrary views are incompatible with each other, and it is impossible the object can at once exist conformable to both of them, their influence becomes mutually destructive, and the mind is determined to the superior only with that force which remains after subtracting the inferior.

I am sensible how abstruse all this reasoning must appear to the generality of readers, who, not being accustomed to such profound reflections on the intellectual faculties of the mind, will be apt to reject as chimerical whatever strikes not in with the common received notions, and with the easiest and most obvious principles of philosophy. And, no doubt, there are some pains required to enter into these arguments; though perhaps very little are necessary to perceive the imperfection of every vulgar hypothesis on this subject, and the little light, which philosophy can yet afford us in such sublime and such curious speculations. Let men be once fully persuaded of these two principles, *that there is nothing in any object, considered in itself, which can afford us a reason for drawing a conclusion beyond it;* and, *that even after the observation of the frequent or constant conjunction of objects, we have no reason to draw any inference concerning any object beyond those of which we have had experience;* I say, let men be once fully convinced of these two principles, and this will throw them so loose from all common systems, that they will make no difficulty of receiving any, which may appear the most extraordinary. These principles we have found to be sufficiently convincing, even with regard to our most certain reasonings from causation: but I shall venture to affirm, that with regard to these conjectural or probable reasonings they still acquire a new degree of evidence.

First, it is obvious that, in reasonings of this kind, it is not the object presented to us, which, considered in itself, affords us any reason to draw a conclusion concerning any other object or event. For as this latter object is supposed uncertain, and as the uncertainty is derived from a concealed contrariety of causes in the former, were any of the causes placed in the known qualities of that object, they would no longer be concealed, nor would our conclusion be uncertain.

But, *secondly*, it is equally obvious in this species of reasoning, that if the transference of the past to the future were founded merely on a conclusion of the understanding, it could never occasion any belief or assurance. When we transfer contrary experiments to the future; we can only repeat these contrary experiments with their particular proportions; which could not produce assurance in any single event upon which we reason, unless the fancy melted together all those images that concur, and extracted from them one single idea or image, which is intense and lively in proportion to the number of experiments from which it is derived, and their superiority above their antagonists. Our past experience presents no determinate object; and as our belief, however faint, fixes itself on a determinate object, it is evident that the belief arises not merely from the transference of past to future, but from some operation of the *fancy* conjoined with it. This may lead us to conceive the manner in which that faculty enters into all our reasonings.

I shall conclude this subject with two reflections which may deserve our attention. The *first* may be explained after this manner: When the mind forms a reasoning concerning any matter of fact, which is only probable, it casts its eye backward upon past experience, and, transferring it to the future, is presented with so many contrary views of its object, of which those that are of the same kind uniting together and running into one act of the mind, serve to fortify and enliven it. But suppose that this multitude of views or glimpses of an object proceeds not from experience, but from a voluntary act of the imagination; this effect does not follow, or, at least, follows not in the same degree. For though custom and education produce belief by such a repetition as is not derived from experience, yet this requires a long tract of time, along with a very frequent and *undesigned* repetition. In general we may pronounce that a person, who would *voluntarily* repeat any idea in his mind, though supported by one past experience, would be no more inclined to believe the existence of its object, than if he had contented himself with one survey of it. Beside the effect of design, each act of the mind, being separate and independent, has a separate influence, and joins not its force with that of its fellows. Not being united by any common object producing them, they have no relation to each other; and consequently make no transition or union of forces. This phenomenon we shall understand better afterwards.

My *second* reflection is founded on those large probabilities which the mind can judge of, and the minute differences it can observe betwixt them. When the chances or experiments on one side amount to ten thousand, and on the other to ten thousand and one, the judgment gives the preference to the latter on account of that superiority; though it is plainly impossible for the mind to run over every particular view, and distinguish the superior vivacity of the image arising from the superior number, where the difference is so inconsiderable. We have a parallel instance in the affections. It is evident, according to the principles above mentioned, that when an object produces any passion in us, which varies according to the different quantity of the object; I say, it is evident, that the passion, properly speaking, is not a simple emotion, but a compounded one, of a great number of weaker passions, derived from a view of each part of the object; for otherwise it were impossible the passion should increase by the increase of these parts. Thus a man who desires a thousand pounds has, in reality, a thousand or more desires, which, uniting together, seem to make only one passion; though the composition evidently betrays itself upon every alteration of the object, by the preference he gives to the larger number, if superior only by an unit. Yet nothing can be more certain that that so small a difference would not be discernible in the passions, nor could render them distinguishable from each other. The difference, therefore, of our conduct in preferring the greater number depends not upon our passions, but upon custom and *general rules*. We have found in a multitude of instances that the augmenting the numbers of any sum augments the passion, where the numbers are precise and the difference sensible. The mind can perceive, from its immediate feeling, that three guineas produce a greater passion than two; and *this* it transfers to larger numbers, because of the resemblance; and by a general rule assigns to a thousand guineas a stronger passion than to nine hundred and ninety-nine. These general rules we shall explain presently.

But besides these two species of probability, which are derived from an *imperfect* experience and from *contrary causes*, there is a third arising from *analogy*, which differs from them in some material circumstances. According to the hypothesis above explained, all kinds of reasoning from causes or effects are founded on two particulars, viz., the constant conjunction of any two objects in all past experience, and the resemblance of a present object to any one of them. The effect of these two particulars is, that the present object invigorates and enlivens the imagination; and the resemblance, along with the constant union, conveys this force and vivacity to the related idea; which we are therefore said to believe or assent to. If you weaken either the union or resemblance, you weaken the principle of transition, and of consequence that belief which arises from it. The vivacity of the first impression cannot be fully conveyed to the related idea, either where the conjunction of their objects is not constant, or where the present impression does not perfectly resemble any of those whose union we are accustomed to observe. In those probabilities of chance and causes above explained, it is the constancy of the union which is diminished; and in the probability derived from analogy, it is the resemblance only which is affected. Without some degree of resemblance, as well as union, it is impossible there can be any reasoning. But as this resemblance admits of many different degrees, the reasoning becomes proportionably more or less firm and certain. An experiment loses of its force when transferred to instances which are not exactly resembling; though it is evident it may still retain as much as may be the foundation of probability, as long as there is any resemblance remaining.

SECTION XII

OF UNPHILOSOPHICAL PROBABILITY

ALL these kinds of probability are received by philosophers, and allowed to be reasonable foundations of belief and opinion. But there are others that are derived from the same principles, though they have not had the good fortune to obtain the same sanction. The *first* probability of this kind may be accounted for thus. The diminution of the union and of the resemblance, as above explained, diminishes the facility of the transition, and by that means weakens the evidence; and we may further observe, that the same diminution of the evidence will follow from a diminution of the impression, and from the shading of those colours under which it appears to the memory or senses. The argument which we found on any matter of fact we remember is more or less convincing, according as the fact is recent or remote; and though the difference in these degrees of evidence be not received by philosophy as solid and legitimate; because in that case an argument must have a different force to-day from what it shall have a month hence; yet, notwithstanding the opposition of philosophy, it is certain this circumstance has a considerable influence on the understanding, and secretly changes the authority of the same argument, according to the different times in which it is proposed to us. A greater force and vivacity in the impression naturally conveys a greater to the related idea; and it is on the degrees of force and vivacity that the belief depends, according to the foregoing system.

There is a *second* difference which we may frequently observe in our degrees of belief and assurance, and which never fails to take place, though disclaimed by philosophers. An experiment that is recent and fresh in the memory affects us more than one that is in some measure obliterated; and has a superior influence on the judgment as well as on the passions. A lively impression produces more assurance than a faint one, because it has more original force to communicate to the related idea, which thereby acquires a greater force and vivacity. A recent observation has a like effect; because the custom and transition is there more entire, and preserves better the original force in the communication. Thus a drunkard, who has seen his companion die of a debauch, is struck with that instance for some time, and dreads a like accident for himself; but as the memory of it decays away by degrees, his former security returns, and the danger seems less certain and real.

I add, as a *third* instance of this kind, that though our reasonings from proofs and from probabilities be considerably different from each other, yet the former species of reasoning often degenerates insensibly into the latter, by nothing but the multitude of connected arguments. It is certain that when an inference is drawn immediately from an object, without any intermediate cause or effect, the conviction is much stronger, and the persuasion more lively, than when the imagination is carried through a long chain of connected arguments, however infallible the connection of each link may be esteemed. It is from the original impression that the vivacity of all the ideas is derived, by means of the customary transition of the imagination; and it is evident this vivacity must gradually decay in proportion to the distance, and must lose somewhat in each transition. Sometimes this distance has a greater influence than even contrary experiments would have; and a man may receive a more lively conviction from a probable reasoning which is close and immediate, than from a long chain of consequences, though just and conclusive in each part. Nay, it is seldom such reasonings produce any conviction; and one must have a very strong and firm imagination to preserve the evidence to the end, where is passes through so many stages.

But here it may not be amiss to remark a very curious phenemenon which the present subject suggests to us. It is evident there is no point of ancient history, of which we can have any assurance, but by passing through many millions of causes and effects, and through a chain of arguments of almost an immeasurable length. Before the knowledge of the fact could come to the first historian, it must be conveyed through many mouths; and after it is committed to writing, each new copy is a new object, of which the connection with the foregoing is known only by experience and observation. Perhaps therefore it may be concluded, from the precedent reasoning, that the evidence of all ancient history must now be lost, or at least will be lost in time, as the chain of causes increases, and runs on to a greater length. But as it seems contrary to common sense to think, that if the republic of letters and the art of printing continue on the same footing as at present, our posterity, even after a thousand ages, can ever doubt if there has been such a man as Julius Cæsar; this may be considered as an objection to the present system. If belief consisted only in a certain vivacity, conveyed from an original impression, it would decay by the length of the transition, and must at last be utterly extinguished. And, *vice versa*, if belief, on some occasions, be not capable of such an extinction, it must be something different from that vivacity.

Before I answer this objection I shall observe, that from this topic there has been borrowed a very celebrated argument against the *Christian Religion;* but with this difference, that the connection betwixt each link of the chain in human testimony has been there supposed not to go beyond probability, and to be liable to a degree of doubt and uncertainty. And indeed it must be confessed, that in this manner of considering the subject (which, however, is not a true one), there is no history or tradition but what must in the end lose all its force and evidence. Every new probability diminishes the original conviction; and, however great that conviction may be supposed, it is impossible it can subsist under such reiterated diminutions. This is true in general, though we shall find afterwards,[1] that there is one very memorable exception, which is of vast consequence in the present subject of the understanding.

Meanwhile, to give a solution of the preceding objection upon the supposition that historical evidence amounts at first to an entire proof, let us consider that, though the links are innumerable that connect any original fact with the present impression, which is the foundation of belief, yet they are all of the same kind, and depend on the fidelity of printers and copyists. One edition passes into another, and that into a third, and so on, till we come to that volume we peruse at present. There is no variation in the steps. After we know one, we know all of them; and after we have made one, we can have no scruple as to the rest. This circumstance

[1] Part IV. Sect. 1.

alone preserves the evidence of history, and will perpetuate the memory of the present age to the latest posterity. If all the long chain of causes and effects, which connect any past event with any volume of history, were composed of parts different from each other, and which it were necessary for the mind distinctly to conceive, it is impossible we should preserve to the end any belief or evidence. But as most of these proofs are perfectly resembling, the minds runs easily along them, jumps from one part to another with facility, and forms but a confused and general notion of each link. By this means a long chain of argument has as little effect in diminishing the original vivacity, as a much shorter would have if composed of parts which were different from each other, and of which each required a distinct consideration.

A fourth unphilosophical species of probability is that derived from *general rules,* which we rashly form to ourselves, and which are the source of what we properly call *prejudice.* An Irishman cannot have wit, and a Frenchman cannot have solidity; for which reason, though the conversation of the former in any instance be visibly very agreeable, and of the latter very judicious, we have entertained such a prejudice against them, that they must be dunces or fops in spite of sense and reason. Human nature is very subject to errors of this kind, and perhaps this nation as much as any other.

Should it be demanded why men form general rules, and allow them to influence their judgment, even contrary to present observation and experience, I should reply, that in my opinion it proceeds from those very principles on which all judgments concerning causes and effects depend. Our judgments concerning cause and effect are derived from habit and experience; and when we have been accustomed to see one object united to another, our imagination passes from the first to the second by a natural transition, which precedes reflection, and which cannot be prevented by it. Now, it is the nature of custom not only to operate with its full force, when objects are presented that are exactly the same with those to which we have been accustomed, but also to operate in an inferior degree when we discover such as are similar; and though the habit loses somewhat of its force by every difference, yet it is seldom entirely destroyed where any considerable circumstances remain the same. A man who has contracted a custom of eating fruit by the use of pears or peaches, will satisfy himself with melons where he cannot find his favourite fruit; as one, who has become a drunkard by the use of red wines, will be carried almost with the same violence to white, if presented to him. From this principle I have accounted for that species of probability, derived from analogy, where we transfer our experience in past instances to objects which are resembling, but are not exactly the same with those concerning which we have had experience. In proportion as the resemblance decays, the probability diminishes, but still has some force as long as there remain any traces of the resemblance.

This observation we may carry further, and may remark, that though custom be the foundation of all our judgments, yet sometimes it has an effect on the imagination in opposition to the judgment, and produces a contrariety in our sentiments concerning the same object. I explain myself. In almost all kinds of causes there is a complication of circumstances, of which some are essential and others superfluous; some are absolutely requisite to the production of the effect, and others are only conjoined by accident. Now we may observe, that when these superfluous circumstances are numerous and remarkable, and frequently conjoined with the essential, they have such an influence on the imagination, that even in the absence of the latter they carry us on to the conception of the usual effect, and give to that conception a force and vivacity which make it superior to the mere fictions of the fancy. We may correct this propensity by a reflection on the nature of those circumstances; but it is still certain that custom takes the start, and gives a bias to the imagination.

To illustrate this by a familiar instance, let us consider the case of a man, who, being hung out from a high tower in a cage of iron, cannot forbear trembling when he surveys the precipice below him, though he knows himself to be perfectly secure from falling, by his experience of the solidity of the iron which supports him, and though the ideas of fall and descent, and harm and death, be derived solely from custom and experience. The same custom goes beyond the instances from which it is derived, and to which it perfectly corresponds; and influences his ideas of such objects as are in some respect resembling, but fall not precisely under the same rule. The circumstances of depth and descent strike so strongly upon him, that their influence cannot be destroyed by the contrary circumstances of support and solidity, which ought to give him a perfect security. His imagination runs away with its object, and excites a passion proportioned to it. That passion returns back upon the imagination, and enlivens the idea; which lively idea has a new influence on the passion, and in its turn augments its force and violence; and both his fancy and affections, thus mutually supporting each other, cause the whole to have a very great influence upon him.

But why need we seek for other instances, while the present subject to philosophical probabilities offers us so obvious a one, in the opposition betwixt the judgment and imagination, arising from these effects of custom? According to my system, all reasonings are nothing but the effects of custom, and custom has no influence, but by enlivening the imagination, and giving us a strong conception of any object. It may therefore be concluded that our judgment and imagination can never be contrary, and that custom cannot operate on the latter faculty after such a manner, as to render it opposite to the former. This difficulty we can remove after no other manner than by supposing the influence of general rules. We shall afterwards[1] take notice of some general rules, by which we ought to regulate our judgment concerning causes and effects; and these rules are formed on the nature of our understanding, and on our experience of its operations in the judgments we form concerning objects. By them we learn to distinguish the accidental circumstances from the efficacious causes; and when we find that an effect can be produced without the concurrence of any particular circumstance, we conclude that that circumstance makes not a part of the efficacious cause, however frequently conjoined with it. But as this frequent conjunction necessarily makes it have some effect on the imagination, in spite of the opposite conclusion from general rules, the opposition of these two principles produces a contrariety in our thoughts, and causes us to ascribe the one inference to our judgment, and the other to our imagination. The general rule is attributed to our judgment, as being more extensive and constant; the exception to the imagination, as being more capricious and uncertain.

Thus our general rules are in a manner set in opposition to each other. When an object appears, that resembles any cause in very considerable circumstances, the imagination naturally carries us to a lively conception of the usual effect, though the object be different in the most material and most efficacious circumstances from that cause. Here is the first influence of general rules. But when we take a review of this act of the mind, and compare it with the more general and authentic operations of the understanding, we find it to be of an irregular nature, and destructive of all the most established principles of reasonings, which is the cause of

<hr>

[1] Sect. 15.

our rejecting it. This is a second influence of general rules, and implies the condemnation of the former. Sometimes the one, sometimes the other prevails, according to the disposition and character of the person. The vulgar are commonly guided by the first, and wise men by the second. Meanwhile the sceptics may here have the pleasure of observing a new and signal contradiction in our reason, and of seeing all philosophy ready to be subverted by a principle of human nature, and again saved by a new direction of the very same principle. The following of general rules is a very unphilosophical species of probability; and yet it is only by following them that we can correct this and all other unphilosophical probabilities.

Since we have instances where general rules operate on the imagination, even contrary to the judgment, we need not be surprised to see their effects increase, when conjoined with that latter faculty, and to observe that they bestow on the ideas they present to us a force superior to what attends any other. Every one knows there is an indirect manner of insinuating praise or blame, which is much less shocking than the open flattery or censure of any person. However he may communicate his sentiments by such secret insinuations, and make them known with equal certainty as by the open discovery of them, it is certain that their influence is not equally strong and powerful. One who lashes me with concealed strokes of satire, moves not my indignation to such a degree, as if he flatly told me I was a fool and a coxcomb; though I equally understand his meaning if he did. This difference is to be attributed to the influence of general rules.

Whether a person openly abuses me, or slily intimates his contempt, in neither case do I immediately perceive his sentiment or opinion; and it is only by signs, that is, by its effects, I become sensible of it. The only difference then, betwixt these two cases, consists in this, that in the open discovery of his sentiments he makes use of signs, which are general and universal; and in the secret intimation employs such as are more singular and uncommon. The effect of this circumstance is, that the imagination, in running from the present impression to the absent idea, makes the transition with greater facility, and consequently conceives the object with greater force, where the connection is common and universal, than where it is more rare and particular. Accordingly, we may observe, that the open declaration of our sentiments is called the taking off the mask, as the secret intimation of our opinions is said to be the veiling of them. The difference betwixt an idea produced by a

BRITISH EMPIRICAL PHILOSOPHERS

general connection, and that arising from a particular one, is here compared to the difference betwixt an impression and an idea. This difference in the imagination has a suitable effect on the passions, and this effect is augmented by another circumstance. A secret intimation of anger or contempt shows that we still have some consideration for the person, and avoid the directly abusing him. This makes a concealed satire less disagreeable, but still this depends on the same principle. For if an idea were not more feeble, when only intimated, it would never be esteemed a mark of greater respect to proceed in this method than in the other.

Sometimes scurrility is less displeasing than delicate satire, because it revenges us in a manner for the injury at the very time it is committed, by affording us a just reason to blame and contemn the person who injures us. But this phenomenon likewise depends upon the same principle. For why do we blame all gross and injurious language, unless it be because we esteem it contrary to good breeding and humanity? And why is it contrary, unless it be more shocking than any delicate satire? The rules of good breeding condemn whatever is openly disobliging, and gives a sensible pain and confusion to those with whom we converse. After this is once established, abusive language is universally blamed, and gives less pain upon account of its coarseness and incivility, which render the person despicable that employs it. It becomes less disagreeable, merely because originally it is more so; and it is more disagreeable, because it affords an inference by general and common rules that are palpable and undeniable.

To this explication of the different influence of open and concealed flattery or satire, I shall add the consideration of another phenomenon, which is analogous to it. There are many particulars in the point of honour, both of men and women, whose violations, when open and avowed, the world never excuses, but which it is more apt to overlook, when the appearances are saved, and the transgression is secret and concealed. Even those who know with equal certainty that the fault is committed, pardon it more easily, when the proofs seem in some measure oblique and equivocal, than when they are direct and undeniable. The same idea is presented in both cases, and, properly speaking, is equally assented to by the judgment; and yet its influence is different, because of the different manner in which it is presented

Now, if we compare these two cases, of the *open* and *concealed* violations of the laws of honour, we shall find that the difference betwixt them consists in this, that in the first case the sign, from which we infer the blamable action, is single, and suffices alone to be the foundation of our reasoning and judgment; whereas in the latter the signs are numerous, and decide little or nothing when alone and unaccompanied with many minute circumstances, which are almost imperceptible. But it is certainly true, that any reasoning is always the more convincing the more single and united it is to the eye, and the less exercise it gives to the imagination to collect all its parts, and run from them to the correlative idea, which forms the conclusion. The labour of the thoughts disturbs the regular progress of the sentiments, as we shall observe presently.[1] The idea strikes not on us with such vivacity, and consequently has no such influence on the passion and imagination.

From the same principles we may account for those observations of the Cardinal de Retz, *that there are many things in which the world wishes to be deceived, and that it more easily excuses a person in acting than in talking contrary to the decorum of his profession and character.* A fault in words is commonly more open and distinct than one in actions, which admit of many palliating excuses, and decide not so clearly concerning the attention and views of the actor.

Thus it appears, upon the whole, that every kind of opinion or judgment which amounts not to knowledge, is derived entirely from the force and vivacity of the perception, and that these qualities constitute in the mind what we call the *belief* of the existence of any object. This force and this vivacity are most conspicuous in the memory; and therefore our confidence in the veracity of that faculty is the greatest imaginable, and equals in many respects the assurance of a demonstration. The next degree of these qualities is that derived from the relation of cause and effect; and this too is very great, especially when the conjunction is found by experience to be perfectly constant, and when the object, which is present to us, exactly resembles those of which we have had experience. But below this degree of evidence there are many others which have an influence on the passions and imagination, proportioned to that degree of force and vivacity which they communicate to the ideas. It is by habit we make the transition from cause to effect; and it is from some present impression we borrow that vivacity which we diffuse over the correlative idea. But when we have not observed a sufficient number of instances to produce a strong habit; or when these instances are contrary to

[1] Part. IV. Sect. 1.

each other; or when the resemblance is not exact; or the present impression is faint and obscure; or the experience in some measure obliterated from the memory; or the connection dependent on a long chain of objects; or the inference derived from general rules, and yet not conformable to them: in all these cases the evidence diminishes by the diminution of the force and intenseness of the idea. This therefore is the nature of the judgment and probability.

What principally gives authority to this system is, beside the undoubted arguments, upon which each part is founded, the agreement of these parts, and the necessity of one to explain another. The belief which attends our memory is of the same nature with that which is derived from our judgments: nor is there any difference betwixt that judgment which is derived from a constant and uniform connection of causes and effects, and that which depends upon an interrupted and uncertain. It is indeed evident, that in all determinations where the mind decides from contrary experiments, it is first divided within itself, and has an inclination to either side in proportion to the number of experiments we have seen and remember. This contest is at last determined to the advantage of that side where we observe a superior number of these experiments; but still with a diminution of force in the evidence correspondent to the number of the opposite experiments. Each possibility, of which the probability is composed, operates separately upon the imagination; and it is the larger collection of possibilities which at last prevails, and that with a force proportionable to its superiority. All these phenomena lead directly to the precedent system; nor will it ever be possible upon any other principles to give a satisfactory and consistent explication of them. Without considering these judgments as the effects of custom on the imagination, we shall lose ourselves in perpetual contradiction and absurdity.

SECTION XIV

OF THE IDEA OF NECESSARY CONNECTION[1]

HAVING thus explained the manner *in which we reason beyond our immediate impressions, and conclude that such particular causes*

[1] See also Enquiry, Sect. VII. Part 1, page 509.

must have such particular effects; we must now return upon our
footsteps to examine that question[1] which first occurred to us, and
which we dropped in our way, viz., *What is our idea of necessity,
when we say that two objects are necessarily connected together?*
Upon this head I repeat, what I have often had occasion to observe,
that as we have no idea that is not derived from an impression,
we must find some impression that gives rise to this idea of necessity, if we assert we have really such an idea.   In order to this, I
consider in what objects necessity is commonly supposed to lie; and,
finding that it is always ascribed to causes and effects, I turn my
eye to two objects supposed to be placed in that relation, and
examine them in all the situations of which they are susceptible.
I immediately perceive that they are *contiguous* in time and place,
and that the object we call cause *precedes* the other we call effect.
In no one instance can I go any further, nor is it possible for me
to discover any third relation betwixt these objects.   I therefore
enlarge my view to comprehend several instances, where I find like
objects always existing in like relations of contiguity and succession.
At first sight this seems to serve but little to my purpose.   The
reflection on several instances only repeats the same objects; and
therefore can never give rise to a new idea.   But upon further
inquiry I find that the repetition is not in every particular the same,
but produces a new impression, and by that means the idea which I
at present examine.   For, after a frequent repetition, I find that
upon the appearance of one of the objects the mind is *determined*
by custom to consider its usual attendant, and to consider it in a
stronger light upon account of its relation to the first object.   It is
this impression, then, or *determination*, which affords me the idea
of necessity.

I doubt not but these consequences will at first sight be received
without difficulty, as being evident deductions from principles which
we have already established, and which we have often employed
in our reasonings.   This evidence, both in the first principles and
in the deductions, may seduce us unwarily into the conclusion, and
make us imagine it contains nothing extraordinary, nor worthy of
our curiosity.   But though such an inadvertence may facilitate the
reception of this reasoning, it will make it be the more easily
forgot; for which reason I think it proper to give warning, that I
have just now examined one of the most sublime questions in
philosophy, viz., *that concerning the power and efficacy of causes*
where all the sciences seem so much interested.   Such a warning

[1] Sect. 2.

will naturally rouse up the attention of the reader, and make him desire a more full account of my doctrine, as well as of the arguments on which it is founded. This request is so reasonable that I cannot refuse complying with it; especially as I am hopeful that these principles, the more they are examined, will acquire the more force and evidence.

There is no question which, on account of its importance, as well as difficulty, has caused more disputes both among ancient and modern philosophers, than this concerning the efficacy of causes, or that quality which makes them be followed by their effects. But before they entered upon these disputes, methinks it would not have been improper to have examined what idea we have of that efficacy, which is the subject of the controversy. This is what I find principally wanting in their reasonings, and what I shall here endeavour to supply.

I begin with observing that the terms of *efficacy, agency, power, force, energy, necessity, connection,* and *productive quality,* are all nearly synonymous; and therefore it is an absurdity to employ any of them in defining the rest. By this observation we reject at once all the vulgar definitions which philosophers have given of power and efficacy; and instead of searching for the ideas in these definitions, must look for it in the impressions from which it is originally derived. If it be a compound idea, it must arise from compound impressions. If simple, from simple impressions.

I believe the most general and most popular explication of this matter, is to say,[1] that finding from experience that there are several new productions in matter, such as the motions and variations of body, and concluding that there must somewhere be a power capable of producing them, we arrive at last by this reasoning at the idea of power and efficacy. But to be convinced that this explication is more popular than philosophical, we need but reflect on two very obvious principles. *First,* that reason alone can never give rise to any original idea; and, *secondly,* that reason, as distinguished from experience, can never make us conclude that a cause or productive quality is absolutely requisite to every beginning of existence. Both these considerations have been sufficiently explained; and therefore shall not at present be any further insisted on.

I shall only infer from them, that since reason can never give rise to the idea of efficacy, that idea must be derived from

---

[1] See Mr. Locke; chapter of Power.

experience, and from some particular instances of this efficacy, which make their passage into the mind by the common channels of sensation or reflection.   Ideas always represent their objects or impressions; and *vice versa*, there are some objects necessary to give rise to every idea.   If we pretend, therefore, to have any just idea of this efficacy, we must produce some instance wherein the efficacy is plainly discoverable to the mind, and its operations obvious to our consciousness or sensation.   By the refusal of this, we acknowledge that the idea is impossible and imaginary; since the principle of innate ideas, which alone can save us from this dilemma, has been already refuted, and is now almost universally rejected in the learned world.   Our present business, then, must be to find some natural production, where the operation and efficacy of a cause can be clearly conceived and comprehended by the mind, without any danger of obscurity or mistake.

In this research we meet with very little encouragement from that prodigious diversity which is found in the opinions of those philosophers who have pretended to explain the secret force and energy of causes.[1]   There are some who maintain that bodies operate by their substantial form; others, by their accidents or qualities; several, by their matter and form; some, by their form and accidents; others, by certain virtues and faculties distinct from all this.   All these sentiments, again, are mixed and varied in a thousand different ways, and form a strong presumption that none of them have any solidity or evidence, and that the supposition of an efficacy in any of the known qualities of matter is entirely without foundation.   This presumption must increase upon us when we consider that these principles of substantial forms, and accidents, and faculties, are not in reality any of the known properties of bodies, but are perfectly unintelligible and inexplicable.   For it is evident philosophers would never have had recourse to such obscure and uncertain principles, had they met with any satisfaction in such as are clear and intelligible; especially in such an affair as this, which must be an object of the simplest understanding, if not of the senses.   Upon the whole, we may conclude that it is impossible, in any one instance, to show the principle in which the force and agency of a cause is placed; and that the most refined and most vulgar understandings are equally at a loss in this particular.   If any one think proper to refute this assertion, he need not put himself to the trouble of inventing any long reasonings, but may

[1] See Father Malbranche, Book VI. Part II. Chap. 3, and the illustrations upon it.

at once show us an instance of a cause where we discover the power or operating principle. This defiance we are obliged frequently to make use of, as being almost the only means of proving a negative in philosophy.

The small success which has been met with in all the attempts tc fix this power, has at last obliged philosophers to conclude that the ultimate force and efficacy of nature is perfectly unknown to us, and that it is in vain we search for it in all the known qualities of matter. In this opinion they are almost unanimous; and it is only in the inference they draw from it that they discover any difference in their sentiments. .For some of them, as the Cartesians in particular, having established it as a principle that we are perfectly acquainted with the essence of matter, have very naturally inferred that it is endowed with no efficacy, and that it is impossible for it of itself to communicate motion, or produce any of those effects which we ascribe to it. As the essence of matter consists in extension, and as extension implies not actual motion, but only mobility; they conclude that the energy which produces the motion cannot lie in the extension.

This conclusion leads them into another, which they regard as, perfectly unavoidable. Matter, say they, is in itself entirely unactive and deprived of any power by which it may produce, or continue, or communicate motion: but since these effects are evident to our senses, and since the power that produces them must be placed somewhere, it must lie in the Deity, or that Divine Being who contains in his nature all excellency and perfection. It is the Deity, therefore, who is the prime mover of the universe, and who not only first created matter, and gave it its original impulse, but likewise, by a continued exertion of omnipotence, supports its existence, and successively bestows on it all those motions, and configurations, and qualities, with which it is endowed.

This opinion is certainly very curious, and well worth our attention; but it will appear superfluous to examine it in this place, if we reflect a moment on our present purpose in taking notice of it. We have established it as a principle, that as all ideas are derived from impressions, or some precedent *perceptions*, it is impossible we can have any idea of power and efficacy, unless some instances can be produced, wherein this power *is perceived* to exert itself. Now, as these instances can never be discovered in body, the Cartesians, proceeding upon their principle of innate ideas, have had recourse to a Supreme Spirit or Deity, whom they consider as the only active being in the universe, and as the immediate cause of every alteration in matter. But the principle of innate ideas being allowed to be false, it follows, that the supposition of a Deity can serve us in no stead, in accounting for that idea of agency, which we search for in vain in all the objects which are presented to our senses, or which we are internally conscious of in our own minds. For if every idea be derived from an impression, the idea of a Deity proceeds from the same origin; and if no impression, either of sensation or reflection, implies any force or efficacy, it is equally impossible to discover or even imagine any such active principle in the Deity. Since these philosophers, therefore, have concluded that matter cannot be endowed with any efficacious principle, because it is impossible to discover in it such a principle, the same course of reasoning should determine them to exclude it from the Supreme Being. Or, if they esteem that opinion absurd and impious, as it really is, I shall tell them how they may avoid it; and that is, by concluding from the very first, that they have no adequate idea of power or efficacy in any object; since neither in body nor spirit, neither in superior nor inferior natures are they able to discover one single instance of it.

The same conclusion is unavoidable upon the hypothesis of those who maintain the efficacy of second causes, and attribute a derivative, but a real power and energy to matter. For as they confess that this energy lies not in any of the known qualities of matter, the difficulty still remains concerning the origin of its idea. If we have really an idea of power, we may attribute power to an unknown quality: but as it is impossible that that idea can be derived from such a quality, and as there is nothing in known qualities which can produce it, it follows that we deceive ourselves when we imagine we are possessed of any idea of this kind, after the manner we commonly understand it. All ideas are derived from and represent impressions. We never have any impression that contains any power or efficacy. We never, therefore, have any idea of power.

Some have asserted that we feel an energy or power in our own mind; and that, having in this manner acquired the idea of power, we transfer that quality to matter, where we are not able immediately to discover it. The motions of our body, and the thoughts and sentiments of our mind (say they) obey the will; nor do we seek any further to acquire a just notion of force or power. But to convince us how fallacious this reasoning is, we need only consider, that the will being here considered as a cause has no more a discoverable connection with its effects than any material cause has with its proper effect. So far from perceiving the connection betwixt an act of volition and a motion of the body, it is allowed that no effect is more inexplicable from the powers and essence of thought and matter. Nor is the empire of the will over our mind more intelligible. The effect is there distinguishable and separable from the cause, and could be foreseen without the experience of their constant conjunction. We have command over our mind to a certain degree, but beyond *that* lose all empire over it: and it is evidently impossible to fix any precise bounds to our authority, where we consult not experience. In short, the actions of the mind are, in this respect, the same with those of matter. We perceive only their constant conjunction; nor can we ever reason beyond it. No internal impression has an apparent energy, more than external objects have. Since, therefore, matter is confessed by philosophers to operate by an unknown force, we should in vain hope to attain an idea of force by consulting our own minds.[1]

It has been established as a certain principle, that general or abstract ideas are nothing but individual ones taken in a certain light, and that, in reflecting on any object, it is as impossible to exclude from our thought all particular degrees of quantity and quality as from the real nature of things. If we be possessed, therefore, of any idea of power in general, we must also be able to conceive some particular species of it; and as power cannot subsist alone, but is always regarded as an attribute of some being or existence, we must be able to place this power in some particular being, and conceive that being as endowed with a real force and energy, by which such a particular effect necessarily results from its operation. We must distinctly and particularly conceive the connection betwixt the cause and effect, and be able to pronounce, from a simple view of the one, that it must be followed or preceded by the other. This is the true manner of conceiving a particular power in a particular body: and a general idea being impossible without an individual; where the latter is impossible, it is certain the former can never exist. Now nothing is more evident than that the human mind cannot form such an idea of two objects, as to conceive any connection betwixt them, or comprehend distinctly that power or efficacy by which they are united. Such a

[1] The same imperfection attends our ideas of the Deity; but this can have no effect either on religion or morals. The order of the universe proves an omnipotent mind; that is, a mind whose will is *constantly attended* with the obedience of every creature and being. Nothing more is requisite to give a foundation to all the articles of religion; nor it is necessary we should form a distinct idea of the force and energy of the Supreme Being.

connection would amount to a demonstration, and would imply the absolute impossibility for the one object not to follow, or to be conceived not to follow upon the other: which kind of connection has already been rejected in all cases. If any one is of a contrary opinion, and thinks he has attained a notion of power in any particular object, I desire he may point out to me that object. But till I meet with such a one, which I despair of, I cannot forbear concluding, that since we can never distinctly conceive how any particular power can possibly reside in any particular object, we deceive ourselves in imagining we can form any such general idea.

Thus, upon the whole, we may infer, that when we talk of any being, whether of a superior or inferior nature, as endowed with a power or force, proportioned to any effect; when we speak of a necessary connection betwixt objects, and suppose that this connection depends upon an efficacy or energy, with which any of these objects are endowed; in all the expressions, *so applied,* we have really no distinct meaning, and make use only of common words, without any clear and determinate ideas. But as it is more probable that these expressions do here lose their true meaning by being *wrong applied,* than that they never have any meaning; it will be proper to bestow another consideration on this subject, to see if possibly we can discover the nature and origin of those ideas we annex to them.

Suppose two objects to be presented to us, of which the one is the cause and the other the effect; it is plain that, from the simple consideration of one or both these objects, we never shall perceive the tie by which they are united, or be able certainly to pronounce, that there is a connection betwixt them. It is not, therefore, from any one instance, that we arrive at the idea of cause and effect, of a necessary connection of power, of force, of energy, and of efficacy. Did we never see any but particular conjunctions of objects, entirely different from each other, we should never be able to form any such ideas.

But, again, suppose we observe instances in which the same objects are always conjoined together, we immediately conceive a connection betwixt them, and begin to draw an inference from one to another. This multiplicity of resembling instances, therefore, constitutes the very essence of power or connection, and is the source from which the idea of it arises. In order, then, to understand the idea of power, we must consider that multiplicity; nor do I ask more to give a solution of that difficulty which has so long perplexed us. For thus I reason. The repetition of perfectly similar instances can never *alone* give rise to an original idea, different from what is to be found in any particular instance, as has been observed, and as evidently follows from our fundamental principle, *that all ideas are copied from impressions.* Since, therefore, the idea of power is a new original idea, not to be found in any one instance, and which yet arises from the repetition of several instances, it follows that the repetition *alone* has not that effect, but must either *discover* or *produce* something new, which is the source of that idea. Did the repetition neither discover nor produce anything new, our ideas might be multiplied by it, but would not be enlarged above what they are upon the observation of one single instance. Every enlargement, therefore (such as the idea of power or connection), which arises from the multiplicity of similar instances, is copied from some effects of the multiplicity, and will be perfectly understood by understanding these effects. Wherever we find anything new to be discovered or produced by the repetition, there we must place the power, and must never look for it in any other object.

But it is evident, in the first place, that the repetition of like objects in like relations of succession and contiguity, *discovers* nothing new in any one of them; since we can draw no inference from it, nor make it a subject either of our demonstrative or probable reasonings; as has been already proved.[1] Nay, suppose we could draw an inference, it would be of no consequence in the present case; since no kind of reasoning can give rise to a new idea, such as this of power is; but wherever we reason, we must antecedently be possessed of clear ideas, which may be the objects of our reasoning. The conception always precedes the understanding; and where the one is obscure, the other is uncertain; where the one fails, the other must fail also.

Secondly, it is certain that this repetition of similar objects in similar situations, *produces* nothing new either in these objects, or in any external body. For it will readily be allowed, that the several instances we have of the conjunction of resembling causes and effects, are in themselves entirely independent, and that the communication of motion, which I see result at present from the shock of two billiard balls, is totally distinct from that which I saw result from such an impulse a twelvemonth ago. These impulses have no influence on each other. They are entirely divided

---

[1] Sect. 6.

by time and place; and the one might have existed and communicated motion, though the other never had been in being.

There is, then, nothing new either discovered or produced in any
objects by their constant conjunction, and by the uninterrupted
resemblance of their relations of succession and contiguity. But it
is from this resemblance that the ideas of necessity, of power, and
of efficacy, are derived. These ideas, therefore, represent not
anything that does or can belong to the objects which are constantly
conjoined. This is an argument which, in every view we can
examine it, will be found perfectly unanswerable. Similar instances
are still the first source of our idea of power or necesity; at the
same time that they have no influence by their similarity either on
each other, or on any external object. We must, therefore, turn
ourselves to some other quarter to seek the origin of that idea.

Though the several resembling instances, which give rise to the
idea of power, have no influence on each other, and can never
produce any new quality *in the object*, which can be the model
of that idea, yet the *observation* of this resemblance produces a
new impression *in the mind*, which is its real model. For after we
have observed the resemblance in a sufficient number of instances,
we immediately feel a determination of the mind to pass from one
object to its usual attendant, and to conceive it in a stronger light
upon account of that relation. This determination is the only effect
of the resemblance; and, therefore, must be the same with power
or efficacy, whose idea is derived from the resemblance. The
several instances of resembling conjunctions lead us into the notion
of power and necessity. These instances are in themselves totally
distinct from each other, and have no union but in the mind, which
observes them, and collects their ideas. Necessity, then, is the
effect of this observation, and is nothing but an internal impression
of the mind, or a determination to carry our thoughts from one
object to another. Without considering it in this view, we can
never arrive at the most distant notion of it, or be able to attribute
it either to external or internal objects, to spirit or body, to causes
or effects.

The necessary connection betwixt causes and effects is the foundation of our inference from one to the other. The foundation
of our inference is the transition arising from the accustomed union.
These are, therefore, the same.

The idea of necessity arises from some impression. There is no
impression conveyed by our senses, which can give rise to that
idea. It must, therefore, be derived from some internal impression,

or impression of reflection. There is no internal impression which has any relation to the present business, but that propensity, which custom produces, to pass from an object to the idea of its usual attendant. This, therefore, is the essence of necessity. Upon the whole, necessity is something that exists in the mind, not in objects; nor is it possible for us ever to form the most distant idea of it, considered as a quality in bodies. Either we have no idea of necessity, or necessity is nothing but that determination of the thought to pass from causes to effects, and from effects to causes, according to their experienced union.

Thus, as the necessity, which makes two times two equal to four, or three angles of a triangle equal to two right ones, lies only in the act of the understanding, by which we consider and compare these ideas; in like manner the necessity of power, which unites causes and effects, lies in the determination of the mind to pass from the one to the other. The efficacy or energy of causes is neither placed in the causes themselves, nor in the Deity, nor in the concurrence of these two principles; but belongs entirely to the soul, which considers the union of two or more objects in all past instances. It is here that the real power of causes is placed, along with their connection and necessity.

I am sensible that of all the paradoxes which I have had, or shall hereafter have occasion to advance in the course of this Treatise, the present one is the most violent, and that it is merely by dint of solid proof and reasoning I can ever hope it will have admission, and overcome the inveterate prejudices of mankind. Before we are reconciled to this doctrine, how often must we repeat to ourselves, *that* the simple view of any two objects or actions, however related, can never give us any idea of power, or of a connection betwixt them: *that* this idea arises from the repetition of their union: *that* the repetition neither discovers nor causes anything in the objects, but has an influence only on the mind, by that customary transition it produces: *that* this customary transition is therefore the same with the power and necessity; which are consequently qualities of perceptions, not of objects, and are internally felt by the soul, and not perceived externally in bodies? There is commonly an astonishment attending everything extraordinary; and this astonishment changes immediately into the highest degree of esteem or contempt, according as we approve or disapprove of the subject. I am much afraid, that though the foregoing reasoning appears to me the shortest and most decisive imaginable, yet, with the generality of readers, the bias of the mind will prevail, and give them a prejudice against the present doctrine.

This contrary bias is easily accounted for. It is a common observation, that the mind has a great propensity to spread itself on external objects, and to conjoin with them any internal impressions which they occasion, and which always make their appearance at the same time that these objects discover themselves to the senses. Thus, as certain sounds and smells are always found to attend certain visible objects, we naturally imagine a conjunction, even in place, betwixt the objects and qualities, though the qualities be of such a nature as to admit of no such conjunction, and really exist nowhere. But of this more fully hereafter.[1] Meanwhile, it is sufficient to observe, that the same propensity is the reason why we suppose necessity and power to lie in the objects we consider, not in our mind, that considers them; notwithstanding it is not possible for us to form the most distant idea of that quality, when it is not taken for the determination of the mind, to pass from the idea of an object to that of its usual attendant.

But though this be the only reasonable account we can give of necessity, the contrary notion is so riveted in the mind from the principles above mentioned, that I doubt not but my sentiments will be treated by many as extravagant and ridiculous. What! the efficacy of causes lie in the determination of the mind! As if causes did not operate entirely independent of the mind, and would not continue their operation, even though there was no mind existent to contemplate them, or reason concerning them. Thought may well depend on causes for its operation, but not causes on thought. This is to reverse the order of nature, and make that secondary, which is really primary. To every operation there is a power proportioned; and this power must be placed on the body that operates. If we remove the power from one cause, we must ascribe it to another; but to remove it from all causes, and bestow it on a being that is noways related to the cause or effect, but by perceiving them, is a gross absurdity, and contrary to the most certain principles of human reason.

I can only reply to all these arguments, that the case is here much the same, as if a blind man should pretend to find a great many absurdities in the supposition, that the colour of scarlet is not the same with the sound of a trumpet, nor light the same with solidity. If we have really no idea of a power or efficacy in any object, or of any real connection betwixt causes and effects, it will be to little purpose to prove that an efficacy is necessary in

[1] Part IV. Sect. 5.

all operations. We do not understand our own meaning in talking so, but ignorantly confound ideas which are entirely distinct from each other. I am, indeed, ready to allow, that there may be several qualities, both in material and immaterial objects, with which we are utterly unacquainted; and if we please to call these *power* or *efficacy*, it will be of little consequence to the world. But when, instead of meaning these unknown qualities, we make the terms of power and efficacy signify something, of which we have a clear idea, and which is incompatible with those objects to which we apply it, obscurity and error begin then to take place, and we are led astray by a false philosophy. This is the case when we transfer the determination of the thought to external objects, and suppose any real intelligible connection betwixt them; that being a quality which can only belong to the mind that considers them.

As to what may be said, that the operations of nature are independent of our thought and reasoning, I allow it; and accordingly have observed, that objects bear to each other the relations of contiguity and succession; that like objects may be observed, in several instances, to have like relations; and that all this is independent of, and antecedent to, the operations of the understanding. But if we go any further, and ascribe a power or necessary connection to these objects, this is what we can never observe in them, but must draw the idea of it from what we feel internally in contemplating them. And this I carry so far, that I am ready to convert my present reasoning into an instance of it, by a subtilty which it will not be difficult to comprehend.

When any object is presented to us, it immediately conveys to the mind a lively idea of that object which is usually found to attend it; and determination of the mind forms the necessary connection of these objects. But when we change the point of view from the objects to the perceptions, in that case the impression is to be considered as the cause, and the lively idea as the effect; and their necessary connection is that new determination, which we feel to pass from the idea of the one to that of the other. The uniting principle among our internal perceptions is as unintelligible as that among external objects, and is not known to us any other way than by experience. Now, the nature and effects of experience have been already sufficiently examined and explained. It never gives us any insight into the internal structure or operating principle of objects, but only accustoms the mind to pass from one to another.

It is now time to collect all the different parts of this reasoning, and, by joining them together, form an exact definition of the relation of cause and effect, which makes the subject of the present inquiry. This order would not have been excusable, of first examining our inference from the relation before we had explained the relation itself, had it been possible to proceed in a different method. But as the nature of the relation depends so much on that of the inference, we have been obliged to advance in this seemingly preposterous manner, and make use of terms before we were able exactly to define them, or fix their meaning. We shall now correct this fault by giving a precise definition of cause and effect.

There may two definitions be given of this relation, which are ony different by their presenting a different view of the same object, and making us consider it either as a *philosophical* or as a *natural* relation; either as a comparison of two ideas, or as an association betwixt them. We may define a *cause* to be " An object precedent and contiguous to another, and where all the objects resembling the former are placed in like relations of precedency and contiguity to those objects that resemble the latter." If this definition be esteemed defective, because drawn from objects foreign to the cause, we may substitute this other definition in its place, viz., " A *cause* is an object precedent and contiguous to another, and so united with it that the idea of the one determines the mind to form the idea of the other, and the impression of the one to form a more lively idea of the other." Should this definition also be rejected for the same reason, I know no other remedy, than that the persons who express this delicacy should substitute a juster definition in its place. But, for my part, I must own my incapacity for such an undertaking. When I examine, with the utmost accuracy, those objects which are commonly denominated causes and effects, I find, in considering a single instance, that the one object is precedent and contiguous to the other; and in enlarging my view to consider several instances, I find only that like objects are constantly placed in like relations of succession and contiguity. Again, when I consider the influence of this constant conjunction, I perceive that such a relation can never be an object of reasoning, and can never operate upon the mind but by means of custom, which determines the imagination to make a transition from the idea of one object to that of its usual attendant, and from the impression of one to a more lively idea of the other. However extraordinary these sentiments may appear, I think it fruitless to trouble myself with any further inquiry or reasoning upon the subject, but shall repose myself on them as on established maxims.

It will only be proper, before we leave this subject, to draw some corollaries from it, by which we may remove several prejudices and popular errors that have very much prevailed in philosophy. First, we may learn, from the foregoing doctrine, that all causes are of the same kind, and that, in particular, there is no foundation for that distinction which we sometimes make betwixt efficient causes, and causes *sine qua non;* or betwixt efficient causes, and formal, and material, and exemplary, and final causes. For as our idea of efficiency is derived from the constant conjunction of two objects, wherever this is observed, the cause is efficient; and where it is not, there can never be a cause of any kind. For the same reason we must reject the distinction betwixt *cause* and *occasion*, when supposed to signify anything essentially different from each other. If constant conjunction be implied in what we call occasion, it is a real cause; if not, it is no relation at all, and cannot give rise to any argument or reasoning.

Secondly, the same course of reasoning will make us conclude, that there is but one kind of *necessity*, as there is but one kind of cause, and that the common distinction betwixt *moral* and *physical* necessity is without any foundation in nature. This clearly appears from the precedent explication of necessity. It is the constant conjunction of objects, along with the determination of the mind, which constitutes a physical necessity: and the removal of these is the same thing with *chance*. As objects must either be conjoined or not, and as the mind must either be determined or not to pass from one object to another, it is impossible to admit of any medium betwixt chance and an absolute necessity. In weakening this conjunction and determination you do not change the nature of the necessity; since even in the operation of bodies these have different degrees of constancy and force, without producing a different species of that relation.

The distinction, which we often make betwixt *power* and the *exercise* of it, is equally without foundation.

Thirdly, we may now be able fully to overcome all that repugnance, which it is so natural for us to entertain against the foregoing reasoning, by which we endeavoured to prove, that the necessity of a cause to every beginning of existence is not founded on any arguments either demonstrative or intuitive. Such an opinion will not appear strange after the foregoing definitions. If we define a cause to be *an object precedent and contiguous to another, and where all the objects resembling the former are placed in a like relation of priority and contiguity to those objects that resemble the latter;* we may easily conceive that there is no absolute nor metaphysical necessity, that every beginning of existence should be attended with such an object. If we define a cause to be, *an object precedent and contiguous to another, and so united with it in the imagination, that the idea of the one determines the mind to form the idea of the other, and the impression of the one to form a more lively idea of the other;* we shall make still less difficulty of assenting to this opinion. Such an influence on the mind is in itself perfectly extraordinary and incomprehensible; nor can we be certain of its reality, but from experience and observation.

I shall add as a fourth corollary, that we can never have reason to believe that any object exists, of which we cannot form an idea. For, as all our reasonings concerning existence are derived from causation, and as all our reasonings concerning causation are derived from the experienced conjunction of objects, not from any reasoning or reflection, the same experience must give us a notion of these objects, and must remove all mystery from our conclusions. This is so evident that it would scarce have merited our attention, were it not to obviate certain objections of this kind which might arise against the following reasonings concerning *matter* and *substance.* I need not observe, that a full knowledge of the object is not requisite, but only of those qualities of it which we believe to exist.

SECTION XV

RULES BY WHICH TO JUDGE OF CAUSES AND EFFECTS

ACCORDING to the precedent doctrine, there are no objects which, by the mere survey, without consulting experience, we can determine to be the causes of any other; and no objects which we can certainly determine in the same manner not to be the causes. Anything may produce anything. Creation, annihilation, motion, reason, volition; all these may arise from one another, or from any other object we can imagine. Nor will this appear strange if we compare two principles explained above, *that the constant conjunction of objects determines their causation,*[1] *and that, properly*

[1] Part I. Sect. 5.

speaking, no objects are contrary to each other but existence and non-existence. Where objects are not contrary, nothing hinders them from having that constant conjunction on whioh the relation of cause and effect totally depends.

Since, therefore, it is possible for all objects to become causes or effects to each other, it may be proper to fix some general rules by which we may know when they really are so.

1. The cause and effect must be contiguous in space and time.

2. The cause must be prior to the effect.

3. There must be a constant union betwixt the cause and effect. It is chiefly this quality that constitutes the relation.

4. The same cause always produces the same effect, and the same effect never arises but from the same cause. This principle we derive from experience, and is the source of most of our philosophical reasonings. For when by any clear experiment we have discovered the causes or effects of any phenomenon, we immediately extend our observation to every phenomenon of the same kind, without waiting for that constant repetition, from which the first idea of this relation is derived.

5. There is another principle which hangs upon this, viz., that where several different objects produce the same effect, it must be by means of some quality which we discover to be common amongst them. For as like effects imply like causes, we must always ascribe the causation to the circumstance wherein we discover the resemblance.

6, The following principle is founded on the same reason. The difference in the effects of two resembling objects must proceed from that particular in which they differ. For as like causes always produce like effects, when in any instance we find our expectation to be disappointed, we must conclude that this irregularity proceeds from some difference in the causes.

7. When any object increases or diminishes with the increase or diminution of its cause, it is to be regarded as a compounded effect, derived from the union of the several different effects which arise from the several different parts of the cause. The absence or presence of one part of the cause is here supposed to be always attended with the absence or presence of a proportionable part of the effect. This constant conjunction sufficiently proves that the one part is the cause of the other. We must, however, beware not to draw such a conclusion from a few experiments. A certain degree of heat gives pleasure; if you diminish that heat, the pleasure diminishes; but it does not follow, that if you augment it beyond

a certain degree, the pleasure will likewise augment; for we find that it degenerates into pain.

8. The eighth and last rule I shall take notice of is, that an object, which exists for any time in its full perfection without any effect, is not the sole cause of that effect, but requires to be assisted by some other principle, which may forward its influence and operation. For as like effects necessarily follow from like causes, and in a contiguous time and place, their separation for a moment shows that these causes are not complete ones.

Here is all the logic I think proper to employ in my reasoning; and perhaps even this was not very necessary, but might have been supplied by the natural principles of our understanding. Our scholastic headpieces and logicians show no such superiority above the mere vulgar in their reason and ability, as to give us any inclination to imitate them in delivering a long system of rules and precepts to direct our judgment in philosophy. All the rules of this nature are very easy in their invention, but extremely difficult in their application; and even experimental philosophy, which seems the most natural and simple of any, requires the utmost stretch of human judgment. There is no phenomenon in nature but what is compounded and modified by so many different circumstances, that, in order to arrive at the decisive point, we must carefully separate whatever is superfluous, and inquire, by new experiments, if every particular circumstance of the first experiment was essential to it. These new experiments are liable to a discussion of the same kind; so that the utmost constancy is required to make us persevere in our inquiry, and the utmost sagacity to choose the right way among so many that present themselves. If this be the case even in natural philosophy, how much more in moral, where there is a much greater complication of circumstances, and where those views and sentiments, which are essential to any action of the mind, are so implicit and obscure, that they often escape our strictest attention, and are not only unaccountable in their causes, but even unknown in their existence? I am much afraid, lest the small success I meet with in my inquiries, will make this observation bear the air of an apology rather than of boasting.

If anything can give me security in this particular, it will be the enlarging the sphere of my experiments as much as possible; for which reason, it may be proper, in this place, to examine the reasoning faculty of brutes, as well as that of human creatures.

PART IV

OF THE SCEPTICAL AND OTHER SYSTEMS OF PHILOSOPHY

I—OF SCEPTICISM WITH REGARD TO REASON. II—OF SCEPTICISM WITH REGARD TO THE SENSES. III—OF THE ANCIENT PHILOSOPHY. IV—OF THE MODERN PHILOSOPHY. VI—OF PERSONAL IDENTITY. VII—CONCLUSION OF THIS BOOK

SECTION I

OF SCEPTICISM WITH REGARD TO REASON

IN all demonstrative sciences the rules are certain and infallible; but when we apply them, our fallible and uncertain faculties are very apt to depart from them, and fall into error. We must, therefore, in every reasoning form a new judgment, as a check or control on our first judgment or belief; and must enlarge our view to comprehend a kind of history of all the instances, wherein our understanding has deceived us, compared with those wherein its testimony was just and true. Our reason must be considered as a kind of cause, of which truth is the natural effect; but such a one as, by the irruption of other causes, and by the inconstancy of our mental powers, may frequently be prevented. By this means all knowledge degenerates into probability; and this probability is greater or less, according to our experience of the veracity or deceitfulness of our understanding, and according to the simplicity or intricacy of the question.

There is no algebraist nor mathematician so expert in his science, as to place entire confidence in any truth immediately upon his discovery of it, or regard it as anything but a mere probability. Every time he runs over his proofs, his confidence increases; but still more by the approbation of his friends; and is raised to its utmost perfection by the universal assent and applauses of the learned word. Now, it is evident that this gradual increase of assurance is nothing but the addition of new probabilities, and is derived from the constant union of causes and effects, according to past experience and observation.

In accounts of any length or importance, merchants seldom trust to the infallible certainty of numbers for their security; but by the artificial structure of the accounts, produce a probability beyond what is derived from the skill and experience of the accountant. For that is plainly of itself some degree of probability; though uncertain and variable, according to the degrees of his experience and length of the account. Now as none will maintain that our assurance in a long numeration exceeds probability, I may safely affirm, that there scarce is any proposition concerning numbers of which we can have a fuller security. For it is easily possible, by gradually diminishing the numbers, to reduce the longest series of addition to the most simple question which can be formed, to an addition of two single numbers; and upon this supposition we shall find it impracticable to show the precise limits of knowledge and of probability, or discover that particular number at which the one ends and the other begins. But knowledge and probability are of such contrary and disagreeing natures, that they cannot well run insensibly into each other, and that because they will not divide, but must be either entirely present, or entirely absent. Besides, if any single addition were certain, every one would be so, and consequently the whole or total sum; unless the whole can be different from all its parts. I had almost said that this was certain; but I reflect that it must reduce *itself*, as well as every other reasoning, and from knowledge degenerate into probability.

Since, therefore, all knowledge resolves itself into probability, and becomes at last of the same nature with that evidence which we employ in common ife, we must now examine this latter species of reasoning, and see on what foundation it stands.

In every judgment which we can form concerning probability, as well as concerning knowledge, we ought always to correct the first judgment, derived from the nature of the object, by another judgment, derived from the nature of the understanding. It is certain a man of solid sense and long experience ought to have, and usually has, a greater assurance in his opinions than one that is foolish and ignorant, and that our sentiments have different degrees of authority, even with ourselves, in proportion to the degrees of our reason and experience. In the man of the best sense and longest experience, this authority is never entire; since even such a one must be conscious of many errors in the past, and must still dread the like for the future. Here then arises a new species of probability to correct and regulate the first, and fix its just standard and proportion. As demonstration is subject to the control of probability, so is probability liable to a new correction by a reflex act of the mind, wherein the nature of our understanding, and our reasoning from the first probability, become our objects.

Having thus found in every probability, beside the original uncertainty inherent in the subject, a new uncertainty, derived from the weakness of that faculty which judges, and having adjusted these two together, we are obliged by our reason to add a new doubt, derived from the possibility of error in the estimation we make of the truth and fidelity of our faculties. This is a doubt which immediately occurs to us, and of which, if we would closely pursue our reason, we cannot avoid giving a decision. But this decision, though it should be favourable to our preceding judgment, being founded only on probability, must weaken still further our first evidence, and must itself be weakened by a fourth doubt of the same kind, and so on *in infinitum;* till at last there remain nothing of the original probability, however great we may suppose it to have been, and however small the diminution by every new uncertainty. No finite object can subsist under a decrease repeated *in infinitum*; and even the vastest quantity which can enter into human imagination, must in this manner be reduced to nothing. Let our first belief be never so strong, it must infallibly perish, by passing through so many new examinations, of which each diminishes somewhat of its force and vigour. When I reflect on the natural fallibility of my judgment, I have less confidence in my opinions than when I only consider the objects concerning which I reason; and when I proceed still further, to turn the scrutiny against every successive estimation I make of my faculties, all the rules of logic require a continual diminution, and at last a total extinction of belief and evidence.

Should it here be asked me, whether I sincerely assent to this argument, which I seem to take such pains to inculcate, and whether I be really one of those sceptics who hold that all is uncertain, and that our judgment is not in *any* thing possessed of *any* measures of truth and falsehood; I should reply, that this question is entirely superfluous, and that neither I, nor any other person, was ever sincerely and constantly of that opinion. Nature, by an absolute and uncontrollable necessity, has determined us to judge as well as to breathe and feel; nor can we any more forbear viewing certain objects in a stronger and fuller light, upon account of their customary connection with a present impression, than we can hinder ourselves from thinking, as long as we are awake, or seeing the surrounding bodies, when we turn our eyes towards them in broad sunshine. Whoever has taken the pains to refute the cavils of this *total* scepticism, has really disputed without an antagonist, and endeavoured by arguments to establish a faculty, which nature has antecedently implanted in the mind, and rendered unavoidable.

My intention then in displaying so carefully the arguments of that fantastic sect, is only to make the reader sensible of the truth of my hypothesis, *that all our reasonings concerning causes and effects, are derived from nothing but custom; and that belief is more properly an act of the sensitive, than of the cogitative part of our natures.* I have here proved, that the very same principles, which make us form a decision upon any subject, and correct that decision by the consideration of our genius and capacity, and of the situation of our mind, when we examined that subject; I say, I have proved that these same principles, when carried further, and applied to every new reflex judgment, must, by continually diminishing the original evidence, at last reduce it to nothing, and utterly subvert all belief and opinion. If belief, therefore, were a simple act of the thought, without any peculiar manner of conception, or the addition of a force and vivacity, it must infallibly destroy itself, and in every case terminate in a total suspense of judgment. But as experience will sufficiently convince any one, who thinks it worth while to try, that though he can find no error in the foregoing arguments, yet he still continues to believe, and think, and reason, as usual, he may safely conclude that his reasoning and belief is some sensation or peculiar manner of conception, which it is impossible for mere ideas and reflections to destroy.

But here, perhaps, it may be demanded, how it happens, even upon my hypothesis, that these arguments above explained produce not a total suspense of judgment, and after what manner the mind ever retains a degree of assurance in any subject? For as these new probabilities, which, by their repetition, perpetually diminish the original evidence, are founded on the very same principles, whether of thought or sensation, as the primary judgment, it may seem unavoidable, that in either case they must equally subvert it, and by the opposition, either of contrary thoughts or sensations, reduce the mind to a total uncertainty. I suppose there is some question proposed to me, and that, after revolving over the impressions of my memory and senses, and carrying my thoughts from them to such objects as are commonly conjoined with them, I feel a stronger and more forcible conception on the one side than on the other. This strong conception forms my first decision. I suppose, that afterwards I examine my judgment itself, and observing, from experience, that it is sometimes just and sometimes erroneous, I consider it as regulated by contrary principles or causes, of which some lead to truth, and some to error; and in balancing these contrary causes, I diminish, by a new probability, the assurance of my first decision. This new probability is liable to the same diminution as the foregoing, and so on, *in infinitum*. It is therefore demanded, *how it happens, that, even after all, we retain a degree of belief, which is sufficient for our purpose, either in philosophy or common life?*

I answer, that after the first and second decision, as the action of the mind becomes forced and unnatural, and the ideas faint and obscure, though the principles of judgment, and the balancing of opposite causes be the same as at the very beginning, yet their influence on the imagination, and the vigour they add to, or diminish from, the thought, is by no means equal. Where the mind reaches not its objects with easiness and facility, the same principles have not the same effect as in a more natural conception of the ideas; nor does the imagination feel a sensation, which holds any proportion with that which arises from its common judgments and opinions. The attention is on the stretch; the posture of the mind is uneasy; and the spirits being diverted from their natural course, are not governed in their movements by the same laws, at least not to the same degree, as when they flow in their usual channel.

If we desire similar instances, it will not be very difficult to find them. The present subject of metaphysics will supply us abundantly. The same argument, which would have been esteemed convincing in a reasoning concerning history or politics, has little or no influence in these abstruser subjects, even though it be perfectly comprehended; and that because there is required a study and an effort of thought, in order to its being comprehended: and this effort of thought disturbs the operation of our sentiments, on which the belief depends. The case is the same in other subjects. The straining of the imagination always hinders the regular flowing of the passions and sentiments. A tragic poet, that would represent his heroes as very ingenious and witty in their misfortunes, would never touch the passions. As the emotions of the soul prevent any subtle reasoning and reflection, so these latter actions of the mind are equally prejudicial to the former. The mind, as well as the body, seems to be endowed with a certain precise degree of force and activity, which it never employs in one action, but at the expense of all the rest. This is more evidently true, where the actions are of quite different natures; since in that case the force of the mind is not only diverted, but even the disposition changed, so as to render us incapable of a sudden transition from one action to the other, and still more of performing both at once. No wonder, then, the conviction, which arises from a subtile reasoning, diminishes in proportion to the efforts which the imagination makes to enter into the reasoning, and to conceive it in all its parts. Belief, being a lively conception, can never be entire, where it is not founded on something natural and easy.

This I take to be the true state of the question, and cannot approve of that expeditious way, which some take with the sceptics, to reject at once all their arguments without inquiry or examination. If the sceptical reasonings be strong, say they, it is a proof that reason may have some force and authority; if weak, they can never be sufficient to invalidate all the conclusions of our understanding. This argument is not just; because the sceptical reasonings, were it possible for them to exist, and were they not destroyed by their subtilty, would be successively both strong and weak, according to the successive dispositions of the mind. Reason first appears in possession of the throne, prescribing laws, and imposing maxims, with an absolute sway and authority. Her enemy, therefore, is obliged to take shelter under her protection, and by making use of rational arguments to prove the fallaciousness and imbecility of reason, produces, in a manner, a patent under her hand and seal. This patent has at first an authority, proportioned to the present and immediate authority of reason, from which it is derived. But as it is supposed to be contradictory to reason, it gradually diminishes the force of that governing power and its own at the same time: till at last they both vanish away into nothing, by a regular and just diminution. The sceptical and dogmatical reasons are of the same kind, though contrary in their operation and tendency; so that where the latter is strong, it has an enemy of equal force in the former to encounter; and as their forces were at first equal, they still continue so, as long as either of them subsists; nor does one of them lose any force in the contest, without taking as much from its antagonist. It is happy, therefore, that nature breaks the force of all sceptical arguments in time, and keeps them from having any considerable influence on the understanding.

Were we to trust entirely to their self-destruction, that can never take place, until they have first subverted all conviction, and have totally destroyed human reason.

SECTION II

OF SCEPTICISM WITH REGARD TO THE SENSES

THUS the sceptic still continues to reason and believe, even though he asserts that he cannot defend his reason by reason; and by the same rule he must assent to the principle concerning the existence of body, though he cannot pretend, by any arguments of philosophy, to maintain its veracity.   Nature has not left this to his choice, and has doubtless esteemed it an affair of too great importance, to be trusted to our uncertain reasonings and speculations.   We may well ask, *What causes induce us to believe in the existence of body?* but it is in vain to ask, *Whether there be body or not?*   That is a point which we must take for granted in all our reasonings.

The subject, then, of our present inquiry, is concerning the *causes* which induce us to believe in the existence of body: and my reasonings on this head I shall begin with a distinction, which at first sight may seem superfluous, but which will contribute very much to the perfect understanding of what follows.   We ought to examine apart those two questions, which are commonly confounded together, viz., Why we attribute a *continued* existence to objects, even when they are not present to the senses; and why we suppose them to have an existence *distinct* from the mind and perception?   Under this last head I comprehend their situation as well as relations, their *external* position as well as the *independence* of their existence and operation.   These two questions concerning the continued and distinct existence of body are intimately connected together.   For if the objects of our senses continue to exist, even when they are not perceived, their existence is of course independent of and distinct from the perception; and *vice versa,* if their existence be independent of the perception, and distinct from it, they must continue to exist, even though they be not perceived.   But though the decision of the one question decides the other; yet that we may the more easily discover the principles of human nature, from whence the decision arises, we shall carry along with us this distinction, and shall consider, whether it be the *senses*, *reason*, or the *imagination*, that produces the opinion of a *continued* or of a *distinct* existence. These are the only questions that are intelligible on the present subject. For as to the notion of external existence, when taken for something specifically different from our perceptions, we have already shown its absurdity.[1]

To begin with the *senses*, it is evident these faculties are incapable of giving rise to the notion of the *continued* existence of their objects, after they no longer appear to the senses. For that is a contradiction in terms, and supposes that the senses continue to operate, even after they have ceased all manner of operation. These faculties, therefore, if they have any influence in the present case, must produce the opinion of a distinct, not of a continued existence; and in order to that, must present their impressions either as images and representations, or as these very distinct and external existences.

That our senses offer not their impressions as the images of something *distinct*, or *independent*, and *external*, is evident; because they convey to us nothing but a single percepiton, and never give us the least intimation of anything beyond. A single perception can never produce the idea of a double existence, but by some inference either of the reason or imagination. When the mind looks further than what immediately appears to it, its conclusions can never be put to the account of the senses; and it certainly looks further, when from a single perception it infers a double existence, and supposes the relations of resemblance and causation betwixt them.

If our senses, therefore, suggest any idea of distinct existences, they must convey the impressions as those very existences, by a kind of fallacy and illusion. Upon this head we may observe that all sensations are felt by the mind, such as they really are, and that, when we doubt whether they present themselves as distinct objects, or as mere impressions, the difficulty is not concerning their nature, but concerning their relations and situation. Now, if the senses presented our impressions as external to, and independent of ourselves, both the objects and ourselves must be obvious to our senses, otherwise they could not be compared by these faculties. The difficulty then is, how far we are *ourselves* the objects of our senses.

It is certain there is no question in philosophy more abstruse

[1] Part II. Sect. 6.

than that concerning identity, and the nature of the uniting principle, which constitutes a person. So far from being able by our senses merely to determine this question, we must have recourse to the most profound metaphysics to give a satisfactory answer to it; and in common life it is evident these ideas of self and person are never very fixed nor determinate. It is absurd therefore to imagine the senses can ever distinguish betwixt ourselves and external objects.

Add to this, that every impression, external and internal, passions, affections, sensations, pains, and pleasures, are originally on the same footing; and that whatever other differences we may observe among them, they appear, all of them, in their true colours, as impressions or perceptions. And indeed, if we consider the matter aright, it is scarce possible it should be otherwise; nor is it conceivable that our senses should be more capable of deceiving us in the situation and relations, than in the nature of our impressions. For since all actions and sensations of the mind are known to us by consciousness, they must necessarily appear in every particular what they are, and be what they appear. Everything that enters the mind, being in *reality* as the perception, it is impossible anything should to *feeling* appear different. This were to suppose, that even where we are most intimately conscious, we might be mistaken.

But not to lose time in examining, whether it is possible for our senses to deceive us, and represent our perceptions as distinct from ourselves, that is, as *external* to and *independent* of us; let us consider whether they really do so, and whether this error proceeds from an immediate sensation, or from some other causes.

To begin with the question concerning *external* existence, it may perhaps be said, that setting aside the metaphysical question of the identity of a thinking substance, our own body evidently belongs to us; and as several impressions appear exterior to the body, we suppose them also exterior to ourselves. The paper on which I write at present is beyond my hand. The table is beyond the paper. The walls of the chamber beyond the table. And in casting my eye towards the window, I perceive a great extent of fields and buildings beyond my chamber. From all this it may be inferred, that no other faculty is required, beside the senses, to convince us of the external existence of body. But to prevent this inference, we need only weigh the three following considerations. *First*, that, properly speaking, it is not our body we perceive when we regard our limbs and members, but certain impressions, which enter by the senses; so that the ascribing a real and corporeal existence to these impressions, or to their objects, is an act of the mind as difficult to explain as that which we examine at present. *Secondly*, sounds, and tastes, and smells, though commonly regarded by the mind as continued independent qualities, appear not to have any existence in extension, and consequently cannot appear to the senses as situated externally to the body. The reason why we ascribe a place to them shall be considered afterwards.[1] *Thirdly*, even our sight informs us not of distance or outness (so to speak), immediately and without a certain reasoning and experience, as is acknowledged by the most rational philosophers.

As to the *independency* of our perceptions on ourselves, this can never be an object of the senses; but any opinion we form concerning it must be derived from experience and observation: and we shall see afterwards, that our conclusions from experience are far from being favourable to the doctrine of the independency of our perceptions. Meanwhile we may observe, that when we talk of real distinct existences, we have commonly more in our eye their independency than external situation in place, and think an object has a sufficient reality, when its being is uninterrupted, and independent of the incessant revolutions, which we are conscious of in ourselves.

Thus to resume what I have said concerning the senses; they give us no notion of continued existence, because they cannot operate beyond the extent, in which they really operate. They as little produce the opinion of a distinct existence, because they neither can offer it to the mind as represented, nor as original. To offer it as represented, they must present both an object and an image. To make it appear as original, they must convey a falsehood; and this falsehood must lie in the relations and situation: in order to which, they must be able to compare the object with ourselves; and even in that case they do not, nor is it possible they should deceive us. We may therefore conclude with certainty, that the opinion of a continued and of a distinct existence never arises from the senses.

To confirm this, we may observe that there are three different kinds of impressions conveyed by the senses. The first are those of the figure, bulk, motion, and solidity of bodies. The second, those of colours, tastes, smells, sounds, heat, and cold. The third are the pains and pleasures that arise from the application of objects to our bodies, as by the cutting of our flesh with steel.

[1] Sect. 5.

and such like. Both philosophers and the vulgar suppose the first of these to have a distinct continued existence. The vulgar only regard the second as on the same footing. Both philosophers and the vulgar, again, esteem the third to be merely perceptions; and, consequently, interrupted and dependent beings.

Now, it is evident, that whatever may be our philosophical opinion, colour, sounds, heat, and cold, as far as appears to the senses, exist after the same manner with motion and solidity; and that the difference we make betwixt them, in this respect, arises not from the mere perception. So strong is the prejudice for the distinct continued existence of the former qualities, that when the contrary opinion is advanced by modern philosophers, people imagine they can almost refute it from their feeling and experience, and that their very senses contradict this philosophy. It is also evident, that colours, sounds, etc., are originally on the same footing with the pain that arises from steel, and pleasure that proceeds from a fire; and that the difference betwixt them is founded neither on perception nor reason, but on the imagination. For as they are confessed to be, both of them, nothing but perceptions arising from the particular configurations and motions of the parts of body, wherein possibly can their difference consist? Upon the whole, then, we may conclude that, as far as the senses are judges, all perceptions are the same in the manner of their existence.

We may also observe, in this instance of sounds and colours, that we can attribute a distinct continued existence to objects without ever consulting *reason*, or weighing our opinions by any philosophical principles. And, indeed, whatever convincing arguments philosophers may fancy they can produce to establish the belief of objects independent of the mind, it is obvious these arguments are known but to very few; and that it is not by them that children, peasants, and the greatest part of mankind, are induced to attribute objects to some impressions, and deny them to others. Accordingly, we find that all the conclusions which the vulgar form on this head, are directly contrary to those which are confirmed by philosophy. For philosophy informs us that everything which appears to the mind is nothing but a perception, and is interrupted and dependent on the mind; whereas the vulgar confound perceptions and objects, and attribute a distinct continued existence to the very things they feel or see. This sentiment, then, as it is entirely unreasonable, must proceed from some other faculty than the understanding. To which we may add, that, as long as we take our perceptions and objects to be the same, we can never infer the existence of the one from that of the other, nor form any argument from the relation of cause and effect; which is the only one that can assure us of matter of fact. Even after we distinguish our perceptions from our objects, it will appear presently that we are still incapable of reasoning from the existence of one to that of the other: so that, upon the whole, our reason neither does, nor is it possible it ever should, upon any supposition give us an assurance of the continued and distinct existence of body. That opinion must be entirely owing to the *imagination*: which must now be the subject of our inquiry.

Since all impressions are internal and perishing existences, and appear as such, the notion of their distinct and continued existence must arise from a concurrence of some of their qualities with the qualities of the imagination; and since this notion does not extend to all of them, it must arise from certain qualities peculiar to some impressions. It will, therefore, be easy for us to discover these qualities by a comparison of the impressions, to which we attribute a distinct and continued existence, with those which we regard as internal and perishing.

We may observe, then, that it is neither upon account of the involuntariness of certain impressions, as is commonly supposed, nor of their superior force and violence, that we attribute to them a reality and continued existence, which we refuse to others that are voluntary or feeble. For it is evident our pains and pleasures, our passions and affections, which we never suppose to have any existence beyond our perception, operate with greater violence, and are equally involuntary, as the impressions of figure and extension, colour and sound, which we suppose to be permanent beings. The heat of a fire, when moderate, is supposed to exist in the fire; but the pain which it causes upon a near approach is not taken to have any being except in the perception.

These vulgar opinions, then, being rejected, we must search for some other hypothesis, by which we may discover those peculiar qualities in our impressions, which makes us attribute to them a distinct and continued existence.

After a little examination, we shall find that all those objects, to which we attribute a continued existence, have a peculiar *constancy*, which distinguishes them from the impressions whose existence depends upon our perception. Those mountains, and houses, and trees, which lie at present under my eye, have always appeared to me in the same order; and when I lose sight of them by shutting my eyes or turning my head, I soon after find them

return upon me without the least alteration. My bed and table,
my books and papers, present themselves in the same uniform
manner, and change not upon account of any interruption in my
seeing or perceiving them. This is the case with all the impressions
whose objects are supposed to have an external existence; and is
the case with no other impressions, whether gentle or violent,
voluntary or involuntary.

This constancy, however, is not so perfect as not to admit of
very considerable exceptions. Bodies often change their position
and qualities, and, after a little absence or interruption, may
become hardly knowable. But here it is observable, that even in
these changes they preserve a *coherence*, and have a regular
dependence on each other; which is the foundation of a kind of
reasoning from causation, and produces the opinion of their continued existence. When I return to my chamber after an hour's
absence, I find not my fire in the same situation in which I left it;
but then I am accustomed, in other instances, to see a like alteration
produced in a like time, whether I am present or absent, near or
remote. This coherence, therefore, in their changes, is one of the
characteristics of external objects, as well as their constancy.

Having found that the opinion of the continued existence of body
depends on the *coherence* and *constancy* of certain impressions, I
now proceed to examine after what manner these qualities give
rise to so extraordinary an opinion. To begin with the coherence;
we may observe, that though those internal impressions, which we
regard as fleeting and perishing, have also a certain coherence or
regularity in their appearances, yet it is of somewhat a different
nature from that which we discover in bodies. Our passions are
found by experience to have a mutual connection with and
dependence on each other; but on no occasion is it necessary to
suppose that they have existed and operated, when they were not
perceived, in order to preserve the same dependence and connection, of which we have had experience. The case is not the same
with relation to external objects. Those require a continued
existence, or otherwise lose, in a great measure, the regularity of
their operation. I am here seated in my chamber, with my face
to the fire; and all the objects that strike my senses are contained
in a few yards around me. My memory, indeed, informs me of
the existence of many objects; but, then, this information extends
not beyond their past existence, nor do either my senses or memory
give any testimony to the continuance of their being. When,
therefore, I am thus seated, and revolve over these thoughts, I

hear on a sudden a noise as of a door turning upon its hinges; and a little after see a porter who advances towards me. This gives occasion to many new reflections and reasonings. First, I never have observed that this noise could proceed from anything but the motion of a door; and therefore conclude that the present phenomenon is a contradiction to all past experience, unless the door, which I remember on the other side the chamber, be still in being. Again, I have always found, that a human body was possessed of a quality which I call gravity, and which hinders it from mounting in the air, as this porter must have done to arrive at my chamber, unless the stairs I remember be not annihilated by my absence. But this is not all. I receive a letter, which, upon opening it, I perceive by the handwriting and subscription to have come from a friend, who says he is two hundred leagues distant. It is evident I can never account for this phenomenon, conformable to my experience in other instances, without spreading out in my mind the whole sea and continent between us, and supposing the effects and continued existence of posts and ferries, according to my memory and observation. To consider these phenomena of the porter and letter in a certain light, they are contradictions to common experience, and may be regarded as objections to those maxims which we form concerning the connections of causes and effects. I am accustomed to hear such a sound, and see such an object in motion at the same time. I have not received, in this particular instance, both these perceptions. These observations are contrary, unless I suppose that the door still remains, and that it was opened without my perceiving it: and this supposition, which was at first entirely arbitrary and hypothetical, acquires a force and evidence by its being the only one upon which I can reconcile these contradictions. There is scarce a moment of my life wherein there is not a similar instance presented to me, and I have not occasion to suppose the continued existence of objects, in order to connect their past and present appearances, and give them such a union with each other, as I have found, by experience, to be suitable to their particular natures and circumstances. Here, then, I am naturally led to regard the world as something real and durable, and as preserving its existence, even when it is no longer present to my perception.

But, though this conclusion, from the coherence of appearances, may seem to be of the same nature with our reasonings concerning causes and effects, as being derived from custom, and regulated by past experience, we shall find, upon examination, that they are at the bottom considerably different from each other, and that this inference arises from the understanding and from custom, in an indirect and oblique manner. For it will readily be allowed, that since nothing is ever really present to the mind, besides its own perceptions, it is not only impossible that any habit should ever be acquired otherwise than by the regular succession of these perceptions, but also that any habit should ever exceed that degree of regularity. Any degree, therefore, of regularity in our perceptions, can never be a foundation for us to infer a greater degree of regularity in some objects which are not perceived, since this supposes a contradiction, viz., a habit acquired by what was never present to the mind. But it is evident that, whenever we infer the continued existence of the objects of sense from their coherence, and the frequency of their union, it is in order to bestow on the objects a greater regularity than what is observed in our mere perceptions. We remark a connection betwixt two kinds of objects in their past appearance to the senses, but are not able to observe this connection to be perfectly constant, since the turning about of our head, or the shutting of our eyes, is able to break it. What, then, do we suppose in this case, but that these objects still continue their usual connection, notwithstanding their apparent interruption, and that the irregular appearances are joined by something of which we are insensible? But as all reasoning concerning matters of fact arises only from custom, and custom can only be the effect of repeated perceptions, the extending of custom and reasoning beyond the perceptions can never be the direct and natural effect of the constant repetition and connection, but must arise from the co-operation of some other principles.

I have already observed,[1] in examining the foundation of mathematics, that the imagination, when set into any train of thinking, is apt to continue even when its object fails it, and, like a galley put in motion by the oars, carries on its course without any new impulse. This I have assigned for the reason, why, after considering several loose standards of equality, and correcting them by each other, we proceed to imagine so correct and exact a standard of that relation as is not liable to the least error or variation. The same principle makes us easily entertain this opinion of the continued existence of body. Objects have a certain coherence even as they appear to our senses; but this coherence is much greater and more uniform if we suppose the objects to have a continued existence; and as the mind is once in the train of

[1] Part II. Sect. 4.

observing a uniformity among objects, it naturally continues till it renders the uniformity as complete as possible. The simple supposition of their continued existence suffices for this purpose, and gives us a notion of a much greater regularity among objects, than what they have when we look no further than our senses.

But whatever force we may ascribe to this principle, I am afraid it is too weak to support alone so vast an edifice as is that of the continued existence of all external bodies; and that we must join the *constancy* of their appearance to the *coherence*, in order to give a satisactory account of that opinion. As the explication of this will lead me into a considerable compass of very profound reasoning, I think it proper, in order to avoid confusion, to give a short sketch or abridgment of my system, and afterwards draw out all its parts in their full compass. This inference from the constancy of our perceptions, like the precedent from their coherence, gives rise to the opinion of the *continued* existence of body, which is prior to that of its *distinct* existence, and produces that latter principle.

When we have been accustomed to observe a constancy in certain impressions, and have found that the perception of the sun or ocean, for instance, returns upon us, after an absence or annihilation, with like parts and in a like order as at its first appearance, we are not apt to regard these interrupted perceptions as different (which they really are), but on the contrary consider them as individually the same, upon account of their resemblance. But as this interruption of their existence is contrary to their perfect identity, and makes us regard the first impression as annihilated, and the second as newly created, we find ourselves somewhat at a loss, and are involved in a kind of contradiction. In order to free ourselves from this difficulty, we disguise, as much as possible, the interruption, or rather remove it entirely, by supposing that these interrupted perceptions are connected by a real existence, of which we are insensible. This supposition, or idea of continued existence, acquires a force and vivacity from the memory of these broken impressions, and from that propensity which they give us to suppose them the same; and according to the precedent reasoning, the very essence of belief consists in the force and vivacity of the conception.

In order to justify this system, there are four things requisite. *First*, to explain the *principium individuationis*, or principle of identity. *Secondly*, give a reason why the resemblance of our broken and interrupted perceptions induces us to attribute an identity to them. *Thirdly*, account for that propensity, which this illusion gives, to unite these broken appearances by a continued existence. *Fourthly*, and lastly, explain that force and vivacity of conception which arises from the propensity.

First, as to the principle of individuation, we may observe, that the view of any one object is not sufficient to convey the idea of identity. For in that proposition, *an object is the same with itself*, if the idea expressed by the word *object* were noways distinguished from that meant by *itself*; we really should mean nothing, nor would the proposition contain a predicate and a subject, which, however, are implied in this affirmation. One single object conveys the idea of unity, not that of identity.

On the other hand, a multiplicity of objects can never convey this idea, however resembling they may be supposed. The mind always pronounces the one not to be the other, and considers them as forming two, three, or any determinate number of objects, whose existences are entirely distinct and independent.

Since then both number and identity are incompatible with the relation of identity, it must lie in something that is neither of them. But to tell the truth, at first sight this seems utterly impossible. Betwixt unity and number there can be no medium; no more than betwixt existence and non-existence. After one object is supposed to exist, we must either suppose another also to exist; in which case we have the idea of number: or we must suppose it not to exist; in which case the first object remains at unity.

To remove this difficulty, let us have recourse to the idea of time or duration. I have already observed,[1] that time, in a strict sense, implies succession, and that, when we apply its idea to any unchangeable object, it is only by a fiction of the imagination by which the unchangeable object is supposed to participate of the changes of the coexisting objects, and in particular of that of our perceptions. This fiction of the imagination almost universally takes place; and it is by means of it that a single object, placed before us, and surveyed for any time without our discovering in it any interruption or variation, is able to give us a notion of identity. For when we consider any two points of this time, we may place them in different lights: we may either survey them at the very same instant; in which case they give us the idea of number, both by themselves and by the object; which must be multiplied in order to be conceived at once, as existent in these two different points of time: or, on the other hand, we may trace the succession of

[1] Part II. Sect. 5.

time by a like succession of ideas, and conceiving first one moment,
along with the object then existent, imagine afterwards a change
in the time without any *variation* or *interruption* in the object; in
which case it gives us the idea of unity. Here then is an idea,
which is a medium betwixt unity and number; or, more properly
speaking, is either of them, according to the view in which we take
it: and this idea we call that of identity. We cannot, in any
propriety of speech, say that an object is the same with itself,
unless we mean that the object existent at one time is the same with
itself existent at another. By this means we make a difference
betwixt the idea meant by the word *object*, and that meant by
itself, without going the length of number, and at the same time
without restraining ourselves to a strict and absolute unity.

Thus the principle of individuation is nothing but the *invariableness* and *uninterruptedness* of any object, through a supposed
variation of time, by which the mind can trace it in the different
periods of its existence, without any break of the view, and without
being obliged to form the idea of multiplicity or number.

I now proceed to explain the *second* part of my system, and
show why the constancy of our perceptions makes us ascribe to
them a perfect numerical identity, though there be very long intervals betwixt their appearance, and they have only one of the
essential qualities of identity, viz., *invariableness*. That I may
avoid all ambiguity and confusion on this head, I shall observe,
that I here account for the opinions and belief of the vulgar with
regard to the existence of body; and therefore must entirely conform
myself to their manner of thinking and of expressing themselves.
Now, we have already observed, that however philosophers may
distinguish betwixt the objects and perceptions of the senses; which
they suppose coexistent and resembling; yet this is a distinction
which is not comprehended by the generality of mankind, who,
as they perceive only one being, can never assent to the opinion
of a double existence and representation. Those very sensations
which enter by the eye or ear are with them the true objects, nor
can they readily conceive that this pen or paper, which is immediately perceived, represents another which is different from, but
resembling it. In order, therefore, to accommodate myself to their
notions, I shall at first suppose that there is only a single existence,
which I shall call indifferently *object* or *perception*, according as
it shall seem best to suit my purpose, understanding by both of
them what any common man means by a hat, or shoe, or stone,
or any other impression conveyed to him by his senses. I shall

be sure to give warning when I return to a more philosophical way of speaking and thinking.

To enter therefore upon the question concerning the source of the error and deception with regard to identity, when we attribute it to our resembling perceptions, notwithstanding their interruption, I must here recall an observation which I have already proved and explained.[1] Nothing is more apt to make us mistake one idea for another, than any relation betwixt them, which associates them together in the imagination, and makes it pass with facility from one to the other. Of all relations, that of resemblance is in this respect the most efficacious; and that because it not only causes an association of ideas, but also of dispositions, and makes us conceive the one idea by an act or operation of the mind, similar to that by which we conceive the other. This circumstance I have observed to be of great moment; and we may establish it for a general rule, that whatever ideas place the mind in the same disposition or in similar ones, are very apt to be confounded. The mind readily passes from one to the other, and perceives not the change without a strict attention, of which, generally speaking, it is wholly incapable.

In order to apply this general maxim, we must first examine the disposition of the mind in viewing any object which preserves a perfect identity, and then find some other object that is confounded with it, by causing a similar disposition. When we fix our thought on any object, and suppose it to continue the same for some time, it is evident we suppose the change to lie only in the time, and never exert ourselves to produce any new image or idea of the object. The faculties of the mind repose themselves in a manner, and take no more exercise than what is necessary to continue that idea of which we were formerly possessed, and which subsists without variation or interruption. The passage from one moment to another is scarce felt, and distinguishes not itself by a different perception or idea, which may require a different direction of the spirits, in order to its conception.

Now, what other objects, besides identical ones, are capable of placing the mind in the same disposition, when it considers them, and of causing the same uninterrupted passage of the imagination from one idea to another? This question is of the last importance. For if we can find any such objects, we may certainly conclude, from the foregoing principle, that they are very naturally confounded with identical ones, and are taken for them in most of

[1] Part II. Sect. 5.

our reasonings. But though this question be very important, it is not very difficult nor doubtful. For I immediately reply, that a succession of related objects places the mind in this disposition, and is considered with the same smooth and uninterrupted progress of the imagination, as attends the view of the same invariable object. The very nature and essence of relation is to connect our ideas with each other, and upon the appearance of one, to facilitate the transition to its correlative. The passage betwixt related ideas is therefore so smooth and easy, that it produces little alteration on the mind, and seems like the continuation of the same action; and as the continuation of the same action is an effect of the continued view of the same object, it is for this reason we attribute sameness to every succession of related objects. The thought slides along the succession with equal facility, as if it considered only one object; and therefore confounds the succession with the identity.

We shall afterwards see many instances of this tendency of relation to make us ascribe an *identity* to *different* objects; but shall here confine ourselves to the present subject. We find by experience that there is such a *constancy* in almost all the impressions of the senses, that their interruption produces no alteration on them, and hinders them not from returning the same in appearance and in situation as at their first existence. I survey the furniture of my chamber; I shut my eyes, and afterwards open them; and find the new perceptions to resemble perfectly those which formerly struck my senses. This resemblance is observed in a thousand instances, and naturally connects together our ideas of these interrupted perceptions by the strongest relation, and conveys the mind with an easy transition from one to another. An easy transition or passage of the imagination, along the ideas of these different and interrupted perceptions, is almost the same disposition of mind with that in which we consider one constant and uninterrupted perception. It is therefore very natural for us to mistake the one for the other.[1]

---

[1] This reasoning, it must be confessed, is somewhat abstruse and difficult to be comprehended; but it is remarkable, that this very difficulty may be converted into a proof of the reasoning. We may observe that there are two relations, and both of them resemblances, which contribute to our mistaking the succession of our interrupted perceptions for an identical object. The first is, the resemblance of the perceptions: the second is, the resemblance which the act of the mind, in surveying a succession of resembling objects, bears to that in surveying an identical object. Now these resemblances we are apt to confound with each other; and it is natural we should, according to this very reasoning. But let us keep them distinct, and we shall find no difficulty in conceiving the precedent argument.

The persons who entertain this opinion concerning the identity of our resembling perceptions, are in general all the unthinking and unphilosophical part of mankind (that is, all of us at one time or another), and, consequently, such as suppose their perceptions to be their only objects, and never think of a double existence internal and external, representing and represented. The very image which is present to the senses is with us the real body; and it is to these interrupted images we ascribe a perfect identity. But as the interruption of the appearance seems contrary to the identity, and naturally leads us to regard these resembling perceptions as different from each other, we here find ourselves at a loss how to reconcile such opposite opinions. The smooth passage of the imagination along the ideas of the resembling perceptions makes us ascribe to them a perfect identity. The interrupted manner of their appearance makes us consider them as so many resembling, but still distinct beings, which appear after certain intervals. The perplexity arising from this contradiction produces a propension to unite these broken appearances by the fiction of a continued existence, which is the *third* part of that hypothesis I proposed to explain.

Nothing is more certain from experience than that any contradiction either to the sentiments or passions, gives a sensible uneasiness, whether it proceeds from without or from within; from the opposition of external objects, or from the combat of internal principles. On the contrary, whatever strikes in with the natural propensities, and either externally forwards their satisfaction, or internally concurs with their movements, is sure to give a sensible pleasure. Now, there being here an opposition betwixt the notion of the identity of resembling perceptions, and the interruption of their appearance, the mind must be uneasy in that situation, and will naturally seek relief from the uneasiness. Since the uneasiness arises from the opposition of two contrary principles, it must look for relief by sacrificing the one to the other. But as the smooth passage of our thought along our resembling perceptions makes us ascribe to them an identity, we can never, without reluctance, yield up that opinion. We must therefore turn to the other side, and suppose that our perceptions are no longer interrupted, but preserve a continued as well as an invariable existence, and are by that means entirely the same. But here the interruptions in the appearance of these perceptions are so long and frequent, that it is impossible to overlook them: and as the *appearance* of a perception in the mind and its *existence* seem at first sight entirely the same, it may be doubted whether we can ever assent to so palpable a contradiction, and suppose a perception to exist without being present to the mind. In order to clear up this matter, and learn how the interruption in the appearance of a perception implies not necessarily an interruption in its existence, it will be proper to touch upon some principles which we shall have occasion to explain more fully afterwards.[1]

We may begin with observing, that the difficulty in the present case is not concerning the matter of fact, or whether the mind forms such a conclusion concerning the continued existence of its perceptions, but only concerning the manner in which the conclusion is formed, and principles from which it is derived. It is certain that almost all mankind, and even philosophers themselves, for the greatest part of their lives, take their perceptions to be their only objects, and suppose that the very being which is intimately present to the mind, is the real body or material existence. It is also certain that this very perception or object is supposed to have a continued uninterrupted being, and neither to be annihilated by our absence, nor to be brought into existence by our presence. When we are absent from it, we say it still exists, but that we do not feel, we do not see it. When we are present, we say we feel or see it. Here then may arise two questions; *first*, how we can satisfy ourselves in supposing a perception to be absent from the mind without being annihilated. *Secondly*, after what manner we conceive an object to become present to the mind, without some new creation of a perception or image; and what we mean by this *seeing*, and *feeling*, and *perceiving*.

As to the first question, we may observe, that what we call a *mind*, is nothing but a heap or collection of different perceptions, united together by certain relations, and supposed, though falsely, to be endowed with a perfect simplicity and identity. Now, as every perception is distinguishable from another, and may be considered as separately existent; it evidently follows, that there is no absurdity in separating any particular perception from the mind; that is, in breaking off all its relations with that connected mass of perceptions which constitute a thinking being.

The same reasoning affords us an answer to the second question. If the name of *perception* renders not this separation from a mind absurd and contradictory, the name of *object*, standing for the same thing, can never render their conjunction impossible. External objects are seen and felt, and become present to the mind; that is,

[1] Sect. 6.

they acquire such a relation to a connected heap of perceptions as
to influence them very considerably in augmenting their number
by present reflections and passions, and in storing the memory
with ideas. The same continued and uninterrupted being may,
therefore, be sometimes present to the mind and sometimes absent
from it without any real or essential change in the being itself.
An interrupted appearance to the senses implies not necessarily an
interruption in the existence. The supposition of the continued
existence of sensible objects or perceptions involves no contradiction. We may easily indulge our inclination to that supposition.
When the exact resemblance of our perceptions makes us ascribe
to them an identity, we may remove the seeeming interruption by
feigning a continued being, which may fill those intervals, and
preserve a perfect and entire identity to our perceptions.

But as we here not only *feign* but *believe* this continued existence,
the question is, *from whence arises such a belief?* and this question
leads us to the *fourth* member of this system. It has been proved
already, that belief, in general, consists in nothing but the vivacity
of an idea; and that an idea may acquire this vivacity by its relation
to some present impression. Impressions are naturally the most
vivid perceptions of the mind; and this quality is in part conveyed
by the relation to every connected idea. The relation causes a
smooth passage from the impression to the idea, and even gives a
propensity to that passage. The mind falls so easily from the one
perception to the other, that it scarce perceives the change, but
retains in the second a considerable share of the vivacity of the
first. It is excited by the lively impression, and this vivacity is
conveyed to the related idea, without any great diminution in the
passage, by reason of the smooth transition and the propensity of
the imagination.

But suppose that this propensity arises from some other principle,
besides that of relation; it is evident it must still have the same
effect, and convey the vivacity from the impression to the idea.
Now, this is exactly the present case. Our memory presents us
with a vast number of instances of perceptions perfectly resembling
each other, that return at different distances of time, after considerable interruptions. This resemblance gives us a propension to
consider these interrupted perceptions as the same; and also a
propension to connect them by a continued existence, in order to
justify this identity, and avoid the contradiction in which the interrupted appearance of these perceptions seems necessarily to involve
us. Here then we have a propensity to feign the continued existence

oi all sensible objects; and as this propensity arises from some lively impressions of the memory, it bestows a vivacity on that fiction; or, in other words, makes us believe the continued existence of body. If sometimes we ascribe a continued existence to objects, which are perfectly new to us, and of whose constancy and coherence we have no experience, it is because the manner, in which they present themselves to our senses, resembles that of constant and coherent objects; and this resemblance is a source of reasoning and analogy, and leads us to attribute the same qualities to the similar objects.

I believe an intelligent reader will find less difficulty to assent to this system, than to comprehend it fully and distinctly, and will allow, after a little reflection, that every part carries its own proof along with it. It is indeed evident, that as the vulgar *suppose*, their perceptions to be their only objects, and at the same time *believe* the continued existence of matter, we must account for the origin of the belief upon that supposition. Now, upon that supposition, it is a false opinion that any of our objects, or perceptions, are identically the same after an interruption; and consequently the opinion of their identity can never arise from reason, but must arise from the imagination. The imagination is seduced into such an opinion only by means of the resemblance of certain perceptions; since we find they are only our resembling perceptions, which we have a propension to suppose the same. This propension to bestow an identity on our resembling perceptions, produces the fiction of a continued existence; since that fiction, as well as the identity, is really false, as is acknowledged by all philosophers, and has no other effect than to remedy the interruption of our perceptions, which is the only circumstance that is contrary to their identity. In the last place, this propension causes belief by means of the present impressions of the memory; since, without the remembrance of former sensations, it is plain we never should have any belief of the continued existence of body. Thus, in examining all these parts, we find that each of them is supported by the strongest proofs; and that all of them together form a consistent system, which is perfectly convincing. A strong propensity or inclination alone, without any present impression, will sometimes cause a belief or opinion. How much more when aided by that circumstance!

But though we are led after this manner, by the natural propensity of the imagination, to ascribe a continued existence to those sensible objects or perceptions, which we find to resemble each other in their interrupted appearance; yet a very little reflection and philosophy is sufficient to make us perceive the fallacy of that opinion. I have already observed that there is an intimate connection betwixt those two principles, of a *continued* and of a *distinct* or *independent* existence, and that we no sooner establish the one than the other follows as a necessary consequence. It is the opinion of a continued existence, which first takes place, and without much study or reflection draws the other along with it, wherever the mind follows its first and most natural tendency. But when we compare experiments, and reason a little upon them, we quickly perceive that the doctrine of the independent existence of our sensible perceptions is contrary to the plainest experience. This leads us backward upon our footsteps to perceive our error in attributing a continued existence to our perceptions, and is the origin of many very curious opinions, which we shall here endeavour to account for.

It will first be proper to observe a few of those experiments, which convince us that our perceptions are not possessed of any independent existence. When we press one eye with a finger, we immediately perceive all the objects to become double, and one half of them to be removed from their common and natural position. But as we do not attribute a continued existence to both these perceptions, and as they are both of the same nature, we clearly perceive that all our perceptions are dependent on our organs and the disposition of our nerves and animal spirits. This opinion is confirmed by the seeming increase and diminution of objects according to their distance; by the apparent alterations in their figure; by the changes in their colour and other qualities, from our sickness and distempers, and by an infinite number of other experiments of the same kind; from all which we learn that our sensible perceptions are not possessed of any distinct or independent existence.

The natural consequence of this reasoning should be, that our perceptions have no more a continued than an independent existence; and, indeed, philosophers have so far run into this opinion, that they change their system, and distinguish (as we shall do for the future) betwixt perceptions and objects, of which the former are supposed to be interrupted and perishing, and different at every different return; the latter to be uninterrupted, and to preserve a continued existence and identity. But however philosophical this new system may be esteemed, I assert that it is only a palliative remedy, and that it contains all the difficulties of the vulgar system, with some others that are peculiar to itself. There are no principles either of the understanding or fancy, which lead us directly to embrace this opinion of the double existence of perceptions and objects, nor can we arrive at it but by passing through the common hypothesis of the identity and continuance of our interrupted perceptions. Were we not first persuaded that our perceptions are our only objects, and continue to exist even when they no longer make their appearance to the senses, we should never be led to think that our perceptions and objects are different, and that our objects alone preserve a continued existence. " The latter hypothesis has no primary recommendation either to reason or the imagination, but acquires all its influence on the imagination from the former." This proposition contains two parts which we shall endeavour to prove as distinctly and clearly as such abstruse subjects will permit.

As to the first part of the proposition, *that this philosophical hypothesis has no primary recommendation, either to reason or the imagination,* we may soon satisfy ourselves with regard to *reason,* by the following reflections. The only existences, of which we are certain, are perceptions, which, being immediately present to us by consciousness, command our strongest assent, and are the first foundation of all our conclusions. The only conclusion we can draw from the existence of one thing to that of another, is by means of the relation of cause and effect, which shows that there is a connection betwixt them, and that the existence of one is dependent on that of the other. The idea of this relation is derived from past experience, by which we find that two beings are constantly conjoined together, and are always present at once to the mind. But as no beings are ever present to the mind but perceptions, it follows that we may observe a conjunction or a relation of cause and effect between different perceptions, but can never observe it between perceptions and objects. It is impossible, therefore, that from the existence or any of the qualities of the former, we can ever form any conclusion concerning the existence of the latter, or ever satisfy our reason in this particular.

It is no less certain that this philosophical system has no primary recommendation to the *imagination,* and that that faculty would never, of itself, and by its original tendency, have fallen upon such a principle. I confess it will be somewhat difficult to prove this to the full satisfaction of the reader; because it implies a negative, which in many cases will not admit of any positive proof. If any one would take the pains to examine this question, and would invent a system to account for the direct origin of this opinion from the imagination, we should be able, by the examination of that system, to pronounce a certain judgment in the present subject. Let it be taken for granted, that our perceptions are broken and interrupted, and, however like, are still different from each other; and let any one, upon this supposition, show why the fancy, directly and immediately, proceeds to the belief of another existence, resembling these perceptions in their nature, but yet continued, and uninterrupted, and identical; and after he has done this to my satisfaction, I promise to renounce my present opinion. Meanwhile I cannot forbear concluding, from the very abstractedness and difficulty of the first supposition, that it is an improper subject for the fancy to work upon. Whoever would explain the origin of the *common* opinion concerning the continued and distinct existence of body, must take the mind in its *common* situation, and must proceed upon the supposition, that our perceptions are our only objects, and continue to exist even when they are not perceived. Though this opinion be false, it is the most natural of any, and has alone any primary recommendation to the fancy.

As to the second part of the proposition, *that the philosophical system acquires all its influence on the imagination from the vulgar one;* we may observe that this is a natural and unavoidable consequence of the foregoing conclusion, *that it has no primary recommendation to reason or the imagination.* For as the philosophical system is found by experience to take hold of many minds, and, in particular, of all those who reflect ever so little on this subject, it must derive all its authority from the vulgar system, since it has no original authority of its own. The manner in which these two systems, though directly contrary, are connected together, may be explained as follows.

The imagination naturally runs on in this train of thinking. Our perceptions are our only objects: resembling perceptions are the same, however broken or uninterrupted in their appearance: this appearing interruption is contrary to the identity: the interruption consequently extends not beyond the appearance, and the perception or object really continues to exist, even when absent from us: our sensible perceptions have, therefore, a continued and uninterrupted existence. But as a little reflection destroys this conclusion, that our perceptions have a continued existence, by showing that they have a dependent one, it would naturally be expected that we must altogether reject the opinion, that there is such a thing in nature as a continued existence, which is preserved even when it no longer appears to the senses. The case, however,

is otherwise. Philosophers are so far from rejecting the opinion
of a continued existence upon rejecting that of the independence
and continuance of our sensible perceptions, that though all sects
agree in the latter sentiment, the former, which is in a manner its
necessary consequence, has been peculiar to a few extravagant
sceptics; who, after all, maintained that opinion in words only
and were never able to bring themselves sincerely to believe it.

There is a great difference betwixt such opinions as we form
after a calm and profound reflection, and such as we embrace by
a kind of instinct or natural impulse, on account of their suitable-
ness and conformity to the mind. If these opinions become contrary,
it is not difficult to foresee which of them will have the advantage.
As long as our attention is bent upon the subject, the philosophical
and studied principle may prevail; but the moment we relax our
thoughts, nature will display herself, and draw us back to our
former opinion. Nay she has sometimes such an influence, that
she can stop our progress, even in the midst of our most profound
reflections, and keep us from running on with all the consequences
of any philosophical opinion. Thus, though we clearly perceive
the dependence and interruption of our perceptions, we stop short
in our career, and never upon that account reject the notion of an
independent and continued existence. That opinion has taken
such deep root in the imagination, that it is impossible ever to
eradicate it, nor will any strained metaphysical conviction of the
dependence of our perceptions be sufficient for that purpose.

But though our natural and obvious principles here prevail above
our studied reflections, it is certain there must be some struggle and
opposition in this case; at least so long as these reflections retain
any force or vivacity. In order to set ourselves at ease in this
particular, we contrive a new hypothesis, which seems to comprehend both these principles of reason and imagination. This
hypothesis is the philosophical one of the double existence of
perceptions and objects; which pleases our reason, in allowing that
our dependent perceptions are interrupted and different, and at the
same time is agreeable to the imagination, in attributing a continued existence to something else, which we call *objects*. This
philosophical system, therefore, is the monstrous offspring of two
principles, which are contrary to each other, which are both at
once embraced by the mind, and which are unable mutually to
destroy each other. The imagination tells us that our resembling
perceptions have a continued and uninterrupted existence, and are
not annihilated by their absence. Reflection tells us, that even our

resembling perceptions are interrupted in their existence, and different from each other. The contradiction betwixt these opinions we elude by a new fiction, which is conformable to the hypothesis both of reflection and fancy, by ascribing these contrary qualities to different existences; the *interruption* to perceptions, and the *continuance* to objects. Nature is obstinate, and will not quit the field, however strongly attacked by reason; and at the same time reason is so clear in the point that there is no possibility of disguising her. Not being able to reconcile these two enemies, we endeavour to set ourselves at ease as much as possible, by successively granting to each whatever it demands, and by feigning a double existence, where each may find something that has all the conditions it desires. Were we fully convinced that our resembling perceptions are continued, and identical, and independent, we should never run into this opinion of a double existence; since we should find satisfaction in our first supposition, and would not look beyond. Again, were we fully convinced that our perceptions are dependent, and interrupted, and different, we should be as little inclined to embrace the opinion of a double existence; since in that case we should clearly perceive the error of our first supposition of a continued existence, and would never regard it any further. It is therefore from the intermediate situation of the mind that this opinion rises, and from such an adherence to these two contrary principles, as makes us seek some pretext to justify our receiving both; which happily at last is found in the system of a double existence.

Another advantage of this philosophical system is its similarity to the vulgar one, by which means we can humour our reason for a moment, when it becomes troublesome and solicitous; and yet upon its least negligence or inattention, can easily return to our vulgar and natural notions. Accordingly we find that philosophers neglect not this advantage, but, immediately upon leaving their closets, mingle with the rest of mankind in those exploded opinions, that our perceptions are our only objects, and continue identically and uninterruptedly the same in all their interrupted appearances.

There are other particulars of this system, where we may remark its dependence on the fancy, in a very conspicuous manner. Of these, I shall observe the two following. *First*, we suppose external objects to resemble internal perceptions. I have already shown that the relation of cause and effect can never afford us any just conclusion from the existence or qualities of our perceptions to the existence of external continued objects: and I shall further add, that even though they could afford such a conclusion, we should never have any reason to infer that our objects resemble our perceptions. That opinion, therefore is derived from nothing but the quality of the fancy above explained, *that it borrows all its ideas from some precedent perception.* We never can conceive anything but perceptions, and therefore must make everything resemble them.

Secondly, as we suppose our objects in general to resemble our perceptions, so we take it for granted that every particular object resembles that perception which it causes. The relation of cause and effect determines us to join the other of resemblance; and the ideas of these existences being already united together in the fancy by the former relation, we naturally add the latter to complete the union. We have a strong propensity to complete every union by joining new relations to those which we have before observed betwixt any ideas, as we shall have occasion to observe presently.[1]

Having thus given an account of all the systems, both popular and philosophical, with regard to external existences, I cannot forbear giving vent to a certain sentiment which arises upon reviewing those systems. I begun this subject with premising that we ought to have an implicit faith in our senses, and that this would be the conclusion I should draw from the whole of my reasoning. But to be ingenuous, I feel myself *at present* of a quite contrary sentiment, and am more inclined to repose no faith at all in my senses, or rather imagination, than to place in it such an implicit confidence. I cannot conceive how such trivial qualities of the fancy, conducted by such false suppositions, can ever lead to any solid and rational system. They are the coherence and constancy of our perceptions, which produce the opinion of their continued existence; though these qualities of perceptions have no perceivable connection with such an existence. The constancy of our perceptions has the most considerable effect, and yet is attended with the greatest difficulties. It is a gross illusion to suppose that our resembling perceptions are numerically the same; and it is this illusion which leads us into the opinion that these perceptions are uninterrupted, and are still existent, even when they are not present to the senses. This is the case with our popular system. And as to our philosophical one, it is liable to the same difficulties; and is, over and above, loaded with this absurdity, that it at once denies and establishes the vulgar supposition. Philosophers deny our resembling perceptions to be identically the

[1] Sect. 5.

same, and uninterrupted; and yet have so great a propensity to
believe them such, that they arbitrarily invent a new set of perceptions, to which they attribute these qualities. I say, a new set of
perceptions: for we may well suppose in general, but it is impossible
for us distinctly to conceive, objects to be in their nature anything
but exactly the same with perceptions. What then can we look
for from this confusion of groundless and extraordinary opinions
but error and falsehood? And how can we justify to ourselves any
belief we repose in them?

This sceptical doubt, both with respect to reason and the senses,
is a malady which can never be radically cured, but must return
upon us every moment, however we may chase it away, and
sometimes may seem entirely free from it. It is impossible, upon
any system, to defend either our understanding or senses; and we
but expose them further when we endeavour to justify them in
that manner. As the sceptical doubt arises naturally from a
profound and intense reflection on those subjects, it always
increases the further we carry our reflections, whether in opposition
or conformity to it. Carelessness and inattention alone can afford
us any remedy. For this reason I rely entirely upon them; and
take it for granted, whatever may be the reader's opinion at this
present moment, that an hour hence he will be persuaded there is
both an external and internal world; and, going upon that
supposition, I intend to examine some general systems, both ancient
and modern, which have been proposed of both, before I proceed
to a more particular inquiry concerning our impressions. This will
not, perhaps, in the end, be found foreign to our present purpose.

SECTION III

OF THE ANCIENT PHILOSOPHY

SEVERAL moralists have recommended it as an excellent method
of becoming acquainted with our own hearts, and knowing our
progress in virtue, to recollect our dreams in a morning, and
examine them with the same rigour that we would our most serious
and most deliberate actions. Our character is the same throughout,
say they, and appears best where artifice, fear, and policy, have
no place, and men can neither be hypocrites with themselves nor
others. The generosity or baseness of our temper, our meekness

or cruelty, our courage or pusillanimity, influence the fictions of the imagination with the most unbounded liberty, and discover themselves in the most glaring colours. In like manner, I am persuaded, there might be several useful discoveries made from a criticism of the fictions of the ancient philosophy concerning *substances, and substantial forms, and accidents, and occult qualities,* which, however unreasonable and capricious, have a very intimate connection with the principles of human nature.

It is confessed by the most judicious philosophers, that our ideas of bodies are nothing but collections formed by the mind of the ideas of the several distinct sensible qualities, of which objects are composed, and which we find to have a constant union with each other. But however these qualities may in themselves be entirely distinct, it is certain we commonly regard the compound, which they form, as *one* thing, and as continuing the *same* under very considerable alterations. The acknowledged composition is evidently contrary to this supposed simplicity, and the variation to the *identity*. It may therefore be worth while to consider the *causes*, which make us almost universally fall into such evident contradictions, as well as the means by which we endeavour to conceal them.

It is evident that as the ideas of the several distinct *successive* qualities of objects are united together by a very close relation, the mind, in looking along the succession, must be carried from one part of it to another by an easy transition, and will no more perceive the change than if it contemplated the same unchangeable object. This easy transition is the effect, or rather essence of relation; and as the imagination readily takes one idea for another, where their influence on the mind is similar; hence it proceeds, that any such succession of related qualities is readily considered as one continued object, existing without any variation. The smooth and uninterrupted progress of the thought, being alike in both cases, readily deceives the mind, and makes us ascribe an identity to the changeable succession of connected qualities.

But when we alter our method of considering the succession, and, instead of tracing it gradually through the successive points of time, survey at once any two distinct periods of its duration, and compare the different conditions of the successive qualities; in that case the variations, which were insensible when they arose gradually, do now appear of consequence, and seem entirely to destroy the identity. By this means there arises a kind of contrariety in our method of thinking, from the different points of view, in which we survey the object, and from the nearness or remoteness of those instants of time, which we compare together. When we gradually follow an object in its successive changes, the smooth progress of the thought makes us ascribe an identity to the succcession; because it is by a similar act of the mind we consider an unchangeable object. When we compare its situation after a considerable change the progress of the thought is broke; and consequently we are presented with the idea of diversity; in order to reconcile which contradictions the imagination is apt to feign something unknown and invisible, which it supposes to continue the same under all these variations; and this unintelligible something it calls a *substance, or original and first matter*.

We entertain a like notion with regard to the *simplicity* of substances, and from like causes. Suppose an object perfectly simple and indivisible to be presented, along with another object, whose *coexistent* parts are connected together by a strong relation, it is evident the actions of the mind, in considering these two objects, are not very different. The imagination conceives the simple object at once, with facility, by a single effort of thought, without change or variation. The connection of parts in the compound object has almost the same effect, and so unites the object within itself, that the fancy feels not the transition in passing from one part to another. Hence the colour, taste, figure, solidity, and other qualities, combined in a peach or melon, are conceived to form *one thing*; and that on account of their close relation, which makes them affect the thought in the same manner, as if perfectly uncompounded. But the mind rests not here. Whenever it views the object in another light, it finds that all these qualities are different and distinguishable, and separable from each other; which view of things being destructive of its primary and more natural notions, obliges the imagination to feign an unknown something, or *original* substance and matter, as a principle of union or cohesion among these qualities, and as what may give the compound object a title to be called one thing, notwithstanding its diversity and composition.

The Peripatetic philosophy asserts the *original* matter to be perfectly homogeneous in all bodies, and considers fire, water, earth, and air, as of the very same substance, on account of their gradual revolutions and changes into each other. At the same time it assigns to each of these species of objects a distinct *substantial form*, which it supposes to be the source of all those different qualities they possess, and to be a new foundation of simplicity and identity to each particular species. All depends on our manner of viewing the objects. When we look along the insensible changes of bodies, we suppose all of them to be of the same substance or essence. When we consider their sensible differences, we attribute to each of them a substantial and essential difference. And in order to indulge ourselves in both these ways of considering our objects, we suppose all bodies to have at once a substance and a substantial form.

The notion of *accidents* is an unavoidable consequence of this method of thinking with regard to substances and substantial forms; nor can we forbear looking upon colours, sounds, tastes, figures, and other properties of bodies, as existences which cannot subsist apart, but require a subject of inhesion to sustain and support them. For having never discovered any of these sensible qualities, where, for the reasons above mentioned, we did not likewise fancy a substance to exist; the same habit, which makes us infer a connection betwixt cause and effect, makes us here infer a dependence of every quality on the unknown substance. The custom of imagining a dependence has the same effect as the custom of observing it would have. This conceit, however, is no more reasonable than any of the foregoing. Every quality being a distinct thing from another, may be conceived to exist apart, and may exist apart not only from every other quality, but from that unintelligible chimera of a substance.

But these philosophers carry their fictions still further in their sentiments concerning *occult qualities,* and both suppose a substance supporting, which they do not understand, and an accident supported, of which they have as imperfect an idea. The whole system, therefore, is entirely incomprehensible, and yet is derived from principles as natural as any of these above explained.

In considering this subject, we may observe a gradation of three opinions that rise above each other, according as the persons who form them acquire new degrees of reason and knowledge. These opinions are that of the vulgar, that of a false philosophy, and that of the true; where we shall find upon inquiry, that the true philosophy approaches nearer to the sentiments of the vulgar than to those of a mistaken knowledge. It is natural for men, in their common and careless way of thinking, to imagine they perceive a connection betwixt such objects as they have constantly found united together; and because custom has rendered it difficult to separate the ideas, they are apt to fancy such a separation to be in itself impossible and absurd. But philosophers, who abstract from the effects of custom, and compare the ideas of objects, immediately perceive the falsehood of these vulgar sentiments, and discover that there is no known connection among objects. Every different object appears to them entirely distinct and separate; and they perceive that it is not from a view of the nature and qualities of objects we infer one from another, but only when in several instances we observe them to have been constantly conjoined. But these philosophers, instead of drawing a just inference from this observation, and concluding that we have no idea of power or agency, separate from the mind and belonging to causes; I say, instead of drawing this conclusion, they frequently search for the qualities in which this agency consists, and are displeased with every system which their reason suggests to them in order to explain it. They have sufficient force of genius to free them from the vulgar error, that there is a natural and perceivable connection betwixt the several qualities and actions of matter, but not sufficient to keep them from ever seeking for this connection in matter or causes. Had they fallen upon the just conclusion, they would have returned back to the situation of the vulgar, and would have regarded all these disquisitions with indolence and indifference. At present they seem to be in a very lamentable condition, and such as the poets have given us but a faint notion of in their descriptions of the punishment of Sisyphus and Tantalus. For what can be imagined more tormenting than to seek with eagerness what for ever flies us, and seek for it in a place where it is impossible it can ever exist?

But as Nature seems to have observed a kind of justice and comprehension in everything, she has not neglected philosophers more than the rest of the creation, but has reserved them a consolation amid all their disappointments and afflictions. This consolation principally consists in their invention of the words *faculty* and *occult quality*. For it being usual, after the frequent use of terms, which are really significant and intelligible, to omit the idea which we would express by them, and preserve only the custom by which we recall the idea at pleasure; so it naturally happens, that after the frequent use of terms which are wholly insignificant and unintelligible, we fancy them to be on the same footing with the precedent, and to have a secret meaning which we might discover by reflection. The resemblance of their appearance deceives the mind, as is usual, and makes us imagine a thorough resemblance and conformity. By this means these philosophers set themselves at ease, and arrive at last, by an illusion, at the same indifference which the people attain by their stupidity, and true philosophers by their moderate scepticism. They need only say, that any phenomenon which puzzles them arises from a faculty or an occult quality, and there is an end of all dispute and inquiry upon the matter.

But among all the instances wherein the Peripatetics have shown they were guided by every trivial propensity of the imagination, no one is more remarkable than their *sympathies, antipathies, and horrors of a vacuum.* There is a very remarkable inclination in human nature to bestow on external objects the same emotions which it observes in itself, and to find everywhere those ideas which are most present to it. This inclination, it is true, is suppressed by a little reflection, and only takes place in children, poets, and the ancient philosophers. It appears in children, by their desire of beating the stones which hurt them; in poets by their readiness to personify everything; and in the ancient philosophers, by these fictions of sympathy and antipathy. We must pardon children, because of their age; poets, because they profess to follow implicitly the suggestions of their fancy; but what excuse shall we find to justify our philosophers in so signal a weakness?

SECTION IV

OF THE MODERN PHILOSOPHY

BUT here it may be objected, that the imagination, according to my own confession, being the ultimate judge of all systems of philosophy, I am unjust in blaming the ancient philosophers for making use of that faculty, and allowing themselves to be entirely guided by it in their reasonings. In order to justify myself, I must distinguish in the imagination betwixt the principles which are permanent, irresistible, and universal; such as the customary transition from causes to effects, and from effects to causes: and the principles, which are changeable, weak, and irregular; such as those I have just now taken notice of. The former are the foundation of all our thoughts and actions, so that upon their removal, human nature must immediately perish and go to ruin. The latter are neither unavoidable to mankind, nor necessary, or so much as useful in the conduct of life; but, on the contrary, are observed only to take place in weak minds, and being opposite to the other principles of custom and reasoning, may easily be subverted by a due contrast and opposition. For this reason, the former are received by philosophy, and the latter rejected. One who concludes somebody to be near him, when he hears an articulate voice in the dark, reasons justly and naturally; though that conclusion be derived from nothing but custom, which infixes and enlivens the idea of a human creature, on account of his usual conjunction with the present impression. But one who is tormented he knows not why, with the apprehension of spectres in the dark, may perhaps be said to reason, and to reason naturally too: but then it must be in the same sense that a malady is said to be natural; as arising from natural causes, though it be contrary to health, the most agreeable and most natural situation of man.

The opinions of the ancient philosophers, their fictions of substance and accident, and their reasonings concerning substantial forms and occult qualities, are like the spectres in the dark, and are derived from principles, which, however common, are neither universal nor unavoidable in human nature. The *modern philosophy* pretends to be entirely free from this defect, and to arise only from the solid, permanent, and consistent principles of the imagination. Upon what grounds this pretension is founded must now be the subject of our inquiry.

The fundamental principle of that philosophy is the opinion concerning colours, sounds, tastes, smells, heat, and cold; which it asserts to be nothing but impressions in the mind, derived from the operation of external objects, and without any resemblance to the qualities of the objects. Upon examination, I find only one of the reasons commonly produced for this opinion to be satisfactory, viz., that derived from the variations of those impressions, even while the external object, to all appearance, continues the same. These variations depend upon several circumstances. Upon the different situations of our health: a man in a malady feels a disagreeable taste in meats, which before pleased him the most. Upon the different complexions and constitutions of men: that seems bitter to one, which is sweet to another. Upon the difference of their external situation and position: colours reflected from the clouds change according to the distance of the clouds, and according to the angle they make with the eye and luminous body. Fire also communicates the sensation of pleasure at one distance, and that of pain at another. Instances of this kind are very numerous and frequent.

The conclusion drawn from them is likewise as satisfactory as can possibly be imagined. It is certain that when different impressions of the same sense arise from any object, every one of these impressions has not a resembling quality existent in the object. For as the same object cannot, at the same time, be endowed with different qualities of the same sense, and as the same quality cannot resemble impressions entirely different; it evidently follows, that many of our impressions have no external model or archetype. Now, from like effects we presume like causes. Many of the impressions of colour, sound, etc., are confessed to be nothing but internal existences, and to arise from causes which noways resemble them. These impressions are in appearance nothing different from the other impressions of colour, sound, etc. We conclude, therefore, that they are, all of them, derived from a like origin.

This principle being once admitted, all the other doctrines of that philosophy seem to follow by an easy consequence. For, upon the removal of sounds, colours, heat, cold, and other sensible qualities, from the rank of continued independent existences, we are reduced merely to what are called primary qualities, as the only real ones, of which we have any adequate notion. These primary qualities are extension and solidity, with their different mixtures and modifications; figure, motion, gravity, and cohesion. The generation, increase, decay, and corruption of animals and vegetables, are nothing but changes of figure and motion; as also the operations of all bodies on each other; of fire, of light, water, air, earth, and of all the elements and powers of nature. One figure and motion produces another figure and motion; nor does there remain in the material universe any other principle, either active or passive, of which we can form the most distant idea.

I believe many objections might be made to this system; but at present I shall confine myself to one, which is, in my opinion, very decisive. I assert, that instead of explaining the operations of external objects by its means, we utterly annihilate all these objects, and reduce ourselves to the opinions of the most extravagant scepticism concerning them. If colours, sounds, tastes, and smells be merely perceptions, nothing, we can conceive, is possessed of a real, continued, and independent existence; not even motion, extension, and solidity, which are the primary qualities chiefly insisted on.

To begin with the examination of motion; it is evident this is a quality altogether inconceivable alone, and without a reference to some other object. The idea of motion necessarily supposes that of a body moving. Now, what is our idea of the moving body, without which motion is incomprehensible ? It must resolve itself into the idea of extension or of solidity; and consequently the reality of motion depends upon that of these other qualities.

This opinion, which is universally acknowledged concerning motion, I have proved to be true with regard to extension; and have shown that it is impossible to conceive extension but as composed of parts, endowed with colour or solidity. The idea of extension is a compound idea; but as it is not compounded of an infinite number of parts or inferior ideas, it must at last resolve itself into such as are perfectly simple and indivisible. These simple and indivisible parts not being ideas of extension, must be nonentities, unless conceived as coloured or solid. Colour is excluded from any real existence. The reality therefore of our idea of extension depends upon the reality of that of solidity; nor can the former be just while the latter is chimerical. Let us then lend our attention to the examination of the idea of solidity.

The idea of solidity is that of two objects, which, being impelled by the utmost orce, cannot penetrate each other, but still maintain a separate and distinct existence. Solidity therefore is perfectly incomprehensible alone, and without the conception of some bodies which are solid, and maintain this separate and distinct existence. Now, what idea have we of these bodies? The ideas of colours, sounds, and other secondary qualities, are excluded. The idea of motion depends on that of extension, and the idea of extension on that of solidity. It is impossible, therefore, that the idea of solidity can depend on either of them. For that would be to run in a circle, and make one idea depend on another, while, at the same time, the latter depends on the former. Our modern philosophy, therefore, leaves us no just nor satisfactory idea of solidity, nor consequently of matter.

This argument will appear entirely conclusive to every one tnat comprehends it; but because it may seem abstruse and intricate to the generality of readers, I hope to be excused if I endeavour to render it more obvious by some variation of the expression. In order to form an idea of solidity, we must conceive two bodies pressing on each other without any penetration; and it is impossible to arrive at this idea when we confine ourselves to one object, much more without conceiving any. Two nonentities cannot exclude each other from their places, because they never possess any place, nor can be endowed with any quality. Now I ask, what idea do we form of these bodies or objects to which we suppose solidity to belong? To say that we conceive them merely as solid, is to run on *in infinitum*. To affirm that we paint them out to ourselves as extended, either resolves all into a false idea, or returns in a circle. Extension must necessarily be considered either as coloured, which is a false idea, or as solid, which brings us back to the first question. We may make the same observation concerning mobility and figure; and, upon the whole, must conclude that after the exclusion of colours, sounds, heat, and cold, from the rank of external existences, there remains nothing which can afford us a just and consistent idea of body.

Add to this, that, properly speaking, solidity or impenetrability is nothing but an impossibility of annihilation, as has been already observed:[1] for which reason it is the more necessary for us to form some distinct idea of that object whose annihilation we suppose impossible. An impossibility of being annihilated cannot exist, and can never be conceived to exist, by itself, but necessarily requires some object or real existence to which it may belong. Now, the difficulty still remains how to form an idea of this object or existence, without having recourse to the secondary and sensible qualities.

Nor must we omit, on this occasion, our accustomed method of examining ideas by considering those impressions from which they are derived. The impressions which enter by the sight and hearing, the smell and taste, are affirmed by modern philosophy to be without any resembling objects; and consequently the idea of solidity, which is supposed to be real, can never be derived from any of these senses. There remains, therefore, the feeling as the only sense that can convey the impression which is original to the idea of solidity; and, indeed, we naturally imagine that we feel the solidity of bodies, and need but touch any object in order to perceive this quality. But this method of thinking is more popular than philosophical, as will appear from the following reflections.

First, it is easy to observe, that though bodies are felt by means of their solidity, yet the feeling is a quite different thing from the solidity, and that they have not the least resemblance to each other. A man who has the palsy in one hand has as perfect an idea of impenetrability, when he observes that hand to be supported by the table, as when he feels the same table with the other hand. An object that presses upon any of our members meets with resistance; and that resistance, by the motion it gives to the nerves and animal spirits, conveys a certain sensation to the mind; but it does not follow that the sensation, motion, and resistance are any ways resembling.

[1] Part II. Sect. 4.

Secondly, the impressions of touch are simple impressions, except when considered with regard to their extension; which makes nothing to the present purpose: and from this simplicity I infer that they neither represent solidity, nor any real object. For let us put two cases, viz., that of a man who presses a stone or any solid body with his hand, and that of two stones which press each other; it will readily be allowed that these two cases are not in in every respect alike, but that in the former there is conjoined with the solidity a feeling or sensation of which there is no appearance in the latter. In order, therefore, to make these two cases alike, it is necessary to remove some part of the impression which the man feels by his hand, or organ of sensation; and that being impossible in a simple impression, obliges us to remove the whole, and proves that this whole impression has no archetype or model in external objects; to which we may add, that solidity necessarily supposes two bodies, along with contiguity and impulse; which being a compound object, can never be represented by a simple impression. Not to mention, that, though solidity continues always invariably the same, the impressions of touch change every moment upon us, which is a clear proof that the latter are not representations of the former.

Thus there is a direct and total opposition betwixt our reason and our senses; or, more properly speaking, betwixt those conclusions we form from cause and effect, and those that persuade us of the continued and independent existence of body. When we reason from cause and effect, we conclude that neither colour, sound, taste, nor smell have a continued and independent existence. When we exclude these sensible qualities, there remains nothing in the universe which has such an existence.

SECTION VI

OF PERSONAL IDENTITY

THERE are some philosophers who imagine we are every moment intimately conscious of what we call our *self*; that we feel its existence and its continuance in existence; and are certain, beyond the evidence of a demonstration, both of its perfect identity and simplicity. The strongest sensation, the most violent passion, say they, instead of distracting us from this view, only fix it the more intensely, and make us consider their influence on *self* either by their pain or pleasure. To attempt a further proof of this were to weaken its evidence; since no proof can be derived from any fact of which we are so intimately conscious; nor is there anything of which we can be certain if we doubt of this.

Unluckily all these positive assertions are contrary to that very experience which is pleaded for them; nor have we any idea of *self*, after the manner it is here explained. For, from what impression could this idea be derived? This question it is impossible to answer without a manifest contradiction and absurdity; and yet it is a question which must necessarily be answered, if we would have the idea of self pass for clear and intelligible. It must be some one impression that gives rise to every real idea. But self or person is not any one impression, but that to which our several impressions and ideas are supposed to have a reference. If any impression gives rise to the idea of self, that impression must continue invariably the same, through the whole course of our lives; since self is supposed to exist after that manner. But there is no impression constant and invariable. Pain and pleasure, grief and joy, passions and sensations succeed each other, and never all exist at the same time. It cannot therefore be from any of these impressions, or from any other, that the idea of self is derived; and consequently there is no such idea.

But further, what must become of all our particular perceptions upon this hypothesis? All these are different, and distinguishable, and separable from each other, and may be separately considered, and may exist separately, and have no need of anything to support their existence. After what manner therefore do they belong to self, and how are they connected with it? For my part, when I enter most intimately into what I call *myself*, I always stumble on some particular perception or other, of heat or cold, light or shade, love or hatred, pain or pleasure. I never can catch *myself* at any time without a perception, and never can observe anything but the perception. When my perceptions are removed for any time, as by sound sleep, so long am I insensible of *myself*, and may truly be said not to exist. And were all my perceptions removed by death, and could I neither think, nor feel, nor see, nor love, nor hate, after the dissolution of my body, I should be entirely annihilated, nor do I conceive what is further requisite to make me a perfect nonentity. If any one, upon serious and unprejudiced reflection, thinks he has a different notion of *himself*, I must confess I can reason no longer with him. All I can allow him is, that he may be in the right as well as I, and that we are

essentially different in this particular He may, perhaps, perceive
something simple and continued, which he calls *himself*; though I
am certain there is no such principle in me.

But setting aside some metaphysicians of this kind, I may venture
to affirm of the rest of mankind, that they are nothing but a bundle
or collection of different perceptions, which succeed each other
with an inconceivable rapidity, and are in a perpetual flux and
movement. Our eyes cannot turn in their sockets without varying
our perceptions. Our thought is still more variable than our sight;
and all our other senses and faculties contribute to this change;
nor is there any single power of the soul, which remains unalterably
the same, perhaps for one moment. The mind is a kind of theatre,
where several perceptions successively make their appearance; pass,
repass, glide away, and mingle in an infinite variety of postures and
situations. There is properly no *simplicity* in it at one time, nor
identity in different, whatever natural propension we may have to
imagine that simplicity and identity. The comparison of the
theatre must not mislead us. They are the successive perceptions
only, that constitute the mind; nor have we the most distant notion
of the place where these scenes are represented, or of the materials
of which it is composed.

What then gives us so great a propension to ascribe an identity
to these successive perceptions, and to suppose ourselves possessed
of an invariable and uninterrupted existence through the whole
course of our lives? In order to answer this question we must
distinguish betwixt personal identity, as it regards our thought
or imagination, and as it regards our passions or the concern we
take in ourselves. The first is our present subject; and to explain
it perfectly we must take the matter pretty deep, and account for
that identity, which we attribute to plants and animals; there being
a great analogy betwixt it and the identity of a self or person.

We have a distinct idea of an object that remains invariable and
uninterrupted through a supposed variation of time; and this idea
we call that of *identity* or *sameness*. We have also a distinct idea
of several different objects existing in succession, and connected
together by a close relation; and this to an accurate view affords
as perfect a notion of *diversity* as if there was no manner of relation
among the objects. But though these two ideas of identity, and
a succession of related objects, be in themselves perfectly distinct,
and even contrary, yet it is certain that, in our common way of
thinking, they are generally confounded with each other. That
action of the imagination, by which we consider the uninterrupted

and invariable object, and that by which we reflect on the succession of related objects, are almost the same to the feeling; nor is there much more effort of thought required in the latter case than in the former. The relation facilitates the transition of the mind from one object to another, and renders its passage as smooth as if it contemplated one continued object. This resemblance is the cause of the confusion and mistake, and makes us substitute the notion identity, instead of that of related objects. However at one instant we may consider the related succession as variable or interrupted, we are sure the next to ascribe to it a perfect identity, and regard it as invariable and uninterrupted. Our propensity to this mistake is so great from the resemblance above mentioned, that we fall into it before we are aware; and though we incessantly correct ourselves by reflection, and return to a more accurate method of thinking, yet we cannot long sustain our philosophy, or take off this bias from the imagination. Our last resource is to yield to it, and boldly assert that these different related objects are in effect the same, however interrupted and variable. In order to justify to ourselves this absurdity, we often feign some new and unintelligible principle, that connects the objects together, and prevents their interruption or variation. Thus we feign the continued existence of the perceptions of our senses, to remove the interruption; and run into the notion of a *soul*, and *self*, and *substance*, to disguise the variation. But, we may further observe, that where we do not give rise to such a fiction, our propension to confound identity with relation is so great, that we are apt to imagine something unknown and mysterious,[1] connecting the parts, beside their relation; and this I take to be the case with regard to the identity we ascribe to plants and vegetables. And even when this does not take place, we still feel a propensity to confound these ideas, though we are not able fully to satisfy ourselves in that particular, nor find anything invariable and uninterrupted to justify our notion of identity.

Thus the controversy concerning identity is not merely a dispute of words. For when we attribute identity, in an improper sense, to variable or interrupted objects, our mistake is not confined to the expression, but is commonly attended with a fiction, either of something invariable and uninterrupted, or of something mysterious

[1] If the reader is desirous to see how a great genius may be influenced by these seemingly trivial principles of the imagination, as well as the mere vulgar, let him read my Lord Shaftesbury's reasonings concerning the uniting principle of the universe, and the identity of plants and animals. See his *Moralists, or Philosophical Rhapsody*.

and inexplicable, or at least with a propensity to such fictions. What will suffice to prove this hypothesis to the satisfaction of every fair inquirer, is to show, from daily experience and observation, that the objects which are variable or interrupted, and yet are supposed to continue the same, are such only as consist of a succession of parts, connected together by resemblance, contiguity, or causation. For as such a succession answers evidently to our notion of diversity, it can only be by mistake we ascribe to it an identity; and as the relation of parts, which leads us into this mistake, is really nothing but a quality, which produces an association of ideas, and an easy transition of the imagination from one to another, it can only be from the resemblance, which this act of the mind bears to that by which we contemplate one continued object, that the error arises. Our chief business, then, must be to prove, that all objects, to which we ascribe identity, without observing their invariableness and uninterruptedness, are such as consist of a succession of related objects.

In order to this, suppose any mass of matter, of which the parts are contiguous and connected, to be placed before us; it is plain we must attribute a perfect identity to this mass, provided all the parts continue uninterruptedly and invariably the same, whatever motion or change of place we may observe either in the whole or in any of the parts. But supposing some very *small* or *inconsiderable* part to be added to the mass, or subtracted from it; though this absolutely destroys the identity of the whole, strictly speaking, yet as we seldom think so accurately, we scruple not to pronounce a mass of matter the same, where we find so trivial an alteration. The passage of the thought from the object before the change to the object after it, is so smooth and easy, that we scarce perceive the transition, and are apt to imagine, that it is nothing but a continued survey of the same object.

There is a very remarkable circumstance that attends this experiment; which is, that though the change of any considerable part in a mass of matter destroys the identity of the whole, yet we must measure the greatness of the part, not absolutely, but by its *proportion* to the whole. The addition or diminution of a mountain would not be sufficient to produce a diversity in a planet; though the change of a very few inches would be able to destroy the identity of some bodies. It will be impossible to account for this, but by reflecting that objects operate upon the mind, and break or interrupt the continuity of its actions, not according to their real greatness, but according to their proportion to each other;

and therefore, since this interruption makes an object cease to appear the same, it must be the uninterrupted progress of the thought which constitutes the imperfect identity.

This may be confirmed by another phenomenon. A change in any considerable part of a body destroys its identity; but it is remarkable, that where the change is produced *gradually* and *insensibly,* we are less apt to ascribe to it the same effect. The reason can plainly be no other, than that the mind, in following the successive changes of the body, feels an easy passage from the surveying its condition in one moment, to the viewing of it in another, and in no particular time perceives any interruption in its actions. From which continued perception, it ascribes a continued existence and identity to the object.

But whatever precaution we may use in introducing the changes gradually, and making them proportionable to the whole, it is certain, that where the changes are at last observed to become considerable, we make a scruple of ascribing identity to such different objects. There is, however, another artifice, by which we may induce the imagination to advance a step further; and that is, by producing a reference of the parts to each other, and a combination to some *common end* or purpose. A ship, of which a considerable part has been changed by frequent reparations, is still considered as the same; nor does the difference of the materials hinder us from ascribing an identity to it. The common end, in which the parts conspire, is the same under all their variations, and affords an easy transition of the imagination from one situation of the body to another.

But this is still more remarkable, when we add a *sympathy* of parts to their *common end,* and suppose that they bear to each other the reciprocal relation of cause and effect in all their actions and operations. This is the case with all animals and vegetables; where not only the several parts have a reference to some general purpose, but also a mutual dependence on, and connection with, each other. The effect of so strong a relation is, that though every one must allow, that in a very few years both vegetables and animals endure a *total* change, yet we still attribute identity to them, while their form, size, and substance, are entirely altered. An oak that grows from a small plant to a large tree is still the same oak, though there be not one particle of matter or figure of its parts the same. An infant becomes a man, and is sometimes fat, sometimes lean, without any change in his identity.

We may also consider the two following phenomena, which are

remarkable in their kind. The first is, that though we commonly be able to distinguish pretty exactly betwixt numerical and specific identity, yet it sometimes happens that we confound them, and in our thinking and reasoning employ the one for the other. Thus, a man who hears a noise that is frequently interrupted and renewed, says it is still the same noise, though it is evident the sounds have only a specific identity or resemblance, and there is nothing numerically the same but the cause which produced them. In like manner it may be said, without breach of the propriety of language, that such a church, which was formerly of brick, fell to ruin, and that the parish rebuilt the same church of freestone, and according to modern architecture. Here neither the form nor materials are the same, nor is there anything common to the two objects but their relation to the inhabitants of the parish; and yet this alone is sufficient to make us denominate them the same. But we must observe, that in these cases the first object is in a manner annihilated before the second comes into existence; by which means, we are never presented, in any one point of time, with the idea of difference and multiplicity; and for that reason are less scrupulous in calling them the same.

Secondly, we may remark, that though, in a succession of related objects, it be in a manner requisite that the change of parts be not sudden nor entire, in order to preserve the identity, yet where the objects are in their nature changeable and inconstant, we admit of a more sudden transition than would otherwise be consistent with that relation. Thus, as the nature of a river consists in the motion and change of parts, though in less than four-and-twenty hours these be totally altered, this hinders not the river from continuing the same during several ages. What is natural and essential to anything is, in a manner, expected; and what is expected makes less impression, and appears of less moment than what is unusual and extraordinary. A considerable change of the former kind seems really less to the imagination than the most trivial alteration of the latter; and by breaking less the continuity of the thought, has less influence in destroying the identity.

We now proceed to explain the nature of *personal identity*, which has become so great a question in philosophy, especially of late years, in England, where all the abstruser sciences are studied with a peculiar ardour and application. And here it is evident the same method of reasoning must be continued which has so successfully explained the identity of plants, and animals, and ships, and houses, and of all compounded and changeable productions either of art or nature. The identity which we ascribe to the mind of man is only a fictitious one, and of a like kind with that which we ascribe to vegetable and animal bodies. It cannot therefore have a different origin, but must proceed from a like operation of the imagination upon like objects.

But lest this argument should not convince the reader, though in my opinion perfectly decisive, let him weigh the following reasoning, which is still closer and more immediate. It is evident that the identity which we attribute to the human mind, however perfect we may imagine it to be, is not able to run the several different perceptions into one, and make them lose their characters of distinction and difference, which are essential to them. It is still true that every distinct perception which enters into the composition of the mind, is a distinct existence, and is different, and distinguishable, and separable from every other perception, either contemporary or successive. But as, notwithstanding this distinction and separability, we suppose the whole train of perceptions to be united by identity, a question naturally arises concerning this relation of identity, whether it be something that really binds our several perceptions together, or only associates their ideas in the imagination; that is, in other words, whether, in pronouncing concerning the identity of a person, we observe some real bond among his perceptions, or only feel one among the ideas we form of them. This question we might easily decide, if we would recollect what has already been proved at large, that the understanding never observes any real connection among objects, and that even the union of cause and effect, when strictly examined, resolves itself into a customary association of ideas. For from thence it evidently follows, that identity is nothing really belonging to these different perceptions, and uniting them together, but is merely a quality which we attribute to them, because of the union of their ideas in the imagination when we reflect upon them. Now, the only qualities which can give ideas a union in the imagination, are these three relations above mentioned. These are the uniting principles in the ideal world, and without them every distinct object is separable by the mind, and may be separately considered, and appears not to have any more connection with any other object than if disjoined by the greatest difference and remoteness. It is therefore on some of these three relations of resemblance, contiguity and causation, that identity depends; and as the very essence of these relations consists in their producing an easy transition of ideas, it follows that our notions of personal identity proceed entirely from the smooth and uninterrupted progress of the thought along a train of connected ideas, according to the principles above explained.

The only question, therefore, which remains is, by what relations this uninterrupted progress of our thought is produced, when we consider the successive existence of a mind or thinking person. And here it is evident we must confine ourselves to resemblance and causation, and must drop contiguity, which has little or no influence in the present case.

To begin with *resemblance*; suppose we could see clearly into the breast of another, and observe that succession of perceptions which constitutes his mind or thinking principle, and suppose that he always preserves the memory of a considerable part of past perceptions, it is evident that nothing could more contribute to the bestowing a relation on this succession amidst all its variations. For what is the memory but a faculty, by which we raise up the images of past perceptions? And as an image necessarily resembles its object, must not the frequent placing of these resembling perceptions in the chain of thought, convey the imagination more easily from one link to another, and make the whole seem like the continuance of one object? In this particular, then, the memory not only discovers the identity, but also contributes to its production, by producing the relation of resemblance among the perceptions. The case is the same, whether we consider ourselves or others.

As to *causation*; we may observe that the true idea of the human mind, is to consider it as a system of different perceptions or different existences, which are linked together by the relation of cause and effect, and mutually produce, destroy, influence, and modify each other. Our impressions give rise to their correspondent ideas; and these ideas, in their turn, produce other impressions. One thought chases another, and draws after it a third, by which it is expelled in its turn. In this respect, I cannot compare the soul more properly to anything than to a republic or commonwealth, in which the several members are united by the reciprocal ties of government and subordination, and give rise to other persons who propagate the same republic in the incessant changes of its parts. And as the same individual republic may not only change its members, but also its laws and constitutions; in like manner the same person may vary his character and disposition, as well as his impressions and ideas without losing his identity. Whatever changes he endures, his several parts are still connected by the relation of causation. And in this view our identity with regard to the passions serves to corroborate that with regard to the imagination, but the making our distant perceptions influence each other, and by giving us a present concern for our past or future pains or pleasures.

As memory alone acquaints us with the continuance and extent of this succession of perceptions, it is to be considered, upon that account chiefly, as the source of personal identity. Had we no memory, we never should have any notion of causation, nor consequently of that chain of causes and effects, which constitute our self or person. But having once acquired this notion of causation from the memory, we can extend the same chain of causes, and consequently the identity of our persons beyond our memory, and can comprehend times, and circumstances, and actions, which we have entirely forgot, but suppose in general to have existed. For how few of our past actions are there, of which we have any memory? Who can tell me, for instance, what were his thoughts and actions on the first of January, 1715, the eleventh of March, 1719, and the third of August, 1733? Or will he affirm, because he has entirely forgot the incidents of these days, that the present self is not the same person with the self of that time; and by that means overturn all the most established notions of personal identity? In this view, therefore, memory, does not so much *produce* as *discover* personal identity, by showing us the relation of cause and effect among our different perceptions. It will be incumbent on those who affirm that memory produces entirely our personal identity, to give a reason why we can thus extend our identity beyond our memory.

The whole of this doctrine leads us to a conclusion, which is of great importance in the present affair, viz., that all the nice and subtile questions concerning personal identity can never possibly be decided, and are to be regarded rather as grammatical than as philosophical difficulties. Identity depends on the relation of ideas; and these relations produce identity, by means of that easy transition they occasion. But as the relations, and the easiness of the transition may diminish by insensible degrees, we have no just standard by which we can decide any dispute concerning the time when they acquire or lose a title to the name of identity. All the disputes concerning the identity of connected objects are merely verbal, except so far as the relation of parts gives rise to some fiction or imaginary principle of union, as we have already observed.

What I have said concerning the first origin and uncertainty of our notion of identity, as applied to the human mind, may be extended with little or no variation to that of *simplicity*. An object, whose different coexistent parts are bound together by a close relation, operates upon the imagination after much the same manner as one perfectly simple and indivisible, and requires not a much greater stretch of thought in order to its conception. From this similarity of operation we attribute a simplicity to it, and feign a principle of union as the support of this simplicity, and the centre of all the different parts and qualities of the object.

Thus we have finished our examination of the several systems of philosophy, both of the intellectual and moral world; and, in our miscellaneous way of reasoning, have been led into several topics, which will either illustrate and confirm some preceding part of this discourse, or prepare the way for our following opinions. It is now time to return to a more close examination of our subject, and to proceed in the accurate anatomy of human nature, having fully explained the nature of our judgment and understanding.

SECTION VII

CONCLUSION OF THIS BOOK

BUT before I launch out into those immense depths of philosophy which lie before me, I find myself inclined to stop a moment in my present station, and to ponder that voyage which I have undertaken, and which undoubtedly requires the utmost art and industry to be brought to a happy conclusion. Methinks I am like a man, who, having struck on many shoals, and having narrowly escaped shipwreck in passing a small frith, has yet the temerity to put out to sea in the same leaky weather-beaten vessel, and even carries his ambition so far as to think of compassing the globe under these disadvantageous circumstances. My memory of past errors and perplexities makes me diffident for the future. The wretched condition, weakness, and disorder of the faculties, I must employ in my inquiries, increase my apprehensions. And the impossibility of amending or correcting these faculties, reduces me almost to despair, and makes me resolve to perish on the barren rock, on which I am at present, rather than venture myself upon that boundless ocean which runs out into immensity. This sudden view of my danger strikes me with melancholy; and, as it is usual for that passion, above all others, to indulge itself, I cannot forbear feeding my despair with all those desponding reflections which the present subject furnishes me with in such abundance.

I am at first affrighted and confounded with that forlorn solitude in which I am placed in my philosophy, and fancy myself some strange uncouth monster, who, not being able to mingle and unite in society, has been expelled all human commerce, and left utterly abandoned and disconsolate. Fain would I run into the crowd for shelter and warmth, but cannot prevail with myself to mix with such deformity. I call upon others to join me, in order to make a company apart, but no one will hearken to me. Every one keeps at a distance, and dreads that storm which beats upon me from every side. I have exposed myself to the enmity of all metaphysicians, logicians, mathematicians, and even theologians; and can I wonder at the insults I must suffer? I have declared my disapprobation of their systems; and can I be surprised if they should express a hatred of mine and of my person? When I look abroad, I foresee on every side dispute, contradiction, anger, calumny, and detraction. When I turn my eye inward, I find nothing but doubt and ignorance. All the world conspires to oppose and contradict me; though such is my weakness, that I feel all my opinions loosen and fall of themselves, when unsupported by the approbation of others. Every step I take is with hesitation, and every new reflection makes me dread an error and absurdity in my reasoning.

For with what confidence can I venture upon such bold enterprises, when, beside those numberless infirmities peculiar to myself, I find so many which are common to human nature? Can I be sure that, in leaving all established opinions, I am following truth? and by what criterion shall I distinguish her, even if fortune should at last guide me on her footsteps? After the most accurate and exact of my reasonings, I can give no reason why I should assent to it, and feel nothing but a *strong* propensity to consider objects *strongly* in that view under which they appear to me. Experience is a principle which instructs me in the several conjunctions of objects for the past. Habit is another principle which determines me to expect the same for the future; and both of them conspiring to operate upon the imagination, make me form certain ideas in a more intense and lively manner than others which are not attended with the same advantages. Without this quality, by which the mind enlivens some ideas beyond others (which seemingly is so trivial, and so little founded on reason), we could never assent to any argument, nor carry our view beyond those few objects which are present to our senses. Nay, even to these objects we could never attribute any existence but what was dependent on the senses, and must comprehend them entirely in that succession of perceptions which constitutes our self or person. Nay, further, even with relation to that succession, we could only admit of those perceptions which are immediately present to our consciousness; nor could those lively images, with which the memory presents us, be ever received as true pictures of past perceptions. The memory, senses, and understanding are therefore all of them founded on the imagination, or the vivacity of our ideas.

No wonder a principle so inconstant and fallacious should lead us into errors when implicitly followed (as it must be) in all its variations. It is this principle which makes us reason from cause and effect; and it is the same principle which convinces us of the continued existence of external objects when absent from the senses. But though these two operations be equally natural and necessary in the human mand, yet in some circumstances they are directly contrary;[1] nor is it possible for us to reason justly and regularly from causes and effects, and at the same time believe the continued existence of matter? How shall we adjust those principles together? Which of them shall we prefer? Or in case we prefer neither of them, but successively assent to both, as is usual among philosophers, with what confidence can we afterwards usurp that glorious title, when we thus knowingly embrace a manifest contradiction?

This contradiction[2] would be more excusable were it compensated by any degree of solidity and satisfaction in the other parts of our reasoning. But the case is quite contrary. When we trace up the human understanding to its first principles, we find it to lead us into such sentiments as seem to turn into ridicule all our past pains and industry, and to discourage us from future inquiries. Nothing is more curiously inquired after by the mind of man than the causes of every phenomenon; nor are we content with knowing the immediate causes, but push on our inquiries till we arrive at the original and ultimate principle. We would not willingly stop before we are acquainted with that energy in the cause by which it operates on its effect; that tie, which connects them together; and that efficacious quality on which the tie depends. This is our aim in all our studies and reflections: and how must we be disappointed when we learn that this connection, tie, or energy lies merely in ourselves, and is nothing but that determination of the mind which

[1] Sect. 4.   [2] Part III. Sect. 14.

is acquired by custom, and causes us to make a transition from an object to its usual attendant, and from the impression of one to the lively idea of the other?   Such a discovery not only cuts off all hope of ever attaining satisfaction, but even prevents our very wishes; since it appears, that when we say we desire to know the ultimate and operating principle as something which resides in the external object, we either contradict ourselves, or talk without a meaning.

This deficiency in our ideas is not indeed perceived in common life, nor are we sensible that, in the most usual conjunctions of cause and effect, we are as ignorant of the ultimate principle which binds them together, as in the most unusual and extraordinary. But this proceeds merely from an illusion of the imagination; and the question is, how far we ought to yield to these illusions.   This question is very difficult, and reduces us to a very dangerous dilemma, whichever way we answer it.   For if we assent to every trivial suggestion of the fancy, beside that these suggestions are often contrary to each other, they lead us into such errors, absurdities, and obscurities, that we must at last become ashamed of our credulity.   Nothing is more dangerous to reason than the flights of the imagination, and nothing has been the occasion of more mistakes among philosophers.   Men of bright fancies may in this respect be compared to those angels, whom the Scripture represents as covering their eyes with their wings.   This has already appeared in so many instances, that we may spare ourselves the trouble of enlarging upon it any further.

But, on the other hand, if the consideration of these instances makes us take a resolution to reject all the trivial suggestions of the fancy, and adhere to the understanding, that is, to the general and more established properties of the imagination; even this resolution, if steadily executed, would be dangerous, and attended with the most fatal consequences.   For I have already shown,[1] that the understanding, when it acts alone, and according to its most general principles, entirely subverts itself, and leaves not the lowest degree of evidence in any proposition, either in philosophy or common life.   We save ourselves from this total scepticism only by means of that singular and seemingly trivial property of the fancy, by which we enter with difficulty into remote views of things, and are not able to accompany them with so sensible an impression, as we do those which are more easy and natural. Shall we, then, establish it for a general maxim that no refined

[1] Sect. 1.

or elaborate reasoning is ever to be received? Consider well the consequences of such a principle. By this means you cut off entirely all science and philosophy: you proceed upon one singular quality of the imagination, and by a parity of reason must embrace all of them; and you expressly contradict yourself; since this maxim must be built on the preceding reasoning, which will be allowed to be sufficiently refined and metaphysical. What party, then, shall we choose among these difficulties? If we embrace this principle, and condemn all refined reasoning, we run into the most manifest absurdities. If we reject in favour of these reasonings, we subvert entirely the human understanding. We have therefore no choice left, but betwixt a false reason and none at all. For my part, I know not what ought to be done in the present case. I can only observe what is commonly done; which is, that this difficulty is seldom or never thought of; and even where it has once been present to the mind, is quickly forgot, and leaves but a small impression behind it. Very refined reflections have little or no influence upon us; and yet we do not, and cannot establish it for a rule, that they ought not to have any influence; which implies a manifest contradiction.

But what have I here said, that reflections very refined and metaphysical have little or no influence upon us? This opinion I can scarce forbear retracting, and condemning from my present feeling and experience. The *intense* view of these manifold contradictions and imperfections in human reason has so wrought upon me, and heated my brain, that I am ready to reject all belief and reasoning, and can look upon no opinion even as more probable or likely than another. Where am I, or what? From what causes do I derive my existence, and to what condition shall I return? Whose favour shall I court, and whose anger must I dread? What beings surround me? and on whom have I any influence, or who have any influence on me? I am confounded with all these questions, and begin to fancy myself in the most deplorable condition imaginable, environed with the deepest darkness, and utterly deprived of the use of every member and faculty.

Most fortunately it happens, that since reason is incapable of dispelling these clouds, Nature herself suffices to that purpose, and cures me of this philosophical melancholy and delirium, either by relaxing this bent of mind, or by some avocation, and lively impression of my senses, which obliterate all these chimeras. I dine, I play a game of backgammon, I converse, and am merry with my friends; and when, after three or four hours' amusement, I would return to these speculations, they appear so cold, and strained, and ridiculous, that I cannot find in my heart to enter into them any further.

Here, then, I find myself absolutely and necessarily determined to live, and talk, and act like other people in the common affairs of life. But notwithstanding that my natural propensity, and the course of my animal spirits and passions reduce me to this indolent belief in the general maxims of the world, I still feel such remains of my former disposition, that I am ready to throw all my books and papers into the fire, and resolve never more to renounce the pleasures of life for the sake of reasoning and philosophy. For those are my sentiments in that splenetic humour which governs me at present. I may, nay I must yield to the current of nature, in submitting to my senses and understanding; and in this blind submission I show most perfectly my sceptical disposition and principles. But does it follow that I must strive against the current of nature, which leads me to indolence and pleasure; that I must seclude myself, in some measure, from the commerce and society of men, which is so agreeable; and that I must torture my brain with subtilties and sophistries, at the very time that I cannot satisfy myself concerning the reasonableness of so painful an application, nor have any tolerable prospect of arriving by its means at truth and certainty? Under what obligation do I lie of making such an abuse of time? And to what end can it serve, either for the service of mankind, or for my own private interest? No: if I must be a fool, as all those who reason or believe anything *certainly* are, my follies shall at least be natural and agreeable. Where I strive against my inclination, I shall have a good reason for my resistance; and will be no more be led a wandering into such dreary solitudes, and rough passages, as I have hitherto met with.

These are the sentiments of my spleen and indolence; and indeed I must confess, that philosophy has nothing to oppose to them, and expects a victory more from the returns of a serious good-humoured disposition, than from the force of reason and conviction. In all the incidents of life, we ought still to preserve our scepticism. If we believe that fire warms, or water refreshes, it is only because it costs us too much pains to think otherwise. Nay, if we are philosophers, it ought only to be upon sceptical principles, and from an inclination which we feel to the employing ourselves after that manner. Where reason is lively, and mixes itself with some propensity, it ought to be assented to. Where it does not, it never can have any title to operate upon us.

At the time, therefore, that I am tired with amusement and company, and have indulged a *reverie* in my chamber, or in a solitary walk by a river side, I feel my mind all collected within itself, and am naturally *inclined* to carry my view into all those subjects, about which I have met with so many disputes in the course of my reading and conversation. I cannot forbear having a curiosity to be acquainted with the principles of moral good and evil, the nature and foundation of government, and the cause of those several passions and inclinations which actuate and govern me. I am uneasy to think I approve of one object, and disapprove of another; call one thing beautiful, and another deformed; decide concerning truth and falsehood, reason and folly, without knowing upon what principles I proceed. I am concerned for the condition of the learned world, which lies under such a deplorable ignorance in all these particulars. I feel an ambition to arise in me of contributing to the instruction of mankind, and of acquiring a name by my inventions and discoveries. These sentiments spring up naturally in my present disposition; and should I endeavour to banish them, by attaching myself to any other business or diversion, I *feel* I should be a loser in point of pleasure; and this is the origin of my philosophy.

But even to suppose this curiosity and ambition should not transport me into speculations without the sphere of common life, it would necessarily happen that from my very weakness I must be led into such inquiries. It is certain that superstition is much more bold in its systems and hypotheses than philosophy; and while the latter contents itself with assigning new causes and principles to the phenomena which appear in the visible world, the former opens a world of its own, and presents us with scenes, and beings, and objects, which are altogether new. Since, therefore, it is almost impossible for the mind of man to rest, like those of beasts, in that narrow circle of objects, which are the subject of daily conversation and action, we ought only to deliberate concerning the choice of our guide, and ought to prefer that which is safest and most agreeable. And in this respect I make bold to recommend philosophy, and shall not scruple to give it the preference to superstition of every kind or denomination. For as superstition arises naturally and easily from the popular opinions of mankind, it seizes more strongly on the mind, and is often able to disturb us in the conduct of our lives and actions. Philosophy, on the contrary, if just, can present us only with mild and moderate sentiments; and if false and extravagant, its opinions are merely the objects of a cold and general speculation, and seldom go so far as to interrupt the course of our natural propensities. The *Cynics* are an extraordinary instance of philosophers, who, from reasonings purely philosophical, ran into as great extravagancies of conduct as any *monk* or *dervise* that ever was in the world. Generally speaking, the errors in religion are dangerous; those in philosophy only ridiculous.

I am sensible that these two cases of the strength and weakness of the mind will not comprehend all mankind, and that there are in England, in particular, many honest gentlemen, who, being always employed in their domestic affairs, or amusing themselves in common recreations, have carried their thoughts very little beyond those objects, which are every day exposed to their senses. And indeed, of such as these I pretend not to make philosophers, nor do I expect them either to be associates in these researches, or auditors of these discoveries. They do well to keep themselves in their present situation; and, instead of refining them into philosophers, I wish we could communicate to our founders of systems, a share of this gross earthy mixture, as an ingredient, which they commonly stand much in need of, and which would serve to temper those fiery particles, of which they are composed. While a warm imagination is allowed to enter into philosophy, and hypotheses embraced merely for being specious and agreeable, we can never have any steady principles, nor any sentiments, which will suit with common practice and experience. But were these hypotheses once removed, we might hope to establish a system or set of opinions, which if not true (for that, perhaps, is too much to be hoped for), might at least be satisfactory to the human mind, and might stand the test of the most critical examination. Nor should we despair of attaining this end, because of the many chimerical systems, which have successively arisen and decayed away among men, would we consider the shortness of that period, wherein these questions have been the subjects of inquiry and reasoning. Two thousand years with such long interruptions, and under such mighty discouragements, are a small space of time to give any tolerable perfection to the sciences; and perhaps we are still in too early an age of the world to discover any principles which will bear the examination of the latest posterity. For my part, my only hope is, that I may contribute a little to the advancement of knowledge, by giving in some particulars a different turn to the speculations of philosophers, and pointing out to them more distinctly those subjects where alone they can expect assurance and conviction. Human Nature is the only science of man; and yet has been hitherto

the most neglected. It will be sufficient for me, if I can bring it a
little more into fashion; and the hope of this serves to compose my
temper from that spleen, and invigorate it from that indolence,
which sometimes prevail upon me. If the reader finds himself in
the same easy disposition, let him follow me in my future speculations. If not, let him follow his inclination, and wait the returns
of application and good humour. The conduct of a man who
studies philosophy in this careless manner, is more truly sceptical
than that of one who, feeling in himself an inclination to it, is yet
so overwhelmed with doubts and scruples, as totally to reject it.
A true sceptic will be diffident of his philosophical doubts, as well
as of his philosophical convictions; and will never refuse any
innocent satisfaction which offers itself, upon account of either
of them.

Nor is it only proper we should in general indulge our inclination
in the most elaborate philosophical researches, notwithstanding our
sceptical principles, but also that we should yield to that propensity,
which inclines us to be positive and certain in *particular points,*
according to the light in which we survey them in any *particular
instant.* It is easier to forbear all examination and inquiry, than
to check ourselves in so natural a propensity, and guard against
that assurance, which always arises from an exact and full survey
of an object. On such an occasion we are apt not only to forget
our scepticism, but even our modesty too; and make use of such
terms as these, *it is evident, it is certain, it is undeniable*; which a
due deference to the public ought, perhaps, to prevent. I may
have fallen into this fault after the example of others; but I here
enter a *caveat* against any objections which may be offered on that
head; and declare that such expressions were extorted from me by
the present view of the object, and imply no dogmatical spirit, nor
conceited idea of my own judgment, which are sentiments that I am
sensible can become nobody, and a sceptic still less than any other.

AN APPENDIX TO THE TREATISE

I had entertained some hopes, that however deficient our theory
of the intellectual world might be, it would be free from those
contradictions, and absurdities, which seem to attend every explication, that human reason can give of the material world. But upon
a more strict review of the section concerning *personal identity,* I
find myself involved in such a labyrinth, that, I must confess, I

neither know how to correct my former opinions, nor how to render them consistent. If this be not a good *general* reason for scepticism, 'tis at least a sufficient one (if I were not already abundantly supplied) for me to entertain a diffidence and modesty in all my decisions. I shall propose the arguments on both sides, beginning with those that induced me to deny the strict and proper identity and simplicity of a self or thinking being.

When we talk of *self* or *substance,* we must have an idea annexed to these terms, otherwise they are altogether unintelligible. Every idea is derived from preceding impressions; and we have no impression of self or substance, as something simple and individual. We have, therefore, no idea of them in that sense.

Whatever is distinct, is distinguishable; and whatever is distinguishable, is separable by the thought or imagination. All perceptions are distinct. They are, therefore, distinguishable and separable, and may be conceived as separately existent, and may exist separately, without any contradiction or absurdity.

When I view this table and that chimney, nothing is present to me but particular perceptions, which are of a like nature with all the other perceptions. This is the doctrine of philosophers. But this table, which is present to me, and that chimney, may and do exist separately. This is the doctrine of the vulgar, and implies no contradiction. There is no contradiction, therefore, in extending the same doctrine to all the perceptions.

In general, the following reasoning seems satisfactory. All ideas are borrowed from preceding perceptions. Our ideas of objects, therefore, are derived from that source. Consequently no proposition can be intelligible or consistent with regard to objects, which is not so with regard to perceptions. But 'tis intelligible and consistent to say, that objects exist distinct and independent, without any common *simple* substance or subject of inhesion. This proposition, therefore, can never be absurd with regard to perceptions.

When I turn my reflection on *myself,* I never can perceive this *self* without some one or more perceptions; nor can I ever perceive any thing but the perceptions. 'Tis the composition of these, therefore, which forms the self.

We can conceive a thinking being to have either many or few perceptions. Suppose the mind to be reduced even below the life of an oyster. Suppose it to have only one perception, as of thirst or hunger. Consider it in that situation. Do you conceive any thing but merely that perception? Have you any notion of *self* or *substance?* If not, the addition of other perceptions can never give you that notion.

The annihilation, which some people suppose to follow upon death, and which entirely destroys this self, is nothing but an extinction of all particular perceptions; love and hatred, pain and pleasure, thought and sensation. These therefore must be the same with self; since the one cannot survive the other.'

Is *self* the same with *substance?* If it be, how can that question have place, concerning the subsistence of self, under a change of substance? If they be distinct, what is the difference betwixt them? For my part, I have a notion of neither, when conceived distinct from particular perceptions.

Philosophers begin to be reconciled to the principle, *that we have no idea of external substance, distinct from the idea of particular qualities.* This must pave the way for a like principle with regard to the mind, *that we have no notion of it, distinct from the particular perceptions.*

So far I seem to be attended with sufficient evidence. But having thus loosened all our particular perceptions, when I proceed to explain the principle of connection, which binds them together, and makes us attribute to them a real simplicity and identity; I am sensible, that my account is very defective, and that nothing but the seeming evidence of the precedent reasonings could have induced me to receive it. If perceptions are distinct existences, they form a whole only by being connected together. But no connections among distinct existences are ever discoverable by human understanding. We only *feel* a connection or determination of the thought, to pass from one object to another. It follows, therefore, that the thought alone finds personal identity, when reflecting on the train of past perceptions, that compose a mind, the ideas of them are felt to be connected together, and naturally introduce each other. However extraordinary this conclusion may seem, it need not surprise us. Most philosophers seem inclined to think, that personal identity *arises* from consciousness; and consciousness is nothing but a reflected thought or perception. The present philosophy, therefore, has so far a promising aspect. But all my hopes vanish, when I come to explain the principles, that unite our successive perceptions in our thought or consciousness. I cannot discover any theory, which gives me satisfaction on this head.

In short there are two principles, which I cannot render consistent; nor is it in my power to renounce either of them, viz., *that all our distinct perceptions are distinct existences,* and *that the mind never perceives any real connection among distinct existences.* Did our perceptions either inhere in something simple and individual, or did the mind perceive some real connection among them, there would be no difficulty in the case. For my part I must plead the privilege of a sceptic, and confess, that this difficulty is too hard for my understanding. I pretend not, however, to pronounce it absolutely insuperable. Others, perhaps, or myself, upon more mature reflections, may discover some hypothesis, that will reconcile those contradictions.

AN ENQUIRY
CONCERNING HUMAN UNDERSTANDING

IV—Sceptical Doubts concerning the Operations of the Understanding. VII—Of the Idea of Necessary Connection. XII—Of the Academical or Sceptical Philosophy.

SECTION IV

SCEPTICAL DOUBTS CONCERNING THE OPERATIONS OF THE UNDERSTANDING

ALL the objects of human reason or enquiry may naturally be divided into two kinds, to wit, *Relations of Ideas,* and *Matters of Fact.* Of the first kind are the sciences of Geometry, Algebra, and Arithmetic; and in short, every affirmation which is either intuitively or demonstratively certain. *That the square of the hypothenuse is equal to the square of the two sides,* is a proposition which expresses a relation between these figures. *That three times five is equal to the half of thirty,* expresses a relation between these numbers. Propositions of this kind are discoverable by the mere operation of thought, without dependence on what is anywhere existent in the universe. Though there never were a circle or triangle in nature, the truths demonstrated by Euclid would for ever retain their certainty and evidence.

Matters of fact, which are the second objects of human reason, are not ascertained in the same manner; nor is our evidence of their truth, however great, of a like nature with the foregoing. The contrary of every matter of fact is still possible; because it can never imply a contradiction, and is conceived by the mind with the same facility and distinctness, as if ever so conformable to reality. *That the sun will not rise to-morrow* is no less intelligible a proposition, and implies no more contradiction than the affirmation, *that it will rise.* We should in vain, therefore, attempt to demonstrate its falsehood. Were it demonstratively false, it would imply a contradiction, and could never be distinctly conceived by the mind.

All reasonings concerning matter of fact seem to be founded on the relation of *Cause and Effect*. By means of that relation alone we can go beyond the evidence of our memory and senses. If you were to ask a man, why he believes any matter of fact, which is absent; for instance, that his friend is in the country, or in France; he would give you a reason; and this reason would be some other fact; as a letter received from him, or the knowledge of his former resolutions and promises. A man finding a watch or any other machine in a desert island, would conclude that there had once been men in that island. All our reasonings concerning fact are of the same nature. And here it is constantly supposed that there is a connection between the present fact and that which is inferred from it. Were there nothing to bind them together, the inference would be entirely precarious. The hearing of an articulate voice and rational discourse in the dark assures us of the presence of some person: Why? because these are the effects of the human make and fabric, and closely connected with it. If we anatomize all the other reasonings of this nature, we shall find that they are founded on the relation of cause and effect, and that this relation is either near or remote, direct or collateral. Heat and light are collateral effects of fire, and the one effect may justly be inferred from the other.

If we would satisfy ourselves, therefore concerning the nature of that evidence, which assures us of matters of fact, we must enquire how we arrive at the knowledge of cause and effect.

I shall venture to affirm, as a general proposition, which admits of no exception, that the knowledge of this relation is not, in any instance, attained by reasonings *a priori*; but arises entirely from experience, when we find that any particular objects are constantly conjoined with each other. Let an object be presented to a man of ever so strong natural reason and abilities; if that object be entirely new to him, he will not be able, by the most accurate examination of its sensible qualities, to discover any of its causes or effects. Adam, though his rational faculties be supposed, at the very first, entirely perfect, could not have inferred from the fluidity and transparency of water that it would suffocate him, or from the light and warmth of fire that it would consume him. No object ever discovers, by the qualities which appear to the senses, either the causes which produced it, or the effects which will arise from it; nor can our reason, unassisted by experience, ever draw any inference concerning real existence and matter of fact.

This proposition, *that causes and effects are discoverable, not by reason but by experience,* will readily be admitted with regard to such objects, as we remember to have once been altogether unknown to us; since we must be conscious of the utter inability, which we then lay under, of foretelling what would arise from them. Present two smooth pieces of marble to a man who has no tincture of natural philosophy; he will never discover that they will adhere together in such a manner as to require great force to separate them in a direct line, while they make so small a resistance to a lateral pressure. Such events, as bear little analogy to the common course of nature, are also readily confessed to be known only by experience; nor does any man imagine that the explosion of gun-powder, or the attraction of a loadstone, could ever be discovered by arguments *a priori.* In like manner, when an effect is supposed to depend upon an intricate machinery or secret structure of parts, we make no difficulty in attributing all our knowledge of it to experience. Who will assert that he can give tthe ultimate reason, why milk or bread is proper nourishment for a man, not for a lion or a tiger?

But the same truth may not appear, at first sight, to have the same evidence with regard to events, which have become familiar to us from our first appearance in the world, which bear a close analogy to the whole course of nature, and which are supposed to depend on the simple qualities of objects, without any secret structure of parts. We are apt to imagine that we could discover these effects by the mere operation of our reason, without experience. We fancy, that were we brought on a sudden into this world, we could at first have inferred that one billiard-ball would communicate motion to another upon impulse; and that we needed not to have waited for the event, in order to pronounce with certainty concerning it. Such is the influence of custom that, where it is strongest, it not only covers our natural ignorance, but even conceals itself, and seems not to take place, merely because it is found in the highest degree.

But to convince us that all the laws of nature, and all the opera-tions of bodies without exception, are known only by experience, the following reflections may, perhaps, suffice. Were any object presented to us, and were we required to pronounce concerning the effect, which will result from it, without consulting past observation; after what manner, I beseech you, must the mind proceed in this operation? It must invent or imagine some event, which it ascribes to the object as its effect; and it is plain that this invention must be entirely arbitrary. The mind can never possibly find the effect in the supposed cause, by the most accurate scrutiny and examination. For the effect is totally different from the cause, and consequently can never be discovered in it. Motion in the second billiard-ball is a quite distinct event from motion in the first; nor is there anything in the one to suggest the smallest hint of the other. A stone or piece of metal raised into the air, and left without any support, immediately falls: but to consider the matter *a priori*, is there anything we discover in this situation which can beget the idea of a downward, rather than an upward, or any other motion, in the stone or metal?

And as the first imagination or invention of a particular effect, in all natural operations, is arbitrary, where we consult not experience; so must we also esteem the supposed tie or connection between the cause and effect, which binds them together, and renders it impossible that any other effect could result from the operation of that cause. When I see, for instance, a billiard-ball moving in a straight line towards another; even suppose motion in the second ball should be accident be suggested to me, as the result of their contact or impulse; may I not conceive, that a hundred different events might as well follow from that cause? May not both these balls remain at absolute rest? May not the first ball return in a straight line, or leap off from the second in any line or direction? All these suppositions are consistent and conceivable. Why then should we give the preference to one, which is no more consistent or conceivable than the rest? All our reasonings *a priori* will never be able to show us any foundation for this preference.

In a word, then, every effect is a distinct event from its cause. It could not, therefore, be discovered in the cause, and the first invention or conception of it, *a priori*, must be entirely arbitrary. And even after it is suggested, the conjunction of it with the cause must appear equally arbitrary; since there are always many other effects, which, to reason, must seem fully as consistent and natural. In vain, therefore, should we pretend to determine any single event, or infer any cause or effect, without the existence of observation and experience.

Hence we may discover the reason why no philosopher, who is rational and modest, has ever pretended to assign the ultimate cause of any natural operation, or to show distinctly the action of that power, which produces any single effect in the universe. It is confessed, that the utmost effort of human reason is to reduce the principles, productive of natural phenomena, to a greater simplicity, and to resolve the many particular effects into a few general causes, by means of reasonings from analogy, experience, and observation. But as to the causes of these general causes, we should in vain attempt their discovery; nor shall we ever be able to satisfy ourselves, by any particular explication of them. These ultimate springs and principles are totally shut up from human curiosity and enquiry. Elasticity, gravity, cohesion of parts, communication of motion by impulse; these are probably the ultimate causes and principles which we shall ever discover in nature; and we may esteem ourselves sufficiently happy, if, by accurate enquiry and reasoning, we can trace up the particular phenomena to, or near to, these general principles. The most perfect philosophy of the natural kind only staves off our ignorance a little longer: as perhaps the most perfect philosophy of the moral or metaphysical kind serves only to discover larger portions of it. Thus the observation of human blindness and weakness is the result of all philosophy, and meets us at every turn, in spite of our endeavours to elude or avoid it.

Nor is geometry, when taken into the assistance of natural philosophy, ever able to remedy this defect, or lead us into the knowledge of ultimate causes, by all that accuracy of reasoning for which it is so justly celebrated. Every part of mixed mathematics proceeds upon the supposition that certain laws are established by nature in her operations; and abstract reasonings are employed, either to assist experience in the discovery of these laws, or to determine their influence in particular instances, where it depends upon any precise degree of distance and quantity. Thus, it is a law of motion, discovered by experience, that the moment or force of any body in motion is in the compound ratio or proportion of its solid contents and its velocity; and consequently, that a small force may remove the greatest obstacle or raise the greatest weight, if, by any contrivance or machinery, we can increase the velocity of that force, so as to make it an overmatch for its antagonist. Geometry assists us in the application of this law, by giving us the just dimensions of all the parts and figures which can enter into any species of machine; but still the discovery of the law itself is owing merely to experience, and all the abstract reasonings in the world could never lead us one step towards the knowledge of it. When we reason *a priori*, and consider merely any object or cause, as it appears to the mind, independent of all observation, it never could suggest to us the notion of any distinct object, such as its effect; much less, show us the inseparable and inviolable connection between them. A man must be very sagacious who could discover by reasoning that crystal is the effect of heat, and ice of cold, without being previously acquainted with the operation of these qualities.

SECTION VII

OF THE IDEA OF NECESSARY CONNECTION

To be fully acquainted with the idea of power or necessary connection, let us examine its impression; and in order to find the impression with greater certainty, let us search for it in all the sources, from which it may possibly be derived.

When we look about us towards external objects, and consider the operation of causes, we are never able, in a single instance, to discover any power or necessary connection; any quality, which binds the effect to the cause, and renders the one an infallible consequence of the other. We only find, that the one does actually. in fact, follow the other. The impulse of one billiard-ball is attended with motion in the second. This is the whole that appears to the *outward* senses. The mind feels no sentiment or *inward* impression from this succession of objects: Consequently, there is not, in any single, particular instance of cause and effect, any thing which can suggest the idea of power or necessary connection.

From the first appearance of an object, we never can conjecture what effect will result from it. But were the power or energy of any cause discoverable by the mind, we could foresee the effect, even without experience; and might, at first, pronounce with certainty concerning it, by mere dint of thought and reasoning.

In reality, there is no part of matter, that does ever, by its sensible qualities, discover any power or energy, or give us ground to imagine, that it could produce any thing, or be followed by any other object, which we could denominate its effect. Solidity, extension, motion; these qualities are all complete in themselves, and never point out any other event which may result from them. The scenes of the universe are continually shifting, and one object follows another in an uninterrupted succession; but the power of force, which actuates the whole machine, is entirely concealed from us, and never discovers itself in any of the sensible qualities of body. We know, that, in fact, heat is a ·constant attendant of flame; but what is the connection between them, we have no room so much as to conjecture or imagine. It is impossible, therefore, that the idea of power can be derived from the contemplation of bodies, in single instances of their operation; because no bodies ever discover any power, which can be the original of this idea.[1]

Since, therefore, external objects as they appear to the senses, give us no idea of power or necessary connection, by their operation in particular instances, let us see, whether this idea be derived from reflection on the operations of our own minds, and be copied from any internal impression. It may be said, that we are every moment conscious of internal power; while we feel, that, by the simple command of our will, we can move the organs of our body, or direct the faculties of our mind. An act of volition produces motion in our limbs, or raises a new idea in our imagination. This influence of the will we know by consciousness. Hence we acquire the idea of power or energy; and are certain, that we ourselves and all other intelligent beings are possessed of power. This idea, then, is an idea of reflection, since it arises from reflecting on the operations of our own mind, and on the command which is exercised by will, both over the organs of the body and faculties of the soul.

We shall proceed to examine this pretension; and first with regard to the influence of volition over the organs of the body. This influence, we may observe, is a fact, which, like all other natural events, can be known only by experience, and can never be foreseen from any apparent energy or power in the cause, which connects it with the effect, and renders the one an infallible consequence of the other. The motion of our body follows upon the command of our will. Of this we are every moment conscious. But the means, by which this is effected; the energy, by which the will performs so extraordinary an operation; of this we are so far from being immediately conscious, that it must for ever escape our most diligent enquiry.

For *first*; is there any principle in all nature more mysterious than the union of soul with body; by which a supposed spiritual substance acquires such an influence over a material one, that the most refined thought is able to actuate the grossest matter? Were we empowered, by a secret wish, to remove mountains, or control the planets in their orbit; this extensive authority would not be more extraordinary, nor more beyond our comprehension. But

---

[1] Mr. Locke, in his chapter of power, says that, finding from experience, that there are several new productions in matter, and concluding that there must somewhere be a power capable of producing them, we arrive at last by this reasoning at the idea of power. But no reasoning can ever give us a new, original, simple idea; as this philosopher himself confesses. This, therefore, can never be the origin of that idea.

if by consciousness we perceived any power or energy in the will, we must know this power; we must know its connection with the effect; we must know the secret union of soul and body, and the nature of both these substances; by which the one is able to operate, in so many instances, upon the other.

Secondly, We are not able to move all the organs of the body with a like authority; though we cannot assign any reason besides experience, for so remarkable a difference between one and the other. Why has the will an influence over the tongue and fingers, not over the heart or liver? This question would never embarrass us, were we conscious of a power in the former case, not in the latter. We should then perceive, independent of experience, why the authority of will over the organs of the body is circumscribed within such particular limits. Being in that case fully acquainted with the power or force, by which it operates, we should also know, why its influence reaches precisely to such boundaries, and no farther.

A man, suddenly struck with palsy in the leg or arm, or who had newly lost those members, frequently endeavours at first to move them, and employ them in their usual offices. Here he is as much conscious of power to command such limbs, as a man in perfect health is conscious of power to actuate any member which remains in its natural state and condition. But consciousness never deceives. Consequently, neither in the one case nor in the other, are we ever conscious of any power. We learn the influence of our will from experience alone. And experience only teaches us, how one event constantly follows another; without instructing us in the secret connection, which binds them together, and renders them inseparable.

Thirdly, We learn from anatomy, that the immediate object of power in voluntary motion, is not the member itself which is moved, but certain muscles, and nerves, and animal spirits, and, perhaps, something still more minute and more unknown, through which the motion is successively propagated, ere it reach the member itself whose motion is the immediate object of volition. Can there be a more certain proof, that the power, by which this whole operation is performed, so far from being directly and fully known by an inward sentiment or consciousness, is, to the last degree, mysterious and unintelligible? Here the mind wills a certain event: immediately another event, unknown to ourselves, and totally different from the one intended, is produced: this event produces another, equally unknown: till at last, through a long succession, the desired event is produced. But if the original power were felt, it must be known: were it known, its effect must also be known; since all power is relative to its effect. And *vice versa*, if the effect be not known, the power cannot be known nor felt. How indeed can we be conscious of a power to move our limbs, when we have no such power; but only that to move certain animal spirits, which, though they produce at last the motion of our limbs, yet operate in such a manner as is wholly beyond our comprehension?

We may, therefore, conclude from the whole, I hope, without any temerity, though with assurance; that our idea of power is not copied from any sentiment or consciousness of power within ourselves, when we give rise to animal motion, or apply our limbs to their proper use and office. That their motion follows the command of the will is a matter of common experience, like other natural events: but the power or energy by which this is effected, like that in other natural events, is unknown and inconceivable.

Shall we then assert, that we are conscious of a power or energy in our own minds, when, by an act or command of our will, we raise up a new idea, fix the mind to the contemplation of it, turn it on all sides, and at last dismiss it for some other idea, when we think that we have surveyed it with sufficient accuracy? I believe the same arguments will prove, that even this command of the will gives us no real idea of force or energy.

First, It must be allowed, that, when we know a power, we know that very circumstance in the cause, by which it is enabled to produce the effect: for these are supposed to be synonimous. We must, therefore, know both the cause and effect, and the relation between them. But do we pretend to be acquainted with the nature of the human soul and the nature of an idea, or the aptitude of the one to produce the other? This is a real creation; a production of

---

¹ It may be pretended, that the resistance which we meet with in bodies, obliging us frequently to exert our force, and call up all our power, this gives us the idea of force and power. It is this *nisus*, or strong endeavour, of which this idea is copied. But, first, we attribute power to a vast number of objects, where we never can suppose this resistance or exertion of force to take place; to the Supreme Being, who never meets with any resistance; to the mind in its command over its ideas and limbs, in common thinking and motion, where the effect follows immediately upon the will, without any exertion or summoning up of force; to inanimate matter, which is not capable of this sentiment. *Secondly,* This sentiment of an endeavour to overcome resistance has no known connection with any event: What follows it we know by experience; but could not know it *a priori*. It must, however, be confessed, that the animal *nisus*, which we experience, though it can afford no accurate precise idea of power, enters very much into that vulgar, inaccurate idea, which is formed of it.

something out of nothing: which implies a power so great, that it may seem, at first sight, beyond the reach of any being, less than infinite. At least it must be owned, that such a power is not felt, nor known, nor even conceivable by the mind. We only feel the event, namely, the existence of an idea, consequent to a command of the will: but the manner in which this operation is performed, the power by which it is produced, is entirely beyond our comprehension.

Secondly, The command of the mind over itself is limited, as well as its command over the body; and these limbs are not known by reason, or any acquaintance with the nature of cause and effect, but only by experience and observation, as in all other natural events and in the operation of external objects. Our authority over our sentiments and passions is much weaker than that over our ideas; and even the latter authority is circumscribed within very narrow boundaries. Will any one pretend to assign the ultimate reason of these boundaries, or show why the power is deficient in one case, not in another.

Thirdly, This self-command is very different at different times. A man in health possesses more of it than one languishing with sickness. We are more master of our thoughts in the morning than in the evening: fasting, than after a full meal. Can we give any reason for these variations, except experience? Where then is the power, of which we pretend to be conscious? Is there not here, either in a spiritual or material substance, or both, some secret mechanism or structure of parts, upon which the effect depends, and which, being entirely unknown to us, renders the power or energy of the will equally unknown and incomprehensible?

Volition is surely an act of the mind, with which we are sufficiently acquainted. Reflect upon it. Consider it on all sides. Do you find anything in it like this creative power, by which it raises from nothing a new idea, and with a kind of *Fiat*, imitates the omnipotence of its Maker, if I may be allowed so to speak, who called forth into existence all the various scenes of nature? So far from being conscious of this energy in the will, it requires as certain experience as that of which we are possessed, to convince us that such extraordinary effects do ever result from a simple act of volition.

SECTION XII

OF THE ACADEMICAL OR SCEPTICAL PHILOSOPHY

IT seems to me, that the only objects of the abstract science or of demonstration are quantity and number, and that all attempts to extend this more perfect species of knowledge beyond these bounds are mere sophistry and illusion. As the component parts of quantity and number are entirely similar, their relations become intricate and involved; and nothing can be more curious, as well as useful, than to trace, by a variety of mediums, their equality or inequality, through their different appearances. But as all other ideas are clearly distinct and different from each other, we can never advance farther, by our utmost scrutiny, than to observe this diversity, and, by an obvious reflection, pronounce one thing not to be another. Or if there be any difficulty in these decisions, it proceeds entirely from the undeterminate meaning of words, which is corrected by juster definitions. That *the square of the hypothenuse is equal to the squares of the other two sides,* cannot be known, let the terms be ever so exactly defined, without a train of reasoning and enquiry. But to convince us of this proposition, *that where there is no property, there can be no injustice,* it is only necessary to define the terms, and explain injustice to be a violation of property. This proposition is, indeed, nothing but a more imperfect definition. It is the same case with all those pretended syllogistical reasonings, which may be found in every branch of learning, except the sciences of quantity and number; and these may safely, I think, be pronounced the only proper objects of knowledge and demonstration.

All other enquiries of men regard only matter of fact and existence; and these are evidently incapable of demonstration. Whatever *is* may *not be.* No negation of a fact can involve a contradiction. The non-existence of any being, without exception, is as clear and distinct an idea as its existence. The proposition, which affirms it not to be, however false, is no less conceivable and intelligible, than that which affirms it to be. The case is different with the sciences, properly so called. Every proposition, which is not true, is there confused and unintelligible. That the cube root of 64 is equal to the half of 10, is a false proposition, and can never be distinctly conceived. But that the Cæsar, or the angel Gabriel, or any being never existed, may be a false proposition, but still is perfectly conceivable, and implies no contradiction.

The existence, therefore, of any being can only be proved by arguments from its cause or its effect; and these arguments are founded entirely on experience. If we reason *a priori*, anything may appear able to produce anything. The falling of a pebble may, for aught we know, extinguish the sun; or the wish of a man control the planets in their orbits. It is only experience, which teaches us the nature and bounds of cause and effect, and enables us to infer the existence of one object from that of another.[1] Such is the foundation of moral reasoning, which forms the greater part of human knowledge, and is the source of all human action and behaviour.

Moral reasonings are either concerning particular or general facts. All deliberations in life regard the former; as also all disquisitions in history, chronology, geography, and astronomy.

The sciences, which treat of general facts, are politics, natural philosophy, physic, chemistry, etc., where the qualities, causes and effects of a whole species of objects are enquired into.

Divinity or Theology, as it proves the existence of a Deity, and the immortality of souls, is composed partly of reasonings concerning particular, partly concerning general facts. It has a foundation in *reason*, so far as it is supported by experience. But its best and most solid foundation is *faith* and divine revelation.

Morals and criticism are not so properly objects of the understanding as of taste and sentiment. Beauty, whether moral or natural, is felt, more properly than perceived. Or if we reason concerning it, and endeavour to fix its standard, we regard a new fact, to wit, the general tastes of mankind, or some such fact, which may be the object of reasoning and enquiry.

When we run over libraries, persuaded of these principles, what havoc must we make? If we take in our hand any volume; of divinity or school metaphysics, for instance; let us ask, *Does it contain any abstract reasoning concerning quantity or number?* No. *Does it contain any experimental reasoning concerning matter of fact and existence?* No. Commit it then to the flames: for it can contain nothing but sophistry and illusion.

[1] That impious maxim of the ancient philosophy, *Ex nihilo, nihil fit,* by which the creation of matter was excluded, ceases to be a maxim, according to this philosophy. Not only the will of the supreme Being may create matter; but, for aught we know *a priori*, the will of any other being might create it, or any other cause, that the most whimsical imagination can assign.

THOMAS REID

Born in Kincardineshire in 1710. Studied philosophy and divinity and took holy orders. Presented to a living near Aberdeen in 1737. Lecturer at King's College, Aberdeen, 1751. Succeeded Adam Smith as Professor of Moral Philosophy at the University of Glasgow, 1764. Died in 1792.

Philosophical works include Inquiry into the Human Mind, 1764, Essay on the Intellectual Powers of Man, 1785, *and* Essay on the Active Powers of Man, 1788.

THE PASSAGES which follow are excerpts from three chapters of the *Essay on the Intellectual Powers of Man*. They have been chosen not so much to illustrate Reid's own philosophical views as for the bearing that they have on certain doctrines of Locke, Berkeley and Hume.

ON THE
INTELLECTUAL POWERS OF MAN

ESSAY II

XIV—Reflections on the Common Theory of Ideas. XVI—
Of Sensation. XVII—Of the Objects of Perception; and
First, of Primary and Secondary Qualities

CHAPTER XIV

REFLECTIONS ON THE COMMON THEORY OF IDEAS

AFTER so long a detail of the sentiments of philosophers, ancient and modern, concerning ideas, it may seem presumptuous to call in question their existence. But no philosophical opinion, however ancient, however generally received, ought to rest upon authority. There is no presumption in requiring evidence for it, or in regulating our belief by the evidence we can find.

To prevent mistakes, the reader must again be reminded, that if by ideas are meant only the acts or operations of our minds in perceiving, remembering, or imagining objects, I am far from calling in question the existence of those acts; we are conscious of them every day and every hour of life; and I believe no man of a sound mind ever doubted of the real existence of the operations of mind, of which he is conscious. Nor is it to be doubted that, by the faculties which God has given us, we can conceive things that are absent, as well as perceive those that are within the reach of our senses; and that such conceptions may be more or less distinct, and more or less lively and strong. We have reason to ascribe to the all-knowing and all-perfect Being distinct conceptions of all things existent and possible, and of all their relations; and if these conceptions are called his eternal ideas, there ought to be no dispute among philosophers about a word.

The ideas, of whose existence I require the proof, are not the operations of any mind, but supposed objects of those operations.

They are not perception, remembrance, or conception, but things that are said to be perceived, or remembered, or imagined.

Nor do I dispute the existence of what the vulgar call the objects of perception. These, by all who acknowledge their existence, are called real things, not ideas. But philosophers maintain that, besides these, there are immediate objects of perception in the mind itself; that, for instance, we do not see the sun immediately, but an idea; or, as Mr. Hume calls it, an impression in our own minds. This idea is said to be the image, the resemblance, the representative of the sun, if there be a sun. It is from the existence of the idea that we must infer the existence of the sun. But the idea, being immediately perceived, there can be no doubt, as philosophers think, of its existence.

In like manner, when I remember, or when I imagine anything, all men acknowledge that there must be something that is remembered, or that is imagined; that is, some object of those operations. The object remembered must be something that did exist in time past; the object imagined may be something that never existed. But, say the philosophers, besides these objects which all men acknowledge, there is a more immediate object which really exists in the mind at the same time we remember or imagine. This object is an idea or image of thing remembered or imagined.

The *first* reflection I would make on this philosophical opinion is, that it is directly contrary to the universal sense of men who have not been instructed in philosophy. When we see the sun or moon, we have no doubt that the very objects which we immediately see are very far distant from us, and from one another. We have not the least doubt that this is the sun and moon which God created some thousands of years ago, and which have continued to perform their revolutions in the heavens ever since. But how are we astonished when the philosopher informs us that we are mistaken in all this; that the sun and moon which we see are not, as we imagine, many miles distant from us, and from each other, but that they are in our own mind; that they had no existence before we saw them, and will have none when we cease to perceive and to think of them; because the objects we perceive are only ideas in our own minds, which can have no existence a moment longer than we think of them!

If a plain man, uninstructed in philosophy, has faith to receive these mysteries, how great must be his astonishment! He is brought into a new world, where everything he sees, tastes, or touches, is an idea—a fleeting kind of being which he can conjure into existence, or can annihilate in the twinkling of an eye.

After his mind is somewhat composed, it will be natural for him to ask his philosophical instructor, Pray, sir, are there then no substantial and permanent beings called the sun and moon, which continue to exist whether we think of them or not?

Here the philosophers differ. Mr. Locke, and those that were before him, will answer to this question, that it is very true there are substantial and permanent beings called the sun and moon; but they never appear to us in their own person, but by their representatives, the ideas in our own minds, and we know nothing of them but what we can gather from those ideas.

Bishop Berkeley and Mr. Hume would give a different answer to the question proposed. They would assure the querist that it is a vulgar error, a mere prejudice of the ignorant and unlearned, to think that there are any permanent and substantial beings called the sun and moon; that the heavenly bodies, our own bodies, and all bodies whatsoever, are nothing but ideas in our minds; and that there can be nothing like the ideas of one mind, but the ideas of another mind.

There is nothing in nature but minds and ideas, says the Bishop; nay, says Mr. Hume, there is nothing in nature but ideas only; for what we call a mind is nothing but a train of ideas connected by certain relations between themselves.

In this representation of the theory of ideas, there is nothing exaggerated or misrepresented, as far as I am able to judge; and surely nothing farther is necessary to show that, to the uninstructed in philosophy, it must appear extravagant and visionary, and most contrary to the dictates of common understanding.

There is the less need of any farther proof of this, that it is very amply acknowledged by Mr. Hume in his Essay on the Academical or Sceptical Philosophy. "It seems evident," says he, "that men are carried, by a natural instinct or prepossession, to repose faith in their senses; and that, without any reasoning, or even almost before the use of reason, we always suppose an external universe, which depends not on our perception, but would exist though we and every sensible creature were absent or annihilated. Even the animal creation are governed by a like opinion, and preserve this belief of external objects in all their thoughts, designs, and actions."

"It seems also evident that, when men follow this blind and powerful instinct of nature, they always suppose the very images presented by the senses to be the external objects, and never entertain any suspicion that the one are nothing but representations of the other. This very table which we see white, and feel hard, is believed to exist independent of our perception, and to be something external to the mind which perceives it; our presence bestows not being upon it; our absence annihilates it not; it preserves its existence uniform and entire, independent of the situation of intelligent beings who perceive or contemplate it.

" But this universal and primary notion of all men is soon destroyed by the slightest philosophy, which teaches us that nothing can ever be present to the mind, but an image or perception; and that the senses are only the inlets through which these images are received, without being ever able to produce any immediate intercourse between the mind and the object.''

It is therefore acknowledged by this philosopher, to be a natural instinct or prepossession, an universal and primary opinion of all men, a primary instinct of nature, that the objects which we immediately perceive by our senses, are not images in our minds, but external objects, and that their existence is independent of us and our perception.

In this acknowledgment, Mr. Hume indeed seems to me more generous, and even more ingenuous than Bishop Berkeley, who would persuade us that his opinion does not oppose the vulgar opinion, but only that of the philosophers; and that the external existence of a material world is a philosophical hypothesis, and not the natural dictate of our perceptive powers. The Bishop shows a timidity of engaging such an adversary, as a primary and universal opinion of all men. He is rather fond to court its patronage. But the philosopher intrepidly gives a defiance to this antagonist, and seems to glory in a conflict that was worthy of his arm. *Optat aprum aut fulvum descendere monte leonem.* After all, I suspect that a philosopher who wages war with this adversary, will find himself in the same condition as a mathematician who should undertake to demonstrate that there is no truth in the axioms of mathematics.

A *second* reflection upon this subject is—that the authors who have treated of ideas, have generally taken existence for granted, as a thing that could not be called in question; and such arguments as they have mentioned incidentally, in order to prove it, seem too weak to support the conclusion.

Mr. Locke, in the introduction to his Essay, tells us, that he uses the word idea to signify whatever is the immediate object of thought; and then adds, '' I presume it will be easily granted me that there are such ideas in men's minds; every one is conscious of them in himself; and men's words and actions will satisfy him that they are in others." I am indeed conscious of perceiving, remembering, imagining; but that the objects of these operations are images in my mind, I am not conscious. I am satisfied by men's words and actions, that they often perceive the same objects which I perceive, which could not be, if those objects were ideas in their own minds.

There is an argument which is hinted at by several authors, which deserves to be more seriously considered. As I find it most clearly expressed and most fully urged by Dr. Samuel Clarke, I shall give it in his words, in his second reply to Leibnitz, "The soul, without being present to the images of the things perceived, could not possibly perceive them. A living substance can only there perceive, where it is present, either to the things themselves (as the omni-present God is to the whole universe) or to the images of things, as the soul is in its proper *sensorium*."

That nothing can act immediately where it is not, I think must be admitted; for I agree with Sir Isaac Newton, that power without substance is inconceivable. It is a consequence of this, that nothing can be acted upon immediately where the agent is not present; let this, therefore, be granted. To make the reasoning conclusive, it is farther necessary, that, when we perceive objects, either they act upon us, or we act upon them. This does not appear self-evident, nor have I ever met with any proof of it. I shall briefly offer the reasons why I think it ought not to be admitted.

When we say that one being acts upon another, we mean that some power or force is exerted by the agent, which produces, or has a tendency to produce, a change in the thing acted upon. If this be the meaning of the phrase, as I conceive it is, there appears no reason for asserting that, in perception, either the object acts upon the mind, or the mind upon the object.

An object, in being perceived, does not act at all. I perceive the walls of the room where I sit; but they are perfectly inactive, and therefore act not upon the mind. To be perceived, is what logicians call an external denomination, which implies neither action nor quality in the object perceived. Nor could men ever have gone into this notion, that perception is owing to some action of the object upon the mind, were it not that we are so prone to form our notions of the mind from some similitude we conceive between it and body. Thought in the mind is conceived to have some analogy to motion in a body; and, as a body is put in motion, by being acted upon by some other body; so we are apt to think the mind is made to perceive, by some impulse it receives from the object. But reasonings, drawn from such analogies, ought never to be trusted. They are, indeed, the cause of most of our errors with regard to the mind. And we might as well conclude, that minds may be measured by feet and inches, or weighed by ounces and drachms, because bodies have those properties.

I see as little reason, in the second place, to believe that in perception the mind acts upon the object. To perceive an object is one thing, to act upon it is another; nor is the last at all included in the first. To say that I act upon the wall by looking at it, is an abuse of language, and has no meaning. Logicians distinguish two kinds of operations of mind: the first kind produces no effect without the mind; the last does. The first they call *immanent acts*, the second *transitive*. All intellectual operations belong to the first class; they produce no effect upon any external object. But, without having recourse to logical distinctions, every man of common sense knows, that to think of an object, and to act upon it, are very different things.

As we have, therefore, no evidence that, in perception, the minds acts upon the object, or the object upon the mind, but strong reasons to the contrary, Dr. Clarke's argument against our perceiving external objects immediately falls to the ground.

There remains only one other argument that I have been able to find urged against our perceiving external objects immediately. It is proposed by Mr. Hume, who, in the essay already quoted, after acknowledging that it is an universal and primary opinion of all men, that we perceive external objects immediately, subjoins what follows: —

" But this universal and primary opinion of all men is soon destroyed by the slightest philosophy, which teaches us that nothing can ever be present to the mind but an image or perception; and that the senses are only the inlets through which these images are received, without being ever able to produce any immediate intercourse between the mind and the object. The table, which we see, seems to diminish as we remove farther from it; but the real table, which exists independent of us, suffers no alteration. It was, therefore, nothing but its image which was present to the mind. These are the obvious dictates of reason; and no man who reflects ever doubted that the existences which we consider, when we say *this house* and *that tree*, are nothing but perceptions in the mind, and fleeting copies and representations of other existences, which remain uniform and independent. So far, then, we are necessitated, by reasoning, to depart from the primary instincts of nature, and to embrace a new system with regard to the evidence of our senses." We have here a remarkable conflict between two contradictory opinions, wherein all mankind are engaged. On the one side stand all the vulgar, who are unpractised in philosophical researches, and guided by the uncorrupted primary instincts of nature. On the other side stand all the philosophers, ancient and modern; every man, without exception, who reflects. In this division, to my great humiliation, I find myself classed with the vulgar.

The passage now quoted is all I have found in Mr. Hume's writings upon this point; and, indeed, there is more reasoning in it than I have found in any other author; I shall, therefore, examine it minutely.

First, he tells us that " this universal and primary opinion of all men is soon destroyed by the slightest philosophy, which teaches us that nothing can ever be present to the mind but an image or perception."

The phrase of being present to the mind has some obscurity; but I conceive he means being an immediate object of thought; and immediate object, for instance, of perception, of memory, or of imagination. If this be the meaning (and it is the only pertinent one I can think of) there is no more in this passage but an assertion of the proposition to be proved, and an assertion that philosophy teaches it. If this be so, I beg leave to dissent from philosophy till she gives me reason for what she teaches.

He tells us, in the next place, " That the senses are only the inlets through which these images are received."

I know that Aristotle and the schoolmen taught that images or species flow from objects, and are let in by the senses, and strike upon the mind; but this has been so effectually refuted by Des Cartes, by Malebranche, and many others, that nobody now pretends to defend it. Reasonable men consider it as one of the most unintelligible and unmeaning parts of the ancient system. To what cause is it owing that modern philosophers are so prone to fall back into this hypothesis, as if they really believed it? For, of this proneness I could give many instances besides this of Mr. Hume; and I take the cause to be, that images in the mind, and images let in by the senses, are so nearly allied, and so strictly connected, that they must stand or fall together. The old system consistently maintained both: but the new system has rejected the doctrine of images let in by the senses, holding, nevertheless, that there are images in the mind; and, having made this unnatural divorce of two doctrines which ought not to be put asunder, that which they have retained often leads them back involuntarily to that which they have rejected.

Mr. Hume surely did not seriously believe that an image of sound is let in by the ear, an image of smell by the nose, an image of hardness and softness, of solidity and resistance, by the touch. For, besides the absurdity of the thing, which has often been shown, Mr. Hume, and all modern philosophers, maintain that the images which are the immediate objects of perception have no existence when they are not perceived; whereas, if they were let in by the senses, they must be, before they are perceived, and have a separate existence.

He tells us, farther, that philosophy teaches that the senses are unable to produce any immediate intercourse between the mind and the object. Here, I still require the reasons that philosophy gives for this; for, to my apprehension, I immediately perceive external objects, and this, I conceive, is the immediate intercourse here meant.

Hitherto I see nothing that can be called an argument. Perhaps it was intended only for illustration. The argument, the only argument, follows:—

The table which we see, seems to diminish as we remove farther from it; but the real table, which exists independent of it, suffers no alteration. It was, therefore, nothing but its image which was presented to the mind. These are obvious dictates of reason.

To judge of the strength of this argument, it is necessary to attend to a distinction which is familiar to those who are conversant in the mathematical sciences—I mean the distinction between real and apparent magnitude. The real magnitude of a line is measured by some known measure of length—as inches, feet, or miles; the real magnitude of a surface or solid, by known measures of surface or of capacity. This magnitude is an object of touch only, and not of sight; nor could we even have had any conception of it, without the sense of touch; and Bishop Berkeley, on that account, calls it *tangible magnitude*.

Apparent magnitude is measured by the angle which an object subtends at the eye. Supposing two right lines drawn from the eye to the extremities of the object making an angle, of which the object is the subtense, the apparent magnitude is measured by this angle. This apparent magnitude is an object of sight, and not of touch. Bishop Berkeley calls it *visible magnitude*.

If it is asked what is the apparent magnitude of the sun's diameter, the answer is, that it is about thirty-one minutes of a degree. But, if it is asked what is the real magnitude of the sun's diameter, the answer must be, so many thousand miles, or so many diameters of the earth. From which it is evident that the real magnitude, and apparent magnitude, are things of a different nature, though the name of magnitude is given to both. The first has three dimensions, the last only two; the first is measured by a line, the last by an angle.

From what has been said, it is evident that the real magnitude of a body must continue unchanged, while the body is unchanged. This we grant. But is it likewise evident, that the apparent magnitude must continue the same while the body is unchanged? So far otherwise, that every man who knows anything of mathematics can easily demonstrate, that the same individual object, remaining in the same place, and unchanged, must necessarily vary in its apparent magnitude, according as the point from which it is seen is more or less distant; and that its apparent length or breadth will be nearly in a reciprocal proportion to the distance of the spectator. This is as certain as the principles of geometry.

We must likewise attend to this—that, though the real magnitude of a body is not originally an object of sight, but of touch, yet we learn by experience to judge of the real magnitude in many cases by sight. We learn by experience to judge of the distance of a body from the eye within certain limits; and, from its distance and apparent magnitude taken together, we learn to judge of its real magnitude.

And this kind of judgment, by being repeated every hour and almost every minute of our lives, becomes, when we are grown up, so ready and so habitual, that it very much resembles the original perceptions of our senses, and may not improperly be called *acquired perception*.

Whether we call it judgment or acquired perception is a verbal difference. But it is evident that, by means of it, we often discover by one sense things which are properly and naturally the objects of another. Thus I can say, without impropriety, I hear a drum, I hear a great bell, or I hear a small bell; though it is certain that the figure or size of the sounding body is not originally an object of hearing. In like manner, we learn by experience how a body of such a real magnitude and at such a distance appears to the eye. But neither its real magnitude, nor its distance from the eye are properly objects of sight, any more than the form of a drum or the size of a bell, are properly objects of hearing.

If these things be considered, it will appear that Mr. Hume's argument hath no force to support his conclusion—nay, that it leads to a contrary conclusion. The argument is this: the table we see seems to diminish as we remove farther from it; that is, its apparent magnitude is diminished; but the real table suffers no alteration—to wit, in its real magnitude; therefore, it is not the real table we see. I admit both the premises in this syllogism, but I deny the conclusion. The syllogism has what the logicians call two middle terms; apparent magnitude is the middle term in the first premise; real magnitude in the second. Therefore, according to the rules of logic, the conclusion is not justly drawn from the premises; but, laying aside the rules of logic, let us examine it by the light of common sense.

Let us, suppose, for a moment, that it is the real table we see: must not this real table seem to diminish as we remove farther from it? It is demonstrable that it must. How then can this apparent diminution be an argument that it is not the real table? When that which must happen to the real table, as we remove farther from it, does actually happen to the table we see, it is absurd to conclude from this, that it is not the real table we see. It is evident, therefore, that this ingenious author has imposed upon himself by confounding real magnitude with apparent magnitude, and that his argument is a mere sophism.

I observed that Mr. Hume's argument not only has no strength to support his conclusion, but that it leads to the contrary conclusion—to wit, that it is the real table we see; for this plain reason, that the table we see has precisely that apparent magnitude which it is demonstrable the real table must have when placed at that distance.

This argument is made much stronger by considering that the real table may be placed successively at a thousand different distances, and, in every distance, in a thousand different positions; and it can be determined demonstratively, by the rules of geometry and perspective, what must be its apparent magnitude and apparent figure, in each of those distances and positions. Let the table be placed successively in as many of those different distances and different positions as you will, or in them all; open your eyes and you will see a table precisely of that apparent magnitude, and that apparent figure, which the real table must have in that distance and in that position. Is not this a strong argument that it is the real table you see?

In a word, the appearance of a visible object is infinitely diversified, according to its distance and position. The visible appearances are innumerable, when we confine ourselves to one object, and they are multiplied according to the variety of objects. Those appearances have been a matter of speculation of ingenious men, at least since the time of Euclid. They have accounted for all this variety, on the supposition that the objects we see are external, and not in the mind itself. The rules they have demonstrated about the various projections of the sphere, about the appearances of the planets in their progressions, stations, and retrogradations, and all the rules of perspective, are built on the supposition that the objects of sight are external. They can each of them be tried in thousands of instances. In many arts and professions, innumerable trials are daily made; nor were they ever found to fail in a single instance. Shall we say that a false supposition, invented by the rude vulgar, has been so lucky in solving an infinite number of phenomena of nature? This, surely, would be a greater prodigy than philosophy ever exhibited; add to this, that, upon the contrary hypothesis—to wit, that the objects of sight are internal—no account can be given of any one of those appearances, nor any physical cause assigned why a visible object should, in any one case, have one apparent figure and magnitude rather than another.

Thus, I have considered every argument I have found advanced to prove the existence of ideas, or images of external things, in the mind; and, if no better arguments can be found, I cannot help thinking that the whole history of philosophy has never furnished an instance of an opinion so unanimously entertained by philosophers upon so slight grounds.

A *third* reflection I would make upon this subject is, that philosophers, notwithstanding their unanimity as to the existence of ideas, hardly agree in any one thing else concerning them. If ideas be not a mere fiction, they must be, of all objects of human knowledge, the things we have best access to know, and to be acquainted with; yet there is nothing about which men differ so much.

Some have held them to be self-existent, others to be in the Divine mind, others in our own minds, and others in the brain or *sensorium*. I considered the hypothesis of images in the brain, in the fourth chapter of this essay. As to images in the mind, if anything more is meant by the image of an object in the mind than the thought of that object, I know not what it means. The distinct conception of an object may, in a metaphorical or analogical sense, be called an *image* of it in the mind. But this image is only the conception of the object, and not the object conceived. It is an act of the mind, and not the object of that act.

Some philosophers will have our ideas, or a part of them, to be innate; others will have them all to be adventitious; some derive them from the senses alone; others from sensation and reflection: some think they are fabricated by the mind itself; others that they are produced by external objects; others that they are the immediate operation of the Deity; others say, that impressions are the causes of ideas, and that the causes of impressions are unknown: some think that we have ideas only of material objects, but none of minds, of their operations, or of the relations of things; others will have the immediate object of every thought to be an idea: some think we have abstract ideas, and that by this chiefly we are distinguished from the brutes; others maintain an abstract idea to be an absurdity, and that there can be no such thing: with some they are the immediate objects of thought, with others the only objects.

A *fourth* reflection is, that ideas do not make any of the operations of the mind to be better understood, although it was probably with that view that they have been first invented, and afterwards so generally received.

We are at a loss to know how we perceive distant objects; how we remember things past; how we imagine things that have no existence. Ideas in the mind seem to account for all these operations: they are all by the means of ideas reduced to one operation —to a kind of feeling, or immediate perception of things present and in contact with the percipient; and feeling is an operation so familiar that we think it needs no explication, but may serve to explain other operations.

But this feeling, or immediate perception, is as difficult to be comprehended as the things which we pretend to explain by it. Two things may be in contact without any feeling or perception; there must therefore be in the percipient a power to feel or to perceive. How this power is produced, and how it operates, is quite beyond the reach of our knowledge. As little can we know whether this power must be limited to things present, and in contact with us. Nor can any man pretend to prove that the Being who gave us the power to perceive things present, may not give us the power to perceive things that are distant, to remember things past, and to conceive things that never existed.

CHAPTER XVI

OF SENSATION

ALMOST all our perceptions have corresponding sensations which constantly accompany them, and, on that account, are very apt to be confounded with them. Neither ought we to expect that the sensation, and its corresponding perception, should be distinguished in common language, because the purposes of common life do not require it. Language is made to serve the purposes of ordinary conversation; and we have no reason to expect that it should make distinctions that are not of common use. Hence it happens, that a quality perceived, and the sensation corresponding to that perception, often go under the same name.

This makes the names of most of our sensations ambiguous, and this ambiguity hath very much perplexed philosophers. It will be necessary to give some instances, to illustrate the distinction between our sensations and the objects of perception.

When I smell a rose, there is in this operation both sensation and perception. The agreeable odour I feel, considered by itself, without relation to any external object, is merely a sensation. It affects the mind in a certain way; and this affection of the mind may be conceived, without a thought of the rose, or any other object. This sensation can be nothing else than it is felt to be. Its very essence consists in being felt; and, when it is not felt, it is not. There is no difference between the sensation and the feeling of it—they are one and the same thing. It is for this reason that we before observed that, in sensation, there is no object distinct from that act of the mind by which it is felt—and this holds true with regard to all sensations.

Let us next attend to the perception which we have in smelling a rose. Perception has always an external object; and the object of my perception, in this case, is that quality in the rose which I discern by the sense of smell. Observing that the agreeable sensation is raised when the rose is near, and ceases when it is removed, I am led, by my nature, to conclude some quality to be in the rose, which is the cause of this sensation. This quality in the rose is the object perceived; and that act of my mind by which I have the conviction and belief of this quality, is what in this case I call perception.

But it is here to be observed, that the sensation I feel, and the quality in the rose which I perceive, are both called by the same name. The smell of a rose is the name given to both; so that this name hath two meanings; and the distinguishing its different meanings removes all perplexity, and enables us to give clear and distinct answers to questions about which philosophers have held much dispute.

Thus, if it is asked, whether the smell be in the rose, or in the mind that feels it, the answer is obvious: that there are two different things signified by the smell of a rose; one of which is in the mind, and can be in nothing but in a sentient being; the other is truly and properly in the rose. The sensation which I feel is in my mind. The mind is the sentient being; and, as the rose is insentient, there can be no sensation, nor anything resembling sensation in it. But this sensation in my mind is occasioned by a certain quality in the rose, which is called by the same name with the sensation, not on account of any similitude, but because of their constant concomitancy.

All the names we have for smells, tastes, sounds, and for the various degrees of heat and cold, have a like ambiguity; and what has been said of the smell of a rose may be applied to them. They signify both a sensation, and a quality perceived by means of that sensation. The first is the sign, the last the thing signified. As both are conjoined by nature, and as the purposes of common life do not require them to be disjoined in our thoughts, they are both expressed by the same name; and this ambiguity is to be found in all languages, because the reason of it extends to all.

The same ambiguity is found in the names of such diseases as are indicated by a particular painful sensation; such as the toothache, the headache. The toothache signifies a painful sensation, which can only be in a sentient being; but it signifies also a disorder in the body, which has no similitude to a sensation, but is naturally connected with it.

Pressing my hand with force against the table, I feel pain, and I feel the table to be hard. The pain is a sensation of the mind, and there is nothing that resembles it in the table. The hardness is in the table, nor is there anything resembling it in the mind. Feeling is applied to both; but in a different sense; being a word common to the act of sensation, and to that of perceiving by the sense of touch.

I touch the table gently with my hand, and I feel it to be smooth, hard, and cold. These are qualities of the table perceived by touch;

but I perceive them by means of a sensation which indicates them. This sensation not being painful, I commonly give no attention to it. It carries my thought immediately to the thing signified by it, and is itself forgot, as if it had never been. But, by repeating it, and turning my attention to it, and abstracting my thought from the thing signified by it, I find it to be merely a sensation, and that it has no similitude to the hardness, smoothness, or coldness of the table, which are signified by it.

It is indeed difficult, at first, to disjoin things in our attention which have always been conjoined, and to make that an object of reflection which never was so before; but some pains and practice will overcome this difficulty in those who have got the habit of reflecting on the operations of their own minds.

Although the present subject leads us only to consider the sensations which we have by means of our external senses, yet it will serve to illustrate what has been said, and, I apprehend, is of importance in itself, to observe, that many operations of mind, to which we give one name, and which we always consider as one thing, are complex in their nature, and made up of several more simple ingredients; and of these ingredients sensation very often makes one. Of this we shall give some instances.

The appetite of hunger includes an uneasy sensation, and a desire of food. Sensation and desire are different acts of mind. The last. from its nature, must have an object; the first has no object. These two ingredients may always be separated in thought—perhaps they sometimes are, in reality; but hunger includes both.

Benevolence towards our fellow-creatures includes an agreeable feeling; but it includes also a desire of the happiness of others. The ancients commonly called it desire. Many moderns choose rather to call it a feeling. Both are right : and they only err who exclude either of the ingredients. Whether these two ingredients are necessarily connected is, perhaps, difficult for us to determine, there being many necessary connections which we do not perceive to be necessary; but we can disjoin them in thought. They are different acts of the mind.

If we thus analyse the various operations of our minds, we shall find that many of them which we consider as perfectly simple, because we have been accustomed to call them by one name, are compounded of more simple ingredients; and that sensation, or feeling, which is only a more refined kind of sensation, makes one ingredient, not only in the perception of external objects, but in most operations of the mind.

I shall conclude this chapter by observing that, as the confounding our sensations with that perception of external objects which is constantly conjoined with them, has been the occasion of most of the errors and false theories of philosophers with regard to the senses; so the distinguishing these operations seems to me to be the key that leads to a right understanding of both.

Sensation, taken by itself, implies neither the conception nor belief of any external object. It supposes a sensient being, and a certain manner in which that being is affected; but it supposes no more. Perception implies an immediate conviction and belief of something external—something different both from the mind that perceives, and from the act of perception. Things so different in their nature ought to be distinguished; but, in our constitution, they are always united. Every different perception is conjoined with a sensation that is proper to it. The one is the sign, the other the thing signified. They coalesce in our imagination. They are signified by one name, and are considered as one simple operation. The purposes of life do not require them to be distinguished.

It is the philosopher alone who has occasion to distinguish them, when he would analyse the operation compounded of them. But he has no suspicion that there is any composition in it; and to discover this requires a degree of reflection which has been too little practised even by philosophers.

In the old philosophy, sensation and perception were perfectly confounded. The sensible species coming from the object, and impressed upon the mind, was the whole; and you might call it sensation or perception as you pleased.

Des Cartes and Locke, attending more to the operations of their own minds, say, that the sensations by which we have notice of secondary qualities have no resemblance to anything that pertains to body; but they did not see that this might, with equal justice, be applied to the primary qualities. Mr. Locke maintains, that the sensations we have from primary qualities are resemblances of those qualities. This shows how grossly the most ingenious men may err with regard to the operations of their minds. It must, indeed, be acknowledged, that it is much easier to have a distinct notion of the sensations that belong to secondary than of those that belong the primary qualities. The reason of this will appear in the next chapter.

But, had Mr. Locke attended with sufficient accuracy to the sensations which he was every day and every hour receiving from primary qualities, he would have seen that they can as little resemble any quality of an inanimated being as pain can resemble a cube or a circle.

What had escaped this ingenious philosopher, was clearly discerned by Bishop Berkeley. He had a just notion of sensations, and saw that it was impossible that anything in an insentient being could resemble them; a thing so evident in itself, that it seems wonderful that it should have been so long unknown. But let us attend to the consequences of this discovery. Philosophers, as well as the vulgar, had been accustomed to comprehend both sensation and perception under one name, and to consider them as one uncompounded operation. Philosophers, even more than the vulgar, gave the name of sensation to the whole operation of the senses; and all the notions we have of material things were called ideas of sensation. This led Bishop Berkeley to take one ingredient of a complex operation for the whole; and, having clearly discovered the nature of sensation, taking for granted that all that the senses present to the mind is sensation, which can have no resemblance to anything material, he concluded that there is no material world.

If the senses furnished us with no materials of thought but sensations, his conclusion must be just; for no sensation can give us the conception of material things, far less any argument to prove their existence. But, if it is true that by our senses we have not only a variety of sensations, but likewise a conception and an immediate natural conviction of external objects, he reasons from a false supposition, and his arguments fall to the ground.

CHAPTER XVII

OF THE OBJECTS OF PERCEPTION; AND, FIRST, OF PRIMARY AND SECONDARY QUALITIES

THE objects of perception are the various qualities of bodies. Intending to treat of these only in general, and chiefly with a view to explain the notions which our senses give us of them, I begin with the distinction between primary and secondary qualities. These were distinguished very early. The Peripatetic system confounded them, and left no difference. The distinction was again revived by Des Cartes and Locke, and a second time abolished by Berkeley and Hume. If the real foundation of this distinction can be pointed out, it will enable us to account for the various revolutions in the sentiments of philosophers concerning it.

Every one knows that extension, divisibility, figure, motion, solidity, hardness, softness, and fluidity, were by Mr. Locke called *primary qualities of body*; and that sound, colour, taste, smell, and heat or cold, were called *secondary qualities*. Is there a just foundation for this distinction? Is there anything common to the primary which belongs not to the secondary? And what is it?

I answer, that there appears to me to be a real foundation for the distinction; and it is this—that our senses give us a direct and a distinct notion of the primary qualities, and inform us what they are in themselves. But of the secondary qualities, our senses give us only a relative and obscure notion. They inform us only, that they are qualities that affect us in a certain manner—that is, produce in us a certain sensation; but as to what they are in themselves, our senses leave us in the dark.

Every man capable of reflection may easily satisfy himself that he has a perfectly clear and distinct notion of extension, divisibility, figure, and motion. The solidity of a body means no more but that it excludes other bodies from occupying the same place at the same time. Hardness, softness, and fluidity are different degrees of cohesion in the parts of a body. It is fluid when it has no sensible cohesion; soft, when the cohesion is weak; and hard, when it is strong. Of the cause of this cohesion we are ignorant, but the thing itself we understand perfectly, being immediately informed of it by the sense of touch. It is evident, therefore, that of the primary qualities we have a clear and distinct notion; we know what they are, though we may be ignorant of their causes.

I observed, farther, that the notion we have of primary qualities is direct, and not relative only. A relative notion of a thing, is strictly speaking, no notion of the thing at all, but only of some relation which it bears to something else.

Thus, gravity sometimes signifies the tendency of bodies towards the earth; sometimes it signifies the cause of that tendency. When it means the first, I have a direct and distinct notion of gravity; I see it, and feel it, and know perfectly what it is; but this tendency must have a cause. We give the same name to the cause; and that cause has been an object of thought and of speculation. Now, what notion have we of this cause when we think and reason about it? It is evident we think of it as an unknown cause, of a known effect. This is a relative notion; and it must be obscure, because it gives us no conception of what the thing is, but of what relation it bears to something else. Every relation which a thing unknown bears to something that is known, may give a relative notion of it; and there are many objects of thought and of discourse of which our faculties can give no better than a relative notion.

Having premised these things to explain what is meant by a relative notion, it is evident that our notion of primary qualities is not of this kind; we know what they are, and not barely what relation they bear to something else.

It is otherwise with secondary qualities. If you ask me, what is that quality or modification in a rose which I call its smell, I am at a loss to answer directly. Upon reflection, I find, that I have a distinct notion of the sensation which it produces in my mind. But there can be nothing like to this sensation in the rose, because it is insentient. The quality in the rose is something which occasions the sensation in me; but what that something is, I know not. My senses give me no information upon this point. The only notion, therefore, my senses give is this—that smell in the rose is an unknown quality or modification, which is the cause or occasion of a sensation which I know well. The relation which this unknown quality bears to the sensation with which nature hath connected it, is all I learn from the sense of smelling; but this is evidently a relative notion. The same reasoning will apply to every secondary quality.

Thus, I think it appears that there is a real foundation for the distinction of primary from second qualities; and that they are distinguished by this—that of the primary we have by our senses a direct and distinct notion; but of the secondary only a relative notion, which must, because it is only relative, be obscure; they are conceived only as the unknown causes or occasions of certain sensations with which we are well acquainted.

The account I have given of this distinction is founded upon no hypothesis. Whether our notions of primary qualities are direct and distinct, those of the secondary relative and obscure, is a matter of fact, of which every man may have certain knowledge by attentive reflection upon them. To this reflection I appeal, as the proper test of what has been advanced, and proceed to make some reflections on this subject.

1. The primary qualities are neither sensations, nor are they resemblances of sensations. This appears to me self-evident. I have a clear and distinct notion of each of the primary qualities. I have a clear and distinct notion of sensation. I can compare the one with the other; and, when I do so, I am not able to discern a

resembling feature. Sensation is the act or the feeling (I dispute not which) of a sentient being. Figure, divisibility, solidity, are neither acts nor feelings. Sensation supposes a sentient being as its subject; for a sensation that is not felt by some sentient being, is an absurdity. Figure and divisibility supposes a subject that is figured and divisible, but not a subject that is sentient.

2. We have no reason to think that any of the secondary qualities resemble any sensation. The absurdity of this notion has been clearly shown by Des Cartes, Locke, and many modern philosophers. It was a tenet of the ancient philosophy, and is still by many imputed to the vulgar, but only as a vulgar error. It is too evident to need proof, that the vibrations of a sounding body do not resemble the sensation of sound, nor the effluvia of an odorous body the sensation of smell.

3. The distinctness of our notions of primary qualities prevents all questions and disputes about their nature. There are no different opinions about the nature of extension, figure, or motion, or the nature of any primary quality. Their nature is manifest to our senses, and cannot be unknown to any man, or mistaken by him, though their causes may admit of dispute.

The primary qualities are the object of the mathematical sciences; and the distinctness of our notions of them enables us to reason demonstratively about them to a great extent. Their various modifications are precisely defined in the imagination, and thereby capable of being compared, and their relations determined with precision and certainty.

It is not so with secondary qualities. Their nature not being manifest to the sense, may be a subject of dispute. Our feeling informs us that the fire is hot; but it does not inform us what that heat of the fire is. But does it not appear a contradiction, to say we know that the fire is hot, but we know not what that heat is? I answer, there is the same appearance of contradiction in many things that must be granted. We know that wine has an inebriating quality; but we know not what that quality is. It is true, indeed, that, if we had not some notion of what is meant by the heat of fire, and by an inebriating quality, we could affirm nothing of either with understanding. We have a notion of both; but it is only a relative notion. We know that they are the causes of certain known effects.

4. The nature of secondary qualities is a proper subject of philosophical disquisition; and in this philoosphy has made some progress. It has been discovered, that the sensation of smell is

occasioned by the effluvia of bodies; that of sound by their vibration. The disposition of bodies to reflect a particular kind of light, occasions the sensation of colour. Very curious discoveries have been made of the nature of heat, and an ample field of discovery in these subjects remains.

5. We may see why the sensations belonging to secondary qualities are an object of our attention, while those which belong to the primary are not.

The first are not only signs of the object perceived, but they bear a capital part in the notion we form of it. We conceive it only as that which occasions such a sensation, and therefore cannot reflect upon it without thinking of the sensation which it occasions; we have no other mark whereby to distinguish it. The thought of a secondary quality, therefore, always carries us back to the sensation which it produces. We give the same name to both, and are apt to confound them together.

But having a clear and distinct conception of primary qualities, we have no need, when we think of them, to recall their sensations. When a primary quality is perceived, the sensation immediately leads our thought to the quality signified by it, and is itself forgot. We have no occasion afterwards to reflect upon it; and so we come to be as little acquainted with it as if we had never felt it. This is the case with the sensations of all primary qualities, when they are not so painful or pleasant as to draw our attention.

When a man moves his hand rudely against a pointed hard body, he feels pain, and may easily be persuaded that this pain is a sensation, and that there is nothing resembling it in the hard body; at the same time he perceives the body to be hard and pointed, and he knows that these qualities belong to the body only. In this case, it is easy to distinguish what he feels from what he perceives.

Let him again touch the pointed body gently, so as to give him no pain; and now you can hardly persuade him that he feels anything but the figure and hardness of the body; so difficult it is to attend to the sensations belonging to primary qualities, when they are neither pleasant nor painful. They carry the thought to the external object, and immediately disappear and are forgot. Nature intended them only as signs; and when they have served that purpose they vanish.

We are now to consider the opinions both of the vulgar and of philosophers upon this subject. As to the former, it is not to be expected that they should make distinctions which have no connection with the common affairs of life; they do not, therefore, distinguish the primary from the secondary qualities, but speak of both as being equally qualities of the external object. Of the primary qualities they have a distinct notion, as they are immediately and distinctly, perceived by the senses; of the secondary, their notions, as I apprehend, are confused and indistinct, rather than erroneous. A secondary quality is the unknown cause or occasion of a well-known effect; and the same name is common to the cause and the effect. Now, to distinguish clearly the different ingredients of a complex notion, and, at the same time, the different meanings of an ambiguous word, is the work of a philosopher; and is not to be expected of the vulgar, when their occasions do not require it.

I grant, therefore, that the notion which the vulgar have of secondary qualities, is indistinct and inaccurate. But there seems to be a contradiction between the vulgar and the philosopher upon this subject, and each charges the other with a gross absurdity. The vulgar say, that fire is hot, and snow cold, and sugar sweet; and that to deny this is a gross absurdity, and contradicts the testimony of our senses. The philosopher says that heat, and cold, and sweetness, are nothing but sensations in our minds; and it is absurd to conceive that these sensations are in the fire, or in the snow, or in the sugar.

I believe this contradiction, between the vulgar and the philosopher, is more apparent than real; and that it is owing to an abuse of language on the part of the philosopher, and to indistinct notions on the part of the vulgar. The philosopher says, there is no heat in the fire, meaning that the fire has not the sensation of heat. His meaning is just, and the vulgar will agree with him, as soon as they understand his meaning: but his language is improper; for there is really a quality in the fire, of which the proper name is heat, and the name of heat is given to this quality, both by philosophers and by the vulgar, much more frequently than to the sensation of heat. This speech of the philosopher, therefore, is meant by him in one sense; it is taken by the vulgar in another sense. In the sense in which they take it, it is indeed absurd, and so they hold it to be. In the sense in which he means it, it is true; and the vulgar, as soon as they are made to understand that sense, will acknowledge it to be true. They know, as well as the philosopher, that the fire does not feel heat; and this is all that he means by saying there is no heat in the fire.

The external senses have a double province—to make us feel,

and to make us perceive. They furnish us with a variety of sensations, some pleasant, others painful, and others indifferent; at the same time, they give us a conception and an invincible belief of the existence of external objects. This conception of external objects is the work of nature; so likewise is the sensation that accompanies it. This conception and belief which nature produces by means of the senses, we call *perception*. The feeling which goes along with the perception, we call *sensation*. The perception and its corresponding sensation are produced at the same time. In our experience we never find them disjoined. Hence, we are led to consider them as one thing, to give them one name, and to confound their different attributes. It becomes very difficult to separate them in thought, to attend to each by itself, and to attribute nothing to it which belongs to the other.

To do this, requires a degree of attention to what passes in our own minds, and a talent of distinguishing things that differ, which is not to be expected in the vulgar, and is even rarely found in philosophers; so that the progress made in a just analysis of the operations of our senses has been very slow. The hypothesis of ideas, so generally adopted, hath, as I apprehend, greatly retarded this progress, and we might hope for a quicker advance, if philosophers could so far humble themselves as to believe that, in every branch of the philosophy of nature, the productions of human fancy and conjecture will be found to be dross; and that the only pure metal that will endure the test, is what is discovered by patient observation and chaste induction.

JOHN STUART MILL

Born in London in 1806. Son of James Mill, the philosophic radical, and friend and disciple of Jeremy Bentham. Intensively educated by his father. Founded Utilitarian Society in 1822. Wrote widely on political, economic and philosophical subjects. Entered the office of the East India Company in 1823. Early contributor to Westminster Review. Attended University College, London, 1828-1830. Appointed Examiner of India correspondence in 1856, a position held previously by his father. Resigned in 1858 when the Crown took over the government of India. Liberal M.P. for Westminster, 1865-68. Died 1873. His Autobiography *was published by his step-daughter after his death.*

Philosophical works include A System of Logic, 1843, On Liberty, 1859, Considerations on Representative Government, 1861, Utilitarianism, 1863, *and* Examination of Sir William Hamilton's Philosophy, 1865.

PHILOSOPHICALLY, Mill's most important work was his *System of Logic*, but its contents fall largely outside the scope of this volume. The following two chapters from his *Examination of Sir W. Hamilton's Philosophy* have been selected because of the topics with which they deal. They have both been slightly abridged.

AN EXAMINATION OF
SIR WILLIAM HAMILTON'S PHILOSOPHY

XI—THE PSYCHOLOGICAL THEORY OF THE BELIEF IN AN EXTERNAL
WORLD. XII—THE PSYCHOLOGICAL THEORY OF THE BELIEF IN
MATTER, HOW FAR APPLICABLE TO MIND

CHAPTER XI

THE PSYCHOLOGICAL THEORY OF THE BELIEF IN AN EXTERNAL WORLD

I PROCEED to state the case of those who hold that the belief in
an external world is not intuitive, but an acquired product.

This theory postulates the following psychological truths, all of
which are proved by experience.

It postulates, first, that the human mind is capable of Expectation. In other words, that after having had actual sensations, we
are capable of forming the conception of Possible sensations;
sensations which we are not feeling at the present moment, but
which we might feel, and should feel if certain conditions were
present, the nature of which conditions we have, in many cases,
learnt by experience.

It postulates, secondly, the laws of the Association of Ideas. So
far as we are here concerned, these laws are the following: 1st.
Similar phenomena tend to be thought of together. 2nd. Phenomena
which have either been experienced or conceived in close
contiguity to one another, tend to be thought of together. The
contiguity is of two kinds; simultaneity, and immediate succession.
Facts which have been experienced or thought of simultaneously,
recall the thought of one another. Of facts which have been
experienced or thought of in immediate succession, the antecedent,
or the thought of it, recalls the thought of the consequent, but not
conversely. 3rd. Associations produced by contiguity become more
certain and rapid by repetition. When two phenomena have been
very often experienced in conjunction, and have not, in any single

instance, occurred separately either in experience or in thought, there is produced between them what has been called Inseparable, or less correctly, Indissoluble Association: by which is not meant that the association must inevitably last to the end of life—that no subsequent experience or process of thought can possibly avail to dissolve it; but only that as long as no such experience or process of thought has taken place, the association is irresistible; it is impossible for us to think the one thing disjoined from the other. 4th. When an association has acquired this character of inseparability—when the bond between the two ideas has been thus firmly riveted, not only does the idea called up by association become, in our consciousness, inseparable from the idea which suggested it, but the facts or phenomena answering to those ideas come at last to seem inseparable in existence: things which we are unable to conceive apart, appear incapable of existing apart; and the belief we have in their co-existence, though really a product of experience, seems intuitive.   Innumerable examples might be given of this law. One of the most familiar, as well as the most striking, is that of our acquired perceptions of sight.   Even those who, with Mr. Bailey, consider the perception of distance by the eye as not acquired, but intuitive, admit that there are many perceptions of sight which, though instantaneous and unhesitating, are not intuitive.   What we see is a very minute fragment of what we think we see.   We see artificially that one thing is hard, another soft.   We see artificially that one thing is hot, another cold.   We see artificially that what we see is a book, or a stone, each of these being not merely an inference, but a heap of inferences, from the signs which we see, to things not visible.   We see, and cannot help seeing, what we have learnt to infer, even when we know that the inference is erroneous, and that the apparent perception is deceptive.   We cannot help seeing the moon larger when near the horizon, though we know that she is of precisely her usual size.   We cannot help seeing a mountain as nearer to us and of less height, when we see it through a more than ordinarily transparent atmosphere.

Setting out from these premises, the Psychological Theory maintains, that there are associations naturally and even necessarily generated by the order of our sensations and of our reminiscences of sensation, which, supposing no intuition of an external world to have existed in consciousness, would inevitably generate the belief, and would cause it to be regarded as an intuition.

What is it we mean, or what is it which leads us to say, that the objects we perceive are external to us, and not a part of our own thoughts? We mean, that there is concerned in our perceptions something which exists when we are not thinking of it; which existed before we had ever thought of it, and would exist if we were annihilated; and further, that there exist things which we never saw, touched, or otherwise perceived, and things which never have been perceived by man. This idea of something which is distinguished from our fleeting impressions by what, in Kantian language, is called Perdurability; something which is fixed and the same, while our impressions vary; something which exists whether we are aware of it or not, and which is always square (or of some other given figure) whether it appears to us square or round — constitutes altogether our idea of external substance. Whoever can assign an origin to this complex conception, has accounted for what we mean by the belief in matter. Now all this, according to the Psychological Theory, is but the form impressed by the known laws of association, upon the conception or notion, obtained by experience, of Contingent Sensations; by which are meant, sensations that are not in our present consciousness, and individually never were in our consciousness at all, but which in virtue of the laws to which we have learnt by experience that our sensations are subject, we know that we should have felt under given supposable circumstances, and under these same circumstances, might still feel.

I see a piece of white paper on a table. I go into another room. If the phenomenon always followed me, or if, when it did not follow me, I believed it to disappear *e rerum natura*, I should not believe it to be an external object. I should consider it as a phantom— a mere affection of my senses: I should not believe that there had been any body there. But, though I have ceased to see it, I am persuaded that the paper is still there. I no longer have the sensations which it gave me; but I believe that when I again place myself in the circumstances in which I had those sensations, that is, when I go again into the room, I shall again have them; and further, that there has been no intervening moment at which this would not have been the case. Owing to this property of my mind, my conception of the world at any given instant consists, in only a small proportion, of present sensations. Of these I may at the time have none at all, and they are in any case a most insignificant portion of the whole which I apprehend. The conception I form of the world existing at any moment, comprises, along with the sensations I am feeling, a countless variety of possibilities of sensation: namely, the whole of those which past observation tells me that I could, under any supposable circumstances, experience at this moment, together with an indefinite and illimitable multitude of others which though I do not know that I could, yet it is possible that I might, experience in circumstances not known to me. These various possibilities are the important thing to me in the world. My present sensations are generally of little importance, and are moreover fugitive: the possibilities, on the contrary, are permanent, which is the character that mainly distinguishes our idea of Substance or Matter from our notion of sensation. These possibilities, which are conditional certainties, need a special name to distinguish them from mere vague possibilities, which experience gives no warrant for reckoning upon. Now, as soon as a distinguishing name is given, though it be only to the same thing regarded in a different aspect, one of the most familiar experiences of our mental nature teaches us, that the different name comes to be considered as the name of a different thing.

There is another important peculiarity of these certified or guaranteed possibilities of sensation; namely, that they have reference, not to single sensations, but to sensations joined together in groups. When we think of anything as a material substance, or body, we either have had, or we think that on some given supposition we should have, not some *one* sensation, but a great and even an indefinite number and variety of sensations, generally belonging to different senses, but so linked together, that the presence of one announces the possible presence at the very same instant of any or all of the rest. In our mind, therefore, not only is this particular Possibility of sensation invested with the quality of permanence when we are not actually feeling any of the sensations at all; but when we are feeling some of them, the remaining sensations of the group are conceived by us in the form of Present Possibilities, which might be realised at the very moment. And as this happens in turn to all of them, the group as a whole presents itself to the mind as permanent, in contrast not solely with the temporariness of my bodily presence, but also with the temporary character of each of the sensations composing the group; in other words, as a kind of permanent substratum, under a set of passing experiences or manifestations: which is another leading character of our idea of substance or matter, as distinguished from sensation.

Let us now take into consideration another of the general characters of our experience, namely, that in addition to fixed groups, we also recognise a fixed Order in our sensations; an Order of succession, which, when ascertained by observation, gives rise to the ideas of Cause and Effect, according to what I hold to be the true theory of that relation, and is on any theory the source of all our knowledge what causes produce what effects. Now, of what nature is this fixed order among our sensations? It is a constancy of antecedence and sequence. But the constant antecedence and sequence do not generally exist between one actual sensation and another. Very few such sequences are presented to us by experience. In almost all the constant sequences which occur in Nature, the antecedence and consequence do not obtain between sensations, but between the groups we have been speaking about, of which a very small portion is actual sensation, the greater part being permanent possibilities of sensation, evidenced to us by a small and variable number of sensations actually present. Hence, our ideas of causation, power, activity, do not become connected in thought with our sensations as *actual* at all, save in the few physiological cases where these figure by themselves as the antecedents in some uniform sequence. Those ideas become connected, not with sensations, but with groups of possibilities of sensation. The sensations conceived do not, to our habitual thoughts, present themselves as sensations actually experienced, inasmuch as not only any one or any number of them may be supposed absent, but none of them need be present. We find that the modifications which are taking place more or less regularly in our possibilities of sensation, are mostly quite independent of our consciousness, and of our presence or absence. Whether we are asleep or awake the fire goes out, and puts an end to one particular possibility of warmth and light. Whether we are present or absent the corn ripens, and brings a new possibility of food. Hence we speedily learn to think of Nature as made up solely of these groups of possibilities, and the active force in Nature as manifested in the modification of some of these by others. The sensations, though the original foundation of the whole, come to be looked upon as a sort of accident depending on us, and the possibilities as much more real than the actual sensations, nay, as the very realities of which these are only the representations, appearances, or effects. When this state of mind has been arrived at, then, and from that time forward, we are never conscious of a present sensation without instantaneously referring it to some one of the groups of possibilities into which a sensation of that particular description enters; and if we do not yet know to what group to refer it, we at least feel an irresistible conviction that it must belong to some group or other; *i.e.*, that its presence proves the existence, here and now, of a great number and variety of possibilities of sensation, without which it would not have been. The whole set of sensations as possible, form a permanent background to any one or more of them that are, at a given moment, actual; and the possibilities are conceived as standing to the actual sensations in the relation of a cause to its effects, or of canvas to the figures painted on it, or of a root to the trunk, leaves, and flowers, or of a substratum to that which is spread over it, or, in transcendental language, of Matter to Form.

When this point has been reached, the Permanent Possibilities in question have assumed such unlikeness of aspect, and such difference of apparent relation to us, from any sensations, that it would be contrary to all we know of the constitution of human nature that they should not be conceived as, and believed to be, at least as different from sensations as sensations are from one another. Their groundwork in sensation is forgotten, and they are supposed to be something intrinsically distinct from it. We can withdraw ourselves from any of our (external) sensations, or we can be withdrawn from them by some other agency. But though the sensations cease, the possibilities remain in existence; they are independent of our will, our presence, and everything which belongs to us. We find, too, that they belong as much to other human or sentient beings as to ourselves. We find other people grounding their expectations and conduct upon the same permanent possibilities on which we ground ours. But we do not find them experiencing the same actual sensations. Other people do not have our sensations exactly when and as we have them : but they have our possibilities of sensation; whatever indicates a present possibility of sensations to ourselves, indicates a present possibility of similar sensations to them, except so far as their organs of sensation may vary from the type of ours. This puts the final seal to our conception of the groups of possibilities as the fundamental reality in Nature. The permanent possibilities are common to us and to our fellow-creatures; the actual sensations are not. That which other people become aware of when, and on the same grounds, as I do, seems more real to me than that which they do not know of unless I tell them. The world of Possible Sensations succeeding one another according to laws, is as much in other beings as it is in me; it has therefore an existence outside me; it is an External World.

Matter, then, may be defined, a Permanent Possibility of Sensation. If I am asked, whether I believe in matter, I ask whether the questioner accepts this definition of it. If he does, I believe in matter : and so do all Berkeleians. In any other sense than this, I do not. But I affirm with confidence, that this conception of Matter includes the whole meaning attached to it by the common world, apart from philosophical, and sometimes from theological, theories. The reliance of mankind on the real existence of visible and tangible objects, means reliance on the reality and permanence of Possibilities of visual and tactual sensations, when no such sensations are actually experienced. We are warranted in believing that this is the meaning of Matter in the minds of many of its most esteemed metaphysical champions, though they themselves would not admit as much: for example, of Reid, Stewart, and Brown. For these three philosophers alleged that all mankind, including Berkeley and Hume, really believed in Matter, inasmuch as unless they did, they would not have turned aside to save themselves from running against a post. Now all which this manœuvre really proved is, that they believed in Permanent Possibilities of Sensation. We have therefore the unintentional sanction of these three eminent defenders of the existence of matter, for affirming, that to believe in Permanent Possibilities of Sensation is believing in Matter. It is hardly necessary, after such authorities, to mention Dr. Johnson, or any one else who resorts to the *argumentum baculinum* of knocking a stick against the ground. Sir W. Hamilton, a far subtler thinker than any of these, never reasons in this manner. He never supposes that a disbeliever in what he means by Matter, ought in consistency to act in any different mode from those who believe in it. He knew that the belief on which all the practical consequences depend, is the belief in Permanent Possibilities of Sensation, and that if nobody believed in a material universe in any other sense, life would go on exactly as it now does. He, however, did believe in more than this, but, I think, only because it had never occurred to him that mere Possibilities of Sensation could, to our artificialised consciousness, present the character of objectivity which, as we have now shown, they not only can, but unless the known laws of the human mind were suspended, must necessarily, present.

Perhaps it may be objected, that the very possibility of framing such a notion of Matter as Sir W. Hamilton's—the capacity in the human mind of imagining an external world which is anything more than what the Psychological Theory makes it—amounts to a disproof of the theory. If (it may be said) we had no revelation in consciousness, of a world which is not in some way or other identified with sensation, we should be unable to have the notion of such a world. If the only ideas we had of external objects were ideas of our sensations, supplemented by an acquired notion of permanent possibilities of sensation, we must (it is thought) be incapable of conceiving, and therefore still more incapable of fancying that we perceive, things which are not sensations at all. It being evident however that some philosophers believe this, and it being maintainable that the mass of mankind do so, the existence of a perdurable basis of sensations, distinct from sensations themselves, is proved, it might be said, by the possibility of believing it.

Let me first restate what I apprehend the belief to be. We believe that we perceive a something closely related to all our sensations, but different from those which we are feeling at any particular minute; and distinguished from sensations altogether, by being permanent and always the same, while these are fugitive, variable, and alternately displace one another. But these attributes of the object of perception are properties belonging to all the possibilities of sensation which experience guarantees. The belief in such permanent possibilities seems to me to include all that is essential or characteristic in the belief in substance. I believe that Calcutta exists, though I do not perceive it, and that it would still exist if every percipient inhabitant were suddenly to leave the place, or be struck dead. But when I analyse the belief, all I find in it is, that were these events to take place, the Permanent Possibility of Sensation which I call Calcutta would still remain; that if I were suddenly transported to the banks of the Hoogly, I should still have the sensations which, if now present, would lead me to affirm that Calcutta exists here and now. We may infer, therefore, that both philosophers and the world at large, when they think of matter, conceive it really as a Permanent Possibility of Sensation. But the majority of philosophers fancy that it is something more; and the world at large, though they have really, as I conceive, nothing in their minds but a Permanent Possibility of Sensation, would, if asked the question, undoubtedly agree with the philosophers: and though this is sufficiently explained by the tendency of the human mind to infer difference of things from difference of names, I acknowledge the obligation of showing how it can be possible to believe in an existence transcending all possibilities of sensation, unless on the hypothesis that such an existence actually is, and that we actually perceive it.

The explanation, however, is not difficult. It is an admitted fact, that we are capable of all conceptions which can be formed by generalising from the observed laws of our sensations. Whatever relation we find to exist between any one of our sensations and something different from *it*, that same relation we have no difficulty in conceiving to exist between the sum of all our sensations and

something different from *them*. The differences which our consciousness recognises between one sensation and another, give us
the general notion of difference, and inseparably associate with
every sensation we have, the feeling of its being different from
other things: and when once this association has been formed, we
can no longer conceive anything, without being able, and even being
compelled, to form also the conception of something different from
it. This familiarity with the idea of something different from *each*
thing we know, makes it natural and easy to form the notion of
something different from *all* things that we know, collectively
as well as individually. It is true we can form no conception of
what such a thing can be; our notion of it is merely negative; but
the idea of a substance, apart from its relation to the impressions
which we conceive it as making on our senses, *is* a merely negative
one. There is thus no psychological obstacle to our forming the
notion of a something which is neither a sensation nor a possibility
of sensation, even if our consciousness does not testify to it; and
nothing is more likely than that the Permanent Possibilities of
sensation, to which our consciousness does testify, should be confounded in our minds with this imaginary conception. All
experience attests the strength of the tendency to mistake mental
abstractions, even negative ones, for substantive realities; and the
Permanent Possibilities of sensation which experience guarantees,
are so extremely unlike in many of their properties to actual
sensations, that since we are capable of imagining something which
transcends sensation, there is a great natural probability that we
should suppose these to be it.

But this natural probability is converted into certainty, when
we take into consideration that universal law of our experience
which is termed the law of Causation, and which makes us mentally
connect with the beginning of everything, some antecedent condition, or Cause. The case of Causation is one of the most marked
of all the cases in which we extend to the sum total of our
consciousness, a notion derived from its parts. It is a striking
example of our power to conceive, and our tendency to believe, that
a relation which subsists between every individual item of our
experience and some other item, subsists also between our experience
as a whole, and something not within the sphere of experience.
By this extension to the sum of all our experiences, of the internal
relations obtaining between its several parts, we are led to consider
sensation itself—the aggregate whole of our sensations—as deriving
its origin from antecedent existences transcending sensation. That

we should do this, is a consequence of the particular character of the uniform sequences, which experience discloses to us among our sensations. As already remarked, the constant antecedent of a sensation is seldom another sensation, or set of sensations, actually felt. It is much oftener the existence of a group of possibilities, not necessarily including any actual sensations, except such as are required to show that the possibilities are really present. Nor are actual sensations indispensable even for this purpose; for the presence of the object (which is nothing more than the immediate presence of the possibilities) may be made known to us by the very sensation which we refer to it as its effect. Thus, the real antecedent of an effect—the only antecedent which, being invariable and unconditional, we consider to be the cause—may be, not any sensation really felt, but solely the presence, at that or the immediately preceding moment, of a group of possibilities of sensation. Hence it is not with sensations as actually experienced, but with their Permanent Possibilities, that the idea of cause comes to be identified: and we, by one and the same process, acquire the habit of regarding Sensation in general, like all our individual sensations, as an Effect, and also that of conceiving as the causes of most of our individual sensations, not other sensations, but general possibilities of sensation. If all these considerations put together do not completely explain and account for our conceiving these Possibilities as a class of independent and substantive entities, I know not what psychological analysis can be conclusive.

It may perhaps be said, that the preceding theory gives, indeed, some account of the idea of Permanent Existence which forms part of our conception of matter, but gives no explanation of our believing these permanent objects to be external, or out of ourselves. I apprehend, on the contrary, that the very idea of anything out of ourselves is derived solely from the knowledge experience gives us of the Permanent Possibilities. Our sensations we carry with us wherever we go, and they never exist where we are not; but when we change our place we do not carry away with us the Permanent Possibilities of Sensation: they remain until we return, or arise and cease under conditions with which our presence has in general nothing to do. And more than all—they are, and will be after we have ceased to feel, Permanent Possibilities of sensation to other beings than ourselves. Thus our actual sensations and the permanent possibilities of sensation, stand out in obtrusive contrast to one another: and when the idea of Cause has been acquired, and extended by generalisation from the parts of our experience to its aggregate whole, nothing can be more natural than that the Permanent Possibilities should be classed by us as existences generically distinct from our sensations, but of which our sensations are the effect.

The same theory which accounts for our ascribing to an aggregate of possibilities of sensation, a permanent existence which our sensations themselves do not possess, and consequently a greater reality than belongs to our sensations, also explains our attributing greater objectivity to the Primary Qualities of bodies than to the Secondary. For the sensations which correspond to what are called the Primary Qualities (as soon at least as we come to apprehend them by two senses, the eye as well as the touch) are always present when any part of the group is so. But colours, tastes, smells, and the like, being, in comparison, fugacious, are not, in the same degree, conceived as being always there, even when nobody is present to perceive them. The sensations answering to the Secondary qualities are only occasional, those to the Primary, constant. The Secondary, moreover, vary with different persons, and with the temporary sensibility of our organs; the Primary, when perceived at all, are, as far as we know, the same to all persons and at all times.

CHAPTER XII

THE PSYCHOLOGICAL THEORY OF THE BELIEF IN MATTER, HOW FAR APPLICABLE TO MIND

It is evident, in the first place, that our knowledge of mind, like that of matter, is entirely relative. We have no conception of mind itself, as distinguished from its conscious manifestations. We neither know nor can imagine it, except as represented by the succession of manifold feelings which metaphysicians call by the name of States or Modifications of Mind. It is nevertheless true that our notion of Mind, as well as of Matter, is the notion of a permanent something, contrasted with the perpetual flux of the sensations and other feelings or mental states which we refer to it; a something which we figure as remaining the same, while the particular feelings through which it reveals its existence, change. This attribute of Permanence, supposing that there were nothing else to be considered, would admit of the same explanation when predicated of Mind, as of Matter. The belief I entertain that my mind exists when it is not feeling, nor thinking, nor conscious of its own existence, resolves itself into the belief of a Permanent Possibility of these states. If I think of myself as in dreamless sleep, or in the sleep of death, and believe that I, or in other words my mind, is or will be existing through these states, though not in conscious feeling, the most scrupulous examination of my belief will not detect in it any fact actually believed, except that my capability of feeling is not, in that interval, permanently destroyed, and is suspended only because it does not meet with the combination of conditions which would call it into action: the moment it did meet with that combination it would revive, and remains, therefore, a Permanent Possibility. Thus far, there seems no hindrance to our regarding Mind as nothing but the series of our sensations (to which must now be added our internal feelings), as they actually occur, with the addition of infinite possibilities of feeling requiring for their actual realisation conditions which may or may not take place, but which as possibilities are always in existence, and many of them present.

In order to the further understanding of the bearings of this theory of the Ego, it is advisable to consider it in its relation to three questions, which may very naturally be asked with reference to it, and which often have been asked, and sometimes answered very erroneously. If the theory is correct, and my mind is but a series of feelings, or, as it has been called, a thread of consciousness, however supplemented by believed Possibilities of consciousness which are not, though they might be, realised; if this is all that Mind, or Myself, amounts to, what evidence have I (it is asked) of the existence of my fellow-creatures? What evidence of a hyperphysical world, or, in one word, of God? and, lastly, what evidence of immortality?

Dr. Reid unhesitatingly answers, None. If the doctrine is true, I am alone in the universe.

I hold this to be one of Reid's most palpable mistakes. Whatever evidence to each of the three points there is on the ordinary theory, exactly that same evidence is there on this.

In the first place, as to my fellow-creatures. Reid seems to have imagined that if I myself am only a series of feelings, the proposition that I have any fellow-creatures, or that there are any Selves except mine, is but words without a meaning. But this is a misapprehension. All that I am compelled to admit if I receive this theory, is that other people's Selves also are but series of feelings, like my own. Though my Mind, as I am capable of conceiving it, be nothing but the succession of my feelings, and though Mind itself may be merely a possibility of feelings, there is nothing in that doctrine to prevent my conceiving, and believing, that there are other successions of feelings besides those of which I am conscious, and that these are as real as my own. The belief is completely consistent with the metaphysical theory. Let us now see whether the theory takes away the grounds of it.

What are those grounds? By what evidence do I know, or by what considerations am I led to believe, that there exist other sentient creatures; that the walking and speaking figures which I see and hear, have sensations and thoughts, or in other words, possess Minds? The most strenuous Intuitionist does not include this among the things that I know by direct intuition. I conclude it from certain things, which my experience of my own states of feeling proves to me to be marks of it. These marks are of two kinds, antecedent and subsequent; the previous conditions requisite for feeling, and the effects of consequences of it. I conclude that other human beings have feelings like me, because, first, they have bodies like me, which I know, in my own case, to be the antecedent condition of feelings; and because, secondly, they exhibit the acts, and other outward signs, which in my own case I know by experience to be caused by feelings. I am conscious in myself of a series of facts connected by an uniform sequence, of which the beginning is modifications of my own body, the middle is feelings, the end is outward demeanour. In the case of other human beings I have the evidence of my senses for the first and last links of the series, but not for the intermediate link. I find, however, that the sequence between the first and last is as regular and constant in those other cases as it is in mine. In my own case I know that the first link produces the last through the intermediate link, and could not produce it without. Experience, therefore, obliges me to conclude that there must be an intermediate link; which must either be the same in others as in myself, or a different one: I must either believe them to be alive, or to be automatons: and by believing them to be alive, that is, by supposing the link to be of the same nature as in the case of which I have experience, and which is in all other respects similar, I bring other human beings, as phenomena, under the same generalisations which I know by experience to be the true theory of my own existence. And in doing so I conform to the legitimate rules of experimental enquiry. The process is exactly parallel to that by which Newton proved that the force which keeps the planets in their orbits is identical with that by which an apple falls to the ground. It was not incumbent on Newton to prove the impossibility of its being any other force; he was thought to have made out his point when he had simply

shown, that no other force need be supposed. We know the existence of other beings by generalisation from the knowledge of our
own : the generalisation merely postulates that what experience
shows to be a mark of the existence of something within the sphere
of our consciousness, may be concluded to be a mark of the same
thing beyond that sphere.

This logical process loses none of its legitimacy on the supposition
that neither Mind nor Matter is anything but a permanent possibility
of feeling. Whatever sensation I have, I at once refer it to one
of the permanent groups of possibilities of sensation which I call
material objects. But among these groups I find there is one (my
own body) which is not only composed, like the rest, of a mixed
multitude of sensations and possibilities of sensations, but is also
connected, in a peculiar manner, with all my sensations. Not only
is this special group always present as an antecedent condition of
every sensation I have, but the other groups are only enabled to
convert their respective possibilities of sensation into actual sensations, by means of some previous change in that particular one. I
look about me, and though there is only one group (or body) which
is connected with all my sensations in this peculiar manner, I observe
that there is a great multitude of other bodies, closely resembling
in their sensible properties (in the sensations composing them as
groups) this particular one, but whose modifications do not call up,
as those of my own body do, a world of sensations in my consciousness. Since they do not do so in my consciousness, I infer that
they do it out of my consciousness, and that to each of them belongs
a world of consciousness of its own, to which it stands in the same
relation in which what I call my own body stands to mine. And
having made this generalisation, I find that all other facts within
my reach accord with it. Each of these bodies exhibits to my
senses a set of phenomena (composed of acts and other manifestations) such as I know, in my own case, to be effects of consciousness,
and such as might be looked for if each of the bodies has really
in connection with it a world of consciousness. All this is as good
and genuine an inductive process on the theory we are discussing,
as it is the common theory. Any objection to it in the one case
would be an equal objection in the other. I have stated the
postulate required by the one theory : the common theory is in
need of the same. If I could not, from my personal knowledge
of one succession of feelings, infer the existence of other successions
of feelings, when manifested by the same outward signs, I could
just as little, from my personal knowledge of a single spiritual
substance, infer by generalisation, when I find the same outward

indications, the existence of other spiritual substances.

As the theory leaves the evidence of the existence of my fellow-creatures exactly as it was before, so does it also with that of the existence of God. Supposing me to believe that the Divine Mind is simply the series of the Divine thoughts and feelings prolonged through eternity, that would be, at any rate, believing God's existence to be as real as my own. And as for evidence, the argument of Paley's Natural Theology, or, for that matter, of his Evidences of Christianity, would stand existly where it does. The Design argument is drawn from the analogy of human experience. From the relation which human works bear to human thoughts and feelings, it infers a corresponding relation between works, more or less similar but superhuman, and superhuman thoughts and feelings. If it proves these, nobody but a metaphysician needs care whether or not it proves a mysterious substratum for them. Again, the arguments for Revelation undertake to prove by testimony, that within the sphere of human experience works were done requiring a greater than human power and words said requiring a greater than human wisdom. These positions, and the evidences of them, neither lose nor gain anything by our supposing that the wisdom only means wise thoughts and volitions, and that the power means thoughts and volitions followed by imposing phenomena.

As to immortality, it is precisely as easy to conceive that a succession of feelings, a thread of consciousness, may be prolonged to eternity, as that a spiritual substance for ever continues to exist: and any evidence which would prove the one, will prove the other. Metaphysical theologians may lose the *a priori* argument by which they have sometimes flattered themselves with having proved that a spiritual substance, by the essential constitution of its nature, *cannot* perish. But they had better drop this argument in any case. To do them justice, they seldom insist on it now

The theory, therefore, which resolves Mind into a series of feelings, with a background of possibilities of feeling, can effectually withstand the most invidious of the arguments directed against it. But, groundless as are the extrinsic objections, the theory has intrinsic difficulties which we have not yet set forth, and which it seems to me beyond the power of metaphysical analysis to remove. Besides present feelings, and possibilities of present feeling, there is another class of phenomena to be included in an enumeration of the elements making up our conception of Mind. The thread of consciousness which composes the mind's phenomenal life, consists not only of present sensations, but likewise, in part, of memories and expectations. Now what are these? In themselves, they are present feelings, states of present consciousness, any in that respect not distinguished from sensations. They all, moreover, resemble some given sensations or feelings, of which we have previously had experience. But they are attended with the peculiarity, that each of them involves a belief in more than its own present existence. A sensation involves only this: but a remembrance of sensation, even if not referred to any particular date, involves the suggestion and belief that a sensation, of which it is a copy or representation, actually existed in the past: and an expectation involves the belief, more or less positive, that a sensation or other feeling to which it directly refers, will exist in the future. Nor can the phenomena involved in these two states of consciousness be adequately expressed, without saying that the belief they include is, that I myself formerly had, or that I myself, and no other, shall hereafter have, the sensations remembered or expected. The fact believed is, that the sensations did actually form, or will hereafter form, part of the self-same series of states, or thread of consciousness, of which the remembrance or expectation of those sensations is the part now present. If, therefore, we speak of the Mind as a series of feelings, we are obliged to complete the statement by calling it a series of feelings which is aware of itself as past and future; and we are reduced to the alternative of believing that the Mind, or Ego, is something different from any series of feelings, or possibilities of them, or of accepting the paradox, that something which *ex hypothesi* is but a series of feelings, can be aware of itself as a series.

The truth is, that we are here face to face with that final inexplicability, at which we inevitably arrive when we reach ultimate facts; and in general, one mode of stating it only appears more incomprehensible than another, because the whole of human language is accommodated to the one, and is so incongruous with the other, that it cannot be expressed in any terms which do not deny its truth. The real stumbling block is perhaps not in any theory of the fact, but in the fact itself. The true incomprehensibility perhaps is, that something which has ceased, or is not yet in existence, can still be, in a manner, present: that a series of feelings, the infinitely greater part of which is past or future, can be gathered up, as it were, into a single present conception, accompanied by a belief of reality. I think, by far the wisest thing we can do, is to accept the inexplicable fact, without any theory of how it takes place; and when we are obliged to speak of it in terms which assume a theory, to use them with a reservation as to their meaning.